What Every Borland C++™ 4 Programmer Should Know

WHAT EVERY
BORLAND® C++ 4
PROGRAMMER SHOULD
KNOW

NAMIR CLEMENT SHAMMAS

SAMS
PUBLISHING

A Division of Prentice Hall Computer Publishing
201 West 103rd Street, Indianapolis, Indiana 46290

To my new and dear friends Bob and Marie Heckmann.

Copyright © 1994 by Sams Publishing

FIRST EDITION

All rights reserved. No part of this book shall be reproduced, stored in a retrieval system, or transmitted by any means, electronic, mechanical, photocopying, recording, or otherwise, without written permission from the publisher. No patent liability is assumed with respect to the use of the information contained herein. Although every precaution has been taken in the preparation of this book, the publisher and author assume no responsibility for errors or omissions. Neither is any liability assumed for damages resulting from the use of the information contained herein. For information, address Sams Publishing, A division of Prentice Hall Computer Publishing, 201 W. 103rd St., Indianapolis, IN 46290.

International Standard Book Number: 0-672-30409—0

Library of Congress Catalog Card Number: 93-86951

97 96 95 94   4 3 2 1

Interpretation of the printing code: the rightmost double-digit number is the year of the book's printing; the rightmost single-digit, the number of the book's printing. For example, a printing code of 94-1 shows that the first printing of the book occurred in 1994.

Composed in **Goudy** and MCPdigital by Prentice Hall Computer Publishing

Printed in the United States of America

Trademarks

OVERVIEW

CONTENTS

ACKNOWLEDGMENTS

I wish to thank many people at Sams for their encouragement. First, I would like to thank Publisher Richard Swadley and Associate Publisher Jordan Gold for their support and vision for this book. Many thanks to Greg Croy and Stacy Hiquet for kicking the idea around. I would also like to thank Dean Miller, Sandy Doell, Deborah Frisby, and Jim Grass for their first-class work and above first-class patience. I would like to thank the technical editor, Andrew Rieger, for his valuable comments. Many thanks to Nan Borreson and Karen Giles at Borland for their support. Finally, I'd like to thank all those who worked on this book and made it tangible. Let's do it again, folks!

About the Author

Namir Shammas is a full-time author of programming books and an expert in object-oriented programming. He has written and co-authored over 30 books on programming languages such as Visual Basic, Pascal, C, and C++. Among his many books are *Advanced C++* and *Teach Yourself Visual C++ in 21 Days*.

INTRODUCTION

Programming in Windows is far more involved and sophisticated than programming in MS-DOS. The C and C++ compiler packages on the market today offer comprehensive development tools and include extensive on-line help, powerful programming environments, versatile debuggers, programming tools, and various kinds of software development kits (SDKs). The new Borland C++ 4.0 is no exception. Windows programmers like you are faced with an explosion of information that must be mastered. The learning curve for programming in Windows is much steeper than that of DOS. The vast information found in the C and C++ compiler packages (including Borland C++) make it impossible for any *single* book to present every aspect of programming related to these packages.

This book is designed to show you the new and necessary aspects of programming with Borland C++ 4.0. Though OWL 2.0 leads the list of new components in Borland C++, I chose to leave the task of focusing on OWL 2.0 to other SAMS authors. Instead, this book offers a balance of OWL basics, using the new AppExpert and ClassExpert utilities, and using the tools like WinSpector, WinSight, and Grep.

WHO SHOULD READ THIS BOOK

This book is aimed at readers who program Windows applications in C or C++. Prior knowledge of C++ or previous versions of Borland C++ compilers is not vital, but it certainly helps.

CONVENTIONS USED IN THIS BOOK

The following typographic conventions are used in this book:

- Code lines, commands, statements, variables, and any text you see on the screen appears in a `computer` typeface.

- Command output and anything that you type appears in a bold **`computer`** typeface.

- Placeholders in syntax descriptions appear in an *italic computer* typeface. Replace the placeholder with the actual filename, parameter, or whatever element it represents.

- *Italics* highlight technical terms when they first appear in the text, and are sometimes used to emphasize important points.

Within each chapter you will encounter several icons that help you pinpoint the current topic's direction.

 indicates that the current topic is new to Borland C++ 4.0.

 indicates that the current topic is new to OWL 2.0.

 indicates that the topic being discussed has slightly changed in OWL 2.0.

GETTING STARTED

The book has thirteen chapters and three appendixes. Chapter 1 looks at the basics of OWL. The chapter presents a brief overview of the OWL classes, a brief overview of Windows messages, and a discussion of sending, responding to, and defining messages. The examples in the chapter include a minimally operating OWL-based program, a minimal menu-driven program, and simple interactive programs.

Chapter 2 focuses on visual programming using the Resource Workshop. The text uses a hands-on approach in working with the Resource Workshop in creating menus, icons, and dialog boxes. Several examples show diverse kinds of dialog boxes, including ones that use VBX controls.

Chapter 3 presents the various text and button controls. These controls include the static text, edit box, pushbutton, group box, check box, and radio button controls. The examples in the chapter present different versions of a command-oriented calculator.

Chapter 4 discusses the scroll bar, list box, and combo box controls. The chapter offers various examples for these controls and discusses topics such as

handling single-selection list boxes, handling multiple-selection list boxes, and synchronized lists scrolling.

Chapter 5 presents the dialog box class and discusses how to create and invoke modal and modeless dialog boxes. The chapter also focuses on transferring data between a dialog box and its parent window.

Chapter 6 offers the Windows common dialog boxes. These dialog boxes include the color selection, font selection, print, print setup, file open, file save, find, and replace dialog boxes. The chapter presents the classes and supporting data structures for each common dialog box, along with examples that show how to invoke them and retrieve data from these dialog boxes.

Chapter 7 looks at MDI windows and discusses the MDI frame, client, and child classes. The text offers examples that show MDI child windows with their own controls.

Chapter 8 presents the IDE for Borland C++ 4.0 and its menu options. The chapter covers important options such as the Search, View, Project, and Options.

Chapter 9 introduces you to the versatile AppExpert utility. The text discusses invoking this utility and looks at the options involved in fine-tuning the generated application. The chapter also presents three single document interface (SDI) compliant text editors that vary in features.

Chapter 10 picks up where Chapter 9 leaves off and presents four versions of multiple document interface (MDI) compliant text editors.

Chapter 11 presents the ClassExpert utility, which complements the AppExpert utility. ClassExpert enables you to add new member functions and classes to your application. The text discusses these features and offers examples for adding new member functions and adding a new dialog box class.

Chapter 12 discusses the Windows programming tools called WinSight, WinSpector, and Grep. The text shows you to use the WinSight utility to monitor all or some of the Windows messages. The chapter also discusses using the WinSpector utility to examine postmortem runtime errors. Finally, the text discusses using the Grep utility from within the IDE.

Chapter 13 focuses on the debugger that is part of the IDE. The text discusses using unconditional breakpoints, logging expressions, using conditional breakpoints, and browsing at symbols.

Appendix A is aimed at readers who are relatively new to C++. The text looks at the basics of OOP and the basics of declaring classes. The appendix also discusses working with constructors, destructors, virtual member functions, friend functions, operators, static members, and creating class hierarchy.

Appendix B presents the control resource script used in menus and dialog box resources. This chapter is aimed at the novice Windows programmer.

Appendix C discusses the new string class that complies with the proposed standard submitted to the ANSI C++ committee. The text looks at the declaration of the class and discusses the various member functions, grouped by their tasks. The appendix also offers a Windows program that tests many of the member functions and operators of class string.

I would like to point out that the source code listings generated by the AppExpert, ClassExpert, and the Resource Workshop contain many lines that exceed 80 characters. These long lines end up wrapping to the next line. The book uses the code-continuation character (➡) to indicate that a line is wrapping.

I hope that you find this book with its hands-on approach valuable in learning about Borland C++ and valuable in your work as a Windows programmer.

Happy Programming!

Namir Clement Shammas

The programs in *What Every Borland C++ 4 Programmer Should Know* are available on disk from the author at the following address:

Namir C. Shammas
3928 Margate Drive
Richmond, VA 23235

Please enclose a check for $10.00 with your request for a copy. Outside the U.S., please enclose a check for $14.00 in U.S. currency, drawn on a U.S. bank. Please make the check payable to **Namir C. Shammas**. Include your name, your company name, and a complete address and indicate whether you prefer a 5.25- or 3.5-inch disk format.

To download the files from CompuServe, type: GO SAMS. The files can be found in the Sams Programming Library.

OBJECTWINDOWS BASICS

The ObjectWindows library provides a powerful tool that assists you in developing Windows applications. Without such a library, coding Windows applications becomes a more difficult, frustrating, and increasingly code-intensive process. The ObjectWindows library succeeds in combining object-oriented and event-driven programming concepts, and it demonstrates how well these two programming disciplines work together. This chapter introduces you to the ObjectWindows class library and some basic information related to Windows. In this chapter, you will learn about the following:

- The ObjectWindows hierarchy

- Responding to Windows messages

- Sending messages

- The user-defined messages

- Examples of simple OWL-based Windows programs

THE OBJECTWINDOWS HIERARCHY

The ObjectWindows hierarchy enables you to significantly reduce the amount of coding involved in creating the user-interface of Windows applications. This section presents selected class declarations of the various ObjectWindows members and briefly discusses the functionality supported by each category of classes. The ObjectWindows library supports the following categories of classes:

- Module and application classes
- Window classes
- Control classes
- Dialog box classes
- Document and view classes
- Printing classes
- Graphics classes
- Miscellaneous classes

The hierarchy of the ObjectWindows library is relatively intricate and involves the use of multiple inheritance. The hierarchy has two base root classes, namely TEventHandler and TStreamableBase. These classes support the event-handling features and streamability of the various window classes.

The Module and Application Classes

This category involves the TModule class and its descendant, the TApplication class. The TModule class is a descendant of the classes TEventHandler and TStreamableBase. This very modest OWL subhierarchy has the vital task of initializing Windows and managing the flow of Windows messages to their proper recipient. Here is the declaration of the TApplication class:

```
class _OWLCLASS TApplication : public TModule {
  public:
    class _OWLCLASS TXInvalidMainWindow : public TXOwl {
      public:
        TXInvalidMainWindow();
        TXOwl* Clone();
        void Throw();
    };
```

```
    HINSTANCE        hPrevInstance;
    int              nCmdShow;

    TDocManager*     DocManager;
    TFrameWindow*    MainWindow;
    HACCEL           HAccTable;

    TApplication(const char far* name = 0);
    TApplication(const char far* name,
                 HINSTANCE         hInstance,
                 HINSTANCE         hPrevInstance,
                 const char far* cmdLine,
                 int               cmdShow);

  ~TApplication();

    static void      SetWinMainParams(HINSTANCE         hInstance,
                                      HINSTANCE         hPrevInstance,
                                      const char far* cmdLine,
                                      int               cmdShow);

    void             GetWinMainParams();


    virtual BOOL     CanClose();
    virtual int      Run();

#if defined(__WIN32__)
    TMutex& GetMutex();

    class _OWLCLASS TAppLock : public TMutex::Lock {
      public:
        TAppLock(TApplication &app);
    };

    //
    // override TEventHandler::Dispatch() to handle multi-thread
    // synchronization
    //
    virtual LRESULT  Dispatch(TEventInfo& info, WPARAM wp, LPARAM lp = 0);
#endif

    BOOL             PumpWaitingMessages(); // pumps all waiting msgs
    virtual int      MessageLoop();          // Loops until break or WM_QUIT
    virtual BOOL     ProcessAppMsg(MSG& msg);
    void             SuspendThrow(xalloc& x); // saves xalloc exception info
    void             SuspendThrow(xmsg& x);   // saves xmsg exception info
    void             SuspendThrow(TXOwl& x);  // saves copy of TXOwl exception
    void             SuspendThrow(int);       // set bit flag to log exception
    void             ResumeThrow(); // checks and rethrows suspended exceptions
```

continues

continued

```
int              QueryThrow() {return XState;}   // return suspend flags
enum {
  xsUnknown   = 1,
  xsBadCast   = 2,
  xsBadTypeid = 4,
  xsMsg       = 8,
  xsAlloc     = 16,
  xsOwl       = 32,
};

//
// begin and end of a modal window's modal message loop
//
int              BeginModal(TWindow* window, int flags=MB_APPLMODAL);
void             EndModal(int result);
virtual void     PreProcessMenu(HMENU);   // called from MainWindow

//
// Dead TWindow garbage collection
//
void             Condemn(TWindow* win);

//
// Call this function after each msg dispatch if TApplication's message
// loop is not used.
//
void             PostDispatchAction();

//
// TApplication has no event table itself, defers event handling to
// DocManager if it has been installed.
//
BOOL  Find(TEventInfo&, TEqualOperator = 0);

// Obsolete
static HINSTANCE GetLibInstance(TModule* module) {return *module;}

void             EnableBWCC(BOOL enable = TRUE, UINT language = 0);
BOOL             BWCCEnabled() const {return BWCCOn;}
TModule*         GetBWCCModule() const {return BWCCModule;}

void             EnableCtl3d(BOOL enable = TRUE);
void             EnableCtl3dAutosubclass(BOOL enable);
BOOL             Ctl3dEnabled() const {return Ctl3dOn;}
TModule*         GetCtl3dModule() const { return Ctl3dModule;}

protected:
  BOOL      BreakMessageLoop;
  int       MessageLoopResult;
```

```
    virtual void      InitApplication();  // "first"-instance initialization
    virtual void      InitInstance();     // each-instance initialization
    virtual void      InitMainWindow();   // init application main window
    virtual int       TermInstance(int status); // each-instance termination

    //
    // (re)set a new main window sometime later, after construction
    //
    TFrameWindow*     SetMainWindow(TFrameWindow* window);

    //
    // called each time there are no messages in the queue. idle count is
    // incremented each time, & zeroed when messages are pumped. Return
    // whether or not more processing needs to be done.
    //
    // default behavior is to give the main window an opportunity to do idle
    // processing by invoking its IdleAction() member function when
    // "idleCount" is 0
    //
    virtual BOOL      IdleAction(long idleCount);

  private:
    BOOL              BWCCOn;
    TModule*          BWCCModule;

    BOOL              Ctl3dOn;
    TModule*          Ctl3dModule;

#if defined(__WIN32__)
    TMutex            Mutex;
#endif

    static HINSTANCE        InitHInstance;
    static HINSTANCE        InitHPrevInstance;
    static const char far*  InitCmdLine;
    static int              InitCmdShow;

    //
    // exception handling state
    //
    int     XState;
    string XString;
    size_t XSize;
    TXOwl* XOwl;

    //
    // Condemned TWindow garbage collection
    //
    void              DeleteCondemned();
    TWindow*          CondemnedWindows;
```

continues

continued

```
//
// hidden to prevent accidental copying or assignment
//
TApplication(const TApplication&);
TApplication& operator =(const TApplication&);
};
```

The preceding declaration shows you that the TApplication class is not a skeleton class. Instead, it encapsulates powerful operations, most notably the Run member function that is used to run your application classes. You always derive your application class from the TApplication class, which supports the following kinds of operations:

- Initializing the Windows applications and their instances

- Processing messages

- Managing the message loop of a modal window

- Collecting garbage

The Window Classes

The category of Window classes has the TWindow class as its root. This class is a descendant of the TEventHandler and TStreamableBase case. Here is the outline that represents the subhierarchy of the Window classes:

```
+ TWindow
    + TFrameWindow
        - TFloatingFrame (also a descendant of TTinyCaption)
        * TMDIFrame
        * TDecoratedFrame
            - TDecoratedMDIFrame
        - TMDIChild
```

The * character indicates that the class is a coparent for the descendant class shown below it.

The TWindow Class

The TWindow class is the base class for all windows (including controls, dialog boxes, MDI windows, and so on) and encapsulates the basic and common operations shared by all of these classes. Here is the declaration of the TWindow class:

```
class _OWLCLASS TWindow : virtual public TEventHandler,
                          virtual public TStreamableBase {
  public:
    class _OWLCLASS TXWindow : public TXOwl {
      public:
        TXWindow(TWindow* win = 0, UINT resourceId = IDS_INVALIDWINDOW);
        TXWindow(const TXWindow& src);
        int Unhandled(TModule* app, unsigned promptResId);
        TXOwl* Clone();
        void Throw() {throw *this;}
        TWindow*      Window;
        static string Msg(TWindow* wnd, UINT resourceid);
    };

    TStatus         Status;
    HWND            HWindow;  // handle to associated MS-Windows window
    char far*       Title;
    TWindow*        Parent;
    TWindowAttr     Attr;
    WNDPROC         DefaultProc;
    TScrollerBase*  Scroller;

    TWindow(TWindow*      parent,
            const char far* title = 0,
            TModule*      module = 0);

    TWindow(HWND hWnd, TModule* module = 0);

    virtual ~TWindow();

    //
    // two iterators that take function pointers
    //
    TWindow*        FirstThat(TCondFunc test, void* paramList = 0);
    void            ForEach(TActionFunc action, void* paramList = 0);

    //
    // two iterators that take pointers to member functions
    //
    TWindow*        FirstThat(TCondMemFunc test, void* paramList = 0);
    void            ForEach(TActionMemFunc action, void* paramList = 0);

    //
    // other functions for iteration
    //
    TWindow*        Next() {return SiblingList;}
    void            SetNext(TWindow* next) {SiblingList = next;}
    TWindow*        GetFirstChild()
                        {return ChildList ? ChildList->SiblingList : 0;}
    TWindow*        GetLastChild() {return ChildList;}
```

continues

continued

```
TWindow*          Previous();
unsigned          NumChildren();   // number of child windows


//
// query and set the flags
//
void              SetFlag(TWindowFlag mask) {Flags |= DWORD(mask);}
void              ClearFlag(TWindowFlag mask) {Flags &= DWORD(~mask);}
BOOL              IsFlagSet(TWindowFlag mask) {return (Flags & mask) ? 1 : 0;}


//
// sets/clears flag which indicates that the TWindow should be
// created if a create is sent while in the parent's child list
//
void              EnableAutoCreate() {SetFlag(WB_AUTOCREATE);}
void              DisableAutoCreate() {ClearFlag(WB_AUTOCREATE);}


//
// sets flag which indicates that the TWindow can/will transfer data
// via the transfer mechanism
//
void              EnableTransfer() {SetFlag(WB_TRANSFER);}
void              DisableTransfer() {ClearFlag(WB_TRANSFER);}


//
// Window's default module access functions
//
TModule*          GetModule() const {return Module;}
void              SetModule(TModule* module) {Module = module;}

// Obsolete library id functions
//
HINSTANCE         GetLibInstance(const TModule* module=0)
                     const {return module ? *module : *GetModule();}


TApplication*     GetApplication() const {return Application;}
WNDPROC           GetThunk() const {return Thunk;}
virtual BOOL      Register();


//
// create/destroy an MS_Windows element to be associated with an OWL window
//
virtual BOOL      Create();
virtual void      PerformCreate(int menuOrId);
BOOL              CreateChildren();
virtual void      Destroy(int retVal = 0);


//
// suggest an Owl window to close itself
//
```

```
    virtual void       CloseWindow(int retVal = 0);

    //
    // This function is obsolete. Destroy() should be called directly, & then
    // the window destructed (using delete, etc).
    //
    void               ShutDownWindow(int retVal = 0);

#if defined( __WIN32__ )
    //
    // override TEventHandler::Dispatch() to handle multi-thread
    // synchronization
    //
    virtual LRESULT  Dispatch(TEventInfo& info, WPARAM wp, LPARAM lp = 0);
#endif

    //
    // called from TApplication::ProcessAppMsg() to give the window an
    // opportunity to perform preprocessing of the Windows message
    //
    // if you return TRUE, further processing of the message is halted
    //
    // if you override this method in a derived class, make sure to call this
    // routine because it handles translation of accelerators...
    //
    virtual BOOL       PreProcessMsg(MSG& msg);
    virtual BOOL       IdleAction(long idleCount);
    virtual BOOL       HoldFocusHWnd(HWND hWndLose, HWND hWndGain);

    int                GetId() const {return Attr.Id;}
    TWindow*           ChildWithId(int id) const;

    virtual void       SetParent(TWindow* newParent);
    virtual BOOL       SetDocTitle(LPCSTR docname, int index);

    void               Show(int showCmd);
    void               SetCaption(const char far* title);
    void               GetWindowTextTitle();
    void               GetHWndState();
    BOOL               SetCursor(TModule* module, TResId resId);

    void               SetBkgndColor(DWORD color) {BkgndColor = color;}

    virtual BOOL       CanClose();

    //
    // forwards the current event to "hWnd" using either PostMessage() or
    // SendMessage(). Owl window version calls directly to window proc on send.
    //
    LRESULT            ForwardMessage(HWND hWnd, BOOL send = TRUE);
```

continues

continued

```
    LRESULT             ForwardMessage(BOOL send = TRUE);


    //
    // send message to all children
    //
    void                ChildBroadcastMessage(UINT msg, WPARAM wParam=0, LPARAM
lParam=0);


    //
    // Called from StdWndProc to allow exceptions to be caught and suspended.
    // Calls HandleMessage from within try block. Catches and suspends all
    // exceptions before returning to Windows (Windows is not exception safe).
    //
    LRESULT             ReceiveMessage(UINT   msg,
                                WPARAM wParam = 0,
                                LPARAM lParam = 0);


    //
    // Call a Window's window proc to handle a message. Similar to SendMessage
    // but more direct.
    //
    LRESULT             HandleMessage(UINT   msg,
                                WPARAM wParam = 0,
                                LPARAM lParam = 0);


    //
    // virtual functions called to handle a message, and to deal with an
    // unhandled message in a default way.
    //
    virtual LRESULT   WindowProc(UINT msg, WPARAM wParam, LPARAM lParam);
    virtual LRESULT   DefWindowProc(UINT msg, WPARAM wParam, LPARAM lParam);


    //
    // called by WindowProc() to handle WM_COMMANDs
    //
    // "id"          - specifies the identifier of the menu item or control
    //
    // "hWndCtl"     - specifies the control sending the message if the message
    //                 is from a control; otherwise it is 0
    //
    // "notifyCode" - specifies the notification message if the message is from
    //                 a control. if the message is from an accelerator, it is 1.
    //                 if the message is from a menu, it is 0
    //
    virtual LRESULT   EvCommand(UINT id, HWND hWndCtl, UINT notifyCode);


    //
    // called by WindowProc() to handle WM_COMMAND_ENABLE
    //
    virtual void      EvCommandEnable(TCommandEnabler& ce);
```

```
//
// default processing, deals with special cases or calling DefWindowProc
//
LRESULT          DefaultProcessing();


//
// Paint function called by base classes when responding to WM_PAINT
//
virtual void     Paint(TDC& dc, BOOL erase, TRect& rect);


//
// transfer buffer
//
void             SetTransferBuffer(void* transferBuffer)
                     {TransferBuffer = transferBuffer;}
virtual UINT     Transfer(void* buffer, TTransferDirection direction);
virtual void     TransferData(TTransferDirection direction);


//
// installs the thunk as the window function and saves the previous window
// function in "DefaultProc"
//
void             SubclassWindowFunction();


//
// Encapsulated HWND functions inline
//


//
// allow a TWindow& to be used as an HWND in Windows API calls
//
operator         HWND() const {return HWindow;}
BOOL             IsWindow() const {return ::IsWindow(HWindow);}


//
// messages
//
LRESULT          SendMessage(UINT    msg,
                             WPARAM wParam = 0,
                             LPARAM lParam = 0);
LRESULT          SendDlgItemMessage(int     childId,
                                    UINT    msg,
                                    WPARAM wParam = 0,
                                    LPARAM lParam = 0);
BOOL             PostMessage(UINT    msg,
                             WPARAM wParam = 0,
                             LPARAM lParam = 0);
static HWND      GetCapture();
HWND             SetCapture();
static void      ReleaseCapture();
```

continues

continued

```
static HWND     GetFocus();
HWND            SetFocus();
BOOL            IsWindowEnabled() const;
BOOL            EnableWindow(BOOL enable);
void            SetRedraw(BOOL redraw);


//
// window coordinates, dimensions...
//
void            ScreenToClient(TPoint& point) const;
void            MapWindowPoints(HWND    hWndTo,
                                TPoint* points,
                                int     count) const;
void            GetClientRect(TRect& rect) const;
TRect           GetClientRect() const;
static HWND     WindowFromPoint(const TPoint& point);
HWND            ChildWindowFromPoint(const TPoint& point) const;
void            ClientToScreen(TPoint& point) const;
void            GetWindowRect(TRect& rect) const;
TRect           GetWindowRect() const;
static void     AdjustWindowRect(TRect& rect, DWORD style, BOOL menu);
static void     AdjustWindowRectEx(TRect& rect, DWORD style,
                                BOOL  menu,  DWORD exStyle);


//
// window and class Words and Longs, window properties
//
long            GetClassName(char far* className, int maxCount) const;
long            GetClassLong(int index) const;
long            SetClassLong(int index, long newLong);
WORD            GetClassWord(int index) const;
WORD            SetClassWord(int index, WORD newWord);
long            GetWindowLong(int index) const;
long            SetWindowLong(int index, long newLong);
WORD            GetWindowWord(int index) const;
WORD            SetWindowWord(int index, WORD newWord);
int             EnumProps(PROPENUMPROC proc);
HANDLE          GetProp(WORD atom) const;
HANDLE          RemoveProp(WORD atom) const;
BOOL            SetProp(WORD atom, HANDLE data) const;
HANDLE          GetProp(const char far* str) const;
HANDLE          RemoveProp(const char far* str) const;
BOOL            SetProp(const char far* str, HANDLE data) const;


//
// window placement(X,Y) and display
//
BOOL            MoveWindow(int x, int y, int w, int h, BOOL repaint = FALSE);
BOOL            MoveWindow(const TRect& rect, BOOL repaint = FALSE);
BOOL            ShowWindow(int cmdShow);
```

```
    void            ShowOwnedPopups(BOOL show);
    BOOL            IsWindowVisible() const;
    BOOL            IsZoomed() const;
    BOOL            IsIconic() const;
    int             GetWindowTextLength() const;
    int             GetWindowText(char far* str, int maxCount) const;
    void            SetWindowText(const char far* str);
    BOOL            GetWindowPlacement(WINDOWPLACEMENT* place) const;
    BOOL            SetWindowPlacement(const WINDOWPLACEMENT* place);

    //
    // window positioning(Z), sibling relationships
    //
    void            BringWindowToTop();
    static HWND     GetActiveWindow();
    HWND            SetActiveWindow();
    static HWND     GetDesktopWindow();
#if !defined(__WIN32__)
    static HWND     GetSysModalWindow();
    HWND            SetSysModalWindow();
#endif
    HWND            GetLastActivePopup() const;
    HWND            GetNextWindow(UINT dirFlag) const;
    HWND            GetTopWindow() const;
    HWND            GetWindow(UINT cmd) const;
    BOOL            SetWindowPos(HWND          hWndInsertAfter,
                                const TRect& rect,
                                UINT         flags);
    BOOL            SetWindowPos(HWND hWndInsertAfter,
                                int x, int y, int w, int h,
                                UINT flags);

    //
    // window painting: invalidating, validating & updating
    //
    void            Invalidate(BOOL erase = TRUE);
    void            InvalidateRect(const TRect& rect, BOOL erase = TRUE);
    void            InvalidateRgn(HRGN hRgn, BOOL erase = TRUE);
    void            Validate();
    void            ValidateRect(const TRect& rect);
    void            ValidateRgn(HRGN hRgn);
    void            UpdateWindow();
    BOOL            FlashWindow(BOOL invert);
    BOOL            GetUpdateRect(TRect& rect, BOOL erase = TRUE) const;
    BOOL            GetUpdateRgn(TRegion& rgn, BOOL erase = TRUE) const;
    BOOL            LockWindowUpdate();
    BOOL            RedrawWindow(TRect* update,
                                HRGN   hUpdateRgn,
                                UINT   redrawFlags = RDW_INVALIDATE |
RDW_UPDATENOW | RDW_ERASE);
```

continues

continued

```
//
// scrolling and scrollbars
//
int             GetScrollPos(int bar) const;
int             SetScrollPos(int bar, int pos, BOOL redraw = TRUE);
void            GetScrollRange(int bar, int& minPos, int& maxPos) const;
void            SetScrollRange(int  bar,
                              int  minPos,
                              int  maxPos,
                              BOOL redraw = TRUE);
void            ShowScrollBar(int bar, BOOL show = TRUE);
void            ScrollWindow(int          dx,
                             int          dy,
                             const TRect far* scroll = 0,
                             const TRect far* clip = 0);
void            ScrollWindowEx(int              dx,
                               int              dy,
                               const TRect far* scroll = 0,
                               const TRect far* clip = 0,
                               HRGN             hUpdateRgn = 0,
                               TRect far*       update = 0,
                               UINT             flags = 0);


//
// parent/child with Ids
//
int             GetDlgCtrlID() const;
HWND            GetDlgItem(int childId) const;
UINT            GetDlgItemInt(int   childId,
                             BOOL* translated = 0,
                             BOOL  isSigned = TRUE) const;
void            SetDlgItemInt(int   childId,
                             UINT value,
                             BOOL isSigned = TRUE) const;
int             GetDlgItemText(int        childId,
                              char far* text,
                              int        max) const;
void            SetDlgItemText(int childId, const char far* text) const;
UINT            IsDlgButtonChecked(int buttonId) const;
HWND            GetParent() const;
BOOL            IsChild(HWND) const;
HWND            GetNextDlgGroupItem(HWND hWndCtrl,
                                  BOOL previous = FALSE) const;
HWND            GetNextDlgTabItem(HWND HWndCtrl,
                                 BOOL previous = FALSE) const;
void            CheckDlgButton(int buttonId, UINT check);
void            CheckRadioButton(int firstButtonId,
                               int lastButtonId,
                               int checkButtonId);
```

```
//
// menus and menubar
//
HMENU           GetMenu() const;
HMENU           GetSystemMenu(BOOL revert = FALSE) const;
BOOL            SetMenu(HMENU hMenu);
BOOL            HiliteMenuItem(HMENU hMenu, UINT idItem, UINT hilite);
void            DrawMenuBar();

//
// clipboard
//
TClipboard&     OpenClipboard();

//
// timer
//
BOOL            KillTimer(UINT timerId);
UINT            SetTimer(UINT timerId, UINT timeout, TIMERPROC proc = 0);

//
// caret, cursor, font
//
void            CreateCaret(HBITMAP hBitmap);
void            CreateCaret(BOOL isGray, int width, int height);
static UINT     GetCaretBlinkTime();
static void     GetCaretPos(TPoint& point);
void            HideCaret();
static void     SetCaretBlinkTime(WORD milliSecs);
static void     SetCaretPos(int x, int y);
static void     SetCaretPos(const TPoint& pos);
void            ShowCaret();
static void     DestroyCaret();
static void     GetCursorPos(TPoint& pos);
void            SetWindowFont(HFONT font, BOOL redraw);
HFONT           GetWindowFont();

//
// hot keys
//
#if defined(__WIN32__)
  BOOL          RegisterHotKey(int  idHotKey,
                               UINT modifiers,
                               UINT virtKey);
  BOOL          UnregisterHotKey(int idHotKey);
#endif

//
// Misc
//
```

continues

continued

```
  BOOL              WinHelp(const char far* helpFile,
                        UINT            command,
                        DWORD           data);
  int               MessageBox(const char far* text,
                           const char far* caption = 0,
                           UINT           type = MB_OK);
#if defined(__WIN32__)
  HANDLE            GetWindowTask() const;
#else
  HTASK             GetWindowTask() const;
#endif
  void              DragAcceptFiles(BOOL accept);

protected:
  //
  // these events are processed by TWindow
  //
  void              EvClose();
  int               EvCreate(CREATESTRUCT far& createStruct);
  void              EvDestroy();
  LRESULT           EvCompareItem(UINT ctrlId, COMPAREITEMSTRUCT far&
compareInfo);
  void              EvDeleteItem(UINT ctrlId, DELETEITEMSTRUCT far&
deleteInfo);
  void              EvDrawItem(UINT ctrlId, DRAWITEMSTRUCT far& drawInfo);
  void              EvMeasureItem(UINT ctrlId, MEASUREITEMSTRUCT far&
measureInfo);
  void              EvHScroll(UINT scrollCode, UINT thumbPos, HWND hWndCtl);
  void              EvVScroll(UINT scrollCode, UINT thumbPos, HWND hWndCtl);
  void              EvMove(TPoint& clientOrigin);
  void              EvNCDestroy();
  BOOL              EvQueryEndSession();
  void              EvSize(UINT sizeType, TSize& size);
  void              EvLButtonDown(UINT modKeys, TPoint& point);
  BOOL              EvEraseBkgnd(HDC);
  void              EvPaint();
  void              EvSysColorChange();
  LRESULT           EvWin32CtlColor(WPARAM, LPARAM);

  void              CmExit();  // CM_EXIT


  //
  // input validation message handler
  //
  void              EvChildInvalid(HWND hWnd);


  //
  // system messages
  //
  void              EvCompacting(UINT compactRatio);
```

```
    void            EvDevModeChange(char far* devName);
    void            EvEnable(BOOL enabled);
    void            EvEndSession(BOOL endSession);
    void            EvFontChange();
    int             EvPower(UINT powerEvent);
    void            EvSysCommand(UINT cmdType, TPoint& point);
    void            EvSystemError(UINT error);
    void            EvTimeChange();
    void            EvTimer(UINT timerId);
    void            EvWinIniChange(char far* section);

    //
    // window manager messages
    //
    void            EvActivate(UINT active,
                               BOOL minimized,
                               HWND hWndOther /* may be 0 */);
#if defined(__WIN32__)
    void            EvActivateApp(BOOL active, HANDLE threadId);
#else
    void            EvActivateApp(BOOL active, HTASK hTask);
#endif
    void            EvCancelMode();
    void            EvGetMinMaxInfo(MINMAXINFO far& minmaxinfo);
    void            EvIconEraseBkgnd(HDC hDC);
    void            EvKillFocus(HWND hWndGetFocus /* may be 0 */);
    UINT            EvMouseActivate(HWND hWndTopLevel,
                                    UINT hitTestCode,
                                    UINT msg);
#if defined(__WIN32__)
    void            EvInputFocus(BOOL gainingFocus);
    void            EvOtherWindowCreated(HWND hWndOther);
    void            EvOtherWindowDestroyed(HWND hWndOther);
    void            EvPaintIcon();
#endif
    void            EvParentNotify(UINT event,
                                   UINT childHandleOrX,
                                   UINT childIDOrY);
    HANDLE          EvQueryDragIcon();
    BOOL            EvQueryOpen();
    BOOL            EvSetCursor(HWND hWndCursor,
                               UINT hitTest,
                               UINT mouseMsg);
    void            EvSetFocus(HWND hWndLostFocus /* may be 0 */);
    void            EvShowWindow(BOOL show, UINT status);
    void            EvWindowPosChanged(WINDOWPOS far& windowPos);
    void            EvWindowPosChanging(WINDOWPOS far& windowPos);

    //
    // keyboard input
```

continues

continued

```
    //
    void            EvChar(UINT key, UINT repeatCount, UINT flags);
    void            EvDeadChar(UINT deadKey, UINT repeatCount, UINT flags);
    void            EvKeyDown(UINT key, UINT repeatCount, UINT flags);
    void            EvKeyUp(UINT key, UINT repeatCount, UINT flags);
    void            EvSysChar(UINT key, UINT repeatCount, UINT flags);
    void            EvSysDeadChar(UINT key, UINT repeatCount, UINT flags);
    void            EvSysKeyDown(UINT key, UINT repeatCount, UINT flags);
    void            EvSysKeyUp(UINT key, UINT repeatCount, UINT flags);

    //
    // hot keys
    //
#if defined(__WIN32__)
    void            EvHotKey(int idHotKey);
#endif

    //
    // controls
    //
    HBRUSH          EvCtlColor(HDC hDC, HWND hWndChild, UINT ctlType);

    //
    // mouse input
    //
    void            EvLButtonDblClk(UINT modKeys, TPoint& point);
    void            EvLButtonUp(UINT modKeys, TPoint& point);
    void            EvMButtonDblClk(UINT modKeys, TPoint& point);
    void            EvMButtonDown(UINT modKeys, TPoint& point);
    void            EvMButtonUp(UINT modKeys, TPoint& point);
    void            EvMouseMove(UINT modKeys, TPoint& point);
    void            EvRButtonDblClk(UINT modKeys, TPoint& point);
    void            EvRButtonDown(UINT modKeys, TPoint& point);
    void            EvRButtonUp(UINT modKeys, TPoint& point);

    //
    // menu related messages
    //
    void            EvInitMenu(HMENU hMenu);
    void            EvInitMenuPopup(HMENU hPopupMenu,
                            UINT  index,
                            BOOL  sysMenu);
    UINT            EvMenuChar(UINT nChar, UINT menuType, HMENU hMenu);
    void            EvMenuSelect(UINT menuItemId, UINT flags, HMENU hMenu);

    //
    // dialog messages
    //
    void            EvEnterIdle(UINT source, HWND hWndDlg);
    UINT            EvGetDlgCode();
```

```
//
// print manager messages
//
void              EvSpoolerStatus(UINT jobStatus, UINT jobsLeft);


//
// clipboard messages
//
void              EvAskCBFormatName(UINT bufLen, char far* buffer);
void              EvChangeCBChain(HWND hWndRemoved, HWND hWndNext);
void              EvDrawClipboard();
void              EvDestroyClipboard();
void              EvHScrollClipboard(HWND hWndCBViewer,
                                UINT scrollCode,
                                UINT pos);
void              EvPaintClipboard(HWND hWnd, HANDLE hPaintStruct);
void              EvRenderAllFormats();
void              EvRenderFormat(UINT dataFormat);
void              EvSizeClipboard(HWND hWndViewer, HANDLE hRect);
void              EvVScrollClipboard(HWND hWndCBViewer,
                                UINT scrollCode,
                                UINT pos);


//
// palette manager messages
//
void              EvPaletteChanged(HWND hWndPalChg);
void              EvPaletteIsChanging(HWND hWndPalChg);
BOOL              EvQueryNewPalette();


//
// drag-n-drop messages
//
void              EvDropFiles(TDropInfo dropInfo);


//
// list box messages
//
int               EvCharToItem(UINT key, HWND hWndListBox, UINT caretPos);
int               EvVKeyToItem(UINT key, HWND hWndListBox, UINT caretPos);


//
// non-client messages
//
BOOL              EvNCActivate(BOOL active);
UINT              EvNCCalcSize(BOOL calcValidRects, NCCALCSIZE_PARAMS far& params);
BOOL              EvNCCreate(CREATESTRUCT far& createStruct);
UINT              EvNCHitTest(TPoint& point);
void              EvNCLButtonDblClk(UINT hitTest, TPoint& point);
void              EvNCLButtonDown(UINT hitTest, TPoint& point);
```

continues

continued

```
    void            EvNCLButtonUp(UINT hitTest, TPoint& point);
    void            EvNCMButtonDblClk(UINT hitTest, TPoint& point);
    void            EvNCMButtonDown(UINT hitTest, TPoint& point);
    void            EvNCMButtonUp(UINT hitTest, TPoint& point);
    void            EvNCMouseMove(UINT hitTest, TPoint& point);
    void            EvNCPaint();
    void            EvNCRButtonDblClk(UINT hitTest, TPoint& point);
    void            EvNCRButtonDown(UINT hitTest, TPoint& point);
    void            EvNCRButtonUp(UINT hitTest, TPoint& point);

protected:
    void*           TransferBuffer;
    HACCEL          hAccel;
    TModule*        CursorModule;
    TResId          CursorResId;
    HCURSOR         HCursor;
    DWORD           BkgndColor;


    //
    // Constructor & subsequent initializer for use with virtual derivations
    // Immediate derivatives must call Init() before constructions are done.
    //
    TWindow();
    void            Init(TWindow* parent, const char far* title, TModule* module);

    virtual void    GetWindowClass(WNDCLASS& wndClass);
    virtual char far* GetClassName();

    virtual void    SetupWindow();
    virtual void    CleanupWindow();

    void            DispatchScroll(UINT scrollCode, UINT thumbPos, HWND hWndCtrl);

    void            LoadAcceleratorTable();
    virtual void    RemoveChild(TWindow* child);

private:
    WNDPROC         Thunk;          // Thunk that load 'this' into registers
    TApplication*   Application;    // Application that this window belongs to
    TModule*        Module;         // default module used for getting resources
    DWORD           Flags;
    WORD            CreateOrder;
    TWindow*        ChildList;
    TWindow*        SiblingList;
    DWORD           UniqueId;

    static DWORD    LastUniqueId;

    void            Init(TWindow* parent, TModule* module);
    BOOL            OrderIsI(TWindow* win, void* position);
    BOOL            CreateZeroChild(TWindow* win, void* );
```

```
    void              AssignCreateOrder();
    void              AddChild(TWindow* child);
    int               IndexOf(TWindow* child);
    TWindow*          At(int position);

    void              SetUniqueId();

    //
    // hidden to prevent accidental copying or assignment
    //
    TWindow(const TWindow&);
    TWindow& operator =(const TWindow&);

  DECLARE_RESPONSE_TABLE(TWindow);
  DECLARE_STREAMABLE(_OWLCLASS, TWindow, 1);
}; // end of class TWindow
```

The TWindow class, with its hefty declaration, supports member functions that
perform the following kinds of operations:

- Iterating through some or all of the child windows to manipulate these
  windows.

- Setting and querying the window's flags.

- Enabling and disabling the automatic creation of child windows, such
  as controls.

- Transferring data to and from a child window.

- Accessing the owner-application class instance.

- Creating and destroying elements of a window.

- Managing the processing of Windows messages sent to windows.

- Manipulating the appearance of the colors and cursor in windows.

- Managing the location, movement, caption, visibility, and appearance
  (minimized, maximized, and normal) of windows.

- Updating, redrawing, and repainting the contents of windows.

- Setting and querying the scrolling of the contents of the windows.

- Obtaining the ID of parent and child windows.

- Setting the values to the child windows (used especially with the
  controls in dialog boxes).

- Managing the menu bar and the menu items.

- Managing the caret, fonts, and cursor in windows.

- Handling a wide variety of events common to all kinds of windows. Among these events are ones involved in creating, closing, destroying, scrolling, moving, repainting, and redrawing windows.

- Managing keyboard and mouse input using sets of special event-handlers.

- Handling Clipboard, palette-management, drag-and-drop, list box, and nonclient messages.

The Frame Windows

The TFrameWindow class is a descendant of TWindow and offers the operations for a frame window. The declaration of the TFrameWindow class is as follows:

```
class _OWLCLASS TFrameWindow : virtual public TWindow {
  public:
    BOOL            KeyboardHandling;

    TFrameWindow(TWindow*        parent,
                 const char far* title = 0,
                 TWindow*        clientWnd = 0,
                 BOOL            shrinkToClient = FALSE,
                 TModule*        module = 0);

    TFrameWindow(HWND hWnd, TModule* module = 0);
    ~TFrameWindow();

    //
    // Menubar manipulating functions
    //
    virtual BOOL        AssignMenu(TResId menuResId);
    virtual BOOL        SetMenu(HMENU newMenu);
    void                SetMenuDescr(const TMenuDescr& menuDescr);
    const TMenuDescr*   GetMenuDescr() const {return MenuDescr;}
    BOOL                MergeMenu(const TMenuDescr& childMenuDescr);
    BOOL                RestoreMenu();

    BOOL                SetIcon(TModule* iconModule, TResId iconResId);

    virtual TWindow*    GetClientWindow();
    virtual TWindow*    SetClientWindow(TWindow* clientWnd);

    //
    // sets flag indicating that the receiver has requested "keyboard
    // handling" (translation of keyboard input into control selections)
```

```
//
void            EnableKBHandler() {KeyboardHandling = TRUE;}

//
// override virtual functions defined by TWindow
//
BOOL            PreProcessMsg(MSG& msg);
BOOL            IdleAction(long idleCount);
BOOL            HoldFocusHWnd(HWND hWndLose, HWND hWndGain);
BOOL            SetDocTitle(LPCSTR docname, int index);

protected:
    HWND        HWndRestoreFocus;
    TWindow*    ClientWnd;
    int         DocTitleIndex;

    //
    // Constructor & subsequent initializer for use with virtual derivations
    // Immediate derivatives must call Init() before constructions are done.
    //
    TFrameWindow();
    void        Init(TWindow* clientWnd, BOOL shrinkToClient);

    //
    // extra processing for commands: starts with the focus window and gives
    // it and its parent windows an opportunity to handle the command
    //
    LRESULT     EvCommand(UINT id, HWND hWndCtl, UINT notifyCode);
    void        EvCommandEnable(TCommandEnabler& ce);

    //
    // message response functions
    //
    void        EvActivate(UINT active, BOOL minimized, HWND hWndOther);
    void        EvInitMenuPopup(HMENU hPopupMenu,
                                UINT  index,
                                BOOL  sysMenu);
    void        EvPaint();
    BOOL        EvEraseBkgnd(HDC);
    HANDLE      EvQueryDragIcon();
    void        EvSetFocus(HWND hWndLostFocus);
    void        EvSize(UINT sizeType, TSize& size);
    void        EvParentNotify(UINT event,
                               UINT childHandleOrX,
                               UINT childIDOrY);

    //
    // override virtual function defined by TWindow
    //
    void        SetupWindow();
```

continues

continued

```
private:
   TMenuDescr*  MenuDescr;
   TModule*     IconModule;
   TResId       IconResId;

   void             Init(TWindow* clientWnd);
   BOOL             ResizeClientWindow(TSize& size);
   TWindow*         FirstChildWithTab();

   //
   // hidden to prevent accidental copying or assignment
   //
   TFrameWindow(const TFrameWindow&);
   TFrameWindow& operator =(const TFrameWindow&);

 DECLARE_RESPONSE_TABLE(TFrameWindow);
 DECLARE_STREAMABLE(_OWLCLASS, TFrameWindow, 1);
};
```

The TFrameWindow class declares member functions to support the following operations:

- Manipulating the menu bar.

- Enabling the keyboard handler, which translates keystrokes into commands that select child controls.

- Offering specific message-processing operations to suit the needs of frame windows.

- Managing responses to events, such as repainting and resizing, in a manner appropriate for frame windows.

The MDI Windows

The OWL classes support the operations of MDI (Multiple Document Interface) windows using the TMDIFrame and TMDIChild classes. These classes work with the TMDIClient class (that is a descendant of TWindow class, but not part of this set of classes) to support MDI frame windows and child windows.

The Decorated Windows

The OWL classes decorate, so to speak, frame windows and MDI frame windows with tool bars, status bars, and message bars. The decorated window classes include TDecoratedFrame and TDecoratedMDIFrame.

The Control Classes

Controls enable you to interact with various kinds of windows. Without controls, the old ways of interacting with DOS programs would still be common. The OWL classes support three kinds of controls: standard controls, widgets, and decorations. Here is the outline that represents the control class subhierarchy:

```
+ TControl
    + TStatic
        + TEdit
            + TEditSearch
                - TEditFile
    + TButton
        + TCheckBox
            - TRadioButton
    - TVbxControl
    - TGroupBox
    - TGauge
    + TScrollBar
        + TSlider
            - THSlider
            - TVSlider
        + TScrollBarData
    + TListBox
        - TListBoxData
        + TComboBox
            - TComboBoxData
```

The Standard Windows Controls

The standard Windows controls include the static text controls, edit boxes, command buttons (also called pushbuttons), list boxes, combo boxes, scroll bars, check boxes, radio controls, and group boxes. This book covers these controls, commonly used in major Windows applications.

The TStatic Class

The TStatic class models static text used to label other controls, such as edit boxes, list boxes, and combo boxes. The declaration of the TStatic class is the following:

```
class _OWLCLASS TStatic : public TControl {
  public:
    UINT  TextLen;
```

continues

continued

```
TStatic(TWindow*        parent,
        int             id,
        const char far* title,
        int x, int y, int w, int h,
        UINT            textLen,
        TModule*        module = 0);

TStatic(TWindow*   parent,
        int        resourceId,
        UINT       textLen,
        TModule*   module = 0);

//
// returns the length of the control's text
//
int   GetTextLen() {return ::GetWindowTextLength(HWindow);}

//
// fills the passed string with the text of the associated text
// control. returns the number of characters copied
//
int   GetText(char far* str, int maxChars)
        {return ::GetWindowText(HWindow, str, maxChars);}

//
// sets the contents of the associated static text control to
// the passed string
//
void  SetText(const char far* str) {::SetWindowText(HWindow, str);}

//
// clears the text of the associated static text control
//
void  Clear() {SetText("");}

//
// Override TWindow virtual member functions
//
UINT  Transfer(void* buffer, TTransferDirection direction);

protected:
//
// Override TWindow virtual member functions
//
char far* GetClassName();

private:
//
// hidden to prevent accidental copying or assignment
//
TStatic(const TStatic&);
```

```
    TStatic& operator =(const TStatic&);

  DECLARE_STREAMABLE(_OWLCLASS, TStatic, 1);
};
```

The TStatic class declares member functions that set and query the control's text and query the length of the control's text.

The TButton Class

The TButton class, a descendant of the TControl class, encapsulates the operations of the command button control. This control is perhaps the most popular control because with it you can make things happen in an application. The declaration of the TButton class is as follows:

```
class _OWLCLASS TButton : public TControl {
  public:
    BOOL  IsDefPB;

    TButton(TWindow*      parent,
            int           id,
            const char far* text,
            int X, int Y, int W, int H,
            BOOL          isDefault = FALSE,
            TModule*      module = 0);

    TButton(TWindow *parent, int resourceId, TModule* module = 0);

  protected:
    BOOL  IsCurrentDefPB;

    //
    // message response functions
    //
    UINT      EvGetDlgCode();
    LRESULT   BMSetStyle(WPARAM, LPARAM);

    //
    // Override TWindow member functions
    //
    char far* GetClassName();
    void      SetupWindow();

  private:
    //
    // hidden to prevent accidental copying or assignment
    //
    TButton(const TButton&);
    TButton& operator=(const TButton&);
```

continues

continued

```
    DECLARE_RESPONSE_TABLE(TButton);
    DECLARE_STREAMABLE(_OWLCLASS, TButton, 1);
};
```

The instances of the TButton class interact with the application by emitting Windows messages that are intercepted and handled by the parent window. You can still manipulate the caption, visibility, and enabled state of a pushbutton using inherited member functions.

The TEdit Class

The TEdit class, a descendant of the TStatic class, encapsulates the operations of single-line and multiline edit controls. The declaration of the TEdit class is as follows:

```
class _OWLCLASS TEdit : public TStatic {
  public:
    TEdit(TWindow*        parent,
          int             id,
          const char far* text,
          int x, int y, int w, int h,
          UINT            textLen = 0,
          BOOL            multiline = FALSE,
          TModule*        module = 0);

    TEdit(TWindow*   parent,
          int        resourceId,
          UINT       textLen = 0,
          TModule*   module = 0);

    ~TEdit();

    //
    // Accessing
    //
    int     GetNumLines() const;
    int     GetLineLength(int lineNumber) const;
    BOOL    GetLine(char far* str, int strSize, int lineNumber) const;
    void    GetSubText(char far* str, UINT startPos, UINT endPos) const;
    void    GetSelection(UINT& startPos, UINT& endPos) const;

    BOOL    IsModified() const;
    void    ClearModify() {HandleMessage(EM_SETMODIFY);}

    int     GetLineFromPos(UINT charPos) const;
    UINT    GetLineIndex(int lineNumber) const;

    //
    // Lock and unlock this edit control's buffer. Allows direct access to the
```

```
// text in the edit control.
//
char far* LockBuffer(UINT newSize = 0);
void    UnlockBuffer(const char far* buffer, BOOL updateHandle = FALSE);

//
// operations
//
BOOL    DeleteSubText(UINT startPos, UINT endPos);
BOOL    DeleteLine(int lineNumber);
BOOL    DeleteSelection();
BOOL    SetSelection(UINT startPos, UINT endPos);

void    Scroll(int horizontalUnit, int verticalUnit);
void    Insert(const char far* str);
int     Search(UINT startPos, const char far* text,
               BOOL caseSensitive=FALSE, BOOL wholeWord=FALSE,
               BOOL up=FALSE);

void    GetRect(TRect& frmtRect) const;
void    SetRect(const TRect& frmtRect);
void    SetRectNP(const TRect& frmtRect);
void    FormatLines(BOOL addEOL);
void    SetTabStops(int numTabs, const int far* tabs);

HLOCAL  GetHandle() const;
void    SetHandle(HLOCAL localMem);

void    SetPasswordChar(UINT ch) {HandleMessage(EM_SETPASSWORDCHAR, ch);}

int     GetFirstVisibleLine() const;
void    SetReadOnly(BOOL readOnly);
UINT    GetPasswordChar() const;

EDITWORDBREAKPROC GetWordBreakProc() const;
void    SetWordBreakProc(EDITWORDBREAKPROC proc);

//
// clipboard operations
//
BOOL    CanUndo() const;
void    EmptyUndoBuffer() {HandleMessage(EM_EMPTYUNDOBUFFER);}
void    Undo() {HandleMessage(WM_UNDO);}
void    Paste() {HandleMessage(WM_PASTE);}
void    Copy() {HandleMessage(WM_COPY);}
void    Cut() {HandleMessage(WM_CUT);}

BOOL    IsValid(BOOL reportErr = FALSE);
void    SetValidator(TValidator* validator);
void    ValidatorError();

protected:
```

continues

continued

```
    //
    // command response functions
    //
    void    CmEditCut()    {Cut();}              // CM_EDITCUT
    void    CmEditCopy()   {Copy();}             // CM_EDITCOPY
    void    CmEditPaste()  {Paste();}            // CM_EDITPASTE
    void    CmEditDelete() {DeleteSelection();}  // CM_EDITDELETE
    void    CmEditClear()  {Clear();}            // CM_EDITCLEAR
    void    CmEditUndo()   {Undo();}             // CM_EDITUNDO


    //
    // command enabler functions
    //
    void CmSelectEnable(TCommandEnabler& commandHandler);
    void CmPasteEnable(TCommandEnabler& commandHandler);
    void CmCharsEnable(TCommandEnabler& commandHandler);
    void CmModEnable(TCommandEnabler& commandHandler);


    //
    // child id notification handled at the child
    //
    void    ENErrSpace();  // EN_ERRSPACE


    //
    // Override TWindow virtual member functions
    //
    char far* GetClassName();
    void      SetupWindow();


    //
    // Input validation object
    //
    TValidator*  Validator;

    void        EvChar(UINT key, UINT repeatCount, UINT flags);
    void        EvKeyDown(UINT key, UINT repeatCount, UINT flags);
    UINT        EvGetDlgCode();
    void        EvKillFocus(HWND hWndGetFocus);
    BOOL        CanClose();


    //
    // handler for input validation message sent by parent
    //
    void        EvChildInvalid(HWND) {ValidatorError();}

private:
    //
    // hidden to prevent accidental copying or assignment
    //
    TEdit(const TEdit&);
    TEdit& operator =(const TEdit&);
```

```
  DECLARE_RESPONSE_TABLE(TEdit);
  DECLARE_STREAMABLE(_OWLCLASS, TEdit, 1);
};
```

The nontrivial declaration of the TEdit class indicates that it brings a lot of editing power. The class has member functions to manipulate selected text or unselected text. The class operations include the popular text editing operations of cut, paste, copy, and clear. In addition, the TEdit class offers member functions that perform nontrivial character and line queries.

The TCheckBox Class

The TCheckBox class, a descendant of TButton, models the three-state (the three states are checked, unchecked, and grayed) check box. This control commonly offers Boolean selections. The declaration of the TCheckBox class is as follows:

```
class _OWLCLASS TCheckBox : public TButton {
  public:
    TGroupBox*  Group;

    TCheckBox(TWindow*         parent,
              int              id,
              const char far* title,
              int x, int y, int w, int h,
              TGroupBox*       group,
              TModule*         module = 0);

    TCheckBox(TWindow*   parent,
              int        resourceId,
              TGroupBox* group = 0,
              TModule*   module = 0);

    void      Check() {SetCheck(BF_CHECKED);}
    void      Uncheck() {SetCheck(BF_UNCHECKED);}
    void      Toggle();

    UINT      GetCheck() const;
    void      SetCheck(UINT check);

    UINT      GetState() const;
    void      SetState(UINT state) {HandleMessage(BM_SETSTATE, state);}

    void      SetStyle(UINT style, BOOL redraw);

    //
    // Override TWindow virtual member functions
    //
    UINT      Transfer(void* buffer, TTransferDirection direction);
```

continues

continued

```
protected:
  //
  // override TButton's processing so drawable check boxes and radio
  // buttons work properly
  //
  UINT        EvGetDlgCode() {return (UINT)DefaultProcessing();}


  //
  // child id notification
  //
  void        BNClicked();   // BN_CLICKED

  char far*  GetClassName();

private:
  //
  // hidden to prevent accidental copying or assignment
  //
  TCheckBox(const TCheckBox&);
  TCheckBox& operator =(const TCheckBox&);

DECLARE_RESPONSE_TABLE(TCheckBox);
DECLARE_STREAMABLE(_OWLCLASS, TCheckBox, 1);
};
```

The TCheckBox class offers member functions that set and query the state of the check box controls and also set the style of the control.

The TRadioButton Class

The TRadioButton class, a descendant of the TCheckBox class, models the radio button controls. Usually, you place two or more radio button controls inside a group box control. With this arrangement, you can logically and visually group radio buttons so that only one is selected at any time; Windows automatically deselects the previously checked radio button. Thus, grouped radio buttons are mutually exclusive. The declaration of the TRadioButton class is as follows:

```
class _OWLCLASS TRadioButton : public TCheckBox {
  public:
    TRadioButton(TWindow*       parent,
                 int            id,
                 const char far* title,
                 int x, int y, int w, int h,
                 TGroupBox*     group,
                 TModule*       module = 0);


    TRadioButton(TWindow*   parent,
                 int        resourceId,
                 TGroupBox* group,
```

```
                        TModule*    module = 0);

  protected:
    //
    // child id notification handled at the child
    //
    void        BNClicked();  // BN_CLICKED

    char far*  GetClassName();

  private:
    //
    // hidden to prevent accidental copying or assignment
    //
    TRadioButton(const TRadioButton&);
    TRadioButton& operator=(const TRadioButton&);

  DECLARE_RESPONSE_TABLE(TRadioButton);
  DECLARE_STREAMABLE(_OWLCLASS, TRadioButton, 1);
};
```

The TRadioButton class interacts with its parent window by sending it notification messages. The parent window then uses the appropriate message-handling function to respond to the updated radio button selection.

The TGroupBox Class

The TGroupBox class, a descendant of the TControl class, models the group box used to group radio buttons (and sometimes check boxes) logically and visually. The declaration of the TGroupBox class is as follows:

```
class _OWLCLASS TGroupBox : public TControl {
  public:
    BOOL  NotifyParent;

    TGroupBox(TWindow*       parent,
             int            id,
             const char far* text,
             int X, int Y, int W, int H,
             TModule*       module = 0);

    TGroupBox(TWindow* parent, int resourceId, TModule*   module = 0);

    virtual void SelectionChanged(int controlId);

  protected:
    char far*    GetClassName();

  private:
```

continues

continued

```
//
// hidden to prevent accidental copying or assignment
//
TGroupBox(const TGroupBox&);
TGroupBox& operator =(const TGroupBox&);

  DECLARE_STREAMABLE(_OWLCLASS, TGroupBox, 1);
};
```

The TGroupBox class interacts with its parent window by sending it notification messages. The parent window then uses the appropriate message-handling function to respond to the updated radio button selection.

The TListBox Class

The TListBox class, a descendant of the TControl class, models single-selection and multiple-selection list boxes. The advantage of the list box control is that you can select from the offered items without having to remember them and their exact spellings. The declaration of the TListBox class is as follows:

```
class _OWLCLASS TListBox : public TControl {
  public:
    TListBox(TWindow*       parent,
             int            id,
             int x, int y, int w, int h,
             TModule*       module = 0);

    TListBox(TWindow* parent, int resourceId, TModule*   module = 0);

    //
    // list box attributes
    //
    virtual int   GetCount() const;
    virtual int   FindString(const char far* str, int index) const;
    int           FindExactString(const char far* str, int searchIndex) const;
    int           GetTopIndex() const;
    int           SetTopIndex(int index);
    BOOL          SetTabStops(int numTabs, int far* tabs);

    int           GetHorizontalExtent() const;
    void          SetHorizontalExtent(int horzExtent);
    void          SetColumnWidth(int width);
    int           GetCaretIndex() const;
    int           SetCaretIndex(int index, BOOL partScrollOk);

    //
    // query individual list items
    //
```

```
virtual int    GetStringLen(int index) const;
virtual int    GetString(char far* str, int index) const;
virtual DWORD GetItemData(int index) const;
virtual int    SetItemData(int index, DWORD itemData);

int            GetItemRect(int index, TRect& rect) const;
virtual int    GetItemHeight(int index) const;
virtual int    SetItemHeight(int index, int height);

//
// operations on the list box itself
//
virtual void   ClearList();
virtual int    DirectoryList(UINT attrs, const char far* fileSpec);

//
// operations on individual list box items
//
virtual int    AddString(const char far* str);
virtual int    InsertString(const char far* str, int index);
virtual int    DeleteString(int index);

//
// single selection list boxes only (combos overload these)
//
virtual int    GetSelIndex() const;
virtual int    SetSelIndex(int index);
       int     GetSelString(char far* str, int maxChars) const;
       int     SetSelString(const char far* str, int searchIndex);

//
// multiple selection list boxes only
//
int            GetSelCount() const;
int            GetSelStrings(char far** strs, int maxCount,
                            int maxChars) const;
int            SetSelStrings(const char far** prefixes, int numSelections,
                            BOOL shouldSet);
int            GetSelIndexes(int* indexes, int maxCount) const;
int            SetSelIndexes(int* indexes, int numSelections, BOOL shouldSet);
BOOL           GetSel(int index) const;
int            SetSel(int index, BOOL select);
int            SetSelItemRange(BOOL select, int first, int last);

//
// Override TWindow virtual member functions
//
UINT           Transfer(void *buffer, TTransferDirection direction);
```

continues

continued

```
protected:
  //
  // Override TWindow virtual member functions
  //
  char far      *GetClassName();

private:
  //
  // hidden to prevent accidental copying or assignment
  //
  TListBox(const TListBox&);
  TListBox& operator =(const TListBox&);

  DECLARE_STREAMABLE(_OWLCLASS, TListBox, 1);
};
```

The TListBox class offers two sets of member functions to manipulate the list box items. The first set manages single-selection list boxes, whereas the second one handles the multiple-selection version of the control. The operations for the single-selection list boxes include adding, inserting, finding, deleting, choosing, and retrieving the selected string. The operations for the multiple-selection list boxes include obtaining the number of selected items, obtaining the selected items, obtaining the indices of the selected items, selecting noncontiguous items, and selecting a range of items.

The TComboBox Class

The TComboBox class, a descendant of the TListBox class, models the combo box control with its edit box and list box components. The combo box control combines the features of the edit box and list box, enabling you either to select an item from the list box part or to type a new item in the edit box part. The declaration of the TComboBox class is as follows:

```
class _OWLCLASS TComboBox : public TListBox {
  public:
    UINT   TextLen;

    TComboBox(TWindow*      parent,
              int           id,
              int x, int y, int w, int h,
              DWORD         style,
              UINT          textLen,
              TModule*      module = 0);

    TComboBox(TWindow*   parent,
              int        resourceId,
              UINT       textLen = 0,
```

```
                TModule*   module = 0);

    //
    // for combo box's edit control
    //
    int            GetTextLen() const {return GetWindowTextLength();}
    int            GetText(char far* str, int maxChars) const;  // num of chars
copied
    void           SetText(const char far* str);

    int            GetEditSel(int& startPos, int& endPos);
    int            SetEditSel(int startPos, int endPos);  //CB_ERR if no edit
control

    void           Clear();  // clear the text

    //
    // for drop down combo boxes
    //
    void           ShowList(BOOL show);
    void           ShowList() {ShowList(TRUE);}
    void           HideList() {ShowList(FALSE);}

    void           GetDroppedControlRect(TRect& Rect) const;
    BOOL           GetDroppedState() const;
    BOOL           GetExtendedUI() const;
    int            SetExtendedUI(BOOL Extended);

    //
    // Combo's List box virtual functions
    //
    virtual int    AddString(const char far* str);
    virtual int    InsertString(const char far* str, int index);
    virtual int    DeleteString(int index);

    virtual void   ClearList();
    virtual int    DirectoryList(UINT attrs, const char far* fileSpec);

    virtual int    GetCount() const;
    virtual int    FindString(const char far* find, int indexStart) const;

    virtual int    GetStringLen(int index) const;
    virtual int    GetString(char far* str, int index) const;

    virtual int    GetSelIndex() const;
    virtual int    SetSelIndex(int index);
    virtual int    SetSelString(const char far* findStr, int indexStart);
    virtual DWORD  GetItemData(int index) const;
    virtual int    SetItemData(int index, DWORD itemData);

    int            GetItemHeight(int index) const;
```

continues

continued

```
    int             SetItemHeight(int index, int height);

    //
    // Override TWindow virtual member functions
    //
    UINT            Transfer(void* buffer, TTransferDirection direction);

  protected:
    //
    // Override TWindow virtual member functions
    //
    char far*       GetClassName();
    void            SetupWindow();

    //
    // message response functions
    //

  private:
    //
    // hidden to prevent accidental copying or assignment
    //
    TComboBox(const TComboBox&);
    TComboBox& operator =(const TComboBox&);

  DECLARE_STREAMABLE(_OWLCLASS, TComboBox, 1);
};
```

The TComboBox class declares member functions that support operations for the
list box and edit box components.

The Widget Classes

The widget classes are controls that do not rely on API Windows functions and
are built using C++ classes. The ObjectWindows library offers the classes
TGauge, TVSlider, and THSlider to model gauges and sliders.

The Decoration Classes

The decoration classes model special controls that interact with the application users. These controls enable you to select a command, offer the location
to present you with information, or support specialized communications.

The Dialog Box Classes

The group of dialog box classes support both custom and common dialog boxes.
Dialog boxes can be modal or modeless. With them you can interact more

intensely with Windows applications. Modal dialog boxes require that you first close them before you can access any other part of the window or windows in the program. Modeless dialog boxes are less attention demanding. With them, you can access other parts of the window or windows in the application. Modal dialog boxes deal with critical data, whereas modeless dialog boxes do not. Here is the outline for the dialog box subhierarchy:

```
+ TDialog
    - TInputDialog
    - TPrinterAbortDlg
    + TCommonDialog
        - TChooseColorDialog
        - TChooseFontDialog
        - TPrintDialog
        + TOpenSaveDialog
            - TFileOpenDialog
            - TFileSaveDialog
        + TFindReplaceDialog
            - TFindDialog
            - TReplaceDialog
```

The preceding outline also indicates that OWL contains classes that model the common dialog boxes. These dialog boxes enable you to choose a color, select a font, print a document, set up your printer, search for text, and replace text. In addition, OWL offers the TInputDialog to support text input.

The TDialog Class

The root of the dialog box subhierarchy is the TDialog class. This class provides its descendants with the common dialog box operations. In addition, you use this class directly, or you can derive from it new descendants to build dialog boxes with specific behaviors. The declaration of the TDialog class is as follows:

```
class _OWLCLASS TDialog : virtual public TWindow {
  public:
    TDialogAttr   Attr;
    BOOL          IsModal;

    TDialog(TWindow* parent, TResId resId, TModule* module = 0);

    ~TDialog();

    //
    // override this to process messages within the dialog function
    // Return TRUE if message handled, FALSE if not.
    //
    // default behavior is to call EvInitDialog & EvSetFont
```

continues

continued

```
//
virtual BOOL    DialogFunction(UINT message, WPARAM wParam, LPARAM lParam);


//
// override this to process WM_INITDIALOG message
//
// default behavior is to call PerformDlgInit & SetupWindow() and return
// TRUE
//
virtual BOOL    EvInitDialog(HWND hWndFocus);


//
// Initialize dialog controls with contents of RT_DLGINIT
//
BOOL            PerformDlgInit();


//
// override this to process WM_SETFONT
//
virtual void    EvSetFont(HFONT);


//
// create a modeless dialog box, and perform actual create call
//
virtual BOOL    Create();
virtual HWND    DoCreate();


//
// create a modal dialog box, and perform actual modal call
//
virtual int     Execute();
virtual int     DoExecute();


//
// override virtual functions defined by class TWindow
//
BOOL            PreProcessMsg(MSG& msg);
void            CloseWindow(int retValue = IDCANCEL);
void            Destroy(int retValue = IDCANCEL);

void            SetCaption(const char far* title);


//
// returns the handle of the dialog's control with the passed Id
// Obsolete- use TWindow::GetDlgItem(Id)
//
HWND            GetItemHandle(int childId) {return GetDlgItem(childId); }


//
// sends the passed message to the dialog's control which has id DlgItemId
// Obsolete- use TWindow::SendDlgItemMessage()
```

```
//
DWORD SendDlgItemMsg(int ChildId, WORD Msg, WORD WParam, DWORD LParam);

UINT            GetDefaultId() const;
void            SetDefaultId(UINT Id) {HandleMessage(DM_SETDEFID, Id, 0);}

//
// message response functions
//
void            EvClose();
void            EvPaint();
HBRUSH          EvCtlColor(HDC, HWND hWndChild, UINT ctlType);

//
// child notifications
//
void            CmOk();       // IDOK
void            CmCancel();  // IDCANCEL

protected:
//
// override virtual functions defined by class TWindow
//
void            SetupWindow();
char far*       GetClassName();
void            GetWindowClass(WNDCLASS& wndClass);

private:
//
// hidden to prevent accidental copying or assignment
//
TDialog(const TDialog&);
TDialog& operator =(const TDialog&);

DECLARE_RESPONSE_TABLE(TDialog);
DECLARE_STREAMABLE(_OWLCLASS, TDialog, 1);
};
```

The TDialog class offers member functions to support creating dialog boxes and managing the user-response of clicking the OK or Cancel button (these buttons are part of every dialog box, though they sometimes have captions other than OK and Cancel). The class offers the Create and Execute functions to build modeless and modal dialog boxes, respectively. The Execute member function returns the value that indicates whether you invoked the OK or Cancel button.

The Document and View Classes

The ObjectWindows library supports classes for document viewing. The classes model documents that may contain one view or more. Each view offers one way

to look at data. For example, a document that opens an ASCII text file can have two views: one to show the characters in the text, the other to display the hexadecimal ASCII codes for the individual characters in the same viewed text. OWL offers the TDocument, TDocManager, and TDocTemplate classes as the base classes to manage documents. The TView class is the base class for the views. The TView and TDocManager classes are descendants of the TEventHandler and TStreamableBase classes. The TDocManager and TDocTemplate classes are descendants of the TStreamableBase class. The OWL hierarchy also offers the classes TWindowView, TEditView, TListView, and TFileDocument as descendants of the previously named base classes.

Printing Classes

The ObjectWindows library offers the TPrinter and TPrintout classes to facilitate printing. The TPrinter class encapsulates the interaction and communication with the printer drivers. The TPrintout class simplifies the printing of a document.

Graphics Classes

The OWL classes offer two sets of graphics-related classes: the device context (DC) classes and the graphics device interface (GDI) classes. The root of the graphics classes subhierarchy is the TGdiBase class. Here is the outline for the GDI classes:

```
+ TGdiBase
    + TGDIObject
        - TRegion
        - TBitmap
        - TFont
        - TPalette
        - TBrush
        - TPen
    - TIcon
    - TCursor
    - TDib
```

The GDI classes model graphics objects such as fonts, pens, brushes, bitmaps, regions, icons, and cursors. The DC class provides the device context for using the previously mentioned GDI objects to draw graphics. Here is the outline for the DC classes:

```
+ TGdibase
    + TDC
```

```
        + TWindowDC
             - TDesktopDC
             - TScreenDC
             - TClientDC
      - TPaintDC
      + TCreatedDC
             - TDibDC
             + TPrintDC
                   - TPrintPreviewDC
             - TIC
             - TMemoryDC
      - TMetafileDC
```

Miscellaneous Classes

This category of classes includes the miscellaneous OWL classes, such as those managing menus (TMenu, TSystemMenu, and TPopMenu), and the Clipboard class, TClipboard.

WINDOWS MESSAGES

Windows applications contain various types of objects that interact with each other with messages and in response to events. The Windows metaphor is that of a working office made up of employees, managers, departments, and material resources (computers, typewriters, photocopying machines, phones, faxes, and so on). Each employee (which, in this metaphor, corresponds to a Windows object) has a role to play as defined by his or her job description (which corresponds to a class declaration). The activities of an office are stimulated by events from the outside world, events directed to the outside world, and internal events. To respond to these events, the various employees and departments need to communicate with each other by messages. In a similar manner, the Windows environment and its applications interact with each other and with the outside world (that is, the input and output devices) using messages. These messages can be generated from the following sources:

1. One source is user-generated events, such as typing on the keyboard, moving the mouse, and clicking the mouse button. These events cause user-generated messages.

2. A Windows application can call Windows functions and cause Windows to send messages back to the application.

3. A Windows application can send internal messages aimed at specific program components.

4. The Windows environment can send messages to a Windows application.

5. Two Windows applications can send dynamic-data exchange (DDE) messages to share data.

Windows 3.1 has the following message categories:

- Windows-management messages: these are sent by Windows to an application when the state of a window is altered. Table 1.1 shows a selection of Windows-management messages.

TABLE 1.1. A SELECTION OF WINDOWS-MANAGEMENT MESSAGES.

Message	Meaning
WM_ACTIVATE	Sent when a window becomes active or inactive.
WM_CLOSE	Sent when a window is closed.
WM_MOVE	Sent when a window is moved.
WM_PAINT	Sent when either Windows or an application requests to repaint part of an application's window.
WM_QUIT	Signifies a request to end an application.
WM_SIZE	Sent after a window is resized.

- Initialization messages: these are sent by Windows when an application constructs a menu or a dialog box. Table 1.2 shows the initialization messages.

TABLE 1.2. THE INITIALIZATION MESSAGES.

Message	Meaning
WM_INITDIALOG	Sent immediately before a dialog box is displayed.
WM_INITMENU	Request to initialize a menu.
WM_INITMENUPOPUP	Sent immediately before a pop-up menu is displayed.

- Input messages: these are emitted by Windows in response to an input through the mouse, keyboard, scroll bars, or system timer. Table 1.3 shows a selection of input messages.

TABLE 1.3. A SELECTION OF INPUT MESSAGES.

Message	Meaning
WM_COMMAND	Sent when you select a menu item.
WM_HSCROLL	Sent when you click the horizontal scroll bar with the mouse.
WM_KEYDOWN	Sent when a nonsystem key is pressed.
WM_KEYUP	Sent when a nonsystem key is released.
WM_LBUTTONDBLCLK	Sent when you double-click the left mouse button.
WM_LBUTTONDOWN	Sent when you press the left mouse button.
WM_LBUTTONUP	Sent when you release the left mouse button.
WM_MOUSEMOVE	Sent when you move the mouse.
WM_RBUTTONDBLCLK	Sent when you double-click the right mouse button.
WM_RBUTTONDOWN	Sent when you press the right mouse button.
WM_RBUTTONUP	Sent when you release the right mouse button.
WM_TIMER	Sent when the timer limit set for a specific timer has elapsed.
WM_VSCROLL	Sent when you click the vertical scroll bar with the mouse.

- The System messages: these are sent by Windows to an application when you access the Windows control-menu, scroll bars, or size box. Most of the Windows applications do not respond to these messages and instead pass them to the DefWindowProc function for default processing.

- Clipboard messages: these are emitted by Windows to an application when other applications attempt to access a Windows clipboard.

- System-information messages: these are sent by Windows when a system-level change is made that affects other Windows applications. Among such changes are ones that affect the fonts, color palette, system color, time, and the contents of the WIN.INI file.

- Control manipulation messages: these are sent by Windows applications to a control object, such as the push down button, list box, combo box, or edit control. The control messages cause both the performance of a specific task and the return of a value that indicates the outcome.

- Control notification messages: these notify a control's parent window of the actions that have occurred within that control.

- Scroll bar notification messages: these include the WM_HSCROLL and WM_VSCROLL messages. The scroll bars send these messages to their parent windows when you click the bars.

- Nonclient-area messages: these are sent by Windows to create and update the nonclient area (that is, the area outside the working or client area of a window). You seldom will be required to override the default responses to these messages in your ObjectWindows application.

- Multiple document interface (MDI) messages: these are sent by an MDI frame window to a child client window. These messages cause operations such as activating, deactivating, creating, removing, arranging, and restoring client windows.

RESPONDING TO MESSAGES

The OWL classes use special sets of macros to map the various kinds of Windows messages onto the member functions that respond to these messages. The following code fragment will be used in the presentation and discussion of these macros:

```
class TMainWindow : public TWindow
{
public:
    TMainWindow();
protected:
    // handle left mouse button click
    void EvLButtonDown(UINT, TPoint&);
    // handle right mouse button click
```

```
    void EvRButtonDown(UINT, TPoint&);
    // handle painting the window
    void EvPaint()
    // handling exiting from the application
    void CmExit();
    // other member functions

    DECLARE_RESPONSE_TABLE(TMainWindow);
};

DEFINE_RESPONSE_TABLE1(TMainWindow, TWindow)
    EV_WM_LBUTTONDOWN,
    EV_WM_RBUTTONDOWN,
    EV_MW_PAINT,
    EV_COMMAND(CM_EXIT, CmExit),
END_RESPONSE_TABLE;
```

The preceding code fragment shows the declaration of the TMainWindow class as a descendant of the TWindow class. The class declaration includes the EvLButtonDown, EvRButtonDown, and EvPaint member functions. These functions handle messages generated by clicking the left mouse button (the WM_LBUTTONDOWN Windows message), clicking the right mouse button (the WM_RBUTTONDOWN Windows message), and repainting of the window (the WM_PAINT Windows message). The class declaration includes the DECLARE_RESPONSE_TABLE(TMainWindow) macro. The DECLARE_RESPONSE_TABLE macro takes one argument; the name of the declared class. This macro tells the compiler to create an empty message mapping table.

The code fragment also contains the DEFINE_RESPONSE_TABLE1 macro, which defines the message response map. The macro name ends with the digit 1 to indicate that the declared class (TMainWindow in this case) has only one parent class. The macro includes the arguments of the declared class along with its parent classes. If you declare a class with two parent classes, then you need to use the DEFINE_RESPONSE_TABLE2 macro. The message mapping macro includes map entries that associate the Windows messages with specific event-handling member functions.

There are two general kinds of map entries: predefined and user-defined. The predefined map entries take no arguments and map specific events to member functions with specific names. For example, the preceding code fragment contains the EV_WM_LBUTTONDOWN, EV_WM_RBUTTONDOWN, and EV_MW_PAINT map entries. These entries are predefined. The map entry EV_WM_LBUTTONDOWN maps the WM_LBUTTONDOWN Windows message with the EvLButtonDown member function; the TMainWindow class declares this function. This member function has two parameters of types UINT and TPoint&. The map entry EV_WM_RBUTTONDOWN maps the WM_RBUTTONDOWN Windows message with the EvRButtonDown member function; the

TMainWindow class also declares this function. Likewise, the map entry EV_PAINT maps the WM_PAINT Windows message with the EvPaint member function, which is also declared in the TMainWindow class.

The preceding message map table also contains the EV_COMMAND map entry. This is a user-defined entry that maps a Windows message command (CM_EXIT in this case) with a member function (CmExit in this case).

The message map table ends with the END_RESPONSE_TABLE macro. Each macro entry ends with a comma. The END_RESPONSE_TABLE macro ends with a semicolon.

The Borland C++ manuals discuss the various kinds of message maps. Consult these manuals for more information.

SENDING MESSAGES

Windows allows your application to send messages to itself, other applications, or to Windows itself. The Windows API functions SendMessage, PostMessage, and SendDlgItemMessage provide important tools for sending messages. The SendMessage function sends a message to a window and requires that window to handle the emitted message. The SendMessage function is declared as follows:

```
DWORD SendMessage(HWND hWnd, WORD wMsg, WORD wParam, LONG lParam);
```

The hWnd parameter is the handle of the window receiving the message. The wMsg parameter specifies the message sent. The wParam and lParam parameters designate additional optional information. You can use the SendMessage function to communicate with other windows and controls (the descendants of TControl).

The PostMessage function is similar to SendMessage, except it lacks the sense of urgency; the message is posted in the window's message queue. The message is handled later by the targeted window when convenient for that window. The declaration of the Boolean PostMessage function is this:

```
BOOL PostMessage(HWND hWnd, WORD wMsg, WORD wParam, LONG lParam);
```

The hWnd parameter is the handle of the window receiving the message. The wMsg parameter specifies the message sent. The wParam and lParam parameters designate additional optional information.

The SendDlgItemMessage function sends a message to a particular item in a dialog box. The declaration of the SendDlgItemMessage function is posted next:

```
DWORD SendDlgItemMessage(HWND hDlg, int nIDDlgItem,
                 WORD wMsg, WORD wParam, LONG lParam);
```

The hDlg parameter is the handle of the dialog box that contains the targeted control. The nIDDlgItem parameter indicates the integer identifier of the dialog box item that receives the message. The wMsg parameter specifies the message sent. The wParam and lParam parameters designate additional optional information.

The TWindow class encapsulates the preceding message-sending API functions. The message-sending member functions of TWindow have default arguments of 0 for the wParam and lParam parameters.

USER-DEFINED MESSAGES

With ObjectWindows, you can define your own messages. The WM_USER constant is associated with the number of the first message. You need to declare constants that represent the offset values for your custom messages. For example, you can use the #define directive to define your own command messages:

```
#define CM_USER1 100
#define CM_USER2 101
#define CM_USER3 102
```

Alternatively, you can use the constant declarations to create similar constants:

```
constant WORD CM_USER1 = 100;
constant WORD CM_USER2 = 101;
constant WORD CM_USER3 = 102;
```

The preceding user-defined command messages can be used in the following example class and its response member functions:

```
class TMainWindow : public TWindow
{
 public:
     TMainWindow();

 protected:
     // declarations of data members
     void CMUser1();
     void CMUser2();
     void CMUser3()
     // other member functions

     DECLARE_RESPONSE_TABLE(TMainWindow);
};
```

continues

continued

```
DEFINE_RESPONSE_TABLE1(TMainWindow, TWindow)
    EV_COMMAND(CM_USER1, CMUser1),
    EV_COMMAND(CM_USER2, CMUser3),
    EV_COMMAND(CM_USER3, CMUser3),
END_RESPONSE_TABLE;
```

To send these preceding user-defined messages, you can use the SendMessage API function. For example, the following statement sends the WM_USER2 message to the parent window (accessed by the predefined Parent pointer):

```
Parent->SendMessage(CM_USER2);
```

THE MINIMAL WINDOWS APPLICATION

Every ObjectWindows application that you develop begins with declaring a descendant of TApplication class. This is a step required by even minor ObjectWindows applications. Extending the other ObjectWindows classes depends on the features of your applications. The other required component for an ObjectWindows application is the WinMain function (which is similar to the main() function in a non-Windows C or C++ program) or the OwlMain function.

The _TWinApp_ class represents any application class that you derive from TApplication. The _WinApp_ variable represents the application instance. This instance is created as a local variable in the OwlMain special function. This function returns the result of sending the C++ Run message to the _WinApp_ object.

```
class _TWinApp_ : public TApplication
{
public:
  // public data members declarations

  _TWinApp_() : TApplication() {}

// other constructors
// class destructors
// other member functions
```

```
protected:
  // protected data members
  virtual void InitMainWindow();
  virtual void InitInstance();      // optional
  virtual void InitApplication();   // optional
  virtual BOOL CanClose();          // optional
  // other protected member functions

private:
  // private data members
  // other private member functions
};

int OwlMain(int /* argc */, char** /* argv[] */)
{
    _TWinApp_ app;
    return app.Run();
}
```

The preceding general template shows that your application classes should declare the member function InitMainWindow. The declarations of the InitInstance, InitApplication, and CanClose member functions are needed only to fine-tune the operations of these inherited functions in your ObjectWindows application. This fact also applies to declaring constructor parameters, data members (public, protected, and private), and member functions (public, protected, and private).

Listing 1.1 shows the contents of the MINWINAP.DEF definition file. Every Windows application requires a definition file that specifies general parameters about the application. Listing 1.2 shows the source code for a minimal ObjectWindows application that uses the preceding template. Notice that the ObjectWindows application class TWinApp declares a constructor and the InitMainWindow member function. The InitMainWindow creates an instance of TWindow, which is accessed by the inherited pointer-typed MainWindow data member. The instances of TWindow can be moved, resized, minimized, maximized, and have a Control menu. Figure 1.1 shows a sample session with the MINWINAPP.EXE application. To close the application window, use the Close option in the Control menu.

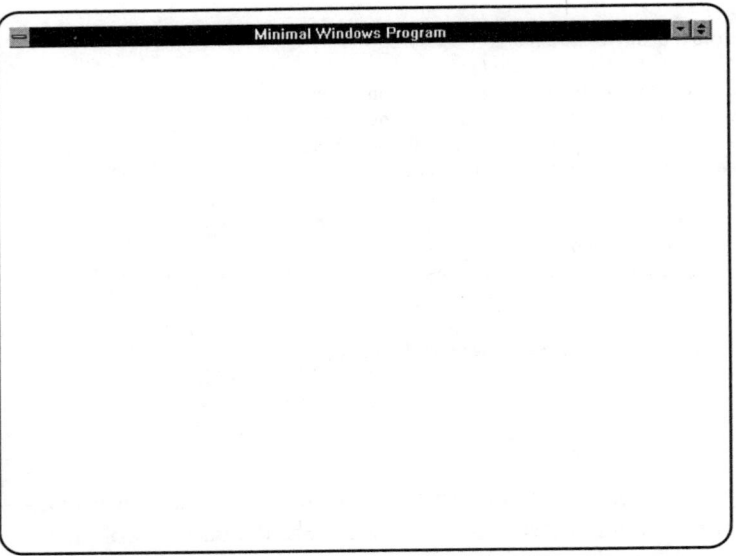

Figure 1.1. A sample session with the MINWINAPP.EXE application.

 To create the MINWINAPP.EXE file, you need to create the MINWINAPP.IDE project file and add the MINIWINAP.CPP and MINWIN.DEF. Please make sure that you create the BC4SAMS subdirectory and attach it to the \BC4 directory. Be sure that you compile using the medium memory model.

LISTING 1.1. THE CONTENTS OF THE MINWINAP.DEF DEFINITION FILE.

```
NAME         MinWinAp
DESCRIPTION  'An OWL Windows Application'
EXETYPE      WINDOWS
CODE         PRELOAD MOVEABLE DISCARDABLE
DATA         PRELOAD MOVEABLE MULTIPLE
HEAPSIZE     1024
STACKSIZE    8192
```

LISTING 1.2. THE SOURCE CODE FOR THE MINWINAP.CPP PROGRAM FILE.

```
/*
  Minimal OWL-based Windows program
*/
```

```
#include <owl\applicat.h>
#include <owl\framewin.h>

// declare the custom application class as
// a subclass of TApplication
class TWinApp : public TApplication
{
public:
  TWinApp() : TApplication() {}

protected:
  virtual void InitMainWindow();
};

void TWinApp::InitMainWindow()
{
  MainWindow = new TFrameWindow(0, "Minimal Windows Program");
}

int OwlMain(int /* argc */, char** /* argv[] */)
{
  TWinApp app;
  return app.Run();
}
```

A SIMPLE INTERACTIVE WINDOWS APPLICATION

After building a minimal ObjectWindows application, you'll write a new application that adds some functionality to the application's window. The .DEF file accompanying the next program is shown in Listing 1.3. The next program, SECAPP.CPP, is itself shown in Listing 1.4. The program performs the following main tasks:

- Responds to the left mouse button click (when the mouse is inside the application window) by displaying a message box with an OK button.

- Responds to the right mouse button click by displaying a message box that asks you whether you want to close the window.

These tasks require that the application declares a descendant of TWindow to implement the desired options. Listing 1.4 shows the declaration of the TMainWindow class, a descendant of TWindow. The new class declares a constructor and two message response member functions. The TMainWindow constructor simply calls the TWindow constructor, because no additional class instantiation is needed. The EvLButtonDown and EvRButtonDown member functions respond to the WM_LBUTTONDOWN and WM_RBUTTONDOWN messages, respectively. The message response table indicates the default association between the member functions and the messages, as previously mentioned and as follows:

```
DEFINE_RESPONSE_TABLE1(TMainWindow, TWindow)
  EV_WM_LBUTTONDOWN,
  EV_WM_RBUTTONDOWN,
END_RESPONSE_TABLE;
```

The EV_WM_LBUTTONDOWN table entry tells the compiler to use the EvLButtonDown member function to handle the Windows message WM_LBUTTONDOWN. Likewise, the table entry EV_WM_RBUTTONDOWN tells the compiler to use the EvRButtonDown member function to handle the WM_RBUTTONDOWN Windows message. The preceding table entries rely on using the specific member function names EvLButtonDown and EvRButtonDown.

The EvLButtonDown member function simply calls the MessageBox function to display the string You clicked the left button! in a message box with the caption Mouse Event. The box has the OK button that you click to resume program execution.

The code for the EvRButtonDown simply sends the WM_CLOSE Windows message to the parent window. The function performs this task by sending the C++ message (not a Windows message) SendMessage to the object accessed by the Parent pointer. The argument of the SendMessage message is WM_CLOSE.

The Boolean member function CanClose serves to check whether or not the window can indeed be closed. For example, if SECAPP.CPP implements a text editor, then you want to make sure that you save updated or new text. The function calls the MessageBox function to display a box with the caption **Query**, the message Want to close this application, Yes and No buttons, and a question mark icon. The function returns the Boolean result generated by comparing the value of the MessageBox function with the IDYES predefined constant.

The application class is very similar to the one in the MINWINAP.CPP file. The exception is that the InitMainWindow member function creates a new instance of TMainWindow, instead of TWindow. Figure 1.2 shows a sample session with the SECAPP.EXE application.

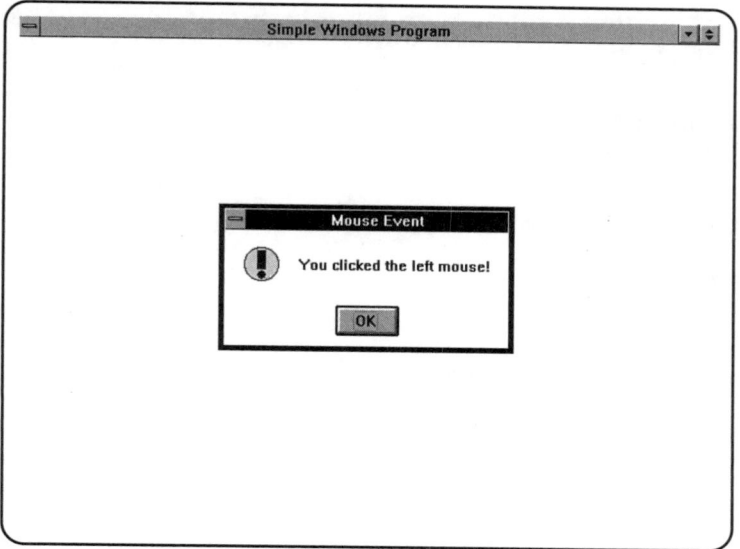

Figure 1.2. A sample session with the SECAPP.EXE program.

LISTING 1.3. THE CONTENTS OF THE SECAPP.DEF DEFINITION FILE.

```
NAME          SecApp
DESCRIPTION   'An OWL Windows Application'
EXETYPE       WINDOWS
CODE          PRELOAD MOVEABLE DISCARDABLE
DATA          PRELOAD MOVEABLE MULTIPLE
HEAPSIZE      1024
STACKSIZE     8192
```

LISTING 1.4. THE SOURCE CODE FOR THE SECAPP.CPP PROGRAM FILE.

```
/*
  Program which responds to mouse button clicks
*/

#include <owl\applicat.h>
#include <owl\framewin.h>
```

continues

LISTING 1.4. CONTINUED

```
// declare the custom application class as
// a subclass of TApplication
class TWinApp : public TApplication
{
public:
  TWinApp() : TApplication() {}

protected:
  virtual void InitMainWindow();
};

class TMainWindow : public TWindow
{
 public:
   TMainWindow() : TWindow(0, 0, 0) {}

 protected:

   // handle clicking the left mouse button
   void EvLButtonDown(UINT, TPoint&);

   // handle clicking the right mouse button
   void EvRButtonDown(UINT, TPoint&);

   // handle confirming closing the window
   virtual BOOL CanClose();

   // declare the response table
   DECLARE_RESPONSE_TABLE(TMainWindow);

};

DEFINE_RESPONSE_TABLE1(TMainWindow, TWindow)
  EV_WM_LBUTTONDOWN,
  EV_WM_RBUTTONDOWN,
END_RESPONSE_TABLE;

void TMainWindow::EvLButtonDown(UINT, TPoint&)
{
  MessageBox("You clicked the left mouse!", "Mouse Event",
          MB_OK | MB_ICONEXCLAMATION);
}

void TMainWindow::EvRButtonDown(UINT, TPoint&)
{
  Parent->SendMessage(WM_CLOSE);
}
```

```
BOOL TMainWindow::CanClose()
{
  return MessageBox("Want to close this application?",
            "Query", MB_YESNO | MB_ICONQUESTION) == IDYES;
}


void TWinApp::InitMainWindow()
{
  MainWindow = new TFrameWindow(0, "Simple Windows Program",
                    new TMainWindow);
}


int OwlMain(int /* argc */, char** /* argv[] */)
{
  TWinApp app;
  return app.Run();
}
```

A MENU SHELL WINDOWS APPLICATION

Most Windows applications include menus. The MINWINAP.EXE and SECAPP.EXE programs have only the Control menu. This section shows you how to attach a menu, defined in a resource file, to the application's window. Appendix B discusses the resource script syntax for the menus and dialog controls, as they relate to the programs in this book.

Listing 1.5 shows the contents of the definition file MENU1.DEF. Listing 1.6 shows declarations for resource script in the header file MENU1.H. Listing 1.7 shows the script for the menu resource file in file MENU1.RC. The file contains a single menu definition with the numeric ID code IDM_OPTIONS (the header file MENU1.H in Listing 1.6 defines the IDM_OPTIONS constant). The menu contains three main menu items, namely, File, Edit, and Help. The File and Edit menu items are pop-up menus. The Edit menu options contain the Delete menu item, which is also a pop-up menu. The menu items include horizontal separator bars. All of the menu names use the ampersand character to define the corresponding hot keys.

The various MENUITEM statements contain CM_*xxxx* constants that define the result of selecting the menu items. The CM_EXIT constant is defined in the WINDOWS.RH file. The other constants are declared in the MENU1.H header file, shown in Listing 1.6.

Listing 1.8 contains the source code for the MENU1.CPP ObjectWindows application. This program was derived from SECAPP.CPP by adding the statement `MainWindow->AssignMenu(TResID(IDM_OPTIONS))` to the `TInitMainWindow` member function. The `AssignMenu` member function loads the menu with the ID `TResID(IDM_OPTIONS)`. If a window is already assigned to `Attr`, the old one is removed. In the MENU1.CPP application, the `AssignMenu` function serves to complete the action of the `TInitMainWindow` member function.

To compile this application, include the following files in the MENU1.IDE project file: MENU1.CPP, MENU1.RC, and MENU1.DEF.

Figure 1.3 shows a sample session with the MENU1.EXE application. The figure shows the nested menus that are defined in the MENU1.RC resource file. The program responds to the left and right mouse button clicks in the same way as does program SECAPP.EXE. The menu items of the MENU1.EXE program are mute, except the Exit menu item to which there is a default response.

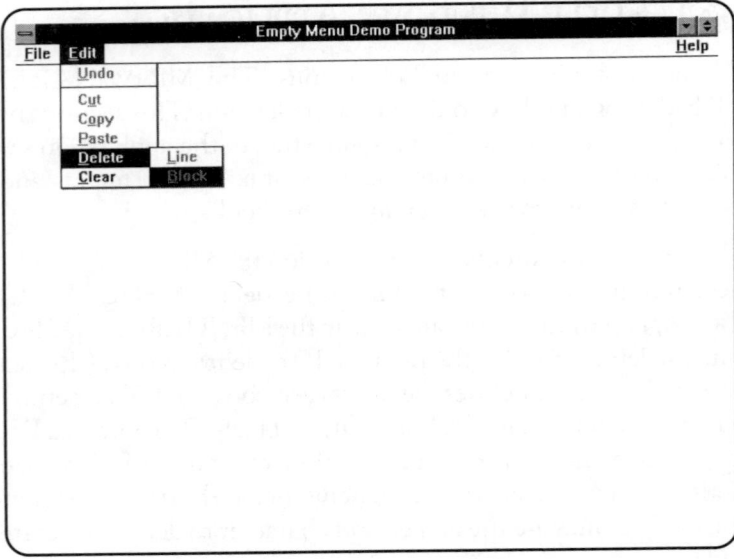

Figure 1.3. A sample session with the MENU1.EXE program.

LISTING 1.5. THE CONTENTS OF THE MENU1.DEF DEFINITION FILE.

```
NAME          Menu1
DESCRIPTION   'An OWL Windows Application'
EXETYPE       WINDOWS
CODE          PRELOAD MOVEABLE DISCARDABLE
DATA          PRELOAD MOVEABLE MULTIPLE
HEAPSIZE      1024
STACKSIZE     8192
```

LISTING 1.6. THE SOURCE CODE FOR THE MENU1.H HEADER FILE.

```
#define CM_FILENEW            100
#define CM_FILEOPEN           101
#define CM_FILESAVE           102
#define CM_FILESAVEAS         103
#define CM_EDITUNDO           104
#define CM_EDITCUT            105
#define CM_EDITCOPY           106
#define CM_EDITPASTE          107
#define CM_EDITDELETE         108
#define CM_EDITDELETE_BLOCK   109
#define CM_EDITCLEAR          110
#define CM_HELP               111
#define IDM_OPTIONS           400
```

LISTING 1.7. THE SCRIPT FOR THE MENU1.RC RESOURCE FILE.

```
#include <windows.h>
#include <owl\window.rh>
#include "menu1.h"

IDM_OPTIONS MENU LOADONCALL MOVEABLE PURE DISCARDABLE
BEGIN
  POPUP "&File"
  BEGIN
    MENUITEM "&New", CM_FILENEW
    MENUITEM "&Open", CM_FILEOPEN
    MENUITEM "&Save", CM_FILESAVE
    MENUITEM "Save&As", CM_FILESAVEAS
    MENUITEM SEPARATOR
    MENUITEM "E&xit", CM_EXIT
  END
```

continues

LISTING 1.7. CONTINUED

```
POPUP "&Edit"
BEGIN
  MENUITEM "&Undo", CM_EDITUNDO
  MENUITEM SEPARATOR
  MENUITEM "C&ut", CM_EDITCUT
  MENUITEM "C&opy", CM_EDITCOPY
  MENUITEM "&Paste", CM_EDITPASTE
  POPUP "&Delete"
  BEGIN
      MENUITEM "&Line", CM_EDITDELETE
      MENUITEM "&Block", CM_EDITDELETE_BLOCK
  END
  MENUITEM "&Clear", CM_EDITCLEAR
END
MENUITEM "&Help", CM_HELP, HELP
END
```

LISTING 1.8. THE SOURCE CODE FOR THE MENU1.CPP PROGRAM FILE.

```
/*
  Program which uses empty nested menus
*/

#include <owl\applicat.h>
#include <owl\framewin.h>
#include "menu1.h"

// declare the custom application class as
// a subclass of TApplication

class TWinApp : public TApplication
{
public:
  TWinApp() : TApplication() {}

protected:
  virtual void InitMainWindow();
};

// expand the functionality of TWindow by deriving class TMainWindow
class TMainWindow : public TWindow
{
 public:
   TMainWindow() : TWindow(0, 0, 0) {}

 protected:
```

```
      // handle clicking the left mouse button
      void EvLButtonDown(UINT, TPoint&);

      // handle clicking the right mouse button
      void EvRButtonDown(UINT, TPoint&);

      // handle confirming closing the window
      virtual BOOL CanClose();

      // declare the response table
      DECLARE_RESPONSE_TABLE(TMainWindow);
};

DEFINE_RESPONSE_TABLE1(TMainWindow, TWindow)
  EV_WM_LBUTTONDOWN,
  EV_WM_RBUTTONDOWN,
END_RESPONSE_TABLE;

void TMainWindow::EvLButtonDown(UINT, TPoint&)
{
  MessageBox("You clicked the left mouse!", "Mouse Event",
        MB_OK | MB_ICONEXCLAMATION);
}

void TMainWindow::EvRButtonDown(UINT, TPoint&)
{
  Parent->SendMessage(WM_CLOSE);
}

BOOL TMainWindow::CanClose()
{
  return MessageBox("Want to close this application?",
            "Query", MB_YESNO | MB_ICONQUESTION) == IDYES;
}

void TWinApp::InitMainWindow()
{
  MainWindow = new TFrameWindow(0, "Empty Menu DemoProgram",
                  new TMainWindow);
  // load the menu resource
  MainWindow->AssignMenu(TResID(IDM_OPTIONS));
}

int OwlMain(int /* argc */, char** /*argv[] */)
{
  TWinApp app;
  return app.Run();
}
```

A MINIMAL MENU WINDOWS APPLICATION

The last program demonstrates how to build a nested menu and to load it in an application. However, selecting the menu items (except for Exit) resulted in no action. This section answers this question: How does an application respond to a menu selection, and can that response load a different menu?

Look at the contents of resource file MENU2.RC, shown in Listing 1.11. The resource file defines two menus, tagged LONGMENU and SHORTMENU. As the names suggest, the first menu is the longer version of the second one. These menus differ from the ones in MENU1.RC in that they are not as nested and use the GRAYED option. Notice that these two options do not appear with every menu item; they are assigned to the menu items that are included but kept inactive. As a result, the names of the menu items appear in a gray color and cannot be selected. From the C++ coding aspect, there are no corresponding message response member functions. By contrast, the menu items that do not have the GRAYED option can be selected and will generate a response, albeit a simple one. Figure 1.4 shows a sample session with the MENU2.EXE program.

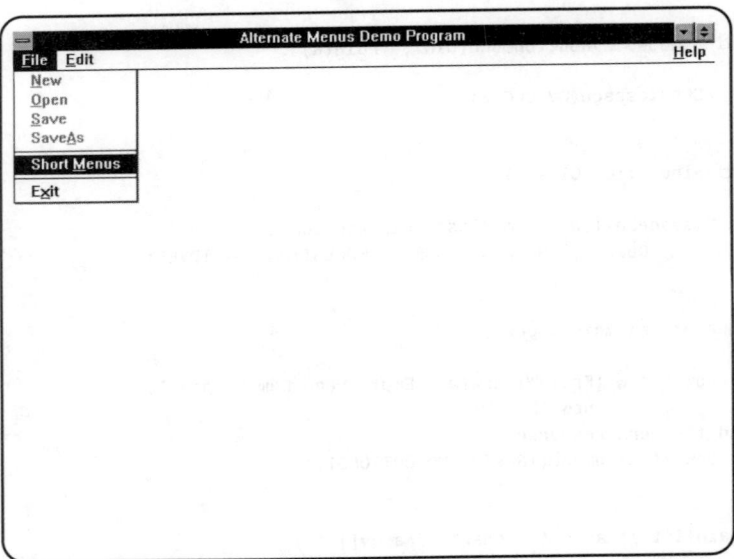

Figure 1.4. A sample session with the MENU2.EXE program.

Listing 1.9 shows the contents of the MENU2.DEF definition file. Listing 1.10 contains the header file MENU2.H which contains the definitions of most of the CM_*xxxx* constants. Listing 1.11 declares that the **Short &Menus** item in the LONGMENU menu results in the CM_SHORTMENU Windows command message that selects the short menu. The SHORTMENU menu has a complimentary menu item, **&Long Menu**, that results in the CM_LONGMENU Windows command message that selects the long menu.

LISTING 1.9. THE CONTENTS OF THE MENU2.DEF DEFINITION FILE.

```
NAME          Menu2
DESCRIPTION   'An OWL Windows Application'
EXETYPE       WINDOWS
CODE          PRELOAD MOVEABLE DISCARDABLE
DATA          PRELOAD MOVEABLE MULTIPLE
HEAPSIZE      1024
STACKSIZE     8192
```

LISTING 1.10. THE SOURCE CODE FOR THE MENU2.H HEADER FILE.

```
#define CM_FILENEW        100
#define CM_FILEOPEN       101
#define CM_FILESAVE       102
#define CM_FILESAVEAS     103
#define CM_EDITUNDO       104
#define CM_EDITCUT        105
#define CM_EDITCOPY       106
#define CM_EDITPASTE      107
#define CM_SHORTMENU      108
#define CM_LONGMENU       109
#define CM_EDITCLEAR      110
#define CM_EDITDELETE     111
#define CM_HELP           112
```

LISTING 1.11. THE SCRIPT FOR THE MENU2.RC RESOURCE FILE.

```
#include <windows.h>
#include <owl\window.rh>
#include "menu2.h"

LONGMENU MENU LOADONCALL MOVEABLE PURE DISCARDABLE
BEGIN
```

continues

LISTING 1.11. CONTINUED

```
  POPUP "&File"
  BEGIN
    MENUITEM "&New", CM_FILENEW, GRAYED
    MENUITEM "&Open", CM_FILEOPEN, GRAYED
    MENUITEM "&Save", CM_FILESAVE, GRAYED
    MENUITEM "Save&As", CM_FILESAVEAS, GRAYED
    MENUITEM SEPARATOR
    MENUITEM "Short &Menus", CM_SHORTMENU
    MENUITEM SEPARATOR
    MENUITEM "E&xit", CM_EXIT
  END
  POPUP "&Edit"
  BEGIN
    MENUITEM "&Undo", CM_EDITUNDO, GRAYED
    MENUITEM SEPARATOR
    MENUITEM "C&ut", CM_EDITCUT
    MENUITEM "C&opy", CM_EDITCOPY
    MENUITEM "&Paste", CM_EDITPASTE
    MENUITEM "&Delete", CM_EDITDELETE, GRAYED
    MENUITEM "&Clear", CM_EDITCLEAR, GRAYED
  END
  MENUITEM "&Help", CM_HELP, HELP
END

SHORTMENU MENU LOADONCALL MOVEABLE PURE DISCARDABLE
BEGIN
  POPUP "&File"
  BEGIN
    MENUITEM "&Open", CM_FILEOPEN, GRAYED
    MENUITEM "Save&As", CM_FILESAVEAS, GRAYED
    MENUITEM SEPARATOR
    MENUITEM "&Long Menus", CM_LONGMENU
    MENUITEM SEPARATOR
    MENUITEM "E&xit", CM_EXIT
  END
  POPUP "&Edit"
  BEGIN
    MENUITEM "C&ut", CM_EDITCUT
    MENUITEM "C&opy", CM_EDITCOPY
    MENUITEM "&Paste", CM_EDITPASTE
  END
  MENUITEM "&Help", CM_HELP, HELP
END
```

```
/*
  Program which uses alternate menus with minimal response
*/

#include <owl\applicat.h>
#include <owl\framewin.h>
#include "menu2.h"

// declare the custom application class as
// a subclass of TApplication

class TWinApp : public TApplication
{
public:
  TWinApp() : TApplication() {}

protected:
  virtual void InitMainWindow();
};

// expand the functionality of TWindow by deriving class TMainWindow
class TMainWindow : public TWindow
{
 public:
   TMainWindow()
     : TWindow(0, 0, 0)
     { LongMenuSelected = TRUE; }

 protected:

   BOOL LongMenuSelected;

   // handle clicking the left mouse button
   void EvLButtonDown(UINT, TPoint&);

   // handle clicking the right mouse button
   void EvRButtonDown(UINT, TPoint&);

   // handle the long menu
   void CMLongMenu();

   // handle the short menu
   void CMShortMenu();

   // handle the help menu
     void CMHelp();
```

continues

LISTING 1.12. CONTINUED

```cpp
    // handle the Edit Copy menu
    void CMEditCopy();

    // handle the Edit Cut menu
    void CMEditCut();

    // handle the Edit Paste
    void CMEditPaste();

    // display a message "Feature not implemented"
    void notImplemented();

    // handle confirming closing the window
    virtual BOOL CanClose();

    // declare the response table
    DECLARE_RESPONSE_TABLE(TMainWindow);

};

DEFINE_RESPONSE_TABLE1(TMainWindow, TWindow)
  EV_WM_LBUTTONDOWN,
  EV_WM_RBUTTONDOWN,
  EV_COMMAND(CM_LONGMENU, CMLongMenu),
  EV_COMMAND(CM_SHORTMENU, CMShortMenu),
  EV_COMMAND(CM_HELP, CMHelp),
  EV_COMMAND(CM_EDITCOPY, CMEditCopy),
  EV_COMMAND(CM_EDITCUT, CMEditCut),
  EV_COMMAND(CM_EDITPASTE, CMEditPaste),
END_RESPONSE_TABLE;

void TMainWindow::EvLButtonDown(UINT, TPoint&)
{
  MessageBox("You clicked the left mouse!", "Mouse Event",
          MB_OK | MB_ICONEXCLAMATION);
}

void TMainWindow::EvRButtonDown(UINT, TPoint&)
{
  if (LongMenuSelected)
    CMShortMenu();
  else
    CMLongMenu();
}

void TMainWindow::CMLongMenu()
{
```

```
    GetApplication()->MainWindow->AssignMenu("LONGMENU");
    LongMenuSelected = TRUE;
    MessageBox("The long menu is now active", "Menu Change",
            MB_OK | MB_ICONINFORMATION);
}

// assign the short menu
void TMainWindow::CMShortMenu()
{
    GetApplication()->MainWindow->AssignMenu("SHORTMENU");
    LongMenuSelected = FALSE;
    MessageBox("The short menu is now active", "Menu Change",
            MB_OK | MB_ICONINFORMATION);}

void TMainWindow::CMEditCut()
{
    notImplemented();
}

void TMainWindow::CMEditCopy()
{
    notImplemented();
}

void TMainWindow::CMEditPaste()
{
    notImplemented();
}

void TMainWindow::CMHelp()
{
    MessageBox(
        "This a sample one line help (that leaves more to be desired)",
        "Help", MB_OK | MB_ICONINFORMATION);
}

void TMainWindow::notImplemented()
{
    MessageBox("This feature is not implemented",
            "Information", MB_OK | MB_ICONEXCLAMATION);
}

BOOL TMainWindow::CanClose()
{
    return MessageBox("Want to close this application?",
                "Query", MB_YESNO | MB_ICONQUESTION) == IDYES;
}

void TWinApp::InitMainWindow()
{
```

continues

Listing 1.12. continued

```
MainWindow = new TFrameWindow(0, "Alternate Menus Demo Program",
                    new TMainWindow);
  // load the menu resource
  MainWindow->AssignMenu("LONGMENU");
}

int OwlMain(int /* argc */, char** /*argv[] */)
{
  TWinApp app;
  return app.Run();
}
```

The source code for the application appears in Listing 1.12. First notice that the MENU2.H header file appears in a #include directive. This inclusion enables the program to use the user-defined CM_*xxxx* constants in the message response table. The source code declares the TWinApp application class and the TMainWindow window class. The second class has the task of responding to the various messages. The TMainWindow class declares a constructor, a data member, and a series of message response member functions. The class constructor assigns TRUE to the BOOL-type data member LongMenuIsSelected. The assigned value is in accord with the fact that the TWinApp::InitMainWIndow member function loads the long menu version.

The TMainWindow class has a message response table to streamline the response for the various messages. The first two entries in the response table are EV_WM_LBUTTONDOWN and EV_WM_RBUTTONDOWN. These entries handle clicking the left and right mouse buttons, respectively. The other table entries are of the EV_COMMAND type and map the various CM_*xxxx* Windows command messages with their respective message handling functions.

The TAppWindow class declares the notImplemented member function, which displays a message box that contains the message This feature is not implemented. In fact, this is the common response to most menu items.

Now look at the message response member functions of TAppWindow. The EvLButtonDown function is the same as the one in the previous program. The EvRButtonDown function has a new behavior. When you click the right mouse button, you toggle between the long and short menu. The function examines the Boolean value in the LongMenuIsSelected member to determine whether to invoke the CMLongMenu function or the CMShortMenu function.

The CMLongMenu member function responds to the user-defined CM_LONGMENU Windows command message. The CMLongMenu calls the AssignMenu with the "LONGMENU" argument to load the long menu. Notice that the function accesses the MainWindow member by using the GetApplication function, which returns a pointer to the application itself. The function then assigns TRUE to the LongMenuIsSelected member. Finally, the function invokes the message dialog box to let you know that the long menu is now active. The CMShortMenu is coded similarly and responds to the CM_SHORTMENU Windows command message to load the short menu.

The CMHelp member function responds to the user-defined CM_HELP command by providing a one-line help message box. The message box appears with an OK button and an information icon (an *i* enclosed in a circle).

The CMEditCut, CMEditCopy, and CMEditPaste member functions each invoke the private notImplemented member function. This is the common (and symbolic) response that is provided for the CM_EDITCUT, CM_EDITCOPY, and CM_EDITPASTE commands.

A Paint Demo Windows Application

Another important basic feature of Windows applications is their ability to repaint or redraw themselves when you move or resize them. This feature is vital in maintaining the visual contents and frame of a window. This section presents a simple non-interactive program that draws text in a window. Figure 1.5 shows a sample session with the MENU3.EXE program. The program draws successive strings leftward and downward. You can resize and move the window and observe how the window clips parts of the strings that do not fit in the current dimensions of the window.

The TWindow::Paint member function is responsible for repainting the client window area, modeled by the descendant of TWindow, that you declare. Who calls the Paint member function? The TFrameWindow::EvPaint member function does, in response to the WM_PAINT Windows message. The declaration of the Paint member function is as follows:

```
void Paint(TDC& dc, BOOL erase, TRect& rect);
```

The dc parameter provides the device context used in drawing graphics or text. The erase parameter specifies whether or not to erase the client area. The rect parameter passes information related to the painted area.

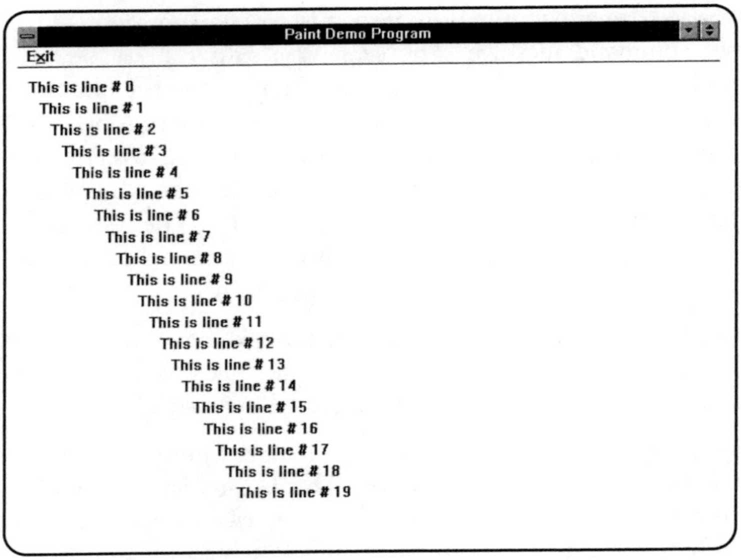

Figure 1.5. A sample session with the MENU3.EXE program.

With the TextOut member function, you can draw text at a specific location. The declaration of the TextOut function is as follows:

```
void TextOut(int x, int y, const char far* text, int textLen);
```

The x and y parameters specify the location for the text output. The text parameter specifies the string that contains the output text. The textLen parameter indicates how many characters appear in parameter text.

Listing 1.13 shows the contents of the MENU3.DEF definition file. Listing 1.14 contains the source code for the MENU3.H header file. Listing 1.15 shows the script for the MENU3.RC resource file. Listing 1.16 contains the source code for the MENU3.CPP program file.

LISTING 1.13. THE CONTENTS OF THE MENU3.DEF DEFINITION FILE.

```
NAME          Menu3
DESCRIPTION   'An OWL Windows Application'
EXETYPE       WINDOWS
CODE          PRELOAD MOVEABLE DISCARDABLE
DATA          PRELOAD MOVEABLE MULTIPLE
HEAPSIZE      1024
STACKSIZE     8192
```

LISTING 1.14. THE SOURCE CODE FOR THE MENU3.H HEADER FILE.

```
#define IDM_MAINMENU 400
```

LISTING 1.15. THE SCRIPT FOR THE MENU3.RC RESOURCE FILE.

```
#include <windows.h>
#include <owl\window.rh>
#include "menu3.h"

MAINMENU MENU LOADONCALL MOVEABLE PURE DISCARDABLE
BEGIN
  MENUITEM "E&xit", CM_EXIT
END
```

LISTING 1.16. THE SOURCE CODE FOR THE MENU3.CPP PROGRAM FILE.

```
/*
  Program which paints text in the window client area
*/

#include <owl\applicat.h>
#include <owl\framewin.h>
#include <owl\dc.h>
#include "menu3.h"
#include <stdio.h>
#include <string.h>

// declare the custom application class as
// a subclass of TApplication

class TWinApp : public TApplication
{
public:
  TWinApp() : TApplication() {}

protected:
  virtual void InitMainWindow();
};

// expand the functionality of TWindow by deriving class TMainWindow
class TMainWindow : public TWindow
{
```

continues

Listing 1.16. continued

```cpp
public:
  TMainWindow() : TWindow(0, 0, 0) { }

protected:

  // handle clicking the left mouse button
  void EvLButtonDown(UINT, TPoint&);

  // handle clicking the right mouse button
  void EvRButtonDown(UINT, TPoint&);

  void Paint(TDC&, BOOL, TRect&);

  // handle confirming closing the window
  virtual BOOL CanClose();

  // declare the response table
  DECLARE_RESPONSE_TABLE(TMainWindow);

};

DEFINE_RESPONSE_TABLE1(TMainWindow, TWindow)
  EV_WM_LBUTTONDOWN,
  EV_WM_RBUTTONDOWN,
END_RESPONSE_TABLE;

void TMainWindow::EvLButtonDown(UINT, TPoint&)
{
  MessageBox("You clicked the left mouse!", "Mouse Event",
          MB_OK | MB_ICONEXCLAMATION);
}

void TMainWindow::EvRButtonDown(UINT, TPoint&)
{
  Parent->SendMessage(WM_CLOSE);
}

void TMainWindow::Paint(TDC& dc, BOOL, TRect&)
{
  char s[81];
  int x = 10;
  int y = 10;
  int deltaY = 20;
  int deltaX = 10;
  int maxLines = 20;

  for(int i = 0; i < maxLines; i++) {
    sprintf(s, "This is line # %d", i);
```

```
      dc.TextOut(x, y, s, strlen(s));
      y += deltaY;
      x += deltaX;
  }
}

BOOL TMainWindow::CanClose()
{
  return MessageBox("Want to close this application?",
               "Query", MB_YESNO | MB_ICONQUESTION) == IDYES;
}

void TWinApp::InitMainWindow()
{
  MainWindow = new TFrameWindow(0, "Paint Demo Program",
                      new TMainWindow);
  // load the menu resource
  MainWindow->AssignMenu("MAINMENU");
}

int OwlMain(int /* argc */, char** /*argv[] */)
{
  TWinApp app;
  return app.Run();
}
```

Listing 1.16 declares the application and window classes. The declaration of
the TMainWindow class resembles that in the SECAPP.CPP program. The paint
demo program contains the Paint member function that performs the sought
painting. This function performs the following tasks:

- Declares and initializes a number of variables.

- Uses a for loop to draw the various lines. The loop statements perform
  the subsequent tasks.

- Builds the formatted output string using the sprintf function. This task
  uses the local variable s to store the formatted string, which includes a
  line number.

- Draws the string s at the location (x, y). This task involves sending the
  C++ message TextOut to the device context object dc. The message
  specifies to output all the characters in string s.

- Increments the value of the local variable y by deltaY.

- Increments the value of the local variable x by deltaX.

SUMMARY

This chapter presented basic information regarding the ObjectWindows class hierarchy as well as Windows-related information. The chapter presented the following sections:

- The ObjectWindows hierarchy: This section presented the various classes that make up the ObjectWindows library.

- The Windows messages: This section presented the various categories of messages.

- Responding to Windows messages: This section illustrated how to respond to messages in your own ObjectWindows applications. This is a process that involves declaring descendant ObjectWindows classes that contain one or more message response member functions. The latter functions provide the required response.

- Sending messages: This section showed how you can use a few Windows API functions to send messages.

- The user-defined messages: This section illustrated how to define your own messages, send these messages, and then respond to them.

VISUAL PROGRAMMING

Windows has ushered in the era of wide-scale use of the graphical user interface (GUI). This interface is easier to use and more consistent across diverse applications than the character-based user interfaces of MS-DOS and PC-DOS. Moreover, software vendors—like Microsoft and Borland—have influenced the evolution of programming by incorporating visual programming tools in their software development programming packages. Though visual programming did exist in the 1980s, it was limited to special university projects. This chapter presents the visual programming aspects of Borland C++ 4.0, which is championed by the Resource Workshop. This utility enables you to rely mainly on visual tools to create a diversity of resources that can be used by all Windows-compliant programming languages, not only Borland C++. In this chapter, you will learn about the following topics:

- Overview of the Resource Workshop

- Types of resources supported by the Resource Workshop

- Resource files

- Creating menu resources
- Creating accelerator resources
- Creating icon resources
- Creating a bare-bones dialog box resource
- Creating resources for a dialog box with non-trivial interfaces
- Creating a fully-functioning dialog box
- Working with VBX (Visual Basic Controls) resources

RESOURCE WORKSHOP OVERVIEW

Resources are special components of Windows applications. Using resources, you can change the text of messages, menus, and icons—and even use different human languages—without having to modify, recompile, or relink the source code. Thus, for example, you can use different resources for different human languages with the same source code. This advantage requires that resources have their own C-like *script* language. Chapter 1 showed you how to use resource scripts to define menus. Appendix B contains the resource statements used by dialog boxes. You can develop resources by typing their script in .RC and .DLG files in a manner that is typical of any programming language.

The Resource Workshop is a powerful tool that enables you to develop resources using visual programming techniques. In other words, you can draw the resources you need using a mouse, visual tools, and a set of menus and dialog boxes. The Resource Workshop then translates your drawings into the proper resource files, such as the script resource .RC files.

The purpose of this chapter is not to discuss the Resource Workshop from A to Z. Instead, I want to show you how to use this valuable tool in creating visually the important (and mostly visual) components of Windows programs.

TYPES OF RESOURCES

The Resource Workshop supports the following kinds of resources:

- Accelerators
- Bit maps

- Cursors
- Dialog boxes
- Fonts
- Icons
- Menus
- String tables
- User-defined and rcdata resources
- VERSIONINFO

In the next subsections, I briefly discuss these resources to alleviate any confusion you might have regarding them.

Accelerators

Accelerators are essentially hot keys that enable you to invoke a menu option without first choosing its parent menu selections and options. Thus, accelerators offer quick and direct ways to perform a task; and and are very useful for invoking nested menu options.

Bit Maps

Bit maps are binary representations of a graphical image. The popular Windows controls—such as pushbuttons, radio buttons, and scroll bars—use bit maps. The Resource Workshop enables you to create bit maps using the Paint editor. This editor supports drawing, coloring, and editing the bit maps.

Cursors

Cursors are special, small bit maps, each being 32 by 32 pixels in size. A cursor displays the location of the mouse on the screen. Windows supports using different cursor shapes to signal various tasks. For example, the hourglass cursor indicates that a Windows application is busy processing data. The Resource Workshop enables you to create cursors using the Paint editor.

Dialog Boxes

Dialog boxes are special windows that interact with the application user. Typically, dialog boxes prompt you to enter or to confirm current data. The

Resource Workshop supports creating dialog box resources and visually draw-ing their controls. This feature is the highlight of this chapter. I will discuss drawing the various controls and using the resulting dialog box resources later in this chapter.

Fonts

Fonts are special bit maps that represent the various characters that appear in a window or are printed. The Resource Workshop enables you to edit existing fonts and create your own fonts.

Icons

Icons are special bit maps, each being 16 by 32, or 32 by 32, or 64 by 64 (for high-resolution devices) pixels in size. Windows uses icons to represent minimized windows, and it supports inserting icons in windows and dialog boxes to incorporate small visual images.

Menus

Menus are resources that offer selections and options for the diverse operations of a Windows application. Because menus are resources, you can create different menu resources in different human languages. This feature enables you to easily distribute your applications to various countries.

String Tables

String tables are resources that contain text for various messages, prompts, and descriptions. Like menu resources, you can create different string tables in different human languages to support multinational versions of your software. This advantage requires that you avoid imbedding string literals in your source code; instead you must rely completely on the string table resources.

User-Defined and rcdata Resources

The user-defined and rcdata resources support special information that is incorporated into the executable files. This kind of information provides read-only data that the host program uses to initialize itself.

VERSIONINFO

The VERSIONINFO resource is a special version of the stamper resource for Windows 3.1 .EXE files.

RESOURCE FILES

The Resource Workshop works with the following kinds of resource files:

- The resource script files with .RC extensions. These text files contain resource statements that define various kinds of resources, such as menus, accelerators, string tables, and dialog boxes.

- The binary .RES files that contain compiled resources. The Resource Workshop can read and produce either .RC or .RES files. In other words, you can ask the Resource Workshop to read a .RES file, decompile it, and then create a corresponding .RC file that you can edit.

- The bit-mapped resource files .BMP, .ICO, .CUR, and .FON that contain bit maps, icons, cursors, and fonts resources. The Resource Workshop also supports font resource files with the .FNT extension.

- The dialog box script resource files .DLG. Typically, these files contain resource script for reusable dialog boxes. You can include the .DLG files (and also other .RC files) in a .RC file using the special directive #rcinclude.

- The executable .EXE and dynamic link library .DLL files contain executable code bound together with compiled resources. The Resource Workshop enables you to read resources in .EXE and .DLL files, decompile them, edit them, and then save the new resources back to the .EXE and .DLL binary files.

- The device driver files .DRV are special .DLL files. As with ordinary .DLL files, the Resource Workshop permits you to edit the resources in a .DRV file.

CREATING MENU RESOURCES

Consider now a hands-on example that illustrates creating a menu resource. In the last chapter, I presented the program MENU2.EXE that enables you to alternate between two minimally functioning menus. I will now present the resource file MENU2.RC in Listing 2.1 to use as a map in creating the same resource using the Resource Workshop. This file declares the LONGMENU and SHORTMENU menu resources. You can think of these menus as a novice menu and an expert menu, respectively.

LISTING 2.1. THE SCRIPT FOR THE MENU2.RC RESOURCE FILE.

```
#include <windows.h>
#include <owl\window.rh>
#include "menu2.h"

LONGMENU MENU LOADONCALL MOVEABLE PURE DISCARDABLE
BEGIN
  POPUP "&File"
  BEGIN
    MENUITEM "&New", CM_FILENEW, GRAYED
    MENUITEM "&Open", CM_FILEOPEN, GRAYED
    MENUITEM "&Save", CM_FILESAVE, GRAYED
    MENUITEM "Save&As", CM_FILESAVEAS, GRAYED
    MENUITEM SEPARATOR
    MENUITEM "Short &Menus", CM_SHORTMENU
    MENUITEM SEPARATOR
    MENUITEM "E&xit", CM_EXIT
  END
  POPUP "&Edit"
  BEGIN
    MENUITEM "&Undo", CM_EDITUNDO, GRAYED
    MENUITEM SEPARATOR
    MENUITEM "C&ut", CM_EDITCUT
    MENUITEM "C&opy", CM_EDITCOPY
    MENUITEM "&Paste", CM_EDITPASTE
    MENUITEM "&Delete", CM_EDITDELETE, GRAYED
    MENUITEM "&Clear", CM_EDITCLEAR, GRAYED
  END
  MENUITEM "&Help", CM_HELP, HELP
END

SHORTMENU MENU LOADONCALL MOVEABLE PURE DISCARDABLE
BEGIN
  POPUP "&File"
```

```
BEGIN
  MENUITEM "&Open", CM_FILEOPEN, GRAYED
  MENUITEM "Save&As", CM_FILESAVEAS, GRAYED
  MENUITEM SEPARATOR
  MENUITEM "&Long Menus", CM_LONGMENU
  MENUITEM SEPARATOR
  MENUITEM "E&xit", CM_EXIT
END
POPUP "&Edit"
BEGIN
  MENUITEM "C&ut", CM_EDITCUT
  MENUITEM "C&opy", CM_EDITCOPY
  MENUITEM "&Paste", CM_EDITPASTE
END
MENUITEM "&Help", CM_HELP, HELP
END
```

Proceed now to creating the menu resource using the Resource Workshop. First, you need to load the Borland C++ IDE and create the new project RWMENU1 with the files RWMENU1.DEF, RWMENU1.CPP, and RWMENU1.RC. You can insert the contents of the MENU2.DEF and MENU2.CPP files in the source code windows of the RWMENU1.DEF and RWMENU1.CPP files, respectively. Later in this section I'll discuss editing the inserted code. For now, focus on creating the menu resources. Here are the general steps involved in this process:

1. Invoke the Resource Workshop option from the Tool menu selection. The Resource Workshop displays a window with a menu, a status bar, and a client area. The client area contains an empty resource window, as shown in Figure 2.1. The resource window has two panes. The first pane lists the current resources. The second pane is the preview pane that shows the contents of the currently selected resource in the first pane.

2. Choose the Resource menu selection and invoke the New... menu option. This option brings up the New Resource dialog box, shown in Figure 2.2, that enables you to choose a new resource. Scroll down through the resource type list box until you find MENU. Click the OK pushbutton in the New Resource dialog box.

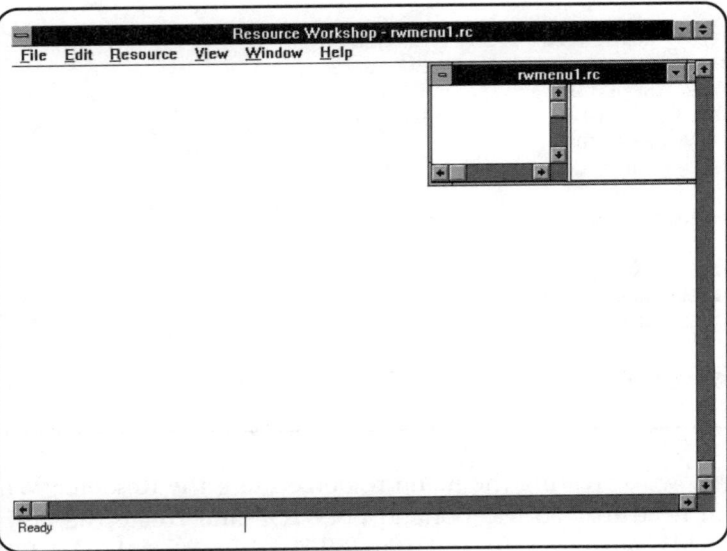

Figure 2.1. The Resource Workshop showing an empty resource window.

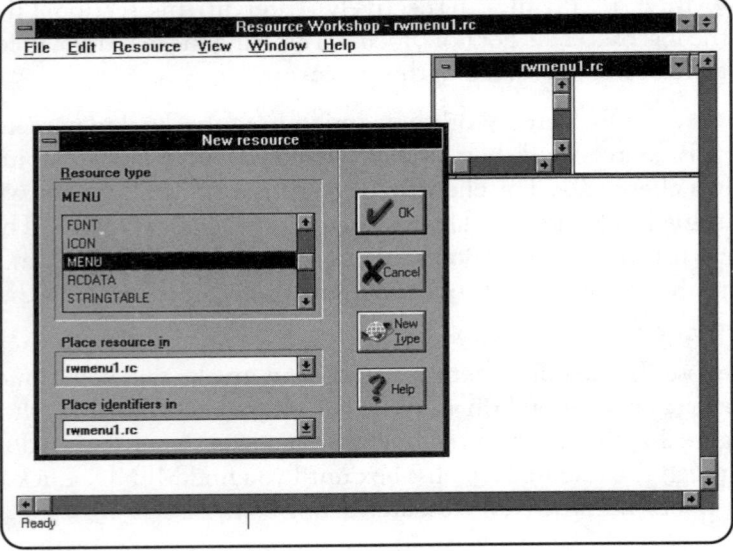

Figure 2.2. A sample session with the New Resource dialog box.

3. The Resource Workshop invokes the MENU:MENU_1 dialog box (see Figure 2.3). The caption of the dialog box incorporates the default name of the new menu resource. The dialog box is made up of three panes: the attribute pane, the outline pane, and the test menu pane. The attribute pane contains the following groups of controls:

- The set of edit boxes labeled Item text, Item help, and Item Id. These controls enable you to enter the caption of a menu item, its corresponding one-line help text (which appears in the status bar when you select the item), and the identifier for the new menu item, respectively.

- The item type diamond-shaped radio buttons: Pop-up, Menu Item, and Separator. If the Pop-up control is enabled, the other two buttons are disabled, and vice versa. The last two controls, when enabled, permit you to select between creating a menu item or a separator.

- The Checked check box; and the three initial state diamond-shaped radio buttons: Enabled, Disabled, and Grayed. These controls enable you to specify the initial state of a menu item.

- The break before diamond-shaped radio buttons: No break, Menu bar break, Menu break, and Help break. Use the last radio button to display the Help menu to the right edge of the menu bar.

- The modifiers check boxes: Alt, Shift, Control, and Invert menu item. These check boxes enable you to fine-tune the hot keys that respond to the menu options.

- The Key edit box and the key type radio buttons: ASCII and Virtual Key. These controls enable you to associate hot keys to menu options.

4. Type in the menu items for the LONGMENU resource (which is currently being created as the resource menu MENU_1), using the following tasks in their appropriate sequence (Listing 2.1 should guide your input and selections):

- To add a new pop-up item as a menu selection, move to the bottom of the menu outline and then invoke the Menu menu selection and select the New pop-up item option. The hot keys for this option are Ctrl+P.

- To add a new menu item, invoke the Menu menu selection and select the New menu item option. The hot key for this option is the Insert key.

- To insert a selector, first insert a new menu item, then click the Menu Item radio button in the item type control group, and then press Enter. You can also use Ctrl+S as hot keys for inserting a separator.

- To insert the Help menu selection, move to the end of the outline and press the Insert key to insert an unnested menu item.

- To make a menu item gray, click the Grayed radio button in the initial state control group.

- Each menu item requires a caption. Place the & character before the hot key character. Use the same hot keys as shown in Listing 2.1.

- Each menu option requires an Id. Enter the CM_*xxxx* ID in the Item Id edit box. Use the same CM_*xxxx* constants as in Listing 2.1.

- The menu selection Menu also has options that spawn standard file, edit, and help selections (including standard options).

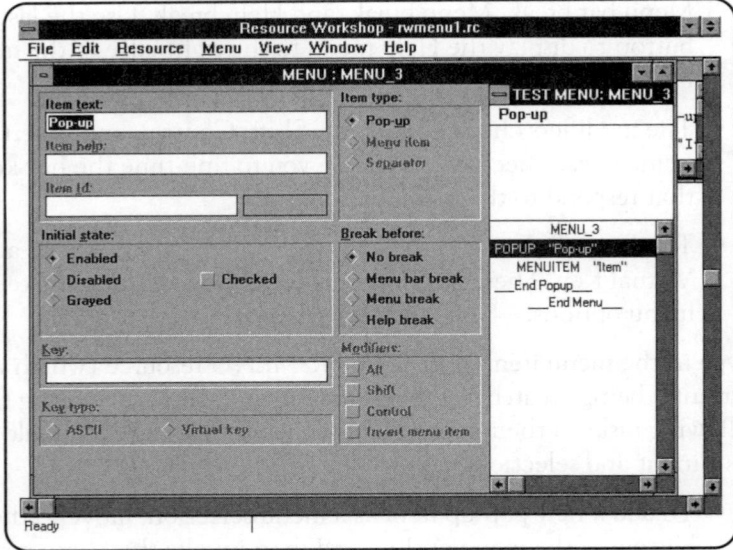

Figure 2.3. The MENU:MENU_1 dialog box, which creates the menu resource.

5. Repeat steps 2 through 4 to create the SHORTMENU menu resource (which is initially created as the resource menu MENU_2). Use Listing 2.1 as a guide for your input. Keep in mind that the two menu resources have few CM_*xxxx* in common. Make sure that these common CM_*xxxx* have the same values.

6. Rename the resources MENU_1 and MENU_2 to LONGMENU and SHORT menu. This task involves using the Identifiers... option in the Resource menu selection. The Resource Workshop displays the Identifiers dialog box, shown in Figure 2.4, which permits you to select a resource, rename it, and renumber it. Select each of these menu resources and click the Rename pushbutton. The Resource Workshop displays a simple input dialog box that enables you to enter the new name for the currently selected resource. Click the Change pushbutton in the Identifiers dialog box to assign numbers 101 and 102 to the menu resources LONGMENU and SHORTMENU.

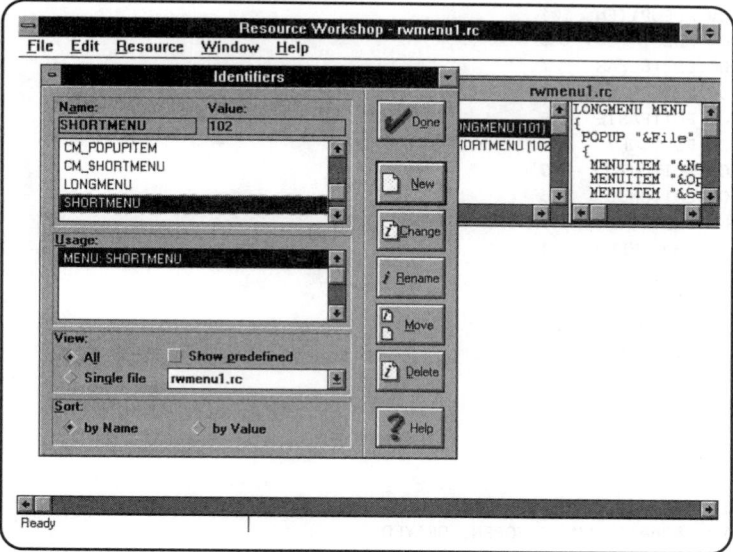

Figure 2.4. A sample session with the Identifiers dialog box.

7. Renumber the value of the identifier CM_SHORTMENU, changing its value from 1 to 9 (or any other integer which does not duplicate the values of the other CM_*xxxx* identifiers). Use the Identifier dialog box for this task.

The Resource Workshop produces the resource file RWMENU1.RC, shown in Listing 2.2.

LISTING 2.2. THE SCRIPT FOR THE RESOURCE FILE RWMENU1.RC THAT IS GENERATED BY THE RESOURCE WORKSHOP.

```
/**************************************************************************


RWMENU1.RC

produced by Borland Resource Workshop



**************************************************************************/
#define LONGMENU        101
#define SHORTMENU       102
#define CM_LONGMENU       1
#define CM_POPUPITEM    101
#define CM_HELP           8
#define CM_EDITCLEAR      7
#define CM_EDITDELETE     6
#define CM_EDITPASTE      5
#define CM_EDITCOPY       4
#define CM_EDITCUT        3
#define CM_EDITUNDO     105
#define CM_EXIT           2
#define CM_SHORTMENU      1
#define CM_FILESAVEAS   104
#define CM_FILESAVE     103
#define CM_FILENEW      101
#define CM_FILEOPEN     102

LONGMENU MENU
{
 POPUP "&File"
 {
  MENUITEM "&New", CM_FILENEW, GRAYED
  MENUITEM "&Open", CM_FILEOPEN, GRAYED
  MENUITEM "&Save", CM_FILESAVE, GRAYED
  MENUITEM "Save&As", CM_FILESAVEAS, GRAYED
  MENUITEM SEPARATOR
  MENUITEM "Short &Menus", CM_SHORTMENU
  MENUITEM SEPARATOR
  MENUITEM "E&xit", CM_EXIT
 }
```

```
POPUP "&Edit"
{
 MENUITEM "&Undo", CM_EDITUNDO, GRAYED
 MENUITEM SEPARATOR
 MENUITEM "C&ut", CM_EDITCUT
 MENUITEM "C&opy", CM_EDITCOPY
 MENUITEM "&Paste", CM_EDITPASTE
 MENUITEM "&Delete", CM_EDITDELETE, GRAYED
 MENUITEM "&Clear", CM_EDITCLEAR, GRAYED
 }

 MENUITEM "&Help", CM_HELP
}


SHORTMENU MENU
{
 POPUP "&File"
 {
 MENUITEM "&Open", CM_FILEOPEN, GRAYED
 MENUITEM "Save&AS", CM_FILESAVEAS, GRAYED
 MENUITEM SEPARATOR
 MENUITEM "&Long Menus", CM_LONGMENU
 MENUITEM SEPARATOR
 MENUITEM "E&xit", CM_EXIT
 }

 POPUP "&Edit"
 {
 MENUITEM "C&ut", CM_EDITCUT
 MENUITEM "C&opy", CM_EDITCOPY
 MENUITEM "&Paste", CM_EDITPASTE
 }

 MENUITEM "&Help", CM_HELP
}
```

Notice that the Listing 2.2 includes the definitions of the cm_xxxx constants and other resource identifiers. The resource script in Listing 2.2 resembles that in Listing 2.1, except the keywords BEGIN and END (in Listing 2.1) are replaced with the open and close brace.

Now, let's focus on editing the projects files. The first task involves creating the empty header file RWMENU1.H and moving the set of #define statements from the resource file RWMENU1.RC to that header file. In addition, you need to delete the definition of the identifier cm_EXIT, because the program needs to use Windows' own definition found in the resource header file WINDOW.H. Listing 2.3 shows the resulting source code for the RWMENU1.H header file.

LISTING 2.3. THE SOURCE CODE FOR THE RWMENU1.H HEADER FILE.

```
#define LONGMENU          101
#define SHORTMENU         102
#define CM_LONGMENU         1
#define CM_POPUPITEM      101
#define CM_HELP             8
#define CM_EDITCLEAR        7
#define CM_EDITDELETE       6
#define CM_EDITPASTE        5
#define CM_EDITCOPY         4
#define CM_EDITCUT          3
#define CM_EDITUNDO       105
#define CM_SHORTMENU        9
#define CM_FILESAVEAS     104
#define CM_FILESAVE       103
#define CM_FILENEW        101
#define CM_FILEOPEN       102
```

Let's work on the resource file RWMEMU1.RC. After removing the set of
#define statements, you need to insert the following #include statements:

```
#include <windows.h>
#include <owl\window.rh>
#include "rwmenu1.h"
```

These statements enable the resource file to access the proper definitions of the
various identifiers. Notice that this version regards the identifiers LONGMENU and
SHORTMENU as constants that have integer values. The MENU2.RC file regards
the same identifiers as string-type names. Listing 2.4 shows the script for the
edited RWMENU1.RC resource file.

LISTING 2.4. THE SCRIPT FOR THE RWMENU1.RC RESOURCE FILE.

```
#include <windows.h>
#include <owl\window.rh>
#include "rwmenu1.h"

LONGMENU MENU
{
 POPUP "&File"
 {
  MENUITEM "&New", CM_FILENEW, GRAYED
  MENUITEM "&Open", CM_FILEOPEN, GRAYED
  MENUITEM "&Save", CM_FILESAVE, GRAYED
  MENUITEM "Save&As", CM_FILESAVEAS, GRAYED
```

```
 MENUITEM SEPARATOR
 MENUITEM "Short &Menus", CM_SHORTMENU
 MENUITEM SEPARATOR
 MENUITEM "E&xit", CM_EXIT
 }

 POPUP "&Edit"
 {
 MENUITEM "&Undo", CM_EDITUNDO, GRAYED
 MENUITEM SEPARATOR
 MENUITEM "C&ut", CM_EDITCUT
 MENUITEM "C&opy", CM_EDITCOPY
 MENUITEM "&Paste", CM_EDITPASTE
 MENUITEM "&Delete", CM_EDITDELETE, GRAYED
 MENUITEM "&Clear", CM_EDITCLEAR, GRAYED
 }

 MENUITEM "&Help", CM_HELP
 }


SHORTMENU MENU
{
 POPUP "&File"
 {
 MENUITEM "&Open", CM_FILEOPEN, GRAYED
 MENUITEM "Save&AS", CM_FILESAVEAS, GRAYED
 MENUITEM SEPARATOR
 MENUITEM "&Long Menus", CM_LONGMENU
 MENUITEM SEPARATOR
 MENUITEM "E&xit", CM_EXIT
 }

 POPUP "&Edit"
 {
 MENUITEM "C&ut", CM_EDITCUT
 MENUITEM "C&opy", CM_EDITCOPY
 MENUITEM "&Paste", CM_EDITPASTE
 }

 MENUITEM "&Help", CM_HELP
}
```

Let's look at the definition file RWMENU1.DEF, in which you inserted the contents of file MENU2.DEF. This file only requires changing the name from Menu2 into RwMenu1 to yield Listing 2.5.

Listing 2.5. The Contents of the RWMENU1.DEF Definition File.

```
NAME          RwMenu1
DESCRIPTION   'An OWL Windows Application'
EXETYPE       WINDOWS
CODE          PRELOAD MOVEABLE DISCARDABLE
DATA          PRELOAD MOVEABLE MULTIPLE
HEAPSIZE      1024
STACKSIZE     8192
```

Finally, let's look at the implementation file RWMENU1.CPP, in which you inserted the contents of file MENU2.CPP. The RWMENU1.CPP file requires the following edits to yield the source code in Listing 2.6:

1. Change the name of the third `#include` file from MENU2.H to RWMENU1.H.

2. Change the first statement in the definition of member function `CMLongMenu` from:

   ```
   GetApplication()->MainWindow->AssignMenu("LONGMENU");
   ```

   to:

   ```
   GetApplication()->MainWindow->AssignMenu(TResID(LONGMENU));
   ```

3. Change the first statement in the definition of member function `CMShortMenu` from:

   ```
   GetApplication()->MainWindow->AssignMenu("SHORTMENU");
   ```

   to:

   ```
   GetApplication()->MainWindow->AssignMenu(TResID(SHORTMENU));
   ```

4. Update the window title as it appears in the first statement inside member function `InitMainWindow`.

5. Change the last statement of member function `InitMainWindow` from:

   ```
   MainWindow->AssignMenu("LONGMENU");
   ```

   to:

   ```
   MainWindow->AssignMenu(TResID(LONGMENU));
   ```

The RWMENU1.EXE program works just like the MENU2.EXE program. The difference between the two is mainly how you created their menu resources.

LISTING 2.6. THE SOURCE CODE FOR THE RWMENU1.CPP IMPLEMENTATION FILE.

```
/*
  Program which uses alternate menus with minimal response
*/

#include <owl\applicat.h>
#include <owl\framewin.h>
#include "rwmenu1.h"

// declare the custom application class as
// a subclass of TApplication

class TWinApp : public TApplication
{
public:
  TWinApp() : TApplication() {}

protected:
  virtual void InitMainWindow();
};

// expand the functionality of TWindow by deriving class TMainWindow
class TMainWindow : public TWindow
{
 public:
   TMainWindow()
     : TWindow(0, 0, 0)
     { LongMenuSelected = TRUE; }

 protected:

   BOOL LongMenuSelected;

   // handle clicking the left mouse button
   void EvLButtonDown(UINT, TPoint&);

   // handle clicking the right mouse button
   void EvRButtonDown(UINT, TPoint&);

   // handle the long menu
   void CMLongMenu();

   // handle the short menu
   void CMShortMenu();

   // handle the help menu
     void CMHelp();
```

continues

LISTING 2.6. CONTINUED

```cpp
    // handle the Edit Copy menu
    void CMEditCopy();

    // handle the Edit Cut menu
    void CMEditCut();

    // handle the Edit Paste
    void CMEditPaste();

    // display a message "Feature not implemented"
    void notImplemented();

    // handle confirming closing the window
    virtual BOOL CanClose();

    // declare the response table
    DECLARE_RESPONSE_TABLE(TMainWindow);
};

DEFINE_RESPONSE_TABLE1(TMainWindow, TWindow)
  EV_WM_LBUTTONDOWN,
  EV_WM_RBUTTONDOWN,
  EV_COMMAND(CM_LONGMENU, CMLongMenu),
  EV_COMMAND(CM_SHORTMENU, CMShortMenu),
  EV_COMMAND(CM_HELP, CMHelp),
  EV_COMMAND(CM_EDITCOPY, CMEditCopy),
  EV_COMMAND(CM_EDITCUT, CMEditCut),
  EV_COMMAND(CM_EDITPASTE, CMEditPaste),
END_RESPONSE_TABLE;

void TMainWindow::EvLButtonDown(UINT, TPoint&)
{
  MessageBox("You clicked the left mouse!", "Mouse Event",
             MB_OK | MB_ICONEXCLAMATION);
}

void TMainWindow::EvRButtonDown(UINT, TPoint&)
{
  if (LongMenuSelected)
    CMShortMenu();
  else
    CMLongMenu();
}

void TMainWindow::CMLongMenu()
{
  GetApplication()->MainWindow->AssignMenu(TResID(LONGMENU));
```

```
  LongMenuSelected = TRUE;
  MessageBox("The long menu is now active", "Menu Change",
           MB_OK | MB_ICONINFORMATION);
}

// assign the short menu
void TMainWindow::CMShortMenu()
{
  GetApplication()->MainWindow->AssignMenu(TResID(SHORTMENU));
  LongMenuSelected = FALSE;
  MessageBox("The short menu is now active", "Menu Change",
           MB_OK | MB_ICONINFORMATION);}

void TMainWindow::CMEditCut()
{
  notImplemented();
}

void TMainWindow::CMEditCopy()
{
  notImplemented();
}

void TMainWindow::CMEditPaste()
{
  notImplemented();
}

void TMainWindow::CMHelp()
{
  MessageBox(
     "This a sample one line help (that leaves more to be desired)",
     "Help", MB_OK | MB_ICONINFORMATION);
}

void TMainWindow::notImplemented()
{
  MessageBox("This feature is not implemented",
           "Information", MB_OK | MB_ICONEXCLAMATION);
}

BOOL TMainWindow::CanClose()
{
  return MessageBox("Want to close this application?",
                "Query", MB_YESNO | MB_ICONQUESTION) == IDYES;
}

void TWinApp::InitMainWindow()
{
  MainWindow = new TFrameWindow(0,
```

continues

LISTING 2.6. CONTINUED

```
                    "Alternate Menus Demo Program (version 2)",
                    new TMainWindow);
  // load the menu resource
  MainWindow->AssignMenu(TResID(LONGMENU));
}

int OwlMain(int /* argc */, char** /*argv[] */)
{
  TWinApp app;
  return app.Run();
}
```

CREATING ACCELERATOR RESOURCES

Let's look at modifying the last project to offer accelerators for the Exit, Cut, Copy, and Paste menu options. The new program offers the accelerators Alt+X, Ctrl+X, Ctrl+C, and Ctrl+V, respectively, for the preceding options. In addition, the program has extended menu text for the preceding menu options to remind you of the accelerator keys (the hot keys).

You can easily create the files of the new project RWMENU2 from those of project RWMENU1. Use the files RWMENU1.IDE, RWMENU1.DEF, RWMENU1.H, RWMENU1.RC, and RWMENU1.CPP to create the files RWMENU2.IDE, RWMENU2.DEF, RWMENU2.H, RWMENU2.RC, and RWMENU2.CPP, respectively. You need to set up the project by making the following changes:

1. In file RMENU2.DEF, change the project name from RwMenu1 to RwMenu2.

2. In files RMENU2.RC and RWMENU2.CPP, change the name of the header file RWMENU1.H into RWMENU2.H.

3. Delete the files for the target RWMENU1 in the project file RWMENU2.IDE and then insert the new target RWMENU2.

The preceding steps prepare the files for editing. Load the Resource Workshop by double-clicking the RWMENU2.RC node in the Project window. The Resource Workshop will load the resources in file RWMENU2.RC.

Resource Workshop permits you to insert accelerators in two ways. First, you can create new accelerator resources that are not explicitly connected with any menu resource. Second, you can incorporate the accelerators resources with the menu. This seems the logical route for the task at hand. Each of the two menu resources perform the following tasks:

1. Select the targeted menu resource to bring up the MENU dialog box.

2. Select one of the targeted menu options (Exit, Cut, Copy, or Paste).

3. Click the Item text edit box and expand the menu text by first adding a few spaces and then typing in the characters for the corresponding accelerators key. This action allows the menu text to show the associated accelerators key.

4. Press the Tab key until you select the Key edit box.

5. The dialog box switches into accelerator input mode and replaces the outline pane with a message pane. This message tells you to enter the accelerator key you want and then press Esc.

6. Enter the accelerator key for the currently selected option. Press Esc when you are done.

7. Repeat steps 2 through 6 for the other targeted menu options.

8. Invoke the Save project option in the menu selection File.

The RWMENU2.RC file now contains two accelerator resources: LONGMENU and SHORTMENU. These resources have the same accelerator keys. In addition, the resource file contains modified menu text for the targeted menu options.

Compile and run the program RWMENU2.EXE. Press the Ctrl+X, Ctrl+C, or Ctr+V keys. Notice the program responds by displaying the message dialog box. This box tells you that the invoked feature is not implemented. These accelerator keys work with either long or short menu versions. To exit the program, press the Alt+X key. The program offers a message dialog box to confirm the request to exit. Figure 2.5 shows a sample session with the RWMENU2.EXE program.

Listing 2.7 shows the contents of the RWMENU2.DEF definition file. Listing 2.8 contains the source code for the RWMENU2.H header file. Listing 2.9 shows the script of the RWMENU2.RC resource file. Listing 2.10 contains the source code for the RWMENU2.CPP implementation file.

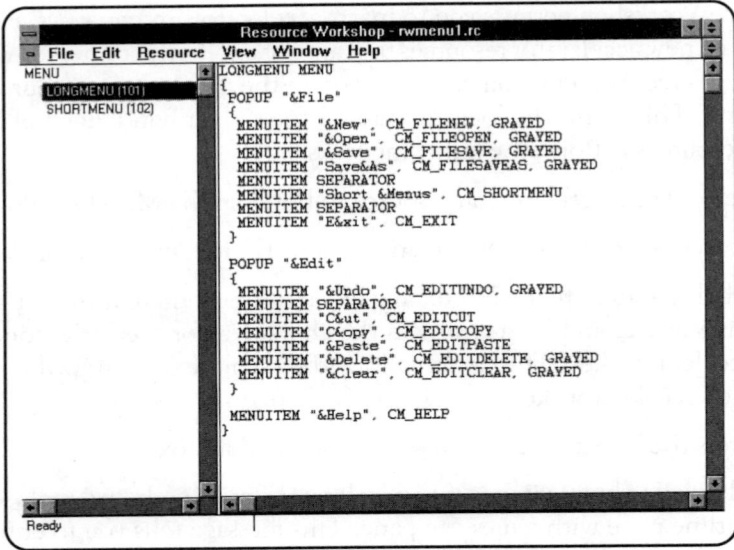

Figure 2.5. A sample session with the RWMENU2.EXE program.

LISTING 2.7. THE CONTENTS OF THE **RWMENU2.DEF** DEFINITION FILE.

```
NAME          RwMenu2
DESCRIPTION   'An OWL Windows Application'
EXETYPE       WINDOWS
CODE          PRELOAD MOVEABLE DISCARDABLE
DATA          PRELOAD MOVEABLE MULTIPLE
HEAPSIZE      1024
STACKSIZE     8192
```

LISTING 2.8. THE SOURCE CODE FOR THE **RWMENU2.H** HEADER FILE.

```
#define LONGMENU       101
#define SHORTMENU      102
#define CM_LONGMENU      1
#define CM_POPUPITEM   101
#define CM_HELP          8
#define CM_EDITCLEAR     7
#define CM_EDITDELETE    6
#define CM_EDITPASTE     5
```

```
#define CM_EDITCOPY        4
#define CM_EDITCUT         3
#define CM_EDITUNDO      105
#define CM_SHORTMENU       9
#define CM_FILENEW       106
#define CM_FILESAVEAS    104
#define CM_FILESAVE      103
#define CM_FILEOPEN      102
```

LISTING 2.9. THE SCRIPT OF THE RWMENU2.RC RESOURCE FILE.

```
#include <windows.h>
#include <owl\window.rh>
#include "rwmenu2.h"

LONGMENU MENU
{
 POPUP "&File"
 {
  MENUITEM "&New", CM_FILENEW, GRAYED
  MENUITEM "&Open", CM_FILEOPEN, GRAYED
  MENUITEM "&Save", CM_FILESAVE, GRAYED
  MENUITEM "Save&As", CM_FILESAVEAS, GRAYED
  MENUITEM SEPARATOR
  MENUITEM "Short &Menus", CM_SHORTMENU
  MENUITEM SEPARATOR
  MENUITEM "E&xit     Alt-X", CM_EXIT
 }

 POPUP "&Edit"
 {
  MENUITEM "&Undo", CM_EDITUNDO, GRAYED
  MENUITEM SEPARATOR
  MENUITEM "C&ut         Ctrl-X", CM_EDITCUT
  MENUITEM "C&opy    Ctrl-C", CM_EDITCOPY
  MENUITEM "&Paste   Ctrl-V", CM_EDITPASTE
  MENUITEM "&Delete", CM_EDITDELETE, GRAYED
  MENUITEM "&Clear", CM_EDITCLEAR, GRAYED
 }

 MENUITEM "&Help", CM_HELP, HELP
}


SHORTMENU MENU
{
```

continues

LISTING 2.9. CONTINUED

```
POPUP "&File"
{
 MENUITEM "&Open", CM_FILEOPEN, GRAYED
 MENUITEM "Save&AS", CM_FILESAVEAS, GRAYED
 MENUITEM SEPARATOR
 MENUITEM "&Long Menus", CM_LONGMENU
 MENUITEM SEPARATOR
 MENUITEM "E&xit    Alt-X", CM_EXIT
}

POPUP "&Edit"
{
 MENUITEM "C&ut        Ctrl-X", CM_EDITCUT
 MENUITEM "C&opy     Ctrl-C", CM_EDITCOPY
 MENUITEM "&Paste    Ctrl-V", CM_EDITPASTE
}

MENUITEM "&Help", CM_HELP, HELP
}


LONGMENU ACCELERATORS
{
 "^X", CM_EDITCUT
 "^C", CM_EDITCOPY
 "^V", CM_EDITPASTE
 "x", CM_EXIT, ASCII, ALT
}

SHORTMENU ACCELERATORS
{
 "x", CM_EXIT, ASCII, ALT
 "^X", CM_EDITCUT
 "^C", CM_EDITCOPY
 "^V", CM_EDITPASTE, ASCII
}
```

LISTING 2.10. THE SOURCE CODE FOR THE RWMENU2.CPP IMPLEMENTATION FILE.

```
/*
  Program which uses alternate menus with minimal response
*/
```

```
#include <owl\applicat.h>
#include <owl\framewin.h>
#include "rwmenu2.h"

// declare the custom application class as
// a subclass of TApplication
class TWinApp : public TApplication
{
public:
  TWinApp() : TApplication() {}

protected:
  virtual void InitMainWindow();
};

// expand the functionality of TWindow by deriving class TMainWindow
class TMainWindow : public TWindow
{
 public:
   TMainWindow()
     : TWindow(0, 0, 0)
     { LongMenuSelected = TRUE; }

 protected:

   BOOL LongMenuSelected;

   // handle clicking the left mouse button
   void EvLButtonDown(UINT, TPoint&);

   // handle clicking the right mouse button
   void EvRButtonDown(UINT, TPoint&);

   // handle the long menu
   void CMLongMenu();

   // handle the short menu
   void CMShortMenu();

   // handle the help menu
     void CMHelp();

   // handle the Edit Copy menu
   void CMEditCopy();

   // handle the Edit Cut menu
   void CMEditCut();

   // handle the Edit Paste
   void CMEditPaste();
```

continues

LISTING 2.10. CONTINUED

```
  // display a message "Feature not implemented"
  void notImplemented();

  // handle confirming closing the window
  virtual BOOL CanClose();

  // declare the response table
  DECLARE_RESPONSE_TABLE(TMainWindow);

};

DEFINE_RESPONSE_TABLE1(TMainWindow, TWindow)
  EV_WM_LBUTTONDOWN,
  EV_WM_RBUTTONDOWN,
  EV_COMMAND(CM_LONGMENU, CMLongMenu),
  EV_COMMAND(CM_SHORTMENU, CMShortMenu),
  EV_COMMAND(CM_HELP, CMHelp),
  EV_COMMAND(CM_EDITCOPY, CMEditCopy),
  EV_COMMAND(CM_EDITCUT, CMEditCut),
  EV_COMMAND(CM_EDITPASTE, CMEditPaste),
END_RESPONSE_TABLE;

void TMainWindow::EvLButtonDown(UINT, TPoint&)
{
  MessageBox("You clicked the left mouse!", "Mouse Event",
            MB_OK | MB_ICONEXCLAMATION);
}

void TMainWindow::EvRButtonDown(UINT, TPoint&)
{
  if (LongMenuSelected)
    CMShortMenu();
  else
    CMLongMenu();
}

void TMainWindow::CMLongMenu()
{
  GetApplication()->MainWindow->AssignMenu(TResID(LONGMENU));
  GetApplication()->MainWindow->Attr.AccelTable = TResID(LONGMENU);
  LongMenuSelected = TRUE;
  MessageBox("The long menu is now active", "Menu Change",
            MB_OK | MB_ICONINFORMATION);
}

// assign the short menu
void TMainWindow::CMShortMenu()
{
```

```
  GetApplication()->MainWindow->AssignMenu(TResID(SHORTMENU));
  GetApplication()->MainWindow->Attr.AccelTable = TResID(SHORTMENU);
  LongMenuSelected = FALSE;
  MessageBox("The short menu is now active", "Menu Change",
             MB_OK | MB_ICONINFORMATION);}

void TMainWindow::CMEditCut()
{
  notImplemented();
}

void TMainWindow::CMEditCopy()
{
  notImplemented();
}

void TMainWindow::CMEditPaste()
{
  notImplemented();
}

void TMainWindow::CMHelp()
{
  MessageBox(
     "This a sample one line help (that leaves more to be desired)",
     "Help", MB_OK | MB_ICONINFORMATION);
}

void TMainWindow::notImplemented()
{
  MessageBox("This feature is not implemented",
             "Information", MB_OK | MB_ICONEXCLAMATION);
}

BOOL TMainWindow::CanClose()
{
  return MessageBox("Want to close this application?",
                    "Query", MB_YESNO | MB_ICONQUESTION) == IDYES;
}

void TWinApp::InitMainWindow()
{
  MainWindow = new TFrameWindow(0,
                       "Alternate Menus Demo Program (version 3)",
                       new TMainWindow);
  // load the menu resource
  MainWindow->AssignMenu(TResID(LONGMENU));
  MainWindow->Attr.AccelTable = TResID(LONGMENU);
}
```

continues

LISTING 2.10. CONTINUED

```
int OwlMain(int /* argc */, char** /*argv[] */)
{
  TWinApp app;
  return app.Run();
}
```

The header file RWMENU2.H has the same declarations as file RWMENU1.H, since the menu systems in projects RWMENU1 and RWMENU2 are the same. The resource file RWMENU2.RC differs from file RWMENU1.RC by the following:

1. The new resource file includes the header file RWMENU2.H, instead of file RWMENU1.H.

2. The menu options Exit, Cut, Copy, and Paste in the new resource file have extended menu text.

3. The LONGMENU accelerators resource, which defines the accelerator keys for the commands CM_EDITCUT, CM_EDITCOPY, CM_EDITPASTE, and CM_EXIT.

4. The SHORTMENU accelerators resource, which defines the accelerator keys for the commands CM_EDITCUT, CM_EDITCOPY, CM_EDITPASTE, and CM_EXIT.

The implementation file RWMENU2.CPP contains the C++ source code for the program. The statements in this file are similar to those in file RWMENU1.CPP. The relevant differences between the two implementation files are :

1. The second statement in member function CMLongMenu is new. This statement loads the accelerators key resource LONGMENU and keeps the selection of the menu and accelerators resource in sync with each other.

2. The second statement in member function CMShortMenu is new. This statement loads the accelerators key resource SHORTMENU and keeps the selection of the menu and accelerators resource in sync with each other.

3. The first statement in member function InitMainWindow has a different window title.

4. The last statement in member function InitMainWindow is new. The function LoadAccelerators loads the accelerators key resource LONGMENU,

CREATING ICON RESOURCES

The Resource Workshop permits you to create icon resources using the following steps.

1. Select the New… options in the Resource menu selection. This menu option brings up the New resource dialog box.

2. Choose the ICON item in the Resource type list box of the New resource dialog box.

3. Click the OK button in the New resource dialog box.

4. The Resource Workshop displays a message dialog box asking whether you want to create the resource in source or binary form. To create the icon resource in source form, click the Source pushbutton. To create the icon resource in binary form, click the Binary pushbutton control. The remaining steps focus on the binary form.

5. The Resource Workshop displays the New file resource dialog box (see Figure 2.6) that enables you to select the following items:

    • Select or enter the resource filename

    • Select the resource file type

    • Select the filename that contains the reference to the resource you are creating.

    • Select the host drive and directory.

6. When you finish working with the New file resource dialog box, click the OK pushbutton.

7. The Resource Workshop displays a relatively small New icon image dialog box which contains two sets of radio buttons. The first set permits you to specify the size of the icon and choose from 32 by 32, 32 by 16, or 64 by 64. The second set of radio buttons enable you to choose from 2, 8, 16, and 256 colors (the latter option may be disabled for your system). Select the size and color settings, and then click the OK pushbutton.

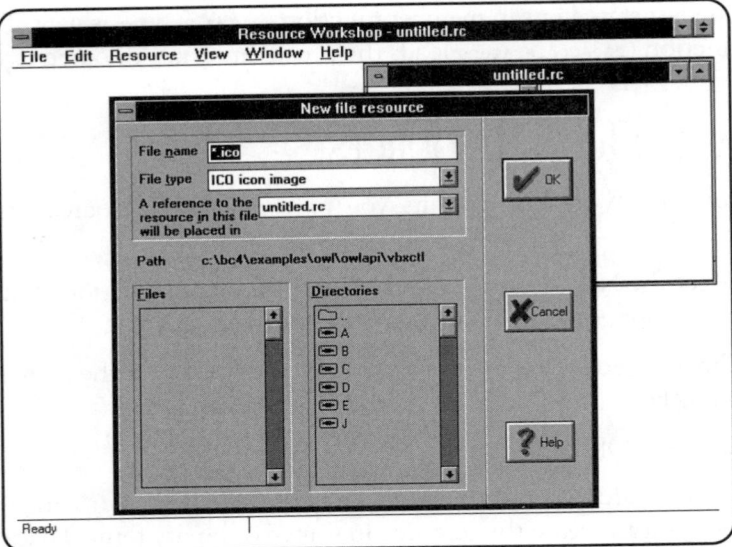

Figure 2.6. A sample session with Resource Workshop showing the New file resource dialog box.

8. The Resource Workshop displays the Paint editor. Figure 2.7 shows a sample session with the Paint editor. The editor has two panes. The edit pane, located to the left, displays the icon at different zoom levels. You can use the Zoom in, Zoom out, and Actual size menu options in the View menu selection, to magnify the icon, demagnify the icon, or view the icon in its actual size. The preview pane, located to the right, always shows the icon in actual size. Initially, the Resource Workshop displays the Colors and Tools palettes in the preview pane. The Colors palette displays the available colors and enables you to select the foreground and background colors. To select the foreground color, move the mouse to the color you want and click the left mouse button. To select the background color, move the mouse to the color you want and click the right mouse button. The Colors palette displays the following color selection indicators:

   • The letters FG appear inside a foreground color.

   • The letters BK appear inside a background color.

   • The letters BF appear inside a color that is in both the foreground and background.

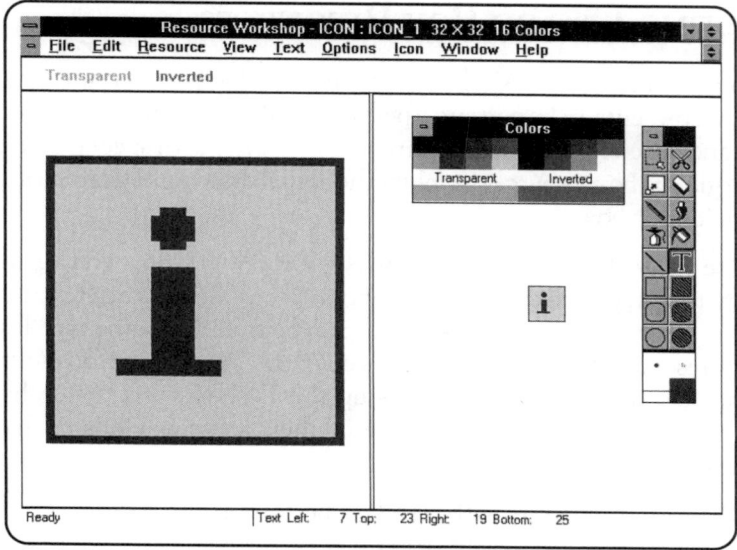

Figure 2.7. A sample session with the Paint editor.

The Tools palette resembles those in Paintbrush and includes the following:

- Tools to cut and move bit maps.

- A tool to erase bit maps.

- Tools to draw pixels, lines, empty rectangles (both sharp and round-edged rectangles), empty circles, filled rectangles (both sharp and round-edged rectangles), and filled circles.

- Airbrush, paintbrush, and paint can tools.

- A tool enter text.

- A zoom tool.

9. Draw the icon using the various colors and tools.

10. Save the icon by saving the project.

I will show you an example of incorporating an icon, along with using the VBX picture control, later in this chapter.

Creating Dialog Box Resources

The ability for Resource Workshop to create dialog boxes containing various controls represents an important aspect of visual programming. While creating menus and accelerators resources involved working with special dialog boxes, creating dialog box resources involves the actual drawing of the controls pasted onto the dialog box.

To create a new dialog box resource in Resource Workshop, you begin as with any new resource: Select the menu option New... from the Resource menu selection. Then select the DIALOG resource type from Resource type list box in the New resource dialog box. Once you click the OK pushbutton of this dialog box, the Resource Workshop brings up the DialogExpert dialog box. This dialog box enables you to create one of the following kinds of dialog box resources:

- Windows dialog box with standard buttons at the bottom
- Windows dialog box with standard buttons near the right edge
- Borland dialog box with standard buttons at the bottom
- Borland dialog box with standard buttons near the right edge
- Child dialog box with no buttons
- Standard window with no buttons

When you click the OK button of the DialogExpert dialog box, the Resource Workshop brings up the Dialog editor. Figure 2.8 shows a sample session with the Dialog editor.

The Dialog editor displays the dialog box resource in its initial state (this includes the default buttons, location, and size), along with the Align palette and Tools palette. You can use the mouse to move and resize the dialog box to accommodate the required size and location.

To rename a resource dialog box (or any other resource), use the Rename... menu option in the Resource menu selection. This option brings up an input dialog box that permits you to enter the new resource name.

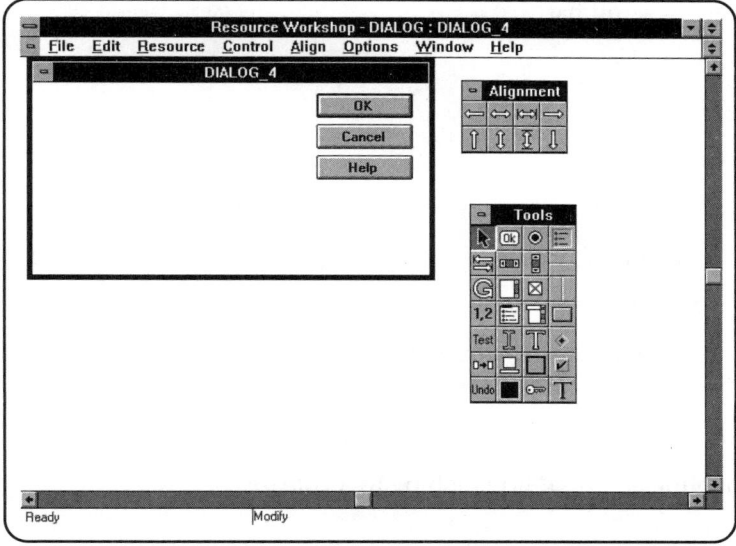

Figure 2.8. A sample session with the Dialog editor.

The Tools Palette

The Tools palette offers the tools to draw and manage the various controls in the dialog box resource. The Tools palette supports the following controls:

- Windows static text
- Borland static text
- Iconic static control
- Black frame static (text) control
- Black rectangle static (text) control
- Windows pushbutton
- Borland pushbutton
- Edit text control
- Group box
- Check box
- Radio button

- Vertical scroll bar
- Horizontal scroll bar
- List box
- Combo box
- Custom controls
- Vertical dip
- Horizontal dip

Other tools enable you to manage the creation of the dialog box resources by supporting the following operations:

- Setting the tab order of the controls
- Enabling and disabling tabbing to a control
- Groups selection and shading
- Duplicating controls
- Undoing the last action
- Testing the dialog box

Using the Dialog editor is fairly intuitive.

The Align Palette

The Align palette contains a set of tools that empowers you to align the controls in the dialog box. In order to align multiple controls, you need to select them. This process involves clicking each of the controls while holding the Shift key down. This process creates a red colored selection frame which defines metrics for the aligned controls. The Align tools support the following operations:

- Aligning the selected controls so their left sides are on the left side of the selection frame.
- Aligning the selected controls so their right sides are on the left side of the selection frame.
- Aligning the selected controls so their horizontal centers are in the center of the selection frame.

- Moving the selection frame horizontally to center it in the dialog box. This operation maintains the relative position of the selected controls in the frame.

- Aligning selected controls so their tops are at the top of the selection frame.

- Aligning the selected controls so their bottoms are at the bottom of the selection frame.

- Aligning the selected controls so their vertical centers are in the center of the selection frame.

- Moving the selection frame vertically, so it is centered in the dialog box. This operation maintains the relative position of the selected controls in the frame.

Creating a Bare-Bones Dialog Box Resource

Let's look at a simple program that brings up bare-bones dialog boxes. The next project, RWDLG1, implements a simple Windows program that responds to the left and right mouse clicks by displaying custom message dialog boxes created by the Resource Workshop.

Let's look at the listings first to make setting up the project a bit easier. Listing 2.11 shows the contents of the RWDLG1.DEF definition file. Listing 2.12 contains the source code for the RWDLG1.H header file. Listing 2.13 shows the script of the RWDLG1.RC resource file. Listing 2.14 contains the source code for the RWDLG1.CPP implementation file.

Prepare the files RWDLG1.DEF, RWDLG1.H, and RWDLG1.CPP by typing the contents shown in their respective listings. By contrast, only type in the #include directive and the menu resource in the RWDLG1.RC. Do not type the dialog box resources. Create the new RWDLG1 project and include the preceding files. Now you are ready to invoke the Resource Workshop.

Use the Resource Workshop to create the IDD_LCKICK_DLG (this resource starts out with the default name DIALOG_1, which you need to rename). Create a Windows dialog box with the buttons located near the bottom edge. The Dialog editor brings up the initial dialog box with the default button set of OK, Cancel, and Help. Delete the latter two by clicking them with the mouse to select them, and then pressing the Delete key.

Create the new dialog box with the Modal frame, Pop-up, Visible, Caption, and System menu styles. The caption of the dialog box is Mouse Event. The dialog box has two controls:

1. The OK pushbutton, which the Resource Workshop inserts by default

2. The static text control with the centered text `You clicked the left button!`

Figure 2.9 shows a session with the Dialog editor while creating the `IDD_LCLICK_DLG` dialog box resource.

Now create the other dialog box resource `IDD_RCLICK_DLG` in a manner similar to the resource `IDD_LCLICK_DLG`. The second dialog box differs from the first in its name and static text message. When you are done, save the new dialog box resources (by saving the project). Compile and run the program. Click in the client window area with the left or right mouse buttons. Observe how the program displays the dialog boxes you created in the Resource Workshop. Figure 2.10 shows a sample session with the RWDLG1.EXE program.

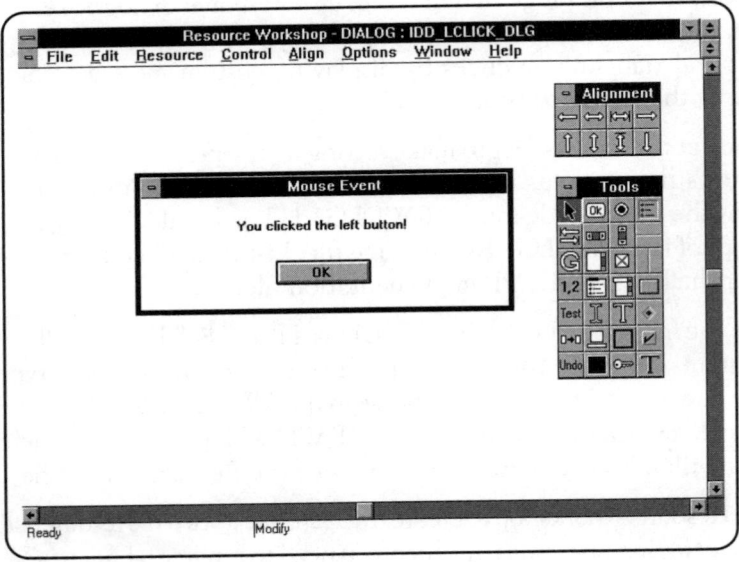

Figure 2.9. This shows a session with the Dialog editor while creating the IDD_LCLICK_DLG dialog box resource.

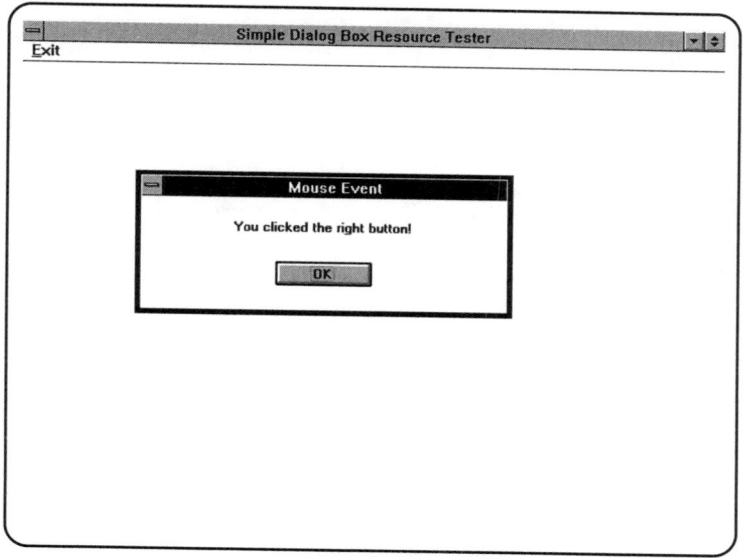

Figure 2.10. A sample session with the RWDLG1.EXE program.

LISTING 2.11. THE CONTENTS OF THE RWDLG1.DEF DEFINITION FILE.

```
NAME          RwDlg1
DESCRIPTION   'An OWL Windows Application'
EXETYPE       WINDOWS
CODE          PRELOAD MOVEABLE DISCARDABLE
DATA          PRELOAD MOVEABLE MULTIPLE
HEAPSIZE      1024
STACKSIZE     8192
```

LISTING 2.12. THE SOURCE CODE FOR THE RWDLG1.H HEADER FILE.

```
#define IDD_LCLICK_DLG   100
#define IDD_RCLICK_DLG   101
#define EXITMENU         102
```

LISTING 2.13. THE SCRIPT OF THE RWDLG1.RC RESOURCE FILE.

```
#include <windows.h>
#include <owl\window.rh>
#include "rwdlg1.h"

IDD_LCLICK_DLG DIALOG 63, 76, 191, 65
STYLE DS_MODALFRAME | WS_POPUP | WS_VISIBLE | WS_CAPTION | WS_SYSMENU
CAPTION "Mouse Event"
FONT 8, "MS Sans Serif"
{
 DEFPUSHBUTTON "OK", IDOK, 70, 37, 50, 14
 CTEXT "You clicked the left button!", -1, 18, 13, 154, 10
}

IDD_RCLICK_DLG DIALOG 63, 76, 191, 65
STYLE DS_MODALFRAME | WS_POPUP | WS_VISIBLE | WS_CAPTION | WS_SYSMENU
CAPTION "Mouse Event"
FONT 8, "MS Sans Serif"
{
 DEFPUSHBUTTON "OK", IDOK, 70, 37, 50, 14
 CTEXT "You clicked the right button!", -1, 18, 13, 154, 10
}

EXITMENU MENU
{
 MENUITEM "&Exit", CM_EXIT
}
```

LISTING 2.14. THE SOURCE CODE FOR THE RWDLG1.CPP IMPLEMENTATION FILE.

```
/*
  Program which uses tests simple dialog resources
*/

#include <owl\applicat.h>
#include <owl\framewin.h>
#include <owl\dialog.h>
#include "rwdlg1.h"

// declare the custom application class as
// a subclass of TApplication

class TWinApp : public TApplication
{
public:
  TWinApp() : TApplication() {}
```

```
protected:
  virtual void InitMainWindow();
};

// expand the functionality of TWindow by deriving class TMainWindow
class TMainWindow : public TWindow
{
 public:
   TMainWindow() : TWindow(0, 0, 0) {}

 protected:

   // handle clicking the left mouse button
   void EvLButtonDown(UINT, TPoint&);

   // handle clicking the right mouse button
   void EvRButtonDown(UINT, TPoint&);

   // handle confirming closing the window
   virtual BOOL CanClose();

   // declare the response table
   DECLARE_RESPONSE_TABLE(TMainWindow);

};

DEFINE_RESPONSE_TABLE1(TMainWindow, TWindow)
  EV_WM_LBUTTONDOWN,
  EV_WM_RBUTTONDOWN,
END_RESPONSE_TABLE;

void TMainWindow::EvLButtonDown(UINT, TPoint&)
{
  TDialog* pDlg = new TDialog(this, TResID(IDD_LCLICK_DLG));

  pDlg->Execute();
}

void TMainWindow::EvRButtonDown(UINT, TPoint&)
{
  TDialog* pDlg = new TDialog(this, TResID(IDD_RCLICK_DLG));

  pDlg->Execute();
}

BOOL TMainWindow::CanClose()
{
  return MessageBox("Want to close this application?",
              "Query", MB_YESNO | MB_ICONQUESTION) == IDYES;
}
```

continues

LISTING 2.14. CONTINUED

```
void TWinApp::InitMainWindow()
{
  MainWindow = new TFrameWindow(0,
                    "Simple Dialog Box Resource Tester",
                    new TMainWindow);
  // load the menu resource
  MainWindow->AssignMenu(TResID(EXITMENU));
}

int OwlMain(int /* argc */, char** /*argv[] */)
{
  TWinApp app;
  return app.Run();
}
```

Listing 2.13 shows the script for the resource file RWDLG1.RC. This file contains the script for the two dialog box resources: IDD_LCLICK_DLG and IDD_RCLICK_DLG. The coordinates, widths, and heights of the dialog boxes and their controls may not match in your own RWDLG1.RC file (in Listing 2.13 they do). To make them match you can edit the resource script (as I did) to duplicate the locations and dimensions of the dialog boxes and their controls. This little trick enables you to smooth the visual design of dialog boxes and their controls.

The implementation source code in Listing 2.14 is simple. The main window class, TMainWindow, responds to the left and right mouse clicks using the member functions EvLButtonDown and EvRButtonDown, respectively. The member function EvLButtonDown creates a dialog box using the OWL class TDialog and the resource IDD_LCLICK_DLG. To invoke the dialog box, the member function sends the C++ message Execute (which invokes a modal dialog box) to the dialog box object, accessed using the local pointer pDlg. The member function EvRButtonDown performs a similar task to invoke the dialog box resource IDD_RCLICK_DLG.

CREATING DIALOG BOX RESOURCES WITH BASIC CONTROLS

Let's look at another example of a dialog box resource. The next project, RWDLG2, creates and displays a dialog box that represents a *dummy* simple calculator. I say *dummy* because the implementation program does not *animate* the custom dialog box class. This means that clicking on the buttons of the calculator does not perform the anticipated operations (what a letdown!). This does not mean that the calculator dialog box does absolutely nothing. The dialog box is reacting minimally by emulating the button down action when you click a button. You can also enter, edit, and select text in the edit box control that emulates the calculator's display. Figure 2.11 shows a sample session with the RWDLG2.EXE program. As the figure shows, the calculator dialog box has the digits, decimal, clear, change of sign, basic math operations, and Close buttons. The latter button is really the OK button appearing under a different caption. You can close the dialog box by clicking the Close button.

Let's peek at the listings first to make setting up the project a bit easier. Listing 2.15 shows the contents of the RWDLG2.DEF definition file. Listing 2.16 contains the source code for the RWDLG2.H header file. Listing 2.17 shows the script of the RWDLG2.RC resource file. Listing 2.18 contains the source code for the RWDLG2.CPP implementation file.

Prepare the files RWDLG2.DEF, RWDLG2.H, and RWDLG2.CPP by typing the contents shown in their respective listings. By contrast, only type in the `#include` directive and the menu resource in the RWDLG2.RC. Do not type the dialog box resources. Create the new RWDLG2 project and include the preceding files. Now you are ready to invoke the Resource Workshop.

Use the Resource Workshop to create the `IDD_CALC_DLG` (this resource starts out with the default name `DIALOG_1`, which you need to rename). Create a Windows dialog box with the buttons located near the bottom edge. The Dialog edit brings up the initial dialog box with the default button set of OK, Cancel, and Help. Delete the latter two by clicking them with the mouse to select them, and then pressing the Delete key.

Create the new dialog box with the Modal frame, Pop-up, Visible, Caption, and System menu styles. The caption of the dialog box is Dummy Calculator. The dialog box has the following sets of controls:

1. The Close pushbutton is really the renamed OK button. This button is the default pushbutton.

2. The edit text control with the text `Major Malfunction!`. This control has the style Tab stop, Border, and Automatic horizontal scroll.

3. The pushbutton controls for the digits and operators. Make each of these buttons into ordinary push buttons (and not the default

pushbutton). Use the identifiers in the file RWDLG2.H for the various controls. For example, the digit button 1 has the identifier IDC_1.

The process of creating the preceding controls involves selecting them from the Tools palette and then drawing them. Since there are many pushbutton controls, you can use the Copy and Paste menu options (in the Edit menu selection) to create these controls. You likely will need to use the Align palette to align the rows and columns of the buttons. Figure 2.9 shows a session with the Dialog editor while creating the IDD_LCLICK_DLG dialog box resource. The figure shows the configuration and location of the various controls. When you are done, save the new dialog box resource (by saving the project). Compile and run the program. Click the Calc menu selection to bring up the calculator resource dialog box. Click the digit and operators push buttons and observe how they simulate pushing these buttons down. You can also type and edit text in the edit text control. When you are done, click the Close pushbutton to close the dialog box. Figure 2.12 shows a sample session with the RWDLG2.EXE program.

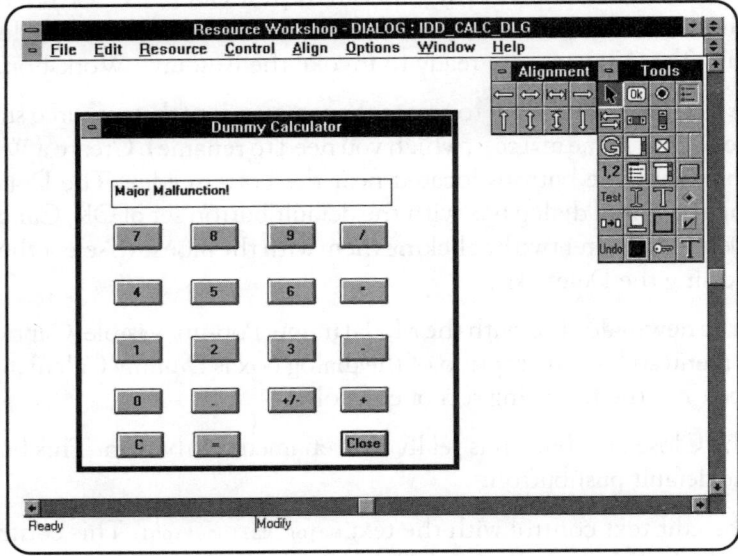

Figure 2.11. A sample session with the Dialog editor while creating the calculator dialog box resource.

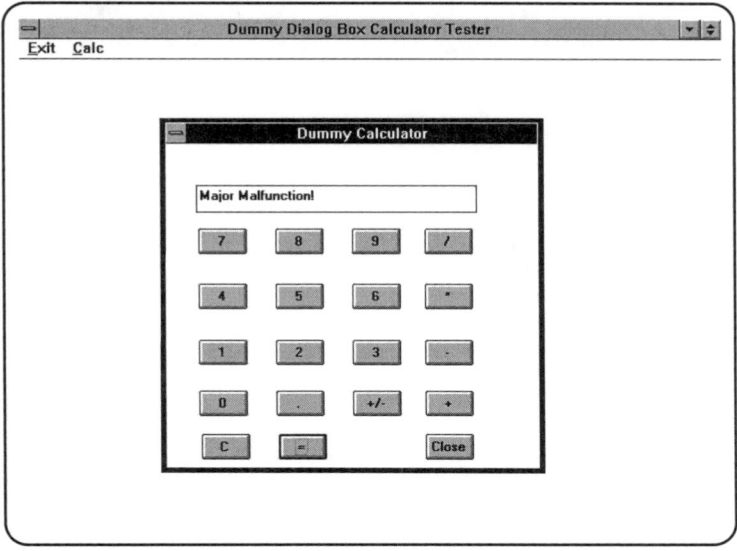

Figure 2.12. A sample session with the RWDLG2.EXE program.

LISTING 2.15. THE CONTENTS OF THE RWDLG2.DEF DEFINITION FILE.

```
NAME          RwDlg2
DESCRIPTION   'An OWL Windows Application'
EXETYPE       WINDOWS
CODE          PRELOAD MOVEABLE DISCARDABLE
DATA          PRELOAD MOVEABLE MULTIPLE
HEAPSIZE      1024
STACKSIZE     8192
```

LISTING 2.16. THE SOURCE CODE FOR THE RWDLG2.H HEADER FILE.

```
#define IDC_0          100
#define IDC_1          101
#define IDC_2          102
#define IDC_3          103
#define IDC_4          104
#define IDC_5          105
#define IDC_6          106
```

continues

LISTING 2.16. CONTINUED

```
#define IDC_7          107
#define IDC_8          108
#define IDC_9          109
#define IDC_CLEAR      110
#define IDC_ADD        111
#define IDC_CHS        112
#define IDC_DOT        113
#define IDC_SUB        114
#define IDC_MUL        115
#define IDC_DIV        116
#define IDC_EQL        117
#define IDC_EDIT1      118
#define CM_CALC        200
#define EXITMENU       201
#define IDD_CALC_DLG   202
```

LISTING 2.17. THE SCRIPT OF THE RWDLG2.RC RESOURCE FILE.

```
#include <windows.h>
#include <owl\window.rh>
#include "rwdlg2.h"

IDD_CALC_DLG DIALOG 6, 15, 194, 189
STYLE DS_MODALFRAME | WS_POPUP | WS_VISIBLE | WS_CAPTION | WS_SYSMENU
CAPTION "Dummy Calculator"
FONT 8, "MS Sans Serif"
{
 DEFPUSHBUTTON "Close", IDOK, 135, 169, 25, 15
 PUSHBUTTON "7", IDC_7, 17, 49, 25, 15
 PUSHBUTTON "8", IDC_8, 57, 49, 25, 15
 PUSHBUTTON "9", IDC_9, 97, 49, 25, 15
 PUSHBUTTON "/", IDC_DIV, 135, 49, 25, 15
 PUSHBUTTON "4", IDC_4, 17, 81, 25, 15
 PUSHBUTTON "5", IDC_5, 57, 81, 25, 15
 PUSHBUTTON "6", IDC_6, 97, 81, 25, 15
 PUSHBUTTON "*", IDC_MUL, 135, 81, 25, 15
 PUSHBUTTON "1", IDC_1, 17, 114, 25, 15
 PUSHBUTTON "2", IDC_2, 57, 114, 25, 15
 PUSHBUTTON "3", IDC_3, 97, 114, 25, 15
 PUSHBUTTON "-", IDC_SUB, 135, 114, 25, 15
 PUSHBUTTON "0", IDC_0, 17, 144, 25, 15
 PUSHBUTTON ".", IDC_DOT, 57, 144, 25, 15
 PUSHBUTTON "+/-", IDC_CHS, 97, 144, 25, 15
 PUSHBUTTON "+", IDC_ADD, 135, 144, 25, 15
```

```
PUSHBUTTON "C", IDC_CLEAR, 18, 169, 25, 15
PUSHBUTTON "=", IDC_EQL, 58, 169, 25, 15
CONTROL "Major Malfunction!", IDC_EDIT1, "EDIT",
        ES_AUTOHSCROLL ¦ WS_BORDER ¦ WS_TABSTOP,
        16, 24, 146, 16
}

EXITMENU MENU
{
 MENUITEM "&Exit", CM_EXIT
 MENUITEM "&Calc", CM_CALC
}
```

LISTING 2.18. THE SOURCE CODE FOR THE RWDLG2.CPP IMPLEMENTATION FILE.

```
/*
  Program which uses tests simple dialog resources
*/

#include <owl\applicat.h>
#include <owl\framewin.h>
#include <owl\dialog.h>
#include "rwdlg2.h"

// declare the custom application class as
// a subclass of TApplication

class TWinApp : public TApplication
{
public:
  TWinApp() : TApplication() {}

protected:
  virtual void InitMainWindow();
};

// expand the functionality of TWindow by deriving class TMainWindow
class TMainWindow : public TWindow
{
 public:
   TMainWindow() : TWindow(0, 0, 0) {}

 protected:

   // handle the Calc menu
   void CMCalc();
```

continues

LISTING 2.18. CONTINUED

```
    // handle confirming closing the window
    virtual BOOL CanClose();

    // declare the response table
    DECLARE_RESPONSE_TABLE(TMainWindow);

};

DEFINE_RESPONSE_TABLE1(TMainWindow, TWindow)
  EV_COMMAND(CM_CALC, CMCalc),
END_RESPONSE_TABLE;

void TMainWindow::CMCalc()
{
  TDialog* pDlg = new TDialog(this, TResID(IDD_CALC_DLG));

  pDlg->Execute();
}

BOOL TMainWindow::CanClose()
{
  return MessageBox("Want to close this application?",
                "Query", MB_YESNO ¦ MB_ICONQUESTION) == IDYES;
}

void TWinApp::InitMainWindow()
{
  MainWindow = new TFrameWindow(0,
                      "Dummy Dialog Box Calculator Tester",
                      new TMainWindow);
  // load the menu resource
  MainWindow->AssignMenu(TResID(EXITMENU));
}

int OwlMain(int /* argc */, char** /*argv[] */)
{
  TWinApp app;
  return app.Run();
}
```

Listing 2.16 shows the RWDLG2.H header file. This file contains the definitions of the identifiers for the dialog box, its controls, and menu resources.

Listing 2.17 contains the RWDLG2.RC resource file, which contains the dialog box and menu resources. The dialog box resources shows that there is one default pushbutton with the label Close and the ID OK. The other pushbutton controls are declared as non-default controls and have appropriate labels and IDs.

Listing 2.18 shows the source code for the implementation file RWDLG2.CPP. The file declares the TWinApp application class and the TMainWindow main window class. The most relevant member function of the latter class is the CMCalc, which responds to the CM_CALC Windows command message sent by the menu selection Calc. The function creates a dynamic instance of dialog class TDialog and specifies the dialog box resource IDD_CALC_DLG. The function then invokes this dialog box by sending the C++ message Execute to the dialog box instance (accessed using the local pointer pDlg).

CREATING DIALOG BOX RESOURCES WITH GROUPED CONTROLS

Let's look at an example of a dialog box resource that contains grouped controls—group boxes, check boxes, and radio buttons. The next project, RWDLG3, creates resource dialog boxes for typical Find and Replace dialog boxes. Such dialog boxes are available in text editor, including the IDE's editor. The Find dialog box implemented in project RWDLG3 contains the following controls:

- The edit text control that holds the search string.
- The static text control that labels the edit control.
- The Options group box that contains the following check boxes:
  - The Whole word check box.
  - The Case sensitive check box.
  - The Prompt check box.
- The Directions group box that contains the following radio buttons:
  - The Forward radio button.
  - The Backward radio button.
  - The Entire radio button.

- The Find Next pushbutton (which is the renamed OK button).

- The Cancel pushbutton.

- The Help button.

The Replace dialog box has all the preceding controls and the following ones:

- The edit text control to enter the replacement string.

- The static text control that labels the preceding control.

- The Replace pushbutton.

- The Replace All pushbutton.

Let's peek at the listings first to make setting up the project a bit easier. Listing 2.19 shows the contents of the RWDLG3.DEF definition file. Listing 2.20 contains the source code for the RWDLG3.H header file. Listing 2.21 shows the script of the RWDLG3.RC resource file. Listing 2.22 contains the source code for the RWDLG3.CPP implementation file.

Prepare the files RWDLG3.DEF, RWDLG3.H, and RWDLG3.CPP by typing the contents shown in their respective listings. By contrast, only type in the #include directive and the menu resource in the RWDLG3.RC. Do not type the dialog box resources. Create the new RWDLG3 project and include the preceding files. Now you are ready to invoke the Resource Workshop.

Use the Resource Workshop to create the IDD_FIND_DLG (this resource starts out with the default name DIALOG_1, which you need to rename). Create a Windows dialog box with the buttons located near the bottom edge. The Dialog edit brings up the initial dialog box with the default buttons OK, Cancel, and Help. Select the OK button and make its caption Find Next.

Create the new Find dialog box with the Modal frame, Pop-up, Visible, Caption, and System menu styles. The caption of the dialog box is Find. Figure 2.13 shows a sample session with the Dialog editor while the Find dialog box is created. Use this figure to guide you in placing the various controls.

The process of creating the preceding controls involves selecting them from the Tools palette and then drawing them. You can use the Copy and Paste menu options (in the Edit menu selection) to create additional check boxes and radio buttons. You most likely will need to use the Align palette to align each set of these controls in the same column. Use the default setting for the group boxes, check boxes, and radio buttons. In the case of the last two controls, the default setting allows automatic checking and selection of the controls.

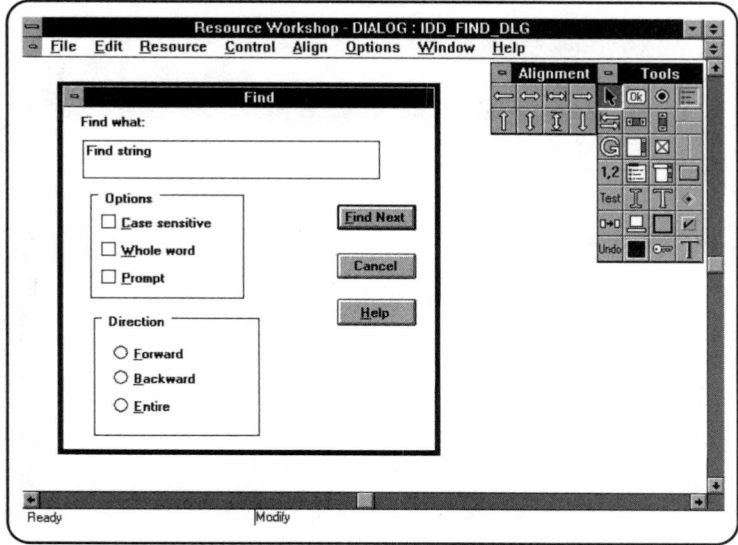

Figure 2.13. A sample session with the Dialog editor in use while the Find dialog box is created.

When you are finished with the Find dialog box, close the Dialog editor, and move to create the Replace dialog box resource. This new resource has the ID of IDD_REPLACE_DLG and the caption Replace.... Make this new dialog box a Borland-style dialog box, with the Modal frame, Pop-up, Visible, Caption, and System menu styles. The dialog box has controls that I mentioned earlier. Figure 2.14 shows a sample session with the Dialog editor while creating the Replace dialog box. Use this figure to guide you in placing the various controls. Include the Borland dips inside the dialog box and inside the group boxes.

When you are done, save the dialog box resources (by saving the project). Compile and run the program. Invoke the Find... menu option in the Search menu selection to bring up the Find dialog box. Experiment with clicking the check boxes, radio buttons, and Find Next button. Notice the dialog box selects only one radio button at a time. Also type in text in the edit box control. When you are done, click the Cancel pushbutton to close the dialog box. Invoke the Replace... menu option to call the Replace dialog box. Experiment with this Borland-style dialog box in a manner similar to the Find dialog box. When you are done, click the Cancel pushbutton to close the dialog box. Figures 2.15 and 2.16 show sample sessions with the RWDLG3.EXE program.

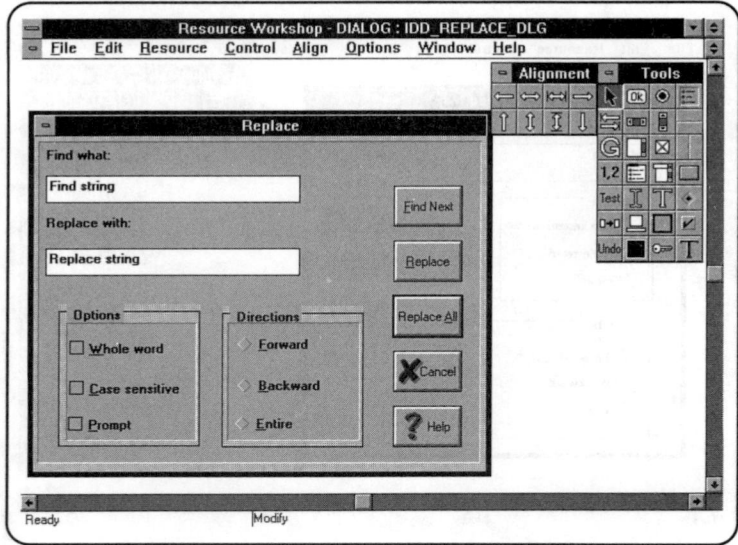

Figure 2.14. A sample session with the Dialog editor while creating the Replace dialog box.

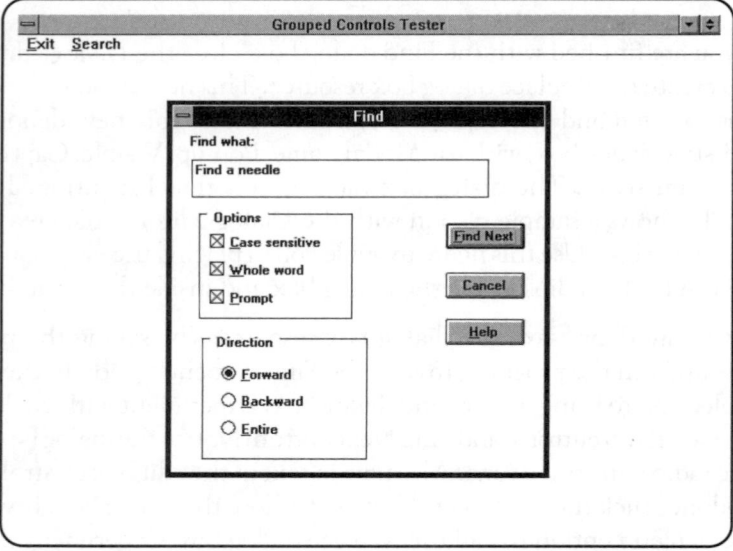

Figure 2.15. A sample session with the RWDLG3.EXE program showing the Find dialog box.

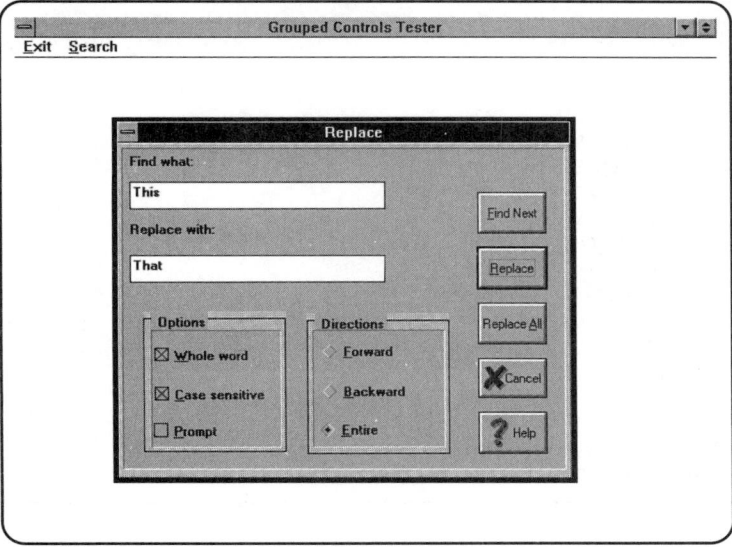

Figure 2.16. A sample session with the RWDLG3.EXE program showing the Replace dialog box.

LISTING 2.19. THE CONTENTS OF THE RWDLG3.DEF DEFINITION FILE.

```
NAME          RwMenu3
DESCRIPTION   'An OWL Windows Application'
EXETYPE       WINDOWS
CODE          PRELOAD MOVEABLE DISCARDABLE
DATA          PRELOAD MOVEABLE MULTIPLE
HEAPSIZE      1024
STACKSIZE     8192
```

LISTING 2.20. THE SOURCE CODE FOR THE RWDLG3.H HEADER FILE.

```
#define IDC_FIND_BOX      100
#define IDC_OPTIONS_GRP   101
#define IDC_WHOLE_CHK     102
#define IDC_CASE_CHK      103
#define IDC_REPLACE_BOX   104
#define IDC_UP_RBT        105
```

continues

Listing 2.20. continued

```
#define IDC_FIND_BTN        106
#define IDC_REPLACE_BTN     107
#define IDC_WHOLEWORD_CHK   108
#define IDC_CASESENSE_CHK   109
#define IDC_CHECKBOX2       110
#define IDC_DIRECTION_GRP   111
#define IDC_PROMPT_CHK      112
#define IDC_DOWN_RBT        113
#define IDC_ALL_RBT         114
#define IDC_DIRECTIONS_GRP  115
#define IDC_REPLACEALL_BTN  116
#define CM_FIND              10
#define CM_REPLACE           11
#define EXITMENU            200
#define IDD_FIND_DLG        301
#define IDD_REPLACE_DLG     302
```

Listing 2.21. The script of the RWDLG3.RC resource file.

```
#include <windows.h>
#include <owl\window.rh>
#include "rwdlg3.h"

EXITMENU MENU
{
 MENUITEM "&Exit", CM_EXIT
 POPUP "&Search"
 {
   MENUITEM "&Find...", CM_FIND
   MENUITEM "&Replace...", CM_REPLACE
 }
}

IDD_FIND_DLG DIALOG 21, -129, 194, 199
STYLE DS_MODALFRAME ¦ WS_POPUP ¦ WS_VISIBLE ¦ WS_CAPTION ¦ WS_SYSMENU
CAPTION "Find"
FONT 8, "MS Sans Serif"
{
 CONTROL "Find string", IDC_FIND_BOX, "EDIT", ES_AUTOHSCROLL ¦
         WS_BORDER ¦ WS_TABSTOP, 10, 19, 155, 22
 LTEXT "Find what:", -1, 9, 4, 51, 13
 DEFPUSHBUTTON "&Find Next", IDC_FIND_BTN, 143, 56, 41, 15
 PUSHBUTTON "Cancel", IDCANCEL, 143, 84, 41, 15
 PUSHBUTTON "&Help", IDHELP, 143, 111, 41, 15
 GROUPBOX " Options ", IDC_OPTIONS_GRP, 14, 47, 80, 64, BS_GROUPBOX
```

```
    CHECKBOX "&Whole word", IDC_WHOLEWORD_CHK, 20, 76, 60, 12,
            BS_AUTOCHECKBOX ¦ WS_TABSTOP
    CHECKBOX "&Prompt", IDC_PROMPT_CHK, 20, 92, 60, 12,
            BS_AUTOCHECKBOX ¦ WS_TABSTOP
    CHECKBOX "&Case sensitive", IDC_CHECKBOX2, 20, 60, 60, 12,
            BS_AUTOCHECKBOX ¦ WS_TABSTOP
    GROUPBOX " Direction ", IDC_DIRECTION_GRP, 16, 118, 86, 73, BS_GROUPBOX
    CONTROL "&Forward", IDC_DOWN_RBT, "BUTTON", BS_AUTORADIOBUTTON,
            26, 135, 50, 15
    CONTROL "&Backward", IDC_DOWN_RBT, "BUTTON", BS_AUTORADIOBUTTON,
            26, 150, 50, 15
    CONTROL "&Entire", IDC_ALL_RBT, "BUTTON", BS_AUTORADIOBUTTON,
            26, 166, 50, 15
}

IDD_REPLACE_DLG DIALOG 6, 15, 236, 195
STYLE DS_MODALFRAME ¦ WS_POPUP ¦ WS_VISIBLE ¦ WS_CAPTION ¦ WS_SYSMENU
CLASS "bordlg"
CAPTION "Replace"
FONT 8, "MS Sans Serif"
{
    CONTROL "Replace &All", IDC_REPLACEALL_BTN, "BorBtn",
            BS_DEFPUSHBUTTON ¦ WS_CHILD ¦ WS_VISIBLE ¦ WS_TABSTOP,
            187, 92, 37, 25
    CONTROL "", IDCANCEL, "BorBtn", BS_PUSHBUTTON ¦ WS_CHILD ¦
            WS_VISIBLE ¦ WS_TABSTOP, 187, 124, 37, 25
    CONTROL "", IDHELP, "BorBtn", BS_PUSHBUTTON ¦ WS_CHILD ¦
            WS_VISIBLE ¦ WS_TABSTOP, 187, 156, 37, 25
    CONTROL "&Find Next", IDC_FIND_BTN, "BorBtn", BS_PUSHBUTTON ¦ WS_CHILD
            ¦ WS_VISIBLE ¦ WS_TABSTOP, 187, 28, 37, 25
    CONTROL "&Replace", IDC_REPLACE_BTN, "BorBtn", BS_PUSHBUTTON ¦ WS_CHILD
            ¦ WS_VISIBLE ¦ WS_TABSTOP, 187, 60, 37, 25
    CONTROL "Find what:", -1, "BorStatic", SS_LEFT ¦ WS_CHILD ¦ WS_VISIBLE
            ¦ WS_GROUP, 6, 7, 73, 10
    CONTROL "Replace with:", -1, "BorStatic", SS_LEFT ¦ WS_CHILD ¦
            WS_VISIBLE ¦ WS_GROUP, 6, 46, 73, 10
    CONTROL "Find string", IDC_FIND_BOX, "EDIT", ES_AUTOHSCROLL ¦ WS_BORDER
            ¦ WS_TABSTOP, 6, 23, 133, 16
    CONTROL "Replace string", IDC_REPLACE_BOX, "EDIT", ES_AUTOHSCROLL ¦
            WS_BORDER ¦ WS_TABSTOP, 6, 65, 133, 16
    GROUPBOX " Options", IDC_OPTIONS_GRP, 13, 98, 74, 82, BS_GROUPBOX
    CHECKBOX "&Whole word", IDC_WHOLE_CHK, 19, 117, 61, 12, BS_AUTOCHECKBOX
            ¦ WS_TABSTOP
    CHECKBOX "&Case sensitive", IDC_CASE_CHK, 19, 140, 61, 12,
            BS_AUTOCHECKBOX ¦ WS_TABSTOP
    CHECKBOX "&Prompt", IDC_PROMPT_CHK, 18, 161, 61, 12, BS_AUTOCHECKBOX ¦
            WS_TABSTOP
    GROUPBOX " Directions", IDC_DIRECTIONS_GRP, 98, 99, 74, 82, BS_GROUPBOX
    CONTROL "&Forward", IDC_DOWN_RBT, "BorRadio", BS_AUTORADIOBUTTON ¦
            WS_CHILD ¦ WS_VISIBLE ¦ WS_TABSTOP, 106, 115, 59, 12
```

continues

```
CONTROL "&Backward", IDC_UP_RBT, "BorRadio", BS_AUTORADIOBUTTON ¦
        WS_CHILD ¦ WS_VISIBLE ¦ WS_TABSTOP, 106, 139, 59, 12
CONTROL "&Entire", IDC_ALL_RBT, "BorRadio", BS_AUTORADIOBUTTON ¦
        WS_CHILD ¦ WS_VISIBLE ¦ WS_TABSTOP, 105, 161, 59, 12
CONTROL "", -1, "BorShade", BSS_GROUP ¦ BSS_CAPTION ¦ BSS_LEFT ¦
        WS_CHILD ¦ WS_VISIBLE, 2, 3, 231, 187
CONTROL "", -1, "BorShade", BSS_GROUP ¦ BSS_CAPTION ¦ BSS_LEFT ¦
        WS_CHILD ¦ WS_VISIBLE, 17, 108, 68, 69
CONTROL "", -1, "BorShade", BSS_GROUP ¦ BSS_CAPTION ¦ BSS_LEFT ¦
        WS_CHILD ¦ WS_VISIBLE, 101, 108, 69, 69
}
```

LISTING 2.22. THE SOURCE CODE FOR THE RWDLG3.CPP IMPLEMENTATION FILE.

```
/*
  Program which uses tests dialog resources with grouped controls
*/

#include <owl\applicat.h>
#include <owl\framewin.h>
#include <owl\dialog.h>
#include "rwdlg3.h"

// declare the custom application class as
// a subclass of TApplication

class TWinApp : public TApplication
{
public:
  TWinApp() : TApplication() {}

protected:
  virtual void InitMainWindow();
};

// expand the functionality of TWindow by deriving class TMainWindow
class TMainWindow : public TWindow
{
 public:
   TMainWindow() : TWindow(0, 0, 0) {}

 protected:

   // handle the Find menu option
   void CMFind();
```

```
    // handle the Replace menu option
    void CMReplace();

    // handle confirming closing the window
    virtual BOOL CanClose();

    // declare the response table
    DECLARE_RESPONSE_TABLE(TMainWindow);

};

DEFINE_RESPONSE_TABLE1(TMainWindow, TWindow)
  EV_COMMAND(CM_FIND, CMFind),
  EV_COMMAND(CM_REPLACE, CMReplace),
END_RESPONSE_TABLE;

void TMainWindow::CMFind()
{
  TDialog* pDlg = new TDialog(this, TResID(IDD_FIND_DLG));

  pDlg->Execute();
}

void TMainWindow::CMReplace()
{
  TDialog* pDlg = new TDialog(this, TResID(IDD_REPLACE_DLG));

  pDlg->Execute();
}

BOOL TMainWindow::CanClose()
{
  return MessageBox("Want to close this application?",
                    "Query", MB_YESNO | MB_ICONQUESTION) == IDYES;
}

void TWinApp::InitMainWindow()
{
  MainWindow = new TFrameWindow(0,
                     "Grouped Controls Tester",
                     new TMainWindow);
  // load the menu resource
  MainWindow->AssignMenu(TResID(EXITMENU));
}

int OwlMain(int /* argc */, char** /*argv[] */)
{
  TWinApp app;
  return app.Run();
}
```

Listing 2.20 shows the RWDLG3.H header file. This file contains the definitions of the identifiers for the dialog box, its controls, and menu resources.

Listing 2.21 contains the RWDLG3.RC resource file, which contains the dialog box and menu resources. The dialog box resource IDD_FIND_DLG contains the resource statements for the various controls. The dialog box resource IDD_REPLACE_DLG is similar to the IDD_FIND_DLG dialog box resource. Notice the following new declarations in the IDD_REPLACE_DLG dialog box resources:

1. The CLASS "borldlg" statement specifies that the dialog box is a Borland-style dialog box.

2. The static text controls are of he type BorStatic.

3. The pushbutton controls are of the type BorBtn.

4. The radio button controls are of type BorRadio.

The preceding BorXXXX control types support the various Borland controls.

Listing 2.22 shows the source code for the implementation file RWDLG3.CPP. The file declares the application class, TWinApp, and the main window class, TMainWindow. The most relevant member functions of the latter class are CMFind and CMReplace, which respond to the CM_FIND and CM_REPLACE Windows command messages sent by the menu options Find… and Replace…, respectively.

The member function CMFind creates a dynamic instance of dialog class TDialog and specifies the dialog box resource IDD_FIND_DLG. The function then invokes this dialog box by sending the C++ message Execute to the dialog box instance (accessed using the local pointer pDlg).

The member function CMReplace creates a dynamic instance of dialog class TDialog and specifies the dialog box resource IDD_REPLACE_DLG. The function then invokes this dialog box by sending the C++ message Execute to the dialog box instance (accessed using the local pointer pDlg).

CREATING A FULLY OPERATIONAL DIALOG BOX

The dummy dialog boxes, which I presented in the last two sections, lack the interaction you have come to expect from dialog boxes. If you have been disappointed (or even downright bored), I have some good news. In this section I present a simple, fully functional dialog box. However, let me point out that breathing life into a dialog box may go beyond your current programming skills. If you think this may be the case, you may choose to skip this section.

The next project, RWDLG4, presents a dialog box that supports a command-line oriented floating-point calculator containing the following controls:

- The Operand 1 edit box in which you type in the first operand.

- The Operator edit box in which you type in an operator. The program supports the operators +, -, /, *, and ^ (raising to powers).

- The Operand 2 edit box in that you type in the second operand.

- The Result edit box that displays the result of a mathematical operation. This control has the read-only style.

- The Error Message edit box that displays any error messages. This control has the read-only style.

- The Calc pushbutton that executes the sought operation using the operands you have entered in the two operands edit boxes.

- The Exit pushbutton that closes the dialog box.

- A set of static text controls that label the preceding edit box controls.

Create the project file and the calculator resource dialog box (with an ID of IDD_CALC_DLG) in a manner similar to the steps mentioned in the last two sections. Figure 2.17 shows a sample session with the RWDLG4.EXE program. Use this figure to guide you in creating the calculator dialog box resource.

Compile and run the program. Click the Calc menu selection to invoke the operational command-oriented calculator dialog box. Enter valid operands and operator in their respective edit boxes and click the Calc pushbutton. Observe the result in the read-only Result edit box. If you enter an invalid operator or attempt to divide by zero, the dialog box displays an error message in the read-only Error Message edit box. When you are finished experimenting with the calculator dialog box, click the Exit button.

Listing 2.23 shows the contents of the RWDLG4.DEF definition file. Listing 2.24 contains the source code for the RWDLG4.H header file. Listing 2.25 shows the script of the RWDLG4.RC resource file. Listing 2.26 contains the source code for the RWDLG4.CPP implementation file.

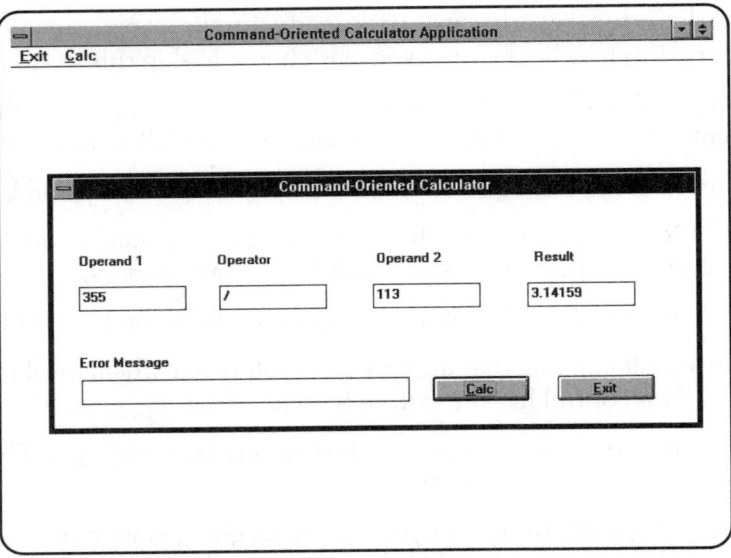

Figure 2.17. A sample session with the RWDLG4.EXE program.

LISTING 2.23. THE CONTENTS OF THE RWDLG4.DEF DEFINITION FILE.

```
NAME          RwDlg4
DESCRIPTION   'An OWL Windows Application'
EXETYPE       WINDOWS
CODE          PRELOAD MOVEABLE DISCARDABLE
DATA          PRELOAD MOVEABLE MULTIPLE
HEAPSIZE      1024
STACKSIZE     8192
```

LISTING 2.24. THE SOURCE CODE FOR THE RWDLG4.H HEADER FILE.

```
#define IDC_OPERAND1_BOX 100
#define IDC_OPERATOR_BOX 101
#define IDC_OPERAND2_BOX 102
#define IDC_RESULT_BOX   103
#define IDC_ERRMSG_BOX   104
#define IDC_CALC_BTN     105
#define CM_CALC          110
#define EXITMENU         201
#define IDD_CALC_DLG     202
```

LISTING 2.25. THE SCRIPT OF THE RWDLG4.RC RESOURCE FILE.

```
#include <windows.h>
#include <owl\window.rh>
#include "rwdlg4.h"

EXITMENU MENU
{
 MENUITEM "&Exit", CM_EXIT
 MENUITEM "&Calc", CM_CALC
}

IDD_CALC_DLG DIALOG 20, 100, 335, 133
STYLE DS_MODALFRAME ¦ WS_POPUP ¦ WS_VISIBLE ¦ WS_CAPTION ¦ WS_SYSMENU
CAPTION "Command-Oriented Calculator"
FONT 8, "MS Sans Serif"
{
 DEFPUSHBUTTON "&Calc", IDC_CALC_BTN, 197, 105, 50, 14
 PUSHBUTTON "&Exit", IDOK, 262, 105, 50, 14
 LTEXT "Operand 1", -1, 13, 32, 58, 13
 LTEXT "Operator", -1, 85, 32, 58, 13
 LTEXT "Operand 2", -1, 168, 32, 58, 13
 LTEXT "Result", -1, 250, 32, 58, 13
 EDITTEXT IDC_OPERAND1_BOX, 13, 51, 56, 14
 EDITTEXT IDC_OPERATOR_BOX, 86, 51, 56, 14
 EDITTEXT IDC_OPERAND2_BOX, 166, 51, 56, 14
 EDITTEXT IDC_RESULT_BOX, 247, 51, 56, 14, ES_READONLY ¦ WS_BORDER ¦
         WS_TABSTOP
 LTEXT "Error Message", -1, 13, 91, 74, 14
 EDITTEXT IDC_ERRMSG_BOX, 14, 105, 171, 14, ES_READONLY ¦ WS_BORDER ¦
         WS_TABSTOP
}
```

LISTING 2.26. THE SOURCE CODE FOR THE RWDLG4.CPP IMPLEMENTATION FILE.

```
/*
  Program to test the resourcs for the static text, edit box,
  and pushbutton controls.
  The program uses these controls to implement a command-line
  oriented calculator application (COCA)
*/

#include <owl\applicat.h>
#include <owl\framewin.h>
#include <owl\dialog.h>
#include <owl\window.rh>
```

continues

LISTING 2.26. CONTINUED

```
#include "rwdlg4.h"
#include <stdlib.h>
#include <stdio.h>
#include <math.h>
#include <string.h>

const MaxEditLen = 40;

// declare the custom application class as
// a subclass of TApplication
class TWinApp : public TApplication
{
public:
  TWinApp() : TApplication() {}

protected:
  virtual void InitMainWindow();
};

// expand the functionality of TWindow by
// deriving class TMainWindow
class TMainWindow : public TWindow
{
public:

  TMainWindow() : TWindow(0, 0, 0) {}

protected:
  //--------------- member functions ------------------

  // handle Calc menu option
  void CMCalc();

  void CMExit()
    { Parent->SendMessage(WM_CLOSE); }

  // handle closing the window
  virtual BOOL CanClose();

  // declare the message map macro
  DECLARE_RESPONSE_TABLE(TMainWindow);

};

class TCalcDialog : public TDialog
{
public:
```

```
  TCalcDialog(TWindow* parent, TResID resID) :
     TWindow(0, 0, 0), TDialog(parent, resID) {}

protected:

  // math error flag
  BOOL InError;

  //--------------- member functions -----------------

  // handle the calculation
  void HandleCalcBtn();

  // declare the message map macro
  DECLARE_RESPONSE_TABLE(TCalcDialog);
};

DEFINE_RESPONSE_TABLE1(TMainWindow, TWindow)
  EV_COMMAND(CM_CALC, CMCalc),
END_RESPONSE_TABLE;


DEFINE_RESPONSE_TABLE1(TCalcDialog, TDialog)
  EV_COMMAND(IDC_CALC_BTN, HandleCalcBtn),
END_RESPONSE_TABLE;

void TCalcDialog::HandleCalcBtn()
{
  double x, y, z;
  char opStr[MaxEditLen+1];
  char s[MaxEditLen+1];

  // obtain the string in the Operand1 edit box
  GetDlgItemText(IDC_OPERAND1_BOX, s, MaxEditLen);
  // convert the string in the edit box
  x = atof(s);

  // obtain the string in the Operand2 edit box
  GetDlgItemText(IDC_OPERAND2_BOX, s, MaxEditLen);
  // convert the string in the edit box
  y = atof(s);

  // obtain the string in the Operator edit box
  GetDlgItemText(IDC_OPERATOR_BOX, opStr, MaxEditLen);

  // clear the error message box
  SetDlgItemText(IDC_ERRMSG_BOX, "");
  InError = FALSE;
```

continues

LISTING 2.26. CONTINUED

```
  // determine the requested operation
  if (strcmp(opStr, "+") == 0)
    z = x + y;
  else if (strcmp(opStr, "-") == 0)
    z = x - y;
  else if (strcmp(opStr, "*") == 0)
    z = x * y;
  else if (strcmp(opStr, "/") == 0) {
    if (y != 0)
        z = x / y;
    else {
      z = 0;
      InError = TRUE;
      SetDlgItemText(IDC_ERRMSG_BOX, "Division-by-zero error");
    }
  }
  else if (strcmp(opStr, "^") == 0) {
    if (x > 0)
      z = exp(y * log(x));
    else {
      InError = TRUE;
          SetDlgItemText(IDC_ERRMSG_BOX,
            "Cannot raise the power of a negative number");
    }
  }
  else {
    InError = TRUE;
    SetDlgItemText(IDC_ERRMSG_BOX, "Invalid operator");
  }
  // display the result if no error has occurred
  if (!InError) {
    sprintf(s, "%g", z);
    SetDlgItemText(IDC_RESULT_BOX, s);
  }
}

void TMainWindow::CMCalc()
{
  TCalcDialog* pDlg = new TCalcDialog(this, TResID(IDD_CALC_DLG));
  pDlg->Execute();
}

BOOL TMainWindow::CanClose()
{
  return MessageBox("Want to close this application?",
                    "Query", MB_YESNO | MB_ICONQUESTION) == IDYES;
}
```

```
void TWinApp::InitMainWindow()
{
  MainWindow = new TFrameWindow(0,
          "Command-Oriented Calculator Application",
          new TMainWindow);
  // load the menu resource
  MainWindow->AssignMenu(TResID(EXITMENU));
  // enable the keyboard handler
  MainWindow->EnableKBHandler();
}

int OwlMain(int /* argc */, char** /*argv[] */)
{
  TWinApp app;
  return app.Run();
}
```

Listing 2.25 contains the script of the RWDLG4.RC resource file. This resource file defines the IDD_CALC_DLG dialog box resource. This resource is a Windows dialog box resource that contains LTEXT, EDITTEXT, DEFPUSHBUTTON, and PUSHBUTTON statements.

Listing 2.26 shows the source code for the RWDLG4.CPP implementation file. This file declares the application class, TWinApp, the TMainWindow main window class, and the TCalcDialog calculator dialog box class.

The TMainWindow Class

The TMainWindow class declares a constructor and a set of member functions. The most relevant member function is CMCalc. This function creates a dynamic instance of class TCalcDialog and specifies the IDD_CALC_DLG dialog box resource. The function pops up the dialog box by sending the C++ message Execute to the dialog box instance. The function accesses this instance using the pDlg local pointer.

The TCalcDialog Class

The TCalcDialog class, which is a descendant of TDialog class, supports the operations of the calculator dialog box. The class declares a constructor, the InError data member, and the member function HandleCalcBtn. The constructor creates the dialog box instance by invoking the ancestors' constructors (both classes TDialog and TWindow). The HandleCalcBtn member function responds to the command message sent by the Calc pushbutton. The member function performs the following tasks:

- Obtains the first operand from the Operand 1 edit box. This task involves the function GetDlgItemText, which obtains the text from the targeted dialog box control. The arguments for calling the function GetDlgItemText are IDC_OPERAND1_BOX, s, and MaxEditLen. The HandleCalcBtn function also uses the atof function to convert the contents of variable s into a double-typed number, and stores that number in the local variable x.

- Obtains the second operand in a manner identical to the first one. The function stores the actual (numeric) second operand in variable y.

- Copies the text in the Operator edit box into the local variable opStr. This task also uses the function GetDlgItemText and specifies the control ID of IDC_OPERATOR_BOX.

- Clears the error message text box and sets the InError data member to FALSE. Clearing the error message edit box involves the SetDlgItemText function, which sets the text for the targeted dialog box control. The arguments for calling the function SetDlgItemText are IDC_ERRMSG_BOX, and the empty literal string.

- Determines the requested operation by using a series of if and if-else statements. The operators supported are +, -, *, /, and ^ (power.) If the function detects an error, it sets the InError data member to TRUE and displays a message in the error message box.

- Displays the result in the Result box if the InError data member is FALSE. The function first converts the result from double to a string and then writes to the Result box using the function SetDlgItemText. The arguments for calling function SetDlgItemText are IDC_RESULT_BOX and the local string variable s.

 INSERTING VBX CONTROLS IN DIALOG BOX RESOURCES

Borland C++ and the Resource Workshop support VBX (Visual Basic) controls. The C++ compiler supports the VBX controls through API functions and OWL classes. The Resource Workshop supports drawing VBX controls using VBX control libraries, which you must first install. These libraries come in either .VBX or .DLL files. As of this writing, the Borland C++ package offers the picture, switch, and gauge VBX controls. These controls are found in the files PICT.VBX, SWITCH.VBX, and GAUGE.VBX. You can find these files in the directories \BC4\WINDOWS\VBDIALOG and \BC4\EXAMPLES\OWL\OWLAPI\VBXCTL.

To install VBX control libraries, use the menu option Install control libraries... in the File menu selection. This option invokes the "Install a new control library" dialog box, which enables you to select the .VBX or .DLL containing the VBX controls. You can use the dialog box to navigate through the available drives and directories to locate the VBX files. Go ahead and install files PICT.VBX, SWITCH.VBX, and GAUGE.VBX using the preceding menu option. Your dialog editor should now show three new VBX tools in the Tools palette.

To remove VBX control libraries, use the menu option Remove control libraries... in the File menu selection. This option invokes the "Remove control library" dialog box, which enables you to select the .VBX or .DLL file to delete.

In the next two sections, I present examples for using the VBX controls in dialog boxes. The first example is very simple and offers the basics of using a VBX control. The second example, which is a neat short program supplied by Borland, shows the three VBX controls in a very interesting demonstration!

Using the Picture VBX Control

The custom message dialog boxes in program RWDLG1.EXE lack a graphics icon. In this section, I present a modified version of program RWDLG1.EXE, which displays a graphics icon in the custom message dialog box. The icon appears in a VBX picture control. To create the new project RWDLG4 you need to perform the following tasks:

1. Copy the file PICT.VBX into the directory \BC4\BC4SAMS, which contains the project files.

2. Create the icon file I.ICO. This file contains the icon for the lower-case letter i. You can use the Resource Workshop for this task or any other icon editor utility. In using the Resource Workshop, you can directly open the Resource Workshop, create the icon, and save it in the file I.ICO.

3. Create the files RWDLG5.DEF, RWDLG5.H, RWDLG5.CPP, and RWDLG5.RC. Listing 2.27 shows the contents of the RWDLG5.DEF definition file. Listing 2.28 contains the source code for the RWDLG5.H header file. Listing 2.29 shows the script of the RWDLG5.RC resource file. Listing 2.30 contains the source code for the RWDLG5.CPP implementation file. Enter the contents of the files RWDLG5.DEF, RWDLG5.H, RWDLG5.CPP as they appear in their respective listings. Regarding the resource file RWDLG5.RC, only enter the #include statements and the menu resource.

4. Create the new RWDLG5.IDE project and include the files RWDLG5.DEF, RWDLG5.H, RWDLG5.CPP, RWDLG5.RC, and \BC4\LIB\BIVBX.LIB. The latter compiled library file provides the support for the VBX controls.

5. Invoke the Resource Workshop from within the IDE to add new dialog box resources. Create the dialog box resources IDD_LCLICK_DLG and IDD_LCLICK_DLG in a manner similar to that in project RWDLG1. However, for each dialog box resource, insert a VBX picture. Double-click the VBX picture control to display the Properties dialog box. Figure 2.18. shows a sample session with the Dialog editor showing the Properties dialog box. Select the icon field in the Properties dialog box. Double-click the icon field. The Resource Workshop displays the Open dialog box to enable you to select the .ICO file. Pick the file I.ICO and click the OK pushbutton. The dialog box resource from that point on shows the icon in the I.ICO file. Moreover, the Resource Workshop creates the DLGINIT resource that incorporates the icon's bitmap image in the resource file RWDLG5.

6. Save the project resources and exit the Resource Workshop.

Compile and run the program RWDLG5.EXE. Click the left or right mouse buttons and observe the custom message dialog box that appears with the icon graphics. Figure 2.19 shows a sample session with the RWDLG5.EXE program.

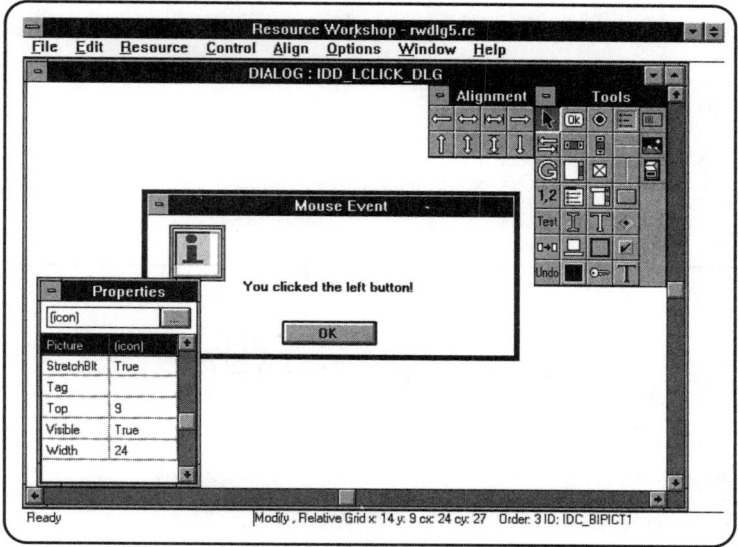

Figure 2.18. A sample session with the Dialog editor showing the Properties dialog box.

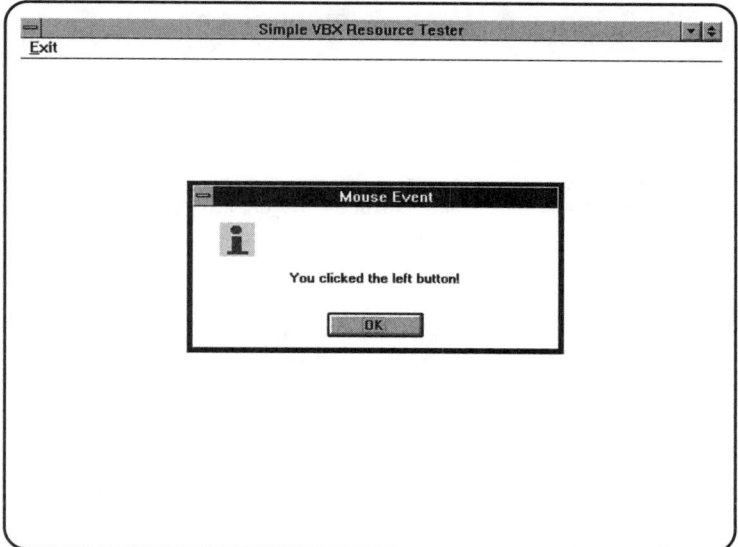

Figure 2.19. A sample session with the RWDLG5.EXE program.

LISTING 2.27. THE CONTENTS OF THE RWDLG5.DEF DEFINITION FILE.

```
NAME          RwDlg4
DESCRIPTION   'An OWL Windows Application'
EXETYPE       WINDOWS
CODE          PRELOAD MOVEABLE DISCARDABLE
DATA          PRELOAD MOVEABLE MULTIPLE
HEAPSIZE      1024
STACKSIZE     8192
```

LISTING 2.28. THE SOURCE CODE FOR THE RWDLG5.H HEADER FILE.

```
#define IDD_LCLICK_DLG  100
#define IDC_BIPICT1     101
#define IDD_RCLICK_DLG  102
#define IDC_BIPICT2     103
#define EXITMENU        102
```

LISTING 2.29. THE SCRIPT OF THE RWDLG5.RC RESOURCE FILE.

```
#include <windows.h>
#include <owl\window.rh>
#include "rwdlg5.h"

IDD_LCLICK_DLG DIALOG 63, 76, 191, 81
STYLE DS_MODALFRAME ¦ WS_POPUP ¦ WS_VISIBLE ¦ WS_CAPTION ¦ WS_SYSMENU
CAPTION "Mouse Event"
FONT 8, "MS Sans Serif"
{
 DEFPUSHBUTTON "OK", IDOK, 70, 61, 50, 14
 CTEXT "You clicked the left button!", -1, 18, 37, 154, 10
 CONTROL "PICT.VBX;BIPICT;", IDC_BIPICT1, "VBControl", 0 ¦ WS_CHILD ¦
         NOT WS_VISIBLE ¦ WS_BORDER ¦ WS_TABSTOP, 14, 9, 24, 27
}

IDD_RCLICK_DLG DIALOG 63, 76, 191, 87
STYLE DS_MODALFRAME ¦ WS_POPUP ¦ WS_VISIBLE ¦ WS_CAPTION ¦ WS_SYSMENU
CAPTION "Mouse Event"
FONT 8, "MS Sans Serif"
{
 DEFPUSHBUTTON "OK", IDOK, 70, 61, 50, 14
 CTEXT "You clicked the right button!", -1, 18, 37, 154, 10
 CONTROL "PICT.VBX;BIPICT;", IDC_BIPICT2, "VBControl", 0 ¦ WS_CHILD ¦
```

```
        NOT WS_VISIBLE ¦ WS_BORDER ¦ WS_TABSTOP, 14, 9, 24, 27
}

EXITMENU MENU
{
 MENUITEM "&Exit", CM_EXIT
}


IDD_LCLICK_DLG DLGINIT
{
    101, 0x0400, 791L,
0x0001, 0x0200, 0xff06, 0x08ff, 0x0a00, 0x0b00, 0x0d00, 0x02fe, 0x0000,
0x0001, 0x0001, 0x2020, 0x0010, 0x0000, 0x0000, 0x02e8, 0x0000, 0x0016,
0x0000, 0x0028, 0x0000, 0x0020, 0x0000, 0x0040, 0x0000, 0x0001, 0x0004,
0x0000, 0x0000, 0x0200, 0x0000, 0x0000, 0x0000, 0x0000, 0x0000, 0x0010,
0x0000, 0x0000, 0x0000, 0x0000, 0x0000, 0x0000, 0x0080, 0x8000, 0x0000,
0x8000, 0x0080, 0x0080, 0x0000, 0x0080, 0x0080, 0x8080, 0x0000, 0x8080,
0x0080, 0xc0c0, 0x00c0, 0x0000, 0x00ff, 0xff00, 0x0000, 0xff00, 0x00ff,
0x00ff, 0x0000, 0x00ff, 0x00ff, 0xffff, 0x0000, 0xffff, 0x00ff, 0xbbbb,
0xbbbb, 0xbbbb, 0xbbbb, 0xbbbb, 0xbbbb, 0xbbbb, 0xbbbb, 0xbbbb, 0xbbbb,
0xbbbb, 0xbbbb, 0xbbbb, 0xbbbb, 0xbbbb, 0xbbbb, 0xbbbb, 0xb9bb, 0x9999,
0x9999, 0x9999, 0x9999, 0xbb99, 0xbbbb, 0xbbbb, 0xb9bb, 0x9999, 0x9999,
0x9999, 0x9999, 0xbb99, 0xbbbb, 0xbbbb, 0xb9bb, 0x9999, 0x9999, 0x9999,
0x9999, 0xbb99, 0xbbbb, 0xbbbb, 0xbbbb, 0xb9bb, 0x9999, 0x9999, 0xbbbb,
0xbbbb, 0xbbbb, 0xbbbb, 0xbbbb, 0xb9bb, 0x9999, 0x9999, 0xbbbb, 0xbbbb,
0xbbbb, 0xbbbb, 0xbbbb, 0xb9bb, 0x9999, 0x9999, 0xbbbb, 0xbbbb, 0xbbbb,
0xbbbb, 0xbbbb, 0xb9bb, 0x9999, 0x9999, 0xbbbb, 0xbbbb, 0xbbbb, 0xbbbb,
0xbbbb, 0xb9bb, 0x9999, 0x9999, 0xbbbb, 0xbbbb, 0xbbbb, 0xbbbb, 0xbbbb,
0xb9bb, 0x9999, 0x9999, 0xbbbb, 0xbbbb, 0xbbbb, 0xbbbb, 0xbbbb, 0xb9bb,
0x9999, 0x9999, 0xbbbb, 0xbbbb, 0xbbbb, 0xbbbb, 0xbbbb, 0xb9bb, 0x9999,
0x9999, 0xbbbb, 0xbbbb, 0xbbbb, 0xbbbb, 0xbbbb, 0xb9bb, 0x9999, 0x9999,
0xbbbb, 0xbbbb, 0xbbbb, 0xbbbb, 0xbbbb, 0xb9bb, 0x9999, 0x9999, 0xbbbb,
0xbbbb, 0xbbbb, 0xbbbb, 0xbbbb, 0xb9bb, 0x9999, 0x9999, 0xbbbb, 0xbbbb,
0xbbbb, 0xbbbb, 0xbbbb, 0xb9bb, 0x9999, 0x9999, 0xbbbb, 0xbbbb, 0xbbbb,
0xbbbb, 0xb9bb, 0x9999, 0x9999, 0xbbbb, 0xbbbb, 0xbbbb, 0xbbbb, 0xbbbb,
0xbbbb, 0xbbbb, 0xbbbb, 0xbbbb, 0xbbbb, 0xbbbb, 0xbbbb, 0xbbbb, 0x9999,
0xbb99, 0xbbbb, 0xbbbb, 0xbbbb, 0xbbbb, 0xbbbb, 0xb9bb, 0x9999, 0x9b99,
0xbbbb, 0xbbbb, 0xbbbb, 0xbbbb, 0xbbbb, 0x99bb, 0x9999, 0x9999, 0xbbbb,
0xbbbb, 0xbbbb, 0xbbbb, 0xbbbb, 0x99bb, 0x9999, 0x9999, 0xbbbb, 0xbbbb,
0xbbbb, 0xbbbb, 0xbbbb, 0x99bb, 0x9999, 0x9999, 0xbbbb, 0xbbbb, 0xbbbb,
0xbbbb, 0xbbbb, 0x99bb, 0x9999, 0x9999, 0xbbbb, 0xbbbb, 0xbbbb, 0xbbbb,
0xbbbb, 0xb9bb, 0x9999, 0x9b99, 0xbbbb, 0xbbbb, 0xbbbb, 0xbbbb, 0xbbbb,
0xbbbb, 0x9999, 0xbb99, 0xbbbb, 0xbbbb, 0xbbbb, 0xbbbb, 0xbbbb, 0xbbbb,
0xbbbb, 0xbbbb, 0xbbbb, 0xbbbb, 0xbbbb, 0xbbbb, 0xbbbb, 0xbbbb, 0xbbbb,
0xbbbb, 0xbbbb, 0xbbbb, 0xbbbb, 0xbbbb, 0xbbbb, 0xbbbb, 0xbbbb, 0xbbbb,
0xbbbb, 0xbbbb, 0xbbbb, 0x0000, 0x0000, 0x0000, 0x0000, 0x0000, 0x0000,
0x0000, 0x0000, 0x0000, 0x0000, 0x0000, 0x0000, 0x0000, 0x0000, 0x0000,
```

continues

LISTING 2.29. CONTINUED

```
0x0000, 0x0000, 0x0000, 0x0000, 0x0000, 0x0000, 0x0000, 0x0000, 0x0000,
0x0000, 0x0000, 0x0000, 0x0000, 0x0000, 0x0000, 0x0000, 0x0000, 0x0000,
0x0000, 0x0000, 0x0000, 0x0000, 0x0000, 0x0000, 0x0000, 0x0000, 0x0000,
0x0000, 0x0000, 0x0000, 0x0000, 0x0000, 0x0000, 0x0000, 0x0000, 0x0000,
0x0000, 0x0000, 0x0000, 0x0000, 0x0000, 0x0000, 0x0000, 0x0000, 0x0000,
0x0000, 0x0000, 0x0000, 0x0000, 0x000e, 0x0f00, 0x1001, 0xffff, "\xff"
    0
}


IDD_RCLICK_DLG DLGINIT
{
    103, 0x0400, 791L,
0x0001, 0x0200, 0xff06, 0x08ff, 0x0a00, 0x0b00, 0x0d00, 0x02fe, 0x0000,
0x0001, 0x0001, 0x2020, 0x0010, 0x0000, 0x0000, 0x02e8, 0x0000, 0x0016,
0x0000, 0x0028, 0x0000, 0x0020, 0x0000, 0x0040, 0x0000, 0x0001, 0x0004,
0x0000, 0x0000, 0x0200, 0x0000, 0x0000, 0x0000, 0x0000, 0x0000, 0x0010,
0x0000, 0x0000, 0x0000, 0x0000, 0x0000, 0x0000, 0x0080, 0x8000, 0x0000,
0x8000, 0x0080, 0x0080, 0x0000, 0x0080, 0x0080, 0x8080, 0x0000, 0x8080,
0x0080, 0xc0c0, 0x00c0, 0x0000, 0x00ff, 0xff00, 0x0000, 0xff00, 0x00ff,
0x00ff, 0x0000, 0x00ff, 0x00ff, 0xffff, 0x0000, 0xffff, 0x00ff, 0xbbbb,
0xbbbb, 0xbbbb, 0xbbbb, 0xbbbb, 0xbbbb, 0xbbbb, 0xbbbb, 0xbbbb, 0xbbbb,
0xbbbb, 0xbbbb, 0xbbbb, 0xbbbb, 0xbbbb, 0xbbbb, 0xbbbb, 0xb9bb, 0x9999,
0x9999, 0x9999, 0x9999, 0xbb99, 0xbbbb, 0xbbbb, 0xb9bb, 0x9999, 0x9999,
0x9999, 0x9999, 0xbb99, 0xbbbb, 0xbbbb, 0xb9bb, 0x9999, 0x9999, 0x9999,
0x9999, 0xbb99, 0xbbbb, 0xbbbb, 0xbbbb, 0xb9bb, 0x9999, 0x9999, 0xbbbb,
0xbbbb, 0xbbbb, 0xbbbb, 0xbbbb, 0xb9bb, 0x9999, 0x9999, 0xbbbb, 0xbbbb,
0xbbbb, 0xbbbb, 0xbbbb, 0xb9bb, 0x9999, 0x9999, 0xbbbb, 0xbbbb, 0xbbbb,
0xbbbb, 0xbbbb, 0xb9bb, 0x9999, 0x9999, 0xbbbb, 0xbbbb, 0xbbbb, 0xbbbb,
0xb9bb, 0x9999, 0x9999, 0xbbbb, 0xbbbb, 0xbbbb, 0xbbbb, 0xbbbb, 0xb9bb,
0x9999, 0x9999, 0xbbbb, 0xbbbb, 0xbbbb, 0xbbbb, 0xbbbb, 0xb9bb, 0x9999,
0x9999, 0xbbbb, 0xbbbb, 0xbbbb, 0xbbbb, 0xbbbb, 0xb9bb, 0x9999, 0x9999,
0xbbbb, 0xbbbb, 0xbbbb, 0xbbbb, 0xbbbb, 0xb9bb, 0x9999, 0x9999, 0xbbbb,
0xbbbb, 0xbbbb, 0xbbbb, 0xbbbb, 0xb9bb, 0x9999, 0x9999, 0xbbbb, 0xbbbb,
0xbbbb, 0xbbbb, 0xbbbb, 0xb9bb, 0x9999, 0x9999, 0xbbbb, 0xbbbb, 0xbbbb,
0xbbbb, 0xbbbb, 0xb9bb, 0x9999, 0x9999, 0xbbbb, 0xbbbb, 0xbbbb, 0xbbbb,
0xbbbb, 0xb9bb, 0x9999, 0x9999, 0xbbbb, 0xbbbb, 0xbbbb, 0xbbbb, 0xbbbb,
0xbbbb, 0xbbbb, 0xbbbb, 0xbbbb, 0xbbbb, 0xbbbb, 0xbbbb, 0xbbbb, 0x9999,
0xbb99, 0xbbbb, 0xbbbb, 0xbbbb, 0xbbbb, 0xbbbb, 0xb9bb, 0x9999, 0x9b99,
0xbbbb, 0xbbbb, 0xbbbb, 0xbbbb, 0xbbbb, 0x99bb, 0x9999, 0x9999, 0xbbbb,
0xbbbb, 0xbbbb, 0xbbbb, 0xbbbb, 0x99bb, 0x9999, 0x9999, 0xbbbb, 0xbbbb,
0xbbbb, 0xbbbb, 0x99bb, 0x9999, 0x9999, 0xbbbb, 0xbbbb, 0xbbbb, 0xbbbb,
0xbbbb, 0x99bb, 0x9999, 0x9999, 0xbbbb, 0xbbbb, 0xbbbb, 0xbbbb, 0xbbbb,
0xbbbb, 0xb9bb, 0x9999, 0x9b99, 0xbbbb, 0xbbbb, 0xbbbb, 0xbbbb, 0xbbbb,
0xbbbb, 0x9999, 0xbb99, 0xbbbb, 0xbbbb, 0xbbbb, 0xbbbb, 0xbbbb, 0xbbbb,
0xbbbb, 0xbbbb, 0xbbbb, 0xbbbb, 0xbbbb, 0xbbbb, 0xbbbb, 0xbbbb, 0xbbbb,
```

```
0xbbbb, 0xbbbb, 0xbbbb, 0xbbbb, 0xbbbb, 0xbbbb, 0xbbbb, 0xbbbb, 0xbbbb,
0xbbbb, 0xbbbb, 0xbbbb, 0x0000, 0x0000, 0x0000, 0x0000, 0x0000, 0x0000,
0x0000, 0x0000, 0x0000, 0x0000, 0x0000, 0x0000, 0x0000, 0x0000, 0x0000,
0x0000, 0x0000, 0x0000, 0x0000, 0x0000, 0x0000, 0x0000, 0x0000, 0x0000,
0x0000, 0x0000, 0x0000, 0x0000, 0x0000, 0x0000, 0x0000, 0x0000, 0x0000,
0x0000, 0x0000, 0x0000, 0x0000, 0x0000, 0x0000, 0x0000, 0x0000, 0x0000,
0x0000, 0x0000, 0x0000, 0x0000, 0x0000, 0x0000, 0x0000, 0x0000, 0x0000,
0x0000, 0x0000, 0x0000, 0x0000, 0x0000, 0x0000, 0x0000, 0x0000, 0x0000,
0x0000, 0x0000, 0x0000, 0x0000, 0x000e, 0x0f00, 0x1001, 0xffff, "\xff"
        101, 0x0400, 791L,
0x0001, 0x0200, 0xff06, 0x08ff, 0x0a00, 0x0b01, 0x0d00, 0x02fe, 0x0000,
0x0001, 0x0001, 0x2020, 0x0010, 0x0000, 0x0000, 0x02e8, 0x0000, 0x0016,
0x0000, 0x0028, 0x0000, 0x0020, 0x0000, 0x0040, 0x0000, 0x0001, 0x0004,
0x0000, 0x0000, 0x0200, 0x0000, 0x0000, 0x0000, 0x0000, 0x0000, 0x0010,
0x0000, 0x0000, 0x0000, 0x0000, 0x0000, 0x0000, 0x0080, 0x8000, 0x0000,
0x8000, 0x0080, 0x0080, 0x0000, 0x0080, 0x0080, 0x8080, 0x0000, 0x8080,
0x0080, 0xc0c0, 0x00c0, 0x0000, 0x00ff, 0xff00, 0x0000, 0xff00, 0x00ff,
0x00ff, 0x0000, 0x00ff, 0x00ff, 0xffff, 0x0000, 0xffff, 0x00ff, 0xbbbb,
0xbbbb, 0xbbbb, 0xbbbb, 0xbbbb, 0xbbbb, 0xbbbb, 0xbbbb, 0xbbbb, 0xbbbb,
0xbbbb, 0xbbbb, 0xbbbb, 0xbbbb, 0xbbbb, 0xbbbb, 0xbbbb, 0xbbbb, 0xbbbb,
0xbbbb, 0xbbbb, 0xbbbb, 0xbbbb, 0xbbbb, 0xbbbb, 0xbbbb, 0xbbbb, 0xbbbb,
0xbbbb, 0xbbbb, 0xbbbb, 0xbbbb, 0xbbbb, 0xbbbb, 0xbbbb, 0xbbbb, 0xbbbb,
0xbbbb, 0xbbbb, 0xbbbb, 0xbbbb, 0xbbbb, 0xbbbb, 0xbbbb, 0xbbbb, 0xbbbb,
0xbbbb, 0xbbbb, 0xbbbb, 0xbbbb, 0xbbbb, 0xbbbb, 0xbbbb, 0xbbbb, 0xbbbb,
0xbbbb, 0xbbbb, 0xbbbb, 0xbbbb, 0xbbbb, 0xbbbb, 0xbbbb, 0xbbbb, 0xbbbb,
0xbbbb, 0xbbbb, 0xbbbb, 0xbbbb, 0xbbbb, 0xbbbb, 0xbbbb, 0xbbbb, 0xbbbb,
0xbbbb, 0xbbbb, 0xbbbb, 0xbbbb, 0xbbbb, 0xbbbb, 0xbbbb, 0xbbbb, 0xbbbb,
0xbbbb, 0xbbbb, 0xbbbb, 0xbbbb, 0xbbbb, 0xbbbb, 0xbbbb, 0xbbbb, 0xbbbb,
0xbbbb, 0xbbbb, 0xbbbb, 0xbbbb, 0xbbbb, 0xbbbb, 0xbbbb, 0xbbbb, 0xbbbb,
0xbbbb, 0xbbbb, 0xbbbb, 0xbbbb, 0xbbbb, 0xbbbb, 0xbbbb, 0xbbbb, 0xbbbb,
0xbbbb, 0xbbbb, 0xbbbb, 0xbbbb, 0xbbbb, 0xbbbb, 0xbbbb, 0xbbbb, 0xbbbb,
0xbbbb, 0xbbbb, 0xbbbb, 0xbbbb, 0xbbbb, 0xbbbb, 0xbbbb, 0xbbbb, 0xbbbb,
0xbbbb, 0xbbbb, 0xbbbb, 0xbbbb, 0xbbbb, 0xbbbb, 0xbbbb, 0xbbbb, 0xbbbb,
0xbbbb, 0xbbbb, 0xbbbb, 0xbbbb, 0xbbbb, 0xbbbb, 0xbbbb, 0xbbbb, 0xbbbb,
0xbbbb, 0xbbbb, 0xbbbb, 0xbbbb, 0xbbbb, 0xbbbb, 0xbbbb, 0xbbbb, 0xbbbb,
0xbbbb, 0xbbbb, 0xbbbb, 0xbbbb, 0xbbbb, 0xbbbb, 0xbbbb, 0xbbbb, 0xbbbb,
0xbbbb, 0xbbbb, 0xbbbb, 0x0000, 0x0000, 0x0000, 0x0000, 0x0000, 0x0000,
0x0000, 0x0000, 0x0000, 0x0000, 0x0000, 0x0000, 0x0000, 0x0000, 0x0000,
0x0000, 0x0000, 0x0000, 0x0000, 0x0000, 0x0000, 0x0000, 0x0000, 0x0000,
0x0000, 0x0000, 0x0000, 0x0000, 0x0000, 0x0000, 0x0000, 0x0000, 0x0000,
```

continues

LISTING 2.29. CONTINUED

```
0x0000, 0x0000, 0x0000, 0x0000, 0x0000, 0x0000, 0x0000, 0x0000,
0x0000, 0x0000, 0x0000, 0x0000, 0x0000, 0x0000, 0x0000, 0x0000,
0x0000, 0x0000, 0x0000, 0x0000, 0x0000, 0x0000, 0x0000, 0x0000,
0x0000, 0x0000, 0x0000, 0x0000, 0x000e, 0x0f00, 0x1001, 0xffff, "\xff"
   0
}
```

LISTING 2.30. THE SOURCE CODE FOR THE **RWDLG5.CPP** IMPLEMENTATION FILE.

```cpp
/*
  Program which uses tests simple dialog resources
*/

#include <owl\applicat.h>
#include <owl\framewin.h>
#include <owl\dialog.h>
#include <owl\vbxctl.h>
#include "rwdlg5.h"

// declare the custom application class as
// a subclass of TApplication

class TWinApp : public TApplication
{
public:
  TWinApp() : TApplication() {}

protected:
  virtual void InitMainWindow();
};

// expand the functionality of TWindow by deriving class TMainWindow
class TMainWindow : public TWindow
{
 public:
  TMainWindow() : TWindow(0, 0, 0) {}

 protected:

   // handle clicking the left mouse button
   void EvLButtonDown(UINT, TPoint&);

   // handle clicking the right mouse button
   void EvRButtonDown(UINT, TPoint&);
```

```
    // handle confirming closing the window
    virtual BOOL CanClose();

    // declare the response table
    DECLARE_RESPONSE_TABLE(TMainWindow);

};

DEFINE_RESPONSE_TABLE1(TMainWindow, TWindow)
  EV_WM_LBUTTONDOWN,
  EV_WM_RBUTTONDOWN,
END_RESPONSE_TABLE;

void TMainWindow::EvLButtonDown(UINT, TPoint&)
{
  TDialog* pDlg = new TDialog(this, TResID(IDD_LCLICK_DLG));

  pDlg->Execute();
}

void TMainWindow::EvRButtonDown(UINT, TPoint&)
{
  TDialog* pDlg = new TDialog(this, TResID(IDD_RCLICK_DLG));

  pDlg->Execute();
}

BOOL TMainWindow::CanClose()
{
  return MessageBox("Want to close this application?",
                "Query", MB_YESNO | MB_ICONQUESTION) == IDYES;
}

void TWinApp::InitMainWindow()
{
  MainWindow = new TFrameWindow(0,
                    "Simple VBX Resource Tester",
                    new TMainWindow);
  // load the menu resource
  MainWindow->AssignMenu(TResID(EXITMENU));
}

int OwlMain(int /* argc */, char** /*argv[] */)
{
  TWinApp app;
  TBIVbxLibrary vbxLib;
  return app.Run();
}
```

Listing 2.29 shows the script of the RWDLG5.RC resource file. The IDD_LCLICK_DLG resource contains the following statement to support the VBX picture control:

```
CONTROL "PICT.VBX;BIPICT;", IDC_BIPICT1, "VBControl", 0 ¦ WS_CHILD ¦
        NOT WS_VISIBLE ¦ WS_BORDER ¦ WS_TABSTOP, 14, 9, 24, 27
```

Likewise, the IDD_RCLICK_DLG resource contains the following statement to support the VBX picture control:

```
CONTROL "PICT.VBX;BIPICT;", IDC_BIPICT2, "VBControl", 0 ¦ WS_CHILD ¦
        NOT WS_VISIBLE ¦ WS_BORDER ¦ WS_TABSTOP, 14, 9, 24, 27
```

Notice that the first argument in the preceding CONTROL statements is a literal string containing the name of the supporting .VBX file and the name of the VBX control resource. The resource file contains the IDD_LCLICK_DLG and IDD_RCLICK_DLG DLGINIT resources. These resources store the bitmap information for the icons used in the dialog box resources.

Listing 2.30 shows the source code for the RWDLG5.CPP implementation file. This file resembles RWDLG1.CPP. The main changes in file RWDLG5.CPP are:

1. The #include <owl\vbxctl.h>, which includes the header file for the VBX control support.

2. The function OwlMain has the following new statement:

   ```
   TBIVbxLibrary vbxLib;
   ```

   The preceding statements declare and initialize the VBX library code.

THE INTERACTIVE VBX CONTROLS EXAMPLE

The Borland C++ examples includes a really neat demonstration for the picture, switch, and gauge VBX controls. The directory \BC4\EXAMPLES \OWL\OWLAPI\VBXCTL contains this example. Open the VBXCTL.IDE project file in the preceding directory. Compile and run the program. The program contains the following sets of controls:

- Three VBX picture controls, two of which contain pictures

- A set of switches

- A set of colored gauges, one for each switch

Compile and run the program. The program enables you to drag and drop either picture into the empty VBX picture control. While dragging either of the existing pictures, the mouse changes into a different bit map (the bit maps are different for each picture). When you click a switch control, the associated gauge becomes active showing repeated cycles of increasing the colors inside the gauge. Figure 2.20 shows a sample session with the VBXCTL.EXE program.

Listing 2.31 contains the source code for the VBXCTL.H header file. Listing 2.32 shows the script of the VBXCTL.RC resource file. Listing 2.33 contains the source code for the VBXCTL.CPP implementation file. I have slightly changed some of the menu items and captions in the resource and implementation files. These changes should not affect the basic operations of the program or the VBX controls. The IDE file for the project contains these files along with the BIVBX.LIB file and a .DEF file.

The discussion of the C++ source code might be more advanced for you. If this is the case, you should read the comments on the source code later, after gaining a better grasp for the OWL classes. Let me also suggest that you obtain one of the SAMS books dedicated to OWL.

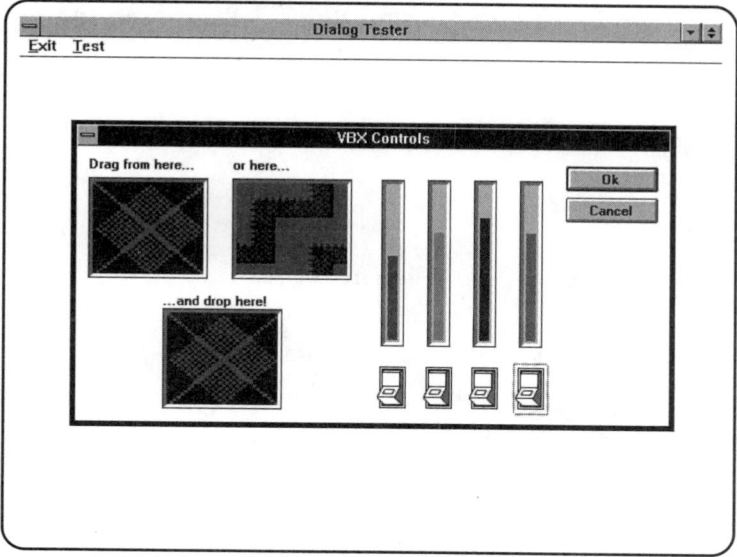

Figure 2.20. A sample session with the VBXCTL.EXE program.

LISTING 2.31. THE SOURCE CODE FOR THE VBXCTL.H HEADER FILE.

```
//---------------------------------------------------------------------
// ObjectWindows - (C) Copyright 1993 by Borland International
//-------------------------------------------------------------#define
CM_TEST     201

#define IDC_BISWITCH1     101
#define IDC_BISWITCH3     104
#define IDC_BISWITCH4     107
#define IDC_BISWITCH2     103
#define IDC_BIGAUGE1      102
#define IDC_BIGAUGE2      105
#define IDC_BIGAUGE3      106
#define IDC_BIGAUGE4      108
#define IDC_BIPICT1      1001
#define IDC_BIPICT2      1002
#define IDC_BIPICT3      1003
#define IDC_GROUPBOX1    1004
#define IDC_GROUPBOX2    1005
```

LISTING 2.32. THE SCRIPT OF THE VBXCTL.RC RESOURCE FILE.

```
//-------------------------------------------------------------------//
ObjectWindows - (C) Copyright 1991, 1993 by Borland International
//-------------------------------------------------------------#ifndef
WORKSHOP_INVOKED
  #include <windows.h>
#endif
#include "vbxctlx.h"

#include <owl\owlapp.rc>              // default owl app icon
#include <owl\window.rh>

COMMANDS MENU LOADONCALL MOVEABLE PURE DISCARDABLE
{
  MENUITEM "&Exit", CM_EXIT
  MENUITEM "&Test VBX", CM_TEST
}

SAMPLES DIALOG 13, 30, 309, 158
STYLE DS_MODALFRAME ¦ WS_POPUP ¦ WS_VISIBLE ¦ WS_CAPTION ¦ WS_SYSMENU
CAPTION "VBX Controls"
FONT 8, "MS Sans Serif"
{
 DEFPUSHBUTTON "Close", IDOK, 255, 9, 48, 14
 LTEXT "Drag from here...", -1, 6, 6, 62, 9
 CONTROL "PICT.VBX;BIPICT;", IDC_BIPICT1, "VBCONTROL", 0 ¦ WS_CHILD ¦
```

```
        WS_VISIBLE | WS_CLIPSIBLINGS | WS_BORDER | WS_TABSTOP,
        6, 18, 62, 58
LTEXT "or here...", -1, 81, 6, 62, 8
CONTROL "PICT.VBX;BIPICT;", IDC_BIPICT2, "VBCONTROL", 0 | WS_CHILD |
        WS_VISIBLE | WS_CLIPSIBLINGS | WS_BORDER | WS_TABSTOP,
        81, 18, 62, 58
LTEXT "...and drop here!", -1, 45, 84, 62, 8
CONTROL "PICT.VBX;BIPICT;", IDC_BIPICT3, "VBCONTROL", 0 | WS_CHILD |
        WS_VISIBLE | WS_CLIPSIBLINGS | WS_BORDER | WS_TABSTOP,
        45, 93, 62, 58
CONTROL "SWITCH.VBX;BISWITCH;", IDC_BISWITCH1, "VBCONTROL",
        0 | WS_CHILD | NOT WS_VISIBLE | WS_TABSTOP, 156, 123, 18, 30
CONTROL "SWITCH.VBX;BISWITCH;", IDC_BISWITCH2, "VBCONTROL",
        0 | WS_CHILD | NOT WS_VISIBLE | WS_TABSTOP, 180, 123, 18, 30
CONTROL "SWITCH.VBX;BISWITCH;", IDC_BISWITCH3, "VBCONTROL",
        0 | WS_CHILD | NOT WS_VISIBLE | WS_TABSTOP, 204, 123, 18, 30
CONTROL "SWITCH.VBX;BISWITCH;", IDC_BISWITCH4, "VBCONTROL",
        0 | WS_CHILD | NOT WS_VISIBLE | WS_TABSTOP, 228, 123, 18, 30
CONTROL "GAUGE.VBX;BIGAUGE;", IDC_BIGAUGE1, "VBCONTROL",
        0 | WS_CHILD | NOT WS_VISIBLE | WS_TABSTOP, 159, 18, 12, 96
CONTROL "GAUGE.VBX;BIGAUGE;", IDC_BIGAUGE2, "VBCONTROL",
        0 | WS_CHILD | NOT WS_VISIBLE | WS_TABSTOP, 183, 18, 12, 96
CONTROL "GAUGE.VBX;BIGAUGE;", IDC_BIGAUGE3, "VBCONTROL",
        0 | WS_CHILD | NOT WS_VISIBLE | WS_TABSTOP, 207, 18, 12, 96
CONTROL "GAUGE.VBX;BIGAUGE;", IDC_BIGAUGE4, "VBCONTROL",
        0 | WS_CHILD | NOT WS_VISIBLE | WS_TABSTOP, 231, 18, 12, 96
}


SAMPLES DLGINIT
{
    1001, 0x0400, 1420L,
0xe901, 0x0203, 0xff06, 0x0008, 0x010a, 0x010b, 0xfe0c, 0x0002, 0x0100,
0x0100, 0x2000, 0x1020, 0x0000, 0x0000, 0xe800, 0x0002, 0x1600, 0x0000,
0x2800, 0x0000, 0x2000, 0x0000, 0x4000, 0x0000, 0x0100, 0x0400, 0x0000,
0x0000, 0x0000, 0x0002, 0x0000, 0x0000, 0x0000, 0x0000, 0x1000, 0x0000,
0x0000, 0x0000, 0x0000, 0x0000, 0x0000, 0x8000, 0x0000, 0x0080, 0x0000,
0x8080, 0x8000, 0x0000, 0x8000, 0x8000, 0x8000, 0x0080, 0xc000, 0xc0c0,
0x8000, 0x8080, 0x0000, 0xff00, 0x0000, 0x00ff, 0x0000, 0xffff, 0xff00,
0x0000, 0xff00, 0xff00, 0xff00, 0x00ff, 0xff00, 0xffff, 0x0000, 0x0000,
0x0000, 0x0000, 0x0000, 0x0000, 0x0000, 0x0000, 0x0000, 0x0000, 0x0000,
0x0000, 0x0000, 0x0000, 0x0000, 0x0000, 0x0000, 0x0000, 0x0000, 0x0000,
0x0000, 0x0000, 0x0000, 0x0000, 0x0000, 0x0000, 0x0000, 0x0000, 0x0000,
0x0000, 0x0000, 0x0000, 0x0000, 0x0000, 0x0000, 0x0000, 0x0000, 0x0000,
0x0088, 0x0000, 0x0000, 0x0000, 0x0000, 0x0000, 0x0000, 0x0000, 0x8008,
0x0000, 0x0000, 0x0000, 0x0000, 0x0000, 0x0000, 0x0000, 0x8880, 0x0000,
0x0000, 0x0000, 0x0000, 0x0000, 0x0000, 0x8f00, 0x0fff, 0x00f0, 0x0000,
0x0000, 0x0000, 0x0000, 0x0000, 0xff8f, 0xf0ff, 0x00ff, 0x0000, 0x0000,
0x0000, 0x0000, 0x8f00, 0xffff, 0xffff, 0xf00f, 0x0000, 0x0000, 0x0000,
0x0000, 0xff08, 0xffff, 0xffff, 0x00f0, 0x0000, 0x0000, 0x0000, 0x0000,
0xffff, 0xffff, 0xffff, 0x0000, 0x0000, 0x0000, 0x0000, 0x0f00, 0x00ff,
```

continues

LISTING 2.32. CONTINUED

```
0xffff, 0xffff, 0x0000, 0x0000, 0x0000, 0x0000, 0x0f00, 0x00f0, 0xff0f,
0xffff, 0x0000, 0x0000, 0x0000, 0x0000, 0x0f00, 0x00f0, 0xff0f, 0xf0ff,
0x0000, 0x0000, 0x0000, 0x0000, 0x0f00, 0xff0f, 0xf0f0, 0x0000, 0x0000,
0x0000, 0x0000, 0x0000, 0xf800, 0xff0f, 0x00f0, 0x0000, 0x0000, 0x0000,
0x0000, 0x0000, 0x0000, 0x0000, 0x0fff, 0x0000, 0x0000, 0x0000, 0x0000,
0x0000, 0x0000, 0x0f00, 0x0fff, 0x0000, 0x0000, 0x0000, 0x0000, 0x0000,
0x0000, 0xff0f, 0x00f0, 0x0000, 0x0000, 0x0000, 0x0000, 0x0000, 0x0000,
0x0000, 0x0000, 0x0000, 0x0000, 0x0000, 0x0000, 0x0000, 0x0000, 0x0000,
0x0000, 0x0000, 0x0000, 0x0000, 0x0000, 0x0000, 0x0000, 0x0000, 0x0000,
0x0000, 0x0000, 0x0000, 0x0000, 0x0000, 0x0000, 0x0000, 0x0000, 0x0000,
0x0000, 0x0000, 0x0000, 0x0000, 0x0000, 0x0000, 0x0000, 0x0000, 0x0000,
0x0000, 0x0000, 0x0000, 0x0000, 0x0000, 0x0000, 0x0000, 0x0000, 0x0000,
0x0000, 0x0000, 0x0000, 0x0000, 0x0000, 0x0000, 0x0000, 0xf008, 0x0000,
0x0000, 0x0000, 0x0000, 0x0000, 0x0000, 0x0000, 0x008f, 0x0000, 0x0000,
0x0000, 0x0000, 0x0000, 0x0000, 0x0800, 0x00f0, 0x0000, 0x0000, 0x0000,
0x0000, 0x0000, 0x0000, 0x0000, 0x0000, 0x0000, 0x0000, 0x0000, 0x0000,
0x0000, 0x0000, 0xff00, 0xffff, 0xffff, 0xffff, 0xff3f, 0xfeff, 0xff1f,
0xfcff, 0xff0f, 0xf8ff, 0xff07, 0xfcff, 0xff03, 0xf0ff, 0xff01, 0xc0ff,
0xff00, 0x00ff, 0xff00, 0x00fe, 0xff01, 0x00fc, 0xff07, 0x00f8, 0xff1f,
0x00f0, 0xff1f, 0x80f0, 0xff1f, 0x00f0, 0xff1f, 0x00e0, 0xff3f, 0x00e0,
0xff7f, 0x00f0, 0xffff, 0x01f0, 0xffff, 0x03e0, 0xffff, 0x1fc0, 0xffff,
0xff87, 0xffff, 0xff0f, 0xfeff, 0xff1f, 0xfcff, 0xff3f, 0xf8ff, 0xff7f,
0xf0ff, 0xffff, 0xe1ff, 0xffff, 0xc3ff, 0xffff, 0x87ff, 0xffff, 0x0fff,
0xffff, 0x9fff, 0xffff, 0x0dff, 0x0276, 0x4d42, 0x0276, 0x0000, 0x0000,
0x0000, 0x0076, 0x0000, 0x0028, 0x0000, 0x0020, 0x0000, 0x0020, 0x0000,
0x0001, 0x0004, 0x0000, 0x0000, 0x0200, 0x0000, 0x0000, 0x0000, 0x0000,
0x0000, 0x0010, 0x0000, 0x0000, 0x0000, 0x0000, 0x0000, 0x0000, 0x0080,
0x8000, 0x0000, 0x8000, 0x0080, 0x0080, 0x0000, 0x0080, 0x0080, 0x8080,
0x0000, 0xc0c0, 0x00c0, 0x8080, 0x0080, 0x0000, 0x00ff, 0xff00, 0x0000,
0xff00, 0x00ff, 0x00ff, 0x0000, 0x00ff, 0x00ff, 0xffff, 0x0000, 0xffff,
0x00ff, 0x444d, 0x4444, 0x4444, 0x4444, 0x4464, 0x4444, 0x4444, 0x4d44,
0xd444, 0x4444, 0x4444, 0x4644, 0x44c6, 0x4444, 0x4444, 0xd444, 0x4d44,
0x4444, 0x4444, 0x6c44, 0x646c, 0x4444, 0x4444, 0x444d, 0x4444, 0x44d4,
0x4444, 0xc646, 0xc6c6, 0x4444, 0x4444, 0x44d4, 0x4444, 0x444d, 0x4444,
0x6c6c, 0x6c6c, 0x4464, 0x4d44, 0x4444, 0x4444, 0xd444, 0x4644, 0xc6c6,
0xc6c6, 0x44c6, 0xd444, 0x4444, 0x4444, 0x4d44, 0x6c44, 0x6c6c, 0x6c6c,
0x646c, 0x444d, 0x4444, 0x4444, 0x4444, 0xc6d6, 0xc6c6, 0xc6c6, 0xc6c6,
0x44d4, 0x4444, 0x4444, 0x4444, 0x6c6d, 0x6c6c, 0x6c6c, 0x6d6c, 0x4464,
0x4444, 0x4444, 0x4644, 0xd6c6, 0xc6c6, 0xc6c6, 0xd6c6, 0x44c6, 0x4444,
0x4444, 0x6c44, 0x6d6c, 0x6c6c, 0x6c6c, 0x6c6d, 0x646c, 0x4444, 0x4444,
0xc646, 0xc6c6, 0xc6d6, 0xc6c6, 0xc6d6, 0xc6c6, 0x4444, 0x4444, 0x6c6c,
0x6c6c, 0x6c6d, 0x6d6c, 0x6c6c, 0x6c6c, 0x4464, 0x4644, 0xc6c6, 0xc6c6,
0xd6c6, 0xd6c6, 0xc6c6, 0xc6c6, 0x44c6, 0x6c44, 0x6c6c, 0x6c6c, 0x6d6c,
0x6c6d, 0x6c6c, 0x6c6c, 0x646c, 0xc646, 0xc6c6, 0xc6c6, 0xc6c6, 0xc6d6,
0xc6c6, 0xc6c6, 0xc6c6, 0x6c44, 0x6c6c, 0x6c6c, 0x6d6c, 0x6c6d, 0x6c6c,
0x6c6c, 0x646c, 0x4644, 0xc6c6, 0xc6c6, 0xd6c6, 0xd6c6, 0xc6c6, 0xc6c6,
0x44c6, 0x4444, 0x6c6c, 0x6c6c, 0x6c6d, 0x6d6c, 0x6c6c, 0x6c6c, 0x4464,
```

```
0x4444, 0xc646, 0xc6c6, 0xc6d6, 0xc6c6, 0xc6d6, 0xc6c6, 0x4444, 0x4444,
0x6c44, 0x6d6c, 0x6c6c, 0x6c6c, 0x6c6d, 0x646c, 0x4444, 0x4444, 0x4644,
0xd6c6, 0xc6c6, 0xc6c6, 0xd6c6, 0x44c6, 0x4444, 0x4444, 0x4444, 0x6c6d,
0x6c6c, 0x6c6c, 0x6d6c, 0x4464, 0x4444, 0x4444, 0x4444, 0x4444, 0xc6d6,
0xc6c6, 0xc6c6, 0x44d4, 0x4444, 0x4444, 0x4d44, 0x6c44, 0x6c6c, 0x6c6c,
0x646c, 0x444d, 0x4444, 0x4444, 0xd444, 0x4644, 0xc6c6, 0xc6c6, 0x44c6,
0xd444, 0x4444, 0x4444, 0x444d, 0x4444, 0x6c6c, 0x6c6c, 0x4464, 0x4d44,
0x4444, 0x4444, 0x44d4, 0x4444, 0xc646, 0xc6c6, 0x4444, 0x4444, 0x44d4,
0x4d44, 0x4444, 0x4444, 0x6c44, 0x646c, 0x4444, 0x4444, 0x444d, 0xd444,
0x4444, 0x4444, 0x4644, 0x44c6, 0x4444, 0x4444, 0xd444, 0x444d, 0x4444,
0x4444, 0x4444, 0x4464, 0x4444, 0x4444, 0x4d44, 0x44d4, 0x4444, 0x4444,
0x4444, 0x4444, 0x4444, 0x4444, 0x4444, 0x030e, 0x0f00, 0xff00,
    1002, 0x0400, 1420L,
0xea01, 0x0203, 0xff06, 0x0008, 0x010a, 0x010b, 0xfe0c, 0x0002, 0x0100,
0x0100, 0x2000, 0x1020, 0x0000, 0x0000, 0xe800, 0x0002, 0x1600, 0x0000,
0x2800, 0x0000, 0x2000, 0x0000, 0x4000, 0x0000, 0x0100, 0x0400, 0x0000,
0x0000, 0x0000, 0x0002, 0x0000, 0x0000, 0x0000, 0x0000, 0x1000, 0x0000,
0x0000, 0x0000, 0x0000, 0x0000, 0x0000, 0x8000, 0x0000, 0x0080, 0x0000,
0x8080, 0x8000, 0x0000, 0x8000, 0x8000, 0x8000, 0x0080, 0xc000, 0xc0c0,
0x8000, 0x8080, 0x0000, 0xff00, 0x0000, 0x00ff, 0x0000, 0xffff, 0xff00,
0x0000, 0xff00, 0xff00, 0xff00, 0x00ff, 0xff00, 0xffff, 0x0000, 0x0000,
0x0000, 0x0000, 0x0000, 0x0000, 0x0000, 0x0000, 0x0000, 0x0000, 0x0000,
0x0000, 0x0000, 0x0000, 0x0000, 0x0000, 0x0000, 0x0003, 0x0000, 0x0000,
0x0000, 0x0000, 0x0000, 0x0000, 0x0000, 0x3000, 0x0000, 0x0000, 0x0000,
0x0000, 0x0000, 0x0000, 0x0000, 0xb300, 0x0000, 0x0000, 0x0000, 0x0000,
0x0000, 0x0000, 0x0000, 0x0b00, 0x0030, 0x0000, 0x0000, 0x0000, 0x0000,
0x0000, 0x0000, 0x0b00, 0x00b3, 0x0000, 0x0000, 0x0000, 0x0000, 0x0000,
0x0000, 0x0000, 0x30bb, 0x0000, 0x0000, 0x0000, 0x0000, 0x0000, 0x0000,
0x0000, 0xb3bb, 0x0000, 0x0000, 0x0000, 0x0000, 0x0000, 0x0000, 0x0000,
0xbb0b, 0x0030, 0x0000, 0x0000, 0x0000, 0x0000, 0x0000, 0x0000, 0xbb0b,
0x00b3, 0x0000, 0x0000, 0x0000, 0x0000, 0x0000, 0x0000, 0xbb00, 0x30bb,
0x0000, 0x0000, 0x0000, 0x0000, 0x0000, 0x0000, 0xbb00, 0xb3bb, 0x0000,
0x0000, 0x0000, 0x0000, 0x0000, 0x0000, 0x0b00, 0xbbbb, 0x0030, 0x0000,
0x0000, 0x0000, 0x0000, 0x0000, 0x0b00, 0xbbbb, 0x00b3, 0x0000, 0x0000,
0x0000, 0x0000, 0x0000, 0xbb0b, 0xbbbb, 0x30bb, 0x0000, 0x0000, 0x0000,
0x0000, 0x0000, 0xbb00, 0xbbbb, 0x3333, 0x0000, 0x0000, 0x0000, 0x0000,
0x0000, 0xbb00, 0xbbbb, 0x0030, 0x0000, 0x0000, 0x0000, 0x0000, 0x0000,
0x0b00, 0xbbbb, 0x00b3, 0x0000, 0x0000, 0x0000, 0x0000, 0x0000, 0x0b00,
0xbbbb, 0x30bb, 0x0000, 0x0000, 0x0000, 0x0000, 0x0000, 0x0000, 0xbbbb,
0xb3bb, 0x0000, 0x0000, 0x0000, 0x0000, 0x0000, 0x0000, 0xbbbb, 0xbbbb,
0x0030, 0x0000, 0x0000, 0x0000, 0x0000, 0x0000, 0xbb0b, 0xbbbb, 0x00b3,
0x0000, 0x0000, 0x0000, 0x0000, 0xbb0b, 0xbbbb, 0x30bb, 0x0000,
0x0000, 0x0000, 0x0000, 0x0000, 0xbb00, 0xbbbb, 0xb3bb, 0x0000, 0x0000,
0x0000, 0x0000, 0x0000, 0xbb00, 0xbbbb, 0xbbbb, 0x0030, 0x0000, 0x0000,
0x0000, 0x0000, 0x0b00, 0xbbbb, 0xbbbb, 0x00b3, 0x0000, 0x0000, 0x0000,
0x0000, 0x0b00, 0xbbbb, 0xbbbb, 0x30bb, 0x0000, 0x0000, 0x0000, 0x0000,
0x0000, 0xbbbb, 0xbbbb, 0xb3bb, 0x0000, 0x0000, 0x0000, 0x0000, 0x0000,
0xbbbb, 0xbbbb, 0xbbbb, 0x0030, 0x0000, 0x0000, 0x0000, 0x0000, 0xbb0b,
0xbbbb, 0xbbbb, 0x00b3, 0x0000, 0x0000, 0x0000, 0x0000, 0x0000, 0x0000,
0x0000, 0x0000, 0xff00, 0xffff, 0xcfff, 0xffff, 0xc7ff, 0xffff, 0xe3ff,
```

continues

LISTING 2.32. CONTINUED

```
0xffff, 0xe1ff, 0xffff, 0xf0ff, 0xffff, 0xf0ff, 0xff7f, 0xf8ff, 0xff3f,
0xf8ff, 0xff1f, 0xfcff, 0xff0f, 0xfcff, 0xff07, 0xfeff, 0xff03, 0xfeff,
0xff01, 0xffff, 0xff00, 0xfcff, 0x7f00, 0xfcff, 0x3f00, 0xfeff, 0x1f00,
0xfeff, 0x0f00, 0xffff, 0x7f00, 0xffff, 0x3f00, 0xffff, 0x1f80, 0xffff,
0x0f80, 0xffff, 0x07c0, 0xffff, 0x03c0, 0xffff, 0x01e0, 0xffff, 0x00e0,
0xffff, 0x00f0, 0xff7f, 0x00f0, 0xff3f, 0x00f8, 0xff1f, 0x00f8, 0xff0f,
0x00fc, 0xff07, 0x00fc, 0x0d03, 0x0276, 0x4d42, 0x0276, 0x0000, 0x0000,
0x0000, 0x0076, 0x0000, 0x0028, 0x0000, 0x0020, 0x0000, 0x0020, 0x0000,
0x0001, 0x0004, 0x0000, 0x0000, 0x0200, 0x0000, 0x0000, 0x0000, 0x0000,
0x0000, 0x0010, 0x0000, 0x0000, 0x0000, 0x0000, 0x0000, 0x0000, 0x0080,
0x8000, 0x0000, 0x8000, 0x0080, 0x0080, 0x0000, 0x0080, 0x0080, 0x8080,
0x0000, 0xc0c0, 0x00c0, 0x8080, 0x0080, 0x0000, 0x00ff, 0xff00, 0x0000,
0xff00, 0x00ff, 0x00ff, 0x0000, 0x00ff, 0x00ff, 0xffff, 0x0000, 0xffff,
0x00ff, 0x6666, 0x6666, 0x6666, 0x6666, 0x6666, 0x546d, 0x5054, 0x6666,
0x6666, 0x6666, 0x6666, 0x6666, 0x6666, 0x4565, 0x4045, 0x6666, 0x6666,
0x6666, 0x6666, 0x6666, 0x6666, 0x546d, 0x5054, 0x6666, 0x6666, 0x6666,
0x6666, 0x6666, 0x6666, 0x4565, 0x4045, 0x6666, 0x0000, 0x0000, 0x0600,
0x6666, 0x6666, 0x546d, 0x5054, 0x0000, 0x4545, 0x4545, 0x0645, 0x6666,
0x6666, 0x4565, 0x4545, 0x4545, 0x5454, 0x5454, 0x0654, 0x6666, 0x6666,
0x546d, 0x5454, 0x5454, 0x4545, 0x4545, 0x0645, 0x6666, 0x6666, 0x4565,
0x4545, 0x4545, 0x5454, 0x5454, 0x0654, 0x6666, 0x6666, 0x546d, 0x5454,
0x5454, 0x4545, 0x4545, 0x0645, 0x6666, 0x6666, 0x4565, 0x4545, 0x4545,
0x5d5d, 0x5454, 0x0654, 0x6666, 0x6666, 0x5d6d, 0x5d5d, 0x5d5d, 0x6666,
0x45d5, 0x0645, 0x6666, 0x6666, 0x6666, 0x6666, 0x6666, 0x6666, 0x5454,
0x0654, 0x6666, 0x6666, 0x6666, 0x6666, 0x6666, 0x6666, 0x45d5, 0x0645,
0x6666, 0x6666, 0x6666, 0x6666, 0x6666, 0x6666, 0x5454, 0x0654, 0x6666,
0x6666, 0x6666, 0x6666, 0x6666, 0x6666, 0x45d5, 0x0645, 0x6666, 0x6666,
0x6666, 0x6666, 0x6666, 0x6666, 0x5454, 0x0654, 0x6666, 0x6666, 0x6666,
0x6666, 0x6666, 0x6666, 0x45d5, 0x0645, 0x6666, 0x6666, 0x6666, 0x6666,
0x6666, 0x6666, 0x5454, 0x0654, 0x6666, 0x6666, 0x6666, 0x6666, 0x6666,
0x6666, 0x45d5, 0x0645, 0x6666, 0x6666, 0x6666, 0x6666, 0x6666, 0x6666,
0x5454, 0x0054, 0x0000, 0x0000, 0x0000, 0x0000, 0x6666, 0x6666, 0x45d5,
0x4545, 0x4545, 0x4545, 0x4545, 0x4045, 0x6666, 0x6666, 0x5454, 0x5454,
0x5454, 0x5454, 0x5454, 0x5054, 0x6666, 0x6666, 0x45d5, 0x4545, 0x4545,
0x4545, 0x4545, 0x4045, 0x6666, 0x6666, 0x5454, 0x5454, 0x5454, 0x5454,
0x5454, 0x5054, 0x6666, 0x6666, 0x45d5, 0x4545, 0x4545, 0x4545, 0x4545,
0x4045, 0x6666, 0x6666, 0x5d5d, 0x5d5d, 0x5d5d, 0x5d5d, 0x545d, 0x5054,
0x6666, 0x6666, 0x6666, 0x6666, 0x6666, 0x6666, 0x4565, 0x4045, 0x6666,
0x6666, 0x6666, 0x6666, 0x6666, 0x6666, 0x546d, 0x5054, 0x6666, 0x6666,
0x6666, 0x6666, 0x6666, 0x6666, 0x4565, 0x4045, 0x6666, 0x6666, 0x6666,
0x6666, 0x6666, 0x6666, 0x546d, 0x5054, 0x6666, 0x6666, 0x6666, 0x6666,
0x6666, 0x6666, 0x4565, 0x4045, 0x6666, 0x030e, 0x0f00, 0xff00,
     1003, 0x0400, 18L,
0xeb01, 0x0203, 0xff06, 0x0008, 0x010a, 0x490b, 0x030e, 0x0f00, 0xff00,
     101, 0x0400, 81L,
0x6501, 0x0200, 0xff06, 0x0908, 0x5369, 0x6977, 0x6374, 0x0168, 0x0a65,
0x0b00, 0x0c00, 0x0d01, 0x0e00, 0x0140, 0x0007, 0x0000, 0x0000, 0x02bc,
0x0000, 0x0000, 0x0201, 0x2202, 0x7953, 0x7473, 0x6d65, 0x3500, 0x4378,
```

```
0x07c4, 0x4380, 0x0000, 0x4ed7, 0x4386, 0x0f01, 0x4096, 0x438c, 0x0000,
0x41bf, 0x4392, 0x0114, 0x0016, "\xff"
     103, 0x0400, 81L,
0x6701, 0x0200, 0xff06, 0x0908, 0x5369, 0x6977, 0x6374, 0x0168, 0x0a67,
0x0b00, 0x0c00, 0x0d01, 0x0e00, 0x0140, 0x0007, 0x0000, 0x0000, 0x02bc,
0x0000, 0x0000, 0x0201, 0x2202, 0x7953, 0x7473, 0x6d65, 0x3500, 0x4378,
0x07c4, 0x4380, 0x0000, 0x4ec7, 0x4386, 0x0f01, 0x5076, 0x438c, 0x0000,
0x41bf, 0x4392, 0x0114, 0x0016, "\xff"
     104, 0x0400, 81L,
0x6801, 0x0200, 0xff06, 0x0908, 0x5369, 0x6977, 0x6374, 0x0168, 0x0a68,
0x0b00, 0x0c00, 0x0d01, 0x0e00, 0x0140, 0x0007, 0x0000, 0x0000, 0x02bc,
0x0000, 0x0000, 0x0201, 0x2202, 0x7953, 0x7473, 0x6d65, 0x3500, 0x4378,
0x07c4, 0x4380, 0x0000, 0x4ecf, 0x4386, 0x0f01, 0x5056, 0x438c, 0x0000,
0x41bf, 0x4392, 0x0114, 0x0016, "\xff"
     107, 0x0400, 81L,
0x6b01, 0x0200, 0xff06, 0x0908, 0x5369, 0x6977, 0x6374, 0x0168, 0x0a6b,
0x0b00, 0x0c00, 0x0d01, 0x0e00, 0x0140, 0x0007, 0x0000, 0x0000, 0x02bc,
0x0000, 0x0000, 0x0201, 0x2202, 0x7953, 0x7473, 0x6d65, 0x3500, 0x4378,
0x07c4, 0x4380, 0x0000, 0x4ef7, 0x4386, 0x0f01, 0x5036, 0x438c, 0x0000,
0x41bf, 0x4392, 0x0114, 0x0016, "\xff"
     102, 0x0400, 37L,
0x6601, 0x0200, 0xff06, 0x0008, 0x010a, 0x000b, 0x000c, 0x0d00, 0x0064,
0x320e, 0x0f00, 0x0002, 0x0110, 0xff11, 0x0000, 0x1200, 0x0003, 0x0013,
"\xff"     105, 0x0400, 37L,
0x6901, 0x0200, 0xff06, 0x0008, 0x010a, 0x000b, 0x000c, 0x0d00, 0x0064,
0x320e, 0x0f00, 0x0002, 0x0110, 0x0011, 0x00ff, 0x1200, 0x0003, 0x0013,
"\xff"     106, 0x0400, 37L,
0x6a01, 0x0200, 0xff06, 0x0008, 0x010a, 0x000b, 0x000c, 0x0d00, 0x0064,
0x320e, 0x0f00, 0x0002, 0x0110, 0x0011, 0xff00, 0x1200, 0x0003, 0x0013,
"\xff"     108, 0x0400, 37L,
0x6c01, 0x0200, 0xff06, 0x0008, 0x010a, 0x000b, 0x000c, 0x0d00, 0x0064,
0x320e, 0x0f00, 0x0002, 0x0110, 0xff11, 0xff00, 0x1200, 0x0003, 0x0013,
"\xff"     0
}
```

LISTING 2.33. THE SOURCE CODE FOR THE VBXCTL.CPP IMPLEMENTATION FILE.

```
//----------------------------------------------------------------------
// ObjectWindows - (C) Copyright 1993 by Borland International
//----------------------------------------------------------------------
#include <owl\owlpch.h>
#include <owl\applicat.h>
#include <owl\dialog.h>
#include <owl\framewin.h>
#include <owl\vbxctl.h>
#include <owl\window.rh>
#include "vbxctlx.h"
```

continues

LISTING 2.33. CONTINUED

```cpp
class TTestDialog : public TDialog, public TVbxEventHandler {
  public:
    TTestDialog(TWindow* parent, const char* name);

  protected:
    void SetupWindow();

    // OWL Aliases for VBX controls in dialog
    //
    TVbxControl* Switch1;
    TVbxControl* Switch2;
    TVbxControl* Switch3;
    TVbxControl* Switch4;
    TVbxControl* Gauge1;
    TVbxControl* Gauge2;
    TVbxControl* Gauge3;
    TVbxControl* Gauge4;

    void EvTimer(UINT timerId);
    void EvDropSrc(VBXEVENT far* event);
    void EvDropDest(VBXEVENT far* event);
    void UpdateGauge(TVbxControl* sw, TVbxControl* ga);

  DECLARE_RESPONSE_TABLE(TTestDialog);
};

DEFINE_RESPONSE_TABLE2(TTestDialog, TDialog, TVbxEventHandler)
  EV_WM_TIMER,
  EV_VBXEVENTNAME(IDC_BIPICT1,"DragDrop",EvDropSrc),
  EV_VBXEVENTNAME(IDC_BIPICT2,"DragDrop",EvDropSrc),
  EV_VBXEVENTNAME(IDC_BIPICT3,"DragDrop",EvDropDest),
END_RESPONSE_TABLE;

TTestDialog::TTestDialog(TWindow* parent, const char* name)
  : TDialog(parent, name), TWindow(parent)
{
  Switch1 = new TVbxControl(this, IDC_BISWITCH1);
  Switch2 = new TVbxControl(this, IDC_BISWITCH2);
  Switch3 = new TVbxControl(this, IDC_BISWITCH3);
  Switch4 = new TVbxControl(this, IDC_BISWITCH4);
  Gauge1  = new TVbxControl(this, IDC_BIGAUGE1);
  Gauge2  = new TVbxControl(this, IDC_BIGAUGE2);
  Gauge3  = new TVbxControl(this, IDC_BIGAUGE3);
  Gauge4  = new TVbxControl(this, IDC_BIGAUGE4);
}

void
TTestDialog::SetupWindow()
{
```

```
  TDialog::SetupWindow();
  SetTimer(1, 1);  // As fast as possible
}

void
TTestDialog::EvTimer(UINT /*timerId*/)
{
  UpdateGauge(Switch1, Gauge1);
  UpdateGauge(Switch2, Gauge2);
  UpdateGauge(Switch3, Gauge3);
  UpdateGauge(Switch4, Gauge4);
}

void
TTestDialog::UpdateGauge(TVbxControl *sw, TVbxControl* ga)
{
  BOOL on=FALSE;
  int val=0;
  if( sw->GetProp("On", on) && on )
    if( ga->GetProp("Value", val) )
      ga->SetProp("Value",  (val + 5)  % 100);
}

void
TTestDialog::EvDropSrc(VBXEVENT far * /*event*/)
{
  MessageBeep(0);
}

void
TTestDialog::EvDropDest(VBXEVENT far * event)
{
  long pic;
  if (VBXGetPropByName(VBX_EVENTARGNUM(event,HCTL,0), "Picture", &pic))
    VBXSetPropByName(event->Control, "Picture", pic);
}

//----------------------------------------------------------------------

class TTestApp : public TApplication {
  public:
    TTestApp() : TApplication() {}

  protected:
    void InitMainWindow() {
      MainWindow = new TFrameWindow(0, "Dialog Tester", 0);
      MainWindow->AssignMenu("COMMANDS");
    }
    void CmTest() {TTestDialog(MainWindow, "SAMPLES").Execute();}
```

continues

LISTING 2.33. CONTINUED

```
  DECLARE_RESPONSE_TABLE(TTestApp);
};

DEFINE_RESPONSE_TABLE(TTestApp)
  EV_COMMAND(CM_TEST, CmTest),
END_RESPONSE_TABLE;

int
OwlMain(int, char**)
{
#if defined(__WIN32__)
  ::MessageBox(0, "This is not a 32 bit example", "OWL Examples", MB_OK);
  return 0;

#else
  TBIVbxLibrary vbxLib;      // constructing this loads & inits the library
  return TTestApp().Run();

#endif
}
```

Listing 2.32 shows the script of the VBXCTL.RC resource file. This file contains the menu and dialog box resources. Notice that the dialog box resources contain various CONTROL statements which specify the VBX picture, switch, and gauge controls. Each such statement starts with the keyword CONTROL and is followed by a special string. This string specifies the name of the .VBX file and the name of the VBX control. Both names are followed by a semicolon. The resource file also contains the SAMPLES DLGINIT resource, which initializes the pictures.

Listing 2.33 shows the source code for the VBXCTL.CPP implementation file. This file declares the dialog box class TTestDialog, and the application class TTestApp. The listing includes the header files needed to support the VBX controls.

The TTestDialog Class

The TTestDialog class is a descendant of the TDialog and TVbxEventHandler classes. The class declares a constructor, a set of data members, and a set of member functions. The data members Switch1 through Switch4, and Gauge1 through Gauge4 are pointers to the VBX switch and gauge controls. These members are all pointers to the class TVbxControl, which models VBX controls. The dialog box class needs these members to access the member function of class TVbxControl.

The constructor has the task of creating the dynamic instances of class TVbxControl and assigning each instance to a SwitchX or GaugeX data member. The arguments for each instance are the pointer this and the ID of the related VBX control.

The dialog box class declares the following member functions:

1. The member function SetupWindow performs two tasks. First it invokes the function SetupWindow of the parent class, TDialog. Second, it invokes the member function SetTimer and supplies with arguments to make the animation run as fast as possible.

2. The member function EvTimer responds to the Windows message WM_TIMER. The function invokes the function UpdateGauge to update the four pairs of switches and gauges.

3. The member function UpdateGauge updates a pair of related VBX switch and gauge controls. The function first determines if the switch control is in the on position. This task involves sending the C++ message GetProp to the targeted switch (accessed by the parameter sw). The arguments for this message are the literal string "On" (which is the name of the examined switch property, or attribute, if you prefer) and the local Boolean variable on. If the switch is on, the function then obtains the value property of the gauge. This task involves sending the C++ message GetProp to the gauge (accessed by pointer ga). The arguments for this message are the name of the examined property "Value" and the local int-type variable val. If the message returns true, the function updated the value in variable val by five and then applies % 100 to the result. The function then sets the new gauge value by sending the C++ message SetProp to the gauge. The arguments for this message are "Value" and the expression (val + 5) % 100.

4. The member function EvDropSrc sounds a beep if you attempt to drag and drop an existing picture into the control of the other existing picture.

5. The member function EvDropDest handles dragging and dropping a picture into its destination. The function uses the VBXGetPropByName function to obtain the handle of the source picture. The function also uses the VBXSetPropByName function to set the picture of the destination VBX picture control.

The TTestApp Class

The `TTestApp` class declares a default constructor, and the `InitMainTest` and `CmTest` member functions. The first function creates the frame window. The second function creates a dynamic instance of `TTestDialog` class and executes it (that is, invokes it as a modal dialog box). The arguments for creating the dynamic dialog box instance are the inherited data member `MainWindow` and the dialog box resource `"SAMPLES"`.

SUMMARY

This chapter discussed visual programming using the Resource Workshop. You learned about the following topics:

- An overview of the Resource Workshop and its support for visual programming techniques in creating various resources.

- The Resource Workshop supports accelerators, bit maps, cursors, dialog boxes, fonts, icons, menus, string tables, user-defined, rcdata, and VERSIONINFO resources.

- The Resource Workshop works with various kinds of files, including the .RC and .DLG script resource files; the .RES compiled resource files; the .BMP, .ICO, .CUR, .FON, and .FNT bit-mapped resource files; the .EXE, .DLL, .DRV binary files, which contain bound resources.

- The Resource Workshop supports creating menu resources using menu options and a special dialog box that enables you to define each menu item and fine-tune its appearance and operations.

- The Resource Workshop enables you to create accelerator resources that are either closely associated with a menu resource or more independent. These resources differ only in the steps used to create them. The final script is of the same nature.

- The Resource Workshop permits you to create and edit icon resources using the Paint editor. This editor contains Colors and Tools palettes, which enable you to select different drawing colors and tools.

- The chapter showed you how to create a bare-bones message dialog box resource and use it to respond to the left and right mouse button clicks. The example used the custom message dialog box in place of the standard message dialog box.

- The chapter also demonstrated creating resources for dialog boxes with non-trivial interfaces. These interfaces included pushbuttons, edit boxes, groups boxes, check boxes, and radio buttons. The chapter illustrated these controls in creating dialog boxes resources for a simple calculator, a Find dialog box, and a Replace dialog box.

- The chapter also showed you how to create a fully-functioning dialog box resource. The example offered an operational command-oriented calculator, which supports the basic four math operations and the exponentiation. The example shows the need to use a dialog box class to animate the calculator dialog box resource.

- The Resource Workshop enables you to work with VBX (Visual Basic Controls) resources. The chapter discussed how to install these controls and use them. Two examples showed you how to work with the picture, switch, and gauge VBX controls.

TEXT AND BUTTON CONTROLS

Using a text editor involves working with dialog boxes that contain various types of controls, such as the list box, edit control (also called edit box), and pushbutton, to name a few. These controls can be included either in windows or, more frequently, in dialog boxes. This chapter treats these controls as they appear in windows and focuses on the basic properties of these controls. The chapter covers the static text, edit text, pushbutton, check box, and radio button controls. These controls appear in typical search and replace dialog boxes and influence certain aspects of the text search or replacement. These aspects include the scope, direction, and case-sensitivity of searching or replacing text.

The Static Text Control

The static text control provides a window or a dialog box with *static text* that the application user cannot easily and readily change. Static text does not necessarily mean text is etched in stone. In fact, static text controls allow your ObjectWindows applications to alter the text as you wish. You can still specify that the text be permanent and unchangeable. The choice is ultimately yours. The TStatic class implements the static text control. Consider now the class constructor and members.

The TStatic Class

The TStatic class, a descendant of TControl, offers static text that is defined by a display area, text to display, and text attributes. Of these three components, you can only alter the displayed text during runtime.

The TStatic class has two public constructors. This section will focus on the constructor that creates a TStatic instance from scratch. This constructor is declared as follows:

```
TStatic(TWindow *parent, int Id, const char far* title, int x,
        int y, int w, int h, UINT textLen,
        TModule module = 0);
```

The parent parameter is the pointer to the parent (or owner, if you prefer) window. The Id parameter is the ID for the static text control. This parameter is available for use with dialog boxes. Passing a -1 argument works with most applications. The title parameter is a pointer to the string that supplies the static text characters. The parameters x, y, w, and h define the location and dimensions for the rectangular area that contains the static text. The textLen parameter specifies the leading number of characters accessed by the title pointer to copy to the static text.

Normally, you create static text in a window or dialog box and need not access it or alter its attributes. In this case, you are not required to maintain a TStatic-pointer data member in the application window class or dialog box. On the other hand, if you want to fine-tune the display attribute or access the static text characters at runtime, then you need such a data member.

As a type of window, the instances of TStatic can redefine the display style by accessing their Attr.Style member. Table 3.1 shows the various static text style values. The default setting of a static text instance is the expression WS_CHILD ¦ WS_VISIBLE ¦ WS_GROUP ¦ SS_LEFT that produces a visible, left-justified static text.

To specify different text alignment attributes, you need to assign a new value to the `Attr.Style` member using a pointer to the static text instance. The assignment statement must be placed inside the window (or dialog box) constructor, after the creation of the static text instance, as shown in the following example:

```
// StaticPtr is a data member of the application window class
StaticPtr = new TStatic(this, -1, textStr, 10, 10,
                        100, 40, strlen(textStr));
StaticPtr->Attr.Style = (Attr.Style & ~SS_LEFT) | SS_CENTER;
```

Normally, accessing the `Attr.Style` outside the constructor of the owner window does not change the display attributes of the static text.

The string accessed by the title pointer in the constructor may include the & (ampersand) character to visually specify a hot key; to actually support the hot key, your application needs to load accelerator keys (more about this later in this chapter). The hot key character appears as an underlined character. The ampersand should be placed before the hot key character. If the string contains multiple ampersand characters, only the last occurrence is effective. The other occurrences of the ampersand are not displayed and are ignored. To display the & character, you need to specify the SS_NOPREFIX style.

Now consider the component of the static text control that you can change during runtime, namely, the text itself. If you specify the `SS_SIMPLE` style during the creation of a `TStatic` instance, then you cannot alter its text. In this sense, the instance of `TStatic` is indeed etched in stone. With the `TStatic` class, you can set, query, and clear the characters of the static text. The following member functions assist in this process:

- The parameterless member function `GetTextLen` returns the length of the control's text.

- With the `GetText` member function, you can access the static text characters. The declaration of the `GetText` function is as follows:

  ```
  inline int GetText(char far* str, int maxChars);
  ```

The `str` parameter is a pointer to the string that receives a copy of the static text characters. The `maxChars` parameter specifies the maximum number of static text characters to copy. The function result returns the actual number of characters copied to the string accessed by the `str` pointer.

- The SetText member function overwrites the current static text characters with those of the string accessed by the far char pointer parameter
  string. The declaration of the SetText function is as follows:

```
void SetText(const char far* string);
```

- The parameterless member function Clear writes a null string to the
  static text buffer. Using the GetText, SetText, and Clear member functions, you can easily toggle between hiding and showing the static text
  at runtime.

TABLE 3.1. THE STATIC TEXT STYLE VALUES.

Value	Meaning
SS_BLACKFRAME	Designates a box with a frame drawn with the color matching that of the window frame. This color is black in the default Windows color scheme.
SS_BLACKRECT	Specifies a rectangle filled with the color matching that of the window frame. This color is black in the default Windows color scheme.
SS_CENTER	Centers the static text characters. The text can be wrapped.
SS_GRAYFRAME	Specifies a box with a frame that has the same color as the screen background. This color is gray in the default Windows color scheme.
SS_GRAYRECT	Selects a rectangle filled with same color as the screen background. This color is gray in the default Windows color scheme.
SS_LEFT	Indicates left-justified text. The text can be wrapped.
SS_LEFTNOWORDWRAP	Indicates left-justified text that cannot be wrapped.
SS_NOPREFIX	Specifies that the ampersand character in the static text string should not be a hot-key designator charac-ter. Instead, the & character appears as part of the static text character.
SS_RIGHT	Selects right-justified text that can be wrapped.

Value	Meaning
SS_SIMPLE	Indicates that the static text characters cannot be altered at runtime. In addition, the static text is displayed on a single line. Line breaks are ignored.
SS_GRAYFRAME	Specifies a box with a frame that has the same color as the window background. This color is white in the default Windows color scheme.
SS_GRAYRECT	Selects a rectangle filled with same color as the window background. This color is white in the default Windows color scheme.

THE EDIT CONTROL

ObjectWindows offers the TEdit class that implements an edit control. With the edit control, you can type in and edit the text in the input dialog box. This section discusses in more detail the operations that support editing, because implementing customized text editors in your ObjectWindows application requires you to become quite familiar with the TEdit member functions.

The TEdit Class

The TEdit class, a child of the TStatic class, implements a versatile edit control that supports single-line and multiline text, as well as the ability to cut, paste, copy, delete, and clear text. The edit control can also undo the last text changes and exchange text with the clipboard. The TEdit class has three constructors, of which two are public and the other is protected. The constructor that enables you to create TEdit instances from scratch is declared as follows:

```
TEdit(TWindow *parent, int Id, const char far* text, int x,
    int y, int w, int h, UINT textLen, BOOL multiline = FALSE,
    TModule* module = 0);
```

The parent parameter is the pointer to the parent (or owner) class. The Id parameter is an integer ID for the edit control. The text parameter is the pointer to the string that supplies the TEdit instance with its initial text. The textLen parameter specifies the number of leading characters accessed by the text pointer and that actually appear in the edit control. The x, y, w, and h parameters specify the coordinates and dimensions of the edit control. The Boolean parameter multiline indicates whether the edit control is single-line (using the default argument FALSE) or multiline (using the argument TRUE).

The TEdit constructor assigns default styles to the instances of the TEdit class. Table 3.2 shows the ES_xxxx style values for the edit control. The default styles for all TEdit instances are WS_CHILD, WS_VISIBLE, WS_TABSTOP, ES_LEFT, ES_AUTOHSCROLL, and WS_BORDER. These styles produce an edit control having a frame and showing left-justified text that can be scrolled horizontally if the entire text does not fit in the frame. When you supply the TRUE argument to the multiline parameter of the constructor, the following styles are included as additional defaults: ES_MULTILINE, ES_AUTOVSCROLL, WS_HSCROLL, and WS_VSCROLL. These additional default styles support multiple text lines, make the text scroll vertically, and include vertical and horizontal scroll bars.

TABLE 3.2. THE VALUES FOR THE EDIT CONTROL STYLES.

Value	Meaning
ES_AUTOHSCROLL	Enables the text to scroll automatically to the right by 10 characters when the user enters a character at the end of the line. When the user presses the Enter key, the text scrolls back all the way to the left.
ES_AUTOVSCROLL	Permits the text to scroll up by one page when the user presses the Enter key on the last visible line.
ES_CENTER	Centers the text in a multiline edit control.
ES_LEFT	Justifies the text to the left.
ES_LOWERCASE	Converts into lowercase all of the letters that the user types.
ES_MULTILINE	Specifies a multiline edit control that recognizes line breaks (designated by the sequence of carriage return and line feed characters).
ES_NOHIDESEL	By default, the edit control hides the selected text when it loses focus, and it shows the selection when it gains focus again. Setting this style prevents the edit control from restoring the selected text.
ES_RIGHT	Justifies the text to the right.

Value	Meaning
ES_UPPERCASE	Converts into uppercase all of the letters that the user types.

The next sections treat the various categories of text editing features supported by the edit control.

Menu-Driven Commands and the Clipboard

The TEdit class includes a set of protected member functions that handle common text editing commands. These commands are available in typical menu options: Cut, Copy, Paste, Clear, Undo, and Delete. Table 3.3 shows the TEdit member functions and the menu commands to which they respond. The table also shows the public member functions of TEdit called by the response member functions.

TABLE 3.3. THE PROTECTED TEDIT MEMBER FUNCTIONS THAT SUPPORT THE BASIC TEXT EDITING MENU COMMANDS.

Response Member Function	Menu Command	Calls Member Function
CMEditCut	CM_EDITCUT	Cut
CMEditCopy	CM_EDITCOPY	Copy
CMEditPaste	CM_EDITPASTE	Paste
CMEditClear	CM_EDITCLEAR	Clear
CMEditDelete	CM_EDITDELETE	DeleteSelection
CMEditUndo	CM_EDITUNDO	Undo

Query of Edit Controls

The TEdit class has a family of text query member functions. These functions enable you to retrieve either the entire control text or parts of it, and permit you to obtain information on the text statistics (number of lines, length of lines, and so on). The relevant query member functions are as follows:

1. The GetText member function is inherited from TStatic. This function enables you to retrieve all or the leading part of the text in an edit control. The following is the declaration of the GetText function:

```
int GetText(char far* str, int maxChars);
```

The maxChars parameter specifies the number of leading control characters to return. The characters are copied to the string accessed by the str pointer. The function result returns the actual number of characters copied.

 When you obtain the text for multiple text lines, you should take into account the pairs of carriage returns and line feed characters at the end of each line. This information is relevant when you are counting the number of characters to process.

2. The GetNumLines member function returns the number of lines in a multiline edit control. This is the declaration of the GetNumLines function:

```
int GetNumLines();
```

The GetNumLines function returns valuable information regarding the number of lines in the multiline edit control. If the edit control has no text (that is, it has one empty line) the function returns 1. If an error occurs, the function returns 0. If you plan to access any line individually, you need to call GetNumLines first.

3. The GetLineLength member function returns the number of characters in a specified line in a multiline edit control. The declaration of the GetLineLength function is as follows:

```
int GetLineLength(int lineNumber);
```

The lineNumber parameter specifies the target line by number. When you pass an argument of -1 to lineNumber, the function returns one of these values:

- The length of the line containing the caret, if no text is selected

- The length of the line minus the number of selected characters, when there is selected text on the line

- The length of the lines minus the number of selected characters, when the selected text stretches across multiple lines

4. The Boolean member function GetLine retrieves the text of a specified line. The declaration of the GetLine function is this:

```
BOOL GetLine(char far* str, int strSize, int lineNumber);
```

The function returns TRUE if the sought text is found and retrieved in its entirety. If either of these conditions fails, the function returns FALSE. The str parameter is the pointer to the string buffer that receives a copy of the specified text line. The strSize parameter specifies the number of characters to copy. The lineNumber parameter selects the target line.

If you are using a static string to retrieve a copy of a text line, then the GetLineLength function should tell you if you have enough string space. If you are using a dynamic string, then the result of GetLineLength helps you in creating an adequately sized dynamic string to copy the target text line.

5. The GetSubText member function enables you to retrieve a copy of the text specified by the starting and ending character positions. The declaration of GetSubText is as follows:

```
void GetSubText(char far* str, UINT startPos, UINT endPos);
```

The str parameter is the pointer to the string receiving the characters from the indices startPos to endPos.

6. The GetSelection member function obtains the starting and ending character positions of the selected text. This is the general declaration of the GetSelection member function:

```
inline void GetSelection(UINT& startPos, UINT& endPos);
```

The startPos and endPos parameters are reference parameters that return the character positions defining the span of the selected text. If no text is selected, the values returned by startPos and endPos are equal and refer to the position of the caret (that is, the current insertion point). Therefore, you can query the existence of any selected text by simply comparing the values of the arguments for the startPos and endPos parameters.

7. The GetLineIndex member function serves two purposes, depending on its argument. The declaration of the GetLineIndex function is as follows:

```
inline UINT GetLineIndex(int lineNumber);
```

The main purpose of the function is to return the number of characters that appear before the lineNumber line number. The second purpose of the function is to return the line number containing the caret when the argument for lineNumber is -1.

8. The GetLineFromPos member function is a versatile function that returns the line number of a character position. This function is valuable in

locating an edited line, given the character position. The declaration of the `GetLineFromPos` function is this:

```
inline int GetLineFromPos(UINT charPos);
```

The `charPos` parameter supplies the character position. If the argument for `charPos` is greater than the actual position of the last character, the function returns the number of the last line. The function returns the line number that contains the first selected character when the argument for `charPos` is -1.

9. The Boolean member function `IsModified` takes no arguments and returns TRUE if the text in the edit control has been changed, and yields FALSE otherwise. The `IsModified` function plays a valuable role in monitoring any text alternations in an edit control. If the text was read from a text file, the application can query the `IsModified` function as to the need for saving the text in the edit control.

10. The `ClearModify` member function takes no arguments and simply resets the text-change flag. Consequently, any previous text changes are ignored by the `IsModified` function, which returns FALSE after calling `ClearModify` (and before making any new text changes).

11. The `Search` member function searches for a specific string in the edit control text. The declaration of the `Search` member function is as follows:

```
int Search(UINT startPos, const char far* text,
        BOOL caseSensitive = FALSE, BOOL wholeWord = FALSE,
        BOOL up = FALSE);
```

The `startPos` parameter specifies the position of the first searched character. If you supply an argument of -1 to `startPos`, the search starts from the end of the currently selected text, or, if no text is selected, from the position of the caret. The `text` parameter is the pointer to the search string. The Boolean parameter `caseSensitive` indicates whether or not the search is case-sensitive. The Boolean parameter `wholeWord` indicates whether or not the search string must match an entire word. The Boolean parameter `up` specifies the search direction. Each of these three Boolean parameters has a default argument of FALSE. Thus, by default, the `Search` function conducts a forward, non-case-sensitive search that matches any text.

Altering the Edit Controls

The member functions of TEdit that alter the edit control text have several operations. The operations of these member functions include deleting text, inserting text, and replacing the selected text.

The TEdit member functions Clear, DeleteLine, DeleteSelection, and DeleteSubText perform various kinds of text deletion, discussed as follows:

- The Clear member function (inherited from the TStatic class) deletes the entire text of an edit control. You can also use the Clear and SetText functions to emulating hiding and showing text in an edit control.

- The Boolean member function DeleteLine deletes a specified line or the current line. The function returns TRUE if the target line was successfully deleted, and yields FALSE if otherwise. The declaration of the DeleteLine function is this:

  ```
  BOOL DeleteLine(int lineNumber);
  ```

The lineNumber parameter specifies the line to delete. If you assign an argument of -1 to lineNumber, the function deletes the current line.

- The parameterless Boolean member function DeleteSelection simply deletes the selected text. The function returns TRUE if a text was selected to delete, and yields FALSE if no text was selected.

- The Boolean member function DeleteSubText deletes a range of characters that you specify. The function returns TRUE if it is successful, and FALSE if otherwise. The declaration of the DeleteSubText function is as follows:

  ```
  BOOL DeleteSubText(UINT startPos, UINT endPos);
  ```

The startPos and endPos parameter specify the character positions that define the text to delete. The DeleteSubText function gives you more control over deleting text than the other functions.

The TEdit class offers the following functions to insert text and overwrite the selected text:

- The Boolean member function SetSelection defines a block of characters as the new selected text. The function returns TRUE if it succeeds in selecting the specified text. The declaration of the `SetSelection` function is as follows:

```
inline BOOL SetSelection(UINT startPos, UINT endPos);
```

The `startPos` and `endPos` parameters define the range of characters that make up the new selected text.

- The `Insert` member function inserts text at the current text insertion position. If a text is selected, the `Insert` function replaces the selected text with the inserted text. The declaration of the `Insert` function is as follows:

```
inline void Insert(const char far* str);
```

The `str` parameter is the pointer to the inserted string. You can use the `Insert` function to replace any portion of the edit control text: you first make that portion the new selected text (using the `SetSelection` function) and then insert the new text.

- The `SetText` member function (which is inherited from the `TStatic` class) assigns a new text to the edit control. This function has the same effect as invoking the `Clear` and `Insert` functions.

THE PUSHBUTTON CONTROL

The pushbutton (also known as the command button) control is perhaps psychologically the most powerful control compared to other controls. The word *button* may remind you of the *nuclear button* in the hand of superpower leaders. You never hear about the *nuclear list box* or the *nuclear check box*. In a sense, the pushbutton control represents the fundamental notion of a control: you click the control and something happens!

The ObjectWindows library implements the `TButton` class whose instances create pushbutton controls. There are basically two types of push button controls: the default and non-default buttons. The default button has slightly thicker edges than non-default buttons. Pressing the Enter key is equivalent to clicking the default button. A group can have only one default button. You can select a new default button by pressing the Tab key. This feature works only when the buttons are in a dialog box. If a non-dialog-box window owns a pushbutton control, the window can only visually display a default button; the functionality is not supported.

The TButton Class

The TButton class is a descendant of TControl and declares a rather small number of member functions. The TButton class declares the public Boolean data member IsDefPB. This member indicates whether or not that pushbutton is the default button.

The most relevant member functions of TButton are its three constructors. This constructor enables you to create a pushbutton control from scratch:

```
TButton(TWindow *parent, int Id, char far* text,
        int x, int y, int w, int h, BOOL isDefault = FALSE,
        TModule* module = 0);
```

The parent parameter is the pointer to the owner window. The Id parameter is a unique ID for the TButton instance. This same ID is used in handling messages sent by the button control to its parent window. The text parameter is the pointer to the button's caption. The x, y, w, and h parameters define the location and dimensions of the TButton instance. The Boolean parameter isDefault specifies whether or not the button is the default button. The default argument for this parameter is FALSE.

Handling Button Messages

When you click a button, the control sends the BN_CLICKED notification message to its parent window. The parent window responds to this message by invoking a message response member function based on the ID of the button. The response table entry for buttons is EV_COMMAND. For example, if you have a button that was created with an ID of ID_EXIT_BTN, then the message handler function is as follows:

```
void HandleExitBtn();
```

The response table entry is this:

```
EV_COMMAND(ID_EXIT_BTN, HandleExitBtn),
```

Manipulating Buttons

You can disable, enable, show, and hide a button by using Windows API functions or their equivalent class-based API wrapper functions. A disabled button has a faded gray caption and does not respond to mouse clicks. Though the TButton class does not implement member functions for this type of visual manipulation, you should know some important points. With the EnableWindow function, you can enable or disable a button. The function accepts two arguments: the handle for the button, and a Boolean argument that specifies whether the button is enabled (when the argument is TRUE) or disabled (when the argument is FALSE). The following shows sample calls to the EnableWindow function:

```
pButton->EnableWindow(FALSE); // disable button
pButton->EnableWindow(TRUE); // enable button
```

You can query the enabled state of a button by using the Boolean IsWindowEnabled function, which takes one argument, the handle for the tested button. The following is a sample call to IsEnabledWindow:

```
// toggle the enabled state of a button
if (pButton->IsWindowEnabled())
    pButton->EnableWindow(FALSE); // disable button
else
    pButton->EnableWindow(TRUE); // enable button
```

You can also hide and show a button using the ShowWindow function. The function takes two arguments: the handle for the button, and either the SW_HIDE constant to hide the button or the SW_SHOW constant to show the button. The Boolean function IsWindowVisible queries the visibility of a button. This function takes one argument, the handle for the queried button. The following shows a sample call to the ShowWindow and IsWindowVisible functions:

```
// toggle the visibility of a button
if (pButton->IsWindowVisible())
    pButton->ShowWindow(SW_HIDE); // hide button
else
    pButton->ShowWindow(SW_SHOW); // show button
```

The preceding short examples manipulate individual pushbuttons by using pointers to the TButton instances. What about manipulating multiple buttons or buttons that meet certain criteria? The answer lies with using the ForEach, FirstThat, LastThat iterator member functions that are declared in the Object class. These iterators work with special functions that have the general declaration:

```
returnType iteratedFunctionName(TWindow* pWin, void* Param)
```

The returnType varies with the function's purpose. The function must typecast the pWin parameter to the pointer of the manipulated window class. The Param parameter is the pointer to the additional information needed by the iterated function. An example for an iterated function that disables a button is the following:

```
void DisableButton(TWindow* pWin, void* Param)
{
    TButton* pBtn = (TButton*)pWin;
    pBtn->EnableWindow(FALSE);
}
```

DisabledButton can then be called in an application window class member function to disable all of the buttons in the window child list. The call might look like the following statement:

```
void TMainWindow::CMDisableAllBtn()
{
    ForEach(DisableButton, NULL);
}
```

A slightly more elaborate code for the CMDisableAllBtn function can exclude certain buttons from being disabled.

The Calculator Application

Let's look now at an application that uses single-line and multiline edit controls. I present the Command-Line Calculator Application (COCA). This application implements a floating-point calculator that uses edit controls instead of buttons. Figure 3.1 shows a sample session with the COCA (version 1) program. This type of interface is somewhat visually inferior to the typical button-populated calculator Windows applications. However, the interface that I present can support more mathematical functions without requiring the addition of the buttons for these extra functions. Another reason I present this application is that I will later replace the menu items and edit controls with the other controls.

As the figure shows, the calculator is made up of the following controls:

- Two edit controls for the first and second operands. These controls accept integers, floating-point numbers, and the names of single-letter variables, A to Z.

- An edit control for the operator. The current version of the calculator supports the four basic math operations and the exponentiation (using the ^ character).

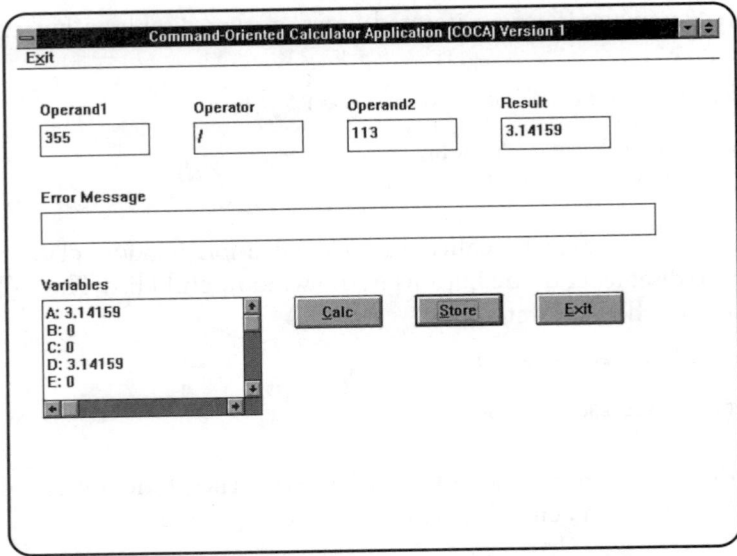

Figure 3.1. A sample session with the COCA (version 1) program.

- An edit control that displays the result of the math operation.

- An edit control that displays any error messages.

- A multiline edit control that enables you to store a number in the Result edit control in one of 26 single-letter variables named A to Z. The multiline edit control displays the current values stored in these variables and enables you to view and edit these numbers. You can use the vertical scroll bar to inspect the values in the different variables.

- Multiple static text controls that serve to label the various edit controls. Of particular interest is the static control for the Error Message box. If you click the accompanying static text, the Error Message is cleared of any text.

- A menu with a single option, Exit.

- The Calc pushbutton, which causes the program to execute the operation you specify in the Operand edit control, uses the operands in the edit controls, Operand1 and Operand2. You can also press Alt+C to invoke this button.

- The Store pushbutton, which causes the program to store the number of the Result edit control in the currently selected line in the Variables edit control. You can press the Alt+S keys to invoke this control. When you store a value in a variable, the program automatically selects the next variable.

- The Exit pushbutton, which assists you in exiting the application.

The calculator application supports the following special features:

1. The Error Message edit control clears its text if you click the left mouse button while positioning the mouse over the label Error Message.

2. The Store pushbutton is disabled if the application attempts to execute an invalid operator. This feature is an example of disabling a pushbutton when a certain condition arises (in this case, a specific calculation error).

3. The Store pushbutton is enabled if you click the Error Message static text. The same button is enabled when you successfully execute a math operation.

The calculator application demonstrates the following:

- The use of single-line edit controls for simple input.

- The use of a multiline edit control to view and edit information.

- The line-oriented text access and editing.

- The simulation of static text that responds to mouse clicks.

- Using pushbuttons.

- Disabling and enabling pushbuttons.

- Associating accelerator keys with pushbuttons. This feature allows the program to maintain the same hot keys used by the menu items of the previous version.

I suggest that you first compile and run the application to get a sense of how the calculator application works. Experiment with typing different numeric operands and the supported operators, then click the Calc pushbutton. Each time, the result appears in the Result box, overwriting the previous result. Try dividing a number by zero to experiment with the error handling features.

Using the single-letter variables is easy. All of these variables are initialized with 0. Therefore, the first step to using them is to store a non-zero value. Perform an operation and then click inside the Variables edit box. Click the Store button (or press Alt+S) and watch the number in the Result box appear in the first line of the Variables edit box. The name of the variable and the colon and space characters that follow reappear with the new text line. Replace the contents of the Operand1 edit box with the variable A, and then click the Calc button. The Result edit box displays the result of the latest operation.

When you store a number in a variable, the insertion point moves to the next line. Thus, you can store the same result in neighboring variables by repeatedly pressing Alt+S.

Listing 3.1 shows the contents of the CTLBTN1.DEF definition file. Listing 3.2 contains the source code for the CTLBTN1.H header file. The file contains the various CM_*xxxx* and ID_*xxxx* constants used by the calculator application. Listing 3.3 contains the script for the CTLBTN1.RC resource file. The resource file reveals a single item menu resource. In addition, the resource file declares the resources of the accelerator keys. These accelerator keys associate the Alt+C, Alt+S, and Alt+E keys with their respective button IDs. Listing 3.4 shows the source code for the CTLBTN1.CPP program file.

LISTING 3.1. THE CONTENTS OF THE CTLBTN1.DEF DEFINITION FILE.

```
NAME          CtlBtn1
DESCRIPTION   'An OWL Windows Application'
EXETYPE       WINDOWS
CODE          PRELOAD MOVEABLE DISCARDABLE
DATA          PRELOAD MOVEABLE MULTIPLE
HEAPSIZE      1024
STACKSIZE     16384
```

LISTING 3.2. THE SOURCE CODE FOR THE CTLBTN1.H HEADER FILE.

```
#define ID_CALC_BTN   100
#define ID_STORE_BTN  101
#define ID_EXIT_BTN   102
#define CM_CALC_BTN   103
#define CM_STORE_BTN  104
#define CM_EXIT_BTN   105
#define IDR_BUTTONS   200
#define IDM_EXITMENU  201
```

LISTING 3.3. THE SCRIPT FOR THE CTLBTN1.RC RESOURCE FILE.

```
#define ID_CALC_BTN   100
#define ID_STORE_BTN  101
#define ID_EXIT_BTN   102
#define CM_CALC_BTN   103
#define CM_STORE_BTN  104
#define CM_EXIT_BTN   105
#define IDR_BUTTONS   200
#define IDM_EXITMENU  201
```

LISTING 3.4. THE SOURCE CODE FOR THE CTLBTN1.CPP PROGRAM FILE.

```
/*
    Program to test the static text, edit box, and push button controls.
    The program uses these controls to implement a command-line
    oriented calculator application (COCA)
*/

#include <owl\applicat.h>
#include <owl\framewin.h>
#include <owl\static.h>
#include <owl\edit.h>
#include <owl\button.h>
#include <owl\window.rh>
#include "ctlbtn1.h"
#include <stdlib.h>
#include <ctype.h>
#include <stdio.h>
#include <math.h>
#include <string.h>

// declare the constants that represent the sizes of the controls
const Wlbl = 100;
const Hlbl = 20;
const LblVertSpacing = 2;
const LblHorzSpacing = 40;
const Wbox = 100;
const Hbox = 30;
const BoxVertSpacing = 30;
const BoxHorzSpacing = 40;
const WLongbox = 4 * (Wbox + BoxHorzSpacing);
const Wvarbox = 2 * Wbox;
const Hvarbox = 3 * Hbox + 20;
const Hbtn = 30;
const Wbtn = 80;
```

continues

LISTING 3.4. CONTINUED

```
const BtnHorzSpacing = 30;
const MaxEditLen = 30;
const MAX_MEMREG = 26;

// declare the ID_XXXX constants for the edit boxes
#define ID_OPERAND1_EDIT 101
#define ID_OPERATOR_EDIT 102
#define ID_OPERAND2_EDIT 103
#define ID_RESULT_EDIT   104
#define ID_ERRMSG_EDIT    105
#define ID_VARIABLE_EDIT 106

// declare the custom application class as
// a subclass of TApplication
class TWinApp : public TApplication
{
public:
  TWinApp() : TApplication() {}

protected:
  virtual void InitMainWindow();
};

// expand the functionality of TWindow by
// deriving class TMainWindow
class TMainWindow : public TWindow
{
public:

  TMainWindow();

protected:

  // pointers to the controls
  TEdit* Operand1Box;
  TEdit* OperatorBox;
  TEdit* Operand2Box;
  TEdit* ResultBox;
  TEdit* ErrMsgBox;
  TEdit* VariableBox;
  TButton* CalcBtn;
  TButton* StoreBtn;
  TButton* ExitBtn;

  // math error flag
  BOOL InError;

  // coordinates for the Error Message static text area
```

```
    int MSG_xulc, MSG_yulc, MSG_xlrc, MSG_ylrc;

    //--------------- member functions -----------------

    // handle clicking the left mouse button
    void EvLButtonDown(UINT, TPoint&);

    // handle the calculation
    void HandleCalcBtn();

    // handle the accelerator key for the Calculate button
    void CMCalcBtn();

    // handle storing the result in a variable
    void HandleStoreBtn();

    // handle the accelerator key for the Store button
    void CMStoreBtn();

    // handle exiting the application
    void HandleExitBtn();

    // handle the accelerator key for the Exit button
    void CMExitBtn();

    // enable a push button control
    void EnableButton(TButton* pBtn)
      { pBtn->EnableWindow(TRUE); }

    // disable a push button control
    void DisableButton(TButton* pBtn)
        { pBtn->EnableWindow(FALSE); }

    // handle closing the window
    virtual BOOL CanClose();

    // obtain a number of a Variable edit box line
    double getVar(int lineNum);

    // store a number in the selected text of
    // the Variable edit box line
    void putVar(double x);

    // declare the message map macro
    DECLARE_RESPONSE_TABLE(TMainWindow);

};

DEFINE_RESPONSE_TABLE1(TMainWindow, TWindow)
  EV_WM_LBUTTONDOWN,
```

continues

LISTING 3.4. CONTINUED

```cpp
  EV_COMMAND(ID_CALC_BTN, HandleCalcBtn),
  EV_COMMAND(CM_CALC_BTN, CMCalcBtn),
  EV_COMMAND(ID_STORE_BTN, HandleStoreBtn),
  EV_COMMAND(CM_STORE_BTN, CMStoreBtn),
  EV_COMMAND(ID_EXIT_BTN, HandleExitBtn),
  EV_COMMAND(CM_EXIT_BTN, CMExitBtn),
END_RESPONSE_TABLE;

TMainWindow::TMainWindow() :
          TWindow(0, 0, 0)
{
  char s[81];
  char bigStr[6 * MAX_MEMREG + 1];
  char c;
  int x0 = 20;
  int y0 = 30;
  int x = x0, y = y0;

  // create the first set of labels for the edit boxes
  strcpy(s, "Operand1");
  new TStatic(this, -1, s, x, y, Wlbl, Hlbl, strlen(s));
  strcpy(s, "Operator");
  x += Wlbl + LblHorzSpacing;
  new TStatic(this, -1, s, x, y, Wlbl, Hlbl, strlen(s));
  strcpy(s, "Operand2");
  x += Wlbl + LblHorzSpacing;
  new TStatic(this, -1, s, x, y, Wlbl, Hlbl, strlen(s));
  x += Wlbl + LblHorzSpacing;
  strcpy(s, "Result");
  new TStatic(this, -1, s, x, y, Wlbl, Hlbl, strlen(s));

  // create the operand1, operator, operand2, and result
  // edit boxes
  x = x0;
  y += Hlbl + LblVertSpacing;
  Operand1Box = new TEdit(this, ID_OPERAND1_EDIT, "", x, y,
                  Wbox, Hbox, 0, FALSE);

  // force conversion of letters to uppercase
  Operand1Box->Attr.Style |= ES_UPPERCASE;
  x += Wbox + BoxHorzSpacing;
  OperatorBox = new TEdit(this, ID_OPERATOR_EDIT, "", x, y,
                  Wbox, Hbox, 0, FALSE);
  x += Wbox + BoxHorzSpacing;
  Operand2Box = new TEdit(this, ID_OPERAND2_EDIT, "", x, y,
                  Wbox, Hbox, 0, FALSE);
  // force conversion of letters to uppercase
  Operand2Box->Attr.Style |= ES_UPPERCASE;
```

```
x += Wbox + BoxHorzSpacing;
ResultBox = new TEdit(this, ID_RESULT_EDIT, "", x, y, Wbox, Hbox,
               0, FALSE);

// create the static text and edit box for the error message
x = x0;
y += Hbox + BoxVertSpacing;
// store the coordinates for the static text area
MSG_xulc = x;
MSG_yulc = y;
MSG_xlrc = x + Wlbl;
MSG_ylrc = y + Hlbl;
strcpy(s, "Error Message");
new TStatic(this, -1, s, x, y, Wlbl, Hlbl, strlen(s));
y += Hlbl + LblVertSpacing;
ErrMsgBox = new TEdit(this, ID_ERRMSG_EDIT, "", x, y,
             WLongbox, Hbox, 0, FALSE);
// create the static text and edit box for the single-letter
// variable selection
y += Hbox + BoxVertSpacing;
strcpy(s, "Variables");
new TStatic(this, -1, s, x, y, Wlbl, Hlbl, strlen(s));
y += Hlbl + LblVertSpacing;
bigStr[0] = '\0';
// build the initial contents of the Variable edit box
for (c = 'A'; c <= 'Z'; c++) {
  sprintf(s, "%c: 0\r\n", c);
  strcat(bigStr, s);
}
VariableBox = new TEdit(this, ID_VARIABLE_EDIT, bigStr, x, y,
               Wvarbox, Hvarbox, 0, TRUE);
// force conversion of letters to uppercase
VariableBox->Attr.Style |= ES_UPPERCASE;

// create the Calc push button
x += Wvarbox + BtnHorzSpacing;
CalcBtn = new TButton(this, ID_CALC_BTN, "&Calc",
             x, y, Wbtn, Hbtn, FALSE);

// create the Store Btn
x += Wbtn + BtnHorzSpacing;
StoreBtn = new TButton(this, ID_STORE_BTN, "&Store",
             x, y, Wbtn, Hbtn, FALSE);

// Create the Exit Btn
x += Wbtn + BtnHorzSpacing;
ExitBtn = new TButton(this, ID_EXIT_BTN, "&Exit",
             x, y, Wbtn, Hbtn, FALSE);

// clear the InError flag
```

continues

LISTING 3.4. CONTINUED

```
  InError = FALSE;

  UpdateWindow();
}

void TMainWindow::EvLButtonDown(UINT, TPoint& point)
{
  if (point.x >= MSG_xulc && point.x <= MSG_xlrc &&
      point.y >= MSG_yulc && point.y <= MSG_ylrc) {
      ErrMsgBox->Clear();
      // enable the Store button
      EnableButton(StoreBtn);
  }
}

void TMainWindow::HandleCalcBtn()
{
  double x, y, z;
  char opStr[MaxEditLen+1];
  char s[MaxEditLen+1];

  // obtain the string in the Operand1 edit box
  Operand1Box->GetText(s, MaxEditLen);
  // does the Operand1Box contain the name
  // of a single-letter variable?
  if (isalpha(s[0]))
    // obtain value from the Variable edit control
      x = getVar(s[0] - 'A');
  else
    // convert the string in the edit box
    x = atof(s);

  // obtain the string in the Operand2 edit box
  Operand2Box->GetText(s, MaxEditLen);
  // does the Operand2Box contain the name
  // of a single-letter variable?
  if (isalpha(s[0]))
    // obtain value from the Variable edit control
      y = getVar(s[0] - 'A');
  else
    // convert the string in the edit box
    y = atof(s);

  // obtain the string in the Operator edit box
  OperatorBox->GetText(opStr, MaxEditLen);

  // clear the error message box
  ErrMsgBox->Clear();
```

```
  InError = FALSE;

  // determine the requested operation
  if (strcmp(opStr, "+") == 0)
    z = x + y;
  else if (strcmp(opStr, "-") == 0)
    z = x - y;
  else if (strcmp(opStr, "*") == 0)
    z = x * y;
  else if (strcmp(opStr, "/") == 0) {
    if (y != 0)
        z = x / y;
    else {
      z = 0;
      InError = TRUE;
      ErrMsgBox->SetText("Division-by-zero error");
    }
  }
  else if (strcmp(opStr, "^") == 0) {
    if (x > 0)
      z = exp(y * log(x));
    else {
      InError = TRUE;
          ErrMsgBox->SetText(
      "Cannot raise the power of a negative number");
    }
  }
  else {
    InError = TRUE;
    ErrMsgBox->SetText("Invalid operator");
  }
  // display the result if no error has occurred
  if (!InError) {
    sprintf(s, "%g", z);
    ResultBox->SetText(s);
    // enable the Store button
    EnableButton(StoreBtn);
  }
  else
    // disable the Store button
    DisableButton(StoreBtn);
}

void TMainWindow::CMCalcBtn()
{
  HandleCalcBtn();
}


void TMainWindow::HandleStoreBtn()
{
```

continues

LISTING 3.4. CONTINUED

```
  char result[MaxEditLen+1];

  // get the string in the Result edit box
  ResultBox->GetText(result, MaxEditLen);

  // store the result in the selected text of
  // the Variable edit box
  putVar(atof(result));
}

void TMainWindow::CMStoreBtn()
{
  HandleStoreBtn();
}

void TMainWindow::HandleExitBtn()
{
  // send a WM_CLOSE message to the parent window
  Parent->SendMessage(WM_CLOSE);
}

void TMainWindow::CMExitBtn()
{
  // send a WM_CLOSE message to the parent window
  Parent->SendMessage(WM_CLOSE);
}

double TMainWindow::getVar(int lineNum)
{
  int lineSize;
  char s[MaxEditLen+1];

  if (lineNum >= MAX_MEMREG) return 0;
  // get the size of the target line
  lineSize = VariableBox->GetLineLength(lineNum);
  // get the line
  VariableBox->GetLine(s, lineSize+1, lineNum);
  // delete the first three characters
  strcpy(s, (s+3));
  // return the number stored in the target line
  return atof(s);
}

void TMainWindow::putVar(double x)
{
```

```
  UINT startPos, endPos;
  int lineNum;
  int lineSize;
  char s[MaxEditLen+1];

  // locate the character position of the cursor
  VariableBox->GetSelection(startPos, endPos);
  // turn off the selected text
  if (startPos != endPos)
    VariableBox->SetSelection(startPos, startPos);
  // get the line number where the cursor is located
  lineNum = VariableBox->GetLineFromPos(startPos);
  // get the line size of line lineNum
  lineSize = VariableBox->GetLineLength(lineNum);
  // obtain the text of line lineNum
  VariableBox->GetLine(s, lineSize+1, lineNum);
  // delete line lineNum
  VariableBox->DeleteLine(lineNum);
  // build the new text line
  sprintf(s, "%c: %g\r\n", s[0], x);
  // insert new text line
  VariableBox->Insert(s);
}


BOOL TMainWindow::CanClose()
{
  return MessageBox("Want to close this application?",
                "Query", MB_YESNO | MB_ICONQUESTION) == IDYES;
}


void TWinApp::InitMainWindow()
{
  MainWindow = new TFrameWindow(0,
            "Command-Oriented Calculator Application (COCA) Version 1",
            new TMainWindow);
  // load the keystroke resources
  MainWindow->Attr.AccelTable = IDR_BUTTONS;
  // load the menu resource
  MainWindow->AssignMenu(TResID(IDM_EXITMENU));
  // enable the keyboard handler
  MainWindow->EnableKBHandler();
}


int OwlMain(int /* argc */, char** /*argv[] */)
{
  TWinApp app;
  return app.Run();
}
```

The COCA program declares a set of constants, the TWinApp application class, and the TMainWindow main window class. The set of constants define the control locations, sizes, and dimensions. The TMainWindow window class is the owner of the static text and edit controls. The class declares a number of data members and member functions.

The TMainWindow class contains the following groups of data members:

- Pointers to the various TEdit instances. Each pointer accesses one of the edit controls that appear in the program.

- Pointers to the various TButton instances. Each pointer accesses one of the pushbutton controls that appear in the program.

- The Boolean data member InError flags any error.

- The MSG_xxxx data members that store the coordinates for the rectangle containing the Error Message static text. The mouse-click response member function EvLButtonDown examines whether or not the mouse is clicked inside that rectangle. If so, the member function clears the Error Message edit control text.

The TMainWindow class contains a constructor and a number of message response member functions that handle the mouse click and the response to the menu options.

The window class constructor performs the following tasks:

- Creates the static text controls that label the Operand1, Operator, Operand2, and Result edit controls by invoking the TStatic constructor. The local variable *x* is increased by (Wlbl + LblHorzSpacing) to calculate the X-coordinate for the next static text control. This approach is easier than plugging in numbers in the TStatic constructor.

- Creates the edit boxes for the operands, operator, and the result. The instances for these controls are accessed by the Operand1Box, OperatorBox, Operand2Box, and ResultBox data members. Each TEdit instance is created with its own ID_xxxx constant, and an empty edit box. The edit boxes have the same size. The constructor modifies the style of the operand edit controls to include the ES_UPPERCASE style. This style results in automatically converting into uppercase the single-letter variable names that you type in these edit controls. The argument for the text parameter in the single-line controls is 0 to indicate that there is no limit on the amount of text to store. The argument for the multiLine parameter is FALSE to indicate that these controls are single-line edit boxes.

- Calculates the upper-left corner and lower-right corner of the rectangle containing the Error Message text and stores them in the MSG_*xxxx* data members.

- Creates the error message static text control and edit control.

- Creates the Variables multiline edit control. This task begins with building the contents of the Variables box using the bigStr string variable. The TEdit constructor uses the bigStr variable as the initial text for the control. The argument for the text parameter is 0 to indicate that there is no limit on the amount of text to store. The argument for the multiLine parameter is TRUE to indicate that the control is a multiline edit box. The style of the Variables edit control is also set to force the conversion of letters into uppercase.

- Creates the pushbutton instances, using the following statements:

```
CalcBtn = new TButton(this, ID_CALC_BTN, "&Calc",
                      x, y, Wbtn, Hbtn, FALSE);


StoreBtn = new TButton(this, ID_STORE_BTN, "&Store",
                       x, y, Wbtn, Hbtn, FALSE);


ExitBtn = new TButton(this, ID_EXIT_BTN, "&Exit",
                      x, y, Wbtn, Hbtn, FALSE);
```

The constructor creates each TButton instance with a unique ID and caption. The caption uses the ampersand character to underline the hot key. The last argument in all of the preceding three statements supplies FALSE to the isDefault parameter. Though these argument values explicitly specify that neither button is the default button, they are not really relevant, because the buttons are created in a non-dialog window. You can use a TRUE value in either constructor and still have the same result.

- Sets the InError data member to FALSE.

The constructor uses the local variables *x* and *y* and the control-size constants to simplify the calculation of the coordinates of the various controls. With this approach, you can modify the application without being lost in a trail of numbers.

The program uses the response table macro to map the various events and commands onto their respective handlers. The program uses the EV_WM_LBUTTONDOWN macro, with the EvLButtonDown member function, to handle clicking the left mouse button. The other map entry is EV_COMMAND, which relates the various CM_XXXX_BTN and ID_XXXX_BTN commands with their corresponding CMXXXXBtn and HandleIXXXXBtn member functions.

The EnableButton and DisableButton member functions enable and disable a pushbutton, respectively, by calling the EnableWindow function. The functions are called by other member functions with the StoreBtn argument. The following is a code snippet for the EvLButtonDown member function:

```
void TMainWindow::EvLButtonDown(UINT, TPoint& point)
{
  if (point.x >= MSG_xulc && point.x <= MSG_xlrc &&
      point.y >= MSG_yulc && point.y <= MSG_ylrc) {
      ErrMsgBox->Clear();
      // enable the Store button
      EnableButton(StoreBtn);
  }
}
```

The EvLButtonDown member function, represented in the preceding lines, performs a simple task. It checks whether or not the mouse click occurs in the rectangle occupied by the error message static text control. If this condition is true, the function clears the error message box by invoking the Clear function. In addition, the function enables the Store button.

The HandleCalcBtn member function responds to the Calc pushbutton and performs the calculation using the operands and operators that appear in their respective edit controls. The HandleCalcBtn function performs the following tasks:

- Obtains the first operand from the Operand1 edit box. The control may contain the name of a single-letter variable (A to Z) or a floating point number. The function uses the GetText function to store a copy of the edit control text in the local variable s. The function then examines the first character in variable s. If that character is a letter, then the first operand is a single-letter variable. Consequently, the function calls the protected member function getVar to obtain the value associated with that variable. If the first character is not a letter, the function uses the atof function to convert the contents of variable s into a double-typed number. In both cases, the function stores the actual (numeric) first operand in variable x.

- Obtains the second operand in a manner identical to the first one. The function stores the actual (numeric) second operand in variable y.

- Copies the text in the Operator edit box into the opStr local variable.

- Clears the error message text box and sets the InError data member to FALSE.

- Determines the requested operation by using a series of if and if-else statements. The operators supported are +, -, *, /, and ∧ (power). If the function detects an error, it sets the InError data member to TRUE and displays a message in the error message box.

- Displays the result in the Result box if the InError data member is FALSE. The function first converts the result from double to a string and then writes to the Result box using the setText function. If the InError member is TRUE, the function disables the Store button by using the DisableButton member function.

The CMCalcBtn member function responds to the CM_CALC_BTN command generated by pressing the Alt+C keys. The function merely calls the HandleCalcBtn member function.

The HandleStoreBtn member function responds to the ID_STORE_BTN command by storing the contents of the Result box in a single-letter variable. The function first obtains the string in the Result edit box by calling the GetText function. Then, the function invokes the protected member function putVar to actually store the result string at the current insertion point in the Variables edit box.

The CMStoreBtn member function responds to the CM_STORE_BTN command generated by pressing the Alt+S keys. The function merely calls the HandleStoreBtn member function.

The HandleExitBtn and CMExitBtn member functions close the window by sending the Windows message WM_CLOSE to the parent window. As explained later, the application uses an instance of TMainWindow as a client window in an instance of TFrameWindow.

The getVar member function returns the number stored at the lineNum line number of the Variables edit box. The function performs the following tasks:

- Exits and returns 0, if the parameter lineNum is greater than or equal to the constant MAX_MEMREG.

- Obtains the size of the target line by making the GetLineLength(lineNum) call.

- Retrieves the strings of the lineNum line number by calling the GetLine function.

- Deletes the first three characters of the retrieved line. This step should leave the string with the number stored in the target line.

- Returns the double-typed number obtained by calling the atof function and supplying it with the s argument.

The putVar member function stores the number in the Result box in the variable that is located on the same line containing the text insert position. The function performs the following tasks:

- Locates the character position of the cursor by calling the GetSelection function. The function returns the start and end character positions in the startPos and endPos local variables.

- Turns off any selected text. The function compares the values in the startPos and endPos variables. If these values do not match, the function invokes the SetSelection function and supplies it with the startPos as both the first and second arguments. This invocation of SetSelection turns off the selected text.

- Obtains the line number of the cursor's location using the GetLineFromPos function.

- Obtains the size of the target line using the GetLineLength function.

- Retrieves the text in the target line by calling the GetLine function.

- Deletes the target line using the DeleteLine function.

- Builds the string for the new line.

- Inserts the new line by calling the Insert function.

The TWinApp application class declares the InitMainWindow member function, which performs the following tasks:

- Creates the main window as an instance of TFrameWindow. This task also specifies the window's title and uses an instance of the TMainWindow class as the client window. The function assigns the address of the TFrameWindow instance to the inherited data member MainWindow.

- Loads the keystroke resources identifier by the ID IDR_BUTTONS.

- Loads the IDM_EXITMENU menu resource. This task sends the AssignMenu message to the main window component of the application.

- Enables the keyboard handler by sending the EnableKBHandler message to the main window part of the application.

THE CHECK BOX CONTROL

The check box control is a special button that toggles a check mark. The control instances appear with a small rectangular button and a title that appears, by default, to the right side of the square. When you click the square, you toggle the control's check mark. Think of the check box as a binary digit that can be either set or cleared. The instances of a check box can appear inside or outside a group box and are mutually non-exclusive; toggling any check box does not affect the check state of other check boxes.

Placing check boxes inside groups serves two purposes. First, the group box provides a visual grouping that clarifies the purpose of the check boxes to the application user. Second, when you place check boxes in a group box, your ObjectWindows application can detect any change in the checked state of the check boxes.

Earlier, I compared the check box control with a binary digit that can be set or cleared. Actually, with Windows, you can specify a check box with three states: checked, unchecked, and grayed. Table 2.4 shows the styles for the check box control. The grayed state fills the control's rectangular button with a gray color. This third state can serve to indicate that the check box control is either disabled or in a don't-care state.

The TCheckBox Class

ObjectWindows offers the TCheckBox class, a descendant of TButton, as the class that provides the instances of check box controls. The TCheckBox class has three constructors and a small number of member functions that set and query the check state of each TCheckBox instance. The following constructor enables you to create a TCheckBox instance from scratch:

```
TCheckBox(TWindow* parent, int Id, const char far* title,
        int x, int y, int w, int h, TGroupBox* group,
        TModule* module = 0);
```

The parent parameter is the pointer to the parent window or dialog box. The Id parameter specifies the unique ID for the control. The title parameter is the pointer to the string that contains the control's title. The x, y, w, and h parameters define the location and size of the control. The group parameter is the pointer to the group box that contains the check box instance. If the check box is not located inside a group box, this parameter is supplied a NULL argument. The constructor creates the TCheckBox instances with the BS_AUTOCHECK style and an unchecked box. You can override this style by specifying another style shown in Table 3.4. Examples of overriding the default check box style are as follows:

```
// make the title appear to the left of the button
Check1->Attr.Style |= BS_LEFTTEXT;

// make the check box non-automatic
Check2->Attr.Style &= ~BS_AUTOCHECK;
Check2->Attr.Style |= BS_CHECK;

// make the check box a three-state control with
// text that appears to the left of the button
Check2->Attr.Style &= ~BS_AUTOCHECK;
Check2->Attr.Style |= BS_AUTO3STATE | BS_LEFTTEXT;
```

The check box styles shown in Table 3.4 indicate that there are two basic modes for managing the check state of a check box control: automatic and non-automatic (manual, if you prefer). In the automatic mode (specified by BS_AUTOCHECK and BS_AUTO3STATE), the check state Windows toggles the check state when you click the control. In manual mode, your application code is responsible for managing the check state of the check box.

TABLE 3.4. THE CHECK BOX CONTROL STYLES.

Style	Meaning
BS_CHECKBOX	Specifies a check box with the title to the right of the rectangular button.
BS_AUTOCHECKBOX	Same as BS_CHECKBOX, except the button is automatically toggled when you click it.
BS_3STATE	Same as BS_CHECKBOX, except that the control has three states: checked, unchecked, and grayed.
BS_AUTO3STATE	Same as BS_3STATE, except the button is automatically toggled when you click it.
BS_LEFTTEXT	Sets the control's title to the left of the button.

The TCheckBox class provides member functions to set and query the state of the check box. The GetCheck member function returns a state of the check box control and is declared as follows:

```
inline UINT GetCheck() const;
```

The function returns a UINT-typed result that can be compared with the predefined constants BF_CHECKED, BF_UNCHECKED, or BF_GRAYED to conclude the check state of the control.

The TCheckBox class offers four member functions to set the check state of a check box control. They are the Check, Uncheck, Toggle, and SetCheck member functions. The first three functions return a void type and are parameterless. The Check member function forces the state of the check box to be checked. The Uncheck function performs the reverse action. The Toggle function toggles the check state of a check box control. For a dual-state control, the Toggle function toggles the state between checked and unchecked. For a three-state control, the Toggle function changes the check state as follows: from unchecked to checked, from checked to grayed, and from grayed to unchecked.

You can create a descendant of TCheckBox that overrides the Toggle member function to provide your applications with a different sequence of changing the check state for three-state controls.

The SetCheck member function enables you to set the check state to a specific value. The function is more useful with a three-state check box. The declaration of the SetCheck function is as follows:

```
void SetCheck(UINT CheckFlag);
```

The CheckFlag parameter takes one of the predefined constants BF_CHECKED, BF_UNCHECKED, or BF_GRAYED as an argument.

The Check member function, which takes no arguments, forces the check box to be checked. This function is a short form for calling the SetCheck member function with the BF_CHECKED argument. The Check function also notifies the related group box (if one does exist) of the change in state.

The Uncheck member function, which takes no arguments, forces the check box to be unchecked. This function is a short form for calling the SetCheck member function with the BF_UNCHECKED argument. The Uncheck function also notifies the related group box (if one does exist) of the change in state.

The `Toggle` member function, which takes no arguments, toggles the state of the check box. In the case of a two-state check box, the function toggles the state of the control between checked and unchecked. In the case of a three-state check box, the function alters the check state from checked, to unchecked, to gray.

Responding to Check Box Messages

When you click a check box, it sends a notification message to its parent window. The parent window handles the `BN_CLICKED` notification message code using a message response member function based on the check box ID number. The response table entry is `EV_COMMAND`. For example, to respond to the notification message emitted by the check box whose ID is `ID_DEGREE_CHK`, you need the following member function:

```
TMainWindow : public TWindow
{
public:
    double angleFactor;

    // constructors here

    void HandleDegreeChk();

    // other member functions

    DECLARE_RESPONSE_TABLE(TMainWindow);
};


DEFINE_RESPOSE_TABLE1(TMainWindow, TWindow)
    ...other response table entries
    EV_COMMAND(ID_DEGREE_CHK, HandleDegreeChk),
    ...other response table entries
END_RESPONSE_TABLE;

void TMainWindow::HandleDegreeChk()
{
    angleFactor = 4 * atan(1) / 180;
}
```

THE RADIO BUTTON CONTROL

Radio buttons are controls that typically enable you to select an option from two or more options. This kind of control comes with a circular button and a title that appears, by default, to the right of the button. When you check a radio button, a tiny, filled circle appears inside the circular button. Radio buttons must be placed in group boxes that visually and logically group them. In each group of radio buttons, only one button can be selected. Therefore, radio buttons are mutually exclusive.

The TRadioButton Class

ObjectWindows offers the TRadioButton class as a descendant of the TCheckBox class, because the radio button is a more specialized version of the check box. The TRadioButton class has three constructors and a small number of member functions that set and query the check state of each TRadioButton instance. The following constructor enables you to create a TRadioButton instance from scratch:

```
TRadioButton(TWindow* parent, int Id, const char far* title,
             int x, int y, int w, int h, TGroupBox* group,
             TModule* module = 0);
```

The parameters of the preceding constructor are identical to those of the TCheckBox constructor presented in the previous section. Table 3.5 contains the radio button styles. The constructor creates a radio button with the BS_AUTORADIOBUTTON style.

TABLE 3.5. THE RADIO BUTTON CONTROL STYLES.

Style	Meaning
BS_RADIOBUTTON	Specifies a radio button with the title to the right of the circular button.
BS_AUTORADIOBUTTON	Same as BS_RADIOBUTTON, except the button is automatically toggled when you click it.
BS_LEFTTEXT	Sets the control's title to the left of the button.

To query and modify the check state of a radio button, you can use the GetCheck, Check, Uncheck, Toggle, and SetCheck member functions that are inherited from the TCheckBox class.

The radio button controls send the same type of notification messages to their parent windows as do the check box controls. Handling these messages for radio buttons is identical to that of check boxes.

THE GROUP CONTROL

The group box control is a special *container* control that encloses radio buttons and check boxes. The group box performs the following:

- Visually groups radio buttons and check boxes. This grouping makes relating these controls to each other clearer for the application user.

- Logically groups multiple radio buttons so that when you select one radio button, the other buttons in the same group are automatically deselected.

- Sends a group notification message to the parent window when you click any check box or radio button inside a group box. This feature provides your application with a single and centralized notification mechanism.

The TGroupBox Class

ObjectWindows provides the TGroupBox class, a descendant of TControl, as the class that implements the group box controls. The class has three constructors. With the following constructor, you can create a group box control from scratch:

```
TGroupBox(TWindow* parent, int Id, const char far* text, int x,
int y, int w, int h, TModule* module = 0);
```

The parent parameter is the pointer to the parent window or dialog box. The Id parameter specifies the unique ID for the group box control. The text parameter is the pointer to the string that contains the group's title. The x, y, w, and h parameters define the location and size of the group box. The TGroupBox class also declares the Boolean NotifyParent data member. The class constructor sets the NotifyParent member to TRUE and creates the group box with a BS_GROUPBOX style and also removes the WS_TABSTOP style. As a result, group boxes notify their parent windows when a selection change takes place in any control within the boxes. To disable parent notification, you simply assign FALSE to the NotifyParent data member.

Responding to Group Box Messages

The group box controls send notification messages to their parent when the NotifyParent data member is TRUE and when a member control selection is altered. The parent window can process the notification message using the ID of the group control. The response table entry is EV_CHILD_NOTIFY_ALL_CODES. The response member function must have a single parameter of type UINT. This parameter represents the ID of the newly selected control. For example, to respond to the notification message emitted by the group box whose ID is ID_ANGLE_GRP, you need the following member function:

```
TMainWindow : public TWindow
{
public:
    TGroupBox* AngleGrp;  // Angle group box control
    // the following controls are contained in
    // the Angle group box control
    TRadioButton* RadianRbt; // Radian radio button
    TRadioButton* DegreeRbt; // Degree radio button
    TRadioButton* GradianRbt; // Gradian radio button

    double angleFactor;

    // constructors here

    void HandleAngleGrp(UINT);

    // other member functions

    DECLARE_RESPONSE_TABLE(TMainWindow);
};


DEFINE_RESPOSE_TABLE1(TMainWindow, TWindow)
    ...other table entries
    EV_CHILD_NOTIFY_ALL_CODES(ID_ANGLE_GRP, HandleAngleGrp),
    ...other table entries
END_RESPONSE_TABLE;


void TMainWindow::HandleAngleGrp(UINT)
{
    static double pi = 4 * atan(1);

    if (RadianRbt->GetCheck() == BF_CHECKED)
        angleFactor = 1;
    else if (DegreeRbt->GetCheck() == BF_CHECKED)
        angleFactor = pi / 180;
    else if (GradianRbt->GetCHeck() == BF_CHECKED)
        angleFactor = pi / 180 / 0.9;
}
```

The preceding code illustrates how the group notification message response function can replace the individual response function for each of the three radio button controls.

The TGroup class contains the SelectionChanged member function that sends the notification messages to the parent window. You can override this function in a descendant of TGroupBox to handle the selection changes in a different manner.

THE UPDATED CALCULATOR APPLICATION

The operations of the calculator application that I presented earlier in this chapter can be expanded to include trigonometric functions. Using trigonometric function frequently involves the choice of angle modes: radians, degrees, or gradians (100 gradians equal 90 degrees). Using a group box that contains angle mode radio buttons seems suitable to illustrate the operations of these controls. Check boxes are added to fine-tune other operational aspects of the calculator. You will see more about this later in this section.

The Illustrated Aspects

The updated calculator application (COCA Version 2) illustrates the following:

- The basic use of check box controls
- The basic use of radio buttons
- Responding to radio button notification messages
- Responding to a group box notification message
- Using a check box control to alter the action of the response message function that handles the group box notification message
- Manipulating multiple check boxes and edit boxes using the ForEach iterator
- Making initial check box selections
- Making initial radio button selections

The new version of the calculator application contains the following controls (see Figure 3.2):

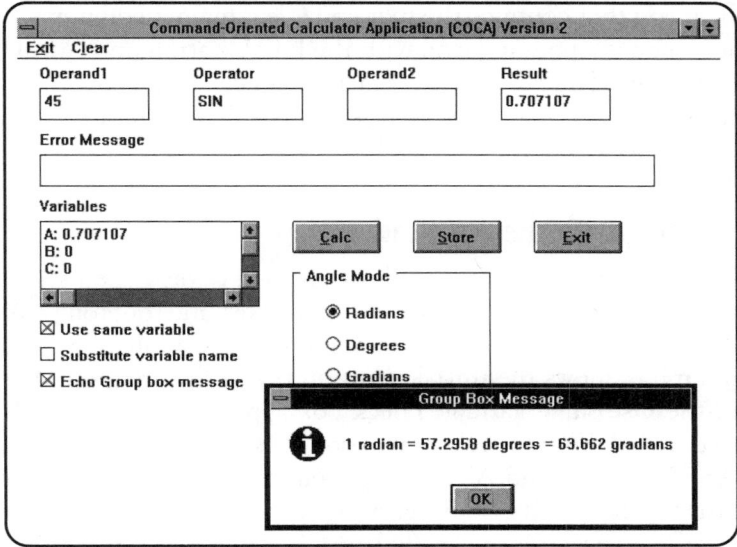

Figure 3.2. A sample session with the CTLGRP1.EXE program.

- The single-line edit controls labeled **Operand1**, **Operator**, **Operand2**, **Result**, and **Error Message**.

- The multiline edit control labeled **Variables**.

- The static text controls that label the previously mentioned edit boxes.

- The **Calc**, **Store**, and **Exit** pushbuttons.

- The **Angle Mode** group box that contains the Radians, Degrees, and Gradians radio buttons.

- The **Use same variable** check box that makes the store commands retain the same variable for storing future results.

- The **Substitute variable name** check box that replaces the names of the single-letter variables, which may appear in either operand edit boxes, with their values. The replacement occurs after you click the Calc pushbutton.

- The **Echo Group box message** check box permits the group notification message handler to display a message box when you select another radio button.

- The menu that contains the Exit and Clear main menu items. The Clear item is a pop-up menu with the Edit Controls and Check Boxes menu items. The Edit Controls menu item clears the contents of the edit controls, except the Variables edit box. The Check Boxes menu item unchecks the three check boxes.

Experimenting with the Application

Compile and run the calculator application to develop a good sense for the features supported by the radio buttons, check boxes, and the group box. When the application's window appears, maximize it to get a full view. The Angle Mode group box shows the initial selection of the Degrees radio button. In addition, the **Use same variable** check box appears checked and the Store button is disabled. The current application version supports the SIN, COS, TAN, ASIN, ACOS, and ATAN trigonometric functions, which you can enter in the Operator edit box. Enter the number 45 in the Operand1 edit box and type in TAN in the Operator edit box. Click the Calc button to obtain the tangent of 45 degrees in the Result edit box (a value of 1). Store the result in variable A by clicking the Store button. Now replace the number 45 with the # character in the Operand1 edit box. Then prepend an A to the string SIN in the Operator box, and click the Calc button. The # character is replaced by 1, the previous number in the Result edit box. The Result edit box now shows the number 45, the arc tangent of 1. Using the # character is a new small feature that I added to the program; by typing in the # character, you can use the result from the previous calculation in either or both operand edit boxes. Now click the Store button again. The application stores the number 45 in variable A, overwriting the previous result. Now click the **Use same variable** check box and click the Store button a few times. Now, the number in the Result edit box is stored in multiple variables.

Check the **Echo Group message box** check box and then click any radio button. The application displays a message box that contains information on converting between different angles. Selecting a different radio button yields a different message. These messages are responses to the `Angle Mode` group notification message.

Experiment with selecting different angle modes. Each time, enter a value in the Operand1 edit box and type in a trigonometric function. Observe how the results differ for the same arguments, whereas the angle mode varies. Keep in mind that the inverse sine and cosine functions accept arguments between -1 and 1. The application detects invalid arguments for these two functions and displays error messages.

Finally, use the Clear | Edit Control and Clear | Check Boxes menu items to clear the edit boxes (except the Variables edit box) and the check boxes.

I have omitted the feature that clears the error message and enables the Store button when you click the Error Message label.

Listing 3.5 shows the contents of CTLGRP1.DEF definition file. Listing 3.6 contains the source code for the CTLGRP1.H header file and Listing 3.7 shows the script for the CTLGRP1.RC resource file. The resource file contains the accelerator keys and the menu resources. Listing 3.8 contains the source code for the CTLGRP1.CPP program file. The program contains #include statements, declaration of constants, iterated functions, and the classes for the application and its window.

LISTING 3.5. THE CONTENTS OF THE CTLGRP1.DEF DEFINITION FILE.

```
NAME         CtlGrp1
DESCRIPTION  'An OWL Windows Application'
EXETYPE      WINDOWS
CODE         PRELOAD MOVEABLE DISCARDABLE
DATA         PRELOAD MOVEABLE MULTIPLE
HEAPSIZE     1024
STACKSIZE    16384
```

LISTING 3.6. THE SOURCE CODE FOR THE CTLGRP1.H HEADER FILE.

```
#define ID_CALC_BTN   100
#define ID_STORE_BTN  101
#define ID_EXIT_BTN   102
#define CM_CALC_BTN   103
#define CM_STORE_BTN  104
#define CM_EXIT_BTN   105
#define CM_CLEARBOX   201
#define CM_CLEARCHK   202
#define IDR_BUTTONS   300
#define IDM_EXITMENU  301
```

LISTING 3.7. THE SCRIPT FOR THE CTLGRP1.RC RESOURCE FILE.

```
#include <windows.h>
#include <owl\window.rh>
#include "ctlgrp1.h"

IRD_BUTTONS ACCELERATORS
BEGIN
  "c", CM_CALC_BTN, ALT
  "s", CM_STORE_BTN, ALT
  "e", CM_EXIT_BTN, ALT
END

IDM_EXITMENU MENU LOADONCALL MOVEABLE PURE DISCARDABLE
BEGIN
    MENUITEM "E&xit", CM_EXIT
    POPUP "C&lear"
    BEGIN
      MENUITEM "&Edit Controls", CM_CLEARBOX
      MENUITEM "&Check Boxes", CM_CLEARCHK
    END
END
```

LISTING 3.8. THE SOURCE CODE FOR THE CTLGRP1.CPP PROGRAM FILE.

```
/*
  Program to test the check box, radio button and group controls.
  The program uses these controls to implement a command-line
  oriented calculator application (COCA) version 2
*/

#include <owl\applicat.h>
#include <owl\framewin.h>
#include <owl\static.h>
#include <owl\edit.h>
#include <owl\button.h>
#include <owl\groupbox.h>
#include <owl\radiobut.h>
#include <owl\checkbox.h>
#include <owl\window.rh>
#include "ctlgrp1.h"
#include <stdlib.h>
#include <ctype.h>
#include <stdio.h>
#include <math.h>
#include <string.h>
```

```
// declare the constants that represent the sizes of the controls
const Wlbl = 100;
const Hlbl = 20;
const LblVertSpacing = 2;
const LblHorzSpacing = 40;
const Wbox = 100;
const Hbox = 30;
const BoxVertSpacing = 10;
const BoxHorzSpacing = 40;
const WLongbox = 4 * (Wbox + BoxHorzSpacing);
const Wvarbox = 2 * Wbox;
const Hvarbox = 3 * Hbox - 10;
const Hbtn = 30;
const Wbtn = 80;
const BtnHorzSpacing = 30;
const BtnVertSpacing = 10;
const Hgrp = 130;
const Wgrp = 180;
const GrpHorzSpacing = 30;
const GrpVertSpacing = 10;
const Hchk = 20;
const Wchk = 200;
const ChkHorzSpacing = 30;
const ChkVertSpacing = 5;
const Hrbt = 30;
const Wrbt = 80;
const RbtHorzSpacing = 30;
const RbtVertSpacing = 30;
const RbtLeftMargin = 30;

const MaxEditLen = 30;
const MAX_MEMREG = 26;

// declare the ID_XXXX constants for the edit boxes
#define ID_OPERAND1_EDIT 200
#define ID_OPERATOR_EDIT 201
#define ID_OPERAND2_EDIT 202
#define ID_RESULT_EDIT   203
#define ID_ERRMSG_EDIT   204
#define ID_VARIABLE_EDIT 205

// include file has IDs for the buttons in the range of 107 to 109
#include "ctlgrp1.h"

#define ID_VAR_CHK      206
#define ID_SUBST_CHK    207
#define ID_ECHO_CHK     208
#define ID_ANGLE_GRP    209
#define ID_RADIAN_RBT   210
#define ID_DEGREE_RBT   211
```

continues

LISTING **3.8.** CONTINUED

```
#define ID_GRADIAN_RBT 212

const double pi = 4 * atan(1);
const double DegToRad = pi / 180;
const double GradToRad = 0.9 * DegToRad;

// declare iterated function to clear the edit controls
// except the Variables edit control
void ClearEditControls(TWindow* pWin, void*)
{
  TEdit* pEdit = (TEdit*)pWin;
  int i = pEdit->Attr.Id;

  // if the instance Id is an edit control (except
  // for the VariableBox control), clear its text
  if (i >= ID_OPERAND1_EDIT && i <= ID_ERRMSG_EDIT)
    pEdit->Clear();
}

// declare the iterated function to clear the check boxes
void ClearCheckBoxes(TWindow* pWin, void*)
{
  TCheckBox* pCheck = (TCheckBox*)pWin;
  int i = pCheck->Attr.Id;

  if (i >= ID_VAR_CHK && i <= ID_ECHO_CHK)
    pCheck->Uncheck();
}

// declare the custom application class as
// a subclass of TApplication
class TWinApp : public TApplication
{
public:
  TWinApp() : TApplication() {}

protected:
  virtual void InitMainWindow();
};

// expand the functionality of TWindow by deriving
// class TMainWindow
class TMainWindow : public TWindow
{
public:

  TMainWindow();
```

```
protected:

  TEdit* Operand1Box;
  TEdit* OperatorBox;
  TEdit* Operand2Box;
  TEdit* ResultBox;
  TEdit* ErrMsgBox;
  TEdit* VariableBox;
  TButton* CalcBtn;
  TButton* StoreBtn;
  TButton* ExitBtn;
  TGroupBox* AngleModeGrp;
  TRadioButton* RadianRbt;
  TRadioButton* DegreeRbt;
  TRadioButton* GradianRbt;
  TCheckBox* AutoVarSubstChk;
  TCheckBox* UseSameVarChk;
  TCheckBox* EchoGroupChk;

  // math error flag
  BOOL InError;

  // the factor that converts between angles the
  // currently selected angle mode and radians
  double angleFactor;

  //------------------- member functions -------------------

  // override window setup to initialize window
  virtual void SetupWindow();

  // handle clearing the edit controls
  void CMClearBox();

  // handle clearing the check box controls
  void CMClearChk();

  // handle the calculation
  void HandleCalcBtn();

  // handle the accelerator key for the Calculate button
  void CMCalcBtn();

  // handle storing the result in a variable
  void HandleStoreBtn();

  // handle the accelerator key for the Store button
  void CMStoreBtn();

  // handle exiting the application
```

continues

LISTING 3.8. CONTINUED

```
void HandleExitBtn();

// handle the accelerator key for the Exit button
void CMExitBtn();

// handle the Angle Mode group box message
void HandleAngleModeGrp(WPARAM);

// handle selecting the Radians radio button
void HandleRadianRbt();

// handle selecting the Degrees radio button
void HandleDegreeRbt();

// handle selecting the Gradians radio button
void HandleGradianRbt();

// enable a push button control
void EnableButton(TButton* pBtn)
{ pBtn->EnableWindow(TRUE); }

// disable a push button control
void DisableButton(TButton* pBtn)
{ pBtn->EnableWindow(FALSE); }

// handle closing the window
virtual BOOL CanClose();

// obtain a number of a Variable edit box line
double getVar(int lineNum);

// store a number in the selected text of
// the Variable edit box line
void putVar(double x);

// declare the message map macro
DECLARE_RESPONSE_TABLE(TMainWindow);

};

DEFINE_RESPONSE_TABLE1(TMainWindow, TWindow)
  EV_COMMAND(CM_CLEARBOX, CMClearBox),
  EV_COMMAND(CM_CLEARCHK, CMClearChk),
  EV_COMMAND(ID_CALC_BTN, HandleCalcBtn),
  EV_COMMAND(CM_CALC_BTN, CMCalcBtn),
  EV_COMMAND(ID_STORE_BTN, HandleStoreBtn),
  EV_COMMAND(CM_STORE_BTN, CMStoreBtn),
  EV_COMMAND(ID_EXIT_BTN, HandleExitBtn),
```

```
  EV_COMMAND(CM_EXIT_BTN, CMExitBtn),
  EV_CHILD_NOTIFY_ALL_CODES(ID_ANGLE_GRP, HandleAngleModeGrp),
  EV_COMMAND(ID_RADIAN_RBT, HandleRadianRbt),
  EV_COMMAND(ID_DEGREE_RBT, HandleDegreeRbt),
  EV_COMMAND(ID_GRADIAN_RBT, HandleGradianRbt),
END_RESPONSE_TABLE;

TMainWindow::TMainWindow() :
          TWindow(0, 0, 0)
{
  char s[81];
  char bigStr[6 * MAX_MEMREG + 1];
  char c;
  int x0 = 20;
  int y0 = 5;
  int x = x0, y = y0;
  int x1, y1;

  // set initialization flag
  //InitFlag = TRUE;

  // create the first set of labels for the edit boxes
  strcpy(s, "Operand1");
  new TStatic(this, -1, s, x, y, Wlbl, Hlbl, strlen(s));
  strcpy(s, "Operator");
  x += Wlbl + LblHorzSpacing;
  new TStatic(this, -1, s, x, y, Wlbl, Hlbl, strlen(s));
  strcpy(s, "Operand2");
  x += Wlbl + LblHorzSpacing;
  new TStatic(this, -1, s, x, y, Wlbl, Hlbl, strlen(s));
  x += Wlbl + LblHorzSpacing;
  strcpy(s, "Result");
  new TStatic(this, -1, s, x, y, Wlbl, Hlbl, strlen(s));

  // create the operand1, operator, operand2, and result
  // edit boxes
  x = x0;
  y += Hlbl + LblVertSpacing;
  Operand1Box = new TEdit(this, ID_OPERAND1_EDIT, "", x, y,
               Wbox, Hbox, 0, FALSE);

  // force conversion of letters to uppercase
  Operand1Box->Attr.Style |= ES_UPPERCASE;
  x += Wbox + BoxHorzSpacing;
  OperatorBox = new TEdit(this, ID_OPERATOR_EDIT, "", x, y,
                         Wbox, Hbox, 0, FALSE);
  // force conversion of letters to uppercase
  OperatorBox->Attr.Style |= ES_UPPERCASE;
  x += Wbox + BoxHorzSpacing;
  Operand2Box = new TEdit(this, ID_OPERAND2_EDIT, "", x, y,
```

continues

LISTING 3.8. CONTINUED

```
                      Wbox, Hbox, 0, FALSE);
// force conversion of letters to uppercase
Operand2Box->Attr.Style |= ES_UPPERCASE;
x += Wbox + BoxHorzSpacing;
ResultBox = new TEdit(this, ID_RESULT_EDIT, "", x, y, Wbox, Hbox,
                      0, FALSE);

// create the static text and edit box for the error message
x = x0;
y += Hbox + BoxVertSpacing;
strcpy(s, "Error Message");
new TStatic(this, -1, s, x, y, Wlbl, Hlbl, strlen(s));
y += Hlbl + LblVertSpacing;
ErrMsgBox = new TEdit(this, ID_ERRMSG_EDIT, "", x, y,
            WLongbox, Hbox, 0, FALSE);
// create the static text and edit box for the single-letter
// variable selection
y += Hbox + BoxVertSpacing;
strcpy(s, "Variables");
new TStatic(this, -1, s, x, y, Wlbl, Hlbl, strlen(s));
y += Hlbl + LblVertSpacing;
bigStr[0] = '\0';
// build the initial contents of the Variable edit box
for (c = 'A'; c <= 'Z'; c++) {
  sprintf(s, "%c: 0\r\n", c);
    strcat(bigStr, s);
}
VariableBox = new TEdit(this, ID_VARIABLE_EDIT, bigStr, x, y,
            Wvarbox, Hvarbox, 0, TRUE);
// force conversion of letters to uppercase
VariableBox->Attr.Style |= ES_UPPERCASE;

// create the Calc push button
x += Wvarbox + BtnHorzSpacing;
x1 = x;
y1 = y;
CalcBtn = new TButton(this, ID_CALC_BTN, "&Calc",
            x, y, Wbtn, Hbtn, FALSE);

// create the Store Btn
x += Wbtn + BtnHorzSpacing;
StoreBtn = new TButton(this, ID_STORE_BTN, "&Store",
            x, y, Wbtn, Hbtn, FALSE);
// disable the Store button control
StoreBtn->EnableWindow(FALSE);

// create the Exit Btn
x += Wbtn + BtnHorzSpacing;
```

```
ExitBtn = new TButton(this, ID_EXIT_BTN, "&Exit",
             x, y, Wbtn, Hbtn, FALSE);

// create the "Use same variable" check box
x = x0;
y += Hvarbox + BoxVertSpacing;
UseSameVarChk = new TCheckBox(this, ID_VAR_CHK,
               "Use same variable",
               x, y, Wchk, Hchk, NULL);

// create the "Substitute variable name" check box
y += Hchk + ChkVertSpacing;
AutoVarSubstChk = new TCheckBox(this, ID_SUBST_CHK,
               "Substitute variable name",
               x, y, Wchk, Hchk, NULL);

// create the "Echo Group box message" check box
y += Hchk + ChkVertSpacing;
EchoGroupChk = new TCheckBox(this, ID_ECHO_CHK,
               "Echo Group box message",
               x, y, Wchk, Hchk, NULL);

// create the Angle Mode group box
y = y1 + Hbtn + BtnVertSpacing;
x = x1;
AngleModeGrp = new TGroupBox(this, ID_ANGLE_GRP, " Angle Mode ",
               x, y, Wgrp, Hgrp);
// create the Radians radio button
y += RbtVertSpacing;
RadianRbt = new TRadioButton(this, ID_RADIAN_RBT, "Radians",
               RbtLeftMargin + x, y, Wrbt, Hrbt,
               AngleModeGrp);
// create the Degrees radio button
y += RbtVertSpacing;
DegreeRbt = new TRadioButton(this, ID_DEGREE_RBT, "Degrees",
               RbtLeftMargin + x, y, Wrbt, Hrbt,
               AngleModeGrp);
// create the Gradians radio button
y += RbtVertSpacing;
GradianRbt = new TRadioButton(this, ID_GRADIAN_RBT, "Gradians",
               RbtLeftMargin + x, y, Wrbt, Hrbt,
               AngleModeGrp);

// clear the InError flag
InError = FALSE;
}

void TMainWindow::SetupWindow()
{
  TWindow::SetupWindow();
```

continues

Listing 3.8. continued

```cpp
  // disable the Store button control
  StoreBtn->EnableWindow(FALSE);
  // check the Degrees radio button
  DegreeRbt->Check();
  angleFactor = DegToRad;
  // check the "Use Same Var" check button
  UseSameVarChk->Check();
}

void TMainWindow::CMClearBox()
{
  ForEach(ClearEditControls, NULL);
}

void TMainWindow::CMClearChk()
{
  ForEach(ClearCheckBoxes, NULL);
}

void TMainWindow::HandleCalcBtn()
{
  double x, y, z, result;
  char opStr[MaxEditLen+1];
  char s[MaxEditLen+1];

  // convert the string in the Result box to a double
  ResultBox->GetText(s, MaxEditLen);
  result = atof(s);

  // obtain the string in the Operand1 edit box
  Operand1Box->GetText(s, MaxEditLen);
  // does the Operand1Box contain the name
  // of a single-letter variable?
  if (isalpha(s[0])) {
    // obtain value from the Variable edit control
    x = getVar(s[0] - 'A');
    // substitute the variable name with its value
    if (AutoVarSubstChk->GetCheck() == BF_CHECKED) {
      sprintf(s, "%g", x);
      Operand1Box->SetText(s);
    }
  }
  // translate the # character into the value in the Result box
  else if (s[0] == '#')
    x = result;
  else
      // convert the string in the edit box
    x = atof(s);
```

```
// obtain the string in the Operand2 edit box
Operand2Box->GetText(s, MaxEditLen);
// does the Operand2Box contain the name
// of a single-letter variable?
if (isalpha(s[0])) {
  // obtain value from the Variable edit control
  y =getVar(s[0] - 'A');
  // substitute the variable name with its value
  if (AutoVarSubstChk->GetCheck() == BF_CHECKED) {
    sprintf(s, "%g", y);
    Operand2Box->SetText(s);
  }
}
// translate the # character into the value in the Result box
else if (s[0] == '#')
  y = result;
else
  // convert the string in the edit box
  y = atof(s);

// obtain the string in the Operator edit box
OperatorBox->GetText(opStr, MaxEditLen);

// clear the error message box
ErrMsgBox->Clear();
InError = FALSE;

// determine the requested operation
if (strlen(opStr) == 1) {
  if (strcmp(opStr, "+") == 0)
    z = x + y;
    else if (strcmp(opStr, "-") == 0)
    z = x - y;
  else if (strcmp(opStr, "*") == 0)
    z = x * y;
  else if (strcmp(opStr, "/") == 0) {
    if (y != 0)
    z = x / y;
    else {
      z = 0;
    InError = TRUE;
    ErrMsgBox->SetText("Division-by-zero error");
    }
  }
  else if (strcmp(opStr, "^") == 0) {
    if (x > 0)
      z = exp(y * log(x));
    else {
    InError = TRUE;
      ErrMsgBox->SetText(
```

continues

LISTING 3.8. CONTINUED

```
            "Cannot raise the power of a negative number");
      }
    }
    else {
      InError = TRUE;
      ErrMsgBox->SetText("Invalid operator");
    }
  }
  else if (strcmp(opStr, "SIN") == 0) {
    z = sin(angleFactor * x);
  }
  else if (strcmp(opStr, "COS") == 0) {
    z = cos(angleFactor * x);
  }
  else if (strcmp(opStr, "TAN") == 0) {
      z = tan(angleFactor * x);
  }
  else if (strcmp(opStr, "ASIN") == 0) {
    if (fabs(x) <= 1)
      z = asin(x) / angleFactor;
    else {
      InError = TRUE;
      ErrMsgBox->SetText(
            "Invalid argument for the asin(x) function");
    }
  }
  else if (strcmp(opStr, "ACOS") == 0) {
    if (fabs(x) <= 1)
      z = acos(x) / angleFactor;
    else {
      InError = TRUE;
      ErrMsgBox->SetText(
            "Invalid argument for the acos(x) function");
    }
  }
  else if (strcmp(opStr, "ATAN") == 0) {
    z = atan(x) / angleFactor;
  }
  else {
    InError = TRUE;
    ErrMsgBox->SetText("Invalid math function");
  }

  // display the result if no error has occurred
  if (!InError) {
    sprintf(s, "%g", z);
    ResultBox->SetText(s);
    // enable the Store button
```

```
    EnableButton(StoreBtn);
  }
  else
    // disable the Store button
    DisableButton(StoreBtn);
}

void TMainWindow::CMCalcBtn()
{
  HandleCalcBtn();
}

void TMainWindow::HandleStoreBtn()
{
  char varName[MaxEditLen+1];
  char result[MaxEditLen+1];

  // get the string in the Result edit box
  ResultBox->GetText(result, MaxEditLen);

  // store the result in the selected text of
  // the Variable edit box
  putVar(atof(result));
}

void TMainWindow::CMStoreBtn()
{
  HandleStoreBtn();
}

void TMainWindow::HandleExitBtn()
{
  // send the WM_CLOSE message to the parent window
  Parent->SendMessage(WM_CLOSE);
}

void TMainWindow::CMExitBtn()
{
  // send the WM_CLOSE message to the parent window
  Parent->SendMessage(WM_CLOSE);
}

void TMainWindow::HandleAngleModeGrp(WPARAM)
{
  char angleStr[81];

  // exit if the EchoGroup check box is not checked
  if (EchoGroupChk->GetCheck() != BF_CHECKED) return;
  // build the text of the message
  if (DegreeRbt->GetCheck() == BF_CHECKED)
```

continues

LISTING 3.8. CONTINUED

```
      sprintf(angleStr, "1 radian = %g degrees", 1 / DegToRad);
  else if (GradianRbt->GetCheck() == BF_CHECKED)
      sprintf(angleStr, "1 radian = %g gradians", 1 / GradToRad);
  else
      sprintf(angleStr, "1 radian = %g degrees = %g gradians",
            1 / DegToRad, 1 / GradToRad);
  MessageBox(angleStr, "Group Box Message",
          MB_OK | MB_ICONINFORMATION);
}

void TMainWindow::HandleRadianRbt()
{
  angleFactor = 1;
}

void TMainWindow::HandleDegreeRbt()
{
  angleFactor = DegToRad;
}

void TMainWindow::HandleGradianRbt()
{
  angleFactor = GradToRad;
}

BOOL TMainWindow::CanClose()
{
  return MessageBox("Want to close this application",
            "Query", MB_YESNO | MB_ICONQUESTION) == IDYES;
}

double TMainWindow::getVar(int lineNum)
{
  int lineSize;
  char s[MaxEditLen+1];

  if (lineNum >= MAX_MEMREG) return 0;
  // get the size of the target line
  lineSize = VariableBox->GetLineLength(lineNum);
  // get the line
  VariableBox->GetLine(s, lineSize+1, lineNum);
  // delete the first three characters
  strcpy(s, (s+3));
  // return the number stored in the target line
  return atof(s);
}
```

```
void TMainWindow::putVar(double x)
{
  UINT startPos, endPos;
  int lineNum;
  int lineSize;
  char s[MaxEditLen+1];

  // locate the character position of the cursor
  VariableBox->GetSelection(startPos, endPos);
  // turn off the selected text
  if (startPos != endPos)
    VariableBox->SetSelection(startPos, startPos);
  // get the line number where the cursor is located
  lineNum = VariableBox->GetLineFromPos(startPos);
  // get the line size of line lineNum
  lineSize = VariableBox->GetLineLength(lineNum);
  // obtain the text of line lineNum
  VariableBox->GetLine(s, lineSize+1, lineNum);
  // delete line lineNum
  VariableBox->DeleteLine(lineNum);
  // build the new text line
  sprintf(s, "%c: %g\r\n", s[0], x);
  // insert it
  VariableBox->Insert(s);
  // use the same variable?
  if (UseSameVarChk->GetCheck())
    // reset insertion point to the original position
    VariableBox->SetSelection(startPos, startPos);
}

void TWinApp::InitMainWindow()
{
  MainWindow = new TFrameWindow(0,
          "Command-Oriented Calculator Application (COCA) Version 2",
          new TMainWindow);
  // load the keystroke resources
  MainWindow->Attr.AccelTable = IDR_BUTTONS;
  // load the menu resource
  MainWindow->AssignMenu(TResID(IDM_EXITMENU));
  // enable the keyboard handler
  MainWindow->EnableKBHandler();
}

int OwlMain(int /* argc */, char** /*argv[] */)
{
  TWinApp app;
  return app.Run();
}
```

The first set of constants specifies the sizes and spacing between the various controls. The macro-based constants define the IDs of the various controls. The last set of constants specifies the value of pi and the angle conversion factors between radians and degrees, and between radians and gradians.

 The program declares the `ClearEditControls` and `ClearCheckBoxes` iterated functions to clear the specified edit boxes and all of the check boxes. You may wonder how to use typecasting for pointers to controls when you have different kinds of controls in the window's child control list. Can straightforward typecasting work? The answer is, fortunately, yes. Consider now the code for each iterated function.

The purpose of the `ClearEditControls` function is to clear all of the edit boxes, except the Variables box. The function performs the following tasks:

- Declares `pEdit` as a `TEdit`-pointer typecast of the `pWin` parameter.

- Declares the local variable `i` (to store the control's ID) by assigning it the expression `pEdit->Attr.Id`. This assignment is critical. If this programming method would have failed, then such an assignment would hang or corrupt the system.

- Tests whether the control's ID is in the range of the ID for the cleared edit boxes. The `if` statement serves two purposes. First, it excludes all controls that are not edit boxes. Second, it also excludes the Variables edit box. When the tested condition is true, the `Clear` member function is applied to clear the text of the client control.

The `ClearCheckBoxes` function works in a manner similar to that of `ClearEditBoxes`. The difference is that `ClearCheckBoxes` invokes the `Uncheck` member function when the control's ID matches that of any check box.

 Coding iterated functions that work on specific controls of a certain type is easier when you declare the ID of these controls using contiguous numbers. This approach creates a suitable range of ID that can be quickly and efficiently examined.

The CTLGRP1.CPP file declares the `TMainWindow` application window class. The class contains several data members. Most of these members are pointers to the instances of the various controls used by the application. The application adds the `angleFactor` data member to store the angle conversion factor between the currently selected angle mode and radians.

The TMainWindow class declares a constructor and a number of member functions to support the nontrivial program operations and special initialization. The constructor loads the menu resource and creates the various controls. Of interest are the statements that create the check boxes, the group box, and the radio buttons. Each instance of TCheckBox involves a unique control ID, title, and coordinates. The last argument for the three constructor invocations is FALSE. This argument value indicates that each check box is created outside a group box. The group box instance is created with its own ID, title, and coordinates. Each radio button control is created with a unique ID, title, and coordinates. The last argument used in each invocation of the TRadioButton constructor is AngleModeGrp. This argument is the pointer to the group box that contains these radio buttons.

The TMainWindow class declares the various member functions needed to implement the program's functionality. The CMClearBox and CMClearChk member functions respond to their respective menu command messages to clear the designated edit boxes and uncheck all of the check boxes. Each function invokes the ForEach operator and specifies the appropriate iterated function.

The HandleCalcBtn member function performs the calculations and any character substitution. The member function performs the following tasks:

- Converts the string in the Result box to a double and stores that value in the local variable result.

- Obtains the value for the first operand stored in variable x. The Operand1 edit box contains either a string image of a number, the name of a single-letter variable, or the # character:

    The statements that support the first option determine whether or not the Operand1 box contains a letter. If this condition is true, the statements invoke the getVar member function and assign the result to variable x. In addition, the code checks whether the **Substitute variable name** check box is checked. If so, the name of the variable in the Operand1 box is replaced with its value.

The statements that support the second option compare the first character in the Operand1 box with the # character. If the two characters match, the value stored in the local variable result is assigned to the variable x.

The statements that support the third option simply convert the string in the Operand1 edit box to a double and assign it to the local variable x.

- Obtains the second operand in a manner similar to the first one. The second operand is stored in the local variable y.

- Acquires the operator or function from the Operator edit box.

- Performs the requested operation or function evaluation. A set of if statements is used to determine the requested operation. The statements also include argument error checking. If there is any error, the function assigns TRUE to the InError data member and displays a message in the error message edit box.

- Displays the result in the Result edit box if no error has occurred.

The member functions CMCalcBtn, HandleStoreBtn, CMStoreBtn, HandleExitBtn, CMExitBtn, putVar, and getVar are the same as in the first version of the COCA program (file CTLBTN1.CPP).

The HandleAngleMode member function responds to the group box notification message. The function first verifies if the **Echo Group box message** check box is not checked. If this condition is true, the member function simply exits. Otherwise, the function determines which radio button is checked and accordingly builds an angle-conversion message. The function then invokes the MessageBox function to display the previously mentioned message.

The HandleRadianRbt, HandleDegreeRbt, and HandleGradianRbt member functions respond to the individual notification messages sent by the three radio buttons. Each member function assigns an angle-conversion factor to the angleFactor data member. Using these member functions is more efficient than systematically examining the check states of the radio buttons in the HandleCalcBtn member function. This approach alters the value in angleFactor *only* when you select a new angle mode.

The TMainWindow class includes the SetupWindow member function that initializes the following controls:

- Invokes the SetupWindow of the parent class.

- Disables the Store button.

- Checks the Degrees radio button.

- Checks the **Use same variable** check box.

The program uses a response table macro to map the various events and Windows messages onto their respective handlers. The table entry EV_CHILD_NOTIFY_ALL_CODES specifies that the HandleAngleModeGrp member function handles selecting a new control in the group box. The other table entries, including the ones emitted by the radio buttons, are of the kind EV_COMMAND. The program has no table entries for the check boxes because the application need not perform a task when you toggle the state of any check box.

SUMMARY

This chapter presented the static text, edit box, pushbutton, check box, radio button, and group box controls. Using these and other controls animates the Windows applications and provides a more consistent user-interface. You learned about the following topics:

- Creating static text controls and manipulating their text at runtime.

- Creating single-line and multiline edit box controls.

- Creating, using, and manipulating pushbutton controls. The control manipulation includes enabling, disabling, showing, and hiding the pushbutton controls at runtime.

- Setting and querying the check state for the check box and radio button controls.

- Responding to notification messages sent by these controls to their parent window.

- Selectively manipulating controls.

- Initializing controls.

## CHAPTER 4

Scroll Bars, List Boxes, and Combo Boxes

List controls are input tools that conveniently provide you items from which to choose. List controls are popular—especially when computer programs expect exact spellings—because list controls absolve you from remembering the list members. The various DOS utilities that display lists of files and directories are far easier and friendlier to use than their counterparts that assume you know all the names of your files and directories. Using list controls has gradually become a routine method for retrieving a large amount of information. In this chapter, I discuss the list box, the combo box (a list box control variant), and the scroll bar control. You will learn about the following topics:

- The scroll bar control

- The list control and its capability to support single or multiple selections

- Synchronized scrolling of list boxes

- Handling multiple-selection list boxes

- The combo box control in its various styles

This chapter covers versatile controls that can be manipulated in various ways. Therefore, I will present a number of test programs to examine most of the functionality supported by the controls discussed in this chapter. The first subject is the scroll bar control.

THE SCROLL BAR CONTROL

Windows allows the scroll bar to exist as a separate control as well as to be incorporated into windows, lists, and combo boxes. The scroll bar control appears and behaves much like the scroll bar of a window. The control has a thumb box that keeps track of the current value and allows mouse clicks to move the thumb box either by single lines or by pages. In addition, the scroll bar responds to cursor control keys, such as Home, End, PageUp, and PageDown. The main purpose of the scroll bar control is to enable you to select quickly and efficiently an integer value in a predefined range of values. Windows, for example, uses scroll bars to fine-tune the color palette, the keyboard rate, and the mouse sensitivity.

The TScrollBar Class

ObjectWindows offers the TScrollBar class, a descendant of TControl, as the class that models the scroll bar controls. The TScrollBar class declares two data members and a number of member functions to set and query the control's current position and range of values. The two data members are LineMagnitude and PageMagnitude. These members store the magnitude of the change in the thumb box position caused when you move the box by a line or a page. The default values for the LineMagnitude and PageMagnitude data members are 1 and 10, respectively.

The TScrollBar class has three constructors. I will focus on the constructor that enables you to create instances of TScrollBar from scratch:

```
TScrollBar(TWindow* parent, int Id, int x, int y,
         int w, int h, BOOL isHScrollBar,
         TModule* module = 0);
```

The parent parameter is the pointer to the parent window. The Id parameter specifies the unique ID for the control. The x, y, w, and h parameters specify the location and dimensions of the control. The Boolean parameter isHScrollBar specifies whether the control is a horizontal or vertical scroll bar. When the argument for parameter isHScrollBar is TRUE, the control is created with the

SBS_HORZ style. By contrast, when the argument for isHScrollBar is FALSE, the control is created with the SBS_VERT style.

The TScrollBar class offers the following member functions to query and set the scroll bar thumb box position:

- The first member function that you most likely use after creating a TScrollBar instance is SetRange. With this function, you can set the range of values for the scroll bar. The declaration of the SetRange function is as follows:

```
inline void SetRange(int min, int max);
```

The arguments for the min and max parameters designate the new range of values for the scroll bar control.

- The GetRange member function enables you to query the current range of values for the scroll bar. The declaration of the GetRange function is this:

```
inline void GetRange(int& min, int& max);
```

The min and max reference parameters return the current range of values for the scroll bar control.

- The parameterless member function GetPosition returns the current position of the thumb box.

- The SetPosition member function moves the thumb box to the specified position. If the requested position is outside the current scroll bar range, the thumb box is moved to the closest position. The SetPosition function is declared as follows:

```
void SetPosition(int thumbPos);
```

The thumbPos parameter specifies the new thumb box position.

- The DeltaPos member function alters the position of the thumb box by a specified magnitude. The declaration of the DeltaPos function is this:

```
int DeltaPos(int delta);
```

The delta parameter specifies the change in the thumb box position. Positive arguments for the delta parameter move the thumb box down in a vertical scroll bar and to the right in a horizontal scroll bar. Negative arguments for the delta parameter move the thumb box up in a vertical scroll bar and to the left in a horizontal scroll bar. The DeltaPos function returns the new thumb box position.

- The group of protected message response member functions— SBLineUp, SBLineDown, SBPageUp, SBPageDown, SBThumbPosition, SBThumbTrack, SBTop, and SBBottom—that handle the thumb box notification messages is shown in Table 4.1.

TABLE 4.1. THE SCROLL BAR NOTIFICATION MESSAGES.

Message	Meaning
SB_LINEUP	Moves the thumb box one line up for a vertical scroll bar and one line to the left for a horizontal scroll bar.
SB_LINEDOWN	Moves the thumb box one line down for a vertical scroll bar and one line to the right for a horizontal scroll bar.
SB_PAGEUP	Moves the thumb box one page up for a vertical scroll bar and one page to the left for a horizontal scroll bar.
SB_PAGEDOWN	Moves the thumb box one page down for a vertical scroll bar and one page to the right for a horizontal scroll bar.
SB_THUMBPOSITION	Moves the thumb box.
SB_THUMBTRACK	Tracks the thumb box.

Responding to Scroll Bar Notification Messages

The parent window of a scroll bar control responds to the notification messages that are based, not on the WM_COMMAND message as with other controls, but on the WM_VSCROLL and WM_HSCROLL messages. The member functions that handle vertical and horizontal scroll bars are EvVScroll and EvHScroll, respectively. Each member function takes three parameters: a UINT parameter that passes the code for the change in the scroll bar, a UINT parameter that passes the current thumb box location, and an HWND parameter for the scroll bar. A sample skeleton response member function that handles vertical scrolling is shown as follows:

```
class TMainWindow : public TWindow
{
public:

    // other declarations

    // handle the scroll bar notification messages
    void EvVScroll(UINT code, UINT pos, HWND wnd);

    // other declarations

    DECLARE_RESPONSE_TABLE(TMainWindow);
};

DEFINE__RESPONSE_TABLE1(TMainWindow, TWindow)
    EV_WM_VSCROLL,
END_RESPONSE_TABLE;

void TMainWindow::EvVScroll(UINT code, UINT pos, HWND wnd)
{
switch (code) {
        case SB_LINEUP:
            // response statements here
            break;
        case SB_LINEDOWN:
            // response statements here
            break;
        case SB_PAGEUP:
            // response statements here
            break;
        case SB_PAGEDOWN:
            // response statements here
            break;
    }
}
```

The Countdown Timer

Consider a small test program that uses the scroll bar control. The countdown timer application, shown in Figure 4.1, contains the following controls:

- The Timer Input Box edit control, which accepts input for the timer and displays the current timer value

- The static text control, which labels the edit box

- The Start button, which triggers the countdown timer

- The Exit button

- The timer scroll bar control, which has a default range of 0 to 600 seconds

- The static text control, which labels the range of values for the timer scroll bar

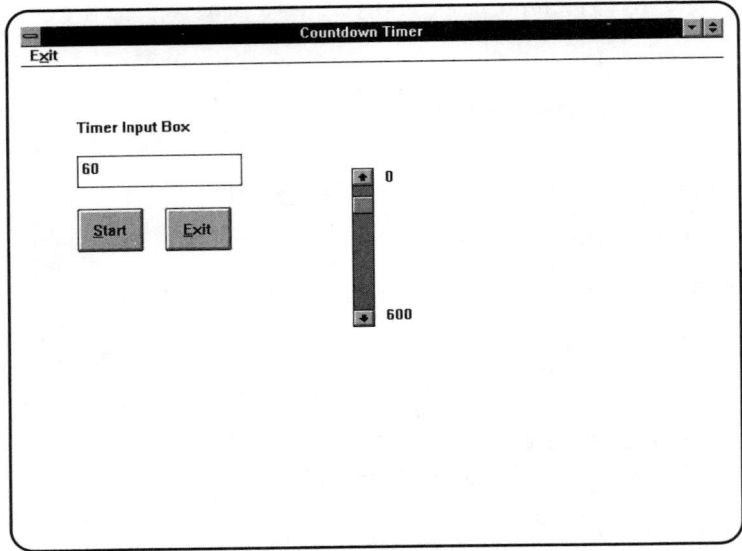

Figure 4.1. A sample session with the CTLLST1.EXE application.

You can set the number of seconds in one of two ways: either you can type that value in the edit box, or you can use the scroll bar. When you move the scroll bar thumb box, the current thumb position appears in the edit box. To trigger the count time process, click the Start button or press the Alt+S keys. The countdown process takes the value stored in the edit box and converts it into the maximum number of seconds to count down. If the edit box is empty, contains 0, or has non-numeric text, the program assigns a default of 15 seconds. The program also assigns that value to the static text that specifies the maximum scroll bar value. During the countdown, the application decrements the number of seconds in the edit box and moves upward the thumb box of the scroll bar. When the countdown ends, the program sounds a beep, restores the maximum limit of the scroll bar, and restores the maximum limit static text.

The countdown timer application illustrates the following aspects of scroll bar manipulation:

- Setting and altering the scroll bar range of values.

- Moving and changing the scroll bar thumb box position. The program illustrates how these tasks are performed either internally or using the mouse.

- Using the scroll bar to supply a value.

Listing 4.1 shows the contents of the CTLLST1.DEF definition file. Listing 4.2 contains the source code for the CTLLST1.H header file. Listing 4.3 shows the script for the CTLLST1.RC resource file. The resource file contains the accelerator keys and menu resources. The program uses a menu with the single menu item Exit. Listing 4.4 includes the source code for the CTLLST1.CPP program file.

LISTING 4.1. THE CONTENTS OF THE CTLLST1.DEF DEFINITION FILE.

```
NAME          CtlLst1
DESCRIPTION   'An OWL Windows Application'
EXETYPE       WINDOWS
CODE          PRELOAD MOVEABLE DISCARDABLE
DATA          PRELOAD MOVEABLE MULTIPLE
HEAPSIZE      1024
STACKSIZE     16384
```

LISTING 4.2. THE SOURCE CODE FOR THE CTLLST1.H HEADER FILE.

```
#define ID_START_BTN 201
#define ID_EXIT_BTN  202
#define CM_START_BTN 203
#define CM_EXIT_BTN  204
#define ID_INPUT_BOX 205
#define ID_TIMER_SCR 206
#define IDR_BUTTONS  400
#define IDM_EXITMENU 401
```

LISTING 4.3. THE SCRIPT FOR THE CTLLST1.RC RESOURCE FILE.

```
#include <windows.h>
#include <owl\window.rh>
#include "ctllst1.h"

IDR_BUTTONS ACCELERATORS
BEGIN
  "s", CM_START_BTN, ALT
  "e", CM_EXIT_BTN, ALT
END

IDM_EXITMENU MENU LOADONCALL MOVEABLE PURE DISCARDABLE
BEGIN
    MENUITEM "E&xit", CM_EXIT
END
```

LISTING 4.4. THE SOURCE CODE FOR THE CTLLST1.CPP PROGRAM FILE.

```
/*
  Program to test the scroll bar control by using it to
  implement a simple timer
*/

#include <owl\applicat.h>
#include <owl\framewin.h>
#include <owl\static.h>
#include <owl\edit.h>
#include <owl\button.h>
#include <owl\scrollba.h>
#include "ctllst1.h"
#include <stdlib.h>
#include <ctype.h>
#include <stdio.h>
#include <math.h>
#include <string.h>

// current timer limit is 10 minutes
const MaxTimer = 600;
const MaxEditLen = 10;

// declare the custom application class as
// a subclass of TApplication
class TWinApp : public TApplication
{
public:
  TWinApp() : TApplication() {}
```

```
protected:
  virtual void InitMainWindow();
};

// expand the functionality of TWindow by deriving class TMainWindow
class TMainWindow : public TWindow
{
public:

  TMainWindow();

protected:
  TEdit* InputBox;
  TButton* StartBtn;
  TButton* ExitBtn;
  TScrollBar* TimerScr;
  TStatic* TimerTxt;

  // set up window
  virtual void SetupWindow();

  // handle starting the timer
  void HandleStartBtn();

  // handle starting the timer
  void CMStartBtn();

  // handle exiting the program
  void HandleExitBtn();

  // handle exiting the program
  void CMExitBtn();

  // handle moving the scroll bar
  void EvVScroll(UINT, UINT, HWND);

  // handle closing the window
  virtual BOOL CanClose();

private:
  // delays the program for about ms milliseconds
  void delay(DWORD ms);

  // declare the message map macro
  DECLARE_RESPONSE_TABLE(TMainWindow);

};

DEFINE_RESPONSE_TABLE1(TMainWindow, TWindow)
  EV_COMMAND(ID_START_BTN, HandleStartBtn),
```

continues

LISTING 4.4. CONTINUED

```
  EV_COMMAND(CM_START_BTN, CMStartBtn),
  EV_COMMAND(ID_EXIT_BTN, HandleExitBtn),
  EV_COMMAND(CM_EXIT_BTN, CMExitBtn),
  EV_WM_VSCROLL,
END_RESPONSE_TABLE;

TMainWindow::TMainWindow() :
        TWindow(0, 0, 0)
{
  char s[81];
  int x = 50, y = 50;

  // create the timer input box and its label
  strcpy(s, "Timer Input Box");
  new TStatic(this, -1, s, x, y, 150, 30, strlen(s));
  y += 30 + 5;
  InputBox = new TEdit(this, ID_INPUT_BOX, "",
                  x, y, 150, 30, 0, FALSE);
  // create the Start button
  y += 30 + 20;
  StartBtn = new TButton(this, ID_START_BTN, "&Start",
                        x, y, 60, 40, FALSE);
  // create the Exit button
  x += 60 + 20;
  ExitBtn  = new TButton(this, ID_EXIT_BTN, "&Exit",
                  x, y, 60, 40, FALSE);
  // create the timer scroll bar
  x = 300;
  y = 100;
  TimerScr = new TScrollBar(this, ID_TIMER_SCR,
                  x, y, 20, 150, FALSE);
  // create the static text controls that label the
  // minimum and maximum values
  x += 20 + 10;
  new TStatic(this, -1, "0", x, y, 80, 20, 2);
  y += 130;
  sprintf(s, "%d", MaxTimer);
  TimerTxt = new TStatic(this, -1, s, x, y,
                  80, 20, strlen(s));
}

void TMainWindow::SetupWindow()
{
  TWindow::SetupWindow();
  TimerScr->SetRange(0, MaxTimer);
}
```

```cpp
void TMainWindow::HandleStartBtn()
{
  char s[MaxEditLen+1];
  int x;

  // get the text in the edit box
  InputBox->GetText(s, MaxEditLen);
  // convert the string into an integer
  x = atoi(s);
  // if x is 0, assign it 15
  x = (x != 0) ? x : 15;
  // set the maximum timer static text
  sprintf(s, "%d", x);
  TimerTxt->SetText(s);
  // set the new range
  TimerScr->SetRange(0, x);
  // set the thumb position to the maximum position
  TimerScr->SetPosition(x);
  // countdown loop
  while (x > 0) {
      delay(980);
      x—;
      // update the thumb position
      TimerScr->DeltaPos(-1);
      sprintf(s, "%d", x);
      // echo thumb position in the edit box
      InputBox->SetText(s);

  }
  MessageBeep(0); // beep
  // restore the default timer limits
  sprintf(s, "%d", MaxTimer);
  TimerScr->SetRange(0, MaxTimer);
  TimerScr->SetPosition(MaxTimer);
  TimerTxt->SetText(s);
}

void TMainWindow::CMStartBtn()
{
  HandleStartBtn();
}

void TMainWindow::HandleExitBtn()
{
  Parent->SendMessage(WM_CLOSE);
}

void TMainWindow::CMExitBtn()
{
  Parent->SendMessage(WM_CLOSE);
```

continues

LISTING 4.4. CONTINUED

```
}

void TMainWindow::EvVScroll(UINT code, UINT pos, HWND wnd)
{
   TWindow::EvVScroll(code, pos, wnd);

     int x = TimerScr->GetPosition();
   char s[MaxEditLen+1];

   // convert the thumb position into a string
   sprintf(s, "%d", x);
   // insert the string in the edit box
   InputBox->SetText(s);
}

BOOL TMainWindow::CanClose()
{
  return MessageBox("Want to close this application",
              "Query", MB_YESNO | MB_ICONQUESTION) == IDYES;
}

void TMainWindow::delay(DWORD ms)
{
  DWORD time1 = GetTickCount();
  do {
    ;
  } while ((GetTickCount() - time1) < ms);
}

void TWinApp::InitMainWindow()
{
  MainWindow = new TFrameWindow(0, "Countdown Timer",
                                new TMainWindow);
  // load the keystroke resources
  MainWindow->Attr.AccelTable = IDR_BUTTONS;
  // load the menu resource
  MainWindow->AssignMenu(TResID(IDM_EXITMENU));
  // enable the keyboard handler
  MainWindow->EnableKBHandler();
}

int OwlMain(int /* argc */, char** /*argv[] */)
{
  TWinApp app;
  return app.Run();
}
```

The program in Listing 4.4 contains the declaration for the application and window classes. The application window class TMainWindow declares a number of data members that are pointers to the controls of the application. In addition, the TMainWindow class declares a constructor and seven member functions.

The TMainWindow class constructor creates the application window and performs the following tasks:

- Creates the timer edit box and the static text that labels it.

- Creates the pushbutton controls marked Start and Exit.

- Creates the timer scroll bar control. The TScrollBar constructor uses the argument ID_TIMER_SCR to specify the ID of the controls. The last argument in the TScrollBar constructor call is FALSE and indicates that the scroll bar is vertical.

- Creates the static text controls that label the range of scroll bar values. The lower value is always 0. The upper limit is initially set using the MaxTimer global constant.

The response table for the TMainWindow class includes a set of EV_COMMAND macros to handle the various buttons and keyboard-based commands. The table also contains the macro EV_WM_VSCROLL, which indicates that the class handles the notification messages of vertical scroll bars by using the EvVScroll member function.

The SetupWindow member function calls the SetupWindow function of the parent class and then sets the range of the scroll bar control to be 0 to MaxTimer.

The HandleStartBtn member function implements the functionality that triggers the timer countdown. The function carries out the following tasks:

- Retrieves the text in the edit box and stores it in the local variable s.

- Converts the characters in variable s into an int type and stores the result in the local variable x.

- Examines the value of x. If it is zero, the function assigns 15 to variable x.

- Sets the maximum timer limit static text to the string image of the value in variable x.

- Sets the range of the timer scroll bar by invoking the TScrollBar::SetRange member function with the arguments of 0 and x.

- Moves the thumb position all the way to the bottom of the scroll bar by using the `TScrollBar::SetPosition` member function. The argument for that function call is `x`.

- Starts the `countdown` loop. This loop invokes the `delay` function and requests that the program waits for 980 milliseconds. This value allows for some processing time. The loop then changes the thumb box position by moving it one value upward. This step involves the `TScrollBar::DeltaPos` member function with an argument of `-1`. The loop then sets a string image of the current thumb box position in the edit box. This task simulates the edit box showing the countdown time in seconds.

- Beeps when the loop terminates.

- Restores the default upper range of the scroll bar timer to 600 and updates the maximum limit static text accordingly.

The `CMStartBtn` member function traps the command message generated by the Alt+S keys. The function merely calls the `HandleStartBtn` member function.

The `HandleExitBtn` and `CMExitBtn` member functions send a `WM_CLOSE` message to the parent window.

The `EvVScroll` member function responds to the notification message that the scroll bar control sends to its parent window. The function converts the current thumb box position into a string and writes it in the edit box. Thus, the `HandleTimerScr` function is responsible for updating the contents of the edit box when you move the thumb box.

The `delay` member function uses the `GetTickCount` API function to simulate the requested delay.

THE LIST BOX CONTROLS

A list box is an input control that enables the application user to choose from a list of items. List boxes typically are framed and include a vertical scroll bar. When you select an item by clicking it, the selection is highlighted. Microsoft suggests the following simple guidelines for making a selection:

- A single mouse click should be used to select a new item or an additional item. A separate button control retrieves the selected item.

- A double-click is a shortcut for selecting an item and retrieving it.

A list box control supports multiple selections only if you specify the multiple-selection style when you create the control. Making a multiple selection is convenient when you want to process the selected items in the same or similar manner. For example, selecting multiple files for deletion speeds up the deletion process and reduces the effort you have to make.

The TListBox Class

ObjectWindows offers a versatile class of TListBox, a descendant of TControl, to implement list box controls. The TListBox class has a rich set of member functions that enable you to easily manipulate and query both the contents of the list box as well as the selected item. Like many other ObjectWindows classes, TListBox has several constructors. The following one enables you to create class instances from scratch:

```
TListBox(TWindows* pParent, int Id, int x, int y,
        int w, int h, TModule* module = 0);
```

The parent parameter is the pointer to the parent window. The Id parameter specifies the unique ID for the control. The x, y, w, and h parameters specify the location and dimensions of the control. The class constructor creates the instance with the LBS_STANDARD style, which sets the WS_BORDER, WS_VSCROLL, LBS_SORT, and LBS_NOTIFY styles. Table 4.2 shows some of the list box styles that are relevant to ObjectWindows.

You can remove the LBS_SORT style from the list box controls to maintain a list of items that are not automatically sorted. With such a list, you can maintain items in a chronological fashion. You can also use such a list actually to maintain the items sorted in a descending way. In this case, you have to preserve the list items in that order. Removing the WS_VSCROLL style gives you a list box without the vertical scroll bar. The next section presents a program that uses this type of list box to implement the synchronized scrolling of multiple list boxes.

	TABLE 4.2. THE LIST BOX CONTROL STYLES.
Style	**Meaning**
LBS_EXTENDESEL	Allows the extension of multiple selections in the list box by using the Shift key.
LBS_MULTICOLUMN	Designates a multicolumn list box that scrolls horizontally. The number of columns is set by sending the message LB_SETCOLUMNWIDTH. Employing this control style requires the use of Windows API functions.
LBS_MULTIPLESEL	Supports multiple selections in a list box.
LBS_NOINTEGRALHEIGHT	Suppresses showing parts of an item.
LBS_NOREDRAW	Prevents the list box from being updated when the selection is changed. The message WM_SETREDRAW alters this style at will.
LBS_NOTIFY	Notifies the parent window when you click or double-click in the list box.
LBS_SORT	Specifies that the items inserted in the list box be automatically sorted in an ascending order.
LBS_STANDARD	Sets the WS_BORDER, WS_VSCROLL, LBS_SORT, and LBS_NOTIFY styles.
LBS_WANTKEYBPARDINPUT	Permits the list box owner to receive WM_VKEYTOITEM or WM_CHARTOITEM messages when you press a key while the list box has the focus. This style allows your application to manipulate the items in the list box.

The TListBox class offers the following member functions to set and to query both ordinary and selected list members:

- The AddString member function adds a string to the list box and is declared as follows:

```
virtual int AddString(const char far* str);
```

The str parameter is the far pointer to the added string. The function also returns the position (list box positions start with 0) of the added string in the control. If there is any error in adding the string, the function yields a -1 value. If the LBS_SORT style is set, the string is inserted such that the list order is maintained. If the LBS_SORT style is removed, the added string is inserted at the end of the list.

- The DeleteString member function removes a list member from a specified position and is declared as follows:

```
inline virtual int DeleteString(int index);
```

The index parameter specifies the position of the item to delete. The function returns the number of remaining list members. If an error occurs, DeleteString yields a negative result.

- The parameterless member function ClearList clears the list of string in the list box control in one swoop. This function serves to reset the contents of a list box before building up a new list.

- The FindExactString member function searches for an item that exactly matches a specified string. The declaration of the FindExactString function is as follows:

```
int FindExactString(const char far* str, int searchIndex) const;
```

The str parameter is the far pointer to the searched string. The searchIndex parameter specifies the first position to be searched. The function then searches the *entire* list, beginning with the SearchIndex position and resuming at the beginning of the list if needed. The search stops either when a list member matches the search string or when the entire list is searched. Passing an argument of -1 to searchIndex forces the function to start searching from the beginning. The function returns the position of the matching list item or returns a negative result if no match is found or if an error occurs.

The interesting search method used by the FindExactString member function enables you to speed up the search by specifying a position that comes closely before the most likely location for a match. The beauty of this method is that if you specify a position actually beyond the position of the string you seek, you will not miss finding the string, because the function resumes searching at the beginning of the list! Another benefit of FindExactString is its capability to find duplicate strings.

- The `FindString` member function is a more relaxed version of the `FindExactString` function. The `FindString` function looks for a list item that starts with the same search string characters. The declaration of the `FindString` function is as follows:

```
inline virtual int FindString(const char far* str,
                              int searchIndex) const;
```

Other aspects of the `FindString` function match those of the `FindExactString` function.

- The parameterless member function `GetCount` returns the number of items in the list box. The function returns a negative value if there is an error.

- The parameterless member function `GetSelCount` returns the number of selected items in the list box. For single-selection list boxes, the function returns either 0 or 1.

- The parameterless member function `GetSelIndex` returns the position of the selected item in a single-selection list box. If there is no selected item, the function yields a negative value. This function is aimed at single-selection list boxes only.

- The `GetSelIndexes` member function returns the number and positions of the selected items in a multiple-selection list box. The declaration of the `GetSelIndexes` function is as follows:

```
int GetSelIndexes(int* indexes, int maxCount) const;
```

The `indexes` parameter is the pointer to an array of integers that stores the positions of the selected items. The `maxCount` parameter specifies the size of the array accessed by the `indexes` pointer. The function returns the current number of selections.

- The `GetSelString` member function obtains part or all of the selected item in a single-selection list box. The declaration for the `GetSelString` function is as follows:

```
int GetSelString(const char far* str, int maxChars) const;
```

The `str` parameter is the far pointer to the string that receives characters from the current selection. The `maxChars` parameter indicates the maximum number of characters to obtain. The function returns either the length of the retrieved string or, if an error occurs, a negative value.

- The GetString member function obtains part or all of an item in a list box. The declaration for the GetString function is as follows:

```
inline int GetString(const char far* str, int index) const;
```

The str parameter is the far pointer to the string that receives characters from the selected items. The index parameter specifies the target list item. The function returns either the length of the retrieved string or, if an error occurs, a negative value.

- The GetStringLen member function returns the length of a list item specified by its position in the list. The declaration of the GetStringLen function is as follows:

```
inline virtual int GetStringLen(int index) const;
```

The index parameter specifies the index of the target list item. The function returns either the length of the target item or, if an error occurs, a negative result.

- The InsertString member function inserts a string in a list box. The declaration of the InsertString function is as follows:

```
virtual int InsertString(const char far* str, int index);
```

The str parameter is the far pointer to the inserted string. The index parameter specifies the requested insertion position. The function returns either the actual insertion position or, if an error occurs, yields a negative value. If the argument for index is -1, the string is simply appended to the end of the list.

> In general, use the InsertString member function with list boxes that have the LBS_SORT style removed. Using this function with ordered list boxes will most likely corrupt the sort order of the list.

- The SetSelIndex member function chooses a list item as the new selection in a single-selection list box. The declaration of the SetSelIndex function is as follows:

```
virtual int SetSelIndex(int index);
```

The index parameter specifies the position of the new selection. To clear a list box from any selection, pass a -1 argument to the index parameter. The function returns a negative value if an error occurs.

- The SetSelIndexes member function makes or clears the selections in a multiple-selection list box. The declaration of the SetSelIndexes function is this:

```
int SetSelIndexes(int* indexes, int numSelections,
                BOOL shouldSet);
```

The indexes parameter is the pointer to the array of integers that store the positions for the multiple selections. The numSelections parameter specifies the number of selections. The Boolean parameter shouldSet indicates whether to select or to deselect the items in the list box. If you assign a TRUE argument to shouldSet, the function selects the items whose positions are indicated by the integer array. By contrast, if you assign FALSE to shouldSet, the indicated items are deselected. The function returns the number of items that were actually selected or deselected. If an error occurs, the function yields a negative value. To select or deselect all of the list items, pass a negative argument to the numSelections parameter.

You can use the GetSelIndexes member function to store specific multiple-selections in different integer arrays. Later, you can restore these multiple selections with the SetSelIndexes member function. Thus, the integer arrays involved in this process serve to define selection sets. This technique assumes that while these snapshots are taken and restored, the list box items remain fixed.

- The SetSelString member function selects the item that matches a search string. The declaration of the SetSelString function is this:

```
int SetSelString(const char far* str, int searchIndex);
```

The str parameter points to the search string. The searchIndex parameter specifies the first list position to search. The SetSelString function works like the FindExactString function with the added feature of selecting the list item that matches the search string. The function returns either the position of the new selection or, if an error occurs, a negative number.

- The SetSelStrings member function selects and deselects multiple-selection list items that match an array of search strings. The declaration of the SetSelStrings function is as follows:

```
int SetSelStrings(const char far** prefixes, int numSelections,
                BOOL shouldSet);
```

The prefixes parameter is a pointer to the array of search strings. The numSelections parameter specifies the number of selections. The Boolean parameter shouldSet indicates whether the list items that match the members of the string search array are selected or deselected. The function searches for a list item that matches each member of the search array. Each time, the function searches the list, starting at the beginning and continuing either until a matching item is found or until the entire list is searched. To select or deselect all of the list items, pass a negative argument to the NumSelections parameter. The function returns the number of list items that were successfully selected or deselected.

Responding to List Box Notification Messages

The changes in a list box result in sending an LBN_*xxxx* notification message to the parent window. To respond to the notification message, the window class must use child-ID response handling member functions. Table 4.3 shows the various list box notification messages and their response table entries. Here is a sample skeleton code for responding to not one, but two list boxes:

```
#define ID_LISTBOX1 101
#define ID_LISTBOX2 102

class TMainWindow : public TWindow
{
public:

    // other declarations

    // handle the selection change in the list box #1
    void EvSelChangeListBox1();

    // handle the double-clicking an item in the list box #1
    void EvDblClkListBox1();

    // handle the selection change in the list box #2
    void EvSelChangeListBox2();

    // handle the double-clicking an item in the list box #2
    void EvDblClkListBox2();

    // other declarations

    DECLARE_RESPONSE_TABLE(TMainWindow);
};

DEFINE_RESPONSE_TABLE1(TMainWindow, TWindow)
    EV_LBN_SELCHANGE(ID_LISTBOX1, EvSelChangeListBox1),
    EV_LBN_DBLCLK(ID_LISTBOX1, EvDblClkListBox1),
```

Borland
4

continues

continued

```
    EV_LBN_SELCHANGE(ID_LISTBOX2, EvSelChangeListBox2),
    EV_LBN_DBLCLK(ID_LISTBOX2, EvDblClkListBox2),
END__RESPONSE_TABLE;

void TMainWindow::EvSelChangeListBox1()
{
    // statements to handle change in selection
}

void TMainWindow::EvDblClkListBox1()
{
    // statements to handle double-clicking a selection
}

void TMainWindow::EvSelChangeListBox2()
{
    // statements to handle change in selection
}

void TMainWindow::EvDblClkListBox2()
{
    // statements to handle double-clicking a selection
}
```

TABLE 4.3. THE LIST BOX NOTIFICATION MESSAGES.

Message	Table Macro	Meaning
LBN_SELCHANGE	EV_LBN_SELCHANGE	A list item is selected with a mouse click.
LBN_DBLCLK	EV_LBN_DBLCLK	A list item is selected with a double mouse click.
LBN_SETFOCUS	EV_LBN_SETFOCUS	The list box has gained focus.
LBN_KILLFOCUS	EV_LBN_KILLFOCUS	The list box has lost focus.

The Simple List Manipulation Tester

Now consider a program that demonstrates how to set and to query both a normal and a selected string, as well as how to set and to query the current selection in a single-selection list box. This section presents a simple list manipulation tester. Figure 4.2 shows the interface of the program and a sample session. The list tester program focuses on illustrating how to use most of the

TListBox member functions presented earlier in this chapter. The program contains the following controls, which offer the indicated test features:

- A List Box control.

- A String Box edit control that enables you to type in and retrieve a list member.

- An Index Box edit control that enables you to key in and retrieve the position of the current selection.

- An Add String pushbutton to add the content of the String Box to the List Box. The program does not enable you to add duplicate names. If you attempt to do so, the program displays a warning message.

- A Delete String pushbutton to delete the current selection in the list box. The program automatically selects another list member.

- A Get Selected String pushbutton that copies the current list selection to the String Box.

- A Set Selected String pushbutton that overwrites the current selection with the string in the String Box.

- A Get Selected Index pushbutton that writes the position of the current selection in the Index Box.

- A Set Selected Index pushbutton that uses the integer value in the Index Box as the position of the new list box selection.

- A Get String by Index pushbutton that copies the string whose position appears in the Index Box into the String Box.

- An Exit pushbutton.

These controls exercise various aspects of manipulating a sorted list box and its members. The program is coded to retain a current selection and to prevent the insertion of duplicate names.

Compile and run the program. When the program starts running, it places a set of names in the list box. Experiment with the various pushbutton controls to add, delete, and obtain strings. The program is straightforward and easy to run.

Listing 4.5 shows the contents of the CTLLST2.DEF definition file. Listing 4.6 contains the source code for the CTLLST2.H header file. Listing 4.7 shows the script for the CTLLST2.RC resource file. Listing 4.8 shows the source code for the CTLLST2.CPP program file.

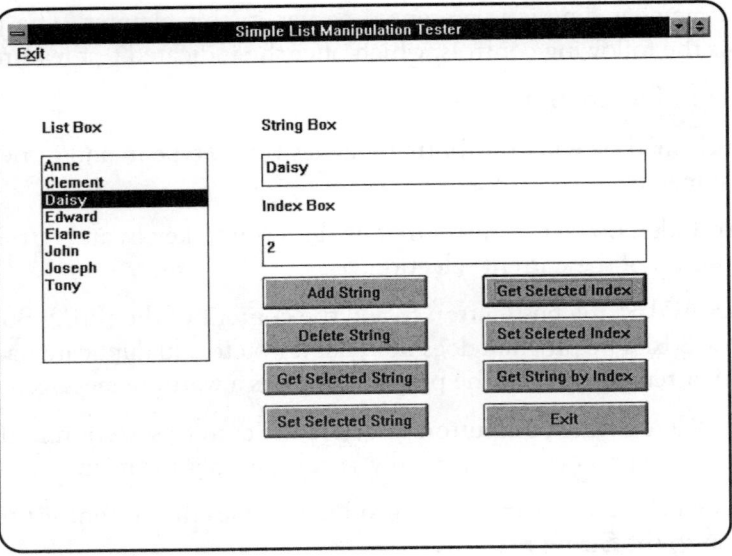

Figure 4.2. A sample session with the CTLLST2.EXE application.

LISTING 4.5. THE CONTENTS OF THE CTLLST2.DEF DEFINITION FILE.

```
NAME          CtlLst2
DESCRIPTION   'An OWL Windows Application'
EXETYPE       WINDOWS
CODE          PRELOAD MOVEABLE DISCARDABLE
DATA          PRELOAD MOVEABLE MULTIPLE
HEAPSIZE      1024
STACKSIZE     16384
```

LISTING 4.6. THE SOURCE CODE FOR THE CTLLST2.H HEADER FILE.

```
#define IDM_EXITMENU 400
```

LISTING 4.7. The script for the CTLLST2.RC resource file.

```
#include <windows.h>
#include <owl\window.rh>
#include "ctllst2.h"

IDM_EXITMENU MENU LOADONCALL MOVEABLE PURE DISCARDABLE
BEGIN
    MENUITEM "E&xit", CM_EXIT
END
```

LISTING 4.8. The source code for the CTLLST2.CPP program file.

```
/*
  Program which illustrates basic manipulation of list box controls
*/

#include <owl\applicat.h>
#include <owl\framewin.h>
#include <owl\static.h>
#include <owl\edit.h>
#include <owl\button.h>
#include <owl\listbox.h>
#include <owl\window.rh>
#include "ctllst2.h"
#include <stdlib.h>
#include <ctype.h>
#include <stdio.h>
#include <string.h>

const LowVertSpacing = 5;
const HiVertSpacing = 10;
const HorzSpacing = 50;
const Wctl = 150;
const Hctl = 30;
const Wbox = 2 * Wctl + HorzSpacing;
const Hlst = Hctl + LowVertSpacing + 4 * (Hctl + HiVertSpacing);
const MaxEditLen = 10;

// declare the ID constants for the various controls
#define ID_STRING_LST    101
#define ID_STRING_EDIT   102
#define ID_INDEX_EDIT    103
#define ID_ADDSTR_BTN    104
#define ID_DELSTR_BTN    105
#define ID_GETSELSTR_BTN 106
```

continues

LISTING 4.8. CONTINUED

```
#define ID_SETSELSTR_BTN 107
#define ID_GETSELIDX_BTN 108
#define ID_SETSELIDX_BTN 109
#define ID_EXIT_BTN      110
#define ID_GETSTR_BTN    111

// declare the custom application class as
// a subclass of TApplication
class TWinApp : public TApplication
{
public:
  TWinApp() : TApplication() {}

protected:
  virtual void InitMainWindow();
};

// expand the functionality of TWindow by deriving class TMainWindow
class TMainWindow : public TWindow
{
public:

  TMainWindow();

protected:

  TListBox* StringLst;
  TEdit* StringBox;
  TEdit* IndexBox;
  TButton* AddStrBtn;
  TButton* DelStrBtn;
  TButton* GetSelStrBtn;
  TButton* SetSelStrBtn;
  TButton* GetSelIdxBtn;
  TButton* SetSelIdxBtn;
  TButton* GetStrBtn;
  TButton* ExitBtn;

  char dataStr[MaxEditLen+1];  // string for StringBox
  char indexStr[MaxEditLen+1]; // string for IndexBox

  // initialize the String list box
  virtual void SetupWindow();

  // handle adding a string to the list box
  void HandleAddStrBtn();

  // handle deleting a string from the list box
  void HandleDelStrBtn();
```

```
  // handle getting the selected text
  void HandleGetSelStrBtn();

  // handle setting the selected text
  void HandleSetSelStrBtn();

  // handle getting the index of the selected text
  void HandleGetSelIdxBtn();

  // handle setting the index of the selected text
  void HandleSetSelIdxBtn();

  // handle getting a string from the list box
  void HandleGetStrBtn();

  // handle setting a string in the list box
  void HandleExitBtn();

  // handle closing the window
  virtual BOOL CanClose();

  // declare the message map macro
  DECLARE_RESPONSE_TABLE(TMainWindow);
};

DEFINE_RESPONSE_TABLE1(TMainWindow, TWindow)
  EV_COMMAND(ID_ADDSTR_BTN, HandleAddStrBtn),
  EV_COMMAND(ID_DELSTR_BTN, HandleDelStrBtn),
  EV_COMMAND(ID_GETSELSTR_BTN, HandleGetSelStrBtn),
  EV_COMMAND(ID_SETSELSTR_BTN, HandleSetSelStrBtn),
  EV_COMMAND(ID_GETSELIDX_BTN, HandleGetSelIdxBtn),
  EV_COMMAND(ID_SETSELIDX_BTN, HandleSetSelIdxBtn),
  EV_COMMAND(ID_GETSTR_BTN, HandleGetStrBtn),
  EV_COMMAND(ID_EXIT_BTN, HandleExitBtn),
  EV_COMMAND(CM_EXIT, HandleExitBtn),
END_RESPONSE_TABLE;

TMainWindow::TMainWindow() :
        TWindow(0, 0, 0)
{
  char s[81];
  int x0 = 30;
  int x1 = x0 + Wctl + HorzSpacing;
  int x2 = x1 + Wctl + HorzSpacing;
  int y0 = 50;
  int x = x0;
  int y = y0;
  int y1;
```

continues

LISTING 4.8. CONTINUED

```
// create the list box and its label
strcpy(s, "List Box");
new TStatic(this, -1, s, x, y, Wctl, Hctl, strlen(s));
y += Hctl + LowVertSpacing;
StringLst = new TListBox(this, ID_STRING_LST, x, y, Wctl, Hlst);

// create the edit boxes and their labels
x = x1;
y = y0;
strcpy(s, "String Box");
new TStatic(this, -1, s, x, y, Wctl, Hctl, strlen(s));
y += Hctl + LowVertSpacing;
StringBox = new TEdit(this, ID_STRING_EDIT, "",
                      x, y, Wbox, Hctl, 0, FALSE);

y += Hctl + HiVertSpacing;
strcpy(s, "Index Box");
new TStatic(this, -1, s, x, y, Wctl, Hctl, strlen(s));
y += Hctl + LowVertSpacing;
IndexBox = new TEdit(this, ID_INDEX_EDIT, "", x, y, Wbox, Hctl,
                     0, FALSE);

// create the button controls
y += Hctl + HiVertSpacing;
y1 = y;
AddStrBtn = new TButton(this, ID_ADDSTR_BTN, "Add String",
                        x, y, Wctl, Hctl, FALSE);

y += Hctl + HiVertSpacing;
DelStrBtn = new TButton(this, ID_DELSTR_BTN, "Delete String",
                        x, y, Wctl, Hctl, FALSE);

y += Hctl + HiVertSpacing;
GetSelStrBtn = new TButton(this, ID_GETSELSTR_BTN,
                           "Get Selected String",
                           x, y, Wctl, Hctl, FALSE);

y += Hctl + HiVertSpacing;
SetSelStrBtn = new TButton(this, ID_SETSELSTR_BTN,
                           "Set Selected String",
                           x, y, Wctl, Hctl, FALSE);

// create the second row of buttons
y  = y1;
x = x2;
GetSelIdxBtn = new TButton(this, ID_GETSELIDX_BTN,
                           "Get Selected Index",
                           x, y, Wctl, Hctl, FALSE);
```

```
  y += Hctl + HiVertSpacing;
  SetSelIdxBtn = new TButton(this, ID_SETSELIDX_BTN,
                             "Set Selected Index",
                             x, y, Wctl, Hctl, FALSE);

  y += Hctl + HiVertSpacing;
  GetStrBtn = new TButton(this, ID_GETSTR_BTN,
                          "Get String by Index",
                          x, y, Wctl, Hctl, FALSE);

  y += Hctl + HiVertSpacing;
  ExitBtn = new TButton(this, ID_EXIT_BTN, "Exit",
                        x, y, Wctl, Hctl, FALSE);

}

void TMainWindow::HandleAddStrBtn()
{
  int i;
  // get the string in the String box
  StringBox->GetText(dataStr, MaxEditLen);
  // exit if the string empty?
  if (dataStr[0] == '\0') return;
  // add the string if it is not already in the list box
  if (StringLst->FindExactString(dataStr, -1) < 0) {
    // add the string and store the position of the new string
    i = StringLst->AddString(dataStr);
    // make the added string the new selection
    StringLst->SetSelIndex(i);
  }
  else
    // handle the duplicate-data error
    MessageBox("Cannot add duplicate names",
            "Bad Data", MB_OK);
}

void TMainWindow::HandleDelStrBtn()
{
  // get the index of the currently selected list member
  int i = StringLst->GetSelIndex();
  // delete the currently selected list member
  StringLst->DeleteString(i);
  // select another list member
  StringLst->SetSelIndex((i > 0) ? (i-1) : 0);
}

void TMainWindow::HandleGetSelStrBtn()
{
  // get the selected list item
  StringLst->GetSelString(dataStr, MaxEditLen);
```

continues

LISTING **4.8.** CONTINUED

```cpp
    /// store it in the String box
    StringBox->SetText(dataStr);
}

void TMainWindow::HandleSetSelStrBtn()
{
  // get the index of the currently selected list member
  int i = StringLst->GetSelIndex();
  // get the string to replace the currently selected list item
  StringBox->GetText(dataStr, MaxEditLen);
  // is the candidate string not in the list?
  if (StringLst->FindExactString(dataStr, -1) < 0) {
    // delete the current selection
    StringLst->DeleteString(i);
    // insert the new selection
    i = StringLst->AddString(dataStr);
    // select the inserted string
    StringLst->SetSelIndex(i);
  }
  else
    MessageBox("Cannot add duplicate names",
               "Bad Data", MB_OK);
}

void TMainWindow::HandleGetSelIdxBtn()
{
  sprintf(indexStr, "%d", StringLst->GetSelIndex());
  IndexBox->SetText(indexStr);
}

void TMainWindow::HandleSetSelIdxBtn()
{
  IndexBox->GetText(indexStr, MaxEditLen);
  StringLst->SetSelIndex(atof(indexStr));
}

void TMainWindow::HandleGetStrBtn()
{
  int i;
  // get the index from the Index box
  IndexBox->GetText(indexStr, MaxEditLen);
  i = atof(indexStr);
  // get the target string from the list box
  StringLst->GetString(dataStr, i);
  // write the list member in the String box
  StringBox->SetText(dataStr);
}
```

```
void TMainWindow::HandleExitBtn()
{
  Parent->SendMessage(WM_CLOSE);
}

BOOL TMainWindow::CanClose()
{
  return MessageBox("Want to close this application",
                    "Query", MB_YESNO | MB_ICONQUESTION) == IDYES;
}

void TMainWindow::SetupWindow()
{
  TWindow::SetupWindow();
  // add data in the list box
  StringLst->AddString("Edward");
  StringLst->AddString("John");
  StringLst->AddString("Anne");
  StringLst->AddString("Elaine");
  StringLst->AddString("Joseph");
  StringLst->AddString("Clement");
  StringLst->AddString("Daisy");
  StringLst->AddString("Tony");
  // select the second item
  StringLst->SetSelIndex(1);
}

void TWinApp::InitMainWindow()
{
  MainWindow = new TFrameWindow(0, "Simple List Manipulation Tester",
                                new TMainWindow);
    // load the menu resource
  MainWindow->AssignMenu(TResID(IDM_EXITMENU));
  // enable the keyboard handler
  MainWindow->EnableKBHandler();
}

int OwlMain(int /* argc */, char** /*argv[] */)
{
  TWinApp app;
  return app.Run();
}
```

The program in Listing 4.8 declares two sets of constants. The first set has the constants used to set the dimensions of the various controls used. The second set of constants specifies the ID for the various controls.

The program listing also declares an application class and a window class. The application window class TMainWindow declares a number of data members that are pointers to the controls owned by the window. The class also declares two strings to handle the contents of the String Box and Index Box edit controls. The TMainWindow class also declares a constructor and a number of member functions that respond to the notification messages emitted by the various pushbutton controls.

The TMainWindow constructor creates the instances for the controls of the application. All of the controls are created with their default styles. For the list box, this means that the control appears with a vertical scroll bar and automatically maintains a sorted list of strings.

The SetupWindow member function initializes the names List Box by adding strings and by selecting the second list item.

The HandleAddStrBtn member function adds the string of the String Box in the List Box control. The function performs the following tasks:

1. Obtains the string in the String Box edit control and stores it in the dataStr data member.

2. Exits if the dataStr member stores an empty string.

3. Verifies that the added string does not already exist in the list box. The function uses the FindExactString function to detect an attempt to add duplicate strings. If the FindExactString function returns a negative number, the HandleAddStrBtn resumes with the subsequent tasks. Otherwise, the function displays a message informing you that you cannot add duplicate strings in the list box.

4. Adds the string of the dataStr member to the list box and assigns the position of the string to the local variable i. The function uses the AddString member to perform this task.

5. Makes the added string the current selection by invoking the SetSelIndex function with the argument i.

The HandleDelStrBtn member function deletes the current selection by carrying out the following tasks:

1. Obtains the position of the current selection by invoking the GetSelIndex function. The function stores the selection position in the local variable i.

2. Deletes the selection by calling the DeleteString function and supplying it the argument i.

3. Selects another list item as the new selection at position i -1. If the variable i already contains 0, the new first list item becomes the new selection.

The HandleGetSelStrBtn member function copies the current selection to the String Box edit control. The function performs the following tasks:

- Copying the current selection to the dataStr member by calling the GetSelString function

- Overwriting the contents of the String Box with the characters of the dataStr member

The HandleSetSelStrBtn member function overwrites the current selection with the string in the String Box edit control. Because the list maintains sorted items, the replacement string will very likely have a different position than the original selection. The function performs the following tasks:

- Obtains the position of the current selection using the GetSelIndex function and assigns that value to the local variable i.

- Copies the text in the String Box to the dataStr member.

- Verifies that the string in dataStr does not already exist in the List Box. This task involves the FindExactString function. If the string in dataStr is new to the list, the function deletes the current selection (using the DeleteString function), adds the dataStr (using the AddString function), and then selects the added string (using the SetSelIndex function). By contrast, if the string in dataStr has a matching list item, the function displays a message informing you that you cannot add duplicate strings in the list box. This warning also appears if you attempt to overwrite the current selection with the same string.

The HandleGetSelIdxBtn member function writes the position of the current selection to the Index Box edit box. The function uses the GetSelIndex function to obtain the sought position.

The HandleSetSelIdxBtn member function reads the value in the Index Box edit control and uses that value to set the new current selection. The function uses the SetSelIndex function to make the new selection.

The HandleGetStrBtn member function enables you to retrieve the list item whose position appears in the Index Box edit control. The function performs the following tasks:

- Copies the characters of the Index Box to the indxStr data member.
- Converts the string in indexStr to the int-typed local variable i.
- Copies the characters of the list item at position i to the dataStr member.
- Writes the characters of dataStr in the String Box edit control.

SYNCHRONIZED LISTS SCROLLING

This section explores a special case of synchronized scrolling of two list boxes. The two lists should meet the following conditions:

- Both lists have the same height and contain the same number of items. An equal number of items enforces the one-to-one correspondence between the items of the two lists.
- At most, one of the two lists can maintain sorted items.
- Changing the selection in one list must result in selecting also the corresponding item in the other list.
- The two lists must scroll simultaneously.

The first condition requires that each item in the two lists has a corresponding item in the other list. Moreover, you should be able to view the same number of items in both lists.

The second condition requires that one list (or both) must be unsorted. When both of the two lists are unsorted, it is easier to insert and delete items from the two list boxes. If one of the list boxes uses the LBS_SORT style, the items of the other unordered list must be added in an order that matches the sort order of the first list.

The third and fourth conditions require that the two lists must maintain the same selection position and the same scroll bar position. Fulfilling this condition provides the application user with a nice interface.

The Synchronized Lists Program

Consider now an ObjectWindows program that demonstrates the synchronized lists feature. Figure 4.3 shows a sample session with the CTLLST3.EXE application that supports the synchronized scrolling of lists. The program has a very simple user interface: two lists boxes and one vertical scroll bar located between the lists. The first list contains the names of capitals and the second list contains the names of the corresponding countries. You cannot add, delete, or modify either list box. When you select a new capital, the corresponding country is also selected, and vice versa. When you move the thumb box of the scroll bar, both lists move simultaneously. If you double-click an item in either list, the application displays a message stating the capital of the currently selected country (which is also the country of the currently selected capital). To exit the program, use the Exit menu item.

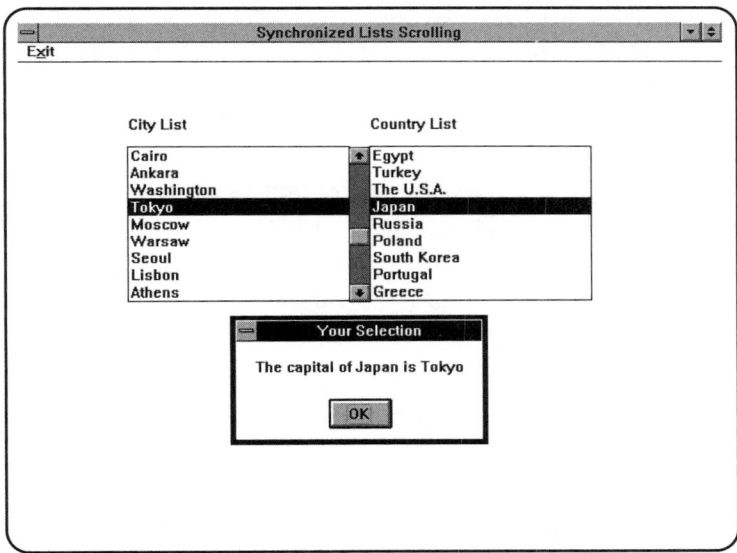

Figure 4.3. A sample session with the CTLLST3.EXE application.

Compile and run the program. Experiment with scrolling the list boxes and making new selections. Experiment with double-clicking items in either list. Also try moving the scroll bar thumb box with the mouse or with the cursor control keys, and watch the two lists move in sync.

Synchronizing the selections in both lists is straightforward. When you make a new selection, the list box notifies the parent window. The parent window in turn sets the same selection position in the other list box.

Synchronizing the scroll bar movement, however, required some doing. The original program version displayed the vertical scroll bars of the list boxes. The problem was that when the thumb boxes of these scroll bars moved, no notification messages were sent to the parent window. After all, the list's own scroll bar is part of the list box and does not have a separate ID. As a result, the two list boxes scrolled independently of each other, while maintaining the corresponding selection. For example, while Tokyo and Japan remained selected, they failed to scroll side by side. This was not good enough. The first step to solve this problem was to remove the ws_vscroll style from both list boxes and maintain a selection at all times. The modified list boxes now scrolled simultaneously at the price of changing the current selections while scrolling. The second part of the solution was to create a vertical scroll bar control and place it between the list boxes. Because the scroll bar control sends a notification message to its parent window, it is possible to move the current list selections in sync with the thumb box movement. Moreover, you can move the thumb box when you scroll through either list. This is the solution that I present here.

Listing 4.9 shows the contents of the CTLLST3.DEF definition file. Listing 4.10 contains the source code for the CTLLST3.H header file. Listing 4.11 shows the script for the CTLLST3.RC resource file. Listing 4.12 shows the source code for the CTLLST3.CPP program file.

LISTING 4.9. THE CONTENTS OF THE CTLLST3.DEF DEFINITION FILE.

```
NAME          CtlLst3
DESCRIPTION   'An OWL Windows Application'
EXETYPE       WINDOWS
CODE          PRELOAD MOVEABLE DISCARDABLE
DATA          PRELOAD MOVEABLE MULTIPLE
HEAPSIZE      1024
STACKSIZE     16384
```

LISTING 4.10. THE SOURCE CODE FOR THE CTLLST3.H HEADER FILE.

```
IDM_EXITMENU 400
```

Listing 4.11. The script for the CTLLST3.RC resource file.

```
#include <windows.h>
#include <owl\window.rh>
#include "ctllst3.h"

IDM_EXITMENU MENU LOADONCALL MOVEABLE PURE DISCARDABLE
BEGIN
    MENUITEM "E&xit", CM_EXIT
END
```

Listing 4.12. The source code for the CTLLST3.CPP program file.

```
/*
  Program which demonstrates how to simultaneously scroll
  two list boxes using a scroll bar control
*/
#include <owl\applicat.h>
#include <owl\framewin.h>
#include <owl\static.h>
#include <owl\scrollba.h>
#include <owl\listbox.h>
#include <owl\window.rh>
#include "ctllst3.h"
#include <stdlib.h>
#include <ctype.h>
#include <stdio.h>
#include <string.h>

const Wtxt = 200;
const Htxt = 20;
const Wlst = 200;
const Hlst = 150;
const Wscr = 20;
const Hscr = Hlst;
const VertSpacing = 10;
const MaxString = 40;

// declare the ID constants for the various controls
#define ID_CITY_LST     101
#define ID_COUNTRY_LST 102
#define ID_SCROLL_SCR  103

// declare the custom application class as
// a subclass of TApplication
```

continues

LISTING 4.12. CONTINUED

```
class TWinApp : public TApplication
{
public:
  TWinApp() : TApplication() {}

protected:
  virtual void InitMainWindow();
};

// expand the functionality of TWindow by deriving class TMainWindow
class TMainWindow : public TWindow
{
public:

  TMainWindow();

protected:
  TListBox* CityLst;
  TListBox* CountryLst;
  TScrollBar* ScrollScr;

  // initialize the city and coutry lists
  virtual void SetupWindow();

  // handle the selecting a new item in the City list box
  void EvSelChangeCityLst();

  // handle double-clicking the City list box
  void EvDblClkCityLst();

  // handle the selecting a new item in the Country list box
  void EvSelChangeCountryLst();

  // handle double-clicking the Country list box
  void EvDblClkCountryLst();

  // handle the scroll bar notification message
  virtual void EvVScroll(UINT code, UINT pos, HWND wnd);

  // handle closing the window
  virtual BOOL CanClose();

  // declare the message map macro
  DECLARE_RESPONSE_TABLE(TMainWindow);

};

DEFINE_RESPONSE_TABLE1(TMainWindow, TWindow)
```

```
    EV_LBN_SELCHANGE(ID_CITY_LST, EvSelChangeCityLst),
    EV_LBN_DBLCLK(ID_CITY_LST, EvDblClkCityLst),
    EV_LBN_SELCHANGE(ID_COUNTRY_LST, EvSelChangeCountryLst),
    EV_LBN_DBLCLK(ID_COUNTRY_LST, EvDblClkCountryLst),
    EV_WM_VSCROLL,
END_RESPONSE_TABLE;

TMainWindow::TMainWindow() :
            TWindow(0, 0, 0)
{
  char s[81];
  int x0 = 100;
  int y0 = 50;
  int x = x0;
  int y = y0;

  // create the city list box and its label
  strcpy(s, "City List");
  new TStatic(this, -1, s, x, y, Wtxt, Htxt, strlen(s));
  y += Htxt + VertSpacing;
  CityLst = new TListBox(this, ID_CITY_LST, x, y, Wlst, Hlst);
  // turn off the automatic sorting of the city list member
  CityLst->Attr.Style &= ~LBS_SORT;
  // hide the vertical scroll bar
  CityLst->Attr.Style &= ~WS_VSCROLL;
  y = y0 + Htxt + VertSpacing;
  x += Wlst;
  ScrollScr = new TScrollBar(this, ID_SCROLL_SCR,
                            x, y, Wscr, Hscr - 4, FALSE);
  x += Wscr;
  y = y0;
  // create the country list box and its label
  strcpy(s, "Country List");
  new TStatic(this, -1, s, x, y, Wtxt, Htxt, strlen(s));
  y += Htxt + VertSpacing;
  CountryLst = new TListBox(this, ID_COUNTRY_LST, x, y, Wlst, Hlst);
  // turn off the automatic sorting of the country list member
  CountryLst->Attr.Style &= ~LBS_SORT;
  // hide the vertical scroll bar
  CountryLst->Attr.Style &= ~WS_VSCROLL;
}

void TMainWindow::SetupWindow()
{
  TWindow::SetupWindow();
  // add data in the city list box
  CityLst->AddString("Paris");
  CityLst->AddString("London");
  CityLst->AddString("Rome");
  CityLst->AddString("Bern");
```

continues

LISTING 4.12. CONTINUED

```
CityLst->AddString("Madrid");
CityLst->AddString("Cairo");
CityLst->AddString("Ankara");
CityLst->AddString("Washington");
CityLst->AddString("Tokyo");
CityLst->AddString("Moscow");
CityLst->AddString("Warsaw");
CityLst->AddString("Seoul");
CityLst->AddString("Lisbon");
CityLst->AddString("Athens");
// add data in the country list box
CountryLst->AddString("France");
CountryLst->AddString("The U.K.");
CountryLst->AddString("Italy");
CountryLst->AddString("Switzerland");
CountryLst->AddString("Spain");
CountryLst->AddString("Egypt");
CountryLst->AddString("Turkey");
CountryLst->AddString("The U.S.A.");
CountryLst->AddString("Japan");
CountryLst->AddString("Russia");
CountryLst->AddString("Poland");
CountryLst->AddString("South Korea");
CountryLst->AddString("Portugal");
CountryLst->AddString("Greece");
// select the first item in both list boxes
CityLst->SetSelIndex(0);
CountryLst->SetSelIndex(0);
// set the range of the scroll bar control
ScrollScr->SetRange(0, CityLst->GetCount()-1);
}

void TMainWindow::EvSelChangeCityLst()
{
  // get the current selection index in the city list
  int i = CityLst->GetSelIndex();
  CountryLst->SetSelIndex(i); // update country selection
  ScrollScr->SetPosition(i);  // update scroll bar control
}

void TMainWindow::EvDblClkCityLst()
{
  char city[MaxString+1];
  char country[MaxString];
  char message[2*MaxString+1];

  // get the selected string in both list boxes
  CityLst->GetSelString(city, MaxString);
```

```
  CountryLst->GetSelString(country, MaxString);
  // build and display a message
  sprintf(message, "The capital of %s is %s", country, city);
  MessageBox(message, "Your Selection", MB_OK);
}

void TMainWindow::EvSelChangeCountryLst()
{
  // get the current selection index in the country list
  int i = CountryLst->GetSelIndex();
  CityLst->SetSelIndex(i); // update city selection
  ScrollScr->SetPosition(i); // update scroll bar control
}

void TMainWindow::EvDblClkCountryLst()
{
  char city[MaxString+1];
  char country[MaxString];
  char message[2*MaxString+1];

  // get the selected string in both list boxes
  CityLst->GetSelString(city, MaxString);
  CountryLst->GetSelString(country, MaxString);
  // build and display a message
  sprintf(message, "The capital of %s is %s", country, city);
  MessageBox(message, "Your Selection", MB_OK);
}

void TMainWindow::EvVScroll(UINT code, UINT pos, HWND wnd)
{
  TWindow::EvVScroll(code, pos, wnd);
  // get the thumb position of the scroll bar control
  int i = ScrollScr->GetPosition();
  // select the city and country items that have the same
  // index as the thumb position
  CityLst->SetSelIndex(i);
  CountryLst->SetSelIndex(i);
}

BOOL TMainWindow::CanClose()
{
  return MessageBox("Want to close this application",
              "Query", MB_YESNO | MB_ICONQUESTION) == IDYES;
}

void TWinApp::InitMainWindow()
{
  MainWindow = new TFrameWindow(0, "Synchronized Lists Scrolling",
                    new TMainWindow);
  // load the menu resource
```

continues

LISTING 4.12. CONTINUED

```
  MainWindow->AssignMenu(TResID(IDM_EXITMENU));
  // enable the keyboard handler
  MainWindow->EnableKBHandler();
}

int OwlMain(int /* argc */, char** /*argv[] */)
{
  TWinApp app;
  return app.Run();
}
```

The program in Listing 4.12 declares two sets of constants. The first set declares the dimensions of the controls used. The second set of constants defines the control ID values.

The program listing also declares an application class and a window class. The application window class TMainWindow declares a number of data members that are pointers to the controls owned by the window. The TMainWindow class also declares a constructor and a number of member functions that respond to the notification messages emitted by the various controls.

The TMainWindow constructor loads the menu resource, creates the instances for the controls of the application, and enables the keyboard handler. Both list boxes are created with the LBS_SORT and WS_VSCROLL styles removed.

The response table includes EV_LBN_SELCHANGE and EV_LBN_DBLCLK entries to handle selecting a new item or double-clicking an item in either list box. The table entry EV_WM_VSCROLL handles scrolling the vertical scroll bar.

The SetupWindow member function initializes the main window controls by performing the following tasks:

- Inserts data in the city and country list boxes.

- Selects the first item in both list boxes.

- Sets the range of the scroll bar control.

The EvSelChangeCityLst member function responds to the LBN_SELCHANGE notification message sent by the city list box, which contains the names of the capitals. The function synchronizes the selections of the two list boxes by performing the following tasks:

- Obtains the position of the new selection in the city list and stores it in the local variable i.

- Selects the country list item at position i as the new selection of that list.

- Updates the position of the scroll bar thumb box to match the selection position common to both list boxes.

The EvDblClkCityLst member function responds to the LBN_DBLCLK notification message sent by the city list box. The function displays a message that uses the currently selected items in both lists.

The EvSelChangeCoutryLst and EvDblClkCountryLst member functions are similar to the EvSelChangeCityLst and EvDblClkCityLst functions, respectively. The functions handle changing the city list selection when you alter the country list selection.

The EvVScroll member function moves the list boxes in sync with the scroll bar thumb box. The function obtains the current thumb box position and then sends the SetPosition message to each of the city and country list boxes.

Handling Multiple-Selection Lists

In this section, I demonstrate the use of multiple-selection lists and focus on getting and setting the selection strings and their indices. Before I introduce the test program and discuss its code, I want to indicate that there are two ways for making multiple selections in a list box. These modes depend on whether you set the LBS_EXTENDEDSEL style when you create a TListBox instance. Setting this style enables you to extend the range of selected items quickly by holding down the Shift key and clicking the mouse. The side effect for this style is that you are committed to selecting manually (that is, using the mouse or cursor keys) blocks of contiguous items in the list box. Using the SetSelIndexes member function, you can make your program select noncontiguous items. However, this approach requires extra effort by the application user and a few extra controls to support this type of selection. By contrast, if you do not set the LBS_EXTENDEDSEL style, you can easily make dispersed selections by clicking the mouse button on the individual items that you want to select. The negative effect of this selection mode is that you must click every item in order to select it, including neighboring items. Choose the selection mode that you feel best meets the user-interface requirements for your ObjectWindows applications.

The Multiple-Selection List Tester

The following program demonstrates how to set and to query multiple selections in a list box. Figure 4.4 shows a sample session with the CTLLST4.EXE application and also indicates the controls used by that application. The controls used by the test program and the operation they support are as follows:

- A multiple-selection list that has the LBS_MULTIPLESEL style selected (but not the LBS_EXTENDEDSEL style). The strings in the list box are sorted in ascending order.

- A multiline edit box control labeled Names Box, which contains the names of the selected strings.

- A pushbutton with the caption Get Names to copy the list box selections in the Names Box edit control. Each selection appears on a separate line in the edit box. Every time you click this button, you loose the previous contents of the Names Box edit control.

- A pushbutton with the caption Set Names to select (or deselect) the list box items that match those in the Names Box edit control. The match need not be exact; the Names Box strings need only match the leading characters of the list items.

- A multiline edit box control labeled Indices Box, which contains the indices of the selected strings.

- A pushbutton with the caption Get Indices to copy the indices of the list box selections in the Indices Box edit control. The index of each selection appears on a separate line in the edit box. Every time you click this button, you lose the previous contents of the Indices Box edit control.

- A pushbutton with the caption Set Indices to select (or deselect) the list box items using the values in the Indices Box edit control.

- A check box control with the caption Deselect Mode, which determines whether the Set Names and Set Indices pushbuttons select or deselect list items.

- The static text controls that label the list and edit boxes.

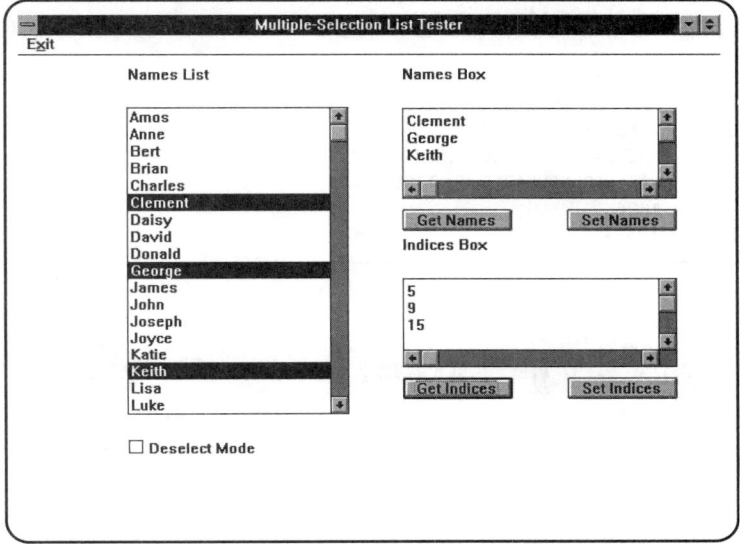

Figure 4.4. A sample session with the CTLLST4.EXE application.

Compile and run the program. The application initializes the list box with several names. This feature saves you the time and effort needed to enter the names yourself. Select a few list items and click the Get Names and Get Indices pushbuttons. The selected string and indices appear in the Names Box and Indices Box edit controls. Now edit the lines on the Names Box by deleting one or two trailing characters from each line to create partial names. Click the Set Names pushbutton. What do you see? The selections have not changed because the strings in the Names Box still match the same list box selection. Now type in a new set of indices in the Indices Box and click the Set Indices pushbutton. The program now displays a new set of selected items in the list box. You can also make a new selection by deleting the text in the Names Box and typing in names that are found in the list box. Now click the Set Names pushbutton and view the new list box selections. When you are done experimenting with the program, click the Exit menu item or press the Alt+X keys.

The multiple-selection list tester application basically drills the GetSelIndexes, GetSelStrings, SetSelIndexes, and SetSelStrings member functions of the TListBox class. Listing 4.13 shows the contents of the CTLLST4.DEF definition file. Listing 4.14 contains the source code for the CTLLST4.H header file. Listing 4.15 shows the script for the CTLLST4.RC resource file. Listing 4.16 shows the source code for the CTLLST4.CPP program file.

LISTING 4.13. THE CONTENTS OF THE CTLLST4.DEF DEFINITION FILE.

```
NAME          CtlLst4
DESCRIPTION   'An OWL Windows Application'
EXETYPE       WINDOWS
CODE          PRELOAD MOVEABLE DISCARDABLE
DATA          PRELOAD MOVEABLE MULTIPLE
HEAPSIZE      1024
STACKSIZE     16384
```

LISTING 4.14. THE SOURCE CODE FOR THE CTLLST4.H HEADER FILE.

```
#define IDM_EXITMENU 400
```

LISTING 4.15. THE SCRIPT FOR THE CTLLST4.RC RESOURCE FILE.

```
#include <windows.h>
#include <owl\window.rh>
#include "ctllst4.h"

IDM_EXITMENU MENU LOADONCALL MOVEABLE PURE DISCARDABLE
BEGIN
    MENUITEM "E&xit", CM_EXIT
END
```

LISTING 4.16. THE SOURCE CODE FOR THE CTLLST4.CPP PROGRAM FILE.

```
/*
  Program which illustrates the multi-item selections
  in a list box control
*/
#include <owl\applicat.h>
#include <owl\framewin.h>
#include <owl\static.h>
#include <owl\edit.h>
#include <owl\button.h>
#include <owl\scrollba.h>
#include <owl\listbox.h>
#include <owl\checkbox.h>
#include "ctllst4.h"
#include <stdlib.h>
```

```
#include <ctype.h>
#include <stdio.h>
#include <string.h>

// declare the constants for the dimensions and spacing
// of the various controls
const Wtxt = 100;
const Htxt = 20;
const TxtVertSpacing = 20;
const Wlst = 200;
const Hlst = 300;
const LstHorzSpacing = 50;
const LstVertSpacing = 10;
const Wbox = 250;
const Hbox = 85;
const BoxVertSpacing = 10;
const Wbtn = 100;
const Hbtn = 20;
const BtnHorzSpacing = 50;
const BtnVertSpacing = 5;
const Wchk = 200;
const Hchk = 20;

const MaxString = 40;
const MaxSelections = 35; // maximum number of selections

// declare the ID constants for the various controls
#define ID_NAMES_LST        101
#define ID_NAMES_EDIT       102
#define ID_INDICES_EDIT     103
#define ID_GETNAMES_BTN     104
#define ID_SETNAMES_BTN     105
#define ID_GETINDICES_BTN 106
#define ID_SETINDICES_BTN 107
#define ID_SELECT_CHK       108

// declare the custom application class as
// a subclass of TApplication
class TWinApp : public TApplication
{
public:
  TWinApp() : TApplication() {}

protected:
  virtual void InitMainWindow();
};

// expand the functionality of TWindow by deriving class TMainWindow
class TMainWindow : public TWindow
{
```

continues

LISTING 4.16. CONTINUED

```
public:

  TMainWindow();

protected:

  TListBox* NamesLst;
  TEdit* NamesBox;
  TEdit* IndicesBox;
  TButton* GetNamesBtn;
  TButton* SetNamesBtn;
  TButton* GetIndicesBtn;
  TButton* SetIndicesBtn;
  TCheckBox* SelectChk;

  // array of string pointers
  char far* names[MaxSelections];

  // array of integers to store the selection indices
  int indices[MaxSelections];

  // initialize the list box
  virtual void SetupWindow();

  // class destructor to deallocate the dynamic space for
  // the names pointers
  ~TMainWindow();

  // handle getting the selections
  virtual void HandleGetNamesBtn();

  // handle setting the selections
  virtual void HandleSetNamesBtn();

  // handle getting the selection indices
  virtual void HandleGetIndicesBtn();

  // handle setting the selection indices
  virtual void HandleSetIndicesBtn();

  // handle closing the window
  virtual BOOL CanClose();

  // declare the message map macro
  DECLARE_RESPONSE_TABLE(TMainWindow);

};
```

```
DEFINE_RESPONSE_TABLE1(TMainWindow, TWindow)
  EV_COMMAND(ID_GETNAMES_BTN, HandleGetNamesBtn),
  EV_COMMAND(ID_SETNAMES_BTN, HandleSetNamesBtn),
  EV_COMMAND(ID_GETINDICES_BTN, HandleGetIndicesBtn),
  EV_COMMAND(ID_SETINDICES_BTN, HandleSetIndicesBtn),
END_RESPONSE_TABLE;

TMainWindow::TMainWindow() :
          TWindow(0, 0, 0)
{
  char s[81];
  int x0 = 100;
  int y0 = 10;
  int x = x0;
  int y = y0;

  // create the name list box and its label
  strcpy(s, "Names List");
  new TStatic(this, -1, s, x, y, Wtxt, Htxt, strlen(s));
  y += Htxt + TxtVertSpacing;
  NamesLst = new TListBox(this, ID_NAMES_LST, x, y, Wlst, Hlst);
  // set the multiple-selection style
  NamesLst->Attr.Style |= LBS_MULTIPLESEL;
  // create the Deselect Mode check box
  y += Hlst + LstVertSpacing;
  SelectChk = new TCheckBox(this, ID_SELECT_CHK, "Deselect Mode",
                    x, y, Wchk, Hchk, NULL);

  x0 += Wlst + LstHorzSpacing;
  x = x0;
  y = y0;
  // creates the multiline Names Box edit control and its label
  strcpy(s, "Names Box");
  new TStatic(this, -1, s, x, y, Wtxt, Htxt, strlen(s));
  y += Htxt + TxtVertSpacing;
  NamesBox = new TEdit(this, ID_NAMES_EDIT, "",
                    x, y, Wbox, Hbox, 0, TRUE);

  // create the Get Names button
  y += Hbox + BoxVertSpacing;
  GetNamesBtn = new TButton(this, ID_GETNAMES_BTN, "Get Names",
                        x, y, Wbtn, Hbtn, FALSE);

  // create the Set Names button
  x += Wbtn + BtnHorzSpacing;
  SetNamesBtn = new TButton(this, ID_SETNAMES_BTN, "Set Names",
                    x, y, Wbtn, Hbtn, FALSE);

  x = x0;
  y += Hbtn + BtnVertSpacing;
```

continues

LISTING 4.16. CONTINUED

```
// create the multiline Indices Box edit control and its label
strcpy(s, "Indices Box");
new TStatic(this, -1, s, x, y, Wtxt, Htxt, strlen(s));
y += Htxt + TxtVertSpacing;
IndicesBox = new TEdit(this, ID_INDICES_EDIT, "",
                x, y, Wbox, Hbox, 0, TRUE);

// create the GetIndices button
y += Hbox + BoxVertSpacing;
GetIndicesBtn = new TButton(this, ID_GETINDICES_BTN, "Get Indices",
                x, y, Wbtn, Hbtn, FALSE);

// create the Set Indices button
x += Wbtn + BtnHorzSpacing;
SetIndicesBtn = new TButton(this, ID_SETINDICES_BTN, "Set Indices",
                x, y, Wbtn, Hbtn, FALSE);

// allocate the dynamic space for the array of strings accessed
// by the array of pointers names
for (int i = 0; i < MaxSelections; i++)
  names[i] = new char far[MaxString + 1];
}

TMainWindow::~TMainWindow()
{
  // deallocate the dynamic string space
  for (int i = 0; i < MaxSelections; i++)
    delete [] (void*)names[i];
}

void TMainWindow::SetupWindow()
{
  TWindow::SetupWindow();
  // add names in the Names list box
  NamesLst->AddString("John");
  NamesLst->AddString("Robert");
  NamesLst->AddString("Melody");
  NamesLst->AddString("Charles");
  NamesLst->AddString("Olivia");
  NamesLst->AddString("Richard");
  NamesLst->AddString("James");
  NamesLst->AddString("Anne");
  NamesLst->AddString("Keith");
  NamesLst->AddString("Brian");
  NamesLst->AddString("Lisa");
  NamesLst->AddString("Margie");
  NamesLst->AddString("Thomas");
  NamesLst->AddString("Joseph");
```

```
    NamesLst->AddString("Donald");
    NamesLst->AddString("Bert");
    NamesLst->AddString("George");
    NamesLst->AddString("Ronald");
    NamesLst->AddString("Katie");
    NamesLst->AddString("Susan");
    NamesLst->AddString("Joyce");
    NamesLst->AddString("David");
    NamesLst->AddString("Paul");
    NamesLst->AddString("Mark");
    NamesLst->AddString("Luke");
    NamesLst->AddString("Amos");
    NamesLst->AddString("Matthew");
    NamesLst->AddString("Mary");
    NamesLst->AddString("Patrick");
    NamesLst->AddString("Clement");
    NamesLst->AddString("Daisy");
}

void TMainWindow::HandleGetNamesBtn()
{
  char s[MaxString+1];
  // get the selected strings
  int n = NamesLst->GetSelStrings(names, MaxSelections, MaxString);
  // exit if n is negative
  if (n < 0) return;
  // clear the Names Box edit control
  NamesBox->SetText("");
  // insert the selected strings in the Names Box control
  for (int i = 0; i < n; i++) {
    sprintf(s, "%s\r\n", names[i]);
    NamesBox->Insert(s);
  }
}

void TMainWindow::HandleSetNamesBtn()
{
  // get the number of lines in the Names Box edit control
  int n = NamesBox->GetNumLines();
  // get the select status from the Deselect Mode check box
  BOOL shouldSet =
    (SelectChk->GetCheck() == BF_UNCHECKED) ? TRUE : FALSE;
  // read the lines from the Names Box control
  for (int i = 0; i < n; i++) {
    NamesBox->GetLine(names[i], MaxString, i);
  }
  // select the strings in the Names List control using the
  // array of pointers names
  NamesLst->SetSelStrings((const char far**)names, n, shouldSet);
}
```

continues

LISTING 4.16. CONTINUED

```
void TMainWindow::HandleGetIndicesBtn()
{
  char s[MaxString+1];
  // get the selected indices
  int n = NamesLst->GetSelIndexes(indices, MaxSelections);
  // exit if n is negative
  if (n < 0) return;
  // clear the Indices Box edit control
  IndicesBox->SetText("");
  // insert the selected indices in the Indices Box control
  for (int i = 0; i < n; i++) {
    sprintf(s, "%d\r\n", indices[i]);
    IndicesBox->Insert(s);
  }
}

void TMainWindow::HandleSetIndicesBtn()
{
  char s[MaxString + 1];
  // get the number of lines in the Indices Box edit control
  // subtract 1 for the extra blank line in the text box
  int n = IndicesBox->GetNumLines() - 1;
  // get the select status from the Deselect Mode check box
  BOOL shouldSet =
    (SelectChk->GetCheck() == BF_UNCHECKED) ? TRUE : FALSE;
  // read the lines from the Names Box control
  for (int i = 0; i < n; i++) {
    IndicesBox->GetLine(s, MaxString, i);
    indices[i] = atoi(s);
  }
  // select the strings in the Names List control using the
  // array of integers indices
  NamesLst->SetSelIndexes(indices, n, shouldSet);
}

BOOL TMainWindow::CanClose()
{
  return MessageBox("Want to close this application",
            "Query", MB_YESNO | MB_ICONQUESTION) == IDYES;
}

void TWinApp::InitMainWindow()
{
  MainWindow = new TFrameWindow(0, "Multiple-Selection List Tester",
                    new TMainWindow);
  // load the menu resource
  MainWindow->AssignMenu(TResID(IDM_EXITMENU));
  // enable the keyboard handler
```

```
  MainWindow->EnableKBHandler();
}

int OwlMain(int /* argc */, char** /*argv[] */)
{
  TWinApp app;
  return app.Run();
}
```

The program in Listing 4.16 declares three sets of constants. The first set specifies the dimensions and spacing for the various application controls. The second set of constants declares the maximum string size and maximum number of selections. The third set of constants establishes the ID numbers for the various controls.

The program also declares an application class and a window class. The TMainWindow class declares two sets of data members. The first set represents pointers to the various controls used in the application. The second set of data members contains the array of string pointers, names; and the array of integers, indices. Both arrays have MaxSelections members.

The TMainWindow class declares a class constructor, a class destructor (something new), and a collection of member functions. The destructor class is needed to remove the dynamic strings created by the constructor.

The TMainWindow constructor creates the various controls and creates the array of dynamic strings. The constructor sets the style for the TListBox instance to include the LBS_MULTIPLESEL style. If you want to make the application extend the list box selections with the Shift key, simply add ¦ LBS_EXTENDEDSEL to the style-setting expression.

The SetupWindow member function initializes the multiline list box by inserting in it a number of names.

The HandleGetNamesBtn member function responds to the notification message sent by clicking the Get Names pushbutton. The function performs the following tasks:

- Invokes the GetSelString function to obtain the list box selections. These selections are copied to the string array accessed by the names array of pointers. The function call also specifies that up to maxSelections can be copied and that up to maxString characters may be copied to each string. The function result is assigned to the local variable n.

- Exits the function if the variable n stores a negative value.

- Clears the text in the Names Box edit control.

- Uses a loop to copy the strings accessed by the names array into separate lines in the Names Box edit control.

The HandleSetNamesBtn member function responds to the notification message of the Set Names pushbutton control. The function carries out the following tasks:

- Obtains the number of lines in the Names Box control.

- Obtains the check state of the Deselect Mode check box. The function assigns a Boolean value, equivalent to the check state, to the local variable shouldSet.

- Copies the lines of the Names Box control to the string array accessed by the array of pointers names.

- Selects the matching list items by calling the SetSelStrings function. The function call specifies the names, n, and shouldSet variables as the arguments for the prefix, numSelections, and shouldSet parameters, respectively.

The HandleGetIndicesBtn member function responds to the notification message sent by the Get Indices pushbutton control. The function performs the following tasks:

- Invokes the GetSelIndexes function to obtain the list box selections. These selections are copied to the indices integer array. The function call also specifies that up to maxSelections indices can be copied to the indices array. The result function is assigned to the local variable n.

- Exits the function if the variable n stores a negative value.

- Clears the text in the Indices Box edit control.

- Uses a loop to convert the selection indices to their string images and displays these string images in the Indices Box edit control.

The HandleSetIndicesBtn member function responds to the notification message of the Set Indices pushbutton control. The function carries out the following tasks:

- Obtains the number of lines in the Indices Box control.

- Obtains the check state of the Deselect Mode check box. The function assigns a Boolean value, equivalent to the check state, to the local variable shouldSet.

- Copies each line of the Indices Box control to a temporary string, converts that string into an int value, and stores that integer in a member of the indices array.

- Selects the matching list items by calling the SetSelIndexes function. The call function specifies the indices, n, and shouldSet variables as the arguments for the indexes, numSelections, and shouldSet parameters, respectively.

The Combo Box Control

Windows supports the combo box control, which combines an edit box with a list box. Thus, with a combo box, you can either select an item in the list box component or type in your own input. In a sense, the list box part of the combo box contains convenient or frequently used selections. A combo box, unlike a list box, does not confine you to choosing items in the list box. There are three kinds of combo boxes: simple, drop-down, and drop-down list. The simple combo box includes the edit box and the list box that is always displayed. The drop-down combo box differs from the simple type by the fact that the list box appears only when you click the down scroll arrow. The drop-down list combo box provides only a drop-down list that appears when you click the down scroll arrow. There is no edit box in this kind of combo box.

The TComboBox Class

ObjectWindows offers the TComboxBox class, a descendant of TListBox, to support the combo box controls. The TComboBox class inherits the list manipulation functionality from the TListBox class. Combo boxes support only the single-selection list boxes. The TComboBox class has three constructors. I will focus on the constructor that enables you to create TComboBox instances from scratch. This constructor has the following declaration:

```
TComboBox(Window* parent, int Id, int x, int y, int w,
        int w, DWORD style, WORD textLen,
        TModule* module = 0);
```

The `parent` parameter is the pointer to the parent window. The `Id` parameter specifies the unique ID of the control. The `x`, `y`, `w`, and `h` parameters specify the location and dimensions of the control. The `style` parameter specifies the combo box style. The arguments for this parameter are `CBS_SIMPLE` for a simple combo box, `CBS_DROPDOWN` for a drop-down combo box, or `CBS_DROPDOWNLIST` for a drop-down list combo box. The instances of `TComboBox` are created with the default styles, including `WS_CHILD`, `WS_VISIBLE`, `WS_GROUP`, `WS_TABSTOP`, `CBS_SORT`, `CBS_AUTOHSCROLL`, and `WS_VSCROLL`. Table 4.4 shows the more frequently used styles for the combo box controls.

TABLE 4.4. THE STYLES FOR THE COMBO BOX CONTROL.	
Style	*Meaning*
`CBS_AUTOHSCROLL`	Automatically scrolls the text in the edit control to the right when you enter a character at the end of the line. Removing this style limits the text to the characters that fit inside the rectangular boundary of the edit control.
`CBS_DROPDOWN`	Specifies a drop-down combo box.
`CBS_DROPDOWNLIST`	Designates a drop-down list combo box.
`CBS_SIMPLE`	Specifies a simple combo box.
`CBS_SORT`	Automatically sorts the items in the list box.

The `TComboBox` implements a number of member functions that manipulate the text in the edit control and show or hide the list box. The `Clear`, `SetText`, `GetText`, `GetTextLen`, `GetEditSel`, and `SetEditSel` member functions manipulate the text in the edit control. The parameterless `ShowList` and `HideList` member functions show and hide the list box component of drop-down and drop-down list combo boxes, respectively.

The edit control manipulation member functions include the following:

1. The parameterless `Clear` member function clears the text in edit control of a combo box.

2. The GetEditSel member function returns the starting and ending positions of the selected text. The declaration of the GetEditSel function is as follows:

```
int GetEditSel(int& startPos, int& endPos);
```

The startPos and endPos are reference parameters that return the starting and ending character positions of the selected text.

3. The GetText member function copies the text in the edit control to a string. The declaration of the GetText function is as follows:

```
inline int GetText(const char far* str, int maxChars) const;
```

The str parameter is the pointer to the string receiving up to maxChars characters from the edit control. The function returns the actual number of characters that were copied.

4. The parameterless member function GetTextLen returns the size of the text in the edit control of a combo box.

5. The SetEditSel member function enables you to define the selected text in the edit control by specifying the starting and ending character positions of the selected text. The declaration of the SetEditSel function is the following:

```
inline int SetEditSel(int startPos, int endPos);
```

The startPos and endPos parameters specify the new selected text.

6. The SetText member function selects the first item in the combo list box that begins with a specified string. The declaration of the SetText function is this:

```
void SetText(const char far* string);
```

The string parameter is the pointer to the search string. The function searches for a list item whose leading characters match the search string. If a match is found, the matching list member is selected. By contrast, if no match is found, the search string appears as selected text in the edit control.

The member functions that show or hide the list box components of a drop-down or drop-down list combo boxes are as follows:

7. The parameterless member function ShowList shows the list box associated with a combo box.

8. The parameterless member function HideList hides the list box associated with a combo box.

 The ShowList and HideList member functions are needed only when you want to manipulate the visibility of the list box though notification messages sent by other controls, such as check boxes or pushbuttons.

Responding to Combo Box Notification Messages

Combo boxes send the same types of notification messages to their parent window as do list boxes. The owner window can respond to the notification messages using child-ID member functions. Use the EV_CBV_*xxxx* message response macros to handle the CBN_*xxxx* notification messages. Table 4.5 shows the combo box notification messages. Here is a sample skeleton code for responding to not one, but two combo boxes:

```
#define ID_COMBOBOX1 101
#define ID_COMBOBOX2 102

class TMainWindow : public TWindow
{
public:

    // other declarations

    // handle the selection change in the combo box #1
    void EvSelChangeComboBox1();

    // handle the double-clicking an item in the combo box #1
    void EvDblClkComboBox1();

    // handle the selection change in the combo box #2
    void EvSelChangeComboBox2();

    // handle the double-clicking an item in the combo box #2
    void EvDblClkComboBox2();

    // other declarations

    DECLARE_RESPONSE_TABLE(TMainWindow);
};

DEFINE_RESPONSE_TABLE1(TMainWindow, TWindow)
    EV_CBN_SELCHANGE(ID_COMBOBOX1, EvSelChangeComboBox1),
    EV_CBN_DBLCLK(ID_COMBOBOX1, EvDblClkComboBox1),
    EV_CBN_SELCHANGE(ID_COMBOBOX2, EvSelChangeComboBox2),
    EV_CBN_DBLCLK(ID_COMBOBOX2, EvDblClkComboBox2),
END__RESPONSE_TABLE;
```

```
void TMainWindow::EvSelChangeComboBox1()
{
    // statements to handle change in selection
}

void TMainWindow::EvDblClkComboBox1()
{
    // statements to handle double-clicking a selection
}

void TMainWindow::EvSelChangeComboBox2()
{
    // statements to handle change in selection
}

void TMainWindow::EvDblClkComboBox2()
{
    // statements to handle double-clicking a selection
}
```

TABLE 4.5. THE COMBO BOX NOTIFICATION MESSAGES.

Message	Table Macro	Meaning
CBN_SELCHANGE	EV_CBN_SELCHANGE	A combo item is selected with a mouse click.
CBN_DBLCLK	EV_CBN_DBLCLK	A combo item is selected with a double mouse click.
CBN_SETFOCUS	EV_CBN_SETFOCUS	The combo box has gained focus.
CBN_KILLFOCUS	EV_CBN_KILLFOCUS	The combo box has lost focus.

Combo Boxes as History List Boxes

A *history list box* is a special combo box that inserts new edit control strings in the list box in chronological order. History list boxes typically follow these rules of operation:

- The combo list box removes the CBS_SORT style to insert the list items in a chronological fashion. New items are inserted at position 0, pushing the older items further down the list. The oldest item is the one at the bottom of the list. Thus, the history list box behaves like a queue structure.

- History boxes usually have a limit on the number of items you can insert; the limit is to prevent bleeding memory. This conservative scheme requires that the oldest list item be removed once the number of list items reaches a maximum limit.

- If the edit control contains a string that does not have an exact match in the accompanying list box, the edit control string is inserted as a new member at position 0.

- If the edit control contains a string that has an exact match in the accompanying list box, the matching list member is moved to position 0, the top of the list. Of course, this process involves first deleting the matching list member from its current position and then reinserting it at position 0.

A history list box is really a combo box that manipulates its edit control and list box items in a certain way. There is no need to drive a descendant of TComboBox to add new member functions.

The COCA Version 3 Application

Let me present the third version of the calculator application (COCA). To reduce the size of the program, I derived this new version from the first version, not the third one (except the feature of substituting the # character in the operand controls with the previous result is also included). Figure 4.5 shows a sample session with the CTLLST5.EXE application and indicates the controls that are used:

- An Operand1 drop-down combo box, which operates like a history list box.

- An Operator simple combo box. This combo box contains the list of supported operators and functions. The functions are log, exp, and sqrt.

- An Operand2 drop-down combo box, which operates like a history list box.

- A Result drop-down combo box, which operates like a history list box.

- The Error Message edit box.

- The Variables list box. This list box supports a new variable-name substitution feature. If you enter the @ character in the Operand edit boxes and double-click a Variables list item, the number stored in that item replaces the @ character in the Operand edit boxes.

- The Calc pushbutton control.

- The Store pushbutton control, which stores the current result (the number in the edit control of the Result combo box) in the currently selected item of the Variables list box.

- The Exit pushbutton control.

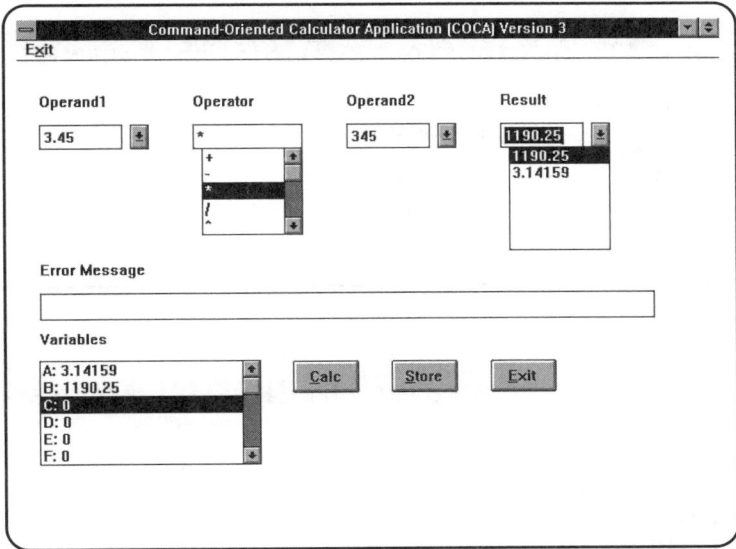

Figure 4.5. A sample session with the CTLLST5.EXE application.

Compile and run the program. Experiment with entering and executing numbers and operators or functions. Notice that the combo boxes for the operands and the result enter in their accompanying list boxes in a chronological order. The Operand combo boxes serve to remind you of the last 35 different operands you entered. The Result combo box serves to remind you of the last 35 different results calculated. In a way, the Result combo box acts as a temporary transient memory. You can select older results and then store them in the Variables list box. Experiment with selecting the supported functions by typing in the first letter of the function's name. In addition, type the @ character in the edit box of either Operand combo box and double-click an item in the Variables list box. This action immediately replaces the @ character with the number in the list box item that you double-clicked.

Look at the code for the COCA version 3 application. Listing 4.17 shows the contents of the CTLST5.DEF definition file. Listing 4.18 shows the source code for the CTLLST5.H header file. Listing 4.19 contains the script for the CTLLST5.RC resource file. The resource file defines the accelerator keys and menu resources. Listing 4.20 shows the source code for the CTLLST5.CPP program file.

LISTING 4.17. THE CONTENTS OF THE CTLLST5.DEF DEFINITION FILE.

```
NAME            CtlLst5
DESCRIPTION     'An OWL Windows Application'
EXETYPE         WINDOWS
CODE            PRELOAD MOVEABLE DISCARDABLE
DATA            PRELOAD MOVEABLE MULTIPLE
HEAPSIZE        1024
STACKSIZE       16384
```

LISTING 4.18. THE SOURCE CODE FOR THE CTLLST5.H HEADER FILE.

```
#define ID_CALC_BTN   110
#define ID_STORE_BTN  111
#define ID_EXIT_BTN   112
#define CM_CALC_BTN   113
#define CM_STORE_BTN  114
#define CM_EXIT_BTN   115
#define IDM_EXITMENU  400
#define IDR_BUTTONS   401
```

LISTING 4.19. THE SCRIPT FOR THE CTLLST5.RC RESOURCE FILE.

```
#include <windows.h>
#include <owl\window.rh>
#include "ctllst5.h"

IDR_BUTTONS ACCELERATORS
BEGIN
  "c", CM_CALC_BTN, ALT
  "s", CM_STORE_BTN, ALT
  "e", CM_EXIT_BTN, ALT
END
```

```
IDM_EXITMENU MENU LOADONCALL MOVEABLE PURE DISCARDABLE
BEGIN
    MENUITEM "E&xit", CM_EXIT
END
```

LISTING 4.20. THE SOURCE CODE FOR THE CTLLST5.CPP PROGRAM FILE.

```cpp
/*
  The COCA version 3 program which uses list boxes and combo boxes
*/
#include <owl\applicat.h>
#include <owl\framewin.h>
#include <owl\static.h>
#include <owl\edit.h>
#include <owl\button.h>
#include <owl\listbox.h>
#include <owl\combobox.h>
#include "ctllst5.h"
#include <stdlib.h>
#include <ctype.h>
#include <stdio.h>
#include <math.h>
#include <string.h>

// declare the constants that represent the sizes of the controls
const Wlbl = 100;
const Hlbl = 20;
const LblVertSpacing = 10;
const LblHorzSpacing = 40;
const Wbox = 100;
const Hbox = 25;
const BoxVertSpacing = 10;
const BoxHorzSpacing = 40;
const WLongbox = 4 * (Wbox + BoxHorzSpacing);
const Wlst = 200;
const Hlst = 100;
const LstVertSpacing = 10;
const LstHorzSpacing = 40;
const Hbtn = 30;
const Wbtn = 60;
const BtnHorzSpacing = 30;
const BtnVertSpacing = 10;
const Wcmb = 100;
const Hcmb = 120;
const CmbVertSpacing = 10;
const CmbHorzSpacing = 40;
```

continues

LISTING 4.20. CONTINUED

```
const MaxEditLen = 30;
// maximum number of items in a combo box that doubles as
// history list box
const MaxHistory = 30;

// declare the ID_XXXX constants for the edit boxes
#define ID_OPERAND1_CMB 101
#define ID_OPERATOR_CMB 102
#define ID_OPERAND2_CMB 103
#define ID_RESULT_CMB   104
#define ID_ERRMSG_EDIT  105
#define ID_VARIABLE_LST 106

// declare the custom application class as
// a subclass of TApplication
class TWinApp : public TApplication
{
public:
  TWinApp() : TApplication() {}

protected:
  virtual void InitMainWindow();
};

// expand the functionality of TWindow by deriving class TMainWindow
class TMainWindow : public TWindow
{
public:

  TMainWindow();

protected:

  TComboBox* Operand1Cmb;
  TComboBox* OperatorCmb;
  TComboBox* Operand2Cmb;
  TComboBox* ResultCmb;
  TEdit* ErrMsgBox;
  TListBox* VariableLst;
  TButton* CalcBtn;
  TButton* StoreBtn;
  TButton* ExitBtn;

  BOOL InError;

  // initialize the instances of TMainWindow
  virtual void SetupWindow();
```

```
// handle the notification messages from the Operator combo box
virtual void EvKillFocusOperatorCmb();

// handle the calculation
void HandleCalcBtn();

// handle the accelerator key for the Calculate button
void CMCalcBtn();

// handle storing the result in a variable
void HandleStoreBtn();

// handle the accelerator key for the Store button
void CMStoreBtn();

// handle exiting the application
void HandleExitBtn();

// handle the accelerator key for the Exit button
void CMExitBtn();

// handle the Variables list box when it gets the focus
void EvDblClkVariableLst();

// enable a push button control
void EnableButton(TButton* pBtn)
  { pBtn->EnableWindow(TRUE); }

// disable a push button control
void DisableButton(TButton* pBtn)
  { pBtn->EnableWindow(FALSE); }

// handle closing the window
virtual BOOL CanClose();

// obtain a number of the Variable list box
double getVar(int lineNum);

// store a number in the selected item of the Variable list box
void putVar(double x);

// update the combo box with the text in the
// accompanying edit box, assuming that the text
// is not already in the box
void updateComboBox(TComboBox* pCombo);

// declare the response table
DECLARE_RESPONSE_TABLE(TMainWindow);
};
```

continues

LISTING 4.20. CONTINUED

```
DEFINE_RESPONSE_TABLE1(TMainWindow, TWindow)
  EV_CBN_KILLFOCUS(ID_OPERATOR_CMB, EvKillFocusOperatorCmb),
  EV_COMMAND(ID_CALC_BTN, HandleCalcBtn),
  EV_COMMAND(CM_CALC_BTN, CMCalcBtn),
  EV_COMMAND(ID_STORE_BTN, HandleStoreBtn),
  EV_COMMAND(CM_STORE_BTN, CMStoreBtn),
  EV_COMMAND(ID_EXIT_BTN, HandleExitBtn),
  EV_COMMAND(CM_EXIT_BTN, CMExitBtn),
  EV_LBN_DBLCLK(ID_VARIABLE_LST, EvDblClkVariableLst),
END_RESPONSE_TABLE;

TMainWindow::TMainWindow() :
            TWindow(0, 0, 0)
{
  char s[81];
  int x0 = 20;
  int y0 = 30;
  int x = x0, y = y0;


  // create the first set of labels for the edit boxes
  strcpy(s, "Operand1");
  new TStatic(this, -1, s, x, y, Wlbl, Hlbl, strlen(s));
  strcpy(s, "Operator");
  x += Wlbl + LblHorzSpacing;
  new TStatic(this, -1, s, x, y, Wlbl, Hlbl, strlen(s));
  strcpy(s, "Operand2");
  x += Wlbl + LblHorzSpacing;
  new TStatic(this, -1, s, x, y, Wlbl, Hlbl, strlen(s));
  x += Wlbl + LblHorzSpacing;
  strcpy(s, "Result");
  new TStatic(this, -1, s, x, y, Wlbl, Hlbl, strlen(s));

  // create the Operand1, Operator, Operand2, and Result
  // combo list boxes
  x = x0;
  y += Hlbl + LblVertSpacing;
  Operand1Cmb = new TComboBox(this, ID_OPERAND1_CMB, x, y,
                              Wcmb, Hcmb, CBS_DROPDOWN, 0);
  Operand1Cmb->Attr.Style &= ~CBS_SORT;
  // create the Operator combo box
  x += Wcmb + CmbHorzSpacing;
  OperatorCmb = new TComboBox(this, ID_OPERATOR_CMB, x, y,
                              Wcmb, Hcmb, CBS_SIMPLE, 0);
  // force conversion of letters to uppercase
  OperatorCmb->Attr.Style &= ~CBS_SORT;
  x += Wcmb + CmbHorzSpacing;
  Operand2Cmb = new TComboBox(this, ID_OPERAND2_CMB, x, y,
                              Wcmb, Hcmb, CBS_DROPDOWN, 0);
```

```
  Operand2Cmb->Attr.Style &= ~CBS_SORT;
  x += Wcmb + CmbHorzSpacing;
  ResultCmb = new TComboBox(this, ID_RESULT_CMB,
                              x, y, Wcmb, Hcmb, CBS_DROPDOWN, 0);
  ResultCmb->Attr.Style &= ~CBS_SORT;
  // create the static text and edit box for the error message
  x = x0;
  y += Hcmb + CmbVertSpacing;
  strcpy(s, "Error Message");
  new TStatic(this, -1, s, x, y, Wlbl, Hlbl, strlen(s));
  y += Hlbl + LblVertSpacing;
  ErrMsgBox = new TEdit(this, ID_ERRMSG_EDIT, "", x, y,
                          WLongbox, Hbox, 0, FALSE);
  // create the static text and list box for the single-letter
  // variable selection
  y += Hbox + BoxVertSpacing;
  strcpy(s, "Variables");
  new TStatic(this, -1, s, x, y, Wlbl, Hlbl, strlen(s));
  y += Hlbl + LblVertSpacing;
  VariableLst = new TListBox(this, ID_VARIABLE_LST,
                              x, y, Wlst, Hlst);
  // create the Calc push button
  x += Wlst + BtnHorzSpacing;
  CalcBtn = new TButton(this, ID_CALC_BTN, "&Calc",
                          x, y, Wbtn, Hbtn, FALSE);

  // create the Store Btn
  x += Wbtn + BtnHorzSpacing;
  StoreBtn = new TButton(this, ID_STORE_BTN, "&Store",
                          x, y, Wbtn, Hbtn, FALSE);

  // Create the Exit Btn
  x += Wbtn + BtnHorzSpacing;
  ExitBtn = new TButton(this, ID_EXIT_BTN, "&Exit",
                          x, y, Wbtn, Hbtn, FALSE);

  // clear the InError flag
  InError = FALSE;

}

void TMainWindow::SetupWindow()
{
  char c;
  char s[MaxEditLen];

  TWindow::SetupWindow();

  Attr.Style |= WS_MAXIMIZE;
  // disable the Store button
```

continues

Listing 4.20. continued

```
StoreBtn->EnableWindow(FALSE);
// build the initial contents of the Variable list box
for (c = 'Z'; c >= 'A'; c—) {
  sprintf(s, "%c: 0", c);
  VariableLst->AddString(s);
}
// select the first item
VariableLst->SetSelIndex(0);

// add the operators in the Operator combo box
OperatorCmb->AddString("+");
OperatorCmb->AddString("-");
OperatorCmb->AddString("*");
OperatorCmb->AddString("/");
OperatorCmb->AddString("^");
OperatorCmb->AddString("log");
OperatorCmb->AddString("exp");
OperatorCmb->AddString("sqrt");
}

void TMainWindow::EvKillFocusOperatorCmb()
{
  char s[MaxEditLen+1];

  // get the text in the Operator combo box edit area
  OperatorCmb->GetText(s, MaxEditLen);
  // use it to search for a matching list item
  OperatorCmb->SetText(s);
}

void TMainWindow::HandleCalcBtn()
{
  int opIndex;
  double x, y, z, result;
  char opStr[MaxEditLen+1];
  char s[MaxEditLen+1];

  // convert the string in the Result combo box to a double
  ResultCmb->GetText(s, MaxEditLen);
  result = atof(s);

  // obtain the string in the Operand1 combo box
  Operand1Cmb->GetText(s, MaxEditLen);
  // does the Operand1Cmb contain the name
  // of a single-letter variable?
  if (isalpha(s[0]))
    // obtain value from the Variable list box control
    x = getVar(toupper(s[0]) - 'A');
```

```
// translate the # character into the value
// in the Result combo box
else if (s[0] == '#')
  x = result;
else
  // convert the string in the edit box area
  x = atof(s);

// obtain the string in the Operand2 combo box
Operand2Cmb->GetText(s, MaxEditLen);
// does the Operand2Cmb contain the name
// of a single-letter variable?
if (isalpha(s[0]))
  // obtain value from the Variable list box
  y =getVar(toupper(s[0]) - 'A');
// translate the # character into the value in
// the Result combo box
else if (s[0] == '#')
  y = result;
else
   // convert the string in the edit box area
  y = atof(s);

// obtain the string in the Operator combo box
OperatorCmb->GetText(opStr, MaxEditLen);

// clear the error message box
ErrMsgBox->Clear();
InError = FALSE;

// determine the requested operation using the FindExactString
// member function of TListBox
opIndex = OperatorCmb->FindExactString(opStr, -1);
switch (opIndex) {
  case 0: // + operator
    z = x + y;
    break;
  case 1: // - operator
    z = x - y;
    break;
  case 2: // * operator
    z = x * y;
    break;
  case 3: // / operator
    if (y != 0)
      z = x / y;
    else {
    z = 0;
      InError = TRUE;
      ErrMsgBox->SetText("Division-by-zero error");
```

continues

LISTING 4.20. CONTINUED

```
      }
      break;
    case 4: // ^ operator
      if (x > 0)
        z = exp(y * log(x));
      else {
        InError = TRUE;
        ErrMsgBox->SetText(
          "Cannot raise the power of a negative number");
      }
      break;
    case 5: // the natural logarithm function
      if (x > 0)
        z = log(x);
      else {
        InError = TRUE;
        ErrMsgBox->SetText(
          "Invalid argument for the log(x) function");
      }
      break;
    case 6: // the exponential function
      if (x < 230)
        z = exp(x);
      else {
        InError = TRUE;
        ErrMsgBox->SetText(
          "Invalid argument for the exp(x) function");
      }
      break;
    case 7: // the square root function
      if (x >= 0)
        z = sqrt(x);
      else {
        InError = TRUE;
        ErrMsgBox->SetText(
          "Invalid argument for the sqrt(x) function");
      }
      break;
    default:
      InError = TRUE;
      ErrMsgBox->SetText("Invalid operator");
      break;
  }

  // display the result if no error has occurred
  if (!InError) {
    sprintf(s, "%g", z);
    ResultCmb->SetText(s);
```

```
    updateComboBox(ResultCmb);
    // enable the Store button
    EnableButton(StoreBtn);
  }
  else
    // disable the Store button
    DisableButton(StoreBtn);

  // update the operand combo boxes
  updateComboBox(Operand1Cmb);
  updateComboBox(Operand2Cmb);
}

void TMainWindow::CMCalcBtn()
{
  HandleCalcBtn();
}

void TMainWindow::HandleStoreBtn()
{
  char varName[MaxEditLen+1];
  char result[MaxEditLen+1];

  // get the string in the edit box of the Result combo box
  ResultCmb->GetText(result, MaxEditLen);

  // store the result in the selected text of
  // the Variable list box
  putVar(atof(result));
}

void TMainWindow::CMStoreBtn()
{
  HandleStoreBtn();
}

void TMainWindow::HandleExitBtn()
{
  Parent->SendMessage(WM_CLOSE);
}

void TMainWindow::CMExitBtn()
{
  Parent->SendMessage(WM_CLOSE);
}

void TMainWindow::EvDblClkVariableLst()
{
  char s[MaxEditLen+1];
  char operandText[MaxEditLen];
```

continues

LISTING 4.20. CONTINUED

```
  VariableLst->GetSelString(s, MaxEditLen);
  strcpy(s, (s+3));
  // get the text in the Operand1 combo box
  Operand1Cmb->GetText(operandText, MaxEditLen);
  // is the first character in the Operand1 combo box a #?
  if (operandText[0] == '@')
  Operand1Cmb->SetText(s);
  // get the text in the Operand2 edit box
  Operand2Cmb->GetText(operandText, MaxEditLen);
  // is the first character in the Operand2 combo box a #?
  if (operandText[0] == '@')
    Operand2Cmb->SetText(s);
}

BOOL TMainWindow::CanClose()
{
  return MessageBox("Want to close this application",
                    "Query", MB_YESNO | MB_ICONQUESTION) == IDYES;
}

double TMainWindow::getVar(int lineNum)
{
  char s[MaxEditLen+1];

  if (lineNum >= VariableLst->GetCount()) return 0;
  VariableLst->GetString(s, lineNum);
  strcpy(s, (s+3));
  // return the number stored in the target line
  return atof(s);
}

void TMainWindow::putVar(double x)
{
  char s[MaxEditLen+1];
  char c;
  int selectIndex = VariableLst->GetSelIndex();

  VariableLst->DeleteString(selectIndex);
  strcpy(s, "A:");
  c = selectIndex + 'A';
  // locate the character position of the cursor
  sprintf(s, "%c: %g", c, x);
  // insert it
  VariableLst->InsertString(s, selectIndex);
  VariableLst->SetSelIndex(selectIndex);
}
```

```
void TMainWindow::updateComboBox(TComboBox* pCombo)
{
  char s[MaxEditLen+1];
  int i;

  pCombo->GetText(s, MaxEditLen);
  // is string s in the combo list
  i = pCombo->FindExactString(s, -1);
  if (i == 0) return;
  else if (i < 0) {
    pCombo->InsertString(s, 0);
    // delete extra history list members?
    while (pCombo->GetCount() >= MaxHistory)
      pCombo->DeleteString(pCombo->GetCount()-1);
  }
  else {
    // delete the current selection
    pCombo->DeleteString(i);
    // insert the string s at the first position
    pCombo->InsertString(s, 0);
    // select the first combo box item
    pCombo->SetSelIndex(0);
  }
}

void TWinApp::InitMainWindow()
{
  MainWindow = new TFrameWindow(0,
      "Command-Oriented Calculator Application (COCA) Version 3",
      new TMainWindow);
  // load the keystroke resources
  MainWindow->Attr.AccelTable = IDR_BUTTONS;
  // load the menu resource
  MainWindow->AssignMenu(TResID(IDM_EXITMENU));
  // enable the keyboard handler
  MainWindow->EnableKBHandler();
}

int OwlMain(int /* argc */, char** /*argv[] */)
{
  TWinApp app;
  return app.Run();
}
```

The program in Listing 4.20 declares three sets of constants. The first set specifies the dimensions and spacing for the various application controls. The second set of constants declares the maximum string size and maximum number of selections. The third set of constants establishes the ID numbers for the various controls.

The calculator program declares an application class and a window class. The TMainWindow class declares two sets of data members. The first set represents pointers to the various controls used in the application. The second set of members contains the InError data member that flags any computational errors.

The TMainWindow class declares a constructor and a collection of member functions to handle the various messages. The TMainWindow constructor performs the following tasks:

- Creates instances for the various controls. The Operand and Result combo boxes are created with the CBS_DROPDOWN style. These same combo boxes remove the CB_SORT style to enable them to work as history list boxes. The Operator combo box is created with the CBS_SIMPLE style and maintains the ordered items in the accompanying list box. The Variables list box is created using the default styles.

- Sets the InError data member to FALSE.

The SetupWindow member function initializes the window instance by performing the following tasks:

1. Disables the Store pushbutton control.

2. Builds the Variables list box.

3. Selects the first item in the Variables list box.

4. Adds the supported operators and math functions in the list box component of the Operator combo box.

The EvKillFocusOperatorCmb member function responds to the LBN_KILLFOCUS notification message sent by the Operator combo box. The function carries out the following tasks:

- Obtains the text from the edit box using the GetText function.

- Invokes the SetText function to search for a list box member that matches the retrieved string. If the SetText call finds a match, the matching item appears as selected text in the edit control area of the combo box.

The HandleCalcBtn member function responds to the notification message of the Calc button and performs the requested calculation. The function performs the subsequent tasks:

1. Obtains the string in the edit box of the Result combo box and converts it into a double type. The function stores the resulting floating point number in the local variable result.

2. Retrieves the string in the edit box of the Operand1 combo box.

3. Examines the operand string to determine if it is a single-letter variable name, the # character (which is substituted by the value in the result variable), or the image of a number. The function performs the necessary conversion and stores the numeric value for the first operand in the local variable x.

4. Retrieves the string in the edit box of the Operand2 combo box. This string is processed in a manner similar to that of the Operand1 combo box. The result, in this task, is stored in variable y.

5. Obtains the string in the edit control of the Operator combo box.

6. Clears the Error Message edit control and assigns FALSE to the InError data member.

7. Finds the position of the invoked operator or math function in the Operator combo box list. The function uses the TListBox::FindExtactString member function for this task.

8. Uses a switch statement to determine the requested operation or math function evaluation. Notice that this is the first time a version of the COCA program uses the switch statement. This decision-making statement should execute faster than the cascaded if statements (that use the strcmp function) found in the earlier versions. The switch statement either performs the requested task and assigns the result to variable z or else flags an error.

9. If no error occurs, the function displays the result of the operation or function evaluation in the edit control box of the Result combo box. In addition, the function inserts the new result in the list box of the Result combo box by calling the updateComboBox member function. The function also enables the Store button control if there is no error, and it disables the button if an error does occur.

10. Inserts the new operands in the list boxes of their respective combo boxes. The function calls the updateComboBox member function twice to update both operand combo boxes. Notice that this update occurs regardless of the error condition. Moreover, if you ask to evaluate a

math function, the list box of the Operand2 combo box remains unchanged, unless you enter a new and superfluous operand in that combo box.

The CMCalcBtn responds to the command message emitted by the Alt+C accelerator key. The function merely calls the HandleCalcBtn member function to provide the needed response.

The HandleStoreBtn member function responds to the notification message sent by the Store pushbutton. The function stores the number found in the edit box of the Result combo box in the currently selected Variables list box item. The function performs the following tasks:

- Retrieves the string in the edit box of the Result combo box using the TComboBox::GetText member function. The obtained string is copied to the result local variable.

- Stores the obtained string in the Variables list box by calling the putVar member function with an argument of atof(result).

The CMStoreBtn member function responds to the command message generated by the accelerator key Alt+S. The function simply calls the HandleStoreBtn member function to provide the required response.

The HandleExitBtn and CMExitBtn member functions offer the same response to the messages sent by the Exit button and the Alt+E accelerator key. Both functions send the WM_CLOSE message to the parent window.

The EvDblClkVariablesLst member function responds to the LBN_DBLCLK notification messages sent by the Variables list box when you double-click a list item. The purpose of double-clicking is to replace the @ character in either Operand edit box with the number in the double-clicked item. The function carries out the following tasks:

- Verifies if the notification message is LBN_DBLCLK by comparing that value with the Msg.LP.HI data member. If the two values match, the function performs these remaining tasks:

- Copies the characters of the new selection (chosen by the double-click action) to the local string variable s. The function calls the GetSelString function for this task.

- Deletes the first three characters of variable s.

- Retrieves a copy of the text in the edit control of the Operand1 combo box and stores it in the local variable operandText.

- If the first character in the string operandText is the @ character, the function sets the edit control of the Operand1 combo box to the string variable s.

- Repeats the last two tasks with the Operand2 combo box.

The protected getVar member function obtains the value from the Variables list box by specifying the item number. The function performs the following tasks:

- Returns a 0 value if the item position exceeds the position of the last item in the Variables list box. This task uses the GetCount function to return the number of items in the list box.

- Obtains the list item at the specified item position using the GetString function.

- Deletes the first three characters of the obtained list item.

- Returns the expression atof(s) that represented the double-typed number stored in the selected list box item.

The protected putVar member function stores the result in the selected Variable list item. The function carries out the following tasks:

- Obtains the index of the current selection by calling the GetSelIndex function. The function stores the retrieved index in the local variable selectIndex.

- Deletes the current selection by invoking the DeleteString function and supplying it the selectIndex argument.

- Creates the string image of the new list item using the sprintf function.

- Inserts the new list item at the selectIndex position. This particular manner of inserting an item in a sorted list box using InsertString does not corrupt the order of the item. Using InsertString in this fashion is the exception and not the rule.

- Selects the newly inserted item. The net effect is that the same item remains selected but now has a different value associated with it.

SUMMARY

This chapter presented the scroll bar, list box, and combo box controls. These controls share the common factor of being input objects. The chapter covered the following topics:

- The scroll bar control, which enables you to select quickly from a wide range of integers.

- The list box control, which provides you with a list of items from which to select.

- Creating synchronized scrolling list boxes. You learned that, at most, one of these lists can be sorted. You also learned that you can use the scroll bar control easily to scroll these lists.

- The multiple-selection list box enables you to select multiple items in a list box for collective processing.

- The combo box control and its various types: simple, drop-down, and drop-down list combo boxes. In addition, you learned about making a history list box from a drop-down combo box.

The list and combo boxes are versatile input devices that benefit from a well-developed functionality supported by ObjectWindows. Consequently, you can do much with these controls. How much you do is a matter of pushing your imagination to the limit.

5

CHAPTER

DIALOG BOXES

Dialog boxes are special child windows that contain controls serving to display information or to input data. Windows applications employ dialog boxes to exchange information with the user. This chapter looks at the modal and modeless dialog boxes supported by Windows. *Modal* dialog boxes require that you close them before you proceed any further with the application, because they are meant to perform a critical exchange of data. In fact, modal dialog boxes disable their parent windows while they have the focus. *Modeless* dialog boxes, on the other hand, need not be closed for the user to continue with the application. In this chapter, you will learn about the following topics:

- Constructing instances of the TDialog class

- Executing a modal dialog box

- Creating a modeless dialog box

- Creating a dialog box as a window

- Basics of transferring control data

- Examples of transferring data for dialog boxes

CONSTRUCTING DIALOG BOXES

The TDialog class has the following constructor:

```
TDialog(TWindow* parent, TResID resID, TModule* module = 0);
```

The parent parameter is the pointer to the parent window. If the dialog box instance is created by the application class, the argument for the parent is 0. The resID parameter specifies the name or ID of the resource that defines the dialog box.

EXECUTING MODAL DIALOG BOXES

Dialog boxes are created and destroyed much more frequently than windows. When a modal dialog box is created, it is immediately activated. We say that the dialog box is *executed*. This process pops up a dialog box that remains active until you click special exit buttons. Typically, these buttons are labeled OK and Cancel, and they send the special IDOK and IDCANCEL notification messages. Clicking the OK button is interpreted as confirming the data in the dialog box controls. Clicking the Cancel button is interpreted as rejecting the control's values and any changes made in these values since the time the dialog box was last executed. You can use alternate captions for the OK and Cancel buttons, but you must retain the same notification messages. Executing a dialog box involves using the TDialog::Execute member function. The general form for executing a modal dialog box is as follows:

```
TMyDialog* pDlg1 = new TMyDialog(this, "AppDialog");
if (pDlg1->Execute() == IDOK) {
    // statements to handle positive response
}


if ((new TMyDialog(this, TResID(ID_DIALOG_BOX))->Execute()
                                   == IDOK) {
    // statements to handle positive response
}
```

The Execute member function returns an integer value that indicates whether you exited the dialog box by pressing the OK button or the Cancel button. If you click the OK button (or an equivalent button that has the predefined IDOK resource ID), the Execute member function returns IDOK. By contrast, if you click the Cancel button (or an equivalent button that has the predefined IDCANCEL resource ID), the Execute function returns IDCANCEL. Normally, you compare the value returned by the Execute function with IDOK (or IDCANCEL, whichever is more convenient for your application) to determine the steps, if any, to take based on your input. Because the ObjectWindows applications delete the dialog box instances after they are closed, dialog boxes must be dynamically created (in the heap). You must avoid using TDialog-type variables to create stack-based instances.

Dialog boxes can certainly contain additional buttons either to manipulate the other controls or to send information to other dialog boxes or the parent window.

Consider a simple ObjectWindows program that uses a dialog box defined in resource files. I'll take the opportunity of using resource files to create alternate forms of the same dialog box—the first uses Modern English, whereas the second uses Old English. The application is simple and is made up of an empty window with a single menu item, Exit. When you click the Exit menu item (or press the Alt+X keys), you get a dialog box that asks you whether you want to exit the application. The dialog box has a title, message, and the two buttons (in fact, I purposely made this dialog box resemble the dialog boxes spawned by the MessageBox function). The program alternates between the two versions of the dialog box. When you first click the Exit menu, you get the Modern English version (with OK and Cancel buttons), shown in Figure 5.1. If you click the Cancel button and then click the Exit menu again, you get the Old English version of the dialog box (with Yea and Nay buttons), shown in Figure 5.2. Every time you select the Cancel or Nay button and then click the Exit menu, you toggle between the two versions of the dialog box. To exit the application, click the OK or Yea button, depending on the current dialog box version.

Listing 5.1 shows the contents of the DIALOG1.DEF definition file. Listing 5.2 contains the source code of the DIALOG1.H header file. Listing 5.3 shows the script for the DIALOG1.RC resource file. Listing 5.4 contains the source code for the DIALOG1.CPP program file.

LISTING 5.1. THE CONTENTS OF THE DIALOG1.DEF DEFINITION FILE.

```
NAME         Dialog1
DESCRIPTION  'An OWL Windows Application'
EXETYPE      WINDOWS
CODE         PRELOAD MOVEABLE DISCARDABLE
DATA         PRELOAD MOVEABLE MULTIPLE
HEAPSIZE     1024
STACKSIZE    8384
```

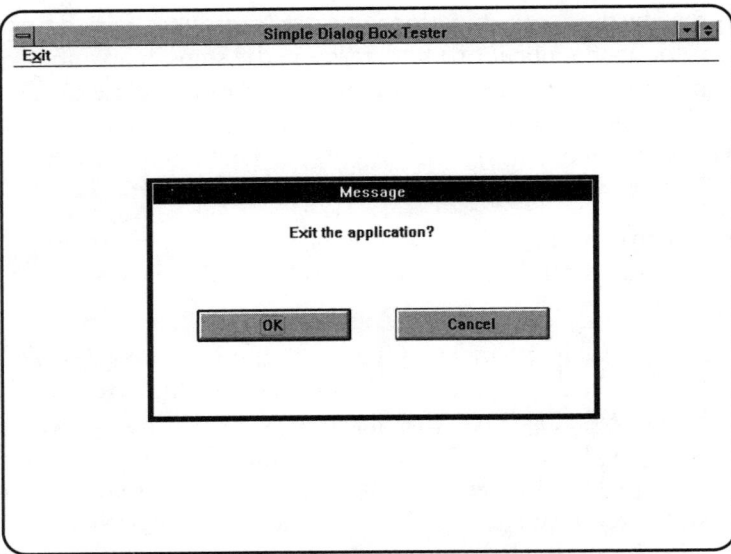

Figure 5.1. A sample session with the DIALOG1.EXE application showing the dialog box with its Modern English wording.

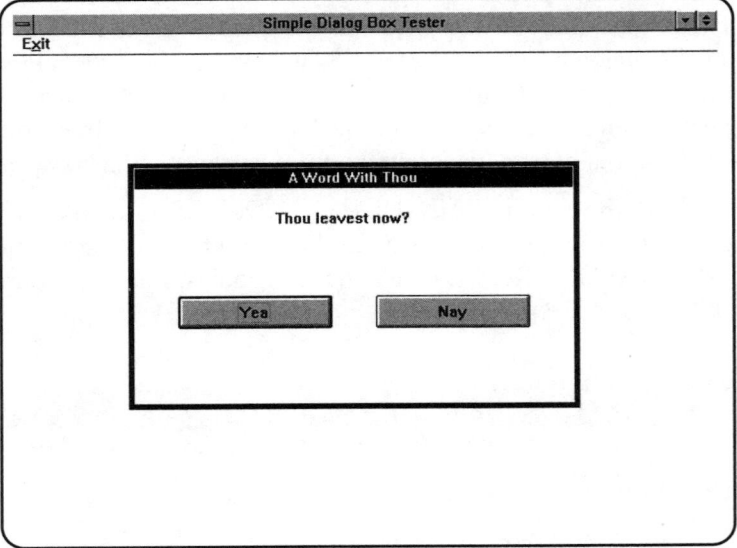

Figure 5.2. A sample session with the DIALOG1.EXE application showing the dialog box with its Old English wording.

LISTING 5.2. THE SOURCE CODE OF THE DIALOG1.H HEADER FILE.

```
#define IDM_EXITMENU    400
#define IDD_OLD         401
#define IDD_NEW         402
```

LISTING 5.3. THE SCRIPT FOR THE DIALOG1.RC RESOURCE FILE.

```
#include <windows.h>
#include <owl\window.rh>
#include "dialog1.h"

IDM_EXITMENU MENU LOADONCALL MOVEABLE PURE DISCARDABLE
BEGIN
    MENUITEM "E&xit", CM_EXIT
END

IDD_NEW DIALOG DISCARDABLE LOADONCALL PURE MOVEABLE 30, 50, 200, 100
STYLE WS_POPUP ¦ DS_MODALFRAME
CAPTION "Message"
BEGIN
  CTEXT "Exit the application?", 1, 10, 10, 170, 15
  CONTROL "OK", IDOK, "BUTTON", WS_CHILD ¦ WS_VISIBLE ¦
    WS_TABSTOP ¦ BS_DEFPUSHBUTTON, 20, 50, 70, 15
  CONTROL "Cancel", IDCANCEL, "BUTTON", WS_CHILD ¦ WS_VISIBLE ¦
    WS_TABSTOP ¦ BS_PUSHBUTTON, 110, 50, 70, 15
END

IDD_OLD DIALOG DISCARDABLE LOADONCALL PURE MOVEABLE 30, 50, 200, 100
STYLE WS_POPUP ¦ DS_MODALFRAME
CAPTION "A Word With Thou"
BEGIN
  CTEXT "Thou leavest now?", 1, 10, 10, 170, 15
  CONTROL "Yea", IDOK, "BUTTON", WS_CHILD ¦ WS_VISIBLE ¦
    WS_TABSTOP ¦ BS_DEFPUSHBUTTON, 20, 50, 70, 15
  CONTROL "Nay", IDCANCEL, "BUTTON", WS_CHILD ¦ WS_VISIBLE ¦
    WS_TABSTOP ¦ BS_PUSHBUTTON, 110, 50, 70, 15
END
```

LISTING 5.4. THE SOURCE CODE FOR THE DIALOG1.CPP PROGRAM FILE.

```
/*
  Program which tests simple modal dialog boxes
*/

#include <owl\applicat.h>
#include <owl\framewin.h>
#include <owl\dialog.h>
#include "dialog1.h"

// declare the custom application class as
// a subclass of TApplication
class TWinApp : public TApplication
{
public:
  TWinApp() : TApplication() {}

protected:
  virtual void InitMainWindow();
};

// expand the functionality of TWindow by deriving class TMainWindow
class TMainWindow : public TWindow
{
public:
  TMainWindow()
    : TWindow(0, 0, 0) {}

protected:

  // Handle closing the window
  virtual BOOL CanClose();

};

BOOL TMainWindow::CanClose()
{
  static BOOL flag = FALSE;
  TDialog* pDlg;

  // toggle flag that selects alternate dialog box resources
  flag = (flag == TRUE) ? FALSE : TRUE;
  if (flag) {
    // use modern English dialog box
    pDlg = new TDialog(this, TResID(IDD_NEW));
    return (pDlg->Execute() == IDOK)
        ? TRUE : FALSE;
  }
  else {
```

```
    // use old English dialog box
    pDlg = new TDialog(this, TResID(IDD_OLD));
    return (pDlg->Execute() == IDOK)
         ? TRUE : FALSE;
  }
}

void TWinApp::InitMainWindow()
{
  MainWindow = new TFrameWindow(0, "Simple Dialog Box Tester",
                                new TMainWindow);
  // load the menu resource
  MainWindow->AssignMenu(TResID(IDM_EXITMENU));
}

int OwlMain(int /* argc */, char** /*argv[] */)
{
  TWinApp app;
  return app.Run();
}
```

Consider now the code behind the application. Listing 5.3 shows the script for the DIALOG1.RC resource file, which defines the following resources:

- The menu resource, named EXITMENU. This resource displays a single menu, with the single item Exit.

- The dialog box resource with the IDD_NEW ID with a defined style, caption, and list of child controls. The specified style indicates that the dialog box is a modal pop-up child window. The caption specified is the Message string. The dialog box contains three controls: a centered static text (for the dialog box message), a default OK pushbutton, and an ordinary Cancel button. The OK button has the resource ID of the predefined IDOK constant. The Cancel button has the resource ID of the predefined IDCANCEL constant.

- The dialog box resource with the IDD_OLD ID that is similar to IDD_NEW resource dialog box, except it uses Old English wording. The Yea button has the resource ID of the predefined IDOK constant. The Nay button has the resource ID of the predefined IDCANCEL constant. These buttons are examples of exit buttons with atypical captions.

Listing 5.4 shows the source code for the DIALOG1.CPP program file. The source code declares three classes: an application class, a window class, and a dialog box class. The latter is actually optional for this program, because it does not add any new functionality to the parent TDialog class.

The most relevant member function is `TMainWindow::CanClose`, which responds to the `WM_CLOSE` command message sent by the Exit menu item. The function uses a Boolean static local variable, `flag`, to toggle between the two dialog box resources `IDD_NEW` and `IDD_OLD`. The Modern English dialog box is invoked in the following statements:

```
// use modern English dialog box
pDlg = new TDialog(this, TResID(IDD_NEW));
return (pDlg->Execute() == IDOK)
    ? TRUE : FALSE;
```

The `CanClose` function sends the `Execute` message to the dialog box object and compares the result of that message with the constant `IDOK`. The outcome of this comparison returns either `TRUE` or `FALSE`.

The instance of the Old English version of the dialog box is similarly created, as shown in the following statement:

```
// use old English dialog box
pDlg = new TDialog(this, TResID(IDD_OLD));
return (pDlg->Execute() == IDOK)
    ? TRUE : FALSE;
```

What about closing the dialog boxes? Who handles that operation? The answer lies with the `TDialog` class itself. When you click the OK (or Yea) button, that button sends the `IDOK` notification message. The `TDialog::CmOk` member function handles closing the window and returning the `IDOK` result for the `Execute` function. By contrast, when you click the CANCEL (or Nay) button, that control emits the `IDCANCEL` notification message. The member function `TDialog::CmCancel` intercepts this notification message and closes the dialog box, causing the `Execute` function to return `IDCANCEL`.

How do the `CmOk` and `CmCancel` member functions in the `TDialog` class work? Their operations can be explained with the help of Listing 5.5, which contains the source code for these functions and the ones that they, in turn, call. These member functions are found in the DIALOG1.CPP file in the SOURCE directory.

The `CmOk` function calls the `TDialog::CloseWindow` member function to close conditionally the dialog box and return an `IDOK` result. The `CmCancel` function invokes the `TDialog::ShutDownWindow` member function to unconditionally close the dialog box. Listing 5.5 also includes the `TDialog::EvClose` member function that responds to the `WM_CLOSE` messages. This function also calls the `ShutDownWindow` member function.

The CloseWindow member function with the int-type parameter first examines whether the dialog box instance is modal or modeless. If the dialog box is modal, the function calls the CanClose function. If the CanClose function returns TRUE, the CloseWindow function transfers the dialog box data (more about this later in this chapter) and calls the ShutDownWindow(int) member function to safely shut down the dialog box. If the dialog box is modeless, the CloseWindow function calls the TWindows::CloseWindow() member function.

The ShutDownWindow(int) member function unconditionally shuts down a dialog box. For a modal dialog box, the function calls the TDialog::Destroy member function and passes its argument to the Destroy function. In the case of a modeless dialog box, the function calls the TWindows::ShutDownWindow() member function.

I presented the preceding member functions to give you a clear idea of how they work and also to show you that these functions do not have extensive code. You can modify the CloseWindow and ShutDownWindow member functions in descendants of the TDialog class to alter the sequence of tasks involved in closing a dialog box.

LISTING 5.5. THE SOURCE CODE FOR THE CMOK, CMCANCEL, EVCLOSE, CLOSEWINDOW, AND SHUTDOWN MEMBER FUNCTIONS OF THE TDIALOG CLASS.

```
//
// responds to an incoming notification message from a button with
// an Id equal to IDOK
//
void
TDialog::CmOk()
{
  CloseWindow(IDOK);
}


//
// conditionally shuts down the dialog box
//
// if this is a modal dialog calls CanClose() and, if CanClose() returns
// TRUE, transfers its data and shuts down, passing retValue(default
// IDCANCEL)
//
// calls TWindow::CloseWindow(retValue) if this is a modeless dialog
//
void
TDialog::CloseWindow(int retValue)
{
```

continues

Listing 5.5. continued

```
  if (IsModal) {
    if (CanClose()) {
      TransferData(tdGetData);
      ShutDownWindow(retValue);
    }

  } else {
    TWindow::CloseWindow(retValue);
  }
}

//
// unconditionally shuts down a dialog box, returning retValue if this
// is a modal dialog
//
void
TDialog::ShutDownWindow(int retValue)
{
  if (IsModal)
    //
    // Note: we can't delete a modal dialog here because we're still in
    // its Execute function
    //
    Destroy(retValue);

  else
    TWindow::ShutDownWindow(retValue);
}
```

Creating Modeless Dialog Boxes

Modeless dialog boxes are less authoritative than modal dialog boxes. You can shift the focus back to the parent window without having to close a modeless dialog box. Modeless dialog boxes are *created* and not executed. Use the Create member function to safely create a modeless dialog box. The general form for creating a modeless dialog box is as follows:

```
TMyDialog* pDlg1 = new TMyDialog(this, "AppDialog")
pDlg1->Create();
pDlg1->ShowWindow(SW_SHOW);

TMyDialog* pDlg2 = new TMyDialog(this, TResID(IDD_DIALOG))
pDlg2->Create();
pDlg2->ShowWindow(SW_SHOW);
```

The preceding general form shows that the Create function must be followed by a call to the ShowWindow function to make the modeless dialog box visible. Modeless dialog boxes do not return a value. To close a modeless dialog box, invoke the TDialog::ShutDownWindow() member function.

DIALOG BOXES AS WINDOWS

A dialog box does not always have to be a child window. In fact, if the nature of your application requires the use of multiple controls and has little use for a typical parent window, you can create a dialog box instance as a direct child of the application class instance. This approach rightfully bypasses the classic parent window, when that window has nothing really to offer to the application. A good example is the category of calculator applications. A calculator is typically heavily populated with controls. Because using dialog boxes is more suitable, calculator applications are often implemented as dialog boxes. Unless you are collecting the results from the various calculator instances in a parent window (or doing some other meaningful management task), there is really no need to have a parent window. Therefore, it is more suitable to use a dialog box as the application window. In the previous chapters, I presented several versions of the Command-Oriented Calculator Application (COCA) that had its controls attached to a window. In this section, I present a calculator version that uses a dialog box. This version is derived from COCA version 1. The two versions offer identical operations. Figure 5.3 shows a sample session with the DIALOG2.EXE program.

Listing 5.6 shows the contents of the DIALOG2.DEF definition file. Listing 5.7 shows the header file DIALOG2.H. Listing 5.8 shows the script for the resource file DIALOG2.RC. The resource file defines the accelerator keys resources and the basic modeless dialog box resource. Listing 5.9 contains the source code for the DIALOG2.CPP program.

LISTING 5.6. THE CONTENTS OF THE DIALOG2.DEF DEFINITION FILE.

```
NAME         Dialog2
DESCRIPTION  'An OWL Windows Application'
EXETYPE      WINDOWS
CODE         PRELOAD MOVEABLE DISCARDABLE
DATA         PRELOAD MOVEABLE MULTIPLE
HEAPSIZE     1024
STACKSIZE    8384
```

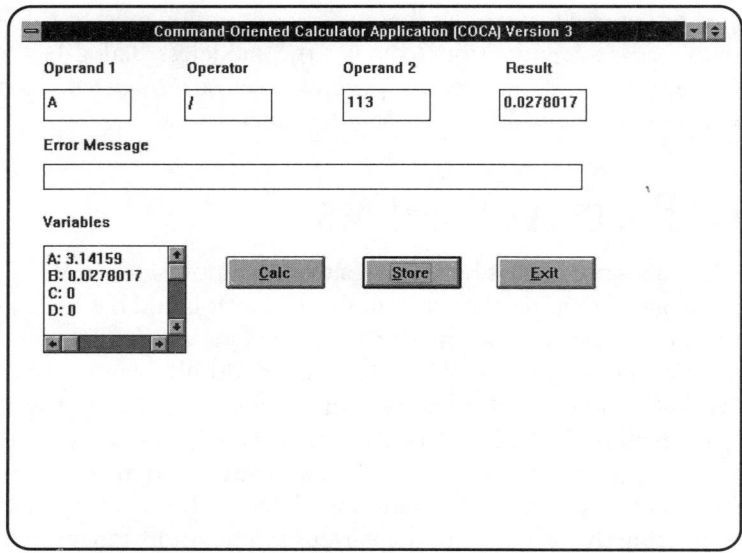

Figure 5.3. A sample session with the DIALOG2.EXE application.

LISTING 5.7. THE SOURCE CODE FOR THE DIALOG2.H HEADER FILE.

```
#define ID_OPERAND1_TXT    100
#define ID_OPERATOR_TXT     101
#define ID_OPERAND2_TXT    102
#define ID_ERRMSG_TXT      103
#define ID_RESULT_TXT      104
#define ID_VARIABLE_TXT    105
#define ID_VARIABLE_BOX    200
#define ID_OPERAND1_BOX    201
#define ID_OPERATOR_BOX    202
#define ID_OPERAND2_BOX    203
#define ID_RESULT_BOX      204
#define ID_ERRMSG_BOX      205
#define ID_CALC_BTN    300
#define ID_STORE_BTN       301
#define IDD_CALCDLG    400
```

LISTING 5.8. THE SCRIPT FOR THE DIALOG2.RC RESOURCE FILE.

```
#include <windows.h>
#include <owl\window.rh>
#include "dialog2.h"


IDD_CALCDLG DIALOG 20, 20, 290, 175
STYLE WS_CHILD | WS_VISIBLE
BEGIN
  LTEXT "Operand 1", ID_OPERAND1_TXT, 10, 8, 49, 8
  LTEXT "Operator", ID_OPERATOR_TXT, 75, 8, 49, 8
  LTEXT "Operand 2", ID_OPERAND2_TXT, 146, 8, 49, 8
  LTEXT "Result", ID_RESULT_TXT, 220, 8, 49, 8
  EDITTEXT ID_OPERAND1_BOX, 10, 22, 40, 15
  EDITTEXT ID_OPERATOR_BOX, 74, 22, 40, 15
  EDITTEXT ID_OPERAND2_BOX, 146, 22, 40, 15
  EDITTEXT ID_RESULT_BOX, 217, 22, 40, 15
  LTEXT "Error Message", ID_ERRMSG_TXT, 10, 44, 60, 8
  EDITTEXT ID_ERRMSG_BOX, 10, 57, 245, 12
  LTEXT "Variables", ID_VARIABLE_TXT, 10, 80, 42, 8
  CONTROL "", ID_VARIABLE_BOX, "EDIT", ES_LEFT | ES_MULTILINE |
      ES_UPPERCASE | WS_CHILD | WS_VISIBLE | WS_BORDER |
      WS_HSCROLL | ES_AUTOHSCROLL | ES_AUTOVSCROLL |
      WS_VSCROLL | WS_TABSTOP, 10, 95, 65, 50
  PUSHBUTTON "&Calc", ID_CALC_BTN, 93, 100, 45, 15
  PUSHBUTTON "&Store", ID_STORE_BTN, 155, 100, 45, 15
  PUSHBUTTON "&Exit", IDOK, 216, 100, 45, 15
END
```

LISTING 5.9. THE SOURCE CODE FOR THE DIALOG2.CPP PROGRAM FILE.

```
/*
  Program demonstrates using a modal dialog box as a main window
*/
#include <owl\applicat.h>
#include <owl\framewin.h>
#include <owl\static.h>
#include <owl\edit.h>
#include <owl\button.h>
#include <owl\dialog.h>
#include "dialog2.h"
#include <stdlib.h>
#include <ctype.h>
#include <stdio.h>
#include <math.h>
#include <string.h>
```

continues

Listing 5.9. continued

```cpp
const UINT MaxEditLen = 30;
const int MAX_MEMREG = 26;

// declare the custom application class as
// a subclass of TApplication
class TWinApp : public TApplication
{
public:
  TWinApp() : TApplication() {}

protected:
  virtual void InitMainWindow();
};

// expand the functionality of TDialog by deriving class TMainWindow
class TMainWindow : public TDialog
{
public:

  TMainWindow(TWindow* parent, TResID resID);

protected:

  TStatic* Operand1Txt;
  TStatic* OperatorTxt;
  TStatic* Operand2Txt;
  TStatic* ResultTxt;
  TStatic* ErrMsgTxt;
  TStatic* VariableTxt;
  TEdit* Operand1Box;
  TEdit* OperatorBox;
  TEdit* Operand2Box;
  TEdit* ResultBox;
  TEdit* ErrMsgBox;
  TEdit* VariableBox;
  TButton* CalcBtn;
  TButton* StoreBtn;
  TButton* ExitBtn;

  // math error flag
  BOOL InError;

  virtual void SetupWindow();

  // handle the calculation
  void HandleCalcBtn();

  // handle storing the result in a variable
  void HandleStoreBtn();
```

```
  // handle exiting the application
  void CmOk();

  // enable a push button control
  void EnableButton(TButton* pBtn)
    { pBtn->EnableWindow(TRUE); }

  // disable a push button control
  void DisableButton(TButton* pBtn)
    { pBtn->EnableWindow(FALSE); }

  // obtain a number of a Variable edit box line
  double getVar(int lineNum);

  // store a number in the selected text of
  // the Variable edit box line
  void putVar(double x);

  // declare the message map macro
  DECLARE_RESPONSE_TABLE(TMainWindow);
};

DEFINE_RESPONSE_TABLE1(TMainWindow, TDialog)
  EV_WM_MOUSEMOVE,
  EV_COMMAND(ID_CALC_BTN, HandleCalcBtn),
  EV_COMMAND(ID_STORE_BTN, HandleStoreBtn),
  EV_COMMAND(IDOK, CmOk),
END_RESPONSE_TABLE;

TMainWindow::TMainWindow(TWindow* parent, TResID resID) :
    TWindow(parent),
    TDialog(parent, resID)
{
  Operand1Txt = new TStatic(this, ID_OPERAND1_TXT, MaxEditLen);
  OperatorTxt = new TStatic(this, ID_OPERATOR_TXT, MaxEditLen);
  Operand2Txt = new TStatic(this, ID_OPERAND2_TXT, MaxEditLen);
  ResultTxt = new TStatic(this, ID_RESULT_TXT, MaxEditLen);
  ErrMsgTxt = new TStatic(this, ID_ERRMSG_TXT, MaxEditLen);
  VariableTxt = new TStatic(this, ID_VARIABLE_TXT, MaxEditLen);
  Operand1Box = new TEdit(this, ID_OPERAND1_BOX, MaxEditLen);
  OperatorBox = new TEdit(this, ID_OPERATOR_BOX, MaxEditLen);
  Operand2Box = new TEdit(this, ID_OPERAND2_BOX, MaxEditLen);
  ResultBox = new TEdit(this, ID_RESULT_BOX, MaxEditLen);
  ErrMsgBox = new TEdit(this, ID_ERRMSG_BOX, MaxEditLen);
  VariableBox = new TEdit(this, ID_VARIABLE_BOX, 1024);
  CalcBtn = new TButton(this, ID_CALC_BTN);
  StoreBtn = new TButton(this, ID_STORE_BTN);
  ExitBtn = new TButton(this, IDOK);
}
```

continues

LISTING 5.9. CONTINUED

```cpp
void TMainWindow::SetupWindow()
{
  char s[81];
  char bigStr[6 * MAX_MEMREG + 1];
  char c;

  TDialog::SetupWindow();
  // build the initial contents of the Variable edit box
  bigStr[0] = '\0';
  for (c = 'A'; c <= 'Z'; c++) {
    sprintf(s, "%c: 0\r\n", c);
    strcat(bigStr, s);
  }
  VariableBox->SetText(bigStr);

  // clear the InError flag
  InError = FALSE;
}

void TMainWindow::HandleCalcBtn()
{
  double x, y, z;
  char opStr[MaxEditLen+1];
  char s[MaxEditLen+1];

  // obtain the string in the Operand1 edit box
  Operand1Box->GetText(s, MaxEditLen);
  strupr(s);
  // does the Operand1Box contain the name
  // of a single-letter variable?
  if (isalpha(s[0]))
    // obtain value from the Variable edit control
    x = getVar(s[0] - 'A');
  else
    // convert the string in the edit box
    x = atof(s);

  // obtain the string in the Operand2 edit box
  Operand2Box->GetText(s, MaxEditLen);
  strupr(s);
  // does the Operand2Box contain the name
  // of a single-letter variable?
  if (isalpha(s[0]))
    // obtain value from the Variable edit control
    y =getVar(s[0] - 'A');
  else
    // convert the string in the edit box
    y = atof(s);
```

```
// obtain the string in the Operator edit box
OperatorBox->GetText(opStr, MaxEditLen);

// clear the error message box
ErrMsgBox->Clear();
InError = FALSE;

// determine the requested operation
if (strcmp(opStr, "+") == 0)
  z = x + y;
else if (strcmp(opStr, "-") == 0)
  z = x - y;
else if (strcmp(opStr, "*") == 0)
  z = x * y;
else if (strcmp(opStr, "/") == 0) {
  if (y != 0)
    z = x / y;
  else {
    z = 0;
    InError = TRUE;
    ErrMsgBox->SetText("Division-by-zero error");
  }
}
else if (strcmp(opStr, "^") == 0) {
  if (x > 0)
    z = exp(y * log(x));
  else {
    InError = TRUE;
    ErrMsgBox->SetText(
      "Cannot raise the power of a negative number");
  }
}
else {
  InError = TRUE;
  ErrMsgBox->SetText("Invalid operator");
}
// display the result if no error has occurred
if (!InError) {
  sprintf(s, "%g", z);
  ResultBox->SetText(s);
  // enable the Store button
  EnableButton(StoreBtn);
}
else
  // disable the Store button
  DisableButton(StoreBtn);
}

void TMainWindow::HandleStoreBtn()
{
```

continues

LISTING 5.9. CONTINUED

```
  char varName[MaxEditLen+1];
  char result[MaxEditLen+1];

  // get the string in the Result edit box
  ResultBox->GetText(result, MaxEditLen);

  // store the result in the selected text of
  // the Variable edit box
  putVar(atof(result));
}

void TMainWindow::CmOk()
{
  Parent->SendMessage(WM_CLOSE);
}

double TMainWindow::getVar(int lineNum)
{
  int lineSize;
  char s[MaxEditLen+1];

  if (lineNum >= MAX_MEMREG) return 0;
  // get the size of the target line
  lineSize = VariableBox->GetLineLength(lineNum);
  // get the line
  VariableBox->GetLine(s, lineSize+1, lineNum);
  // delete the first three characters
  strcpy(s, (s+3));
  // return the number stored in the target line
  return atof(s);
}

void TMainWindow::putVar(double x)
{
  UINT startPos, endPos;
  int lineNum;
  int lineSize;
  char s[MaxEditLen+1];

  // locate the character position of the cursor
  VariableBox->GetSelection(startPos, endPos);
  // turn off the selected text
  if (startPos != endPos)
    VariableBox->SetSelection(startPos, startPos);
  // get the line number where the cursor is located
  lineNum = VariableBox->GetLineFromPos(startPos);
  // get the line size of line lineNum
  lineSize = VariableBox->GetLineLength(lineNum);
```

```
  // obtain the text of line lineNum
  VariableBox->GetLine(s, lineSize+1, lineNum);
  // delete line lineNum
  VariableBox->DeleteLine(lineNum);
  // build the new text line
  sprintf(s, "%c: %g\r\n", s[0], x);
  // insert it
  VariableBox->Insert(s);
}

void TWinApp::InitMainWindow()
{
  MainWindow = new TFrameWindow(0,
      "Command-Oriented Calculator Application (COCA) Version 3",
      new TMainWindow(0, TResID(IDD_CALCDLG)), TRUE);
}


int OwlMain(int /* argc */, char** /*argv[] */)
{
  TWinApp app;
  return app.Run();
}
```

The DIALOG2.H header file declares the constants for the various controls in the dialog box and for the different resources. The DIALOG2.RC resource file declares the IDD_CALCDLG resource. Notice that the style of the dialog box resource has WS_CHILD and WS_VISIBLE and is deliberately void of the WS_POPUP, WS_CAPTION, WS_BORDER, and DS_MODALFRAME styles. These styles interfere with the way the dialog box is linked with its parent TFrameWindow-typed window.

This source code in Listing 5.9 is very similar to that of file CTLBTN1.CPP. Notice that the Listing 5.9 declares the TMainWindow class as a descendant of TDialog. The relevant member functions are as follows:

1. The constructor for the TMainWindow class creates the various controls using their respective resource-related constructors. These constructors require the pointers to the parent window and the ID of the controls. The constructors for the static text and edit controls also require the maximum length of the text of the controls. Notice that the constructor uses the IDOK control ID to create the Exit button, which is handled by the ExitBtn pointer. The dialog box has no Cancel button.

2. The SetupWindow member function initializes the multiline edit control that stores the variables. The application needs the SetupWindow function to perform this task because the task cannot be done in the resource file.

3. The CmOk member function closes the application by sending the Windows message WM_CLOSE to the parent window. This message takes care of closing the parent message and the dialog box itself. Notice that the function does not invoke the inherited member function TDialog::CmOk. This kind of invocation leads to a runtime error because it attempts to delete a dialog box that is already removed.

The other member functions are similar to those in file CTLBTN1.CPP, shown in Listing 3.4. The application class defines the InitMainWindow member function. Notice that this member function creates an instance of TFrameWindow and specifies the dialog box class TMainWindow as the client window.

BASICS OF TRANSFERRING CONTROL DATA

Dialog boxes serve mainly as pop-up windows to request input from the application user. This input often includes a variety of settings that use radio buttons, check boxes, and edit boxes. Because dialog boxes are frequently executed or created, it makes sense to preserve the latest values in the controls of the dialog box for the next time it appears. The Search and Replace dialog boxes that are found in the Borland C++ IDE and many other Windows editors are typical examples. These dialog boxes remember the settings of all or some of their controls from the last time the dialog boxes were executed.

The Transfer Buffer Type

To implement the previously-discussed feature in dialog boxes (and also in windows), Windows offers a data transfer mechanism between the dialog box and a buffer. This buffer is usually a data member of the parent window. Therefore, the first step in supporting data transfer is to define a transfer buffer type. The buffer defines data fields for the controls that you want to make transfer their data. These controls include the static text, edit box, list box, combo box, scroll bar, check box, and radio button. The group box and pushbutton controls have no data to transfer and therefore do not enter in the declaration of the data transfer buffer type. A sample data buffer type that includes a single instance of each allowable control is as follows:

```
struct TAppTransferBuffer {
    char StaticText[MaxSTaticLen];
    char EditBox[MaxEditLen];
    TListBoxData* ListBoxData;
    TComboBoxData* ComboBoxData;
```

```
    TScrollBarData ScrollBarData;
    UINT CheckBox;
    UINT RadioButton;
};
```

You should observe two simple rules regarding the type and sequence of declared data members:

- Include only members for the controls whose data is transferred.

- Declare the buffer type members in the same order that you create the controls in the dialog box constructor.

Look now at the various members of the data transfer buffer type:

- The staticText member helps in transferring data between a static text control and the data buffer. The data member defines a character array that must be equal to the number of characters in the static text control.

- The EditBox member assists in moving data between the edit box control and the data buffer. The data member defines a character array that must be equal to the number of characters in the edit box control.

- The ListBoxData member helps to transfer data between a list box control and the data buffer. The ListBoxData is a pointer to the TListBoxData class shown as follows:

```
class _OWLCLASS TListBoxData {
  public:
    TListBoxData();
    ~TListBoxData();

    TStringArray&   GetStrings() { return Strings; }
    TDwordArray&    GetItemDatas() { return ItemDatas; }
    TIntArray&      GetSelIndices() { return SelIndices; }

    void    AddString(const char* str, BOOL isSelected = FALSE);
    void    AddStringItem(const char* str, DWORD itemData,
                    BOOL isSelected = FALSE);
    void    Clear() { Strings.Flush();
                    ItemDatas.Flush();
                    ResetSelections(); }

    void    Select(int index);
    void    SelectString(const char far* str);
    int     GetSelCount() const
            { return SelIndices.GetItemsInContainer(); }
    void    ResetSelections() { SelIndices.Flush(); }
    int     GetSelStringLength(int index = 0) const;
```

continues

continued

```
void      GetSelString(char far* buffer, int bufferSize,
                       int index=0) const;
void      GetSelString(string& str, int index=0) const;

protected:
  TStringArray    Strings;      // Contains all strings in listbox
  TDwordArray     ItemDatas;    // Contains all item data DWORDS in
                                // listbox
  TIntArray       SelIndices;   // Contains all selection indices
};
```

The TListBoxData class offers the following member functions to query and to manipulate the list box data in the transfer buffer:

1. The GetStrings member function returns the reference to the array of strings in the list box.

2. The GetSelIndices member function returns the reference to the array of selection indices.

3. The AddString member function adds a string to the list box buffer.

4. The Clear member function clears the data items in the list box buffer.

5. The Select member function selects an item by specifying its index.

6. The SelectString member function selects an item that matches its string argument.

7. The GetSelCount member function yields the number of selected items in the associated list box.

8. The ResetSelections member function removes all of the selections.

9. The GetSelStringLength member function returns the length of the string specified by its index.

10. The overloaded member function GetSelString obtains a string from the list box by specifying its index.

    - The ComboBoxData member helps to move data between a combo box control and the data buffer. The ComboBoxData is a pointer to the TComboBoxData class shown as follows:

```
class _OWLCLASS TComboBoxData {
  public:
    TComboBoxData();
    ~TComboBoxData();
```

```
TStringArray&   GetStrings() { return Strings; }
TDwordArray&    GetItemDatas() { return ItemDatas; }
int             GetSelIndex() { return SelIndex; }
string&         GetSelection() { return Selection; }

void    AddString(const char* str, BOOL isSelected = FALSE);
void    AddStringItem(const char* str, DWORD itemData,
                     BOOL isSelected = FALSE);
void    Clear()
        { Strings.Flush();
          ItemDatas.Flush();
          ResetSelections(); }

void    Select(int index);
void    SelectString(const char far* str);
int     GetSelCount() const
        { return SelIndex == CB_ERR ? 0 : 1; }
void    ResetSelections()
        { SelIndex = CB_ERR;
          Selection = ""; }
int     GetSelStringLength() const;
void    GetSelString(char far* buffer, int bufferSize) const;

protected:
  TStringArray    Strings;
  TDwordArray     ItemDatas;
  string          Selection;
  int             SelIndex;
};
```

The TComboBoxData class offers member functions that are similar to that of the TListBoxData class. The TComboBoxData class provides you with the GetSelection member function to obtain the string in the edit control part of the combo box.

- The ScrollBarData member assists in transferring data between a scroll bar control and the data buffer. This member has the TScollBarData structure type, shown as follows:

```
struct TScrollBarData {
  int  LowValue;
  int  HighValue;
  int  Position;
};
```

The LowValue, HighValue, and Position members store the scroll bar range and the current thumb position.

- The CheckBox member stores the current check state of a check box in a UINT type.

- The RadioButton member stores the current check state of a radio button in a UINT type.

The Transfer Member Function

The TStatic, TListBox, TComboBox, TScrollBar, and TCheckBox classes declare their own versions of the virtual Transfer member function. The TEdit class inherits the TStatic::Transfer member function. Similarly, the TRadioButton class inherits the TCheckBox::Transfer member function. The Transfer function contains the code to transfer data to and from the buffer. The general form of the Transfer function is this:

```
UINT Transfer(void* buffer, TTransferDirection direction)
```

The buffer parameter is a pointer to the buffer of the transferred data. The direction parameter specifies the transfer direction flag, which can take the following values:

- tdSetData to move data from the buffer to the control of the dialog box

- tdGetData to move data from the control of the dialog box to the buffer

- tdSizeData simply to return the size of the transferred data, which is systematically supplied by the result type of the function

Listing 5.10 contains the Transfer member functions for various controls. The listing serves to show how the current Transfer member functions are coded and how to write a Transfer member function in general.

LISTING 5.10. THE TRANSFER MEMBER FUNCTIONS FOR VARIOUS CONTROLS.

```
UINT TStatic::Transfer(void *buffer, TTransferDirection direction)
{
  if (direction == tdGetData)
    GetText((char far*)buffer, TextLen);

  else if (direction == tdSetData)
    SetText((char far*)buffer);

  return TextLen;
}


UINT TCheckBox::Transfer(void* buffer, TTransferDirection direction)
{
  if (direction == tdGetData)
```

```
      *(UINT*)buffer = GetCheck();

  else if (direction == tdSetData)
    SetCheck(*(UINT*)buffer);

  return sizeof(UINT);
}

UINT TComboBox::Transfer(void* buffer, TTransferDirection direction)
{
  TComboBoxData* comboBoxData = (TComboBoxData*)buffer;

  if (direction == tdGetData) {
    //
    // Clear out Strings array and fill with contents of list box part
    // Prescan for longest string to allow a single temp allocation
    //
    comboBoxData->Clear();

    int  count = GetCount();
    int  maxStringLen = 0;
    for (int i = 0; i < count; i++) {
      int  stringLen = GetStringLen(i);
      if (stringLen > maxStringLen)
        maxStringLen = stringLen;
    }
    char*  tmpString = new char[maxStringLen+1];
    for (i = 0; i < count; i++) {
      GetString(tmpString, i);
      comboBoxData->AddString(tmpString, FALSE);
      comboBoxData->GetItemDatas()[i] = GetItemData(i);
    }
    delete tmpString;

    //
    // Get the sel string from the list by index, or, if no index, from
    // the edit box
    //
    int selIndex = GetSelIndex();
    if (selIndex >= 0) {
      int  stringLen = GetStringLen(selIndex);
      if (stringLen > 0) {
        char* str = new char[stringLen+1];
        GetString(str, selIndex);
        comboBoxData->SelectString(str);
        delete str;

      } else
        comboBoxData->SelectString("");
```

continues

LISTING 5.10. CONTINUED

```
    } else {
      int  stringLen = GetWindowTextLength();
      if (stringLen > 0) {
        char* str = new char[stringLen+1];
        GetWindowText(str, stringLen+1);
        comboBoxData->SelectString(str);
        delete str;

      } else
        comboBoxData->SelectString("");
    }

  } else if (direction == tdSetData) {
    ClearList();
    comboBoxData->GetStrings().ForEach(DoAddStringToCB, this);
    for (int i = 0;
         i < comboBoxData->GetItemDatas().GetItemsInContainer(); i++)
      SetItemData(i, comboBoxData->GetItemDatas()[i]);

    SetWindowText(comboBoxData->GetSelection().c_str());
    if (comboBoxData->GetSelIndex() >= 0)
      SetSelIndex(comboBoxData->GetSelIndex());
  }

  return sizeof (TComboBoxData);
}

UINT TListBox::Transfer(void* buffer, TTransferDirection direction)
{
  long           style = GetWindowLong(GWL_STYLE);
  TListBoxData*  listBoxData = *(TListBoxData**)buffer;

  if (direction == tdGetData) {
    //
    // first, clear out Strings array and fill with contents of
    // list box
    //
    listBoxData->Strings->Flush();
    listBoxData->ItemDatas->Flush();

    int  count = GetCount();
    int  maxStrLen = 0;
    for (int i = 0; i < count; i++) {
      int  strLen = GetStringLen(i);
      if (strLen > maxStrLen)
        maxStrLen = strLen;
    }
    char  *tmpStr = new char[maxStrLen+1];
```

```
for (i = 0; i < GetCount(); i++) {
  GetString(tmpStr, i);
  listBoxData->AddStringItem(tmpStr, GetItemData(i), FALSE);
}
delete tmpStr;

//
// update transfer data with new selected item or items
//
listBoxData->ResetSelections();

if (!(style & MULTIPLESEL)) {
  //
  // single selection
  //
  listBoxData->Select(GetSelIndex());

} else {
  //
  // multiple selection
  //
  int  selCount = GetSelCount();

  if (selCount > 0) {
    int*  selections = new int[selCount];

    GetSelIndexes(selections, selCount);

    // Select each item by index
    //
    for (int selIndex = 0; selIndex < selCount; selIndex++)
      listBoxData->Select(selections[selIndex]);

    delete selections;
  }
}

} else if (direction == tdSetData) {
  ClearList();

  //
  // add each string and item data in listBoxData to list box
  //
  listBoxData->Strings->ForEach(DoAddForLB, this);
  for (int i = 0;
       i < listBoxData->ItemDatas->GetItemsInContainer();
       i++)
    SetItemData(i, (*listBoxData->ItemDatas)[i]);

  //
```

continues

LISTING 5.10. CONTINUED

```
    // update selected item or items as per listBoxData
    //
    if (!(style & MULTIPLESEL)) {
      //
      // single selection
      //
      if (listBoxData->SelCount) {
        int  selIndex =
          FindExactString((*listBoxData->SelStrings)[0].c_str(), -1);
        if (selIndex > -1)
          SetSelIndex(selIndex);
      }

    } else {
      //
      // multiple selection
      //
      SetSel(-1, FALSE); // deselect all
      for (int i = 0; i < listBoxData->SelCount; i++) {
        int  selIndex =
          FindExactString((*listBoxData->SelStrings)[i].c_str(), -1);
        if (selIndex > -1)
          SetSel(selIndex, TRUE);
      }
    }
  }

  return sizeof(TListBoxData*);
}

UINT TScrollBar::Transfer(void* buffer, TTransferDirection direction)
{
  TScrollBarData* scrollBuff = (TScrollBarData*) buffer;

  if (direction == tdGetData) {
    GetRange(scrollBuff->LowValue, scrollBuff->HighValue);
    scrollBuff->Position = GetPosition();

  } else if (direction == tdSetData) {
    SetRange(scrollBuff->LowValue, scrollBuff->HighValue);
    SetPosition(scrollBuff->Position);
  }

  return sizeof(TScrollBarData);
}
```

Creating the Transfer Buffer

The transfer buffer is typically declared as a member of the parent window. The window class constructor is the member that usually performs the initialization of the transfer buffer. The members of the buffer transfer types are assigned values to set the initial values and states of the controls. The buffer parts for the list box and combo box controls need a few extra steps. This involves at least creating the instances of the TListBoxData and TComboBoxData classes. The additional optional steps involve adding and selecting list items. A simple example is as follows:

```
// create the class instance
AppBuffer.ListBox = new TListBoxData()
// add strings to the list box buffer
AppBuffer.ListBox->AddString("List String #1");
AppBuffer.ListBox->AddString("List String #2");
AppBuffer.ListBox->AddString("List String #3");
// select the second list item
AppBuffer.ListBox->SelString("List String #2");

// create the class instance
AppBuffer.ComboBox = new TComboBoxData()
// add strings to the combo box buffer
AppBuffer.ComboBox->AddString("Combo String #1");
AppBuffer.ComboBox->AddString("Combo String #2");
AppBuffer.ComboBox->AddString("Combo String #3");
```

Once the data buffer is initialized, you assign its address to the predefined pointer member TransferBuffer. An example is as follows:

```
TransferBuffer = &AppBuffer;
```

This assignment establishes the connection between the buffer and the dialog box or window.

Data Transfer Rules

ObjectWindows establishes a protocol for transferring data between a control and its buffer. Here are the rules that make up the transfer protocol:

- The transfer of data for the controls of a dialog box is enabled by default.

- The transfer of data for the controls of a window is disabled by default.

- To disable the transfer mechanism for a dialog box control, use the DisableTransfer member function of that control class. An example is this:

```
pCheckBox = new TCheckBox(this, TResID(ID_CHECK_BOX));
pCheckBox->DisableTransfer();
```

- To enable the transfer mechanism for a window control, use the
  EnableTransfer member function of that control class. An example is
  the following:

```
pWindowCheckBox = new TCheckBox(this, TResID(ID_CHECK_BOX));
pWindowCheckBox->EnableTransfer();
```

- Data is automatically transferred either when a window (with at least
  one control that has enabled data transfer) is created or when a dialog
  box is created or executed.

- The data of a modal dialog box is automatically transferred to the
  buffer when the dialog box receives a notification message of IDOK.
  A notification message of IDCANCEL blocks the transfer of data to the
  buffer.

- The data of a modal dialog box is automatically transferred to the
  buffer if the CloseWindow member function obtains a TRUE result by
  calling the CanClose member function.

- Data must be explicitly transferred out of a window or modeless dialog
  box by using the TransferData member function with a single argument
  tdGetData.

- Data can be transferred to the buffer and from the buffer (to reset the
  controls of a window or dialog box) at will by invoking the TransferData
  member function with the tdGetData or tdSetData arguments.

DATA TRANSFER EXAMPLES

This section presents examples of transferring data between dialog boxes and
their buffers. These examples show how to transfer data with modal dialog
boxes, modeless dialog boxes, and windows.

Simple Modal Dialog Box

Consider a simple example of transferring data between the controls of modal
dialog box and a buffer. I present a simple application that creates a sample
dialog box that is used in replacing text. Figure 5.4 shows the dialog box in

question during a sample session with the DIALOG3.EXE application. The dialog box contains the following controls:

- The Find edit box
- The Replace edit box
- The Scope group box, which contains the Global and Selected Text radio button controls
- The Case Sensitive check box
- The Whole Word check box
- The OK pushbutton control
- The Cancel pushbutton control

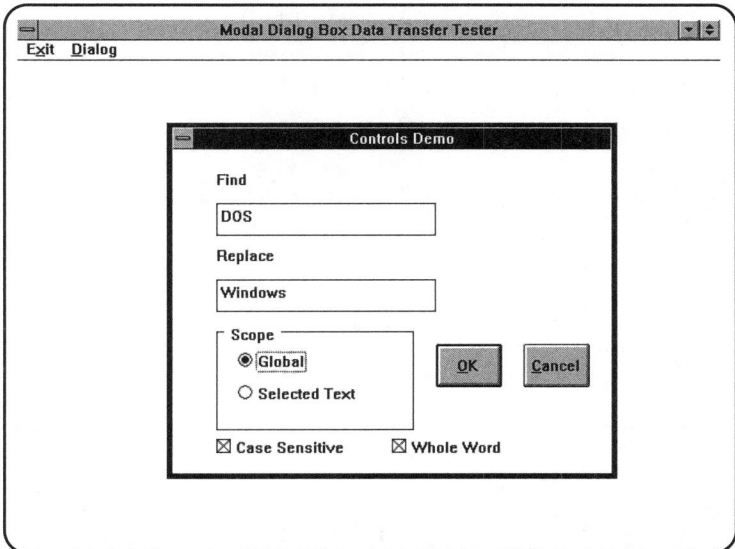

Figure 5.4. A sample session with the DIALOG3.EXE application.

The application has a main menu with the Exit and Dialog menu items. To invoke the dialog box, click the Dialog menu item or press the Alt+D keys. When you invoke the dialog box for the first time, the controls have the following initial values and states:

- The Find edit box contains the string DOS.

- The Replace edit box has the string Windows.

- The Global radio button is checked.

- The Case-Sensitive check box is checked.

- The Whole Word check box is checked.

Type new strings in the edit box and alter the check states of the radio buttons and check boxes. Click the OK button (or press the Alt+O keys) to close the dialog box. Invoke the Dialog menu item again to pop up the dialog box. Notice that the controls of the dialog box have the same values and states as when you last closed the dialog box.

Listing 5.11 shows the contents of the DIALOG3.DEF definition file. Listing 5.12 shows the header file DIALOG3.H. Listing 5.13 shows the script for the resource file DIALOG3.RC. The resource file defines the accelerator keys resources and the basic modeless dialog box resource. Listing 5.14 contains the source code for the DIALOG3.CPP program.

LISTING 5.11. THE CONTENTS OF THE DIALOG3.DEF DEFINITION FILE.

```
NAME          Dialog3
DESCRIPTION   'An OWL Windows Application'
EXETYPE       WINDOWS
CODE          PRELOAD MOVEABLE DISCARDABLE
DATA          PRELOAD MOVEABLE MULTIPLE
HEAPSIZE      1024
STACKSIZE     8384
```

LISTING 5.12. THE SOURCE CODE FOR THE DIALOG3.H HEADER FILE.

```
#define CM_DIALOG       101
#define ID_DIALOG       200
#define ID_FIND_TXT     201
#define ID_FIND_EDIT    202
#define ID_REPLACE_TXT  203
#define ID_REPLACE_EDIT 204
#define ID_SCOPE_GRP    205
#define ID_GLOBAL_RBT   206
#define ID_SELTEXT_RBT  207
#define ID_CASE_CHK     208
```

```
#define ID_WHOLEWORD_CHK 209
#define IDM_MAINMENU     400
#define IDD_DIALOG       401
```

LISTING 5.13. THE SCRIPT FOR THE DIALOG3.RC RESOURCE FILE.

```
#include <windows.h>
#include <owl\window.rh>
#include "dialog3.h"

IDM_MAINMENU MENU LOADONCALL MOVEABLE PURE DISCARDABLE
BEGIN
    MENUITEM "E&xit", CM_EXIT
    MENUITEM "&Dialog", CM_DIALOG
END

IDD_DIALOG DIALOG DISCARDABLE LOADONCALL PURE MOVEABLE 10, 10, 200, 150
STYLE WS_POPUP ¦ WS_CLIPSIBLINGS ¦ WS_CAPTION ¦ WS_SYSMENU ¦
     DS_MODALFRAME
CAPTION "Controls Demo"
BEGIN
  CONTROL "Find", ID_FIND_TXT, "STATIC", WS_CHILD ¦ WS_VISIBLE ¦
    SS_LEFT, 20, 10, 100, 15

  CONTROL "", ID_FIND_EDIT, "EDIT", WS_CHILD ¦ WS_VISIBLE ¦
    WS_BORDER ¦ WS_TABSTOP, 20, 25, 100, 15

  CONTROL "Replace", ID_REPLACE_TXT, "STATIC", WS_CHILD ¦ WS_VISIBLE ¦
    SS_LEFT, 20, 45, 100, 15

  CONTROL "", ID_REPLACE_EDIT, "EDIT", WS_CHILD ¦ WS_VISIBLE ¦
    WS_BORDER ¦ WS_TABSTOP, 20, 60, 100, 15

  CONTROL " Scope ", ID_SCOPE_GRP, "BUTTON", WS_CHILD ¦ WS_VISIBLE
    ¦ WS_GROUP ¦ BS_GROUPBOX, 20, 80, 90, 50

  CONTROL "Global", ID_GLOBAL_RBT, "BUTTON", WS_CHILD ¦ WS_VISIBLE
    ¦ WS_TABSTOP ¦ BS_AUTORADIOBUTTON, 30, 90, 50, 15

  CONTROL "Selected Text", ID_SELTEXT_RBT, "BUTTON", WS_CHILD ¦
    WS_VISIBLE ¦ WS_TABSTOP ¦ BS_AUTORADIOBUTTON, 30, 105, 60, 15

  CONTROL "Case Sensitive", ID_CASE_CHK, "BUTTON", WS_CHILD ¦
    WS_VISIBLE ¦ WS_TABSTOP ¦ BS_AUTOCHECKBOX, 20, 130, 80, 15

  CONTROL "Whole Word", ID_WHOLEWORD_CHK, "BUTTON", WS_CHILD ¦
    WS_VISIBLE ¦ WS_TABSTOP ¦ BS_AUTOCHECKBOX, 100, 130, 80, 15
```

continues

LISTING 5.13. CONTINUED

```
CONTROL, "&OK", IDOK, "BUTTON", WS_CHILD | WS_VISIBLE |
    WS_TABSTOP | BS_DEFPUSHBUTTON, 120, 90, 30, 20

CONTROL "&Cancel", IDCANCEL, "BUTTON", WS_CHILD | WS_VISIBLE |
    WS_TABSTOP | BS_PUSHBUTTON, 160, 90, 30, 20
END
```

LISTING 5.14. THE SOURCE CODE FOR THE DIALOG3.CPP PROGRAM FILE.

```
/*
  Program which tests data transfer with a modal dialog box
*/

#include <owl\framewin.h>
#include <owl\applicat.h>
#include <owl\static.h>
#include <owl\edit.h>
#include <owl\checkbox.h>
#include <owl\groupbox.h>
#include <owl\radiobut.h>
#include <owl\button.h>
#include <owl\dialog.h>
#include "dialog3.h"
#include <string.h>

const UINT MaxEditLen = 30;

struct TAppTransferBuf {
  char FindBoxBuff[MaxEditLen];
  char ReplaceBoxBuff[MaxEditLen];
  UINT GlobalRbtBuff;
  UINT SelTextRbtBuff;
  UINT CaseChkBuff;
  UINT WholeWordChkBuff;
};

// declare the custom application class as
// a subclass of TApplication
class TWinApp : public TApplication
{
public:
  TWinApp() : TApplication() {}
```

```
protected:
  virtual void InitMainWindow();
};

// expand the functionality of TDialog by deriving class TAppDialog
class TAppDialog : public TDialog
{
public:

  TAppDialog(TWindow* parent, TResID resID);

protected:

  TGroupBox* ScopeGrp;
  TStatic* FindTxt;
  TStatic* ReplaceTxt;
  TEdit* FindBox;
  TEdit* ReplaceBox;
  TRadioButton* GlobalRbt;
  TRadioButton* SelTextRbt;
  TCheckBox* CaseChk;
  TCheckBox* WholeWordChk;
  TButton* OKBtn;
  TButton* CancelBtn;
};

// expand the functionality of TWindow by deriving class TMainWindow
class TMainWindow : public TWindow
{
public:

  TAppTransferBuf AppBuffer;

  TMainWindow();

protected:

  // handle the dialog command
  void CMDialog();

  // handle closing the window
  virtual BOOL CanClose();

  // declare the response table
  DECLARE_RESPONSE_TABLE(TMainWindow);
};

DEFINE_RESPONSE_TABLE1(TMainWindow, TWindow)
  EV_COMMAND(CM_DIALOG, CMDialog),
```

continues

Listing 5.14. CONTINUED

```
END_RESPONSE_TABLE;

TMainWindow::TMainWindow()
        : TWindow(0, 0, 0)
{
  // fill buffer with 0's
  memset(&AppBuffer, 0x0, sizeof(AppBuffer));
  strcpy(AppBuffer.FindBoxBuff, "DOS");
  strcpy(AppBuffer.ReplaceBoxBuff, "Windows");
  AppBuffer.GlobalRbtBuff = BF_CHECKED;
  AppBuffer.CaseChkBuff = BF_CHECKED;
  AppBuffer.WholeWordChkBuff = BF_CHECKED;
};

void TMainWindow::CMDialog()
{
  char msgStr[256];
  TAppDialog* pDlg = new TAppDialog(this, TResID(IDD_DIALOG));

  if (pDlg->Execute() == IDOK) {
    strcpy(msgStr, "Find String: ");
    strcat(msgStr, AppBuffer.FindBoxBuff);
    strcat(msgStr, "\n\nReplace String: ");
    strcat(msgStr, AppBuffer.ReplaceBoxBuff);
    MessageBox(msgStr, "Dialog Box Data", MB_OK);
  }
}

BOOL TMainWindow::CanClose()
{
  return MessageBox("Want to close this application",
            "Query", MB_YESNO | MB_ICONQUESTION) == IDYES;
}

TAppDialog::TAppDialog(TWindow* parent, TResID resID)
   : TWindow(parent), TDialog(parent, resID)
{
  FindTxt = new TStatic(this, ID_FIND_TXT, MaxEditLen);
  FindBox = new TEdit(this, ID_FIND_EDIT, MaxEditLen);
  ReplaceTxt = new TStatic(this, ID_REPLACE_TXT, MaxEditLen);
  ReplaceBox = new TEdit(this, ID_REPLACE_EDIT, MaxEditLen);
  ScopeGrp = new TGroupBox(this, ID_SCOPE_GRP);
  GlobalRbt = new TRadioButton(this, ID_GLOBAL_RBT, ScopeGrp);
  SelTextRbt = new TRadioButton(this, ID_SELTEXT_RBT, ScopeGrp);
  CaseChk = new TCheckBox(this, ID_CASE_CHK, NULL);
  WholeWordChk = new TCheckBox(this, ID_WHOLEWORD_CHK, NULL);
  OKBtn = new TButton(this, IDOK);
  CancelBtn = new TButton(this, IDCANCEL);
  // assign the address of the dialog transfer buffer
```

```
  // to member TransferBuffer
  TransferBuffer = (void far*)&(((TMainWindow *)Parent)->
                        AppBuffer);
}

void TWinApp::InitMainWindow()
{
  MainWindow = new TFrameWindow(0,
                      "Modal Dialog Box Data Transfer Tester",
                      new TMainWindow());
  // load the menu resource
  MainWindow->AssignMenu(TResID(IDM_MAINMENU));
}

static TWinApp App;
```

Look at the code that implements the DIALOG3.EXE application. Listing 5.12 shows the source code for the DIALOG3.H header file. This file declares the ID_*xxxx* constants for the various controls as well as the CM_DIALOG constant for the Dialog menu command.

Listing 5.13 contains the script for the DIALOG3.RC resource file. This file defines the resources for the accelerator keys, the menu, and the dialog box, including its controls. This approach is necessary to enable the data transfer mechanism supported by ObjectWindows. Creating the controls, from scratch, inside the dialog box constructor *will not work!* Notice that the controls are created using the CONTROL keyword (which is used to create controls in general). This keyword requires the caption, ID, control class name, style, location, and dimensions of the control. Consult an introductory Windows programming book to learn about keywords involved in defining a dialog box resource. Looking at the dialog box resource definition, you should notice that the OK and Cancel pushbuttons have the predefined IDOK and IDCANCEL IDs, respectively. Also notice that the OK button has the default pushbutton style, while the Cancel button has the normal pushbutton style. In addition, notice that the group box, radio buttons, and check boxes have the BUTTON class name. The styles associated with these controls determine their final form.

Listing 5.14 shows the source code for the DIALOG3.CPP program file. The program declares the data transfer type TAppTransferBuf and includes members for the edit boxes, radio buttons, and check boxes.

The program listing declares three classes: an application class, a window class, and a dialog box class.

The application dialog box class TAppDialog declares a class constructor and a set of pointers to the various controls in the dialog box. The class constructor creates the instances of the various controls in the dialog box using resource-tapping constructors. The order of creating these controls matches the order of their corresponding buffer members in the TAppTransferBuf structure. Using resource-tapping constructors reduces the number of statements and does not require the services of the coordinate-tracking variables. The last statement assigns the address of the data buffer (which is a data member in the parent window class, TMainWindow) to the predefined TransferBuffer pointer. This statement makes the connection between the controls of the dialog box and the data buffer.

The application window class, TMainWindow, declares a public data transfer buffer, AppBuffer, a class constructor, and two member functions. Making the AppBuffer data member public is necessary for the dialog box class constructor to access it.

The TMainWindow constructor initializes the data buffer. The call to the memset function fills the AppBuffer member with zeros. I recommend that you systematically call the memset function to perform a basic initialization of the buffer, before assigning specific values to its controls. The constructor then assigns the "DOS" and "Windows" strings to the Find and Replace edit boxes buffers, respectively. The constructor also assigns BF_CHECKED to the GlobalRbtBuff, CaseChkBuff, and WholeWordChkBuf members.

The TMainWindow class declares the CMDialog member function to handle the command message emitted by the Dialog menu item. This function executes an instance of the application dialog box using the Execute member function and compares the result of that function with IDOK. If the two items match, the CMDialog function builds and displays a message string that reflects the current Find and Replace text.

Complex Modal Dialog Box

The last example shows the data transfer between the simple controls of a modal dialog box. I'll modify the example and use combo boxes instead of the edit boxes. This means that the transfer buffer requires using pointers to the TComboBoxData class to allocate dynamic portions of the buffer. Figure 5.5 shows a sample session with the new version of the dialog box. The Find and Replace dialog boxes allow you to enter text in their edit control areas. If you close the dialog box by clicking the OK button, the text you type in the edit box area is inserted in the corresponding list box component of each combo box. The next time you bring up the dialog box, the list box (and edit area) components of the combo boxes contain the previous input. As you type new strings in the combo boxes and exit the dialog box, the list box components build a list of your previous input. The latest input is always inserted at the top of the list box (at index 0, to be exact).

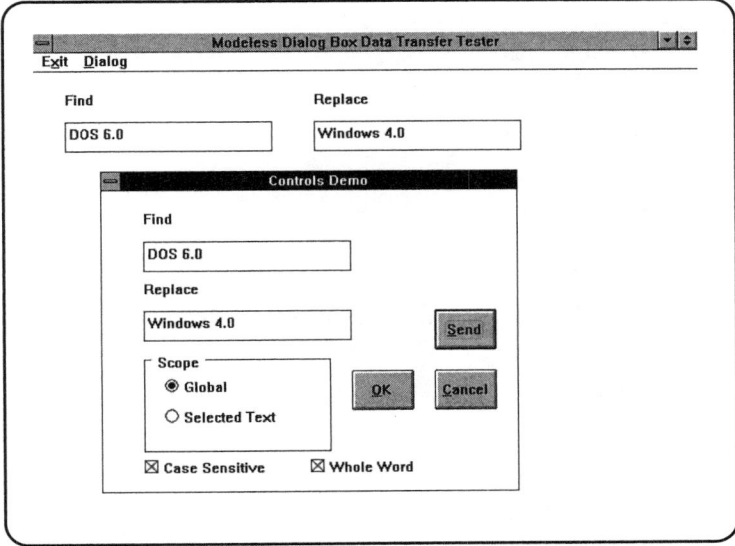

Figure 5.5. A sample session with the DIALOG4.EXE application.

Listing 5.15 shows the contents of the DIALOG4.DEF definition file. Listing 5.16 shows the header file DIALOG4.H. Listing 5.17 shows the script for the resource file DIALOG4.RC. The resource file defines the accelerator keys resources and the basic modeless dialog box resource. Listing 5.18 contains the source code for the DIALOG4.CPP program.

LISTING 5.15. THE CONTENTS OF THE DIALOG4.DEF DEFINITION FILE.

```
NAME          Dialog4
DESCRIPTION   'An OWL Windows Application'
EXETYPE       WINDOWS
CODE          PRELOAD MOVEABLE DISCARDABLE
DATA          PRELOAD MOVEABLE MULTIPLE
HEAPSIZE      1024
STACKSIZE     8384
```

LISTING 5.16. THE SOURCE CODE FOR THE DIALOG4.H HEADER FILE.

```
#define CM_DIALOG 101
#define ID_DIALOG         200
#define ID_FIND_TXT       201
#define ID_FIND_CMB       202
#define ID_REPLACE_TXT    203
#define ID_REPLACE_CMB    204
#define ID_SCOPE_GRP      205
#define ID_GLOBAL_RBT     206
#define ID_SELTEXT_RBT    207
#define ID_CASE_CHK       208
#define ID_WHOLEWORD_CHK 209
#define IDM_MAINMENU      400
#define IDD_DIALOG        401
```

LISTING 5.17. THE SCRIPT FOR THE DIALOG4.RC RESOURCE FILE.

```
#include <windows.h>
#include <owl\window.rh>
#include "dialog4.h"

IDM_MAINMENU MENU LOADONCALL MOVEABLE PURE DISCARDABLE
BEGIN
    MENUITEM "E&xit", CM_EXIT
    MENUITEM "&Dialog", CM_DIALOG
END

IDD_DIALOG DIALOG DISCARDABLE LOADONCALL PURE MOVEABLE 10, 10, 200, 150
STYLE WS_POPUP ¦ WS_CLIPSIBLINGS ¦ WS_CAPTION ¦ WS_SYSMENU ¦ DS_MODALFRAME
CAPTION "Controls Demo"
BEGIN
  CONTROL "Find", ID_FIND_TXT, "STATIC", WS_CHILD ¦ WS_VISIBLE ¦
    SS_LEFT, 20, 10, 100, 15

  CONTROL "", ID_FIND_CMB, "COMBOBOX", WS_CHILD ¦ WS_VISIBLE ¦
    WS_BORDER ¦ WS_TABSTOP ¦ CBS_DROPDOWN, 20, 25, 100, 50

  CONTROL "Replace", ID_REPLACE_TXT, "STATIC", WS_CHILD ¦ WS_VISIBLE ¦
    SS_LEFT, 20, 45, 100, 15

  CONTROL "", ID_REPLACE_CMB, "COMBOBOX", WS_CHILD ¦ WS_VISIBLE ¦
    WS_BORDER ¦ WS_TABSTOP ¦ CBS_DROPDOWN, 20, 60, 100, 50

  CONTROL " Scope ", ID_SCOPE_GRP, "BUTTON", WS_CHILD ¦ WS_VISIBLE
    ¦ WS_GROUP ¦ BS_GROUPBOX, 20, 80, 90, 50
```

```
CONTROL "Global", ID_GLOBAL_RBT, "BUTTON", WS_CHILD ¦ WS_VISIBLE
   ¦ WS_TABSTOP ¦ BS_AUTORADIOBUTTON, 30, 90, 50, 15

CONTROL "Selected Text", ID_SELTEXT_RBT, "BUTTON", WS_CHILD ¦
   WS_VISIBLE ¦ WS_TABSTOP ¦ BS_AUTORADIOBUTTON, 30, 105, 60, 15

CONTROL "Case Sensitive", ID_CASE_CHK, "BUTTON", WS_CHILD ¦
   WS_VISIBLE ¦ WS_TABSTOP ¦ BS_AUTOCHECKBOX, 20, 130, 80, 15

CONTROL "Whole Word", ID_WHOLEWORD_CHK, "BUTTON", WS_CHILD ¦
   WS_VISIBLE ¦ WS_TABSTOP ¦ BS_AUTOCHECKBOX, 100, 130, 80, 15

CONTROL "&OK", IDOK, "BUTTON", WS_CHILD ¦ WS_VISIBLE ¦ WS_TABSTOP
   ¦ BS_DEFPUSHBUTTON, 120, 90, 30, 20

CONTROL "&Cancel", IDCANCEL, "BUTTON", WS_CHILD ¦ WS_VISIBLE
   ¦ WS_TABSTOP ¦ BS_PUSHBUTTON, 160, 90, 30, 20
END
```

LISTING 5.18. THE SOURCE CODE FOR THE DIALOG4.CPP PROGRAM FILE.

```
/*
  Program which demonstrates a modal dialog box with
  combo boxes
*/

#include <owl\framewin.h>
#include <owl\applicat.h>
#include <owl\static.h>
#include <owl\combobox.h>
#include <owl\checkbox.h>
#include <owl\groupbox.h>
#include <owl\radiobut.h>
#include <owl\button.h>
#include <owl\dialog.h>
#include "dialog4.h"
#include <string.h>

const MaxEditLen = 30;

struct TAppTransferBuf {
  TComboBoxData* FindCmbBuff;
  TComboBoxData* ReplaceCmbBuff;
  UINT GlobalRbtBuff;
  UINT SelTextRbtBuff;
```

continues

LISTING 5.18. CONTINUED

```
  UINT CaseChkBuff;
  UINT WholeWordChkBuff;
};

// declare the custom application class as
// a subclass of TApplication
class TWinApp : public TApplication
{
public:
  TWinApp() : TApplication() {}

protected:
  virtual void InitMainWindow();
};

// expand the functionality of TDialog by deriving class TAppDialog
class TAppDialog : public TDialog
{
public:

  TAppDialog(TWindow* parent, TResID resID);

  void CmOk();

protected:

  TGroupBox* ScopeGrp;
  TStatic* FindTxt;
  TStatic* ReplaceTxt;
  TComboBox* FindCmb;
  TComboBox* ReplaceCmb;
  TRadioButton* GlobalRbt;
  TRadioButton* SelTextRbt;
  TCheckBox* CaseChk;
  TCheckBox* WholeWordChk;
  TButton* OKBtn;
  TButton* CancelBtn;

  DECLARE_RESPONSE_TABLE(TAppDialog);
};

DEFINE_RESPONSE_TABLE1(TAppDialog, TDialog)
  EV_COMMAND(IDOK, CmOk),
END_RESPONSE_TABLE;

// expand the functionality of TWindow by deriving class TMainWindow
class TMainWindow : public TWindow
{
```

```
public:
  TAppTransferBuf AppBuffer;

  TMainWindow();
  ~TMainWindow();

protected:

  // handle the dialog command
  void CMDialog();

  // handle closing the window
  virtual BOOL CanClose();

  // declare the response table
  DECLARE_RESPONSE_TABLE(TMainWindow);
};

DEFINE_RESPONSE_TABLE1(TMainWindow, TWindow)
  EV_COMMAND(CM_DIALOG, CMDialog),
END_RESPONSE_TABLE;

TAppDialog::TAppDialog(TWindow* parent, TResID resID)
    : TWindow(parent), TDialog(parent, resID)
{
  FindTxt = new TStatic(this, ID_FIND_TXT, MaxEditLen);
  FindCmb = new TComboBox(this, ID_FIND_CMB, MaxEditLen);
  ReplaceTxt = new TStatic(this, ID_REPLACE_TXT, MaxEditLen);
  ReplaceCmb = new TComboBox(this, ID_REPLACE_CMB, MaxEditLen);
  ScopeGrp = new TGroupBox(this, ID_SCOPE_GRP);
  GlobalRbt = new TRadioButton(this, ID_GLOBAL_RBT, ScopeGrp);
  SelTextRbt = new TRadioButton(this, ID_SELTEXT_RBT, ScopeGrp);
  CaseChk = new TCheckBox(this, ID_CASE_CHK, NULL);
  WholeWordChk = new TCheckBox(this, ID_WHOLEWORD_CHK, NULL);
  OKBtn = new TButton(this, IDOK);
  CancelBtn = new TButton(this, IDCANCEL);
  // assign the address of the dialog transfer buffer
  // to member TransferBuffer
  TransferBuffer = (void far*)&(((TMainWindow *)Parent)->
                     AppBuffer);
}

void TAppDialog::CmOk()
{
  char s[MaxEditLen+1];
  int i;

  // get the string in the edit box
  FindCmb->GetText(s, MaxEditLen);
  // process if not an empty string
```

continues

Listing 5.18. continued

```
  if (s[0] != '\0') {
    // does the string s exist in the list box part
    i = FindCmb->FindString(s, 0);
    if (i >= 0)
      // delete it
      FindCmb->DeleteString(i);
    // insert string s
    FindCmb->InsertString(s, 0);
    // bug: need to rewrite string s to edit control part
    FindCmb->SetText(s);
  }
  // repeat same process with Replace combo box
  ReplaceCmb->GetText(s, MaxEditLen);
  if (s[0] != '\0') {
    i = ReplaceCmb->FindString(s, 0);
    if (i >= 0)
      ReplaceCmb->DeleteString(i);
    ReplaceCmb->InsertString(s, 0);
    ReplaceCmb->SetText(s);
  }
  TDialog::CmOk();
}

TMainWindow::TMainWindow()
        : TWindow(0, 0, 0)
{
  // fill buffer with 0's
  memset(&AppBuffer, 0x0, sizeof(AppBuffer));
  AppBuffer.GlobalRbtBuff = BF_CHECKED;
  AppBuffer.CaseChkBuff = BF_CHECKED;
  AppBuffer.WholeWordChkBuff = BF_CHECKED;
  AppBuffer.FindCmbBuff = new TComboBoxData();
  AppBuffer.FindCmbBuff->AddString("DOS");
  AppBuffer.FindCmbBuff->AddString("DOS 5.0");
  AppBuffer.FindCmbBuff->AddString("DOS 4.0");
  AppBuffer.FindCmbBuff->AddString("DOS 3.3");
  AppBuffer.ReplaceCmbBuff = new TComboBoxData();
  AppBuffer.ReplaceCmbBuff->AddString("Windows");
  AppBuffer.ReplaceCmbBuff->AddString("Windows 3.1");
  AppBuffer.ReplaceCmbBuff->AddString("Windows 3.0");
  AppBuffer.ReplaceCmbBuff->AddString("Windows NT");
};

TMainWindow::~TMainWindow()
{
  delete AppBuffer.FindCmbBuff;
  delete AppBuffer.ReplaceCmbBuff;
}
```

```
void TMainWindow::CMDialog()
{
  char s[MaxEditLen];
  char msgStr[256];
  TAppDialog* pDlg = new TAppDialog(this, TResID(IDD_DIALOG));

  if (pDlg->Execute() == IDOK) {
      strcpy(s, AppBuffer.FindCmbBuff->GetSelection().c_str());
      strcpy(msgStr, "Find String: ");
      strcat(msgStr, s);
      strcat(msgStr, "\n\n");
      strcpy(s, AppBuffer.ReplaceCmbBuff->GetSelection().c_str());
      strcat(msgStr, "Replace String: ");
      strcat(msgStr, s);
      strcat(msgStr, "\n");
      MessageBox(msgStr, "Dialog Box Data",
                         MB_OK | MB_ICONINFORMATION);
  }
}

BOOL TMainWindow::CanClose()
{
  return MessageBox("Want to close this application",
               "Query", MB_YESNO | MB_ICONQUESTION) == IDYES;
}

void TWinApp::InitMainWindow()
{
  MainWindow = new TFrameWindow(0,
                     "Modal Dialog Box Data Transfer Tester",
                     new TMainWindow());
  // load the menu resource
  MainWindow->AssignMenu(TResID(IDM_MAINMENU));
}

int OwlMain(int /* argc */, char** /*argv[] */)
{
  TWinApp app;
  return app.Run();
}
```

Listing 5.16 shows the source code for the DIALOG4.H header file. This file declares the ID_*xxxx* constants for the various controls as well as the CM_DIALOG constant for the Dialog menu command.

Listing 5.17 contains the script for the DIALOG4.RC resource file. The resource file defines the accelerator keys, menu, and dialog box resources. Notice that dialog box resource definition for the new combo boxes uses the class type "COMBOBOX". In addition, the heights of the combo box controls are greater than the heights of the edit boxes they replace. This provides the space for the list box component of each combo box.

Listing 5.18 shows the source code for the DIALOG4.CPP program file. The program listing declares a modified version of the data transfer buffer type. This new version replaces the character array members with two `TComboBoxData*` pointers to access the buffer components for the combo box controls.

The DIALOG4.CPP listing has the same classes and data members as DIALOG3.CPP. The difference is in the code for the constructors and member functions.

The `TAppDialog` class constructor creates the instances for the various controls in the dialog box. Like the `TAppDialog` constructor in DIALOG3.CPP, this version also uses resource-tapping constructors to create the various controls. Once the controls are created, the `TAppDialog` constructor assigns the address of the `AppBuffer` buffer to the `TransferBuffer` pointer.

The application window class constructor loads the menu resource and then initializes the data transfer buffer. This process involves creating two instances of `TComboBoxData` for the Find and Replace combo box buffers. Because these combo boxes are initially empty, the constructor does not use the `TComboBoxData::AddString` member function.

The `CMDialog` member function executes the dialog box and compares the result of the `Execute` function with `IDOK`. If the two values match, the function updates the combo box buffers and displays the selected Find and Replace strings in a separate message box. Updating the combo box controls involves calling the member functions `TComboBox::FindString`, `TComboBox::DeleteString`, and `TComboBox::InsertString`. The function verifies that a selection is in each combo box before performing the update.

A Modeless Dialog Box

In this section, I present an ObjectWindows application that transfers data for a modeless dialog box. The program also shows how to transfer data at will by using a special pushbutton control. The next application uses a modified version of the original Replace dialog box (the one that uses edit boxes), presented earlier in this chapter. This new version, DIALOG5.EXE, is very similar to that presented in DIALOG3.EXE and differs in the follows aspects:

- The dialog box is modeless.
- The dialog box has an extra Send pushbutton.

When you click the Send button (see Figure 5.6), the dialog box copies the text in its Find and Replace edit boxes to the edit boxes in the parent window that are also labeled Find and Replace.

When you click the Dialog menu item in the program, the application pops up a modeless dialog box. The dialog box has the "DOS" and "Windows" strings appear in the Find and Replace edit boxes, respectively. The Global radio button, the Case-Sensitive check box, and the Selected check box are all initially selected. Type new text in either edit box or in both, and click the OK pushbutton. This action closes the dialog box and echoes the text of the dialog box in the edit boxes of the window. Reinvoke the dialog box to check that it does retain your last input. Now type new text in both edit boxes and click the Send button. Watch the text echoed in the edit boxes of the window.

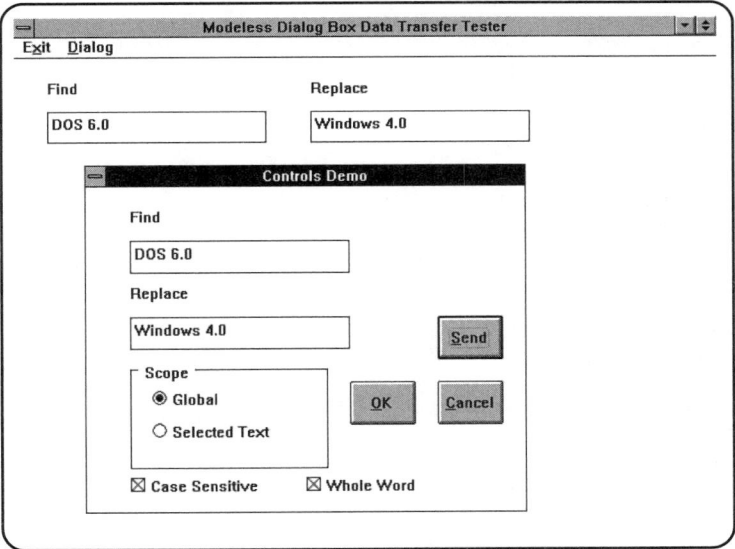

Figure 5.6. A sample session with the DIALOG5.EXE application.

Listing 5.19 shows the contents of the DIALOG5.DEF definition file. Listing 5.20 shows the header file DIALOG5.H. Listing 5.21 shows the script for the resource file DIALOG5.RC. The resource file defines the accelerator keys resources and the basic modeless dialog box resource. Listing 5.22 contains the source code for the DIALOG5.CPP program.

LISTING 5.19. THE CONTENTS OF THE DIALOG5.DEF DEFINITION FILE.

```
NAME          Dialog5
DESCRIPTION   'An OWL Windows Application'
EXETYPE       WINDOWS
CODE          PRELOAD MOVEABLE DISCARDABLE
DATA          PRELOAD MOVEABLE MULTIPLE
HEAPSIZE      1024
STACKSIZE     8384
```

LISTING 5.20. THE SOURCE CODE FOR THE DIALOG5.H HEADER FILE.

```
#define CM_DIALOG           101
#define ID_DIALOG           200
#define ID_FIND_TXT         201
#define ID_FIND_EDIT        202
#define ID_REPLACE_TXT      203
#define ID_REPLACE_EDIT     204
#define ID_SCOPE_GRP        205
#define ID_GLOBAL_RBT       206
#define ID_SELTEXT_RBT      207
#define ID_CASE_CHK         208
#define ID_WHOLEWORD_CHK 209
#define ID_SEND_BTN         210

/* application window control ID */
#define ID_FIND_BOX         301
#define ID_REPLACE_BOX      302

#define IDM_MAINMENU        400
#define IDD_DIALOG          401
```

LISTING 5.21. THE SCRIPT FOR THE DIALOG5.RC RESOURCE FILE.

```
#include <windows.h>
#include <owl\window.rh>
#include "dialog5.h"

IDM_MAINMENU MENU LOADONCALL MOVEABLE PURE DISCARDABLE
BEGIN
    MENUITEM "E&xit", CM_EXIT
    MENUITEM "&Dialog", CM_DIALOG
END
```

```
IDD_DIALOG DIALOG DISCARDABLE LOADONCALL PURE MOVEABLE 10, 10, 200, 150
STYLE WS_POPUP | WS_CLIPSIBLINGS | WS_CAPTION | WS_SYSMENU | WS_DLGFRAME
CAPTION "Controls Demo"
BEGIN
  CONTROL "Find", ID_FIND_TXT, "STATIC", WS_CHILD | WS_VISIBLE |
    SS_LEFT, 20, 10, 100, 15

  CONTROL "", ID_FIND_EDIT, "EDIT", WS_CHILD | WS_VISIBLE |
    WS_BORDER | WS_TABSTOP, 20, 25, 100, 15

  CONTROL "Replace", ID_REPLACE_TXT, "STATIC", WS_CHILD | WS_VISIBLE |
    SS_LEFT, 20, 45, 100, 15

  CONTROL "", ID_REPLACE_EDIT, "EDIT", WS_CHILD | WS_VISIBLE |
    WS_BORDER | WS_TABSTOP, 20, 60, 100, 15

  CONTROL " Scope ", ID_SCOPE_GRP, "BUTTON", WS_CHILD | WS_VISIBLE
    | WS_GROUP | BS_GROUPBOX, 20, 80, 90, 50

  CONTROL "Global", ID_GLOBAL_RBT, "BUTTON", WS_CHILD | WS_VISIBLE
    | WS_TABSTOP | BS_AUTORADIOBUTTON, 30, 90, 50, 15

  CONTROL "Selected Text", ID_SELTEXT_RBT, "BUTTON", WS_CHILD |
    WS_VISIBLE | WS_TABSTOP | BS_AUTORADIOBUTTON, 30, 105, 60, 15

  CONTROL "Case Sensitive", ID_CASE_CHK, "BUTTON", WS_CHILD |
    WS_VISIBLE | WS_TABSTOP | BS_AUTOCHECKBOX, 20, 130, 80, 15

  CONTROL "Whole Word", ID_WHOLEWORD_CHK, "BUTTON", WS_CHILD |
    WS_VISIBLE | WS_TABSTOP | BS_AUTOCHECKBOX, 100, 130, 80, 15

  CONTROL, "&OK", IDOK, "BUTTON", WS_CHILD | WS_VISIBLE | WS_TABSTOP
    | BS_DEFPUSHBUTTON, 120, 90, 30, 20

  CONTROL "&Cancel", IDCANCEL, "BUTTON", WS_CHILD | WS_VISIBLE |
    WS_TABSTOP, 160, 90, 30, 20

  CONTROL "&Send", ID_SEND_BTN, "BUTTON", WS_CHILD | WS_VISIBLE |
    WS_TABSTOP, 160, 60, 30, 20

END
```

LISTING 5.22. THE SOURCE CODE FOR THE DIALOG5.CPP PROGRAM FILE.

```
/*
  Program which tests data transfer with a modeless dialog box
*/
```

continues

LISTING 5.22. CONTINUED

```
#include <owl\framewin.h>
#include <owl\applicat.h>
#include <owl\static.h>
#include <owl\edit.h>
#include <owl\checkbox.h>
#include <owl\groupbox.h>
#include <owl\radiobut.h>
#include <owl\button.h>
#include <owl\dialog.h>
#include "dialog5.h"
#include <string.h>

// declare constants for spacing and dimensioning the
// application window's controls
const Wtxt = 200;
const Htxt = 20;
const TxtVertSpacing = 10;
const Wbox = 200;
const Hbox = 30;
const BoxHorzSpacing = 40;

const MaxEditLen = 30;

// declare the data transfer buffer structure
struct TAppTransferBuf {
  char FindBoxBuff[MaxEditLen];
  char ReplaceBoxBuff[MaxEditLen];
  UINT GlobalRbtBuff;
  UINT SelTextRbtBuff;
  UINT CaseChkBuff;
  UINT WholeWordChkBuff;
};

// declare the custom application class as
// a subclass of TApplication
class TWinApp : public TApplication
{
public:
  TWinApp() : TApplication() {}

protected:
  virtual void InitMainWindow();
};

// expand the functionality of TDialog by deriving class TAppDialog
class TAppDialog : public TDialog
{
public:
```

```
    TAppDialog(TWindow* parent, TResID resID);

protected:

  TGroupBox* ScopeGrp;
  TStatic* FindTxt;
  TStatic* ReplaceTxt;
  TEdit* FindBox;
  TEdit* ReplaceBox;
  TRadioButton* GlobalRbt;
  TRadioButton* SelTextRbt;
  TCheckBox* CaseChk;
  TCheckBox* WholeWordChk;
  TButton* OKBtn;
  TButton* CancelBtn;
  TButton* SendBtn;

  // handle buttons
  void CmOk();
  void CmCancel();
  void HandleSendBtn();

  DECLARE_RESPONSE_TABLE(TAppDialog);
};

DEFINE_RESPONSE_TABLE1(TAppDialog, TDialog)
  EV_COMMAND(IDOK, CmOk),
  EV_COMMAND(IDCANCEL, CmCancel),
  EV_COMMAND(ID_SEND_BTN, HandleSendBtn),
END_RESPONSE_TABLE;

// expand the functionality of TWindow by deriving class TMainWindow
class TMainWindow : public TWindow
{
public:
  BOOL DialogActive;
  TAppTransferBuf AppBuffer;

  TMainWindow();

protected:
  TAppDialog* pDlg;
  TEdit* FindBox;
  TEdit* ReplaceBox;

  // handle the dialog command
  void CMDialog();

  // handle a message sent by the Send button of
  // the dialog box
  void HandleSendBtn();
```

continues

LISTING 5.22. CONTINUED

```
  // handle closing the window
  virtual BOOL CanClose();

  DECLARE_RESPONSE_TABLE(TMainWindow);
};

DEFINE_RESPONSE_TABLE1(TMainWindow, TWindow)
  EV_COMMAND(CM_DIALOG, CMDialog),
  EV_COMMAND(ID_SEND_BTN, HandleSendBtn),
END_RESPONSE_TABLE;

TAppDialog::TAppDialog(TWindow* parent, TResID resID)
    : TWindow(parent), TDialog(parent, resID)
{
  FindTxt = new TStatic(this, ID_FIND_TXT, MaxEditLen);
  FindBox = new TEdit(this, ID_FIND_EDIT, MaxEditLen);
  ReplaceTxt = new TStatic(this, ID_REPLACE_TXT, MaxEditLen);
  ReplaceBox = new TEdit(this, ID_REPLACE_EDIT, MaxEditLen);
  ScopeGrp = new TGroupBox(this, ID_SCOPE_GRP);
  GlobalRbt = new TRadioButton(this, ID_GLOBAL_RBT, ScopeGrp);
  SelTextRbt = new TRadioButton(this, ID_SELTEXT_RBT, ScopeGrp);
  CaseChk = new TCheckBox(this, ID_CASE_CHK, NULL);
  WholeWordChk = new TCheckBox(this, ID_WHOLEWORD_CHK, NULL);
  OKBtn = new TButton(this, IDOK);
  SendBtn = new TButton(this, ID_SEND_BTN);
  CancelBtn = new TButton(this, IDCANCEL);
  // assign the address of the dialog transfer buffer
  // to member TransferBuffer
  TransferBuffer = (void far*)&(((TMainWindow *)Parent)->
                      AppBuffer);
}

void TAppDialog::CmOk()
{
  TMainWindow* pDlg = (TMainWindow*)Parent;
  TransferData(tdGetData);
  Parent->SendMessage(WM_COMMAND, ID_SEND_BTN, NULL);
  pDlg->DialogActive = FALSE;
  TDialog::CmOk();
}

void TAppDialog::CmCancel()
{
  TMainWindow* pDlg = (TMainWindow*)Parent;
  pDlg->DialogActive = FALSE;
  TDialog::CmCancel();
}
```

```
void TAppDialog::HandleSendBtn()
{
  TransferData(tdSetData);
  Parent->SendMessage(WM_COMMAND, ID_SEND_BTN, NULL);
}

TMainWindow::TMainWindow()
        : TWindow(0, 0, 0)
{
  int x0 = 30;
  int y0 = 20;
  int x = x0;
  int y = y0;

  char s[MaxEditLen];

  strcpy(s, "Find");
  new TStatic(this, -1, s, x, y, Wtxt, Htxt, strlen(s));

  y += Htxt + TxtVertSpacing;
  FindBox = new TEdit(this, ID_FIND_BOX, "", x, y, Wbox, Hbox,
                         0, FALSE);

  x += Wbox + BoxHorzSpacing;
  y = y0;
  strcpy(s, "Replace");
  new TStatic(this, -1, s, x, y, Wtxt, Htxt, strlen(s));

  y += Htxt + TxtVertSpacing;
  ReplaceBox = new TEdit(this, ID_REPLACE_BOX, "", x, y,
                            Wbox, Hbox, 0, FALSE);

  // fill buffer with 0's
  memset(&AppBuffer, 0x0, sizeof(AppBuffer));
  strcpy(AppBuffer.FindBoxBuff, "DOS");
  strcpy(AppBuffer.ReplaceBoxBuff, "Windows");
  AppBuffer.GlobalRbtBuff = BF_CHECKED;
  AppBuffer.CaseChkBuff = BF_CHECKED;
  AppBuffer.WholeWordChkBuff = BF_CHECKED;
  // clear active-dialog flag
  DialogActive = FALSE;
};

void TMainWindow::CMDialog()
{
  if (DialogActive) return;
  pDlg = new TAppDialog(this, TResID(IDD_DIALOG));
  pDlg->Create();
  pDlg->ShowWindow(SW_SHOW);
  DialogActive = TRUE;
}
```

continues

LISTING 5.22. CONTINUED

```
void TMainWindow::HandleSendBtn()
{
  FindBox->SetText(AppBuffer.FindBoxBuff);
  ReplaceBox->SetText(AppBuffer.ReplaceBoxBuff);
}

BOOL TMainWindow::CanClose()
{
  return MessageBox("Want to close this application",
                    "Query", MB_YESNO | MB_ICONQUESTION) == IDYES;
}

void TWinApp::InitMainWindow()
{
  MainWindow = new TFrameWindow(0,
          "Modeless Dialog Box Data Transfer Tester",
          new TMainWindow());
  // load the menu resource
  MainWindow->AssignMenu(TResID(IDM_MAINMENU));
}

int OwlMain(int /* argc */, char** /*argv[] */)
{
  TWinApp app;
  return app.Run();
}
```

Examine now the code that implements the application. Listing 5.20 shows the source code for the DIALOG5.H header file. This file declares the constant for the ID_*xxxx* controls in both the modeless dialog box and the parent window.

Listing 5.21 shows the script for the DIALOG5.RC resource file. The resource file defines the resources for the accelerator keys, menu, and modeless dialog box.

Listing 5.22 contains the source code for the DIALOG5.CPP program file. The listing declares a group of constants for sizing and spacing the controls in the window application. The listing also contains the declaration of the data transfer buffer type—this is identical to that shown in the listing of file DIALOG3.CPP.

The application declares three classes: the application class, the window class, and the dialog box class. The TAppDialog class declares a class constructor, the ScopeGrp data member, and a set of member functions.

The TAppDialog constructor in this program is identical to that of the DIALOG3.EXE program. The constructor creates the dialog box controls and sets the TransferBuffer pointer.

The TAppDialog class declares member functions to handle each pushbutton. The virtual CmOk member function responds to the IDOK notification message emitted by the OK button. The function performs the following tasks:

- Transfers the data from the controls to the buffer by calling the TransferData member function with a tdGetData argument

- Sends the Window command message ID_SEND_BTN to the parent window using the SendMessage function

- Sets the parent window data member, DialogActive, to FALSE

- Invokes the parent class CmOk member function.

The CmCancel member function handles the IDCANCEL notification message sent by the Cancel button. The function performs the following two tasks:

- Sets the parent window data member, DialogActive, to FALSE

- Invokes the CmCancel member function of the parent class

The HandleSendBtn member function handles the ID_SEND_BTN notification message emitted by the Send button. The function carries out the following tasks:

- Transfers the data from the controls to the buffer by calling the TransferData member function with a tdGetData argument

- Sends the Windows command message ID_SEND_BTN to the parent window using the SendMessage function

The CMSendBtn member function handles the ID_SEND_BTN command message generated by the accelerator key Alt+S. The function simply calls the HandleSendBtn member function.

The application window class TMainWindow declares two public data members, three protected data members, a constructor, and three member functions. The Boolean DialogActive data member indicates whether or not the dialog box instance exists. Using this flag ensures that there is one instance of the modeless dialog box. The AppBuffer data member is the data transfer buffer. The window class declares three protected pointers. The FindBox and ReplaceBox pointers access the edit box instances. The DlgPtr pointer is the pointer to the dialog box instance.

The TMainWindow constructor performs the following tasks:

- Creates the static text instance that labels the Find edit box
- Creates the Find edit box
- Creates the static text instance that labels the Replace edit box
- Creates the Replace edit box
- Initializes the buffer by filling it with zeros
- Assigns values to the edit box buffers, the check box buffers, and the Global radio button buffer
- Sets the DialogActive data member to FALSE

The application window class declares the CMDialog member function to create a modeless dialog box. The function carries out the subsequent tasks:

- Returns if the DialogActive member is TRUE.
- Creates a TAppDialog instance that is accessed by the DlgPtr pointer.
- Creates the modeless dialog box by invoking the inherited Create member function. The function call uses the DlgPtr pointer as its argument.
- Calls the ShowWindow function to display the dialog box.
- Sets the DialogActive data member to TRUE.

The HandleSendBtn member function responds to the message sent by the Send button in the dialog box by copying the FindBoxBuff and ReplaceBoxBuff buffer members to the Find and Replace edit boxes in the window.

SUMMARY

This chapter presented the powerful dialog boxes that serve as input tools. You learned about:

- Constructing instances of the TDialog class.
- Executing a modal dialog box using the Execute member function.
- Creating, displaying, and closing a modeless dialog box using the Create member function, the ShowWindow function, and the ShutDownWindow member function.

- Creating a command-oriented calculator version using a dialog box as a window. In this case, the dialog box is a child of the application.

- The basics of transferring control data. These include declaring the data transfer buffer type, declaring the buffer, creating the controls in a sequence that matches their buffers, and establishing the buffer link.

- Examples of transferring data for dialog boxes. These examples showed you how to transfer data for modal dialog boxes and for modeless dialog boxes and how to initialize window controls.

COMMON DIALOG BOXES

The last chapter introduced you to building your own dialog boxes. In this chapter, I present six common dialog boxes supported by Windows and the ObjectWindows library. These common dialog boxes, as the name suggests, are commonly used. In this chapter you'll learn the following:

- Software requirements for using the common dialog boxes.

- The TInputDialog ObjectWindows class.

- The TFileOpenDialog file selection dialog box class. This class creates dialog boxes that support opening a file.

- The TFileSaveDialog file selection dialog box class. This class creates dialog boxes that support saving a file.

- The TChooseFontDialog font selection dialog box class.

- The TChooseColorDialog color selection dialog box class.

- The TPrintDialog printer setup dialog box class.

- The `TFindDialog` text search dialog box class. This class creates dialog boxes that support finding text.

- The `TReplaceDialog` text replacement dialog box class. This class creates dialog boxes that support replacing text.

I would like to stress that the common dialog boxes only offer the user interface for their respective tasks. You are responsible for providing the associated functionality based on the information supplied or selected by the dialog box user. Most of the examples in this chapter focus on retrieving data from the common dialog boxes. This approach allows the chapter's programs to be short and to focus on creating, invoking, and then accessing the data of the common dialog boxes.

SOFTWARE REQUIREMENTS

The use of the common dialog boxes requires Windows 3.1 COMMDLG functions to compile. However, these dialog boxes do not require Windows 3.1 to run. You need to observe the following when incorporating the common dialog box in your Windows applications:

- Be sure that the project's .DEF file assigns at least 16K of stack space.

- Include the corresponding header file in the client source files.

- Be sure that the COMMDLG.DLL file is present in the Windows system directory.

THE TINPUTDIALOG CLASS

Some of the programs presented in earlier chapters required input dialog boxes to obtain your input. These programs executed instances of the ObjectWindows `TInputDialog` class. This class declares three data members, a constructor, and a set of member functions. The declaration of `TInputDialog` class follows.

```
class _EXPCLASS TInputDialog : public TDialog {
  public:
    char far* Prompt;
    char far* Buffer;
    int      BufferSize;

    TInputDialog(TWindow       *parent,
                 const char far *title,
```

```
                const char far *prompt,
                char far*       buffer,
                int             bufferSize,
                TLibId          libId = 0);

    //
    // Override TWindow virtual member functions
    //
    void TransferData(TTransferDirection);

  protected:
    //
    // Override TWindow virtual member functions
    //
    void SetupWindow();

  private:
    //
    // hidden to prevent accidental copying or assignment
    //
    TInputDialog(const TInputDialog&);
    TInputDialog& operator=(const TInputDialog&);

  DECLARE_STREAMABLE(TInputDialog, 1);
};
```

The Buffer and Prompt data buffers are pointers to the text buffer and prompting string, respectively. The BufferSize data member stores the size of the buffer that returns the user's input.

The class constructor requires the parameters for the parent window, the pointer to the dialog box title, the pointer to the prompt string, the pointer to the text buffer, and the buffer size. The constructor calls the TDialog constructor to pass the parameter parent, the SD_INPUTDIALOG resource identifier, and the AModule parameter. The SD_INPUTDIALOG identifier is the name of the dialog box resource defined in the INPUTDIA.DLG resource file, which is supplied by Borland.

The most noteworthy TInputDialog member function is perhaps the TransferData function. This function transfers the data between the edit control of the input dialog box and the text buffer. If the caller passes the argument TF_SETDATA to the Direction parameter, the function transfers data from the text buffer to the edit control. The function moves data in the reverse direction when a caller passes the TF_GETDATA argument.

Let's look at a simple number guessing game that uses the input dialog box to prompt you for a new guess. The game has a main menu with the Exit and Game menu items. To start the game, click the Game menu item or press Alt+G. The program generates a secret number between 0 and 1,000 and allows you up to 10 guesses. To assist you in refining your guess, the program displays hints in the dialog box that tells you whether your last guess was higher or lower than the secret number. You can stop the game at any time by clicking the Cancel button. In this case, the program displays the secret number. If you fail to guess the number after 10 tries, the program also displays the secret number. If you do manage to guess the number, the program displays a congratulatory message. Figure 6.1 shows a sample session with the INPUTDLG.EXE application.

Let's look at the source code for the number guessing game. Listing 6.1 shows the contents of the INPUTDLG.DEF definition file. Listing 6.2 shows the source code for the INPUTDLG.H header file that contains a single constant declaration. Listing 6.3 shows the script for the INPUTDLG.RC resource file. The file includes the INPUTDIA.DLG resource file required to define the ObjectWindows input dialog box. Listing 6.4 shows the source code for the INPUTDLG.CPP program file.

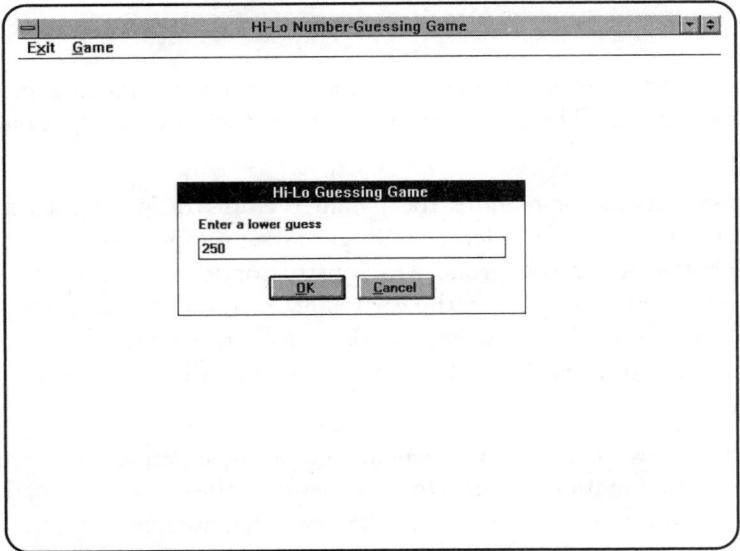

Figure 6.1. A sample session with the INPUTDLG.EXE application.

Listing 6.1. The contents of the INPUTDLG.DEF definition file.

```
NAME          InputDlg
DESCRIPTION   'An OWL Windows Application'
EXETYPE       WINDOWS
CODE          PRELOAD MOVEABLE DISCARDABLE
DATA          PRELOAD MOVEABLE MULTIPLE
HEAPSIZE      1024
STACKSIZE     8384
```

Listing 6.2. The source code for the INPUTDLG.H header file.

```
#define CM_GAME     101
#define IDM_MAINMENU 400
```

Listing 6.3. The script for the INPUTDLG.RC resource file.

```
#include <windows.h>
#include <owl\window.rh>
#include <owl\inputdia.rh>
#include <owl\inputdia.rc>
#include "inputdlg.h"

IDM_MAINMENU MENU LOADONCALL MOVEABLE PURE DISCARDABLE
BEGIN
    MENUITEM "E&xit", CM_EXIT
    MENUITEM "&Game", CM_GAME
END
```

Listing 6.4. The source code for the INPUTDLG.CPP program file.

```
/*
  Program illustrates using the input dialog box in a
  number-guessing game
*/
#include <owl\applicat.h>
#include <owl\framewin.h>
#include <owl\inputdia.h>
#include "inputdlg.h"
```

continues

LISTING 6.4. CONTINUED

```
#include <stdlib.h>
#include <stdio.h>
#include <string.h>

const MaxBuffer = 81;

// declare the custom application class as
// a subclass of TApplication
class TWinApp : public TApplication
{
public:
  TWinApp() : TApplication() {}

protected:
  virtual void InitMainWindow();
};

// expand the functionality of TWindow by deriving class TMainWindow
class TMainWindow : public TWindow
{
public:

  TMainWindow() : TWindow(0, 0, 0) {}

protected:

  // handle the Game menu item
  void CMGame();

  // handle closing the window
  virtual BOOL CanClose();

  DECLARE_RESPONSE_TABLE(TMainWindow);
};

DEFINE_RESPONSE_TABLE1(TMainWindow, TWindow)
  EV_COMMAND(CM_GAME, CMGame),
END_RESPONSE_TABLE;

void TMainWindow::CMGame()
{
  char s[MaxBuffer];
  int n, m;
  int MaxIter = 10;
  int iter = 0;
  BOOL ok = TRUE;
  TInputDialog* pDlg;
```

```
    randomize();
    n = random(1001);

    strcpy(s, "500");
    // execute the opening dialog box
    pDlg = new TInputDialog(this, "Hi-Lo Guessing Game",
                            "Enter a number between 0 and 1000",
                            s, sizeof(s));
    if (pDlg->Execute() == IDOK) {
        m = atoi(s);
        iter++;
        // loop to obtain the other guesses
        while (m != n && iter < MaxIter && ok == TRUE) {
          // is the user's guess higher?
          if (m > n) {
            pDlg = new TInputDialog(this,
                            "Hi-Lo Guessing Game",
                            "Enter a lower guess",
                             s, sizeof(s));
            ok = (pDlg->Execute() == IDOK) ? TRUE : FALSE;

          }
          else {
            pDlg = new TInputDialog(this,
                            "Hi-Lo Guessing Game",
                            "Enter a higher guess",
                             s, sizeof(s));
            ok = (pDlg->Execute() == IDOK) ? TRUE : FALSE;
          }
          m = atoi(s);
          iter++;
        }

        // did the user guess the secret number
        if (iter < MaxIter && ok == TRUE) {
        MessageBeep(MB_ICONEXCLAMATION);
        MessageBeep(MB_ICONEXCLAMATION);
        sprintf(s, "You guessed it! It's %d", n);
        MessageBox(s, "Congratulations!", MB_OK);
        }
        else {
        MessageBeep(-1);
          sprintf(s, "The secret number is %d", n);
          MessageBox(s, "Sorry!", MB_OK);
        }
    }
}

BOOL TMainWindow::CanClose()
{
```

continues

LISTING 6.4. CONTINUED

```
    return MessageBox("Want to close this application",
                      "Query", MB_YESNO | MB_ICONQUESTION) == IDYES;
}

void TWinApp::InitMainWindow()
{
  MainWindow = new TFrameWindow(0, "Hi-Lo Number-Guessing Game",
                                new TMainWindow);
  // load the menu resource
  MainWindow->AssignMenu(TResID(IDM_MAINMENU));
}

int OwlMain(int /* argc */, char** /*argv[] */)
{
  TWinApp app;
  return app.Run();
}
```

The program in Listing 6.4 declares two classes: the application class TWinApp, and the main window class TMainWindow.

The most relevant part of the program is the CMGame member function, which executes the number guessing game. The function performs the following tasks:

- Randomizes the seed for the random-number generating function.

- Obtains a random number in the range of 0 to 1,000 and stores that number in the local variable n.

- Assigns the string "500" to the text buffer (implemented using the s local variable).

- Executes the opening dialog box by calling the Execute member function to create an instance of the TInputDialog class. If the Execute function returns IDOK, the game resumes by executing the next tasks.

- Converts the contents of the text buffer into an int and stores that value in the m local variable.

- Increments the iteration counter variable iter.

- Loops to obtain other guesses while the following conditions are true:

  - The contents of variables m and n differ.

  - The number of iterations is less than the maximum limit.

- The Boolean ok flag is TRUE to indicate that you did not click the Cancel button of the dialog box.

The loop displays one of two dialog box versions depending on whether the last number you entered is less than or greater than the secret number. The loop also converts your input into the integer stored in variable m and increments the loop iteration counter.

- Displays a congratulatory message if you guessed the secret number within the allowed number of iterations. Otherwise, the program displays the secret number.

THE TCOMMONDIALOG CLASS

The classes that model the common dialog boxes in this chapter are descendants of the TDialog class. In addition, these classes, except TInputDialog, are also descendants of the TCommonDialog class. Here is the declaration of the TCommonDialog class.

```
class _OWLCLASS TCommonDialog : public TDialog {
  public:
    TCommonDialog(TWindow* parent, const char far* title = 0,
                  TModule* module = 0);

    HWND DoCreate()
         { return 0; }
    int DoExecute()
         { return IDCANCEL; }

  protected:
    const char far* CDTitle;

    void SetupWindow();

    // Default behavior inline for message response functions
    //
    void CmOkCancel()
         { DefaultProcessing(); } // EV_COMMAND(IDOK or IDCANCEL)
    void EvClose()
         { DefaultProcessing(); } // EV_CLOSE
    void CmHelp()
         { DefaultProcessing(); } // EV_COMMAND(pshHelp,

  private:
    TCommonDialog(const TCommonDialog&);
    TCommonDialog& operator=(const TCommonDialog&);
```

continues

continued

```
  DECLARE_RESPONSE_TABLE(TCommonDialog);
  DECLARE_CASTABLE;
};
```

The `TCommonDialog` class is the root of the common dialog class subhierarchy that models color selection, font selection, input file selection, output file selection, printing, text search, and text replacement dialog boxes.

THE FILE DIALOG CLASSES

The `ObjectWindows` library offers the classes `TOpenSaveDialog` and `TFileOpenDialog`, and `TFileSaveDialog`, which implement the common modal dialog boxes that support opening a file and saving data in a file. The `TOpenSaveDialog` class is a descendant of `TCommonDialog` class and the parent of `TFileOpenDialog` and `TFileSaveDialog` classes. Figure 6.2 shows a standard file dialog box in the open file mode. The Open and Save As dialog boxes have the following controls:

- A filename combo box
- A file filter combo box
- A current directory static text control
- A directory list box that shows the current directory, its sibling directories, and its parent directory
- A drives combo box
- An OK pushbutton
- A Cancel pushbutton
- A Help pushbutton
- A read-only check box to select read-only files

The Supporting Classes and Structures

The `TOpenSaveDialog` class encapsulates the `OPENFILENAME` structure and the `GetOpenFileName` and `GetSaveFileName` Windows API functions. The `OPENFILENAME` structure is declared as follows.

```
typedef struct tagOFN
{
    DWORD     lStructSize;
    HWND      hwndOwner;
    HINSTANCE hInstance;
```

```
    LPCSTR  lpstrFilter;
    LPSTR   lpstrCustomFilter;
    DWORD   nMaxCustFilter;
    DWORD   nFilterIndex;
    LPSTR   lpstrFile;
    DWORD   nMaxFile;
    LPSTR   lpstrFileTitle;
    DWORD   nMaxFileTitle;
    LPCSTR  lpstrInitialDir;
    LPCSTR  lpstrTitle;
    DWORD   Flags;
    UINT    nFileOffset;
    UINT    nFileExtension;
    LPCSTR  lpstrDefExt;
    LPARAM  lCustData;
    UINT    (CALLBACK *lpfnHook)(HWND, UINT, WPARAM, LPARAM);
    LPCSTR  lpTemplateName;
}   OPENFILENAME;
```

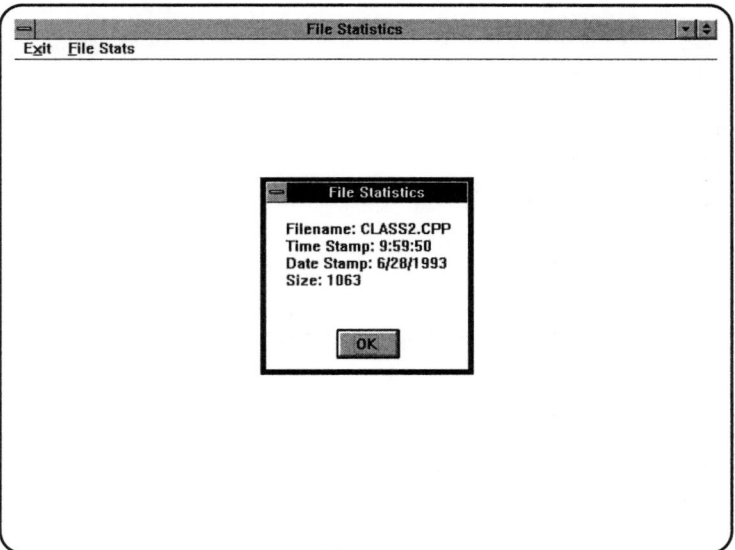

Figure 6.2. A sample session with the COMMDLG1.EXE program.

The OPENFILENAME structure and its related Windows API functions use the following OFN_*xxxx* constants:

```
#define OFN_READONLY              0x00000001
#define OFN_OVERWRITEPROMPT       0x00000002
#define OFN_HIDEREADONLY          0x00000004
#define OFN_NOCHANGEDIR           0x00000008
```

continues

continued

```
#define OFN_SHOWHELP                    0x00000010
#define OFN_ENABLEHOOK                  0x00000020
#define OFN_ENABLETEMPLATE              0x00000040
#define OFN_ENABLETEMPLATEHANDLE        0x00000080
#define OFN_NOVALIDATE                  0x00000100
#define OFN_ALLOWMULTISELECT            0x00000200
#define OFN_EXTENSIONDIFFERENT          0x00000400
#define OFN_PATHMUSTEXIST               0x00000800
#define OFN_FILEMUSTEXIST               0x00001000
#define OFN_CREATEPROMPT                0x00002000
#define OFN_SHAREAWARE                  0x00004000
#define OFN_NOREADONLYRETURN            0x00008000
#define OFN_NOTESTFILECREATE            0x00010000
```

The declaration of the TOpenSaveDialog class is given next:

```
class _OWLCLASS TOpenSaveDialog : public TCommonDialog {
  public:
    class _OWLCLASS TData {
      public:
        DWORD      Flags;
        DWORD      Error;
        char*      FileName;
        char*      Filter;
        char*      CustomFilter;
        int        FilterIndex;
        char*      InitialDir;
        char*      DefExt;

        TData(DWORD flags=0, char* filter=0, char* customFilter=0,
              char* initialDir=0, char* defExt=0);
        ~TData();

        void    SetFilter(const char* filter = 0);

        void    Write(opstream& os);
        void    Read(ipstream& is);
    };

    TOpenSaveDialog(TWindow*      parent,
                    TData&        data,
                    TResId        templateId = 0,
                    const char far* title = 0,
                    TModule*      module = 0);

    static int GetFileTitleLen(const char far* fileName)
        { return ::GetFileTitle((LPSTR)fileName, 0, 0);  //Win32 cast

    static int GetFileTitle(const char far* fileName,
                            char far* fileTitle,
```

```
                          int fileTitleLen) //Win32 casts
           { return ::GetFileTitle((LPSTR)fileName,
                               fileTitle,(WORD)fileTitleLen); }

  protected:
    OPENFILENAME ofn;
    TData&        Data;

    TOpenSaveDialog(TWindow* parent, TData& data, TModule* module = 0);
    void Init(TResId templateId);
    BOOL DialogFunction(UINT message, WPARAM, LPARAM);

    //
    // override TWindow & TDialog virtuals
    //
    int DoExecute() = 0;

    //
    // Virtual function called when a share violation occurs in dlg
    //
    virtual int ShareViolation();

    //
    // Messages registered by the common dialog DLL
    //
    static UINT ShareViMsgId;

    //
    // Default behavior inline for message response functions
    //
    void CmOk()
         { DefaultProcessing(); } // EV_COMMAND(IDOK,
    void CmLbSelChanged()
         { DefaultProcessing(); } // EV_COMMAND(lst1 or lst2)

  private:
    TOpenSaveDialog(const TOpenSaveDialog&);
    TOpenSaveDialog& operator =(const TOpenSaveDialog&);

  DECLARE_RESPONSE_TABLE(TOpenSaveDialog);
};
```

The TOpenSaveDialog class declares the TData nested class. This nested class
contains data members that store information related to the selected file and
other information used in the file selection process. The TOpenSaveDialog::TData
class works with both descendants, TFileOpenDialog and TFileSaveDialog.

Typically you create an instance of the TData class and initialize it when you
create the main window. The creation of the TData instance involves specifying
the values for the TData members Flags, Filter, CustomFilter, InitialDir, and
DefExt.

The argument for the parameter `flags` in the `TData` constructor can have one or more OFN_*xxxx* constants to fine-tune various aspects of the file dialog box. In the case of multiple OFN_*xxxx* constants, you need to use the bitwise or operator to combine their effects. For example, the following expression

```
OFN_HIDEREADONLY ¦ OFN_NOCHANGEDIR ¦ OFN_FILEMUSTEXIST
```

performs the following dialog box operations:

1. Hides the read-only check box in the dialog box.

2. Sets the current directory back to the original one when the dialog box was opened.

3. Permits the user to type in only names of existing files. If this condition is violated, the dialog box displays a warning message dialog box.

The argument for `filter` parameter (in the `TData` constructor) is a specially-formatted string. It contains pairs of substrings. The first pair member contains the wording of the filter—the string `C++ file (*.CPP)`, for example. This wording is selected by the dialog box user and need not include any filename wildcard. The second pair member contains the actual wildcard used in filtering the selected files—*.CPP, for example. The formatting rules to observe are:

- Use the bar character, ¦, to separate the substrings.

- Use pairs of strings, one for wording and one for the corresponding wildcard. The latter is actually used to filter the file selection.

- The string must end with an empty substring. That is, the last two string characters must be a pair of bar characters, ¦¦.

An example of the argument for `lpszFilter` is the following string:

```
char szFilter[] =
"All files (*.*)¦*.*¦C++ files¦*.cpp¦Header files (*.h)¦*.h¦¦";
```

This string displays three file selections. The first one allows you to select all of the files, the second permits you to choose the *.CPP files, and the last one enables you to pick the header files.

The argument for `customFilter` parameter (in the `TData` constructor) is a string that represents a user-specified file filter, such as *.CPP. The argument for the `initialDir` parameter can specify an initial directory other than the current one. The argument for the `defExt` parameter indicates the default file extension. The `Error` data member contains a CDERR_*xxxx* value, which identified the kind of error involved in creating the dialog box.

The declaration of the `TFileOpenDialog` is

```
class _OWLCLASS TFileOpenDialog : public TOpenSaveDialog {
  public:
    TFileOpenDialog(TWindow*        parent,
                    TData&          data,
                    TResId          templateId = 0,
                    const char far* title = 0,
                    TModule*        module = 0);

    //
    // override TDialog virtual functions
    //
    int  DoExecute();

  private:
    TFileOpenDialog(const TOpenSaveDialog&);
    TFileOpenDialog& operator=(const TOpenSaveDialog&);
};
```

The `TFileOpenDialog` class declares a constructor that has a list of five parameters. The `parent` parameter is the pointer to the parent window. The `data` parameter is the reference to the `TData` structure which passes the information for the file I/O operation. The `templateId` is the resource ID. The `title` parameter specifies the dialog box title.

The declaration of `TFileSaveDialog` class is

```
class _OWLCLASS TFileSaveDialog : public TOpenSaveDialog {
  public:
    TFileSaveDialog(TWindow*        parent,
                    TData&          data,
                    TResId          templateId = 0,
                    const char far* title = 0,
                    TModule*        module = 0);

    //
    // override TDialog virtual functions
    //
    int  DoExecute();

  private:
    TFileSaveDialog(const TFileSaveDialog&);
    TFileSaveDialog& operator=(const TFileSaveDialog&);
};
```

The `TFileOpenDialog` class constructor creates a modal dialog box defined by the various parameters. These parameters are similar to those in class `TFileSaveDialog`.

Invoking the File Dialog Box

After the TFileOpenDialog instance is created by the constructor, you can invoke the dialog box using the Execute member function. To accept the dialog box selection, click the OK button. This action makes the Execute function return the IDOK result. To close the dialog box without accepting the current selection, click the Cancel button or select the Close system menu option. Either action causes the Execute function to return IDCANCEL.

The File Statistics Program

Let me present a program that enables you to obtain the basic file statistics (file size and date/time stamp) using the standard file dialog box. Listing 6.5 shows the contents of the COMMDELG1.DEF definition file. Listing 6.6 shows the COMMDLG1.H header file. Listing 6.7 contains the script for the COMMDLG1.RC resource file. Listing 6.8 contains the source code for the COMMDLG1.CPP program file.

Compile and run the COMMDLG1.EXE program. Click the File Stats menu item to invoke the Open dialog box. The file filter combo box has two items: all the files and the .CPP files. You can select a file from the current directory or move to another directory. When you have selected a file, click the OK button. The Open dialog box disappears and a message box appears with the selected filename, size, and date/time stamp.

LISTING 6.5. THE CONTENTS OF THE COMMDLG1.DEF DEFINITION FILE.

```
NAME          CommDlg1
DESCRIPTION   'An OWL Windows Application'
EXETYPE       WINDOWS
CODE          PRELOAD MOVEABLE DISCARDABLE
DATA          PRELOAD MOVEABLE MULTIPLE
HEAPSIZE      1024
STACKSIZE     16384
```

LISTING 6.6. THE SOURCE CODE FOR THE COMMDLG1.H HEADER FILE.

```
#define CM_FILESTAT    100
#define IDM_MAINMENU   400
```

LISTING 6.7. THE SCRIPT FOR THE COMMDLG1.RC RESOURCE FILE.

```
#include <windows.h>
#include <owl\window.rh>
#include "commdlg1.h"


IDM_MAINMENU MENU LOADONCALL MOVEABLE PURE DISCARDABLE
BEGIN
    MENUITEM "E&xit", CM_EXIT
    MENUITEM "&File Stats", CM_FILESTAT
END
```

LISTING 6.8. THE SOURCE CODE FOR THE COMMDLG1.CPP PROGRAM FILE.

```
/*
   Program to test the Open File common dialog box. The program
   displays the basic statistics for the file you select
*/

#include <owl\applicat.h>
#include <owl\framewin.h>
#include <owl\opensave.h>
#include "commdlg1.h"
#include <stdlib.h>
#include <stdio.h>
#include <string.h>
#include <dos.h>
#include <dir.h>

const MaxStringLen = 256;

// declare the custom application class as
// a subclass of TApplication
class TWinApp : public TApplication
{
public:
  TWinApp() : TApplication() {}

protected:
  virtual void InitMainWindow();
};

// expand the functionality of TWindow by
// deriving class TMainWindow
class TMainWindow : public TWindow
```

continues

LISTING 6.8. CONTINUED

```cpp
{
public:

  TMainWindow();

protected:

  // the pointer to the data for the File Open dialog box
  TOpenSaveDialog::TData *FileData;

  // handle the calculation
  void CMFileStat();

  // handle exiting the program
  void CMExit();

  // handle closing the window
  virtual BOOL CanClose();

  // declare the message map macro
  DECLARE_RESPONSE_TABLE(TMainWindow);

};

DEFINE_RESPONSE_TABLE1(TMainWindow, TWindow)
  EV_COMMAND(CM_FILESTAT, CMFileStat),
  EV_COMMAND(CM_EXIT, CMExit),
END_RESPONSE_TABLE;

TMainWindow::TMainWindow()
  : TWindow(0, 0, 0)
{
  FileData = new TOpenSaveDialog::TData(
        DWORD(OFN_HIDEREADONLY | OFN_OVERWRITEPROMPT),
        "All Files (*.*)|*.*|"
        "C++ Programs (*.cpp)|*.cpp|"
        "Batch files (*.bat)|*.bat||",
        "*.cpp", "", "*.cpp");
}

void TMainWindow::CMFileStat()
{
  char selFile[MaxStringLen];
  char s[MaxStringLen];
  char format[MaxStringLen];
  ffblk fileInfo;
  unsigned Hour, Minute, Second, Day, Month, Year,
        uDate, uTime;
```

```
TFileOpenDialog* FileDialog;

FileDialog = new TFileOpenDialog(this, *FileData);

if (FileDialog->Execute() == IDOK) {
  // get the file information
  strcpy(selFile, FileData->FileName);
  findfirst(selFile, &fileInfo, FA_ARCH);
  // build the format string
  strcpy(format, "Filename: %s\n");
  strcat(format, "Time Stamp: %u:%u:%u\n");
  strcat(format, "Date Stamp: %u/%u/%u\n");
  strcat(format, "Size: %ld\n");
  uTime = (unsigned)fileInfo.ff_ftime;
  // get the seconds
  Second = 2 * (uTime & 0x1f);
  // get the minutes
  Minute = (uTime >> 5) & 0x3f;
  // get the hours
  Hour = (uTime >> 11) & 0x1f;
  uDate = (unsigned)fileInfo.ff_fdate;
  // get the day
  Day =  uDate & 0x1f;
  // get the month
  Month = (uDate >> 5) & 0xf;
  // get the year
  Year = (uDate >> 9) & 0x7f;
  sprintf(s, format, fileInfo.ff_name, Hour, Minute, Second,
      Month, Day, Year + 1980U, fileInfo.ff_fsize);
  MessageBox(s, "File Statistics", MB_OK);
  }
}

void TMainWindow::CMExit()
{
  Parent->SendMessage(WM_CLOSE);
}

BOOL TMainWindow::CanClose()
{
  return MessageBox("Want to close this application?",
           "Query", MB_YESNO | MB_ICONQUESTION) == IDYES;
}

void TWinApp::InitMainWindow()
{
  MainWindow = new TFrameWindow(0, "File Statistics",
              new TMainWindow);
  // load the menu resource
  MainWindow->AssignMenu(TResID(IDM_MAINMENU));
```

continues

LISTING 6.8. CONTINUED

```
  // enable the keyboard handler
  MainWindow->EnableKBHandler();
}

int OwlMain(int /* argc */, char** /*argv[] */)
{
  TWinApp app;
  return app.Run();
}
```

Let's now look at the code for the program in Listing 6.4. The window class
TMainWindow declares a constructor, a data member, and three member functions.
The data member FileData is a pointer to the supporting structure
TOpenSaveDialog::TData. The TMainWindow constructor initializes the member FileData
by dynamically allocating a new instance of TOpenSaveDialog::TData. This instance is initialized using the ORed constants OFN_HIDEREADONLY and
OFN_OVERWRITEPROMPT. In addition, the creation of the preceding instance specifies
the arguments for the parameters filter (the long string, which spans more than
three lines), customFilter (the string "*.cpp"), initialDir (the empty string), and
defxt (the string *.cpp).

The most relevant component of the class is the CMFileStat member function.
The function declares a number of local variables, among them is the string
szFilter that contains the two pairs of file filters. The function also declares the
ffblk-typed fileInfo variable. This variable contains the structure for the DOS
file data. In addition, the function declares the FileDialog object as a pointer to
TFileOpenDialog. The function CmFileStat creates a dynamic instance of
TFileOpenDialog using the arguments this and *FileData. The latter argument
passes information to and from the dialog box.

The CMFileStat function invokes the member function Execute in an if statement
that compares the result of Execute with IDOK. If the two values match, the
function obtains the full name of the selected file by using the expression
FileData->FileName. (FileName is a member of structure TOpenSave::TData.) The
result of this function is assigned to the string variable selFile. The function
CMFileStat then uses this string variable in the function findfirst to obtain the
information for the selected file and stores it in the fileInfo variable. The rest
of the statements, in the if statement, obtain the file statistics and build the
output string. The function then displays the text of this output string in a call
to function MessageBox.

THE TCHOOSEFONTDIALOG CLASS

The `TChooseFontDialog` class supports the Font dialog box that enables you to select different fonts. Figure 6.3 shows the Font dialog box, which contains the following controls:

- A font selection combo box

- A font style combo box

- A font size combo box

- An Effects group box that contains the Strikeout check box, the Underline check box, and a color selection combo box

- A Sample group box that displays a sample of the currently selected font

- An OK pushbutton

- A Cancel pushbutton

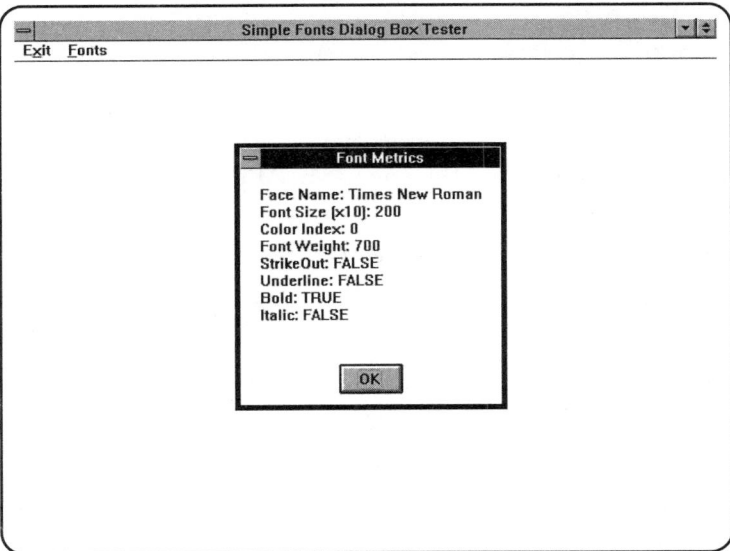

Figure 6.3. A sample session with the COMMDLG2.EXE program.

Supporting Classes and Structures

The TChooseFontDialog class encapsulates the CHOOSEFONT structure and the Windows API function ChooseFont. The CHOOSEFONT structure is declared as follows:

```
typedef struct tagCHOOSEFONT
{
    DWORD lStructSize;
    HWND hwndOwner;  /* caller's window handle */
    HDC hDC; /* printer DC/IC or NULL */
    LOGFONT FAR* lpLogFont;  /* ptr. to a LOGFONT struct */
    int iPointSize; /* 10 * size in points of selected font */
    DWORD Flags; /* enum. type flags */
    COLORREF rgbColors; /* returned text color */
    LPARAM lCustData; /* data passed to hook fn. */
    UINT (CALLBACK* lpfnHook)(HWND, UINT, WPARAM, LPARAM);
                            /* ptr. to hook function */
    LPCSTR lpTemplateName; /* custom template name */
    HINSTANCE hInstance; /* instance handle of.EXE that
                        contains cust. dlg. template */
    LPSTR lpszStyle; /* return the style field here
                    must be LF_FACESIZE or bigger */
    UINT nFontType; /* same value reported to the EnumFonts
                    call back with the extra FONTTYPE_
                    bits added */
    int nSizeMin; /* minimum pt size allowed & */
    int nSizeMax; /* max pt size allowed if
                CF_LIMITSIZE is used */
} CHOOSEFONT;
```

The CHOOSEFONT structure and the ChooseFont API function use the following CF_*xxxx* constants:

```
#define CF_SCREENFONTS            0x00000001
#define CF_PRINTERFONTS           0x00000002
#define CF_BOTH                   (CF_SCREENFONTS | CF_PRINTERFONTS)
#define CF_SHOWHELP               0x00000004L
#define CF_ENABLEHOOK             0x00000008L
#define CF_ENABLETEMPLATE         0x00000010L
#define CF_ENABLETEMPLATEHANDLE   0x00000020L
#define CF_INITTOLOGFONTSTRUCT    0x00000040L
#define CF_USESTYLE               0x00000080L
#define CF_EFFECTS                0x00000100L
#define CF_APPLY                  0x00000200L
#define CF_ANSIONLY               0x00000400L
#define CF_NOVECTORFONTS          0x00000800L
#define CF_NOOEMFONTS             CF_NOVECTORFONTS
#define CF_NOSIMULATIONS          0x00001000L
#define CF_LIMITSIZE              0x00002000L
#define CF_FIXEDPITCHONLY         0x00004000L
```

```
#define CF_WYSIWYG              0x00008000L /* must also have
                                                CF_SCREENFONTS &
                                                CF_PRINTERFONTS */
#define CF_FORCEFONTEXIST       0x00010000L
#define CF_SCALABLEONLY         0x00020000L
#define CF_TTONLY               0x00040000L
#define CF_NOFACESEL            0x00080000L
#define CF_NOSTYLESEL '         0x00100000L
#define CF_NOSIZESEL            0x00200000L

/* these are extra nFontType bits that are added to what is
   returned to the EnumFonts callback routine */

#define SIMULATED_FONTTYPE      0x8000
#define PRINTER_FONTTYPE        0x4000
#define SCREEN_FONTTYPE         0x2000
#define BOLD_FONTTYPE           0x0100
#define ITALIC_FONTTYPE         0x0200
#define REGULAR_FONTTYPE        0x0400
```

The TChooseFontDialog class, a descendant of TCommonDialog, is declared as follows:

```
class _OWLCLASS TChooseFontDialog : public TCommonDialog {
  public:
    class _OWLCLASS TData {
      public:
        DWORD       Flags;
        DWORD       Error;
        HDC         DC;
        LOGFONT     LogFont;
        int         PointSize;
        TColor      Color;
        char far*   Style;
        WORD        FontType;
        int         SizeMin;
        int         SizeMax;
    };

    TChooseFontDialog(TWindow*        parent,
                      TData&          data,
                      TResId          templateId = 0,
                      const char far* title = 0,
                      TModule*        module = 0);

  protected:
    CHOOSEFONT  cf;
    TData&      Data;

    int DoExecute();
    BOOL DialogFunction(UINT message, WPARAM, LPARAM);
```

continues

continued

```
    // Default behavior inline for message response functions
    //
    void CmFontApply()
        { DefaultProcessing(); }   // EV_COMMAND(psh3...

  private:
    TChooseFontDialog(const TChooseFontDialog&);
    TChooseFontDialog& operator=(const TChooseFontDialog&);

  DECLARE_RESPONSE_TABLE(TChooseFontDialog);
  DECLARE_CASTABLE;
};
```

The TChooseFontDialog class declares a constructor that creates instances of modal font selection dialog boxes. The class also declares the nested TData class with data members for storing font-related information, such as font name, size, type, and weight. The member TData::Flags stores the flags used to fine-tune the dialog box appearance and operations. The other members set and query information assigned to and obtained from the Fonts dialog box. The data member Error contains a CDERR_*xxxx* value, which identified the kind of error involved in creating the dialog box.

Invoking a Font dialog box is very similar to invoking an Open or Save As dialog box. The OK button, Cancel button, and the Close system menu item play the same role in influencing the result returned by the Execute member function. The Windows API function CommDlgExtendedError can also be used to detect errors when the Execute function returns IDCANCEL.

A Sample Program

Let me present a simple program that invokes the Font dialog box and then displays the results returned by the various helper functions. Please feel free to further develop the program to actually change the fonts and display text using the current font. For now, I present a simple program that focuses on creating, using, and accessing the data of a Font dialog box.

Listing 6.9 shows the contents of the COMMDLG2.DEF definition file. Listing 6.10 shows the COMMDLG2.H header file. Listing 6.11 contains the script for the COMMDLG2.RC resource file. Listing 6.12 contains the source code for the COMMDLG2.CPP program file.

Compile and run the COMMDLG2.EXE program. Click the Fonts menu item to invoke the Font dialog box. Experiment with selecting different fonts, font styles, font sizes, font colors, and font effects. Click the OK button to close the dialog box. The program then displays a message box that contains the numeric code for the selected font along with its style, color, and other effects.

LISTING 6.9. THE CONTENTS OF THE COMMDLG2.DEF DEFINITION FILE.

```
NAME          CommDlg2
DESCRIPTION   'An OWL Windows Application'
EXETYPE       WINDOWS
CODE          PRELOAD MOVEABLE DISCARDABLE
DATA          PRELOAD MOVEABLE MULTIPLE
HEAPSIZE      1024
STACKSIZE     16384
```

LISTING 6.10. THE SOURCE CODE FOR THE COMMDLG2.H HEADER FILE.

```
#define CM_FONTCHANGE 100
#define IDM_MAINMENU  400
```

LISTING 6.11. THE SCRIPT FOR THE COMMDLG2.RC RESOURCE FILE.

```
#include <windows.h>
#include <owl\window.rh>
#include "commdlg2.h"

IDM_MAINMENU MENU LOADONCALL MOVEABLE PURE DISCARDABLE
BEGIN
    MENUITEM "E&xit", CM_EXIT
    MENUITEM "&Fonts", CM_FONTCHANGE
END
```

LISTING 6.12. THE SOURCE CODE FOR THE COMMDLG2.CPP PROGRAM FILE.

```
/*
  Program to test the Choose Font common dialog box.
*/

#include <owl\applicat.h>
#include <owl\framewin.h>
```

continues

LISTING 6.12. CONTINUED

```
#include <owl\choosefo.h>
#include "commdlg2.h"
#include <stdio.h>
#include <string.h>

const int MaxStrLen = 31;
const int MaxLongStrLen = 1024;

// declare the custom application class as
// a subclass of TApplication
class TWinApp : public TApplication
{
public:
  TWinApp() : TApplication() {}

protected:
  virtual void InitMainWindow();
};

// expand the functionality of TWindow by
// deriving class TMainWindow
class TMainWindow : public TWindow
{
public:

  TMainWindow();

protected:

  LOGFONT MainFontData;

  // the data for the font dialog box
  TChooseFontDialog::TData FontData;

  // handle invoking the font dialog box
  void CMFonts();

  // handle exiting the program
  void CMExit();

  // handle closing the window
  virtual BOOL CanClose();

  // declare the message map macro
  DECLARE_RESPONSE_TABLE(TMainWindow);

};

DEFINE_RESPONSE_TABLE1(TMainWindow, TWindow)
```

```
  EV_COMMAND(CM_FONTCHANGE, CMFonts),
  EV_COMMAND(CM_EXIT, CMExit),
END_RESPONSE_TABLE;

TMainWindow::TMainWindow()
  : TWindow(0, 0, 0)
{
  MainFontData.lfHeight = 26;
  MainFontData.lfWidth = 10;
  MainFontData.lfEscapement = 0;
  MainFontData.lfOrientation = 0;
  MainFontData.lfWeight = FW_BOLD;
  MainFontData.lfItalic = 0;
  MainFontData.lfUnderline = 0;
  MainFontData.lfStrikeOut = 0;
  MainFontData.lfCharSet = ANSI_CHARSET;
  MainFontData.lfOutPrecision = OUT_DEFAULT_PRECIS;
  MainFontData.lfClipPrecision = CLIP_DEFAULT_PRECIS;
  MainFontData.lfQuality = PROOF_QUALITY;
  MainFontData.lfPitchAndFamily = VARIABLE_PITCH | FF_ROMAN;
  strcpy(MainFontData.lfFaceName, "Times New Roman");
}

void TMainWindow::CMFonts()
{
  char s[MaxLongStrLen];
  char StrikeOutStr[MaxStrLen];
  char UnderlineStr[MaxStrLen];
  char BoldStr[MaxStrLen];
  char ItalicStr[MaxStrLen];
  char SizeStr[MaxStrLen];
  char WeightStr[MaxStrLen];
  char ColorStr[MaxStrLen];
  TChooseFontDialog* FontDialog;

  FontData.LogFont = MainFontData;
  FontData.Flags = CF_ANSIONLY | CF_TTONLY | CF_SCREENFONTS |
          CF_INITTOLOGFONTSTRUCT | CF_EFFECTS;
  FontData.FontType = SCREEN_FONTTYPE;
  FontData.SizeMin = 20;
  FontData.SizeMax = 20;
  FontDialog = new TChooseFontDialog(this, FontData);

  if (FontDialog->Execute() == IDOK) {
    MainFontData = FontData.LogFont;
    sprintf(SizeStr, "%d\r\n", FontData.PointSize);
    sprintf(WeightStr, "%d\r\n", FontData.LogFont.lfWeight);
    sprintf(ColorStr, "%lu\r\n", COLORREF(FontData.Color));
    sprintf(StrikeOutStr, "%s\r\n",
          (FontData.LogFont.lfStrikeOut) ? "TRUE" : "FALSE");
```

continues

LISTING 6.12. CONTINUED

```
    sprintf(UnderlineStr, "%s\r\n",
            (FontData.LogFont.lfUnderline) ? "TRUE" : "FALSE");
    sprintf(BoldStr, "%s\r\n",
            (FontData.LogFont.lfWeight >= FW_SEMIBOLD &&
             FontData.LogFont.lfWeight <= FW_EXTRABOLD) ?
             "TRUE" : "FALSE");
    sprintf(ItalicStr, "%s\r\n",
            (FontData.LogFont.lfItalic) ? "TRUE" : "FALSE");
    // begin building output string
    strcpy(s, "Face Name: ");
    strcat(s, FontData.LogFont.lfFaceName);
    strcat(s, "\r\n");
    strcat(s, "Font Size (x10): ");
    strcat(s, SizeStr);
    strcat(s, "Color Index: ");
    strcat(s, ColorStr);
    strcat(s, "Font Weight: ");
    strcat(s, WeightStr);
    strcat(s, "StrikeOut: ");
    strcat(s, StrikeOutStr);
    strcat(s, "Underline: ");
    strcat(s, UnderlineStr);
    strcat(s, "Bold: ");
    strcat(s, BoldStr);
    strcat(s, "Italic: ");
    strcat(s, ItalicStr);
    MessageBox(s, "Font Metrics", MB_OK);
  }
}

void TMainWindow::CMExit()
{
  Parent->SendMessage(WM_CLOSE);
}

BOOL TMainWindow::CanClose()
{
  return MessageBox("Want to close this application?",
              "Query", MB_YESNO ¦ MB_ICONQUESTION) == IDYES;
}

void TWinApp::InitMainWindow()
{
  MainWindow = new TFrameWindow(0, "Simple Fonts Dialog Box Tester",
                  new TMainWindow);
  // load the menu resource
  MainWindow->AssignMenu(TResID(IDM_MAINMENU));
  // enable the keyboard handler
```

```
  MainWindow->EnableKBHandler();
}

int OwlMain(int /* argc */, char** /*argv[] */)
{
  TWinApp app;
  return app.Run();
}
```

Let's look at the source code shown in Listing 6.12. The window class TMainWindow declares a constructor, two data members, and a number of member functions. The data member MainFontData is a LOGFONT structure and the member FontData is a TChooseFontDialog::TData structure. Both members are involved in passing font metrics information to and from the dialog box. The constructor TMainWindow initializes the various fields of the data member MainFontData. This process selects the proof quality of the Times New Roman font. The font size is 26 point and is bold.

The relevant member function is CMFont. It declares a number of strings and a pointer to class TChooseFontDialog, FontDialog. The function assigns values to the nested members of member FontData. This assignment includes copying the member MainFontData to the nested LogFont member of FontData. The function dynamically allocates the dialog box and then invokes it using the Execute function in an if statement. The if statement compares the value returned by function Execute with IDOK. If the two values match, the CMFonts obtains the data from the various members of Fontdata and FontData.LogFont. The function CMFonts converts numerical and BOOL data into strings using the sprintf function. Notice that the statement, which determines if the font is bold, uses a more elaborate Boolean expression. This expression is true if the member FontData.LogFont.lfWeight is in the range FW_SEMIBOLD to FW_EXTRABOLD. The CMFonts function then labels and concatenates the individual results, inserting line breaks between the various individual results. The results string is then displayed in a message box.

THE TChooseColorDialog Class

The TChooseColorDialog class supports the color selection common dialog box. Figure 6.4 shows the Color dialog box. The dialog box contains various controls to select colors, define custom colors, and add to custom colors. As with every other dialog box, the Color dialog box has the OK and Cancel buttons.

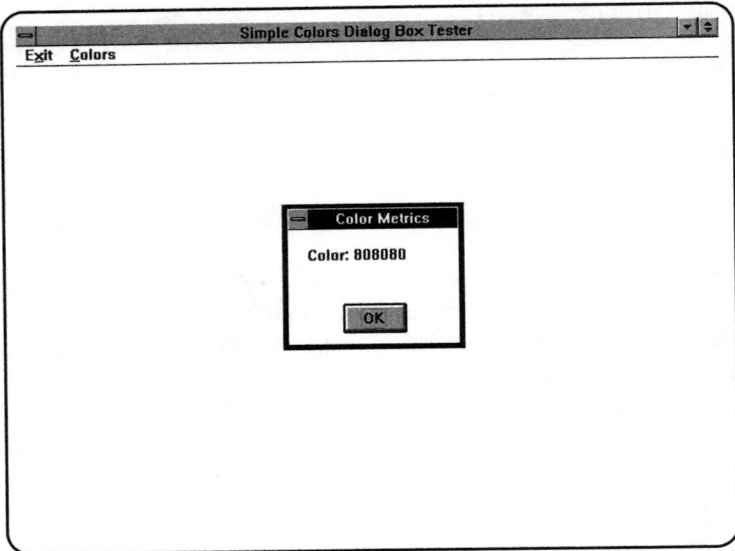

Figure 6.4. A sample session with the COMMDLG3.EXE program.

Supporting Classes and Structures

The TChooseColorDialog class encapsulates the CHOOSECOLOR structure and the Windows API function ChooseColor. The declaration of the CHOOSECOLOR structure is shown below:

```
typedef struct tagCHOOSECOLOR
{
    DWORD    lStructSize;
    HWND     hwndOwner;
    HWND     hInstance;
    COLORREF rgbResult;
    COLORREF FAR* lpCustColors;
    DWORD    Flags;
    LPARAM   lCustData;
    UINT     (CALLBACK* lpfnHook)(HWND, UINT, WPARAM, LPARAM);
    LPCSTR   lpTemplateName;
} CHOOSECOLOR;
```

The CHOOSECOLOR structure uses the following CC_*xxxx* constants:

```
#define CC_RGBINIT              0x00000001
#define CC_FULLOPEN             0x00000002
#define CC_PREVENTFULLOPEN      0x00000004
#define CC_SHOWHELP             0x00000008
#define CC_ENABLEHOOK           0x00000010
```

```
#define CC_ENABLETEMPLATE        0x00000020
#define CC_ENABLETEMPLATEHANDLE  0x00000040
```

The TChooseColorDialog class, a descendant of TCommonDialog, is declared as follows:

```
class _OWLCLASS TChooseColorDialog : public TCommonDialog {
  public:
    class _OWLCLASS TData {
      public:
        DWORD       Flags;
        DWORD       Error;
        TColor      Color;
        TColor*     CustColors;
    };

    TChooseColorDialog(TWindow*       parent,
                       TData&         data,
                       TResId         templateId = 0,
                       const char far* title = 0,
                       TModule*       module = 0);

    //
    // Set the current RGB color in this dialog
    //
    void SetRGBColor(TColor color)
        { SendMessage(SetRGBMsgId,0,color); }

  protected:
    CHOOSECOLOR  cc;
    TData&       Data;

    int DoExecute();
    BOOL DialogFunction(UINT message, WPARAM, LPARAM);

    //
    // Registered messages this class sends (to itself)
    //
    static UINT SetRGBMsgId;

    //
    // Default behavior inline for message response functions
    //
    LPARAM EvSetRGBColor(WPARAM, LPARAM) // EV_REGISTERED(SETRGBSTRING,
            { return DefaultProcessing(); }

  private:
    TChooseColorDialog(const TChooseColorDialog&);
    TChooseColorDialog& operator=(const TChooseColorDialog&);

  DECLARE_RESPONSE_TABLE(TChooseColorDialog);
  DECLARE_CASTABLE;
};
```

The class constructor has five parameters that customize the Color dialog boxes. The parameter parent is the pointer to the parent window. The parameter data is a reference to a `TChooseColorDialog::TData` structure. The parameter `templateId` is the dialog box resource ID. The parameter `title` specifies the title of the Colors dialog box.

The `TChooseColorDialog` declares the protected data members `cc` and `Data`. The member `cc` has the `CHOOSECOLOR` structure type. This data member enables the class instances to exchange data with the supporting API functions. The data member `Data` is a reference to the `TData` structure. This structure contains data members that set and query the color in the dialog box, and set the flags which fine-tune the appearance and operations of the dialog box. The data member `Error` contains a `CDERR_xxxx` value, which identified the kind of error involved in creating the dialog box.

Invoking a Color dialog box is very similar to invoking an Open or Save As dialog box. The OK button, Cancel button, and the Close system menu item play the same role in influencing the result returned by the `Execute` member function. The Windows API function `CommDlgExtendedError` can also be used to detect errors when the Execute function returns `IDCANCEL`.

A Sample Program

Let me present a simple program that invokes the Color dialog box and then displays the numeric value for the selected color. Listing 6.13 shows the contents of the COMMDLG3.DEF definition file. Listing 6.14 shows the COMMDLG3.H header file. Listing 6.15 contains the script for the COMMDLG3.RC resource file. Listing 6.16 contains the source code for the COMMDLG3.CPP program file.

Compile and run the COMMDLG3.EXE program. Click the Colors menu item to invoke the Color dialog box. Experiment with selecting different colors. Click the OK button to close the dialog box. The program then displays a message box that contains the integer code for the currently selected color.

LISTING 6.13. THE CONTENTS OF THE COMMDLG3.DEF DEFINITION FILE.

```
NAME         CommDlg3
DESCRIPTION  'An OWL Windows Application'
EXETYPE      WINDOWS
CODE         PRELOAD MOVEABLE DISCARDABLE
```

```
DATA        PRELOAD MOVEABLE MULTIPLE
HEAPSIZE    1024
STACKSIZE   16384
```

LISTING 6.14. THE SOURCE CODE FOR THE COMMDLG3.H HEADER FILE.

```
#define CM_COLORCHANGE 100
#define IDM_MAINMENU   400
```

LISTING 6.15. THE SCRIPT FOR THE COMMDLG3.RC RESOURCE FILE.

```
#include <windows.h>
#include <owl\window.rh>
#include "commdlg3.h"

IDM_MAINMENU MENU LOADONCALL MOVEABLE PURE DISCARDABLE
BEGIN
    MENUITEM "E&xit", CM_EXIT
    MENUITEM "&Colors", CM_COLORCHANGE
END
```

LISTING 6.16. THE SOURCE CODE FOR THE COMMDLG3.CPP PROGRAM FILE.

```
/*
  Program to test the Choose Color common dialog box.
*/

#include <owl\applicat.h>
#include <owl\framewin.h>
#include <owl\chooseco.h>
#include "commdlg3.h"
#include <stdio.h>
#include <string.h>

const int MaxStrLen = 31;
const int MaxLongStrLen = 1024;

// declare the custom application class as
// a subclass of TApplication
class TWinApp : public TApplication
```

continues

LISTING 6.16. CONTINUED

```
{
public:
  TWinApp() : TApplication() {}

protected:
  virtual void InitMainWindow();
};

// expand the functionality of TWindow by
// deriving class TMainWindow
class TMainWindow : public TWindow
{
public:

  TMainWindow();

protected:

  // the data for the color dialog box
  TChooseColorDialog::TData ColorData;

  // handle invoking the color dialog box
  void CMColors();

  // handle exiting the program
  void CMExit();

  // handle closing the window
  virtual BOOL CanClose();

  // declare the message map macro
  DECLARE_RESPONSE_TABLE(TMainWindow);

};

DEFINE_RESPONSE_TABLE1(TMainWindow, TWindow)
  EV_COMMAND(CM_COLORCHANGE, CMColors),
  EV_COMMAND(CM_EXIT, CMExit),
END_RESPONSE_TABLE;

TMainWindow::TMainWindow()
  : TWindow(0, 0, 0)
{
}

void TMainWindow::CMColors()
{
```

```
    char ColorStr[MaxStrLen];
    static TColor CustColors[16] =
      {
        TColor(0,0,0), TColor(255, 255, 255), TColor(128, 128, 128),
        TColor(255, 0, 0), TColor(0, 255, 0), TColor(0, 0, 255),
        TColor(255, 128, 0), TColor(128, 255, 0), TColor(128, 0, 255),
        TColor(255, 0, 128), TColor(0, 255, 128), TColor(0, 128, 255),
        TColor(255, 128, 128), TColor(128, 255, 128),
        TColor(128, 128, 255), TColor(64, 64, 64)
      };
    TChooseColorDialog* ColorDialog;

    ColorData.Color = TColor(255, 0, 0);
    ColorData.Flags = CC_FULLOPEN | CC_SHOWHELP | CC_RGBINIT;
    ColorData.CustColors = CustColors;
    ColorDialog = new TChooseColorDialog(this, ColorData);

    if (ColorDialog->Execute() == IDOK) {
      sprintf(ColorStr, "Color: %lX\r\n", COLORREF(ColorData.Color));
      MessageBox(ColorStr, "Color Metrics", MB_OK);
    }
}

void TMainWindow::CMExit()
{
  Parent->SendMessage(WM_CLOSE);
}

BOOL TMainWindow::CanClose()
{
  return MessageBox("Want to close this application?",
            "Query", MB_YESNO | MB_ICONQUESTION) == IDYES;
}

void TWinApp::InitMainWindow()
{
  MainWindow = new TFrameWindow(0, "Simple Colors Dialog Box Tester",
                new TMainWindow);
  // load the menu resource
  MainWindow->AssignMenu(TResID(IDM_MAINMENU));
  // enable the keyboard handler
  MainWindow->EnableKBHandler();
}

int OwlMain(int /* argc */, char** /*argv[] */)
{
  TWinApp app;
  return app.Run();
}
```

Let's look at the source code shown in Listing 6.16. The window class TMainWindow declares a constructor, a data member, and a number of member functions. The data member ColorData is a TChooseColorDialog::TData structure and is involved in passing information to and from the color selection dialog box.

The relevant member function is CMColor. This function declares a local string variable, the TColor-typed static array, CustColors, and a pointer to class TChooseColorDialog, ColorDialog. The function initializes the array CustColors. The function invokes the Color dialog box using the Execute function in an if statement. The if statement compares the value returned by function Execute with IDOK. If the two values match, the CMColors function converts the numeric value of the expression ColorData.Color into a string and then displays that string in a message box.

The TPrintDialog Class

The TPrintDialog class supports common dialog boxes for printing files and setting up the printer. Figure 6.5 shows the Print dialog box that assists in printing files. Figure 6.6 shows the Print Setup dialog box that helps in setting up the printer. The Print dialog box contains the following controls:

- A static text control that specifies the current printer.

- A Print Range group box that contains a set of controls. They include the All, Selection, and Pages radio buttons, as well as the From and To edit controls.

- A print Quality combo box.

- A Copies edit control that enables you to specify the number of copies.

- A Collate Copies check box.

- A Print to File check box that enables you to print to a file.

- An OK pushbutton.

- A Cancel pushbutton.

- A Setup pushbutton. Clicking this control leads to the Print Setup dialog box.

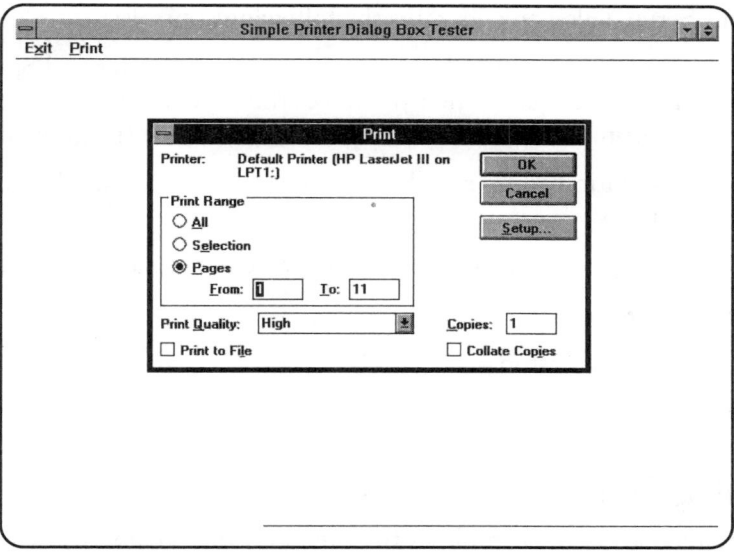

*Figure 6.5. A sample session with program COMMDLG4.EXE
showing the Print dialog box.*

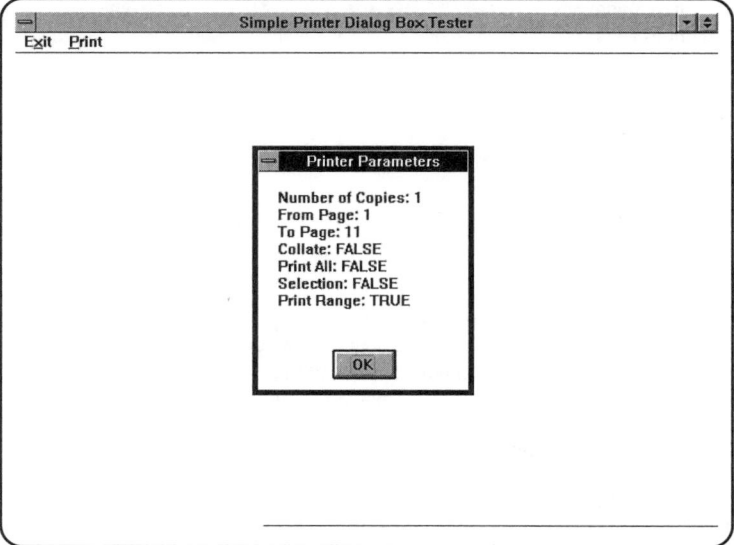

*Figure 6.6. A sample session with program COMMDLG4.EXE
showing the Print Setup dialog box.*

The Print Setup dialog box contains the following controls:

- A Printer group box which contains the Default Printer and Specific Printer radio buttons. When you select the latter control, you can also use the printer selection combo box, which is inside the group box.
- The Orientation group box that contains the Portrait and Landscape radio buttons.
- The Paper group box that contains the Size and Source combo boxes.
- An OK pushbutton.
- A Cancel pushbutton.
- An Options pushbutton.

Supporting Classes and Structures

The TPrintDialog class encapsulates the PRINTDLG structure and the supporting Windows API functions. The declaration of the PRINTDLG structure follows.

```
typedef struct tagPD
{
    DWORD     lStructSize;
    HWND      hwndOwner;
    HGLOBAL   hDevMode;
    HGLOBAL   hDevNames;
    HDC       hDC;
    DWORD     Flags;
    UINT      nFromPage;
    UINT      nToPage;
    UINT      nMinPage;
    UINT      nMaxPage;
    UINT      nCopies;
    HINSTANCE hInstance;
    LPARAM    lCustData;
    UINT      (CALLBACK* lpfnPrintHook)(HWND, UINT,
                                        WPARAM,LPARAM);
    UINT      (CALLBACK* lpfnSetupHook)(HWND, UINT,
                                        WPARAM, LPARAM);
    LPCSTR    lpPrintTemplateName;
    LPCSTR    lpSetupTemplateName;
    HGLOBAL   hPrintTemplate;
    HGLOBAL   hSetupTemplate;
} PRINTDLG;
```

The PRINTDLG structure and the related Windows API functions use the following PD_*xxxx* constants:

```
#define PD_ALLPAGES                        0x00000000
#define PD_SELECTION                       0x00000001
#define PD_PAGENUMS                        0x00000002
#define PD_NOSELECTION                     0x00000004
#define PD_NOPAGENUMS                      0x00000008
#define PD_COLLATE                         0x00000010
#define PD_PRINTTOFILE                     0x00000020
#define PD_PRINTSETUP                      0x00000040
#define PD_NOWARNING                       0x00000080
#define PD_RETURNDC                        0x00000100
#define PD_RETURNIC                        0x00000200
#define PD_RETURNDEFAULT                   0x00000400
#define PD_SHOWHELP                        0x00000800
#define PD_ENABLEPRINTHOOK                 0x00001000
#define PD_ENABLESETUPHOOK                 0x00002000
#define PD_ENABLEPRINTTEMPLATE             0x00004000
#define PD_ENABLESETUPTEMPLATE             0x00008000
#define PD_ENABLEPRINTTEMPLATEHANDLE       0x00010000
#define PD_ENABLESETUPTEMPLATEHANDLE       0x00020000
#define PD_USEDEVMODECOPIES                0x00040000
#define PD_DISABLEPRINTTOFILE              0x00080000
#define PD_HIDEPRINTTOFILE                 0x00100000
```

The TPrintDialog class, a descendant of TCommonDialog, has the following declaration:

```cpp
class _OWLCLASS TPrintDialog : public TCommonDialog {
  public:
    class _OWLCLASS TData {
      public:
        DWORD             Flags;
        DWORD             Error;
        int               FromPage;
        int               ToPage;
        int               MinPage;
        int               MaxPage;
        int               Copies;

        TData();
        ~TData();
        void              Lock();
        void              Unlock();
        void              ClearDevMode();
        const DEVMODE far* GetDevMode() const {return DevMode;}
        void              SetDevMode(const DEVMODE far* devMode);
        void              ClearDevNames();
        const DEVNAMES far* GetDevNames() const {return DevNames;}
        const char far*   GetDriverName() const;
        const char far*   GetDeviceName() const;
        const char far*   GetOutputName() const;
```

continues

continued

```
    void                SetDevNames(const char far* driver,
                                    const char far* device,
                                    const char far* output);
    TPrintDC*           TransferDC();

    void*               Read(ipstream& is, uint32 version);
    void                Write(opstream& os);

  private:
    HGLOBAL      hDevMode;
    HGLOBAL      hDevNames;
    HDC          hDC;

    DEVMODE far* DevMode;
    DEVNAMES far* DevNames;

  friend class TPrintDialog;
  };

  TPrintDialog(TWindow*       parent,
               TData&         data,
               const char far* printTemplateName = 0,
               const char far* setupTemplateName = 0,
               const char far* title = 0,
               TModule*       module = 0);

  BOOL GetDefaultPrinter();

  int DoExecute();

protected:
  PRINTDLG  pd;
  TData&    Data;

  BOOL DialogFunction(UINT message, WPARAM, LPARAM);

  // Default behavior inline for message response functions
  //
  void CmSetup()
       { DefaultProcessing(); } //EV_COMMAND(psh1,

private:
  TPrintDialog(const TPrintDialog&);
  TPrintDialog& operator=(const TPrintDialog&);

DECLARE_RESPONSE_TABLE(TPrintDialog);
DECLARE_CASTABLE;
};
```

The class constructor has six parameters involved in creating the Print and Print Setup dialog boxes. The `parent` parameter is the pointer to the parent window. The `data` parameter is the reference to the nested structure `TPrintDialog::TData`. The `printTemplateName` and `setupTemplateName` parameters specify the names of the resources for the Print and Print Setup dialog boxes, respectively. The default arguments for these parameters invoke their respective standard dialog boxes. The `title` parameter specifies the title of the dialog box. The default argument for this parameter invokes the standard title.

The `TPrintDialog::TData` structure contains data members and member functions that support the Print and Print Setup dialog boxes. The `Flags` data member enables you to tune the appearance and operations of the printing-related dialog boxes. This member takes one or more `PD_xxxx` constants. Most of the other data members set and query printing-related information, such as page range, first and last page to print, and the number of printed copies. The `Error` data member contains a `CDERR_xxxx` value, which identifies the kind of error involved in creating the dialog box.

A Sample Program

Let me present a simple menu-driven test program that uses the standard Print and Print Setup dialog boxes. Listing 6.17 shows the contents of the COMMDLG4.DEF definition file. Listing 6.18 shows the COMMDLG4.H header file. Listing 6.19 contains the script for the COMMDLG4.RC resource file. Listing 6.20 contains the source code for the COMMDLG4.CPP program file.

Compile and run the test COMMDLG4.EXE program. The program has two main menu items, Exit and Print. When you select the Print menu item, a pull-down menu with Print... and SetUp... options appears. The first option invokes the Print dialog box, whereas the second one invokes the Print Setup dialog box. Select either option and experiment with making new selections in the corresponding dialog box. When you click the OK button, the program removes the dialog box and displays the current printer parameter—obtained using the helper functions—in a message box. The program displays the same type of message box for either dialog box.

LISTING 6.17. THE CONTENTS OF THE COMMDLG4.DEF DEFINITION FILE.

```
NAME         CommDlg4
DESCRIPTION  'An OWL Windows Application'
EXETYPE      WINDOWS
CODE         PRELOAD MOVEABLE DISCARDABLE
DATA         PRELOAD MOVEABLE MULTIPLE
HEAPSIZE     1024
STACKSIZE    16384
```

LISTING 6.18. THE SOURCE CODE FOR THE COMMDLG4.H HEADER FILE.

```
#define CM_PRINT       100
#define CM_SETUP       101
#define IDM_MAINMENU   400
```

LISTING 6.19. THE SCRIPT FOR THE COMMDLG4.RC RESOURCE FILE.

```
#include <windows.h>
#include <owl\window.rh>
#include "commdlg4.h"

IDM_MAINMENU MENU LOADONCALL MOVEABLE PURE DISCARDABLE
BEGIN
    MENUITEM "E&xit", CM_EXIT
    POPUP "&Print"
    BEGIN
      MENUITEM "&SetUp...", CM_SETUP
      MENUITEM "&Print...", CM_PRINT
    END
END
```

LISTING 6.20. THE SOURCE CODE FOR THE COMMDLG4.CPP PROGRAM FILE.

```
/*
  Program to test the Print common dialog box.
*/

#include <owl\applicat.h>
#include <owl\framewin.h>
#include <owl\printdia.h>
```

```
#include "commdlg4.h"
#include <stdio.h>
#include <string.h>

const int MaxStrLen = 31;
const int MaxLongStrLen = 1024;

// declare the custom application class as
// a subclass of TApplication
class TWinApp : public TApplication
{
public:
  TWinApp() : TApplication() {}

protected:
  virtual void InitMainWindow();
};

// expand the functionality of TWindow by
// deriving class TMainWindow
class TMainWindow : public TWindow
{
public:

  TMainWindow() : TWindow(0, 0, 0) {}

protected:

  enum PrintState { printAll, printSelection, printRange };

  // the data for the print dialog box
  TPrintDialog::TData PrintData;

  // handle invoking the print dialog box
  void CMPrint();

  // handle the SetUp menu item
  void CmSetup();

  // handle exiting the program
  void CMExit();

  // handle closing the window
  virtual BOOL CanClose();

  // write "TRUE" or "FALSE" in string
  void BoolToStr(DWORD Flag, char* s);

  // display the parameters of the Print dialog box
  void ShowParameters();
```

continues

Listing 6.20. continued

```
  // declare the message map macro
  DECLARE_RESPONSE_TABLE(TMainWindow);

};

DEFINE_RESPONSE_TABLE1(TMainWindow, TWindow)
  EV_COMMAND(CM_PRINT, CMPrint),
  EV_COMMAND(CM_SETUP, CmSetup),
  EV_COMMAND(CM_EXIT, CMExit),
END_RESPONSE_TABLE;

void TMainWindow::CMPrint()
{
  TPrintDialog* PrintDialog;

  PrintData.Flags = PD_ALLPAGES | PD_USEDEVMODECOPIES;
  PrintData.MinPage = 1;
  PrintData.MaxPage = 100;
  PrintDialog = new TPrintDialog(this, PrintData);

  if (PrintDialog->Execute() == IDOK)
    ShowParameters();
}

void TMainWindow::CmSetup()
{
  TPrintDialog* PrintDialog;

  PrintData.Flags = PD_ALLPAGES | PD_USEDEVMODECOPIES | PD_PRINTSETUP;
  PrintData.MinPage = 1;
  PrintData.MaxPage = 100;
  PrintDialog = new TPrintDialog(this, PrintData);

  if (PrintDialog->Execute() == IDOK)
    ShowParameters();
}

void TMainWindow::ShowParameters()
{
  char s[MaxLongStrLen];
  char PrtCollateStr[MaxStrLen];
  char PrtSelectionStr[MaxStrLen];
  char PrtAllStr[MaxStrLen];
  char PrtRangeStr[MaxStrLen];
  char CopiesStr[MaxStrLen];
  char FromPageStr[MaxStrLen];
  char ToPageStr[MaxStrLen];
  PrintState State = printAll;
```

```
  sprintf(CopiesStr, "%u\r\n", PrintData.Copies);
  if (PrintData.FromPage < 0xffff)
    sprintf(FromPageStr, "%u\r\n", PrintData.FromPage);
  else
    strcpy(FromPageStr, "N/A\r\n");
  if (PrintData.ToPage < 0xffff)
    sprintf(ToPageStr, "%u\r\n", PrintData.ToPage);
  else
    strcpy(ToPageStr, "N/A\r\n");
  BoolToStr(PrintData.Flags & PD_COLLATE, PrtCollateStr);
  if (PrintData.Flags & PD_SELECTION)
    State = printSelection;
  else if (PrintData.Flags & PD_PAGENUMS)
    State = printRange;
  BoolToStr(State == printSelection, PrtSelectionStr);
  BoolToStr(State == printAll, PrtAllStr);
  BoolToStr(State == printRange, PrtRangeStr);
  strcpy(s, "Number of Copies: ");
  strcat(s, CopiesStr);
  strcat(s, "From Page: ");
  strcat(s,  FromPageStr);
  strcat(s, "To Page: ");
  strcat(s, ToPageStr);
  strcat(s, "Collate: ");
  strcat(s, PrtCollateStr);
  strcat(s, "Print All: ");
  strcat(s, PrtAllStr);
  strcat(s, "Selection: ");  strcat(s, PrtSelectionStr);
  strcat(s, "Print Range: ");
  strcat(s, PrtRangeStr);
  MessageBox(s, "Printer Parameters", MB_OK);
}

void TMainWindow::CMExit()
{
  Parent->SendMessage(WM_CLOSE);
}

BOOL TMainWindow::CanClose()
{
  return MessageBox("Want to close this application?",
            "Query", MB_YESNO | MB_ICONQUESTION) == IDYES;
}

void TMainWindow::BoolToStr(DWORD Flag, char* s)
{
  strcpy(s, (Flag != 0) ? "TRUE\r\n" : "FALSE\r\n");
}
```

continues

LISTING 6.20. CONTINUED

```
void TWinApp::InitMainWindow()
{
  MainWindow = new TFrameWindow(0, "Simple Printer Dialog Box Tester",
                    new TMainWindow);
  // load the menu resource
  MainWindow->AssignMenu(TResID(IDM_MAINMENU));
  // enable the keyboard handler
  MainWindow->EnableKBHandler();
}

int OwlMain(int /* argc */, char** /*argv[] */)
{
  TWinApp app;
  return app.Run();
}
```

Let's look at the source code in Listing 6.20. The TMainWindow window class declares a constructor, a data member, and a set of member functions. The PrintData data member is a TPrintDialog::TData structure that passes printer-related information to and from the print dialog box.

The member functions CMPrint, CMSetUp, BoolToStr, and ShowParameters are relevant to the test program. The BoolToStr function examines the value in parameter Flag and accordingly assigns the string "TRUE" or "FALSE" to parameter s. The CMPrint and CMSetUp respond to the Print... and SetUp... menu options, respectively. The two functions are short and resemble each other. The function CMPrint initializes the nested members of data member PrintData and then creates an instance of TPrintDialog that specifies the Print dialog box. The CMPrint function invokes the Execute function in an if statement that compares the result of Execute with IDOK. If the two values match, the function invokes the member function ShowParameters.

The function CMSetUp is similar to the CMPrint function. The only difference is in the initializing the nested member PrintData.Flags. This function includes the flag PD_PRINTSETUP.

The ShowParameters member function has the task of displaying the printer status as supplied by the various helper functions. The function declares a number of local string variables to store the results of various printing parameters. The function then concatenates these individual strings in the large string variable s. Each result is labeled and is placed on a separate line. The function uses a message box to display the set of printing-related data.

THE FIND AND REPLACE DIALOG CLASSES

The ObjectWindows library offers the classes TFindReplaceDialog, TFindDialog, and TReplaceDialog to support modeless dialog boxes that are involved in finding and replacing text. The Find dialog box contains the following controls:

- A Find What edit control that contains the search text
- A Match Whole Word Only check box
- A Match Case check box
- A Direction group box that contains the Up and Down radio buttons
- The Find Next pushbutton which acts similar to the OK button of a typical modal dialog box
- The Cancel pushbutton
- The Help pushbutton

The Replace dialog box contains the following controls:

- A Find What edit control that contains the search text
- A Replace With edit control that contains the replacing text
- A Match Whole Word Only check box
- A Match Case check box
- The Find Next pushbutton, which acts similar to the OK button of a typical modal dialog box
- A Replace pushbutton
- A Replace All pushbutton
- The Cancel pushbutton

Supporting Classes and Structures

The TFindReplaceDialog class encapsulates the FINDREPLACE structure and the Windows API functions FindText and ReplaceText. The declaration of the FINDREPLACE structure is shown below:

```
typedef struct tagFINDREPLACE
{
    DWORD lStructSize; /* size of this struct 0x20 */
    HWND hwndOwner; /* handle to owner's window    */
```

continues

continued

```
    HINSTANCE hInstance; /* instance handle of.EXE that
                            contains  cust. dlg. template */

    DWORD Flags; /* one or more of the FR_?? */
    LPSTR lpstrFindWhat; /* ptr. to search string */
    LPSTR lpstrReplaceWith; /* ptr. to replace string */
    UINT wFindWhatLen; /* size of find buffer */
    UINT wReplaceWithLen;  /* size of replace buffer */
    LPARAM lCustData; /* data passed to hook fn. */
    UINT (CALLBACK* lpfnHook)(HWND, UINT, WPARAM, LPARAM);
         /* ptr. to hook fn. or NULL     */
    LPCSTR lpTemplateName; /* custom template name */
} FINDREPLACE;
```

The FINDREPLACE structure and the related Windows API functions use the following FR_*xxxx* constants:

```
#define FR_DOWN                   0x00000001
#define FR_WHOLEWORD              0x00000002
#define FR_MATCHCASE              0x00000004
#define FR_FINDNEXT               0x00000008
#define FR_REPLACE                0x00000010
#define FR_REPLACEALL             0x00000020
#define FR_DIALOGTERM             0x00000040
#define FR_SHOWHELP               0x00000080
#define FR_ENABLEHOOK             0x00000100
#define FR_ENABLETEMPLATE         0x00000200
#define FR_NOUPDOWN               0x00000400
#define FR_NOMATCHCASE            0x00000800
#define FR_NOWHOLEWORD            0x00001000
#define FR_ENABLETEMPLATEHANDLE   0x00002000
#define FR_HIDEUPDOWN             0x00004000
#define FR_HIDEMATCHCASE          0x00008000
#define FR_HIDEWHOLEWORD          0x00010000
```

The TFindReplaceDialog Class

The TFindReplaceDialog class, a descendant of class TCommonDialog, supports the modeless dialog boxes that are typically used to find and replace text. The descendant classes, TFindDialog and TReplaceDialog, offer more specialized operations for searching and replacing text. Making the instances of class TFindDialog modeless makes them easier to use, since their dialog boxes remain visible while the text search takes place. As modeless dialogs, the Find and Replace dialog boxes permit the focus to be shifted to the related window that contains the edited text. At any time you can reselect these dialog boxes and resume another round of text search. There is no need to re-invoke the dialog box from a menu, since they are on stand-by. This flexibility comes at a price—a slightly more elaborate coding requirement. The declaration of the TFindReplaceDialog class is given below:

```
class _OWLCLASS TFindReplaceDialog : public TCommonDialog {
  public:
    class _OWLCLASS TData {
      public:
        DWORD     Flags;
        DWORD     Error;
        char*     FindWhat;
        char*     ReplaceWith;
        int       BuffSize;

        TData(DWORD flags = 0, int buffSize = 81);
        ~TData();

        void      Write(opstream& os);
        void      Read(ipstream& is);
    };

    TFindReplaceDialog(TWindow*        parent,
                       TData&          data,
                       TResId          templateId = 0,
                       const char far* title = 0,
                       TModule*        module = 0);

    void UpdateData(LPARAM lParam = 0);

  protected:
    FINDREPLACE  fr;
    TData&       Data;

    HWND DoCreate() = 0;

    TFindReplaceDialog(TWindow*        parent,
                       TResId          templateId = 0,
                       const char far* title = 0,
                       TModule*        module = 0);

    void Init(TResId templateId);
    BOOL DialogFunction(UINT message, WPARAM, LPARAM);

    //
    // Default behavior inline for message response functions
    //
    void CmFindNext()
         { DefaultProcessing(); }   // EV_COMMAND(IDOK,
    void CmReplace()
         { DefaultProcessing(); }    // EV_COMMAND(psh1,
    void CmReplaceAll()
```

continues

continued

```
          { DefaultProcessing(); }    // EV_COMMAND(psh2,
    void CmCancel()
          { DefaultProcessing(); }      // EV_COMMAND(IDCANCEL,

    void EvNCDestroy();

  DECLARE_RESPONSE_TABLE(TFindReplaceDialog);
  DECLARE_CASTABLE;
};
```

The class TFindReplaceDialog declares the nested class TData. This nested class contains data members that store the dialog box flags, search string, replacement string, error flag, and buffer size. The dialog box flags tune the appearance and operations of the Find and Replace dialog boxes. The TFindReplaceDialog class declares a constructor with five parameters. The parent parameter is the pointer to the parent window. The data parameter is the reference to the nested TData class. The templateID parameter specifies the resource ID for the dialog box. The default argument for this parameter invokes the standard resource for the Find or Replace dialog box. The title parameter designates the title of the dialog box. The default argument for this parameter invokes the standard title for Find or Replace dialog box. The UpdateData member function serves to update the protected Data data member, which is a reference to the nested class TData.

The TFindReplaceDialog class declares a set of protected member functions CmFindNext, CmReplace, CmReplaceAll, and CmCancel to handle clicking the Find Next, Replace, Replace All, and Cancel buttons in the Find or the Replace dialog boxes.

The TFindDialog Class

The declaration of class TFindDialog is as follows:

```
class _OWLCLASS TFindDialog : public TFindReplaceDialog {
  public:
    TFindDialog(TWindow*        parent,
                TData&          data,
                TResId          templateId = 0,
                const char far* title = 0,
                TModule*        module = 0);

  protected:
    HWND DoCreate();

  private:
    TFindDialog();
```

```
      TFindDialog(const TFindDialog&);

   DECLARE_CASTABLE;
};
```

The TFindDialog class constructor has the same number and type of parameters as the constructor of its parent class TFindReplaceDialog. The class also declares two additional private constructor. One is the default constructor and the other is a copy constructor.

The TReplaceDialog Class

The TReplaceDialog class, which models the modeless Replace dialog box, has the following declaration:

```
class _OWLCLASS TReplaceDialog : public TFindReplaceDialog {
   public:
     TReplaceDialog(TWindow*        parent,
                    TData&          data,
                    TResId          templateId = 0,
                    const char far* title = 0,
                    TModule*        module = 0);

   protected:
     HWND      DoCreate();

   private:
     TReplaceDialog(const TReplaceDialog&);
     TReplaceDialog& operator=(const TReplaceDialog&);

   DECLARE_CASTABLE;
};
```

The TReplaceDialog class constructor has the same number and type of parameters as the constructor of its parent class TFindReplaceDialog. The class also declares two additional private constructor. One is the default constructor and the other is a copy constructor.

Notifying the Parent Window

In order for the instances of classes TFindDialog and TReplaceDialog to notify the parent window, you need to define the following:

- A data member that is an instance of the TFindReplaceDialog::TData class.

- A data member that is a pointer to the TFindDialog class. The window class should initialize this data member to NULL or 0.

- A data member that is a pointer to TReplaceDialog class. The window class should initialize this data member to NULL or 0.

In addition, include in your main window class the following member functions:

1. A member function to handle the command that invokes the Find dialog box. This function examines the data member that points to class TFindDialog to determine whether or not to create the Find dialog box.

2. A member function to handle the command that invokes the Replace dialog box. This function examines the data member that points to TReplaceDialog class to determine whether or not to create the Replace dialog box.

3. A member function that handles the messages sent by the Find and Replace dialog boxes. The function examines the pointers to both classes TFindDialog and TReplaceDialog in order to determine which dialog box is sending messages to the main window.

The following code fragment gives you a general idea of how to code and initialize the above members:

```
class TMainWindow : public TWindow
{
public:
    // member declarations

protected:
    TFindReplaceDialog::TData FRdata;
    TFindDialog* pFindDlg;
    TReplaceDialog* pReplaceDlg;

    // other declarations

    // handle invoking the Find dialog box
    void CMFind();

    // handle invoking the Replace dialog box
    void CMReplace();

    // handle the messages
    LRESULT EvFindMsg(WPARAM, LPARAM lParam);

    DECLARE_RESPONSE_TABLE(TMainWindow);
};
```

```
DEFINE_RESPONSE_TABLE1(TMainWindow, TWindow)
    .
    .
    .
    EV_COMMAND(CM_FIND, CMFind),
    EV_COMMAND(CM_REPLACE, CMReplace),
    EV_REGISTERED(FINDMSGSTRING, EvFindMsg),
END_RESPONSE_TABLE;


TMainWindow::TMainWindow()
    : TWindow(0, 0, 0)
{
    pFindDlg = NULL;
    pReplaceDlg = NULL;
    // other statements
}

void TMainWindow::CMFind()
{
    if (!pFindDlg && !pReplaceDlg) {
        // create the Find dialog box
    }
}

void TMainWindow::CMReplace()
{
    if (!pReplaceDlg && !pReplaceDlg) {
        // create the Replace dialog box
    }
}


LRESULT TMainWindow::EvFindMsg(WPARAM, LPARAM lParam)
{
    // handle the Find dialog box
    if (pFindDlg) {
        pFindDlg->UpdateData(lParam);
        // is dialog box terminating?
        if (FRdata.Flags & FR_DIALOGTREM) {
            // statements for dialog box cleanup
        }
        else {
            // statements for continual usage
        }
    }

    // handle the Replace dialog box
    if (pReplaceDlg) {
        pReplaceDlg->UpdateData(lParam);
        // is dialog box terminating?
```

continues

continued

```
        if (FrData.Flags & FR_DIALOGTREM) {
            // statements for dialog box cleanup
        }
        else {
            // clicked Replace button?
            if (FRdata.Flags & FR_REPLACE) {
                // handle Replace button
            }
            // clicked Replace All button?
            else if (FRdata.Flags & FR_REPLACEALL) {
                // handle Replace All button
            }
            else {
                // handle Find Next button
            }
        }

    }
    return 0;
}
```

The above code segment shows the TMainWindow class declaring the following three data members:

1. The member FRdata, an instance of class TFindReplaceDialog::TData.

2. The member pFindDlg, a pointer to class TFindDialog.

3. The member pReplaceDlg, a pointer to class TReplaceDialog.

The above pointers access their respective dynamic dialog boxes. The main window class also declares the member functions CMFind, CMReplace, and EvFindMsg. The first two functions handle the commands that invoke the Find and Replace dialog boxes. The third member function handles the messages sent by either dialog box to the main window. Notice that the response table contains the EV_COMMAND entries to map the CM_FIND and CM_REPLACE commands with member functions CMFind and CMReplace. In addition, the response table contains the registered message map entry EV_RGISTERED to map the FINDMSGSTRING message with the EvFindMsg member function. This is how the main window is able to respond to clicking the various buttons in the Find and Replace dialog boxes.

The constructor for the TMainWindow class initializes the pointers pFindDlg and pReplaceDlg with NULLS. The CMFind member function creates the Find dialog box only if neither the Find or Replace dialog boxes are nonexistent. This condition assumes that the two modeless dialog boxes antagonize each other and should not coexist. If your program can tolerate both dialog boxes (assuming each has its own TData instance), then you can replace the current tested condition with

!pFindDlg. The code fragment defines the CMReplace member function in a manner similar to function CMFind.

The EvFindMsg member function handles responding to the buttons of the Find and Replace dialog boxes. The function takes a WPARAM-type parameter and an LPARAM-type parameter. The latter parameter contains a pointer that must be passed to the Updatedata member function of the dialog box instance. The function returns a LRESULT type. The function has two main if statements that determine if the Find or Replace dialog box is active. If the Find dialog box is active, the function performs the following tasks:

- Sends the C++ message UpdateData to the Find dialog box. The parameter of this message is the argument for the LPARAM-type parameter.

- Determines if the dialog box is not terminating by performing a bitwise and operation between the Flags member and the predefined constant FR_DIALOGTERM. If the result is not zero, the statements in the if clause handle the cleanup operation before closing the dialog box. Otherwise, the function EvFindMsg executes the statements in the else clause to support the ongoing operations of the dialog box.

If the Replace dialog box is active the function performs the following tasks:

- Sends the C++ message UpdateData to the Replace dialog box. The parameter of this message is the argument for the LPARAM-type parameter.

- Determines if the dialog box is not terminating by performing a bitwise and operation between the Flags member and the predefined constant FR_DIALOGTERM. If the result is not zero, the statements in the if clause handle the cleanup operation before closing the dialog box.

- If EvFindMsg executes the else clause, it uses an if-elseif-else statement to determine if you clicked the Replace, Replace All, or the Find Next buttons in the Replace dialog box.

Remember that the above code segment is just one way of managing the Find and Replace dialog boxes. Your application may warrant changing the above code. In fact, the next programming example does just that!

A Sample Program

Let's put all the preceding information to work in a test program. I present a simple menu-driven program that enables you to invoke a Find or Replace dialog box. Listing 6.21 shows the contents of the COMMDLG5.DEF definition file. Listing 6.22 shows the COMMDLG5.H header file. Listing 6.23 contains the script for the COMMDLG5.RC resource file. Listing 6.24 contains the source code for the COMMDLG5.CPP program file.

Compile and run the COMMDLG5.EXE test program. The program has two main menu items: Exit and Search. When you select the Search menu item, a pull-down menu pops up with the Find... and Replace... options. The first option invokes the Find dialog box, whereas the second invokes the Replace dialog box. Select either option and experiment with making new selections and typing new text in the corresponding dialog box. Click the Find Next button (available in both Find and Replace dialog boxes) and watch the program display a message box that contains data for the Find or Replace dialog box. When you finish experimenting with one dialog box, select the other. When you are completely done testing the program, click the Cancel button of the current dialog box to exit. Figure 6.7 shows a sample session with program COMMDLG5.EXE showing the Find dialog box. Figure 6.8 shows a sample session with program COMMDLG5.EXE showing the Replace dialog box.

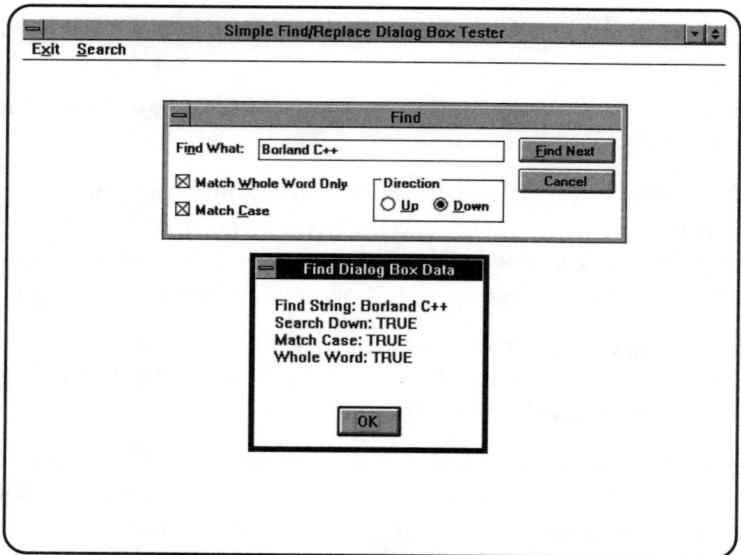

Figure 6.7. A sample session with program COMMDLG5.EXE showing the Find dialog box.

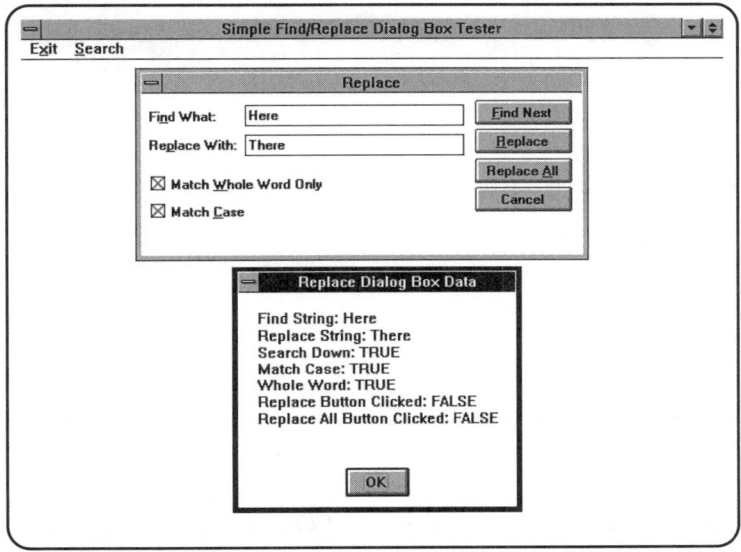

Figure 6.8. A sample session with program COMMDLG5.EXE showing the Replace dialog box.

LISTING 6.21. THE CONTENTS OF THE COMMDLG5.DEF DEFINITION FILE.

```
NAME          CommDlg5
DESCRIPTION   'An OWL Windows Application'
EXETYPE       WINDOWS
CODE          PRELOAD MOVEABLE DISCARDABLE
DATA          PRELOAD MOVEABLE MULTIPLE
HEAPSIZE      1024
STACKSIZE     16384
```

LISTING 6.22. THE SOURCE CODE FOR THE COMMDLG5.H HEADER FILE.

```
#define CM_FIND      100
#define CM_REPLACE   101
#define IDM_MAINMENU 400
```

LISTING 6.23. THE SCRIPT FOR THE COMMDLG5.RC RESOURCE FILE.

```
#include <windows.h>
#include <owl\window.rh>
#include "commdlg5.h"


IDM_MAINMENU MENU LOADONCALL MOVEABLE PURE DISCARDABLE
BEGIN
    MENUITEM "E&xit", CM_EXIT
    POPUP "&Search"
    BEGIN
      MENUITEM "&Find...", CM_FIND
      MENUITEM "&Replace...", CM_REPLACE
    END
END
```

LISTING 6.24. THE SOURCE CODE FOR THE COMMDLG5.CPP PROGRAM FILE.

```
/*
  Program to test the Find and Replace common dialog boxes.
*/

#include <owl\applicat.h>
#include <owl\framewin.h>
#include <owl\findrepl.h>
#include "commdlg5.h"
#include <stdio.h>
#include <string.h>

const int MaxStrLen = 31;
const int MaxLongStrLen = 1024;

// declare the custom application class as
// a subclass of TApplication
class TWinApp : public TApplication
{
public:
  TWinApp() : TApplication() {}

protected:
  virtual void InitMainWindow();
};

// expand the functionality of TWindow by
// deriving class TMainWindow
class TMainWindow : public TWindow
{
public:
```

```
  TMainWindow();

protected:

  TFindReplaceDialog::TData FRdata;
  TFindDialog* pFindDlg;
  TReplaceDialog* pReplaceDlg;

  // handle invoking the Find dialog box
  void CMFind();

  // handle clicking the Find Next button
  LRESULT EvFindMsg(WPARAM, LPARAM);

  // handle the Replace menu item
  void CMReplace();

  // handle exiting the program
  void CMExit();

  // handle closing the window
  virtual BOOL CanClose();

  // write "TRUE" or "FALSE" in string
  void BoolToStr(DWORD Flag, char* s);

  // declare the message map macro
  DECLARE_RESPONSE_TABLE(TMainWindow);

};

DEFINE_RESPONSE_TABLE1(TMainWindow, TWindow)
  EV_COMMAND(CM_FIND, CMFind),
  EV_COMMAND(CM_REPLACE, CMReplace),
  EV_COMMAND(CM_EXIT, CMExit),
  EV_REGISTERED(FINDMSGSTRING, EvFindMsg),
END_RESPONSE_TABLE;

TMainWindow::TMainWindow()
    : TWindow(0, 0, 0)
{
  pFindDlg = NULL;
  pReplaceDlg = NULL;
}

void TMainWindow::CMFind()
{
  if (!pFindDlg && !pReplaceDlg) {
      FRdata.Flags |= FR_DOWN;
```

continues

LISTING 6.24. CONTINUED

```
      pFindDlg = new TFindDialog(this, FRdata);
      pFindDlg->Create();
  }
}

LRESULT TMainWindow::EvFindMsg(WPARAM, LPARAM lParam)
{
  char s[MaxLongStrLen];
  char s2[MaxStrLen];
  if (pFindDlg) {
      pFindDlg->UpdateData(lParam);
      // is the dialog box still opened
      if (!(FRdata.Flags & FR_DIALOGTERM)) {
          strcpy(s, "Find String: ");
          strcat(s, FRdata.FindWhat);
          strcat(s, "\nSearch Down: ");
          BoolToStr(DWORD(FRdata.Flags & FR_DOWN), s2);
          strcat(s, s2);
          strcat(s, "Match Case: ");
          BoolToStr(DWORD(FRdata.Flags & FR_MATCHCASE), s2);
          strcat(s, s2);
          strcat(s, "Whole Word: ");
          BoolToStr(DWORD(FRdata.Flags & FR_WHOLEWORD), s2);
          strcat(s, s2);
          MessageBox(s, "Find Dialog Box Data", MB_OK);
      }
       else
            pFindDlg = NULL;
  }

  if (pReplaceDlg) {
      pReplaceDlg->UpdateData(lParam);
      // is the dialog box still opened
      if (!(FRdata.Flags & FR_DIALOGTERM)) {
          strcpy(s, "Find String: ");
          strcat(s, FRdata.FindWhat);
          strcat(s, "\nReplace String: ");
          strcat(s, FRdata.ReplaceWith);
          strcat(s, "\nSearch Down: ");
          BoolToStr(DWORD(FRdata.Flags & FR_DOWN), s2);
          strcat(s, s2);
          strcat(s, "Match Case: ");
          BoolToStr(DWORD(FRdata.Flags & FR_MATCHCASE), s2);
          strcat(s, s2);
          strcat(s, "Whole Word: ");
          BoolToStr(DWORD(FRdata.Flags & FR_WHOLEWORD), s2);
          strcat(s, s2);
          strcat(s, "Replace Button Clicked: ");
          BoolToStr(DWORD(FRdata.Flags & FR_REPLACE), s2);
```

```
              strcat(s, s2);
              strcat(s, "Replace All Button Clicked: ");
              BoolToStr(DWORD(FRdata.Flags & FR_REPLACEALL), s2);
              strcat(s, s2);
              MessageBox(s, "Replace Dialog Box Data", MB_OK);
       }
        else
             pReplaceDlg = NULL;
  }
  return 0;
}

void TMainWindow::CMReplace()
{
  if (!FindDlg && !pReplaceDlg) {
      FRdata.Flags = FR_DOWN ¦ FR_MATCHCASE ¦ FR_WHOLEWORD;
      pReplaceDlg = new TReplaceDialog(this, FRdata);
      pReplaceDlg->Create();
  }
}

void TMainWindow::CMExit()
{
  Parent->SendMessage(WM_CLOSE);
}

void TMainWindow::BoolToStr(DWORD Flag, char* s)
{
  strcpy(s, (Flag != 0) ? "TRUE\r\n" : "FALSE\r\n");
}

BOOL TMainWindow::CanClose()
{
  return MessageBox("Want to close this application?",
                "Query", MB_YESNO ¦ MB_ICONQUESTION) == IDYES;
}

void TWinApp::InitMainWindow()
{
  MainWindow = new TFrameWindow(0, "Simple Find/Replace Dialog Box Tester",
                    new TMainWindow);
  // load the menu resource
  MainWindow->AssignMenu(TResID(IDM_MAINMENU));
  // enable the keyboard handler
  MainWindow->EnableKBHandler();
}

int OwlMain(int /* argc */, char** /*argv[] */)
{
  TWinApp app;
  return app.Run();
}
```

The COMMDLG5.CPP source code in Listing 6.24 declares the main window class TMainWindow and the application class TWinApp. The main window class has the following three protected data members:

1. The FRdata member, an instance of class TFindReplaceDialog::TData. This member is commonly used by the Find and Replace dialog boxes. This program feature requires that the dialog box should not coexist.

2. The pFindDlg member is a pointer to class TFindDialog. This member is a pointer to the Find dialog box instance that is dynamically created.

3. The pReplaceDlg member is a pointer to class TReplaceDialog. This member is a pointer to the Replace dialog box instance that is dynamically created.

The TMainWindow constructor assigns NULLS to the data members pFindDlg and pReplaceDlg. The class declares the following relevant member functions:

1. The CMFind member function handles invoking the Find dialog box. The function performs the following tasks:

   - Verifies that both pFindDlg and pReplaceDlg pointers are NULLs. If this condition is true, the CMFind function proceeds with the remaining tasks:

   - Includes the downward search flag FR_DOWN to the current set of flags, stored in the FRdata.Flags member.

   - Creates a dynamic instance of class TFindDialog and assigns its pointer to the pFindDlg member. The creation of this instance specifies the pointer this and FRdata as the arguments for the parent window and the TData reference.

   - Invokes the modeless Find dialog box by sending the Create C++ message to the dialog box object.

2. The CMReplace member function handles invoking the Replace dialog box. The function performs the following tasks:

   - Verifies that both pFindDlg and pReplaceDlg pointers are NULLs. If this condition is true, the function CMReplace proceeds with the remaining tasks:

   - Assigns the FR_xxxx flags for downward replacement, case-sensitive replacement, and the replacement of whole words to the FRdata.Flags member.

- Creates a dynamic instance of `TReplaceDialog` class and assigns its pointer to the `pReplaceDlg` member. The creation of this instance specifies the `this` and `FRdata` pointer as the arguments for the parent window and the `TData` reference.

- Invokes the modeless Replace dialog box by sending the `Create` C++ message to the dialog box object.

3. The `EvFindMsg` member function handles the message sent by the Find and Replace dialog boxes to the main window. This function uses two main `if` statement to handle messages sent by either dialog box. If the `pFindDlg` member is not NULL, the function carries out the following tasks:

   - Sends the `UpdateData` C++ message to the Find dialog box. The argument for this message is the `lParam` parameter.

   - Determines if the Find dialog box is not terminating. If this condition is true, the `EvFindMsg` function performs the next tasks. Otherwise, the function executes the `else` clause statement which assigns NULL to the `pFindDlg` member. This assignment allows the program to properly invoke the Find dialog box the next time you invoke the Find menu option.

   - Builds the `s` multiline string, which contains information about the search string, the search direction, the match case state, and the whole word state. This task involves the `BoolToStr` member function, which converts integers into a `"TRUE"` or `"FALSE"` string.

   - Displays the `s` dialog box data string in a message dialog box.

If the `pReplaceDlg` member is not NULL, the function carries out the following tasks:

- Sends the `UpdateData` C++ message to the Replace dialog box. The argument for this message is the parameter `lParam`.

- Determines if the Replace dialog box is not terminating. If this condition is true, the `EvFindMsg` function performs the next tasks. Otherwise, the function executes the `else` clause statement, which assigns NULL to the `pReplaceDlg` member. This assignment allows the program to properly invoke the Replace dialog box the next time you invoke the Replace menu option.

- Builds the s multiline string, which contains information about the search string, the replacement string, the search direction, the match case state, the whole word state, whether or not the user clicked the Replace button, and whether or not the user clicked the Replace All button. This task involves the BoolToStr member function, which converts integers into a "TRUE" or "FALSE" string.

- Displays the s dialog box data string in a message dialog box.

The if statement that handles the message sent by the Replace dialog box is simpler that the code fragment presented earlier. This is due to the fact that the program does not take alternate action if you click the Replace or Replace All button.

SUMMARY

This chapter presented you with powerful dialog boxes that serve as input tools. You learned about:

- The TInputDialog ObjectWindows class that enables you to prompt the user for an input.

- Software requirements for using the common dialog boxes. This included adequate stack space in the .DEF file, making sure that the COMMDLG.DLL file in the Windows system directory, and including the corresponding header files.

- The file selection dialog box classes TSaveOpenDialog, TFileOpenDialog, and TFileSaveDialog. These class create dialog boxes that support either opening or saving a file.

- The TChooseFontDialog font selection dialog box class.

- The TChooseColorDialog color selection dialog box class.

- The TPrintDialog printer setup dialog box class.

- The text find/replace dialog box classes TFindReplaceDialog, TFindDialog, and TReplaceDialog. These classes create dialog boxes that support either finding or replacing text.

MDI WINDOWS

You have probably noticed that many Windows applications—such as the Windows Program Manager, the Windows File Manager, and even the Borland C++ IDE—implement a special Windows interface. This interface is called the Multiple Document Interface (MDI) and is a standard Windows interface. The MDI standard is also part of the Common User Access (CUA) standard set by IBM. Each MDI-compliant application enables you to open child windows for file-specific tasks such as editing text, managing a database, or working with a spreadsheet. In this chapter, you will learn about the following topics on managing MDI windows and objects:

- The basic features and components of an MDI-compliant application

- Basics of building an MDI-compliant application

- The `TMDIFrame` class

- The `TMDIClient` class

- Building MDI client windows

- The `TMDIChild` class

- Building MDI child windows

- Managing messages in an MDI-compliant application

The MDI Application Features and Components

An MDI-compliant application is made up of the following objects:

- The visible *MDI frame window* that contains all other MDI objects. The MDI frame window is an instance of the TMDIFrame class or its descendants. Each MDI application has one MDI frame window.

- The invisible *MDI client window* that performs underlying management of the MDI child windows that are dynamically created and removed. The MDI client window is an instance of the TMDIClient class. Each MDI application has one MDI client window.

- The dynamic and visible *MDI child window*. An MDI application dynamically creates and removes multiple instances of MDI child windows. An MDI child window is an instance of TMDIChild or of its descendant. These windows are located, moved, resized, maximized, and minimized inside the area defined by the MDI frame window. At any given time (and while there is at least one MDI child window), only one MDI child window is active.

When you maximize an MDI child window, it occupies the area defined by the MDI frame window. When you minimize an MDI child window, the icon of that window appears at the bottom area of the MDI frame window.

 The MDI frame window has a menu that manipulates the MDI child windows and their contents. The MDI child windows cannot have a menu, but they may contain controls. In other any respect, you can think of an MDI child window as an instance of TWindow or its descendants.

Basics of Building an MDI Application

Before I discuss in more detail the creation of the various components that make up an MDI application, let me focus on the basic strategy involved. In the last section, you learned that the basic ingredients for an MDI application are the TMDIFrame, TMDIClient, and TWindow (or a TWindow descendant) classes. The TMDIFrame class supports the following tasks:

- The creation and handling of the MDI client window

- The creation and handling of the MDI child windows

- Managing menu selections

The MDIClient class focuses on the underlying management of MDI child windows. The TWindow class offers the functionality for the MDI child windows.

At this stage, you might wonder whether you typically derive descendants for all three classes to create an MDI application. The answer is no. You normally need to derive descendants for the TMDIFrame and TWindow classes only. The functionality of the TMDIClient class is adequate for most MDI-compliant applications.

THE TMDIFRAME CLASS

ObjectWindows offers the TMDIFrame class, a descendant of TWindow, to implement the MDI frame window of an MDI application. The declaration of the TMDIFrame class is as follows:

```
class _OWLCLASS TMDIFrame : virtual public TFrameWindow {
  public:
    TMDIFrame(const char far* title,
              TResId        menuResId,
              TMDIClient&   clientWnd = *new TMDIClient,
              TModule*      module = 0);


    TMDIFrame(HWND hWindow, HWND clientHWnd, TModule* module = 0);

    //
    // override virtual functions defined by TFrameWindow
    //
    BOOL         SetMenu(HMENU);
    TMDIClient*  GetClientWindow();

    //
    // find & return the child menu of an MDI frame's (or anyone's) menu
    // bar
    //
    static HMENU FindChildMenu(HMENU);

  protected:
    //
    // call ::DefFrameProc() instead of ::DefWindowProc()
    //
    LRESULT DefWindowProc(UINT message, WPARAM wParam, LPARAM lParam);
```

continues

continued

```
private:
  //
  // hidden to prevent accidental copying or assignment
  //
  TMDIFrame(const TMDIFrame&);
  TMDIFrame& operator=(const TMDIFrame&);

DECLARE_RESPONSE_TABLE(TMDIFrame);
DECLARE_STREAMABLE(_OWLCLASS, TMDIFrame, 1);
};
```

The TMDIFrame class has public, protected, and private members. The MDI frame window class has three constructors, one of which is private. The first constructor creates a class instance by specifying the title, the associated menu resource ID, and the reference to the associated MDI client window. The second constructor creates a class instance from an existing non-OWL window. The third constructor, which is declared private, creates an instance of the TMDIFrame class using another existing instance.

The TMDIFrame class declares the public member functions SetMenu, GetClientWindow, and FindChildMenu. The SetMenu function searches for the MDI submenu in the menu bar and updates the position, in the MDI window's top-level menu, of the child window submenu. The GetClientWindow function returns the reference to the associated MDI client window. The FindChildMenu function searches for the child menu of the menu bar of an MDI frame.

The TMDIFrame class declares the single protected member function DefWindowProc. This function overrides the inherited function TWindow::DefWindowProc and invokes the Windows API function DefFrameProc. The API function provides the default processing for any incoming Windows message not handled by the MDI frame window.

BUILDING MDI FRAME WINDOWS

The usual approach for creating the objects that make up an ObjectWindows application starts with creating the application instance and then its main window instance. In the case of an MDI-compliant application, the main window of the application is typically a descendant of the TMDIFrame class. The InitMainWindow member function of the application class creates this window. Looking at the first two TMDIFrame constructors, you can tell that creating the main MDI window involves a title and menu resource; there is no pointer to a parent window, because MDI frame windows have no parent windows. The

MDI frame window, unlike most descendants of the TWindow class, must have a menu associated with it. This menu typically includes the items needed, as shown in Table 7.1, to manipulate the MDI children. In addition, the menu of the MDI frame window is dynamically and automatically updated to include the current MDI children.

		TABLE 7.1. THE PREDEFINED MENU COMMAND MESSAGES FOR MANIPULATING MDI CHILDREN.

Action	Menu ID Constant	Responding TMDIClient member function
Tile	CM_TILECHILDREN	CmTileChildren
Cascade	CM_CASCASDECHILDREN	CmCascadeChildren
Arrange Icons	CM_ARRANGEICONS	CmArrangeIcons
Close All	CM_CLOSECHILDREN	CmCloseChildren

The constructor of the descendant of TMDIFrame (call it the application frame class) can, in many cases, simply invoke the parent class constructor. This invocation occurs if the steps taken by the latter are adequate for creating the MDI frame window instance. If you want to modify the behavior of the application frame class, you need to include the required statements. Such statements might assign initial values to data members declared in the application frame class.

The SetupWindow member function invokes InitClientWindow to create the TMDIClient instance. You can modify the SetupWindow function, for example, to create automatically the first child MDI window.

THE TMDICLIENT CLASS

ObjectWindows offers the TMDIClient class, a descendant TWindow, to implement the invisible MDI client window. The declaration of the TMDIClient class is as follows:

```
class _OWLCLASS TMDIClient : public virtual TWindow {
  public:
```

continues

continued

```
  LPCLIENTCREATESTRUCT  ClientAttr;

  TMDIClient(TModule* module = 0);
  ~TMDIClient();

  virtual BOOL CloseChildren();

  TMDIChild* GetActiveMDIChild();

  //
  // member functions to arrange the MDI children
  //
  virtual void ArrangeIcons();
  virtual void CascadeChildren();
  virtual void TileChildren(int tile = MDITILE_VERTICAL);

  //
  // override member functions defined by TWindow
  //
  BOOL PreProcessMsg(MSG& msg);
  BOOL Create();

  virtual TWindow* CreateChild();

  //
  // constructs a new MDI child window object. by default, constructs
  // an instance of TWindow as an MDI child window object
  //
  // will almost always be overridden by derived classes to construct
  // an instance of a user-defined TWindow derived class as an MDI
  // child window object
  //
  virtual TMDIChild* InitChild();

protected:
  char far* GetClassName();

  //
  // menu command handlers & enabler
  //
  void CmCreateChild()
        { CreateChild(); } // CM_CREATECHILD
  void CmTileChildren()
        { TileChildren(); }  // CM_TILECHILDREN
  void CmTileChildrenHoriz()
        { TileChildren(MDITILE_HORIZONTAL); }  // CM_TILECHILDREN
  void CmCascadeChildren()
        { CascadeChildren(); }  // CM_CASCADECHILDREN
  void CmArrangeIcons()
        { ArrangeIcons(); }  // CM_ARRANGEICONS
```

```
    void CmCloseChildren()
          { CloseChildren(); }   // CM_CLOSECHILDREN
    void CmChildActionEnable(TCommandEnabler& commandEnabler);

    LRESULT EvMDICreate(MDICREATESTRUCT far& createStruct);

  private:
    friend class TMDIFrame;
    TMDIClient(HWND hWnd, TModule*   module = 0);

    //
    // hidden to prevent accidental copying or assignment
    //
    TMDIClient(const TMDIClient&);
    TMDIClient& operator =(const TMDIClient&);

  DECLARE_RESPONSE_TABLE(TMDIClient);
  DECLARE_STREAMABLE(_OWLCLASS, TMDIClient, 1);
};
```

The TMDIClient class declares a public constructor and destructor. The MDI client class declares a number of member functions that handle Windows and menu command messages for activating an MDI child window, for arranging the MDI child icons, for cascading and tiling MDI children, for closing MDI children, and for creating an MDI child window. These message response functions use sibling member functions. Table 7.1 shows the predefined menu ID constants and the TMDIClient member functions that respond to them.

You may want to modify a number of member functions in the TMDIFrame class when you create class descendants. The list of such member functions includes CreateChild, SetupWindow, CanClose, and CloseChildren. With these functions, you can modify how to create, set up, and close MDI children.

THE MDI CHILD WINDOW CLASS

The TMDIChild class models the basic operations of all MDI child windows. The declaration for the TMDIChild class is this:

```
class _OWLCLASS TMDIChild : virtual public TFrameWindow {
  public:
    TMDIChild(TMDIClient&    parent,
              const char far* title = 0,
              TWindow*        clientWnd = 0,
              BOOL            shrinkToClient = FALSE,
              TModule*        module = 0);
```

continues

continued

```
    TMDIChild(HWND hWnd, TModule* module = 0);

  ~TMDIChild() {}

  //
  // override method defined by TWindow
  //
  BOOL PreProcessMsg(MSG& msg);

protected:
  void Destroy(int retVal = 0);
  void PerformCreate(int menuOrId);
  LRESULT DefWindowProc(UINT msg, WPARAM wParam, LPARAM lParam);
  void EvMDIActivate(HWND hWndActivated,
                     HWND hWndDeactivated);

private:
  //
  // hidden to prevent accidental copying or assignment
  //
  TMDIChild(const TMDIChild&);
  TMDIChild& operator =(const TMDIChild&);

  DECLARE_RESPONSE_TABLE(TMDIChild);
  DECLARE_STREAMABLE(_OWLCLASS, TMDIChild, 1);
};
```

The TMDIChild class declares three constructors (one of which is private) and a destructor. With the first constructor, you can create a class instance by specifying the parent MDI client window, the MDI child window title, the client window, and whether or not the MDI child window shrinks to fit the client area. The second constructor creates a class instance using an existing non-OWL MDI child window. The third constructor, which is declared private, creates a TMDIChild class instance using an existing instance.

The MDI child window class declares the single public member function PreProcessMsg. This function preprocesses the Windows messages sent to the MDI child windows. The TMDIChild class offers a set of protected functions that create, destroy, and activate MDI child windows. In addition, the class provides its own version of the DefWindowProc function to handle default Windows message processing.

BUILDING MDI CHILD WINDOWS

Building MDI child windows is very similar to building application windows in the programs presented earlier. The differences are as follows:

- An MDI child window cannot have its own menu. The menu of the MDI frame window is the one that manipulates the currently active MDI child window or all of the MDI children.

- The keyboard handler must not be enabled. It causes actually the reverse effect in the MDI children and antagonizes the proper operations of the MDI application.

- An MDI child window can have controls—this is unusual but certainly allowed.

MANAGING MDI MESSAGES

The message loop directs the command messages first to the active MDI child window to allow it to respond. If that window does not respond, the message is then sent to the parent MDI frame window. Of course, the active MDI child window responds to the notification messages sent by its controls, as would any window or dialog box.

SIMPLE TEXT VIEWER

Consider now a simple MDI-compliant application. Because MDI applications are frequently used as text viewers and text editors, the next application emulates a simple text viewer. I say *emulates* because the application actually displays random text, instead of text that you can retrieve from a file. This approach keeps the program simple and helps you to focus on implementing the various MDI objects. Figure 7.1 shows a sample session with the MDIWIN1.EXE program. The MDI application has a simple menu containing the Exit and MDI Children.

Compile and run the application. Experiment with creating MDI children. Notice that the text in odd-numbered MDI child windows is static, though the text in even-numbered windows can be edited. I implemented this feature to illustrate how to create a simple form of text viewer and text editor (with no Save option, to keep the example short). Try to tile, cascade, maximize, and minimize these windows. Also, test closing individual MDI child windows and test closing all of the MDI children.

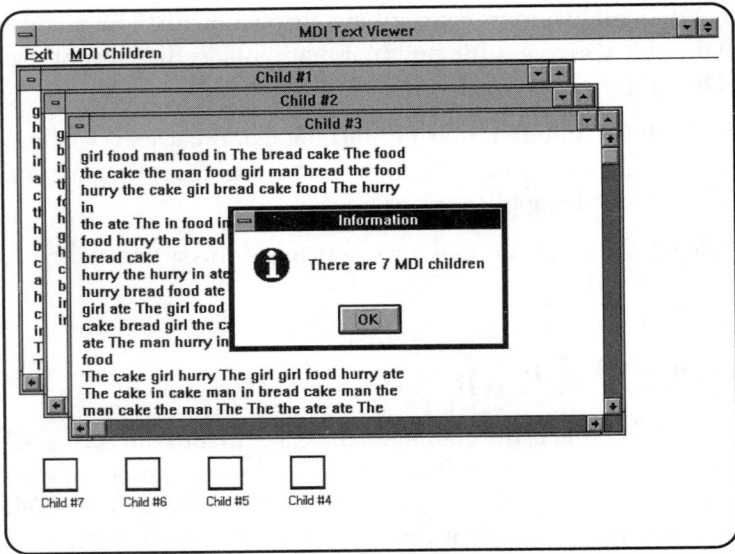

Figure 7.1. A sample session with the MDIWIN1.EXE program.

Examine the code that implements this simple MDI application. Listing 7.1 shows the contents of the MDIWIN1.DEF definition file. Listing 7.2 shows the source code for the MDIWIN1.H header file. This file declares the command message constants and a control ID constant. Listing 7.3 contains the script for the MDIWIN1.RC resource file. The file defines the menu resource required by the MDI frame window. The menu has two menu items, Exit and MDI Children. The latter menu item is a pop-up menu with several options. The menu options, except the Count Children option, use predefined command message constants. Listing 7.4 shows the source code for the MDIWIN1.CPP program file.

LISTING 7.1. THE CONTENTS OF THE MDIWIN1.DEF DEFINITION FILE.

```
NAME          MDIWin1
DESCRIPTION   'An OWL Windows Application'
EXETYPE       WINDOWS
CODE          PRELOAD MOVEABLE DISCARDABLE
DATA          PRELOAD MOVEABLE MULTIPLE
HEAPSIZE      1024
STACKSIZE     8192
```

LISTING 7.2. THE SOURCE CODE FOR THE MDIWIN1.H HEADER FILE.

```
#define CM_COUNTCHILDREN 101
#define ID_TEXT_EDIT     102
#define IDM_COMMANDS     400
```

LISTING 7.3. THE SCRIPT FOR THE MDIWIN1.RC RESOURCE FILE.

```
#include <windows.h>
#include <owl\window.rh>
#include <owl\mdi.rh>
#include "mdiwin1.h"

IDM_COMMANDS MENU LOADONCALL MOVEABLE PURE DISCARDABLE
BEGIN
  MENUITEM "E&xit", CM_EXIT
  POPUP "&MDI Children"
  BEGIN
    MENUITEM  "C&reate", CM_CREATECHILD
    MENUITEM  "&Cascade", CM_CASCADECHILDREN
    MENUITEM  "&Tile", CM_TILECHILDREN
    MENUITEM  "Arrange &Icons", CM_ARRANGEICONS
    MENUITEM  "C&lose All", CM_CLOSECHILDREN
    MENUITEM  "C&ount Children", CM_COUNTCHILDREN
  END
END
```

LISTING 7.4. THE SOURCE CODE FOR THE MDIWIN1.CPP PROGRAM FILE.

```
/*
  Program to demonstrate simple MDI windows
*/

#include <owl\mdi.rh>
#include <owl\applicat.h>
#include <owl\framewin.h>
#include <owl\mdi.h>
#include <owl\static.h>
#include <owl\edit.h>
#include <owl\scroller.h>
#include "mdiwin1.h"
#include <stdio.h>
#include <string.h>
```

continues

LISTING 7.4. CONTINUED

```
const MaxWords = 200;
const WordsPerLine = 10;
const NumWords = 10;
char* Words[NumWords] = { "The ", "man ", "ate ", "the ",
                          "food ", "in ", "hurry ", "girl ",
                          "cake ", "bread " };

BOOL ExpressClose = FALSE;
int NumMDIChild = 0;
int HighMDIindex = 0;

class TWinApp : public TApplication
{
public:
  TWinApp() : TApplication() {}

protected:
  virtual void InitMainWindow();
};

class TAppMDIChild : public TMDIChild
{
public:
  // pointer to the edit box control
  TEdit* TextBox;
  TStatic* TextTxt;

  TAppMDIChild(TMDIClient& parent, int ChildNum);

protected:

  // handle closing the MDI child window
  virtual BOOL CanClose();
};

class TAppMDIClient : public TMDIClient
{
public:

  TAppMDIClient() : TMDIClient() {}

 protected:

  // create a new child
  virtual TMDIChild* InitChild();

  // close all MDI children
  virtual BOOL CloseChildren();
```

```cpp
  // handle the command for counting the MDI children
  void CMCountChildren();

  // handle closing the MDI frame window
  virtual BOOL CanClose();

  // declare response table
  DECLARE_RESPONSE_TABLE(TAppMDIClient);
};

DEFINE_RESPONSE_TABLE1(TAppMDIClient, TMDIClient)
  EV_COMMAND(CM_COUNTCHILDREN, CMCountChildren),
END_RESPONSE_TABLE;

TAppMDIChild::TAppMDIChild(TMDIClient& parent, int ChildNum)
  : TMDIChild(parent),
    TFrameWindow(&parent),
    TWindow(&parent)
{
  char s[1024];

  // set the scrollers in the window
  Attr.Style |= WS_VSCROLL | WS_HSCROLL;
  // create the TScroller instance
  Scroller = new TScroller(this, 200, 15, 10, 50);

  // set MDI child window title
  sprintf(s, "%s%i", "Child #", ChildNum);
  Title = _fstrdup(s);

  // randomize the seed for the random-number generator
  randomize();

  // assign a null string to the variable s
  strcpy(s, "");
  // build the list of random words
  for (int i = 0; i < MaxWords; i++) {
    if (i > 0 && i % WordsPerLine == 0)
      strcat(s, "\r\n");
    strcat(s, Words[random(NumWords)]);
  }
  // create a static text object in the child window if the
  // ChildNum variable stores an odd number. Otherwise,
  // create an edit box control
  if (ChildNum % 2 == 0) {
    // create the edit box
    TextBox = new TEdit(this, ID_TEXT_EDIT, s,
              10, 10, 300, 200, 0, TRUE);
    // remove borders and scroll bars
    TextBox->Attr.Style &= ~WS_BORDER;
```

continues

LISTING 7.4. CONTINUED

```
    TextBox->Attr.Style &= ~WS_VSCROLL;
    TextBox->Attr.Style &= ~WS_HSCROLL;
  }
  else
    // create static text
    TextTxt = new TStatic(this, -1, s, 10, 10, 300, 400, strlen(s));
}

BOOL TAppMDIChild::CanClose()
{
  // return TRUE if the ExpressClose member of the
  // parent MDI frame window is TRUE
  if (ExpressClose == TRUE) {
    NumMDIChild—;
    return TRUE;
  }
  else
    // prompt the user and return the prompt result
    if (MessageBox("Close this MDI window?",
              "Query", MB_YESNO | MB_ICONQUESTION) == IDYES) {
      NumMDIChild—;
      return TRUE;
    }
    else
      return FALSE;
}

TMDIChild* TAppMDIClient::InitChild()
{
  ++NumMDIChild;
  return new TAppMDIChild(*this, ++HighMDIindex);
}

BOOL TAppMDIClient::CloseChildren()
{
  BOOL result;
  // set the ExpressClose flag
  ExpressClose = TRUE;
  // invoke the parent class CloseChildren() member function
  result = TMDIClient::CloseChildren();
  // clear the ExpressClose flag
  ExpressClose = FALSE;
  NumMDIChild = 0;
  HighMDIindex = 0;
  return result;
}

// display a message box that shows the number of children
void TAppMDIClient::CMCountChildren()
```

```
{
  char msgStr[81];

  sprintf(msgStr, "There are %i MDI children", NumMDIChild);
  MessageBox(msgStr, "Information", MB_OK | MB_ICONINFORMATION);
}

BOOL TAppMDIClient::CanClose()
{
  return MessageBox("Close this application",
             "Query", MB_YESNO | MB_ICONQUESTION) == IDYES;
}

void TWinApp::InitMainWindow()
{
  MainWindow = new TMDIFrame("MDI Text Viewer",
                    TResID(IDM_COMMANDS),
                    *new TAppMDIClient);
}

int OwlMain(int /* argc */, char** /*argv[] */)
{
  TWinApp app;
  return app.Run();
}
```

The program in Listing 7.4 declares a set of global constants used in generating the random text in each MDI child window. The global array of pointers Words contains the rather limited vocabulary of the program. The listing also declares the global variables ExpressClose, NumMDIChild, and HighMDIindex. These variables provide a simple solution for sharing information among the descendants of the branched-out OWL classes. The ExpressClose variable assists in closing all of the child MDI windows in one swoop. The NumMDIChild variable maintains the actual number of MDI child windows. The HighMDIindex variable stores the index of the last MDI child window created.

The program listing declares three classes: the TWinApp application class, the TAppMDIClient MDI client class, and the TAppMDIChild MDI child window class. I will discuss these classes in order.

The code for the TWinApp application class looks very similar to that in previous programs, with one exception. The InitMainWindow member function creates an instance of the stock MDI frame class, TMDIFrame. The TMDIFrame constructor call has the following arguments: the title of the application, the menu resource identifier, IDM_COMMANDS; and the pointer to the dynamically allocated instances of TAppMDIClient.

The TAppMDIClient class declares a constructor and a group of protected member functions. The member functions are as follows:

1. The InitChild member function initializes an MDI child window. The function increments the NumMDIChild global variable and then returns a dynamically allocated instance of TAppMDIChild. The arguments of creating this instance are *this and ++HighMDIindex. The second argument pre-increments the HighMDIindex global variable, which keeps track of the highest index for an MDI child window.

2. The CloseChildren member function alters the behavior of the inherited CloseChildren function. The new version performs the following tasks:

   - Assigns TRUE to the ExpressClose global variable.

   - Invokes the CloseChildren parent class and stores the result of that function call in the local variable result.

   - Assigns FALSE to the ExpressClose variable.

   - Assigns 0 to the NumMDIChild global variable.

   - Assigns 0 to the HighMDIindex global variable. This task resets the value in the HighMDIindex variable when you close all of the MDI child windows.

   - Returns the value stored in the variable result.

3. The CMCountChildren member function responds to the Windows command message CM_COUNTCHILDREN generated by the menu selection Count Children. The function displays the number of MDI child windows in a message dialog box. The function first builds the msgStr string to contain the formatted image of the NumMDIChild global variable. Then, the function invokes the MessageBox member function to display the sought information.

4. The virtual member function CanClose prompts you to confirm closing the MDI-compliant application. This function is identical to the versions of CanClose that I included in earlier programs.

The MDI child window class, TAppMDIChild, declares the TextBox and TextTxt data members, a constructor, and the CanClose member function. The TextBox member is the pointer to the TEdit instance created to store the random text in one kind of MDI child windows. The TextTxt member is the pointer to the TStatic instance created to store random text in the other kind of MDI child windows.

The TAppMDIChild constructor performs a variety of tasks. They are the following:

- Sets the window style to include the vertical and horizontal scrolls.

- Creates an instance of TScroller to animate the scroll bars of the window.

- Sets the window title to include the MDI child window number.

- Randomizes the seed for the random-number generator function, random.

- Creates the random text and stores it in the local string variable s.

- If the MDI child window number is even, creates a multiline instance of TEdit. This instance contains a copy of the text stored in variable s. In addition, the constructor disables the border, vertical scroll bar, and horizontal scroll bar styles. These scroll bars are not needed because the MDI child window itself has scroll bars. In the case of an odd-numbered MDI child window number, the constructor creates static text using the characters in variable s.

The CanClose member function regulates the closing of an MDI child window. When you close such a window using the Close option in its own system menu, the function requires your confirmation. If the request to close comes from the Close All menu command in the parent window, the MDI child window closes without confirmation. The function decrements the NumMDIChild global variable in two cases: first, when the ExpressClose global variable is TRUE; and second, when the MessageBox function, which prompts you to confirm closing the window, returns IDYES.

REVISED TEXT VIEWER

I'll expand on the MDIWIN1.EXE program to illustrate other aspects of managing MDI windows. The next application also creates MDI children that contain edit box controls with random text. Each MDI child window has, however, the following additional controls:

- An ->UpperCase pushbutton control that converts the text in the MDI child window into uppercase.

- A ->LowerCase pushbutton control that converts the text in the MDI child window into lowercase.

- A can Close check box. Using this box replaces using the confirmation dialog box that appears when you want to close the MDI child window. With the check box, you can predetermine whether or not the MDI child window can be closed.

The application menu adds a new pop-up menu item, Current MDI Child. This menu item has options that work on the current MDI child window. With the menu options, you can clear, convert to uppercase, convert to lowercase, or reset the characters in the MDI child window. The new pop-up menu shows how you can manipulate MDI children with custom menus.

Compile and run the application. Create a few MDI children and use their pushbutton controls to toggle the case of characters in these windows. Use the Current MDI Child menu options to further manipulate the text in the currently active MDI child window. Try to close the MDI children with the Can Close check box marked and unmarked. Only the MDI children with the Can Close control checked close individually. Use the Close All option in the MDI Children pop-up menu and watch all of the MDI children close, regardless of the check state of the Can Close control. Figure 7.2 shows a sample session with the MDIWIN2.EXE program.

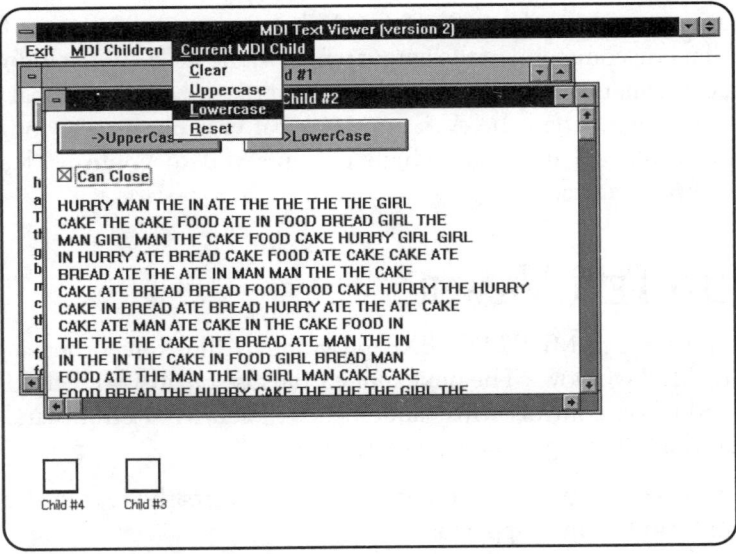

Figure 7.2. A sample session with the MDIWIN2.EXE program.

Listing 7.5 shows the contents of the MDIWIN2.DEF definition file. Listing 7.6 shows the source code for the MDIWIN2.H header file. The file contains the constants for the menu commands and the control IDs. Listing 7.7 contains the script for the MDIWIN2.RC resource file and shows the resource for the expanded menu. Listing 7.8 contains the source code for the MDIWIN2.CPP program file.

LISTING 7.5. THE CONTENTS OF THE MDIWIN2.DEF DEFINITION FILE.

```
NAME         MDIWin2
DESCRIPTION  'An OWL Windows Application'
EXETYPE      WINDOWS
CODE         PRELOAD MOVEABLE DISCARDABLE
DATA         PRELOAD MOVEABLE MULTIPLE
HEAPSIZE     1024
STACKSIZE    8192
```

LISTING 7.6. THE SOURCE CODE FOR THE MDIWIN2.H HEADER FILE.

```
#define CM_COUNTCHILDREN 101
#define CM_CLEAR       102
#define CM_UPPERCASE     103
#define CM_LOWERCASE     104
#define CM_RESET         105
#define ID_TEXT_EDIT     106
#define ID_CANCLOSE_CHK  107
#define ID_UPPERCASE_BTN 108
#define ID_LOWERCASE_BTN 109
#define IDM_COMMANDS     400
```

LISTING 7.7. THE SCRIPT FOR THE MDIWIN2.RC RESOURCE FILE.

```
#include <windows.h>
#include <owl\window.rh>
#include <owl\mdi.rh>
#include "mdiwin2.h"

IDM_COMMANDS MENU LOADONCALL MOVEABLE PURE DISCARDABLE
BEGIN
```

continues

LISTING 7.7. CONTINUED

```
    MENUITEM "E&xit", CM_EXIT
    POPUP "&MDI Children"
    BEGIN
      MENUITEM   "C&reate", CM_CREATECHILD
      MENUITEM   "&Cascade", CM_CASCADECHILDREN
      MENUITEM   "&Tile", CM_TILECHILDREN
      MENUITEM   "Arrange &Icons", CM_ARRANGEICONS
      MENUITEM   "C&lose All", CM_CLOSECHILDREN
      MENUITEM   "C&ount Children", CM_COUNTCHILDREN
    END
    POPUP "&Current MDI Child"
    BEGIN
      MENUITEM   "&Clear", CM_CLEAR
      MENUITEM   "&Uppercase", CM_UPPERCASE
      MENUITEM   "&Lowercase", CM_LOWERCASE
      MENUITEM   "&Reset", CM_RESET
    END
END
```

LISTING 7.8. THE SOURCE CODE FOR THE MDIWIN2.CPP PROGRAM FILE.

```
/*
  Program to demonstrate MDI windows with controls
*/
#include <owl\mdi.rh>
#include <owl\applicat.h>
#include <owl\framewin.h>
#include <owl\button.h>
#include <owl\edit.h>
#include <owl\checkbox.h>
#include <owl\scroller.h>
#include <owl\mdi.h>
#include "mdiwin2.h"
#include <stdio.h>
#include <string.h>

// declare constants for sizing and spacing the controls
// in the MDI child window
const Wbtn = 50 * 3;
const Hbtn = 30;
const BtnHorzSpacing = 20;
const BtnVertSpacing = 10;
const Wchk = 200 * 3;
const Hchk = 20;
```

```
const ChkVertSpacing = 10;
const Wbox = 300 * 3;
const Hbox = 200 * 3;

// declare the constants for the random text that appears
// in the MDI child window
const MaxWords = 200;
const WordsPerLine = 10;
const NumWords = 10;
const BufferSize = 1024;
char AppBuffer[BufferSize];
char* Words[NumWords] = { "The ", "man ", "ate ", "the ",
                          "food ", "in ", "hurry ", "girl ",
                          "cake ", "bread " };


BOOL ExpressClose = FALSE;
int NumMDIChild = 0;
int HighMDIindex = 0;

class TWinApp : public TApplication
{
public:
  TWinApp() : TApplication() {}

protected:
  virtual void InitMainWindow();
};

class TAppMDIChild : public TMDIChild
{
public:


  TAppMDIChild(TMDIClient& parent, int ChildNum);

protected:

  TEdit* TextBox;
  TCheckBox* CanCloseChk;

  // handle the UpperCase button
  void HandleUpperCaseBtn()
    { CMUpperCase(); }

  // handle the LowerCase button
  void HandleLowerCaseBtn()
    { CMLowerCase(); }
```

continues

LISTING 7.8. CONTINUED

```cpp
    // handle clear the active MDI child
    void CMClear()
      { TextBox->Clear(); }

    // handle converting the text of the active
    // MDI child to uppercase
    void CMUpperCase();

    // handle converting the text of the active
    // MDI child to lowercase
    void CMLowerCase();

    // handle resetting the text of the active MDI child
    void CMReset();

    // reset the text in an MDI child window
    void InitText();

    // handle closing the MDI child window
    virtual BOOL CanClose();

    // declare response table
    DECLARE_RESPONSE_TABLE(TAppMDIChild);
};

DEFINE_RESPONSE_TABLE1(TAppMDIChild, TMDIChild)
  EV_COMMAND(ID_UPPERCASE_BTN, HandleUpperCaseBtn),
  EV_COMMAND(ID_LOWERCASE_BTN, HandleLowerCaseBtn),
  EV_COMMAND(CM_CLEAR, CMClear),
  EV_COMMAND(CM_UPPERCASE, CMUpperCase),
  EV_COMMAND(CM_LOWERCASE, CMLowerCase),
  EV_COMMAND(CM_RESET, CMReset),
END_RESPONSE_TABLE;

class TAppMDIClient : public TMDIClient
{
public:


  TAppMDIClient() : TMDIClient() {}

 protected:

  // create a new child
  virtual TMDIChild* InitChild();

  // close all MDI children
  virtual BOOL CloseChildren();
```

```
  // handle the command for counting the MDI children
  void CMCountChildren();

  // handle closing the MDI frame window
  virtual BOOL CanClose();

  // declare response table
  DECLARE_RESPONSE_TABLE(TAppMDIClient);
};

DEFINE_RESPONSE_TABLE1(TAppMDIClient, TMDIClient)
  EV_COMMAND(CM_COUNTCHILDREN, CMCountChildren),
END_RESPONSE_TABLE;

TAppMDIChild::TAppMDIChild(TMDIClient& parent, int ChildNum)
  : TMDIChild(parent),
    TFrameWindow(&parent),
    TWindow(&parent)
{
  char s[41];
  int x0 = 10;
  int y0 = 10;
  int x = x0;
  int y = y0;

  // set the scrollers in the window
  Attr.Style |= WS_VSCROLL | WS_HSCROLL;
  // create the TScroller instance
  Scroller = new TScroller(this, 200, 15, 10, 50);

  // set MDI child window title
  sprintf(s, "%s%i", "Child #", ChildNum);
  Title = _fstrdup(s);

  // create the push button controls
  new TButton(this, ID_UPPERCASE_BTN, "->UpperCase",
              x, y, Wbtn, Hbtn, TRUE);
  x += Wbtn + BtnHorzSpacing;
  new TButton(this, ID_LOWERCASE_BTN, "->LowerCase",
              x, y, Wbtn, Hbtn, FALSE);

  x = x0;
  y += Hbtn + BtnVertSpacing;
  CanCloseChk = new TCheckBox(this, ID_CANCLOSE_CHK, "Can Close",
                             x, y, Wchk, Hchk, NULL);
  y += Hchk + ChkVertSpacing;
  InitText();
  // create the edit box
  TextBox = new TEdit(this, ID_TEXT_EDIT, AppBuffer,
                      x, y, Wbox, Hbox, 0, TRUE);
```

continues

LISTING 7.8. CONTINUED

```
  // remove borders and scroll bars
  TextBox->Attr.Style &= ~WS_BORDER;
  TextBox->Attr.Style &= ~WS_VSCROLL;
  TextBox->Attr.Style &= ~WS_HSCROLL;
}

void TAppMDIChild::CMUpperCase()
{
  TextBox->GetText(AppBuffer, BufferSize);
  strupr(AppBuffer);
  TextBox->SetText(AppBuffer);
}

void TAppMDIChild::CMLowerCase()
{
  TextBox->GetText(AppBuffer, BufferSize);
  strlwr(AppBuffer);
  TextBox->SetText(AppBuffer);
}

void TAppMDIChild::CMReset()
{
  InitText();
  TextBox->SetText(AppBuffer);
}

BOOL TAppMDIChild::CanClose()
{
  // return TRUE if the ExpressClose member of the
  // parent MDI frame window is TRUE
  if (ExpressClose == TRUE) {
    NumMDIChild--;
    return TRUE;
  }
  else
  // do not close the MDi child window if the Can Close is not checked
  if (CanCloseChk->GetCheck() == BF_UNCHECKED)
    return FALSE;
  else {
    NumMDIChild--;
    return TRUE;
  }
}

void TAppMDIChild::InitText()
{
  // randomize the seed for the random-number generator
  randomize();
```

```
    // assign a null string to the buffer
    AppBuffer[0] = '\0';
    // build the list of random words
    for (int i = 0;
         i < MaxWords && strlen(AppBuffer) <= (BufferSize - 10);
         i++) {
      if (i > 0 && i % WordsPerLine == 0)
        strcat(AppBuffer, "\r\n");
      strcat(AppBuffer, Words[random(NumWords)]);
    }
}

TMDIChild* TAppMDIClient::InitChild()
{
  ++NumMDIChild;
  return new TAppMDIChild(*this, ++HighMDIindex);
}

BOOL TAppMDIClient::CloseChildren()
{
  BOOL result;
  // set the ExpressClose flag
  ExpressClose = TRUE;
  // invoke the parent class CloseChildren() member function
  result = TMDIClient::CloseChildren();
  // clear the ExpressClose flag
  ExpressClose = FALSE;
  NumMDIChild = 0;
  HighMDIindex = 0;
  return result;
}

//  display a message box that shows the number of children
void TAppMDIClient::CMCountChildren()
{
  char msgStr[81];

  sprintf(msgStr, "There are %i MDI children", NumMDIChild);
  MessageBox(msgStr, "Information", MB_OK | MB_ICONINFORMATION);
}

BOOL TAppMDIClient::CanClose()
{
  return MessageBox("Close this application",
            "Query", MB_YESNO | MB_ICONQUESTION) == IDYES;
}

void TWinApp::InitMainWindow()
```

continues

LISTING 7.8. CONTINUED

```
{
  MainWindow = new TMDIFrame("MDI Text Viewer (version 2)",
                 TResID(IDM_COMMANDS),
                 *new TAppMDIClient);
}

int OwlMain(int /* argc */, char** /*argv[] */)
{
  TWinApp app;
  return app.Run();
}
```

The program in Listing 7.8 declares two sets of constants. The first set is used for sizing and spacing the controls of each MDI child window. The second set of constants is used to manage the random text. The program also declares the AppBuffer variable as a single 1K text buffer. I chose to make the buffer global instead of a class data member mainly to reduce the buffer space—the application classes need only one shared buffer at any time. The program listing also declares the global variables ExpressClose, NumMDIChild, and HighMDIindex—another set of components carried over from the program in file MDIWIN1.CPP.

The new application maintains the same three classes that I described in the last program. The MDI child class has, however, different members in this program. The new members manage the response to the control notification messages as well as the Current MDI Child menu command messages.

The TAppMDIChild constructor performs the following tasks:

- Sets the window style to include the vertical and horizontal scrolls.

- Creates an instance of TScroller to animate the scroll bars of the window.

- Sets the window title to include the MDI child window number.

- Creates the ->LowerCase and ->UpperCase pushbutton controls.

- Creates the Can Close check box control.

- Calls the InitText member function to generate random text in the AppBuffer application buffer.

- Creates a multiline instance of TEdit. This instance contains a copy of the text stored in the application buffer.

- Disables the border, vertical scroll bar, and horizontal scroll bar styles.

The CMUpperCase member function responds to the command message emitted by the UpperCase menu option. The function copies the text in the MDI child window to the application buffer, converts the characters in the buffer to uppercase, and then writes the buffer back to the MDI child window.

The CMLowerCase member function responds to the command message emitted by the Lowercase menu option. The function performs similar steps to those in CMUpperCase, except that the text is converted into lowercase.

The CanClose member function responds to the WM_CLOSE message emitted by the Close option in the system menu available in each MDI child window. If the MDI frame window's ExpressClose variable is TRUE, the function decrements the NumMDIChild global variable and then returns TRUE. Otherwise, the function returns FALSE if the Can Close check box is unchecked, or it decrements the NumMDIChild global variable and then returns FALSE if the control is not checked.

The InitText member function is an auxiliary routine that fills the application buffer with random text. The function creates up to MaxWords words or creates them until the buffer limit is closely reached (within 10 bytes). Checking the number of characters in the buffer ensures that the program does not corrupt the memory while attempting to add MaxWords words to the buffer.

The HandleUpperCaseBtn and HandleLowerCase member functions respond to the notification messages sent by the pushbuttons of an MDI child window. These functions perform the same tasks of CMUpperCase and CMLowerCase, respectively. Therefore, the notification response functions call their respective command-message response member functions.

The CMClear member function responds to the command message emitted by the Clear menu option in the Current MDI Child menu item. The function simply invokes the TextBox->Clear() function call.

The CMReset member function responds to the command message emitted by the Reset menu option in the Current MDI Child menu item. The function calls the InitText member function to create a new batch of random text and then copies the buffer's text to the edit control of the MDI child window.

The Current MDI Child pop-up menu has four options that manipulate the currently active MDI child window. The command messages emitted by these

options are handled by the MDI child window instances and not—as a window instance normally does regarding its own menu commands—by the MDI frame instance. This order of handling the command messages is preferred and makes use of the fact that the menu-based messages do reach the currently active MDI child window first. You can rewrite the program so that the CMClear, CMUpperCase, CMLowerCase, and CMReset functions appear as member functions of the TAppMDIFrame class.

SUMMARY

This chapter presented the Multiple Document Interface (MDI), an interface standard in Windows. The chapter discussed the following subjects:

- The basic features and components of an MDI-compliant application. These components include the MDI frame window, the invisible MDI client window, and the dynamically created MDI child window.

- Basics of building an MDI application.

- The TMDIFrame class that manages the MDI client window, the MDI child window, and the execution of the menu commands.

- Building MDI frame windows as objects that are owned by the application and that own the MDI children.

- The TMDIClient class.

- Building MDI child windows as an instance of a TWindow descendant.

- Managing messages in an MDI-compliant application. The currently active MDI child window has a higher priority for handling menu-based command messages than its parent, the MDI frame window.

THE BORLAND C++ IDE

The Borland C++ Integrated Development Environment (IDE) is the perhaps the most powerful programming tool in the Borland C++ 4.0 package. The IDE contains a menu system and speed bar buttons, which enable you to manage the various stages of creating your Windows applications. This chapter presents the various options and features of the IDE. You will learn about options of the following menu selections:

- Overview of the IDE
- The File menu selection
- The Edit menu selection
- The Search menu selection
- The View menu selection
- The Project menu selection
- The Debug menu selection
- The Tool menu selection
- The Options menu selection
- The Window menu selection
- The Help menu selection

OVERVIEW OF THE IDE

The Borland C++ IDE is an MDI-compliant window with the following main components:

- The window frame with the menu system, minimize, and maximize icons. You can resize, move, maximize, and minimize the Borland C++ IDE window. This window has a title that reflects the name of the active window.

- The menu system, which offers numerous options.

- The speed bar, which contains special bit-mapped buttons that offer shortcuts to specific menu options. The IDE enables you to customize the bit-mapped buttons in the speed bar. In addition, these buttons are context sensitive. Their number and type change depending on the current task or active window. The IDE supports a nice feature that displays what a bit-mapped button does (the text appears in the status line) when you move the mouse over that button.

- The client area, which contains various windows, such as the source code editing window, the message window, the variable watch window, and so on.

- The status line located at the bottom of the IDE window. This line displays brief on-line help as you move the mouse over the buttons in the speed bar, offers a brief explanation for the various menu items, displays the cursor location, and shows the status of the insert/overwrite mode.

Figure 8.1 shows a sample session with the Borland C++ IDE.

THE FILE MENU SELECTION

The File menu selection provides options to manage files, print text, and exit the IDE. Table 8.1 summarizes the options in the File menu selection. The File menu selection also includes a dynamic list of the most recently opened source code files.

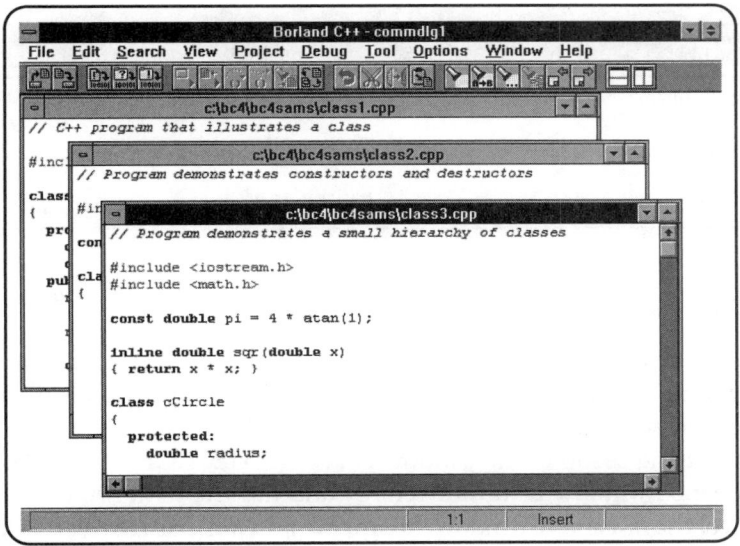

Figure 8.1. The Borland C++ IDE.

TABLE 8.1. THE SUMMARY OF THE OPTIONS IN THE FILE MENU SELECTION.

Menu Option	Shortcut Key(s)	Function
New		Opens a new edit window
Open...		Loads an existing source code file into a new edit window
Save	Ctrl+K, S	Saves the contents of the active edit window
Save as...		Saves the contents of the active edit window using a new filename
Save all		Saves all of the opened source code windows in their respective files
Print...		Prints the contents of a source code window

continues

Menu Option	Shortcut Key(s)	Function
Print setup...		Sets up the printer
Exit		Exits the IDE

TABLE 8.1. CONTINUED

The New Option

The New option opens a new edit window (also known as a source code window) and assigns it a default associated filename. The default filename of the first new window you open is NONAME00.CPP. Likewise, the default filename of the second new window is NONAME01.CPP, and so on. The newly opened window is initially empty and has the same window size and location of the last active window. In other words, if the last active window was maximized, the new window also will be maximized.

The Open... Option

The Open... option enables you to load the contents of an existing source code file into a new edit window. The option invokes the Open a File dialog box, shown in Figure 8.2. The dialog box has several list box and combo box controls which enable you to locate the source code file and select it. These controls permit you to choose the drive, directory, and filename wildcards that help you locate the source code file you seek.

The Save Option

The Save option assists you in saving the contents of the active edit window to its associated file. If you invoke this option with a new edit window, the Save option invokes the Save File As dialog box, shown in Figure 8.3. This dialog box permits you to optionally specify the non-default filename, as well as the destination drive and directory. The shortcut keys for the Save option are Ctrl+K, S.

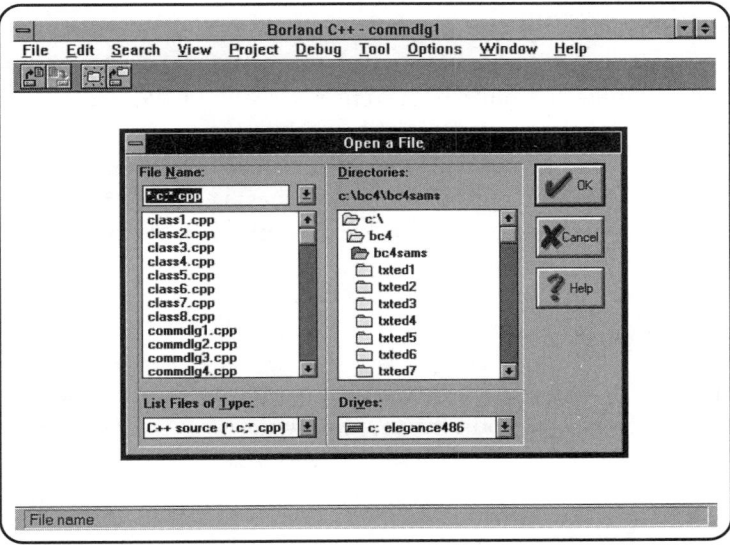

Figure 8.2. The Open a File dialog box.

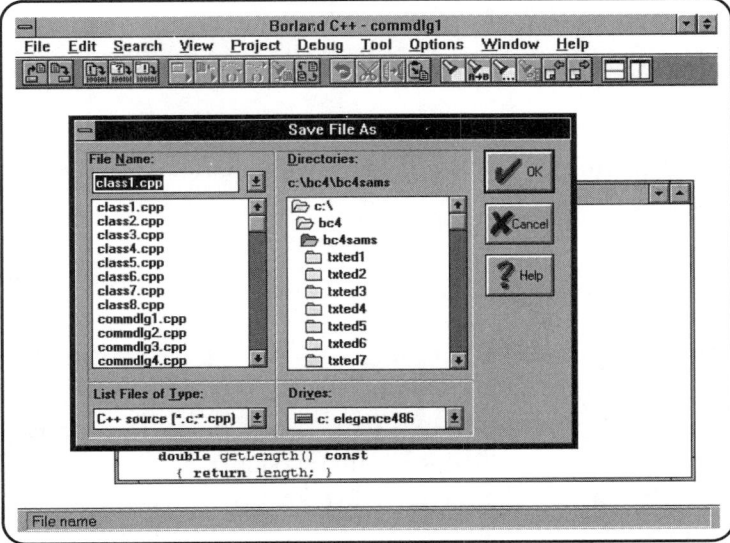

Figure 8.3. The Save File As dialog box.

The Save As... Option

The Save as... option permits you to save the contents of the active edit window in file that is different from the currently associated file. In fact, the new filename becomes the new associated file for the active edit window. The Save As... option invokes the Save File As dialog box, shown in Figure 8.3. If you select an existing file, the option brings up a message dialog box to ask you if you wish to overwrite the contents of the existing file with those of the active edit window.

The Save All Option

The Save all option writes the contents of all the modified edit windows to their associated files. If the IDE contains new edit windows, this option invokes the Save File As dialog box to save these new windows.

The Print... Option

The Print... option enables you to print the contents of the active edit window. The option brings up the Print Options dialog box shown in Figure 8.4. This dialog box has check boxes for the following options:

- Print a header and page numbers
- Print line numbers
- Highlights syntax keywords by printing them in bold characters
- Use color if your printer supports colors
- Wrap lines

The Print Setup... Option

The Print setup... option permits you to set up your printer before you print using the Print... option. The printer setup option brings up the Setup dialog box, shown in Figure 8.5 (the dialog box in this figure is based on my own system which has an HP LaserJet III). This dialog box contains controls that enable you to specify the following items:

- The paper size.

- The paper source.

- The number of copies to print.

- The amount of printer memory.

- The orientation of the printout.

- The selected font cartridges and fonts.

- Page protection to reserve additional memory for printing a page. This option is available only when you have more than one 1M of printer memory.

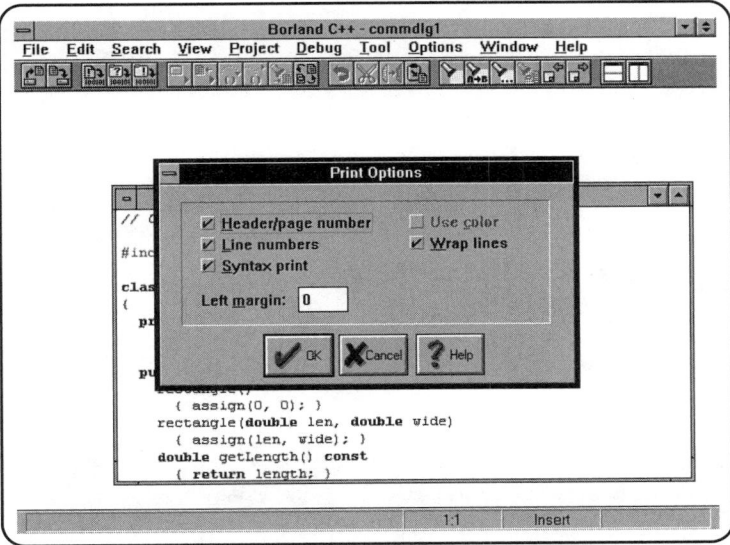

Figure 8.4. The Print Options dialog box.

The Exit Option

The Exit option permits you to exit the Borland C++ IDE altogether. The IDE prompts you for any modified edit window that has not been saved.

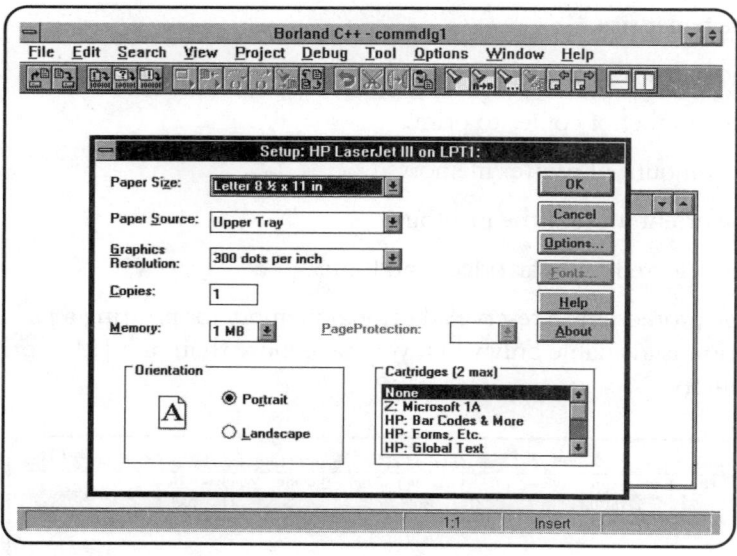

Figure 8.5. The Setup dialog box.

THE EDIT MENU SELECTION

The Edit menu selection contains options that enable you to edit the text in the edit windows. Table 8.2 summarizes the options in the Edit menu selection.

TABLE 8.2. THE SUMMARY OF THE OPTIONS IN THE EDIT MENU SELECTION.

Menu Option	Shortcut Key(s)	Function
Undo	Ctrl+Z	Undoes the last editing action.
Redo	Shift+Ctrl+Z	Reverses the action of the last Undo option.
Cut	Ctrl+X	Deletes the selected text and copies it in the Clipboard. The previous contents of the Clipboard are lost.
Copy	Ctrl+C	Copies the selected text to the Clipboard. The previous contents of the Clipboard are lost.

Menu Option	Shortcut Key(s)	Function
Paste	Ctrl+V	Inserts the contents of the Clipboard at the current cursor location.
Clear	Ctrl+Delete	Deletes selected text but does not write it to the Clipboard.
Select all		Selects all of the text in the active edit window.
Buffer list...		Displays the Buffer List dialog box.

The Undo Option

The Undo option enables you to reverse the effect of the last editing task and restore the contents of the active edit window. The shortcut keys for this option are Ctrl+Z. This option enables you to quickly and efficiently deal with editing errors—especially after working long hours!

The Redo Option

The Redo option enables you to reverse the action of the Undo option. The shortcut keys for the Redo option are Shift+Ctrl+Z. The Redo option enables you to switch between two versions of edited source code. This option also benefits the truly exhausted programmer who cannot make up his mind about the source code!

The Cut Option

The Cut option deletes selected text and places it in the Clipboard. The previous contents of the Clipboard are lost. The shortcut keys for the Cut option are Ctrl+X.

The Copy Option

The Copy option copies the selected text into the Clipboard. The previous contents of the Clipboard are lost. The shortcut keys for the Copy option are Ctrl+C.

The Paste Option

The Paste option inserts the contents of the Clipboard at the current insertion point. The contents of the Clipboard remain unaffected. This means you can use the Cut and Paste options to move text in the same edit window or across different edit windows. You can also use the Copy and Paste options to duplicate blocks of text in the same edit window or across different edit windows. The shortcut keys for the Paste option are Ctrl+V.

The Clear Option

The Clear option clears the selected text without copying it to the Clipboard. This does not mean the deleted text is irreversibly lost, since you can use the Undo option to undelete that text. The shortcut keys for the Clear option are Ctrl+Delete.

The Select All Option

The Select all option selects all of the text in the active edit window. You can then copy this text into the Clipboard by using the Copy option. You can then write the contents of the Clipboard to another edit window with the Paste option.

The Buffer List... Option

The Buffer list... option enables you to examine the list of buffers used with the various edit windows. This option brings up the Buffer List dialog box, shown in Figure 8.6. The dialog box enables you to load a buffer into an edit window. The dialog box contains the list of buffers. Those buffers that have changed since they were last loaded are followed by the word *MODIFIED* (in parentheses). The dialog box permits you to replace the contents of an edit window without closing the associated file. The replaced file is hidden if it is not loaded into another edit window. You may utilize the buffer list later on to load the hidden buffer into an edit window.

You can use the Save pushbutton of the Buffer List dialog box to update the file associated with the selected buffer. This action causes the word *MODIFIED* to disappear from the selected buffer entry. You may also use the Delete pushbutton to remove the selected buffer from memory, if that buffer is not being viewed.

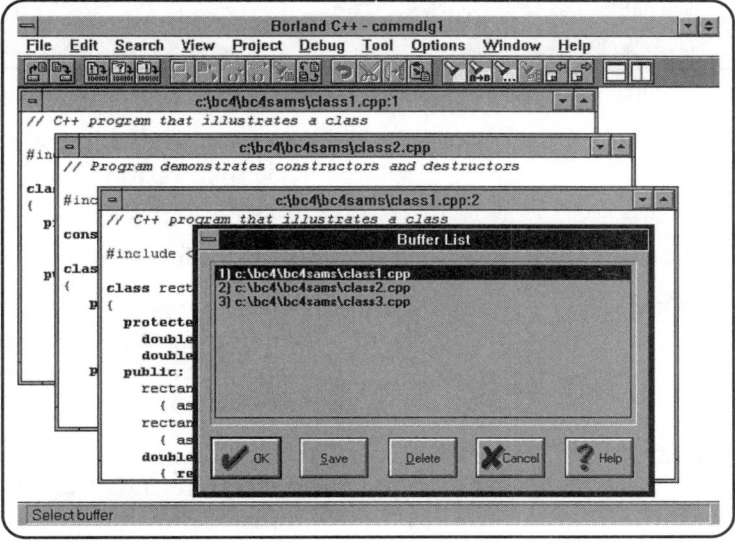

Figure 8.6. The Buffer List dialog box.

THE SEARCH MENU SELECTION

The Search menu selection contains options that enable you to locate various kinds of information, such as text, symbol definitions, function declarations, and program building errors. Table 8.3 offers the summary of the options in the Search menu selection.

TABLE 8.3. THE SUMMARY OF THE OPTIONS IN THE SEARCH MENU SELECTION.

Menu Option	Shortcut Key(s)	Function
Find...	Ctrl+Q, F	Searches for text in the active edit window
Replace...	Ctrl+Q, A	Replaces text in the active source code window
Search again	F3	Repeats the last Find or Replace operation

continues

	TABLE 8.3. CONTINUED	
Menu Option	*Shortcut Key(s)*	*Function*
Browse symbol...		Locates a symbol in any source code that is part of the current project
Locate function...		Locates a function
Previous message	Alt+F7	Selects the previous program building message and places the cursor at the offending line in an edit window
Next message	Alt+F8	Selects the next program building message and places the cursor at the offending line in an edit window

The Find... Option

The Find... option supports search for text in the active edit window. This option, which has the shortcut keys Ctrl+Q, F, brings up the Find Text dialog box, shown in Figure 8.7. This dialog box has the following controls:

- The "Text to find" combo box control, which enables you either to type in the search text or recall recently searched text.

- The Options check boxes which are:

  •The Case sensitive check box, which enables you to select case sensitive or insensitive text search.

  •The Whole words only check box, which enables you to choose between matching entire words or matching any text.

  •The Regular expression check box, which turns on or off the use of the BRIEF editor regular expressions. Such expressions result in using the text in the Text to find control as text pattern.

- The Direction diamond-shaped radio button controls. These controls enable you to choose between forward or backward search.

- The Scope diamond-shaped radio button controls. These controls enable you to choose between searching the entire text or limiting the search to the selected text.

- The Origin diamond-shaped radio button controls. These controls offer you the option of searching the entire edit window or searching from the cursor position on.

- The OK, Cancel, and Help buttons.

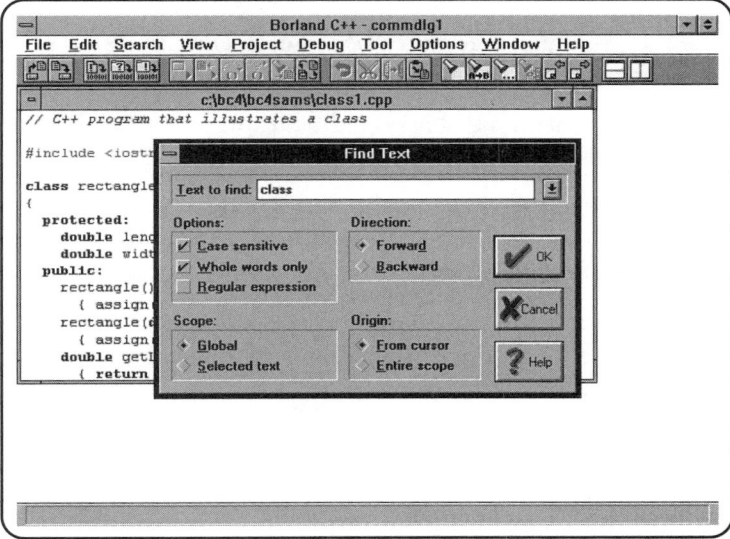

Figure 8.7. The Find Text dialog box.

The Replace... Option

The Replace... option supports replacing text in the active edit window. This option, which has the shortcut keys Ctrl+Q, A, brings up the Replace Text dialog box, shown in Figure 8.8. This dialog box has the following controls:

- The Text to find combo box control, which enables you to either type in the search text or recall recently searched text.

- The New text combo box, which enables you to either enter the replacement text or select recently used replacement text.

- The Options check boxes which are

  - The Case-sensitive check box, which enables you to select case sensitive or insensitive text search.

  - The Whole words only check box, which enables you to choose between matching entire words or matching any text.

  - The Regular expression check box, which turns on or off the use of the BRIEF editor regular expressions. Such expressions result in using the text in the Text to find control as text pattern.

  - The Prompt on replace check box, which enables you to select whether to replace text with or without asking you.

- The Direction diamond-shaped radio button controls. These controls enable you to choose between forward or backward search.

- The Scope diamond-shaped radio button controls. These controls enable you to choose between searching the entire text or limiting the search to the selected text.

- The Origin diamond-shaped radio button controls. These controls offer you the option between searching the entire edit window or searching from the cursor position on.

- The Replace All pushbutton, which enables you to replace all matching text.

- The OK, Cancel, and Help buttons.

The Search Again Option

The Search again option enables you to repeat the last Find... or Replace... option. The shortcut key for this option is the F3 function key.

The Browse Symbol... Option

The Browse symbol... option enables you to browse at the makeup of a symbol, including classes, functions, and variables. These symbols need not be defined in the active edit window, as long as they are defined in one of the current project's source code files. Figure 8.9 shows a sample symbol browsing dialog box. In Chapter 12, I will discuss browsing at symbols in more detail.

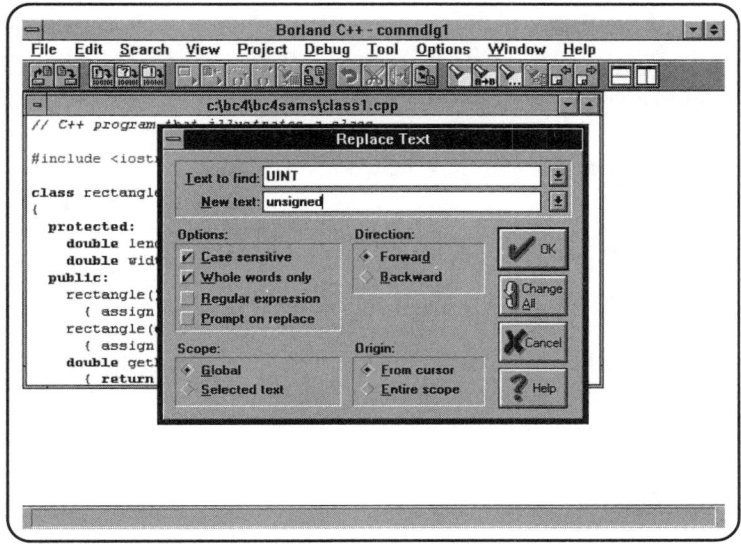

Figure 8.8. The Replace Text dialog box.

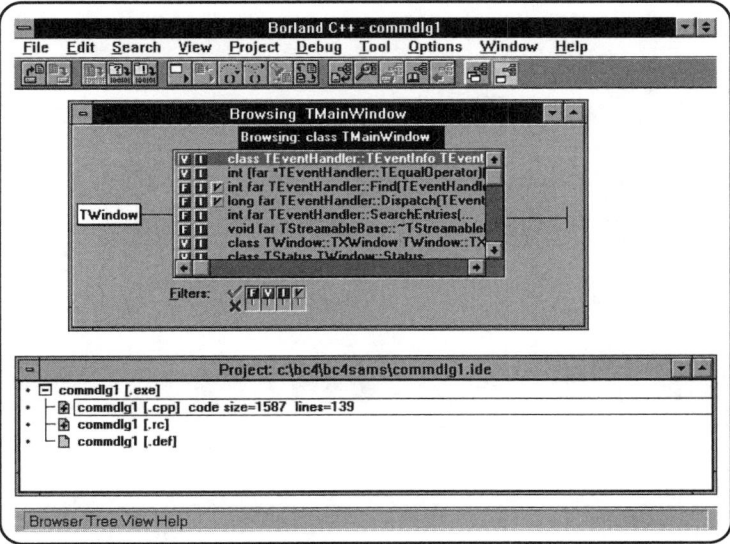

Figure 8.9. A sample Symbol Browsing dialog box.

The Locate Function... Option

The Locate function... option enables you to find where the function is defined. This option brings up the Locate Function dialog box, which prompts you to enter the name of the function you wish to find. The IDE responds by displaying the function definition in a new edit window, if need be.

The Previous Message Option

The Previous message option enables you to zoom in on the offending source code line, which is associated with the previous message in the Message window. The IDE responds to this option by displaying the edit window, which contains the offending source code line. The shortcut keys for this option are Alt+F7.

The Next Message Option

The Next message option enables you to zoom in on the offending source code line which is associated with the next message in the Message window. The IDE responds to this option by displaying the edit window which contains the offending source code line. The shortcut keys for this option are Alt+F8.

THE VIEW MENU SELECTION

The View menu selection contains options that enable you to view and browse at a wide variety of information. This information goes beyond the declarations in the source code files of your project. Table 8.4 contains the summary of the options in the View menu selection.

TABLE 8.4. THE SUMMARY OF THE OPTIONS IN THE VIEW MENU SELECTION.

Menu Option	Shortcut Key(s)	Function
ClassExpert		Invokes the ClassExpert utility, which works with project files generated by AppExpert

Menu Option	Shortcut Key(s)	Function
Project		Displays the Project window
Message		Displays the Message window
Classes		Browses through the classes
Globals		Browses through global data types constants, and variables
Watch		Selects or opens the Watch window
Breakpoint		Selects or opens the Breakpoints window
Call stack		Selects or opens the Call Stack window
Register		Selects or opens the Registers window
Event log		Selects or opens the Event Log window
Information...		Displays compiler information

The ClassExpert Option

The ClassExpert option invokes the ClassExpert utility, which works only with project files created by the AppExpert (which I introduce in the next section). This option invokes the ClassExpert window, which has three panes:

- The Classes pane, which lists the classes involved in the project created using AppExpert. The information in the other two panes are related to the currently-selected class in this pane.

- The Events pane, which lists the command notification, control notifications, virtual functions, Windows messages, and other events that are related to the class selected in the Classes pane.

- The source code window in which the selected class is defined.

Figure 8.10 shows a sample ClassExpert window.

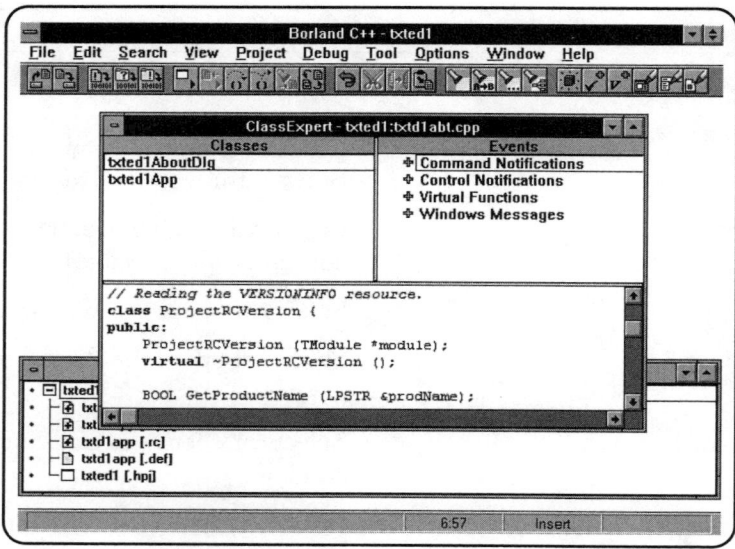

Figure 8.10. A sample ClassExpert window.

The Project Option

The Project option selects or opens the Project window, which lists the targets in the current .IDE file. The Project window displays the files of a target in the form of a tree-like outline. The outline is made up of nodes that you can expand and collapse (if they have sub-nodes). Figure 8.11 shows a sample Project window. Each node has a bit map graphics to its left. If the bit map graphics has a + sign, then the node has sub-nodes, which are currently hidden. If you click the + sign, you expand that node, the IDE replace the + sign with a - sign. The node child with no + or - sign have no subsequent sub-nodes.

If you click the right mouse button while the mouse is inside the Project window, the IDE displays a floating menu, which empowers you to view various components of the project, manage nodes, and edit project-related components.

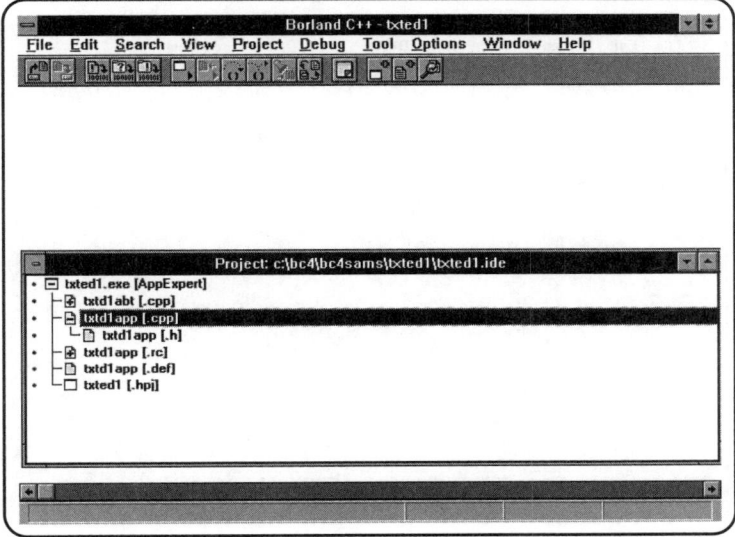

Figure 8.11. A sample Project window.

The Message Option

The Message option displays selects or opens the Message window, which contains the source code compiler, resource compiler, and linker messages. These messages inform you of the progress of building the .EXE program file. In addition, the Message window contains any warning or error messages generated by the compilers or linker.

The Classes Option

The Classes option displays the Browsing Objects window showing a graph of the various classes in the current project and how they are interlinked. Typically, the Browsing Objects has vertical and horizontal scroll bars that enable you to scroll through the various classes involved in the current project. Figure 8.12 shows a sample Browsing Objects window, which displays the TWinApp custom application class and the application's TMainWindow frame window class.

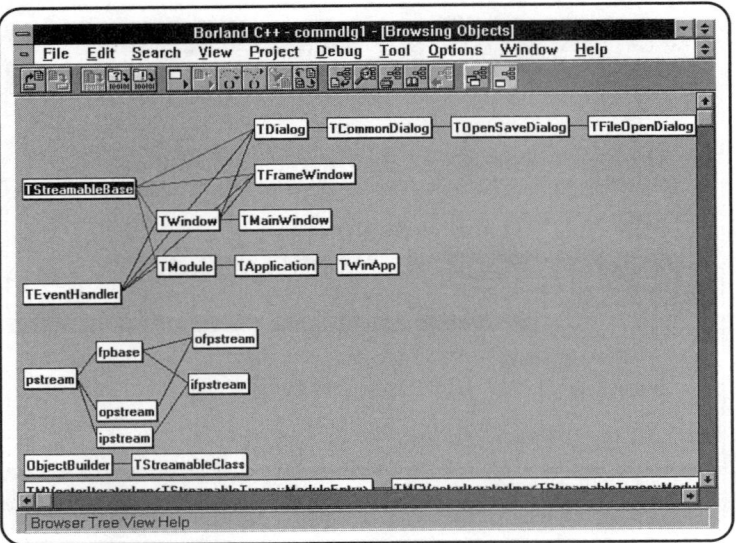

Figure 8.12. A sample Browsing Objects window.

The Globals Option

The Globals option displays the Browsing Globals window, which shows the global data types, constants, variables, and functions. Figure 8.13 shows a sample Browsing Globals window. The window identifies each item by using the following special bit map:

- The bit map T indicates that the symbol is a data type.

- The bit map C signals that the symbol is a constant.

- The bit map F signifies that the symbol is a function.

- The bit map V indicates that the symbol is a variable.

The Browsing Globals window contains switches, which enable you to filter viewing certain global symbols. The window also contains an edit box control that enables you to type in the name of the symbol you want to find. The edit box control filters the symbols with every keystroke you enter.

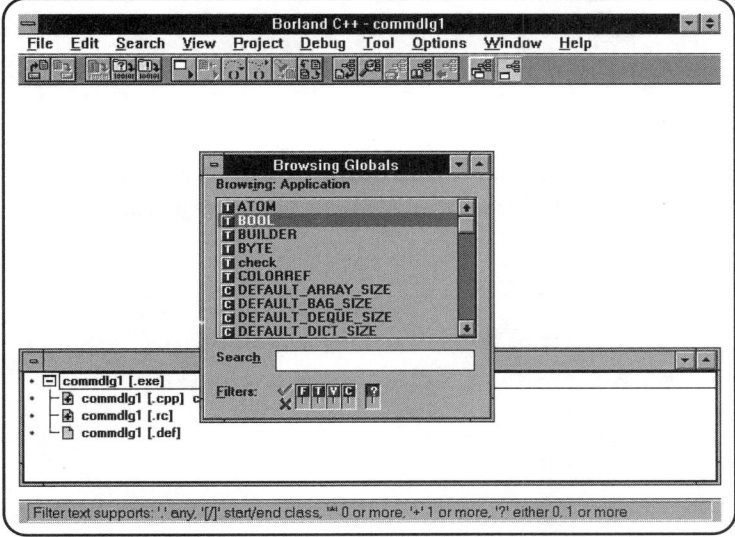

Figure 8.13. A sample Browsing Globals window.

The Watch Option

The Watch option selects or opens the Watch window. This window lists the currently watched variables in your program. Figure 8.14 shows a sample Watch window. The window displays a check box to the left of each variable. The check box is checked by default to display and update the value in the associated variable. You can uncheck the control to temporarily disable displaying the value of a variable. This task is especially meaningful when the watched variable is not defined in the currently traced function. Use the Watch option to monitor the contents of a variable during a debug session. You might want to limit the number of variables to fit inside the Watch window, so you can easily monitor these variables without extensive scrolling up and down in the Watch window.

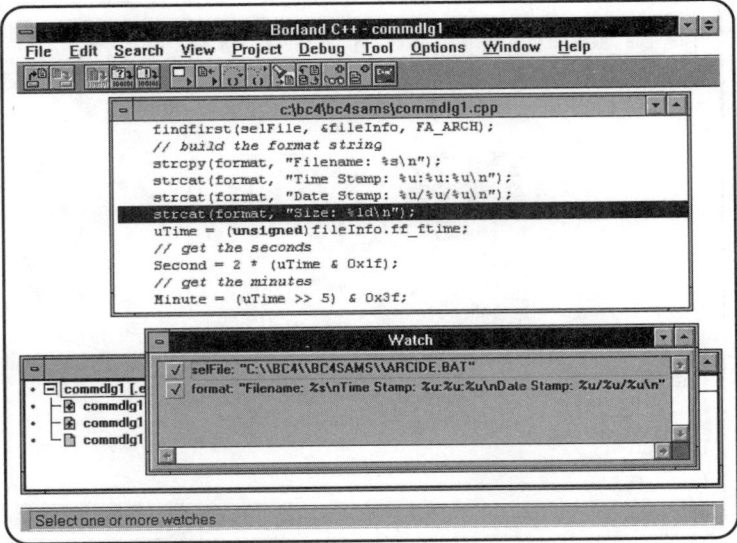

Figure 8.14. A sample Watch window.

The Breakpoint Option

The Breakpoint option displays the Breakpoints window, which lists the location and type of breakpoints. Figure 8.15 shows a sample Breakpoints window. The Breakpoints window displays the following information:

- The filename that contains the breakpoint.
- The line number where the breakpoint is located.
- The state of the breakpoint.
- The number of passes (that is the number of times the statement is executed before the program stops at the breakpoint).

If you double-click any entry in the Breakpoints window, the IDE displays the Breakpoints Properties dialog box. This dialog box enables you to edit the breakpoint's data. I'll cover this dialog box in the Debug menu section.

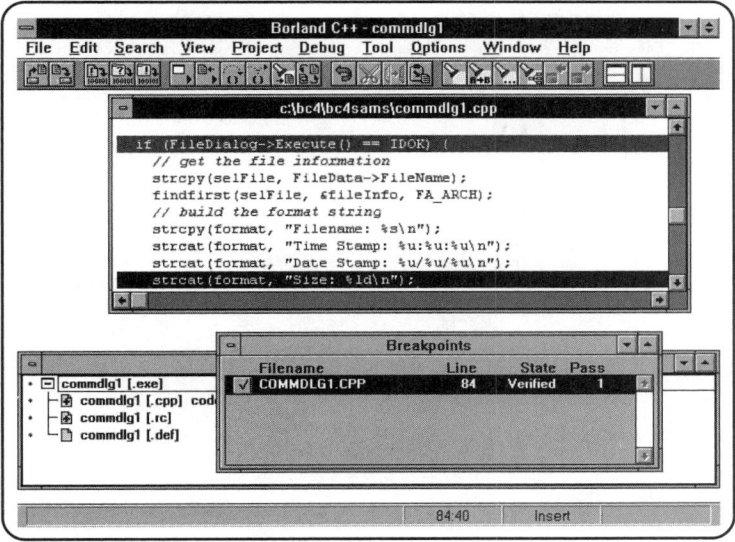

Figure 8.15. The Breakpoints window.

The Call Stack Option

The Call stack option displays the Call Stack window. This window lists the pending program and DLL functions that were called (and not yet returned) when the program reached the current breakpoint or the current single stepped line. Figure 8.16 shows a sample Call Stack window. The DDL functions are referenced by the name of the DLL library followed by the address of the function.

The Register Option

The Register option displays the Registers window. This window reveals the current values in CPU registers. The information in this window helps you perform a low-level debug and trace of a program.

The Event Log Option

The Event log option displays the Event Log window, which lists the sequence of breakpoint events. Each log entry includes the breakpoint address followed by text that identifies the related Windows messages, output messages, or exceptions. Figure 8.17 shows a sample Event Log window.

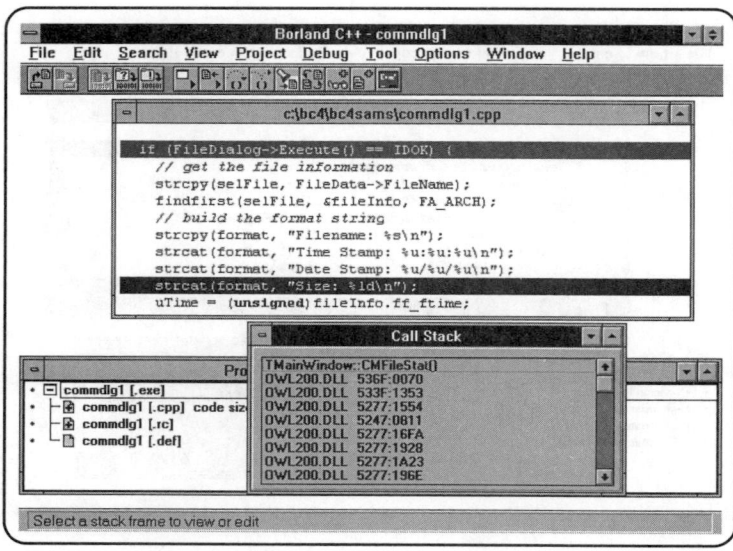

Figure 8.16. A sample Call Stack window.

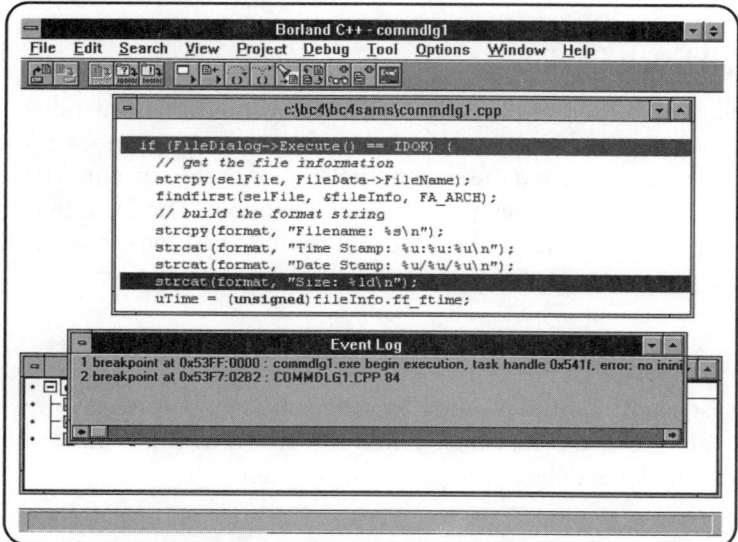

Figure 8.17. A sample Event Log window.

The Information... Option

The Information... option displays the Information dialog box. This dialog box contains the following information:

- The current directory
- The Windows version and mode
- The MS-DOS version
- The total free memory space
- The largest free memory block
- The percent of USER, GDI, and total free heap space

Figure 8.18 shows a sample Information dialog box.

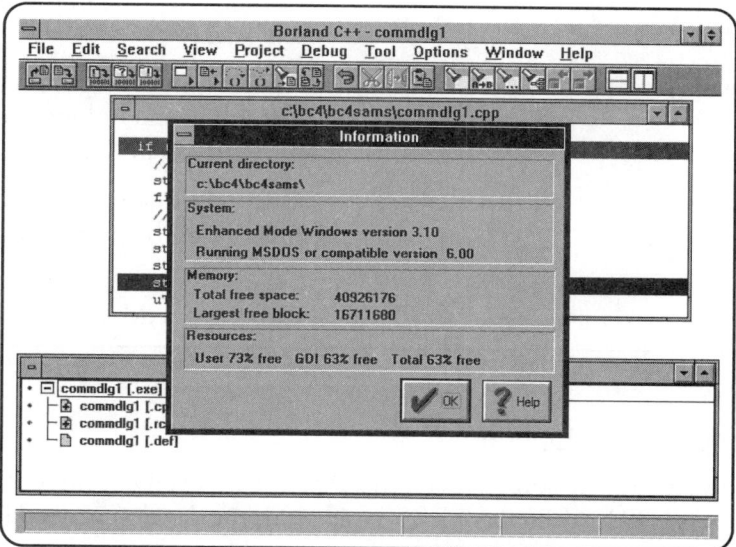

Figure 8.18. A sample Information dialog box.

THE PROJECT MENU SELECTION

The Project menu selection offers options that manage a project to build an executable program or a library. Table 8.5 contains the summary of the options in the Project menu selection.

TABLE 8.5. THE SUMMARY OF THE OPTIONS IN THE PROJECT MENU SELECTION.

Menu Option	Shortcut Key(s)	Function
AppExpert...		Invokes the AppExpert utility to generate the files of a project
New project...		Creates a new project
Open project...		Opens an existing project and closes the current project
Close project		Closes the current project
New target...		Creates a new target in the current project
Compile	Alt+F9	Compiles the file in the active edit window
Make all		Updates the project files by compiling and linking the necessary source code files
Build all		Unconditionally compiles and links all of the project source code files
Generate makefile		Generates a .MAK makefile

The AppExpert... Option

The AppExpert... option invokes the AppExpert utility. This utility is a valuable and sophisticated tool for rapid program development. The next chapter covers working with the AppExpert option.

The New Project... Option

The New project... option triggers the process, which enables you to create a new project without involving the AppExpert utility. This option brings up the New Project dialog box, shown in Figure 8.19. The dialog box enables you to specify the following information:

- The path and name of the new project.
- The target name (that is, the name of the .EXE file).
- The target type, which can be one of the following:
  - A Windows .EXE application
  - A Windows .DLL dynamic library
  - An EasyWin .EXE program
  - A .LIB static library
  - A .LIB import library
  - A Windows .HLP help file
- The application's platform, which can be the 16-bit Windows 3.x or Win32.
- The target's memory model, which can be small, compact, medium, large, or huge.
- A variety of choices related to the libraries included.
- The options to specify sub-node files with .C or .CPP extension along with optional a .RC resource file and a .DEF definition file. The Advanced pushbutton control in the dialog box offers these options through a special dialog box.
- The option to select the path for the project. The Browse pushbutton control in the dialog box offers this option.

The Open Project... Option

The Open project... option permits you to open a new project and automatically close the current one. This option brings up the Open Project File dialog box, which resembles the File Open dialog box. The Project File dialog box enables you to specify the drive, directory, and filename wildcards involved in selecting the .IDE or .PRJ project files. The .IDE project files are new to Borland C++ 4.0 and support multiple targets. The .PRJ project files are available for backward compatibility with previous versions of Borland C++.

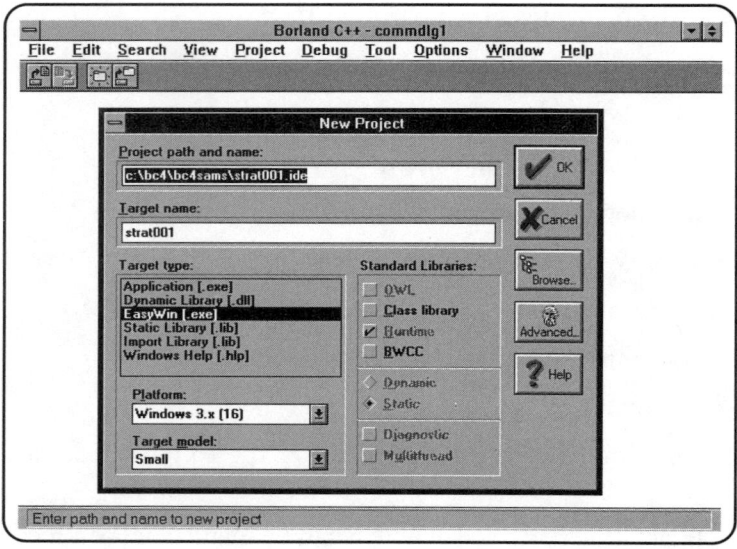

Figure 8.19. A sample New Project dialog box.

The Close Project Option

The Close project option closes the current project and its edit windows.

The New Target... Option

The New target... option enables you to add another target to the project. The option first brings up the New Target dialog box, which enables you to enter the name and type of the target. The target type may be AppExpert, Standard, and SourcePool. If you choose the AppExpert target type, the IDE invokes the AppExpert once you close the New Target dialog box. If you select the Standard target type, the IDE invokes the New Project dialog box. If you choose the SourcePool target type, the IDE quietly adds a SourcePool target node. The Project window reflects the addition of the new target and indicates its type.

A source pool target contains a set of nodes that are not built in the project. Source pools instead play the role of templates for creating reference copies that enable different targets to employ common source code. For example, you can use the source pools in creating a 16-bit .EXE target and a 32-bit .EXE target.

The Compile Option

The Compile option compiles the source code in the active edit window. The option displays the Compile Status dialog box. This dialog box informs you of the files being compiled, the number of lines, the number of warnings, and the number of errors. Once the compilation process ends, the Message window also displays general messages for the compilation steps and includes warnings and error messages as generated by the compiler. The shortcut keys for this option are Alt+F9.

The Make All Option

The Make all option updates the project's target by compiling and linking only those files that have been changed since the previous program creation. The option also uses the Compile Status dialog box to display the progress of the compilation and linking steps. Once this process is terminated, the Message window displays messages that reflect the progress of compiling and linking, along with any warning and error messages.

The Build All Option

The Build all option is similar to the Make all option, except that it systematically recompiles and links all the project's files.

The Generate Makefile Option

The Generate makefile option generates a .MAK file. This option opens a new edit window for the .MAK file, creates the contents of the .MAK file, and then displays the contents of the makefile in the new edit window. Listing 8.1 shows the COMMDLG1.MAK makefile for the COMMDLG1.IDE project (the second example in Chapter 6).

LISTING 8.1. THE COMMDLG1.MAK FILE FOR THE COMMDLG1.IDE PROJECT FILE.

```
#
# Borland C++ IDE generated makefile
#
.AUTODEPEND

IDE_TARGET_NAME = steps
```

continues

LISTING 8.1. CONTINUED

```
#
# Borland C++ tools
#
TLINK   = TLink
TLINK32 = TLink32
IMPLIB  = Implib
TASM    = Tasm
BCC     = Bcc +$(IDE_TARGET_NAME).cfg
BCC32   = Bcc32 +$(IDE_TARGET_NAME).cfg
BRC     = Brc
BRC32   = Brc32


#
# IDE Debug/Release option
#
!if $d(PRJ_DEBUG)

IDE_DBG_LFLAGS = -v
IDE_DBG_CFLAGS = -v

!endif


#
# IDE macros
#


#
# Options
#
IDE_LFLAGS =  -L\BC4\LIB -c -C
IDE_RFLAGS =  -I\BC4\INCLUDE
IDE_BFLAGS =
CLAT_commdlg1dexe =  -ml -WS -D_USEDLL;
LLAT_commdlg1dexe =  -Twe -C -c
RLAT_commdlg1dexe =
BLAT_commdlg1dexe =
CEAT_commdlg1dexe = $(CLAT_commdlg1dexe)
LEAT_commdlg1dexe = $(LLAT_commdlg1dexe)
REAT_commdlg1dexe = $(RLAT_commdlg1dexe)
BEAT_commdlg1dexe = $(BLAT_commdlg1dexe)
CLAT_commdlg1dcpp =
LLAT_commdlg1dcpp =
RLAT_commdlg1dcpp =
BLAT_commdlg1dcpp =
CEAT_commdlg1dcpp = $(CEAT_commdlg1dexe) $(CLAT_commdlg1dcpp)
LEAT_commdlg1dcpp = $(LEAT_commdlg1dexe) $(LLAT_commdlg1dcpp)
REAT_commdlg1dcpp = $(REAT_commdlg1dexe) $(RLAT_commdlg1dcpp)
BEAT_commdlg1dcpp = $(BEAT_commdlg1dexe) $(BLAT_commdlg1dcpp)
```

```
CLAT_commdlg1drc =
LLAT_commdlg1drc =
RLAT_commdlg1drc =
BLAT_commdlg1drc =
CEAT_commdlg1drc = $(CEAT_commdlg1dexe) $(CLAT_commdlg1drc)
LEAT_commdlg1drc = $(LEAT_commdlg1dexe) $(LLAT_commdlg1drc)
REAT_commdlg1drc = $(REAT_commdlg1dexe) $(RLAT_commdlg1drc)
BEAT_commdlg1drc = $(BEAT_commdlg1dexe) $(BLAT_commdlg1drc)

#
# Dependency List
#
Dep_steps = \
   commdlg1.exe

steps : $(IDE_TARGET_NAME).cfg $(Dep_steps)
#  $(MakeNode) steps

Dep_commdlg1dexe = \
   commdlg1.obj\
   commdlg1.res\
   commdlg1.def

commdlg1.exe : $(Dep_commdlg1dexe)
  $(TLINK)    @&&¦
 $(IDE_DBG_LFLAGS) +
 $(IDE_LFLAGS) $(LEAT_commdlg1dexe) +
C:\BC4\LIB\c0wl.obj+
commdlg1.obj
$<,$*
C:\BC4\LIB\bidsi.lib+
C:\BC4\LIB\owlwi.lib+
C:\BC4\LIB\import.lib+
C:\BC4\LIB\crtldll.lib
commdlg1.def
¦
   $(BRC) commdlg1.res $<

commdlg1.obj :  commdlg1.cpp
  $(BCC)   -c $(CEAT_commdlg1dcpp) -o$@ commdlg1.cpp

commdlg1.res :  commdlg1.rc
  $(BRC) $(IDE_RFLAGS) $(REAT_commdlg1drc) -R -FO$@ commdlg1.rc

# Compiler configuration file
$(IDE_TARGET_NAME).cfg :
   Copy &&¦
$(IDE_DBG_CFLAGS)
-I\BC4\INCLUDE
¦ $(IDE_TARGET_NAME).cfg
```

THE DEBUG MENU SELECTION

The Debug menu selection provides you with options that enable you to debug your C or C++ source code. Table 8.6 presents a summary of the options in the Debug menu selection.

TABLE 8.6. THE SUMMARY OF THE OPTIONS IN THE DEBUG MENU SELECTION.

Menu Option	Shortcut Key(s)	Function
Run	Ctrl+F9	Runs the program of the current target. If needed, this option also compiles and links the project source code files
Step over	F8	Single steps through the next statement without tracing the statements of functions that are called in the next statement
Trace into	F7	Single steps through the next statement and also trace the statements of functions that are called in the next statement
Toggle breakpoint	F5	Toggles making the line at the current cursor location an unconditional breakpoint
Find execution point		Shows the source code at the execution point
Pause program		Pauses the program and switches to the debugger
Terminate program	Ctrl+F2	Stops the program and restarts it from the beginning
Add watch...	Ctrl+F5	Opens the Watch Properties dialog box to add a variable to watch

Menu Option	Shortcut Key(s)	Function
Add **b**reakpoint...		Opens the Breakpoint Properties dialog box to add a breakpoint
Evaluate/Modify...		Evaluates an expression and/or modifies the value in a variable
Inspect...	Alt+F5	Inspects the contents of a variable
Load symbol table...		Loads DLL symbol table

Chapter 13 discusses using the various options offered by the Debug menu selection. In addition, the chapter shows sample erroneous programs that are debugged using the Debug menu options.

THE TOOL MENU SELECTION

The Tool menu selection provides access to several programming utilities. The IDE Tools... option in the Options menu selection enables you to customize the list of programming tools that appear in the Tool menu selection. Table 8.7 provides you with the summary of the default options in the Tool menu selection. Chapter 12 discusses some of the Windows programming tools.

TABLE 8.7. THE SUMMARY OF THE DEFAULT OPTIONS IN THE TOOL MENU SELECTION.

Menu Option	Function
TDW	Invokes the Turbo Debugger for Windows to work with the current target node
Resource Workshop	Invokes the Resource Workshop utility
Grep	Runs the Grep utility on the currently selected nodes

continues

TABLE 8.7. CONTINUED	
Menu Option	*Function*
WinSight	Invokes the WinSight utility to monitor Windows messages
WinSpector	Runs the WinSpector utility to perform post-mortem analysis
Key map compiler	Compiles the IDE key map file

THE OPTIONS MENU SELECTION

TABLE 8.8. THE SUMMARY OF THE OPTIONS IN THE OPTIONS MENU SELECTION.	
Menu Option	*Function*
Project...	Inspects and edits the setting of the current project
Environment...	Views and edits the setting of the environment
Tools...	Adds and/or deletes tools in the Tool menu options
St**y**le Sheets...	Edits the options style sheets
Save...	Configures to save the project, desktop, and environment

The Project... Option

The Project... option displays the dialog box with the title "Style Sheet:Default Project Options," shown in Figure 8.20. The project option dialog box contains a list of topics, which influence the appearance of commenting text and the controls for each topic. The project options topics are

- The Directories section, which enables you to specify the directories for the include, library, and source code files, as well as specify the paths for intermediate and final files.

- The Compiler sections, which offer the options to fine-tune compiling C and C++ source code, specify the preprocessor definitions, manage the inclusion of debug information, and manage precompiled header files.

- The 16-bit Compiler sections, which enable you to manage compiling for the 16-bit Windows 3.x applications, select the processor type, and choose the memory model for the compiled files.

- The 32-bit Compiler sections, which enable you to generate 32-bit Windows application (aimed at Win32s and Windows NT) and specify the processor type.

- The C++ Options sections, which assist you in determining how the C++ compiler interprets your source code to manage new and old C++ language features.

- The Optimizations sections, which empower you to fine-tune the generation of the program or library code to make that code smaller or faster, or perform general optimization.

- The Messages sections, which enable you to determine the kind of messages emitted during the creation of the program. The options in the Message sections enable you to choose levels of warnings or errors ranging from very strict to very relaxed.

- The Linker sections, which permit you to control the creation of .OBJ, .LIB, and .RES files, which are united into the executable .EXE files.

- The Librarian section, which enables you to combine a set of .OBJ files into a .LIB file and control this process.

- The Resources section, which enables you to specify the target Windows version in order to create the right kind of .RES compiled resource file.

- The Make section, which offers options that control the integrated make process.

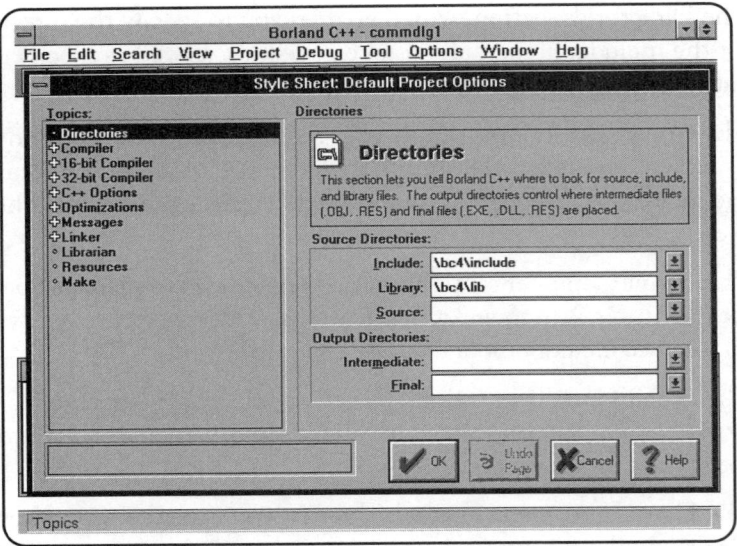

Figure 8.20. A sample session with the Project Options dialog box.

The Environment... Option

The Environment... option brings up the Environment Options dialog box, shown in Figure 8.21, to enable you to customize various aspects of the IDE. These aspects are organized and controlled by the following sections, which appear in the dialog box:

- The Editor sections control the operations of the IDE's text editor. These sections enable you to select the default (wordStar-like) text editor, IDE classical text editor, emulate the BRIEF editor, emulate the Epsilon editor, or customize various aspects of the current text editor.

- The Syntax Highlighting sections enable you to determine both the color and style used by the Editor to display the source code. The syntax sections offer a few predefined sets of colors and styles.

- The Browser section permits you to determine the default filters for the Browser. In addition, the section enables you to request creating new windows as you traverse through the hierarchy of classes.

- The Debugger section enables you to select between hard mode and soft mode debugging (these modes determine how the Windows messages are intercepted by the debugger). In addition, this section enables you to select capturing Windows messages, output messages, and breakpoints.

- The Speedbar sections offer you the ability to customize the location and contents of the speed bar.

- The Preferences section provides you with options related to saving various IDE components, such as the editor files, the environment, the desktop, and the project. The section also provides options to specify which parts of the desktop to save.

- The Project View section provides options which determine the kind of information included in the Project window, including code size, data size, location, name, number of lines, node type, and so on.

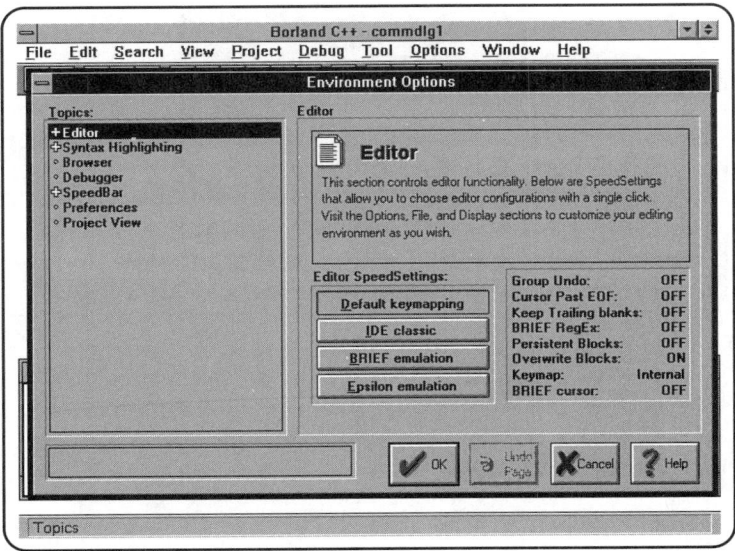

Figure 8.21. A sample session with the Environment Options dialog box.

The Tools... Option

The Tools... option empowers you to add new menu items to the Tool menu selection and delete items from that menu. Figure 8.22 shows the Tools dialog box, which contains a Tools list box that shows you the available tools. If you click the Edit pushbutton, the dialog box brings up the Tools Options dialog box, shown in Figure 8.23. The latter dialog box enables you to specify the name of the tool along with its path, command line, menu text, and help hint (which appears in the status line).

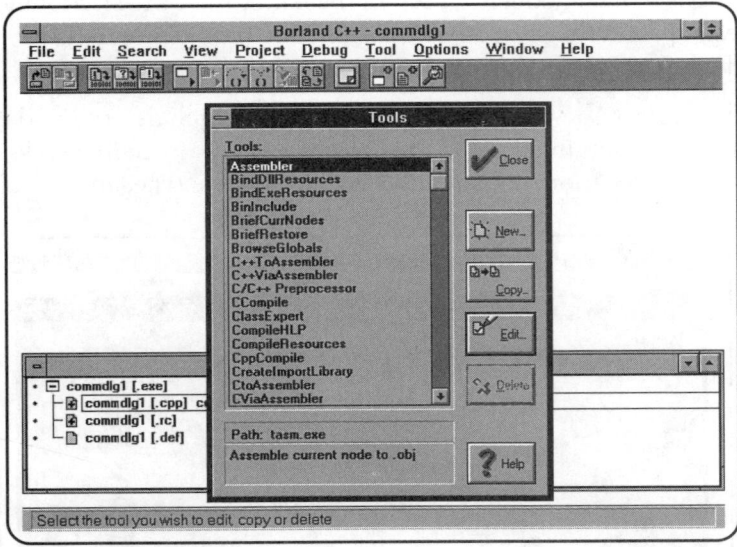

Figure 8.22. The Tools dialog box.

The Style Sheets... Option

The Style Sheets... option displays the Style Sheet dialog box, shown in Figure 8.24, which enables you to select a configuration for the compile and run time settings for a project. Each style sheet is a predefined collection of settings that can be affiliated with a node.

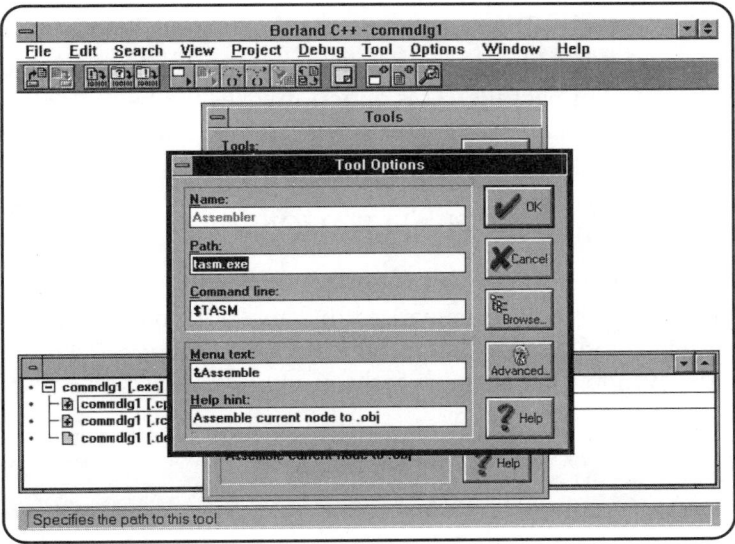

Figure 8.23. The Tools Options dialog box.

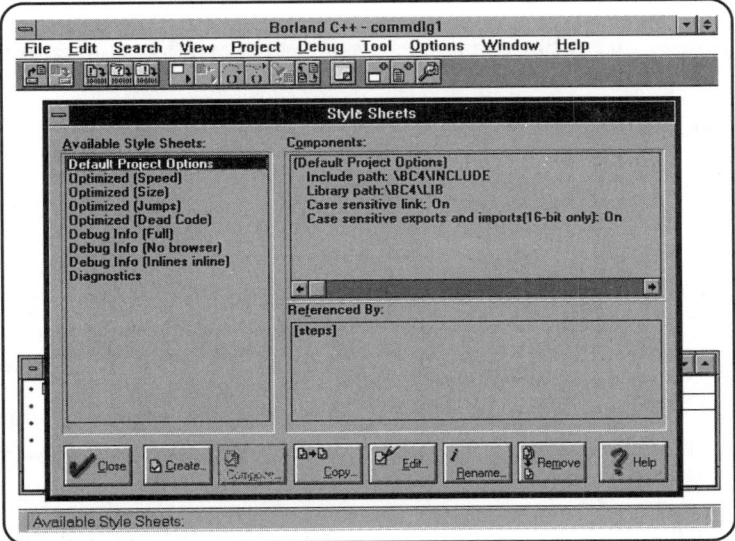

Figure 8.24. The Style Sheets dialog box.

The Save... Option

The Save... option enables you to specify to automatically save the desktop, environment, and project file. This option invokes the Save Options dialog box, which offers check boxes for saving these three IDE components.

THE WINDOW MENU SELECTION

The Window menu selection offers options to manage windows in the IDE client area. These options, summarized in Table 8.9, enable you to arrange, close, minimize, and restore some or all windows. In addition to the standard options, the Window menu also lists the current windows.

TABLE 8.9. THE SUMMARY OF THE OPTIONS IN THE WINDOW MENU SELECTION.

Menu Option	Shortcut Key(s)	Function
Cascade	Shift+F5	Cascades the windows in the client area of the IDE
Tile horizontal	Shift+F4	Tiles the windows horizontally on client area of the IDE
Tile vertical		Tiles the windows vertically on client area of the IDE
Arrange icons		Arranges the icons in the client area of the IDE
Close all		Closes all windows, debugger windows, browser windows, or editor windows
Minimize all		Minimizes all windows, debugger windows, browser windows, or editor windows
Restore all		Restores all windows, debugger windows, browser windows, or editor windows

The Help Menu Selection

The Help menu selection provides you with the kind of on-line help you have become accustomed to.

TABLE 8.10. The summary of the options in the Help menu selection.

Menu Option	Shortcut Key(s)	Function
Contents		Displays the table of contents for the on-line help system
Keyword search	F1	Displays help regarding the keyword where the current cursor is located
Keyboard		Displays information that explains the mapping of the keyboard
Using help		Displays information to assist you in using the on-line help system
About...		Displays information regarding the software version and copyright

Summary

This chapter presented you with a brief overview of the Borland C++ IDE. You learned about the following topics:

- Overview of the IDE as an MDI-compliant application with a powerful menu system, a speed bar, a status line, and a client area that supports various kinds of MDI child windows.

- The File menu selection manages creating new files, opening files, saving files, printing, and exiting the IDE.

- The Edit menu selection offers options to perform popular editing operations (such as undo, cut, copy, paste, and delete).

- The Search menu selection enables you to find and replace text, as well as browse through symbols, locate functions, and visit the offending source code lines.

- The View menu selection permits you to view a wide variety of information. Among the viewed information are the project nodes, the compiler and linker messages, the hierarchy of the project classes, global symbols, watched variables, the stack of called functions, and the CPU registers.

- The Project menu selection provides options to create, open, close, and manage a project. The project options enable you to compile and link project files.

- The Debug menu selection offers options that enable you to debug and single-step in the source code from within the IDE.

- The Tool menu selection presents a quick access to a variety of Windows programming tools, such as the Turbo Debugger for Windows, the message-tracing WinSight utility, and the post-mortem WinSpector utility.

- The Options menu selection empowers you to fine-tune various aspects of your project, environment, tools, and project style sheets.

- The Window menu selection supports managing, arranging, closing, and restoring the windows in the IDE desktop.

- The Help menu selection supplies you with on-line help.

USING THE APPLICATION EXPERT

The AppExpert utility is a versatile tool that enables you to build project source code files systematically and quickly. The utility generates functioning skeleton code that you can customize to meet the needs of your Windows applications. Thus, rather than starting from scratch or adapting similar existing code, you can make the AppExpert utility do much of the systematic work for you, freeing you to concentrate on implementing the code that supports the special features of your application. Using the AppExpert utility along with the ClassExpert utility (covered in Chapter 11) is a subject worthy of a small book; there are many aspects to learn. In this chapter, I focus on the following topics:

- Using the AppExpert utility
- Examining the different source code output generated by selecting various project options in AppExpert

USING THE APPEXPERT UTILITY

To use the AppExpert utility, invoke the AppExpert... option in the Project menu selection. The IDE brings up the project file selection dialog box. This dialog box is very similar to the Open a File dialog box. Select an .IDE filename or type in the name of a new .IDE file and then click the OK button. If you enter the name of a new .IDE file, the AppExpert utility creates a new project file. On the other hand, if you select an existing .IDE file, the AppExpert utility simply adds the new target to that project file. Next, the AppExpert utility brings up the AppExpert Application Generation Options dialog box (which I'll call simply the AppExpert dialog box), shown in Figure 9.1. This dialog box has three option topics: Application, Main Window, and MDI Child/View.

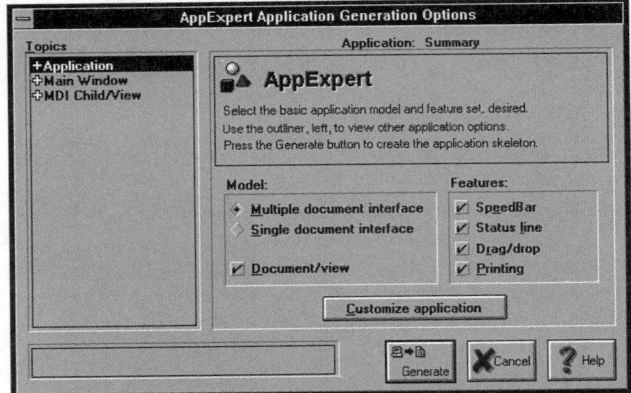

Figure 9.1. The AppExpert Application Generation Options (AppExpert) dialog box.

I would like to point out that the AppExpert dialog box hides and shows different controls based on the currently selected topic or subtopic.

The Application Topic

Figure 9.1 shows the options of the Application topic. I will be working with these options in this chapter and in the next chapter to generate projects with the AppExpert utility. The options of the Application topic are as follows:

- The choice between either an application supporting SDI child windows or an application supporting MDI child windows

- The use of document and view classes in the text editor

- The inclusion of a speed bar
- The inclusion of a status line
- The support for a drag-and-drop feature
- The support for printing and print previewing features

If you click the + sign located to the left of the Application topic (or double-click the Application topic itself), you expand the Application subtopics. Figure 9.2 shows the options offered by the Application subtopics:

- Basic Options
- Advanced Options
- Code Gen Control
- Admin Options

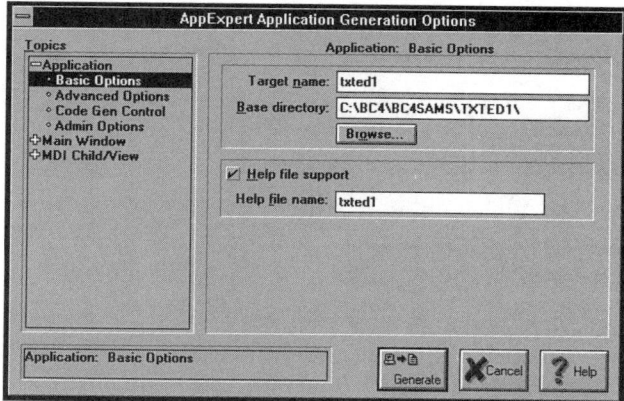

Figure 9.2. The AppExpert dialog box showing the Basic Options subtopic in the Application topic.

The Basic Options Subtopic

Figure 9.2 also shows the options offered by the Basic Options subtopic. These options deal with three basic aspects of the target:

- The name of the target
- The base directory for the target
- The name of the help file

The dialog box offers three edit box controls for you to enter this basic information. In addition, the dialog box shows a Browse... pushbutton that enables you to invoke a dialog box to select a new base directory. As for the help file, the AppExpert dialog box contains a check box that enables you to either support or prevent the creation of the help file.

The Advanced Options Subtopic

If you click the Advanced Options subtopic, the AppExpert dialog box changes to the version appearing in Figure 9.3. There are two kinds of options in this subtopic: Startup and Control style. The dialog box offers a set of radio buttons for the Startup options. These options are Normal, Minimized, and Maximized. The default selection is the Normal setting. The dialog box offers a set of radio buttons for the Control style options. These options are Windows, BWCC, and 3D. The default option is the Windows setting. If you wish to use Borland custom controls or Microsoft 3D controls, select the appropriate radio button.

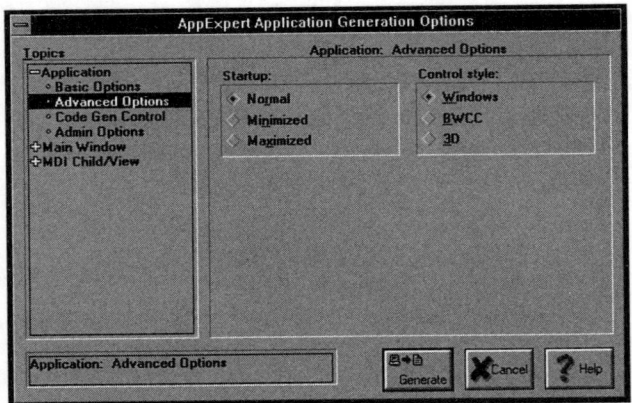

Figure 9.3. The AppExpert dialog box showing the Advanced Options subtopic.

The Code Gen Control Subtopic

The Code Gen Control subtopic offers the options shown in Figure 9.4. When you select this subtopic, the AppExpert dialog box displays the target name and the base directory. In addition, the dialog box offers edit box controls to enable you to select the following:

- The Source directory
- The Header directory

- The Main source file
- The Main header file
- The Application class
- The About dialog class

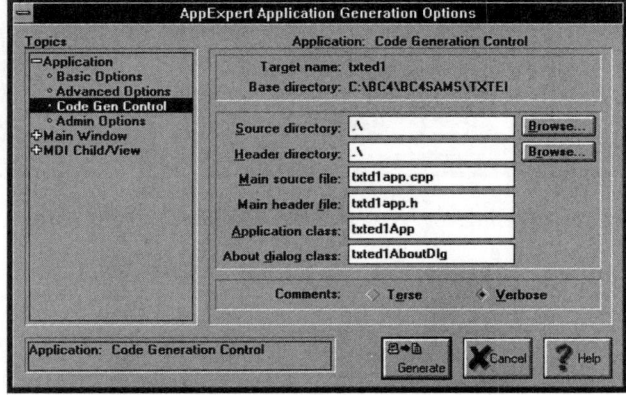

Figure 9.4. The AppExpert dialog box showing the Code Gen Control subtopic.

The dialog box offers browse buttons for these source and header directory options. In addition, the dialog box presents a frame with two radio buttons that enable you to select between terse or verbose comments. The default setting is the verbose comments.

The Admin Options Subtopic
The Admin Options subtopic, shown in Figure 9.5, handles the administrative side of the project. The AppExpert dialog box provides you with edit box controls to enter the following information:

- The Version number. The default is 1.0.
- The Copyright notice. The dialog box offers a default wording for the copyright notice.
- The Description. The default description is the target name.
- The name of the target author.
- The name of the company.

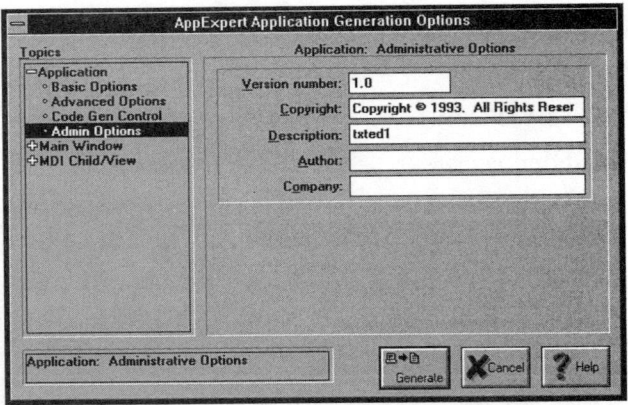

Figure 9.5. The AppExpert dialog box showing the Admin Options subtopic.

The Main Window Topic

The Main Window topic alters the AppExpert dialog box (see Figure 9.6) to offer you options that set the window title and background. The dialog box also presents a Background color... pushbutton to enable you to alter the background color.

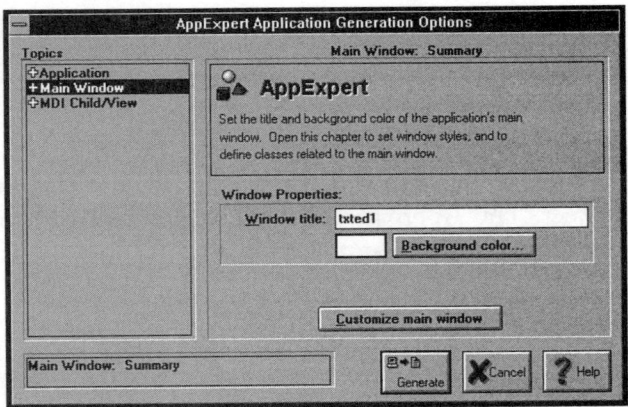

Figure 9.6. The AppExpert dialog box showing the Main Window topic.

The Main Window topic has the following subtopics:

- The Basic Options
- The SDI Client
- The MDI Client

The Basic Options Subtopic

The Basic Options subtopic in the Main Window topic permits you to select the window style. Figure 9.7 shows the options offered by this subtopic:

- Caption: creates a single thin border and a title bar that displays a caption.

- Border: creates a single thin border that has no title bar.

- Max box: adds a maximize button to the right side of the title bar that belongs to the main window of the application.

- Min box: adds a minimize button to the right side of the title bar that belongs to the main window of the application.

- Vertical scroll: includes a vertical scroll on the right side of the main window.

- Horizontal scroll: includes a horizontal scroll on the bottom of the main window.

- System menu: includes the system menu button located to the left side of the title bar in the main window. The Caption option must be selected to make this option available.

- Visible: makes the main window visible.

- Disabled: disables the main window.

- Dialog frame: displays the main window as a dialog box, with a double border. Consequently, you cannot resize the main window.

- Clip siblings: protects the sibling windows of the main window.

- Clip children: ensures that the main window is not painted over by the child windows.

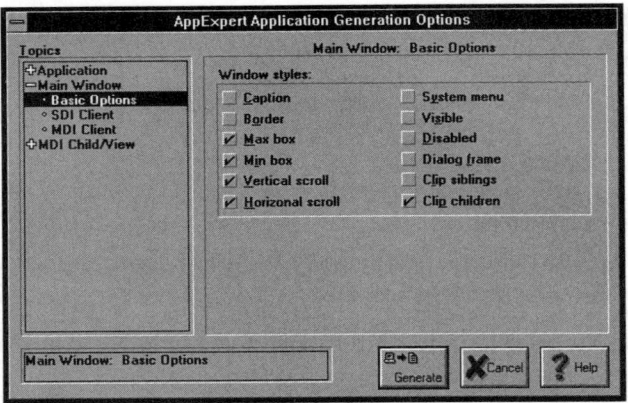

Figure 9.7. The AppExpert dialog box showing the Basic Options subtopic in the Main Window topic.

The SDI Client Subtopic

The SDI Client subtopic offers options that define the class which, in turn, models the client area of an SDI-compliant main window. These options are effective only if you select the Single Document Interface option in the opening AppExpert dialog box. Figure 9.8 presents the AppExpert dialog box showing the SDI Client subtopic with the following options:

- The drop-down combo box that enables you to select the client/view class.

- The drop-down combo box that enables you to select the Document class.

- The three edit boxes to enter the file-type filters. These controls accept the file description, filters, and default extensions.

The MDI Client Subtopic

The MDI Client subtopic offers options defining the class that models the client area of an MDI-compliant main window. These options are effective only if you select the Multiple Document Interface option in the opening AppExpert dialog box. Figure 9.9 presents the AppExpert dialog box showing the MDI Client subtopic with the following options:

- The name of the client class.

- The source (which I call *implementation* in this book, because I use the word *source* in a broad sense) filename.

- The header filename.

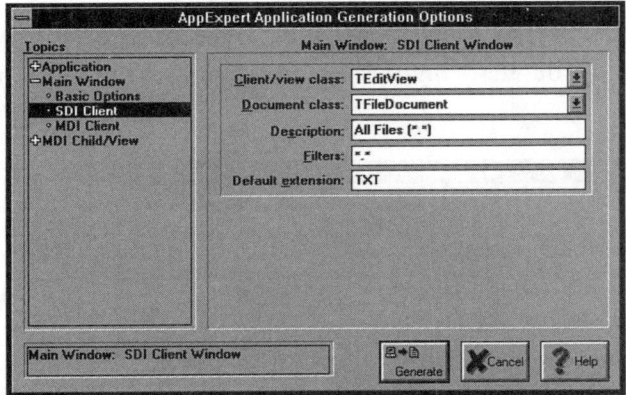

Figure 9.8. The AppExpert dialog box showing the SDI Client subtopic.

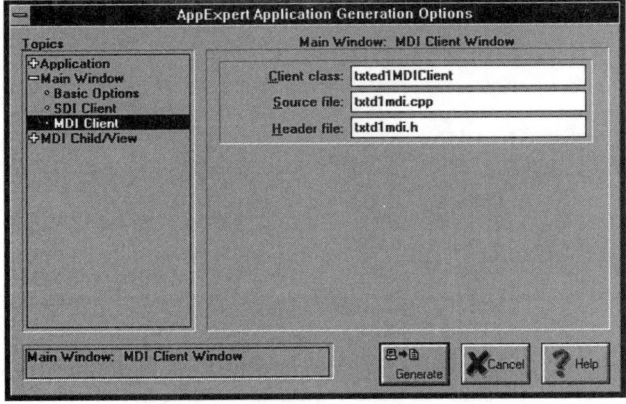

Figure 9.9. The AppExpert dialog box showing the MDI Client subtopic.

The MDI Child/View Topic

The MDI Child/View topic has options, shown in Figure 9.10, that enable you to specify the following:

- The name of the MDI child window class

- The source file that contains the implementation of the MDI child window class

- The header file that contains the declaration of the MDI child window class

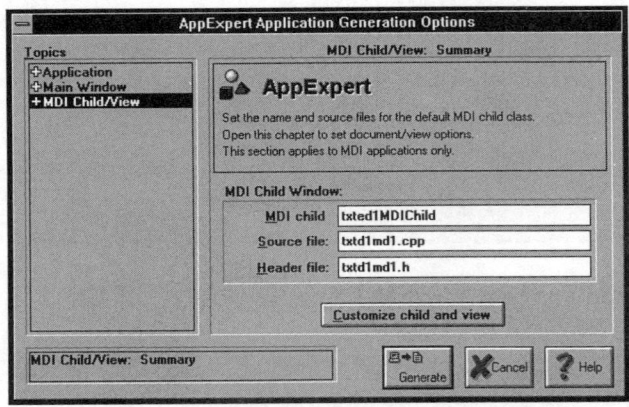

Figure 9.10. The AppExpert dialog box showing the MDI Child/View topic.

The AppExpert dialog box offers the Customize child and view pushbutton control, which simply invokes the Basic Options subtopic.

The Basic Options Subtopic

The Basic Options subtopic offers options that define the class modeling the client area of an MDI child window. These options are effective only if you select the Multiple Document Interface option in the opening AppExpert dialog box. Figure 9.11 presents the AppExpert dialog box showing the basic Options subtopic with the following options:

- The drop-down combo box that enables you to select the MDI client/ view class.

- The drop-down combo box that permits you to select the Document class.

- The three edit boxes to enter the file type filters. These controls accept the file description, filters, and default extensions.

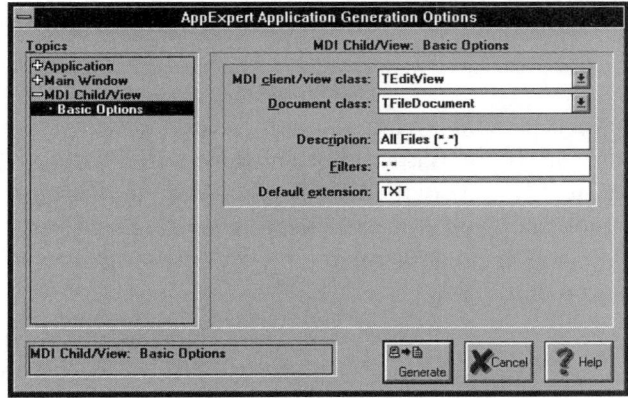

Figure 9.11. The AppExpert dialog box showing the Basic Options subtopic in the MDI Child/View topic.

STUDYING THE APPEXPERT OUTPUT

The last section indicated that the AppExpert utility offers many options which determine the kind of source code files to generate. In the next sections, I present different versions of SDI-compliant projects generated by altering the AppExpert options. In the next chapter, I present the different versions of MDI-compliant projects created by changing the AppExpert options. Because the total number of possible source code listings is large, I will focus on a selection of source code files generated by AppExpert. Table 9.1 shows the SDI-compliant text editor projects that I generate using AppExpert and also the options influencing them.

				Status	Drag &	
Project	MDI/ SDI?	Doc/View?	SpeedBar?	Line?	Drop?	Print?
TXTED1	SDI	No	No	No	No	No
TXTED2	SDI	No	Yes	Yes	No	No
TXTED3	SDI	Yes	Yes	Yes	No	No

TABLE 9.1. THE VARIOUS PROJECTS GENERATED BY APPEXPERT FOR THE CASE STUDIES IN THIS CHAPTER.

Though AppExpert generates a fair amount of source code very quickly, I feel that you need to study the output. Becoming very familiar with the output enables you to quickly and efficiently customize the AppExpert output. This approach shortens the entire process of creating your applications. By contrast, not being familiar with the emitted source code will cost you extra time in debugging your programs.

The ideal study of the source code files generated by AppExpert would include varying each of the AppExpert options, one at a time, and covering all of the possible combinations. Because the total number of these combinations is relatively large, I will examine the output source code generated by changing two options at a time. In addition, I will select a total of three output cases in this chapter and four output cases in the next one. In each case, AppExpert generates a minimally functioning text editor. Please do not take the words *minimally functioning* to mean a *real dud*! In fact, the generated text editors offer an acceptable level of operations, because the various OWL classes used in these editors support these operations.

Keep in mind the following points regarding the source code files presented both in this chapter and in the next one:

1. The projects of Tables 9.1 and 10.1 are generated by changing only the options in the opening AppExpert dialog box. The other settings of AppExpert use the default values. Changing these settings would lead to a greater variation in the different kinds of project files generated by AppExpert.

2. The text editor projects use separate directories for each project.

3. The output source code listings have been edited to fit the page layout of this book, as well as to shorten the listings.

THE TXTED1 PROJECT

Borland
4

The first project, which I consider the ground-zero project, is TXTED1. This project generates an SDI-compliant text editor with no speed bar, no status bar, no drag-and-drop feature support, and no printing-related features. In other words, the TXTED1 project is the simplest text editor generated by AppExpert.

When you invoke the AppExpert utility from the IDE Project menu selection, select the SDI option and turn off the other options in the opening dialog box of AppExpert. The utility generates the following set of files:

```
APPLSDI   ICO              1,086
TXTD1ABD  CPP              4,745
TXTD1ABD  H                  910
TXTD1APP  RC              12,984
TXTD1APP  RH               4,238
TXTD1APP  DEF                509
TXTD1APP  CPP              3,950
TXTD1APP  H                1,346
TXTED1    APX             10,209
TXTED1    IDE             55,086
TXTED1    DSW                250
```

These files contain icon, header, definition, resource header, resource, implementation, and IDE files. Consider the .DEF, .H, .RH, .RC, and .CPP files. Listing 9.1 shows the contents of the TXTED1.DEF definition file. The .DEF definition files for the other projects are similar and differ mainly in the name of the project. Because showing the other .DEF files will not reveal any significant new information, the TXTED1.DEF acts as a representative sample for the other TXTEDx.DEF files.

Build the TXTED1 project and experiment with its text-editing features. Figure 9.12 shows a sample session with the TXTED1.EXE application.

LISTING 9.1. THE CONTENTS OF THE TXTED1.DEF DEFINITION FILE.

```
;--------------------------------------------------
;   Main txted1
;
;   Copyright _ 1993. All Rights Reserved.
;
;   SUBSYSTEM:    txted1.exe Module Definition File
;   FILE:         txtd1app.def
;   AUTHOR:
```

continues

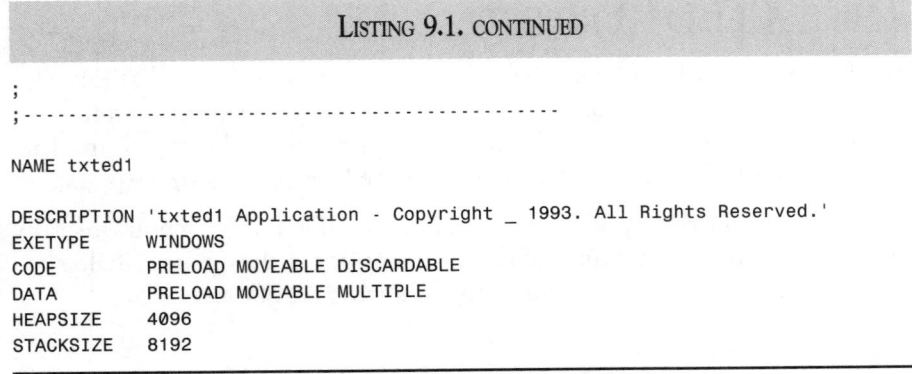

```
;
;------------------------------------------------

NAME txted1

DESCRIPTION 'txted1 Application - Copyright _ 1993. All Rights Reserved.'
EXETYPE     WINDOWS
CODE        PRELOAD MOVEABLE DISCARDABLE
DATA        PRELOAD MOVEABLE MULTIPLE
HEAPSIZE    4096
STACKSIZE   8192
```

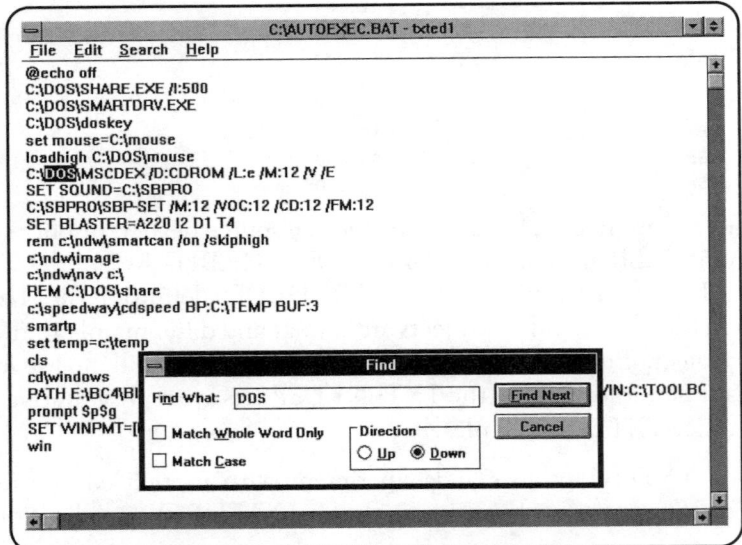

Figure 9.12. A sample session with the TXTED1.EXE application.

Listing 9.2 shows the source code for the TXTED1.RH resource header file. The file contains the definitions of constants used to manage the following menu commands and resources:

- The File menu options

- The Edit menu options

- The Help menu options

- The About dialog box

- The edit file messages

- The general and application exception messages

- The GDI messages

- The input dialog box resources

- The slider bitmaps

- The validation messages

Listing 9.2. The source code for the TXTED1.RH resource header file.

```
//#if !defined(__txtd1app_rh)          // Sentry use file only if it's not
                                        //    already included.

//#define __txtd1app_rh

/*  Main txted1

    Copyright _ 1993. All Rights Reserved.

    SUBSYSTEM:      txted1.exe Application
    FILE:           txtd1app.h
    AUTHOR:


    OVERVIEW
    ========
    Constant definitions for all resources defined in txtd1app.rc.
*/


//
// IDHELP BorButton for BWCC dialogs.
//
#define IDHELP               998         // Id of help button


//
// Application specific definitions:
//
#define IDI_SDIAPPLICATION   1001        // Application icon

#define SDI_MENU             100         // Menu resource ID and Accel-
                                         //    erator IDs
```

continues

LISTING 9.2. CONTINUED

```
//
// CM_FILEnnnn commands (include\owl\editfile.rh except for CM_FILEPRINTPREVIEW)
//
#define CM_FILENEW              24331      // SDI New
#define CM_FILEOPEN             24332      // SDI Open
#define CM_FILECLOSE            24339
#define CM_FILESAVE             24333
#define CM_FILESAVEAS           24334


//
// Window commands (include\owl\windows.rh)
//
#define CM_EXIT                 24310


//
// CM_EDITnnnn commands (include\owl\edit.rh)
//
#define CM_EDITUNDO             24321
#define CM_EDITCUT              24322
#define CM_EDITCOPY             24323
#define CM_EDITPASTE            24324
#define CM_EDITDELETE           24325
#define CM_EDITCLEAR            24326


//
// Search menu commands (include\owl\editsear.rh)
//
#define CM_EDITFIND             24351
#define CM_EDITREPLACE          24352
#define CM_EDITFINDNEXT         24353


//
// Help menu commands.
//
#define CM_HELPABOUT            24389


//
// About Dialogs
//
#define IDD_ABOUT           22000
#define IDC_VERSION           22001
#define IDC_COPYRIGHT         22002
#define IDC_DEBUG             22003
```

```
//
// OWL defined strings
//

// Statusbar
#define IDS_MODES               32530

// EditFile
#define IDS_UNTITLED            32550
#define IDS_UNABLEREAD          32551
#define IDS_UNABLEWRITE         32552
#define IDS_FILECHANGED         32553
#define IDS_FILEFILTER          32554

// EditSearch
#define IDS_CANNOTFIND          32540


//
// General & application exception messages (include\owl\except.rh)
//
#define IDS_UNKNOWNEXCEPTION    32767
#define IDS_OWLEXCEPTION        32766
#define IDS_OKTORESUME          32765
#define IDS_UNHANDLEDXMSG       32764
#define IDS_UNKNOWNERROR        32763
#define IDS_NOAPP               32762
#define IDS_OUTOFMEMORY         32761
#define IDS_INVALIDMODULE       32760
#define IDS_INVALIDMAINWINDOW   32759

//
// Owl 1 compatibility messages
//
#define IDS_INVALIDWINDOW       32756
#define IDS_INVALIDCHILDWINDOW  32755
#define IDS_INVALIDCLIENTWINDOW 32754

//
// TXWindow messages
//
#define IDS_CLASSREGISTERFAIL   32749
#define IDS_CHILDREGISTERFAIL   32748
#define IDS_WINDOWCREATEFAIL    32747
#define IDS_WINDOWEXECUTEFAIL   32746
#define IDS_CHILDCREATEFAIL     32745

#define IDS_MENUFAILURE         32744
#define IDS_VALIDATORSYNTAX     32743
#define IDS_PRINTERERROR        32742
```

continues

LISTING 9.2. CONTINUED

```
#define IDS_LAYOUTINCOMPLETE      32741
#define IDS_LAYOUTBADRELWIN       32740


//
// TXGdi messages
//
#define IDS_GDIFAILURE            32739
#define IDS_GDIALLOCFAIL          32738
#define IDS_GDICREATEFAIL         32737
#define IDS_GDIRESLOADFAIL        32736
#define IDS_GDIFILEREADFAIL       32735
#define IDS_GDIDELETEFAIL         32734
#define IDS_GDIDESTROYFAIL        32733
#define IDS_INVALIDDIBHANDLE      32732


// TInputDialog DIALOG resource (include\owl\inputdia.rh)
#define IDD_INPUTDIALOG           32514
#define ID_PROMPT                 4091
#define ID_INPUT                  4090


// TSlider bitmaps (horizontal and vertical) (include\owl\slider.rh)
#define IDB_HSLIDERTHUMB          32000
#define IDB_VSLIDERTHUMB          32001


// Validation messages (include\owl\validate.rh)
#define IDS_VALPXPCONFORM         32520
#define IDS_VALINVALIDCHAR        32521
#define IDS_VALNOTINRANGE         32522
#define IDS_VALNOTINLIST          32523


//#endif          // __txtd1app_rh sentry.
```

Listing 9.3 shows the source code for the TXTD1APP.H header file. This file declares the text editor application class txted1App as a descendant of TApplication. The class has public, protected, and private members. The public members include the constructor, the destructor, and the InitMainWindow member function. The protected members include the Cm*xxxx* functions that respond to various menu commands. The private members include the following:

- The Client data member, which is a pointer to the OWL class TEditFile. The TEditFile class models the client area for the frame window.

- The `FileData` data member, an instance of the `TOpenSaveDialog::TData` class, which stores the data for the File Open and File Save dialog boxes.

LISTING 9.3. THE SOURCE CODE FOR THE TXTD1APP.H HEADER FILE.

```
#if !defined(__txtd1app_h)          // Sentry, use file only if it's not already
                                    included.
#define __txtd1app_h

/*  Project txted1

    Copyright _ 1993. All Rights Reserved.

    SUBSYSTEM:    txted1.exe Application
    FILE:         txtd1app.h
    AUTHOR:


    OVERVIEW
    ========
    Class definition for txted1App (TApplication).
*/


#include <owl\owlpch.h>
#pragma hdrstop

#include <owl\editfile.h>
#include <owl\opensave.h>

#include "txtd1app.rh"          // Definition of all resources.


//{{TApplication = txted1App}}
class txted1App : public TApplication {
private:
    TEditFile *Client;                  // Client window for the frame.
    TOpenSaveDialog::TData FileData;    // Data to control open/saveas standard
                                        dialog.

public:
    txted1App ();
    virtual ~txted1App ();

    void OpenFile (const char *fileName = 0);
//{{txted1AppVIRTUAL_BEGIN}}
```

continues

LISTING 9.3. CONTINUED

```
public:
    virtual void InitMainWindow();
//{{txted1AppVIRTUAL_END}}

//{{txted1AppRSP_TBL_BEGIN}}
protected:
    void CmFileNew ();
    void CmFileOpen ();
    void CmFileClose ();
    void CmHelpAbout ();
//{{txted1AppRSP_TBL_END}}
  DECLARE_RESPONSE_TABLE(txted1App);
};    //{{txted1App}}


#endif                                     // __txtd1app_h sentry.
```

Listing 9.4. shows the source code for the TXTED1ABD.H header file. This header file contains the declaration of the About dialog box class, txted1AboutDlg. This class is a descendant of the TDialog class and declares a constructor, the destructor, and the SetupWindow member function. Because the other text editor projects use the same kind of About dialog box, the TXTED1ABD.H file is representative of the other TXTEDxABD.H header files. These files differ only in the name of the dialog box class, which is derived from the project name.

LISTING 9.4. THE SOURCE CODE FOR THE TXTED1ABD.H HEADER FILE.

```
#if !defined(__txtd1abd_h)              // Sentry, use file only if it's not
                                        already included.

#define __txtd1abd_h

/*  Project txted1

    Copyright _ 1993. All Rights Reserved.

    SUBSYSTEM:    txted1.exe Application
    FILE:         txtd1abd.h
    AUTHOR:


    OVERVIEW
    ========
    Class definition for txted1AboutDlg (TDialog).
*/
```

```
#include <owl\owlpch.h>
#pragma hdrstop

#include "txtd1app.rh"                    // Definition of all resources.


//{{TDialog = txted1AboutDlg}}
class txted1AboutDlg : public TDialog {
public:
    txted1AboutDlg (TWindow *parent, TResId resId = IDD_ABOUT, TModule *module =
➥0);
    virtual ~txted1AboutDlg ();

//{{txted1AboutDlgVIRTUAL_BEGIN}}
public:
    void SetupWindow ();
//{{txted1AboutDlgVIRTUAL_END}}
};     //{{txted1AboutDlg}}


#endif                                    // __txtd1abd_h sentry.
```

Listing 9.5 contains the script for the TXTD1APP.RC resource file. This file contains the definition of the various menu, key, string, icon, and dialog box resources. The resource files for the other text editor projects contain script that varies somewhat from the one in Listing 9.5. Because the variation is not major, I will not list the .RC files for the other text editor projects. You are welcome to browse through the other .RC files and compare them with file TXTED1.RC.

LISTING 9.5. THE SCRIPT FOR THE TXTD1APP.RC RESOURCE FILE.

```
/*  Main txted1

    Copyright _ 1993. All Rights Reserved.

    SUBSYSTEM:     txted1.exe Application
    FILE:          txtd1app.rc
    AUTHOR:


    OVERVIEW
    ========
    All resources defined here.
*/
```

continues

LISTING 9.5. CONTINUED

```
#if !defined(WORKSHOP_INVOKED)
#include <windows.h>
#endif
#include "txtd1app.rh"

SDI_MENU MENU
BEGIN
    POPUP "&File"
    BEGIN
        MENUITEM "&New", CM_FILENEW
        MENUITEM "&Open...", CM_FILEOPEN
        MENUITEM "&Close", CM_FILECLOSE
        MENUITEM SEPARATOR
        MENUITEM "&Save", CM_FILESAVE, GRAYED
        MENUITEM "Save &As...", CM_FILESAVEAS, GRAYED
        MENUITEM SEPARATOR
        MENUITEM "E&xit\tAlt+F4", CM_EXIT
    END

    POPUP "&Edit"
    BEGIN
        MENUITEM "&Undo\tAlt+BkSp", CM_EDITUNDO, GRAYED
        MENUITEM SEPARATOR
        MENUITEM "Cu&t\tShift+Del", CM_EDITCUT, GRAYED
        MENUITEM "&Copy\tCtrl+Ins", CM_EDITCOPY, GRAYED
        MENUITEM "&Paste\tShift+Ins", CM_EDITPASTE, GRAYED
        MENUITEM SEPARATOR
        MENUITEM "Clear &All\tCtrl+Del", CM_EDITCLEAR, GRAYED
        MENUITEM "&Delete\tDel", CM_EDITDELETE, GRAYED
    END

    POPUP "&Search"
    BEGIN
        MENUITEM "&Find...", CM_EDITFIND, GRAYED
        MENUITEM "&Replace...", CM_EDITREPLACE, GRAYED
        MENUITEM "&Next\aF3", CM_EDITFINDNEXT, GRAYED
    END

    POPUP "&Help"
    BEGIN
        MENUITEM "&About...", CM_HELPABOUT
    END

END


// Accelerator table for short-cut to menu commands. (include\owl\editfile.rc)
SDI_MENU ACCELERATORS
```

```
BEGIN
  VK_DELETE, CM_EDITCUT,      VIRTKEY, SHIFT
  VK_INSERT, CM_EDITCOPY,     VIRTKEY, CONTROL
  VK_INSERT, CM_EDITPASTE,    VIRTKEY, SHIFT
  VK_DELETE, CM_EDITCLEAR,    VIRTKEY, CONTROL
  VK_BACK,   CM_EDITUNDO,     VIRTKEY, ALT
  VK_F3,     CM_EDITFINDNEXT, VIRTKEY
END


//
// Table of help hints displayed in the status bar.
//
STRINGTABLE
BEGIN
    -1,                 "File/document operations"
    CM_FILENEW,         "Creates a new window"
    CM_FILEOPEN,        "Opens a window"
    CM_FILECLOSE,       "Close this document"
    CM_FILESAVE,        "Saves this document"
    CM_FILESAVEAS,      "Saves this document with a new name"
    CM_EXIT,            "Quits txted1App and prompts to save the
                        documents"
    CM_EDITUNDO-1,      "Edit operations"
    CM_EDITUNDO,        "Reverses the last operation"
    CM_EDITCUT,         "Cuts the selection and puts it on the Clip-
                        board"
    CM_EDITCOPY,        "Copies the selection and puts it on the
                        Clipboard"
    CM_EDITPASTE,       "Inserts the clipboard contents at the insertion
                        point"
    CM_EDITDELETE,      "Deletes the selection"
    CM_EDITCLEAR,       "Clear the document"
    CM_EDITFIND-1,      "Search/replace operations"
    CM_EDITFIND,        "Finds the specified text"
    CM_EDITREPLACE,     "Finds the specified text and changes it"
    CM_EDITFINDNEXT,    "Finds the next match"
    CM_HELPABOUT-1,     "Access About"
    CM_HELPABOUT,       "About the txted1 application"
END


//
// OWL string table
//

// EditFile (include\owl\editfile.rc and include\owl\editsear.rc)
STRINGTABLE LOADONCALL MOVEABLE DISCARDABLE
```

continues

LISTING 9.5. CONTINUED

```
BEGIN
    IDS_CANNOTFIND,                  "Cannot find ""%s""."
    IDS_UNTITLED,                    "Untitled"
    IDS_UNABLEREAD,                  "Unable to read file %s from disk."
    IDS_UNABLEWRITE,                 "Unable to write file %s to disk."
    IDS_FILECHANGED,                 "The text in the %s file has changed.\n\nDo you
want to save the changes?"
    IDS_FILEFILTER,                  "Text files (*.TXT)¦*.TXT¦AllFiles (*.*)¦*.*¦"
END


// Exception string resources (include\owl\except.rc)
STRINGTABLE LOADONCALL MOVEABLE DISCARDABLE
BEGIN
    IDS_OWLEXCEPTION,                "ObjectWindows Exception"
    IDS_UNHANDLEDXMSG,               "Unhandled Exception"
    IDS_OKTORESUME,                  "OK to resume?"
    IDS_UNKNOWNEXCEPTION,            "Unknown exception"

    IDS_UNKNOWNERROR,                "Unknown error"
    IDS_NOAPP,                       "No application object"
    IDS_OUTOFMEMORY,                 "Out of memory"
    IDS_INVALIDMODULE,               "Invalid module specified for window"
    IDS_INVALIDMAINWINDOW,           "Invalid MainWindow"

    IDS_INVALIDWINDOW,               "Invalid window %s"
    IDS_INVALIDCHILDWINDOW,          "Invalid child window %s"
    IDS_INVALIDCLIENTWINDOW,         "Invalid client window %s"

    IDS_CLASSREGISTERFAIL,           "Class registration fail for window %s"
    IDS_CHILDREGISTERFAIL,           "Child class registration fail for window %s"
    IDS_WINDOWCREATEFAIL,            "Create fail for window %s"
    IDS_WINDOWEXECUTEFAIL,           "Execute fail for window %s"
    IDS_CHILDCREATEFAIL,             "Child create fail for window %s"

    IDS_MENUFAILURE,                 "Menu creation failure"
    IDS_VALIDATORSYNTAX,             "Validator syntax error"
    IDS_PRINTERERROR,                "Printer error"

    IDS_LAYOUTINCOMPLETE,            "Incomplete layout constraints specified in
                                     window %s"
    IDS_LAYOUTBADRELWIN,             "Invalid relative window specified in layout
                                     constraint in window %s"

    IDS_GDIFAILURE,                  "GDI failure"
    IDS_GDIALLOCFAIL,                "GDI allocate failure"
    IDS_GDICREATEFAIL,               "GDI creation failure"
    IDS_GDIRESLOADFAIL,              "GDI resource load failure"
```

```
        IDS_GDIFILEREADFAIL,        "GDI file read failure"
        IDS_GDIDELETEFAIL,          "GDI object %X delete failure"
        IDS_GDIDESTROYFAIL,         "GDI object %X destroy failure"
        IDS_INVALIDDIBHANDLE,       "Invalid DIB handle %X"
END


// General Window's status bar messages. (include\owl\statusba.rc)
STRINGTABLE
BEGIN
        IDS_MODES               "EXT¦CAPS¦NUM¦SCRL¦OVR¦REC"
        SC_SIZE,                "Changes the size of the window"
        SC_MOVE,                "Moves the window to another position"
        SC_MINIMIZE,            "Reduces the window to an icon"
        SC_MAXIMIZE,            "Enlarges the window to it maximum size"
        SC_RESTORE,             "Restores the window to its previous size"
        SC_CLOSE,               "Closes the window"
        SC_TASKLIST,            "Opens task list"
        SC_NEXTWINDOW,          "Switches to next window"
END


// Validator messages (include\owl\validate.rc)
STRINGTABLE LOADONCALL MOVEABLE DISCARDABLE
BEGIN
        IDS_VALPXPCONFORM       "Input does not conform to picture:\n""%s"""
        IDS_VALINVALIDCHAR      "Invalid character in input"
        IDS_VALNOTINRANGE       "Value is not in the range %ld to %ld."
        IDS_VALNOTINLIST        "Input is not in valid-list"
END


//
// Misc application definitions
//

// Application ICON
IDI_SDIAPPLICATION ICON "applsdi.ico"


// About box.
IDD_ABOUT DIALOG 12, 17, 204, 65
STYLE DS_MODALFRAME ¦ WS_POPUP ¦ WS_CAPTION ¦ WS_SYSMENU
CAPTION "About txted1"
FONT 8, "MS Sans Serif"
BEGIN
    CTEXT "Version", IDC_VERSION, 2, 14, 200, 8, SS_NOPREFIX
    CTEXT "My Application", -1, 2, 4, 200, 8, SS_NOPREFIX
    CTEXT "", IDC_COPYRIGHT, 2, 27, 200, 17, SS_NOPREFIX
    RTEXT "", IDC_DEBUG, 136, 55, 66, 8, SS_NOPREFIX
```

continues

LISTING 9.5. CONTINUED

```
    ICON IDI_SDIAPPLICATION, -1, 2, 2, 16, 16
    DEFPUSHBUTTON "OK", IDOK, 88, 48, 28, 12
END


// TInputDialog class dialog box.
IDD_INPUTDIALOG DIALOG 20, 24, 180, 64
STYLE WS_POPUP ¦ WS_CAPTION ¦ DS_SETFONT
FONT 8, "Helv"
BEGIN
    LTEXT "", ID_PROMPT, 10, 8, 160, 10, SS_NOPREFIX
    CONTROL "", ID_INPUT, "EDIT", WS_CHILD ¦ WS_VISIBLE ¦ WS_BORDER ¦ WS_TABSTOP
¦ ES_AUTOHSCROLL, 10, 20, 160, 12
    DEFPUSHBUTTON "&OK", IDOK, 47, 42, 40, 14
    PUSHBUTTON "&Cancel", IDCANCEL, 93, 42, 40, 14
END


// Horizontal slider thumb bitmap for TSlider and VSlider
(include\owl\slider.rc)
IDB_HSLIDERTHUMB BITMAP PRELOAD MOVEABLE DISCARDABLE
BEGIN
    '42 4D 66 01 00 00 00 00 00 00 76 00 00 00 28 00'
    '00 00 12 00 00 00 14 00 00 00 01 00 04 00 00 00'
    '00 00 F0 00 00 00 00 00 00 00 00 00 00 00 00 00'
    '00 00 10 00 00 00 00 00 00 00 00 00 C0 00 00 C0'
    '00 00 00 C0 C0 00 C0 00 00 00 C0 00 C0 00 C0 C0'
    '00 00 C0 C0 C0 00 80 80 80 00 00 00 FF 00 00 FF'
    '00 00 00 FF FF 00 FF 00 00 00 FF 00 FF 00 FF FF'
    '00 00 FF FF FF 00 BB BB 0B BB BB BB·B0 BB BB 00'
    '00 00 BB B0 80 BB BB BB 08 0B BB 00 00 00 BB 08'
    'F8 0B BB B0 87 70 BB 00 00 00 B0 8F F8 80 BB 08'
    '77 77 0B 00 00 00 08 F8 88 88 00 88 88 87 70 00'
    '00 00 0F F7 77 88 00 88 77 77 70 00 00 00 0F F8'
    '88 88 00 88 88 87 70 00 00 00 0F F7 77 88 00 88'
    '77 77 70 00 00 00 0F F8 88 88 00 88 88 87 70 00'
    '00 00 0F F7 77 88 00 88 77 77 70 00 00 00 0F F8'
    '88 88 00 88 88 87 70 00 00 00 0F F7 77 88 00 88'
    '77 77 70 00 00 00 0F F8 88 88 00 88 88 87 70 00'
    '00 00 0F F7 77 88 00 88 77 77 70 00 00 00 0F F8'
    '88 88 00 88 88 87 70 00 00 00 0F F7 77 88 00 88'
    '77 77 70 00 00 00 0F F8 88 88 00 88 88 87 70 00'
    '00 00 0F F7 77 78 00 88 77 77 70 00 00 00 0F FF'
    'FF FF 00 88 88 88 80 00 00 00 B0 00 00 00 BB 00'
    '00 00 0B 00 00 00'
END
```

```
// Vertical slider thumb bitmap for TSlider and HSlider (include\owl\slider.rc)
IDB_VSLIDERTHUMB BITMAP PRELOAD MOVEABLE DISCARDABLE
BEGIN
        '42 4D 2A 01 00 00 00 00 00 00 76 00 00 00 28 00'
        '00 00 28 00 00 00 09 00 00 00 01 00 04 00 00 00'
        '00 00 B4 00 00 00 00 00 00 00 00 00 00 00 00 00'
        '00 00 10 00 00 00 00 00 00 00 00 00 C0 00 00 C0'
        '00 00 00 C0 C0 00 C0 00 00 00 C0 00 C0 00 C0 C0'
        '00 00 C0 C0 C0 00 80 80 80 00 00 00 FF 00 00 FF'
        '00 00 00 FF FF 00 FF 00 00 00 FF 00 FF 00 FF FF'
        '00 00 FF FF FF 00 B0 00 00 00 00 00 00 00 00 0B'
        'B0 00 00 00 00 00 00 00 0B 0F 88 88 88 88 88 88'
        '88 88 88 80 08 88 88 88 88 88 88 88 88 80 0F 77'
        '77 77 77 77 77 77 80 08 77 77 77 77 77 77 77 77'
        '77 80 0F 77 FF FF FF FF FF FF F7 80 08 77 FF FF'
        'FF FF FF FF F7 80 0F 70 00 00 00 00 00 00 77 80'
        '08 70 00 00 00 00 00 00 77 80 0F 77 77 77 77 77'
        '77 77 77 80 08 77 77 77 77 77 77 77 80 0F 77'
        '77 77 77 77 77 77 80 08 77 77 77 77 77 77 77'
        '77 80 0F FF FF FF FF FF FF FF F0 08 88 88 88'
        '88 88 88 88 88 80 B0 00 00 00 00 00 00 00 0B'
        'B0 00 00 00 00 00 00 00 0B'
END


// Version info.
//
#if !defined(__DEBUG_)
// Non-Debug VERSIONINFO
1 VERSIONINFO LOADONCALL MOVEABLE
FILEVERSION 1, 0, 0, 0
PRODUCTVERSION 1, 0, 0, 0
FILEFLAGSMASK 0
FILEFLAGS VS_FFI_FILEFLAGSMASK
FILEOS VOS__WINDOWS16
FILETYPE VFT_APP
BEGIN
    BLOCK "StringFileInfo"
    BEGIN
        // Language type = U.S. English (0x0409) and Character Set = Windows,
            Multilingual(0x04e4)
        BLOCK "040904E4"                            // Matches VarFileInfo
                                                       Translation hex value.

        BEGIN
            VALUE "CompanyName", "\000"
            VALUE "FileDescription", "txted1 for Windows\000"
            VALUE "FileVersion", "1.0\000"
            VALUE "InternalName", "txted1\000"
            VALUE "LegalCopyright", "Copyright _ 1993. All Rights Reserved.\000"
            VALUE "LegalTrademarks", "Windows /231 is a trademark of Microsoft
                                        Corporation\000"
```

continues

LISTING 9.5. CONTINUED

```
                VALUE "OriginalFilename", "txted1.EXE\000"
                VALUE "ProductName", "txted1\000"
                VALUE "ProductVersion", "1.0\000"
        END
    END

    BLOCK "VarFileInfo"
    BEGIN
        VALUE "Translation", 0x04e4, 0x0409          // U.S. English(0x0409) &
                                                        Windows
                                                        Multilingual(0x04e4) 1252

    END

END
#else

// Debug VERSIONINFO
1 VERSIONINFO LOADONCALL MOVEABLE
FILEVERSION 1, 0, 0, 0
PRODUCTVERSION 1, 0, 0, 0
FILEFLAGSMASK VS_FF_DEBUG ¦ VS_FF_PRERELEASE ¦ VS_FF_PATCHED ¦
VS_FF_PRIVATEBUILD ¦ VS_FF_SPECIALBUILD
FILEFLAGS VS_FFI_FILEFLAGSMASK
FILEOS VOS__WINDOWS16
FILETYPE VFT_APP
BEGIN
    BLOCK "StringFileInfo"
    BEGIN
        // Language type = U.S. English (0x0409) and Character Set = Windows,
Multilingual(0x04e4)
        BLOCK "040904E4"                              // Matches VarFileInfo
                                                        Translation hex value.

        BEGIN
            VALUE "CompanyName", "\000"
            VALUE "FileDescription", "txted1 for Windows\000"
            VALUE "FileVersion", "1.0\000"
            VALUE "InternalName", "txted1\000"
            VALUE "LegalCopyright", "Copyright _ 1993. All Rights Reserved.\000"
            VALUE "LegalTrademarks", "Windows \231 is a trademark of Microsoft
Corporation\000"
            VALUE "OriginalFilename", "txted1.EXE\000"
            VALUE "ProductName", "txted1\000"
            VALUE "ProductVersion", "1.0\000"
            VALUE "SpecialBuild", "Debug Version\000"
            VALUE "PrivateBuild", "Built by \000"
        END
    END
```

```
    BLOCK "VarFileInfo"
    BEGIN
        VALUE "Translation", 0x04e4, 0x0409        // U.S. English(0x0409) &
Windows Multilingual(0x04e4) 1252
    END

END
#endif
```

Listing 9.6 shows the source code for the TXTD1ABD.CPP implementation file. This file defines the txted1AboutDlg class that implements the About dialog box. In addition, the file declares and defines the project resource version class, ProjectRCVersion. Briefly consider this class first. The class declares a constructor, a destructor, a set of public member functions, and two protected data members. The ProjectRCVersion class supports operations that extract the information about the product name, version, and copyright.

The About dialog box class defines the following members:

1. The constructor simply invokes the constructor of the parent class TDialog. The constructor has no executable statements and contains a comment that indicates where to place your code to support additional initialization.

2. The destructor simply calls the inherited member function Destroy. The definition contains a comment that indicates where to place your code to support additional cleanup.

3. The SetupWindow member function sets up the About dialog box by carrying out the following tasks:

   - Creates three static text controls for the version, copyright, and debug information. The function assigns the addresses of these controls to the local pointers versionCtrl, copyrightCtrl, and debugCtrl.

   - Invokes the SetupWindow member function of the parent dialog box class.

   - Creates the applVersion instance of the ProjectRCVersion class.

   - Sends the C++ message GetProductName to the applVersion object to obtain the product name from the dialog box resource.

- Sends the C++ message GetProductVersion to the applVersion object to obtain the product version from the dialog box resource.

- Sends the C++ message GetCopyright to the applVersion object to obtain the copyright information from the dialog box resource.

- Assigns the product name, version name, and version number to the static text control accessed by the versionCtrl pointer. This task invokes sending the C++ messages GetText and SetText to the version static text control. In addition, this task involves calling the wsprintf function.

- Assigns the copyright to the copyright static text control. This task involves sending the C++ message SetText to the copyright static text control.

- Assigns the debug information to the debug static text control, if the C++ message GetDebug, sent to the applVersion object, returns a nonzero value. This task involves sending the C++ message SetText to the debug static text control.

LISTING 9.6. THE SOURCE CODE FOR THE TXTD1ABD.CPP IMPLEMENTATION FILE.

```
/*  Project txted1

    Copyright _ 1993. All Rights Reserved.

    SUBSYSTEM:    txted1.exe Application
    FILE:         txtd1abd.cpp
    AUTHOR:


    OVERVIEW
    ========
    Source file for implementation of txted1AboutDlg (TDialog).
*/


#include <owl\owlpch.h>
#pragma hdrstop

#include <owl\static.h>

#include <ver.h>

#include "txtd1app.h"
```

```
#include "txtd1abd.h"


// Reading the VERSIONINFO resource.
class ProjectRCVersion {
public:
    ProjectRCVersion (TModule *module);
    virtual ~ProjectRCVersion ();

    BOOL GetProductName (LPSTR &prodName);
    BOOL GetProductVersion (LPSTR &prodVersion);
    BOOL GetCopyright (LPSTR &copyright);
    BOOL GetDebug (LPSTR &debug);

protected:
    LPBYTE      TransBlock;
    void FAR    *FVData;

private:
    // Don't allow this object to be copied.
    ProjectRCVersion (const ProjectRCVersion &);
    ProjectRCVersion & operator =(const ProjectRCVersion &);
};


ProjectRCVersion::ProjectRCVersion (TModule *module)
{
    char    appFName[255];
    DWORD   fvHandle;
    UINT    vSize;

    FVData = 0;

    module->GetModuleFileName(appFName, sizeof(appFName));
    DWORD dwSize = GetFileVersionInfoSize(appFName, &fvHandle);
    if (dwSize) {
        FVData = (void FAR *)new char[(UINT)dwSize];
        if (GetFileVersionInfo(appFName, fvHandle, dwSize, FVData))
            if (!VerQueryValue(FVData, "\\VarFileInfo\\Translation", (void FAR*
FAR*)&TransBlock, &vSize)) {
                delete FVData;
                FVData = 0;
            }
    }
}


ProjectRCVersion::~ProjectRCVersion ()
{
```

continues

LISTING 9.6. CONTINUED

```
    if (FVData)
        delete FVData;
}


BOOL ProjectRCVersion::GetProductName (LPSTR &prodName)
{
    UINT    vSize;
    char    subBlockName[255];

    wsprintf(subBlockName, "\\StringFileInfo\\%08lx\\%s", *(DWORD *)TransBlock,
(LPSTR)"ProductName");
    return FVData ? VerQueryValue(FVData, subBlockName, (void FAR*
FAR*)&prodName, &vSize) : FALSE;
}


BOOL ProjectRCVersion::GetProductVersion (LPSTR &prodVersion)
{
    UINT    vSize;
    char    subBlockName[255];

    wsprintf(subBlockName, "\\StringFileInfo\\%08lx\\%s", *(DWORD *)TransBlock,
(LPSTR)"ProductVersion");
    return FVData ? VerQueryValue(FVData, subBlockName, (void FAR*
FAR*)&prodVersion, &vSize) : FALSE;
}


BOOL ProjectRCVersion::GetCopyright (LPSTR &copyright)
{
    UINT    vSize;
    char    subBlockName[255];

    wsprintf(subBlockName, "\\StringFileInfo\\%08lx\\%s", *(DWORD *)TransBlock,
(LPSTR)"LegalCopyright");
    return FVData ? VerQueryValue(FVData, subBlockName, (void FAR*
FAR*)&copyright, &vSize) : FALSE;
}


BOOL ProjectRCVersion::GetDebug (LPSTR &debug)
{
    UINT    vSize;
    char    subBlockName[255];

    wsprintf(subBlockName, "\\StringFileInfo\\%08lx\\%s", *(DWORD *)TransBlock,
```

```
                                (LPSTR)"SpecialBuild");
    return FVData ? VerQueryValue(FVData, subBlockName, (void FAR* FAR*)&debug,
&vSize) : FALSE;
}



//{{txted1AboutDlg Implementation}}



/////////////////////////////////////////////////////////////
// txted1AboutDlg
// ==========
// Construction/Destruction handling.
txted1AboutDlg::txted1AboutDlg (TWindow *parent, TResId resId, TModule *module)
    : TDialog(parent, resId, module)
{
    // INSERT>> Your constructor code here.
}


txted1AboutDlg::~txted1AboutDlg ()
{
    Destroy();

    // INSERT>> Your destructor code here.
}


void txted1AboutDlg::SetupWindow ()
{
    LPSTR prodName, prodVersion, copyright, debug;

    // Get the static text who's value is based on VERSIONINFO.
    TStatic *versionCtrl = new TStatic(this, IDC_VERSION, 255);
    TStatic *copyrightCtrl = new TStatic(this, IDC_COPYRIGHT, 255);
    TStatic *debugCtrl = new TStatic(this, IDC_DEBUG, 255);

    TDialog::SetupWindow();

    // Process the VERSIONINFO.
    ProjectRCVersion applVersion(GetModule());

    // Get the product name, product version and legal copyright strings.
    applVersion.GetProductName(prodName);
    applVersion.GetProductVersion(prodVersion);
    applVersion.GetCopyright(copyright);

    // IDC_VERSION is the product name and version number, the initial value of
       IDC_VERSION is
    // the word Version (in whatever language) product name VERSION product
```

continues

LISTING 9.6. CONTINUED

```
    version.
char    buffer[255];
char    versionName[128];
versionCtrl->GetText(versionName, sizeof(versionName));
wsprintf(buffer, "%s %s %s", prodName, versionName, prodVersion);
versionCtrl->SetText(buffer);

copyrightCtrl->SetText(copyright);

// Only get the SpecialBuild text if the VERSIONINFO resource is there.
if (applVersion.GetDebug(debug))
    debugCtrl->SetText(debug);
}
```

Listing 9.7 shows the source code for the TXTD1APP.CPP implementation file. The listing includes the preceding header file to access the definition of the application and About dialog box classes. In addition, the listing contains the declaration of a class that models a decorated SDI window frame.

The listing contains the definition of the message response table for the txted1App application class. The table includes a set of EV_COMMAND macros to map the various CM_xxxx commands with their respective CmxxxX member functions.

The listing offers the declaration and definition of the SDIDecFrame class. This class, which is a descendant of the TDecoratedFrame class, models the decorated SDI frame window. The AppExpert comments remind you that this class needs to override the member functions that support the printing and print previewing features. The class declares a constructor and a dummy destructor.

The listing contains the definitions of the following members:

1. The constructor that performs the following minimal initialization:

   - Assigns an expression of bitwise ORed OFN_xxxx constants to the Flags member of the FileData data member.

   - Sends the C++ message SetFilter to the FileData data member. This message has the string literal argument that assigns the file type filters to the FileData member.

These two assignments initialize the FileData data member to prepare it for the dialog boxes that open and save files. The constructor contains a comment that indicates where to place statements for additional initialization.

2. The destructor merely contains a comment that indicates where to place statements for application cleanup.

3. The InitMainWindow member function initializes the main window by carrying out the following tasks:

   - Creates a new client area by allocating an instance of the TEditFile class. The function assigns the address of this instance to the Client data member.

   - Creates a new, decorated SDI frame window by allocating an instance of the SDIDecFrame class. The function assigns the address of this instance to the local pointer frame.

   - Assigns a value to the inherited nCmdShow data member, such that the window appears in its normal state.

   - Assigns the application's icon using the icon resource IDI_SDIAPPLICATION. This task involves sending the C++ message SetIcon to the SDI window accessed by pointer frame.

   - Assigns the application's menu using the menu resource SDI_MENU. This task involves sending the C++ message AssignMenu to the SDI window accessed by pointer frame.

   - Assigns the accelerator table SDI_MENU to the frame window.

   - Assigns the address in pointer frame to the inherited data member MainWindow.

4. The CmFileNew member function responds to the New menu option by sending the C++ message NewFile to the window client area accessed by the Client pointer.

5. The CmFileOpen member function responds to the Open... menu option. The function contains nested if statements. The outer if statement sends the C++ message CanClose to the client area (accessed by member Client). If this message returns a nonzero value, the CmFileOpen function executes the nested if statement. The statement creates a dynamic instance of the TFileOpenDialog class and sends it the C++ message Execute. The if statement compares the result of the message with the predefined constant IDOK. If the two values match, the function invokes the OpenFile member function.

6. The OpenFile member function performs two simple tasks. The first task assigns the string in the fileName parameter to the Filename member of the FileData data member. The second task updates the title of the window with the name of the newly opened file. The function performs this task by sending the C++ message ReplaceWith to the window client area object. The argument of this message is the Filename member of the FileData data member.

7. The CmFileClose member function closes the window by sending the C++ message CanClose to the window client area object. If this message returns a nonzero value, the function sends the C++ message DeleteSubText to the client area. The arguments for this message are 0 and UINT (-1), which specify the entire text to text.

8. The CmHelpAbout member function responds to the Help | Contents menu option. The function creates a new instance of the txted1AboutDlg class to invoke the About dialog box. The function invokes this modal dialog box by sending it the C++ message Execute.

LISTING 9.7. THE SOURCE CODE FOR THE **TXTD1APP.CPP** IMPLEMENTATION FILE.

```
/*  Project txted1

    Copyright _ 1993. All Rights Reserved.

    SUBSYSTEM:    txted1.exe Application
    FILE:         txtd1app.cpp
    AUTHOR:


    OVERVIEW
    ========
    Source file for implementation of txted1App (TApplication).
*/


#include <owl\owlpch.h>
#pragma hdrstop


#include "txtd1app.h"
#include "txtd1abd.h"                          // Definition of about dialog.


//{{txted1App Implementation}}
```

```
//
// Build a response table for all messages/commands handled
// by the application.
//
DEFINE_RESPONSE_TABLE1(txted1App, TApplication)
//{{txted1AppRSP_TBL_BEGIN}}
    EV_COMMAND(CM_FILENEW, CmFileNew),
    EV_COMMAND(CM_FILEOPEN, CmFileOpen),
    EV_COMMAND(CM_FILECLOSE, CmFileClose),
    EV_COMMAND(CM_HELPABOUT, CmHelpAbout),
//{{txted1AppRSP_TBL_END}}
END_RESPONSE_TABLE;


//
// FrameWindow must be derived to override Paint for Preview and Print.
//
class SDIDecFrame : public TDecoratedFrame {
public:
    SDIDecFrame (TWindow *parent, const char far *title, TWindow *clientWnd,
BOOL trackMenuSelection = FALSE, TModule *module = 0) :
            TDecoratedFrame(parent, title, clientWnd, trackMenuSelection,
module)
        {  }
    ~SDIDecFrame ()
        {  }
};


////////////////////////////////////////////////////////
// txted1App
// =====
//
txted1App::txted1App () : TApplication("txted1")
{

    // Common file file flags and filters for Open/Save As dialogs. Filename and
directory are
    // computed in the member functions CmFileOpen, and CmFileSaveAs.
    FileData.Flags = OFN_FILEMUSTEXIST | OFN_HIDEREADONLY | OFN_OVERWRITEPROMPT;
    FileData.SetFilter("All Files (*.*)|*.*|");

    // INSERT>> Your constructor code here.

}


txted1App::~txted1App ()
{
    // INSERT>> Your destructor code here.
```

continues

LISTING 9.7. CONTINUED

```
}


////////////////////////////////////////////////////////////
// txted1App
// =====
// Application initialization.
//
void txted1App::InitMainWindow ()
{
    Client = new TEditFile(0, 0, 0);
    SDIDecFrame *frame = new SDIDecFrame(0, GetName(), Client, FALSE);

    nCmdShow = nCmdShow != SW_SHOWMINIMIZED ? SW_SHOWNORMAL : nCmdShow;

    //
    // Assign ICON w/ this application.
    //
    frame->SetIcon(this, IDI_SDIAPPLICATION);

    //
    // Menu associated with window and accelerator table associated with table.
    //
    frame->AssignMenu(SDI_MENU);

    //
    // Associate with the accelerator table.
    //
    frame->Attr.AccelTable = SDI_MENU;


    MainWindow = frame;

}


////////////////////////////////////////////////////////////
// txted1App
// ===========
// Menu File New command
void txted1App::CmFileNew ()
{
    Client->NewFile();
}
```

```
/////////////////////////////////////////////////////////
// txted1App
// ===========
// Menu File Open command
void txted1App::CmFileOpen ()
{
    //
    // Display standard Open dialog box to select a file name.
    //
    *FileData.FileName = 0;
    if (Client->CanClose())
        if (TFileOpenDialog(MainWindow, FileData).Execute() == IDOK)
            OpenFile();
}


void txted1App::OpenFile (const char *fileName)
{
    if (fileName)
        lstrcpy(FileData.FileName, fileName);

    Client->ReplaceWith(FileData.FileName);
}


/////////////////////////////////////////////////////////
// txted1App
// =====
// Menu File Close command
void txted1App::CmFileClose ()
{
    if (Client->CanClose())
        Client->DeleteSubText(0, UINT(-1));
}


/////////////////////////////////////////////////////////
// txted1App
// ===========
// Menu Help About txted1.exe command
void txted1App::CmHelpAbout ()
{
    //
    // Show the modal dialog.
    //
    txted1AboutDlg(MainWindow).Execute();
}
```

continues

LISTING 9.7. CONTINUED

```
int OwlMain (int , char* [])
{
    txted1App       App;
    int             result;

    result = App.Run();

    return result;
}
```

THE TXTED2 PROJECT

The TXTED2 project supports an SDI-compliant editor with a speed bar and a status line. When you invoke AppExpert, check the options for the SDI window, the speed bar, and the status line. Uncheck all of the other options. AppExpert generates the following files:

```
APPLSDI   ICO              1,086
COPY      BMP                358
CUT       BMP                358
FIND      BMP                358
FINDNEXT  BMP                358
NEW       BMP                358
OPEN      BMP                358
PASTE     BMP                358
SAVE      BMP                358
TXTD2ABD  CPP              4,745
TXTD2ABD  H                  910
TXTD2APP  RC              13,383
TXTD2APP  RH               4,238
TXTD2APP  DEF                509
TXTD2APP  CPP              5,400
TXTD2APP  H                1,489
TXTED2    APX             10,209
TXTED2    IDE             55,030
TXTED2    DSW                262
UNDO      BMP                358
```

This list of files exceeds that of project TXTED1 by a few .BMP files, because the speed bar uses additional bit maps to display its buttons.

Build the TXTED2 project and experiment with its text-editing features. Figure 9.13 shows a sample session with the TXTED2.EXE application.

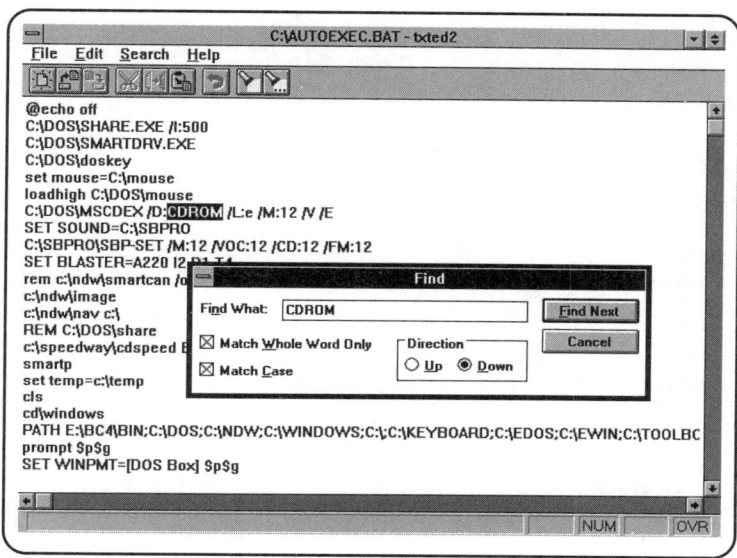

Figure 9.13. A sample session with the TXTED2.EXE application.

Because of the limited space, I'll focus on the header and implementation files, which are fairly different from those in project TXTED1. The TXTD2ABD.H and TXTD2ABD.CPP files are similar to the TXTD1ABD.H and TXTD1ABD.CPP files, respectively. The main differences are in the class names, which are derived from the project name. By contrast, the TXTD2APP.H and TXTD2APP.CPP files have more statements and declarations that the TXTD1APP.H and TXTD1APP.CPP files, respectively.

Listing 9.8 shows the source code for the TXTD2APP.H header file. This file includes more nested header files than TXTD1APP.H in order to support the status bar and the speed bar features. In addition, the TXTD2APP.H header file declares the `txted2App` application class. This class is similar to the `txted1App` class, except it has the additional public member function `SetUpSpeedBar`.

LISTING 9.8. THE SOURCE CODE FOR THE **TXTD2APP.H** HEADER FILE.

```
#if !defined(__txtd2app_h)          // Sentry, use file only if it's not
                                    //    already included.
#define __txtd2app_h
```

continues

LISTING 9.8. CONTINUED

```
/*  Project txted2

    Copyright _ 1993. All Rights Reserved.

    SUBSYSTEM:    txted2.exe Application
    FILE:         txtd2app.h
    AUTHOR:


    OVERVIEW
    ========
    Class definition for txted2App (TApplication).
*/


#include <owl\owlpch.h>
#pragma hdrstop

#include <owl\statusba.h>
#include <owl\controlb.h>
#include <owl\buttonga.h>
#include <owl\editfile.h>
#include <owl\opensave.h>

#include "txtd2app.rh"            // Definition of all resources.


//{{TApplication = txted2App}}
class txted2App : public TApplication {
private:
    TEditFile *Client;                        // Client window for the
                                              // frame.

    TOpenSaveDialog::TData FileData;          // Data to control open/
                                              // saveas standard
                                              // dialog.


private:
    void SetupSpeedBar (TDecoratedFrame *frame);

public:
    txted2App ();
    virtual ~txted2App ();

    void OpenFile (const char *fileName = 0);
//{{txted2AppVIRTUAL_BEGIN}}
public:
    virtual void InitMainWindow();
//{{txted2AppVIRTUAL_END}}
```

```
//{{txted2AppRSP_TBL_BEGIN}}
protected:
    void CmFileNew ();
    void CmFileOpen ();
    void CmFileClose ();
    void CmHelpAbout ();
//{{txted2AppRSP_TBL_END}}
  DECLARE_RESPONSE_TABLE(txted2App);
};    //{{txted2App}}


#endif                              // __txtd2app_h sentry.
```

Listing 9.9 contains the source code for the TXTD2APP.CPP implementation file. The file contains the message response table macro, the declaration of the SDIDecFrame class, and the definition of the members of the txted2App class. The message response macro table and declaration of the SDIDecFrame class are similar to those in the TXTD1APP.CPP file. The following application class member functions are new or different in the TXTD2APP.CPP file:

1. The SetupSpeedBar member function sets up the speed bar of the application by carrying out these tasks:

   - Creates a new instance of the TControlBar class and assigns the address of that instance to the local pointer cb.

   - Inserts the bit-mapped buttons in the speed bar by sending a sequence of the C++ message Insert to the instance accessed by pointer cb. Each message has the appropriate arguments needed to insert a specific bit-mapped button.

   - Includes fly-over help hints by sending the C++ message SetHintMode to the control bar accessed by the pointer cb.

   - Sends the C++ message Insert to the object accessed by the frame pointer-type parameter. This parameter represents the SDI decorated frame window.

2. The InitMainWindow member function initializes the main window by carrying out the following tasks:

   - Creates a new client area by allocating an instance of the TEditFile class. The function assigns the address of this instance to the Client data member.

- Creates a new, decorated SDI frame window by allocating an instance of the `SDIDecFrame` class. The `task` function assigns the address of this instance to the `frame` locate pointer.

- Assign a value to the inherited data member `nCmdShow` such that the window appears in its normal state.

- Assigns the application's icon using the icon resource `IDI_SDIAPPLICATION`. This task involves sending the C++ message `SetIcon` to the SDI window accessed by the `frame` pointer.

- Assigns the application's menu using the menu resource `SDI_MENU`. This task involves sending the C++ message `AssignMenu` to the SDI window accessed by the `frame` pointer.

- Assigns the accelerator table `SDI_MENU` to the frame window.

- Invokes the `SetUpSpeedBar` member function to set up the tool bar. The argument for this member function is the `frame` local pointer.

- Creates a new instance of the `TStatusBar` class. The function assigns the address of the status bar object to the local pointer `sb`.

- Inserts the status bar in the SDI frame window. This task involves sending the C++ message `Insert` to the frame window. The arguments for this message are the speed bar object (represented by the expression `*sb`) and the `TDecoratedFrame::Bottom` value. This value locates the status bar at the bottom of the SDI frame window.

- Assigns the address in the `frame` pointer to the inherited data member `MainWindow`.

LISTING 9.9. THE SOURCE CODE FOR THE TXTD2APP.CPP IMPLEMENTATION FILE.

```
/*  Project txted2

    Copyright _ 1993. All Rights Reserved.

    SUBSYSTEM:    txted2.exe Application
    FILE:         txtd2app.cpp
    AUTHOR:



    OVERVIEW
    ========
```

```
        Source file for implementation of txted2App (TApplication).
*/


#include <owl\owlpch.h>
#pragma hdrstop


#include "txtd2app.h"
#include "txtd2abd.h"                          // Definition of about dialog.


//{{txted2App Implementation}}


//
// Build a response table for all messages/commands handled
// by the application.
//
DEFINE_RESPONSE_TABLE1(txted2App, TApplication)
//{{txted2AppRSP_TBL_BEGIN}}
    EV_COMMAND(CM_FILENEW, CmFileNew),
    EV_COMMAND(CM_FILEOPEN, CmFileOpen),
    EV_COMMAND(CM_FILECLOSE, CmFileClose),
    EV_COMMAND(CM_HELPABOUT, CmHelpAbout),
//{{txted2AppRSP_TBL_END}}
END_RESPONSE_TABLE;


//
// FrameWindow must be derived to override Paint for Preview and Print.
//
class SDIDecFrame : public TDecoratedFrame {
public:
    SDIDecFrame (TWindow *parent, const char far *title, TWindow *clientWnd,
BOOL trackMenuSelection = FALSE, TModule *module = 0) :
            TDecoratedFrame(parent, title, clientWnd, trackMenuSelection,
module)
        {  }
    ~SDIDecFrame ()
        {  }
};


////////////////////////////////////////////////////////////
// txted2App
// =====
//
txted2App::txted2App () : TApplication("txted2")
{
```

continues

Listing 9.9. continued

```
    // Common file file flags and filters for Open/Save As dialogs. Filename and
    // directory are computed in the member functions CmFileOpen, and
    // CmFileSaveAs.
    FileData.Flags = OFN_FILEMUSTEXIST | OFN_HIDEREADONLY | OFN_OVERWRITEPROMPT;
    FileData.SetFilter("All Files (*.*)|*.*|");

    // INSERT>> Your constructor code here.

}


txted2App::~txted2App ()
{
    // INSERT>> Your destructor code here.

}


void txted2App::SetupSpeedBar (TDecoratedFrame *frame)
{
    //
    // Create default toolbar New and associate toolbar buttons with commands.
    //
    TControlBar* cb = new TControlBar(frame);
    cb->Insert(*new TButtonGadget(CM_FILENEW, CM_FILENEW));
    cb->Insert(*new TButtonGadget(CM_FILEOPEN, CM_FILEOPEN));
    cb->Insert(*new TButtonGadget(CM_FILESAVE, CM_FILESAVE));
    cb->Insert(*new TSeparatorGadget(6));
    cb->Insert(*new TButtonGadget(CM_EDITCUT, CM_EDITCUT));
    cb->Insert(*new TButtonGadget(CM_EDITCOPY, CM_EDITCOPY));
    cb->Insert(*new TButtonGadget(CM_EDITPASTE, CM_EDITPASTE));
    cb->Insert(*new TSeparatorGadget(6));
    cb->Insert(*new TButtonGadget(CM_EDITUNDO, CM_EDITUNDO));
    cb->Insert(*new TSeparatorGadget(6));
    cb->Insert(*new TButtonGadget(CM_EDITFIND, CM_EDITFIND));
    cb->Insert(*new TButtonGadget(CM_EDITFINDNEXT, CM_EDITFINDNEXT));

    // Add fly-over help hints.
    cb->SetHintMode(TGadgetWindow::EnterHints);

    frame->Insert(*cb, TDecoratedFrame::Top);
}


//////////////////////////////////////////////////////////////
// txted2App
// =====
// Application initialization.
```

```
//
void txted2App::InitMainWindow ()
{
    Client = new TEditFile(0, 0, 0);
    SDIDecFrame *frame = new SDIDecFrame(0, GetName(), Client, TRUE);

    nCmdShow = nCmdShow != SW_SHOWMINIMIZED ? SW_SHOWNORMAL : nCmdShow;

    //
    // Assign ICON w/ this application.
    //
    frame->SetIcon(this, IDI_SDIAPPLICATION);

    //
    // Menu associated with window and accelerator table associated with table.
    //
    frame->AssignMenu(SDI_MENU);

    //
    // Associate with the accelerator table.
    //
    frame->Attr.AccelTable = SDI_MENU;

    SetupSpeedBar(frame);

    TStatusBar *sb = new TStatusBar(frame, TGadget::Recessed,
                                    TStatusBar::CapsLock    ¦
                                    TStatusBar::NumLock     ¦
                                    TStatusBar::ScrollLock  ¦
                                    TStatusBar::Overtype);
    frame->Insert(*sb, TDecoratedFrame::Bottom);

    MainWindow = frame;

}


////////////////////////////////////////////////////////////
// txted2App
// ===========
// Menu File New command
void txted2App::CmFileNew ()
{
    Client->NewFile();
}


////////////////////////////////////////////////////////////
// txted2App
// ===========
```

continues

LISTING 9.9. CONTINUED

```cpp
// Menu File Open command
void txted2App::CmFileOpen ()
{
    //
    // Display standard Open dialog box to select a file name.
    //
    *FileData.FileName = 0;
    if (Client->CanClose())
        if (TFileOpenDialog(MainWindow, FileData).Execute() == IDOK)
            OpenFile();
}


void txted2App::OpenFile (const char *fileName)
{
    if (fileName)
        lstrcpy(FileData.FileName, fileName);

    Client->ReplaceWith(FileData.FileName);
}


/////////////////////////////////////////////////////////
// txted2App
// =====
// Menu File Close command
void txted2App::CmFileClose ()
{
    if (Client->CanClose())
        Client->DeleteSubText(0, UINT(-1));
}


/////////////////////////////////////////////////////////
// txted2App
// ===========
// Menu Help About txted2.exe command
void txted2App::CmHelpAbout ()
{
    //
    // Show the modal dialog.
    //
    txted2AboutDlg(MainWindow).Execute();
}


int OwlMain (int , char* [])
{
```

```
txted2App      App;
int               result;

result = App.Run();

return result;
}
```

THE TXTED3 PROJECT

The TXTED3 project deals with an SDI-compliant text editor that uses the document and view classes. The editor also has a speed bar and a status line. The AppExpert generates the following set of files:

```
APPLDOCV ICO                          1,086
COPY       BMP                          358
CUT        BMP                          358
FIND       BMP                          358
FINDNEXT BMP                            358
NEW        BMP                          358
OPEN       BMP                          358
PASTE      BMP                          358
SAVE       BMP                          358
TXTD3ABD CPP                          4,745
TXTD3ABD H                              910
TXTD3APP RC                          14,380
TXTD3APP RH                           4,825
TXTD3APP DEF                            509
TXTD3APP CPP                          4,724
TXTD3APP H                            1,299
TXTED3     APX                        10,168
TXTED3     IDE                        55,086
TXTED3     DSW                           262
UNDO       BMP                          358
```

The AppExpert utility generates the same number and kinds of files for both projects TXTED2 and TXTED3. Again the header and implementation files for the About dialog box are similar to those in the last two projects. By contrast, the header and implementation files for the application class have new and modified code.

First, build the TXTED3 project and experiment with its text editing features. Figure 9.14 shows a sample session with the TXTED3.EXE application. Look at the source code listings next.

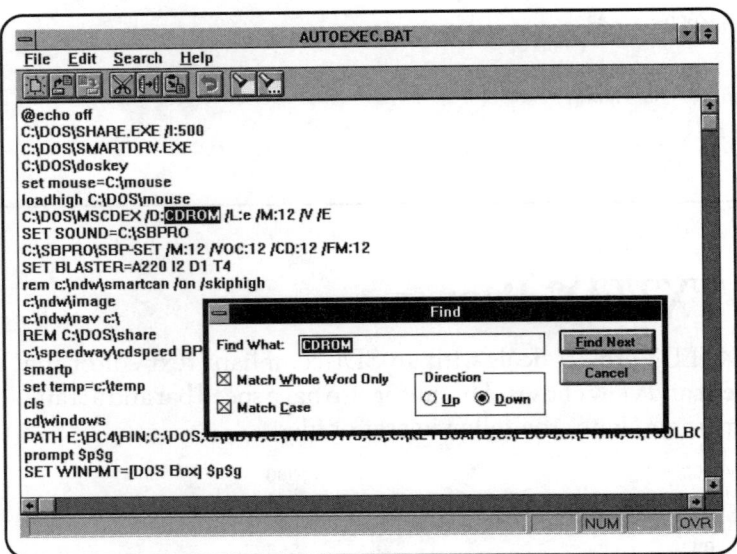

Figure 9.14. A sample session with the TXTED3.EXE application.

Listing 9.10 shows the source code for the TXTD3APP.H header file. This listing contains the declaration of the txted3App application class. The declaration is similar to that of txted2App, except for the declaration of the EvNewView and EvCloseView member functions. These member functions create and close a view.

LISTING **9.10.** THE SOURCE CODE FOR THE **TXTD3APP.H** HEADER FILE.

```
#if !defined(__txtd3app_h)                    // Sentry, use file only if it's not
                                              // already included.

#define __txtd3app_h

/*  Project txted3

    Copyright _ 1993. All Rights Reserved.

    SUBSYSTEM:    txted3.exe Application
    FILE:         txtd3app.h
    AUTHOR:


    OVERVIEW
    ========
    Class definition for txted3App (TApplication).
*/
```

```
#include <owl\owlpch.h>
#pragma hdrstop

#include <owl\statusba.h>
#include <owl\controlb.h>
#include <owl\buttonga.h>
#include <owl\editview.h>
#include <owl\listview.h>
#include <owl\docmanag.h>
#include <owl\filedoc.h>

#include "txtd3app.rh"              // Definition of all resources.


//{{TApplication = txted3App}}
class txted3App : public TApplication {
private:

private:
    void SetupSpeedBar (TDecoratedFrame *frame);

public:
    txted3App ();
    virtual ~txted3App ();

//{{txted3AppVIRTUAL_BEGIN}}
public:
    virtual void InitMainWindow();
//{{txted3AppVIRTUAL_END}}

//{{txted3AppRSP_TBL_BEGIN}}
protected:
    void EvNewView (TView& view);
    void EvCloseView (TView& view);
    void CmHelpAbout ();
//{{txted3AppRSP_TBL_END}}
  DECLARE_RESPONSE_TABLE(txted3App);
};     //{{txted3App}}


#endif                                     // __txtd3app_h sentry.
```

Listing 9.11 shows the source code for the TXTD3APP.CPP implementation file. The listing defines class members, among them the following:

1. The constructor creates a new instance of the TDocManager class and assigns the address of that instance to the inherited member DocManager.

2. The SetUpSpeedBar member function sets up the speed bar. The statements of this function are identical to those in file TXTED2.CPP.

3. The `InitMainWindow` member function initializes the main window by carrying out the following tasks:

- Creates a new, decorated frame window by allocating an instance of the `TDecoratedFrame` class. The function assigns the address of this instance to the local pointer frame.

- Assigns a value to the inherited data member `nCmdShow`, such that the window appears in its normal state.

- Assigns the application's icon using the icon resource `IDI_SDIAPPLICATION`. This task involves sending the C++ message `SetIcon` to the SDI window accessed by pointer `frame`.

- Assigns the application's menu using the menu resource `SDI_MENU`. This task involves sending the C++ message `AssignMenu` to the SDI window accessed by pointer `frame`.

- Assigns the accelerator table `SDI_MENU` to the frame window.

- Invokes the `SetUpSpeedBar` member function to set up the tool bar. The argument for this member function is the local pointer `frame`.

- Creates a new instance of the `TStatusBar` class. The function assigns the address of the status bar object to the local pointer `sb`.

- Inserts the status bar in the SDI frame window. This task involves sending the C++ message `Insert` to the frame window. The arguments for this message are the speed bar object (represented by the expression `*sb`) and the `TDecoratedFrame::Bottom` value. This value locates the status bar at the bottom of the SDI frame window.

- Assigns the address in the pointer `frame` to the inherited data member `MainWindow`.

4. The `EvNewView` member function sets the client area to be that of the view accessed by the parameter `view`.

5. The `EvCloseView` member function selects the default client window.

LISTING 9.11. THE SOURCE CODE FOR THE TXTD3APP.CPP IMPLEMENTATION FILE.

```
/*  Project txted3

    Copyright _ 1993. All Rights Reserved.

    SUBSYSTEM:    txted3.exe Application
    FILE:         txtd3app.cpp
    AUTHOR:


    OVERVIEW
    ========
    Source file for implementation of txted3App (TApplication).
*/


#include <owl\owlpch.h>
#pragma hdrstop


#include "txtd3app.h"
#include "txtd3abd.h"                        // Definition of about dialog.


//{{txted3App Implementation}}

//{{DOC_VIEW}}
DEFINE_DOC_TEMPLATE_CLASS(TFileDocument, TEditView, DocType1);
//{{DOC_VIEW_END}}

//{{DOC_MANAGER}}
DocType1 __dvt1("All Files (*.*)", "*.*", 0, "TXT", dtAutoDelete ¦ dtUpdateDir);
//{{DOC_MANAGER_END}}

//
// Build a response table for all messages/commands handled
// by the application.
//
DEFINE_RESPONSE_TABLE1(txted3App, TApplication)
//{{txted3AppRSP_TBL_BEGIN}}
    EV_OWLVIEW(dnCreate, EvNewView),
    EV_OWLVIEW(dnClose,  EvCloseView),
    EV_COMMAND(CM_HELPABOUT, CmHelpAbout),
//{{txted3AppRSP_TBL_END}}
END_RESPONSE_TABLE;
//
// FrameWindow must be derived to override Paint for Preview and Print.
//
```

continues

Listing 9.11. continued

```
class SDIDecFrame : public TDecoratedFrame {
public:
    SDIDecFrame (TWindow *parent, const char far *title, TWindow *clientWnd,
BOOL trackMenuSelection = FALSE, TModule *module = 0) :
            TDecoratedFrame(parent, title, clientWnd, trackMenuSelection,
module)
      {  }
    ~SDIDecFrame ()
      {  }
};



//////////////////////////////////////////////////////////
// txted3App
// =====
//
txted3App::txted3App () : TApplication("txted3")
{

    DocManager = new TDocManager(dmSDI ¦ dmMenu);

    // INSERT>> Your constructor code here.

}


txted3App::~txted3App ()
{
    // INSERT>> Your destructor code here.

}


void txted3App::SetupSpeedBar (TDecoratedFrame *frame)
{
    //
    // Create default toolbar New and associate toolbar buttons with commands.
    //
    TControlBar* cb = new TControlBar(frame);
    cb->Insert(*new TButtonGadget(CM_FILENEW, CM_FILENEW));
    cb->Insert(*new TButtonGadget(CM_FILEOPEN, CM_FILEOPEN));
    cb->Insert(*new TButtonGadget(CM_FILESAVE, CM_FILESAVE));
    cb->Insert(*new TSeparatorGadget(6));
    cb->Insert(*new TButtonGadget(CM_EDITCUT, CM_EDITCUT));
    cb->Insert(*new TButtonGadget(CM_EDITCOPY, CM_EDITCOPY));
    cb->Insert(*new TButtonGadget(CM_EDITPASTE, CM_EDITPASTE));
    cb->Insert(*new TSeparatorGadget(6));
    cb->Insert(*new TButtonGadget(CM_EDITUNDO, CM_EDITUNDO));
```

```
        cb->Insert(*new TSeparatorGadget(6));
        cb->Insert(*new TButtonGadget(CM_EDITFIND, CM_EDITFIND));
        cb->Insert(*new TButtonGadget(CM_EDITFINDNEXT, CM_EDITFINDNEXT));

        // Add fly-over help hints.
        cb->SetHintMode(TGadgetWindow::EnterHints);

        frame->Insert(*cb, TDecoratedFrame::Top);
}


/////////////////////////////////////////////////////////
// txted3App
// =====
// Application initialization.
//
void txted3App::InitMainWindow ()
{
    TDecoratedFrame *frame = new SDIDecFrame(0, GetName(), 0, TRUE);

    nCmdShow = nCmdShow != SW_SHOWMINIMIZED ? SW_SHOWNORMAL : nCmdShow;

    //
    // Assign ICON w/ this application.
    //
    frame->SetIcon(this, IDI_SDIAPPLICATION);

    //
    // Menu associated with window and accelerator table associated with table.
    //
    frame->AssignMenu(SDI_MENU);

    //
    // Associate with the accelerator table.
    //
    frame->Attr.AccelTable = SDI_MENU;

    SetupSpeedBar(frame);

    TStatusBar *sb = new TStatusBar(frame, TGadget::Recessed,
                                    TStatusBar::CapsLock      |
                                    TStatusBar::NumLock       |
                                    TStatusBar::ScrollLock    |
                                    TStatusBar::Overtype);
    frame->Insert(*sb, TDecoratedFrame::Bottom);

    MainWindow = frame;

}
```

continues

LISTING 9.11. CONTINUED

```cpp
//////////////////////////////////////////////////////////
// txted3App
// =====
// Response Table handlers:
//
void txted3App::EvNewView (TView& view)
{
    MainWindow->SetClientWindow(view.GetWindow());
    if (!view.IsOK())
        MainWindow->SetClientWindow(0);
}


void txted3App::EvCloseView (TView&)
{
    MainWindow->SetClientWindow(0);
    MainWindow->SetCaption("txted3")    ;
}


//////////////////////////////////////////////////////////
// txted3App
// ===========
// Menu Help About txted3.exe command
void txted3App::CmHelpAbout ()
{
    //
    // Show the modal dialog.
    //
    txted3AboutDlg(MainWindow).Execute();
}


int OwlMain (int , char* [])
{
    txted3App      App;
    int            result;

    result = App.Run();

    return result;
}
```

SUMMARY

This chapter introduced you to using the AppExpert utility and offered sample SDI-compliant text editor applications generated using that utility. You learned about the following topics:

- Working with the AppExpert utility, which you invoked from inside the IDE.

- The Application topics that enable you to make main selections about the kind of application you wish AppExpert to generate.

- The Main Window topics that permit you to fine-tune the window styles and the SDI or MDI client windows.

- The MDI Child/View options that enable you to control the creation of the MDI child windows.

- The TXTED1, TXTED2, and TXTED3 projects, which implement SDI-compliant minimally functioning text editors generated by the AppExpert utility. The TXTED1 project implements the simplest kind of text editor that you can create with the AppExpert utility. The TXTED2 project supports an SDI-compliant editor that has a speed bar and a status line. The TXTED3 project supports a version of TXTED2 that uses the document/view classes.

GENERATING MDI APPLICATIONS WITH APPEXPERT

This chapter takes up the subjects treated in the preceding chapter and examines the different versions of the MDI-compliant text editors generated by the AppExpert utility. You will learn about the following minimal MDI editors:

- An editor that contains the speed bar and the status line

- An editor that supports the drag-and-drop and printing features

- An editor that uses the document and views classes

- An editor that combines all of these features

Table 10.1 shows the various projects that create different versions of the MDI-compliant text editors.

The output source code listings have been edited to fit the page layout of this book and to shorten the listings.

	TABLE 10.1. THE VARIOUS MDI-COMPLIANT PROJECTS GENERATED BY APPEXPERT FOR THE CASE STUDIES OF THIS CHAPTER.					
Project	MDI/SDI?	Doc/View?	Speed Bar?	Status Line?	Drag and Drop?	Print?
TXTED4	MDI	No	Yes	Yes	No	No
TXTED5	MDI	No	No	No	Yes	Yes
TXTED6	MDI	Yes	No	No	No	No
TXTED7	MDI	Yes	Yes	Yes	Yes	Yes

THE TXTED4 PROJECT

The TXTED4 project creates an MDI-compliant text editor containing the speed bar and the status line. When you invoke the AppExpert menu option, select the options for the MDI windows, the speed bar, and the status line. Clear the check marks for the remaining options. The AppExpert utility generates the following files:

```
APPLMDI  ICO            1,086
COPY     BMP              358
CUT      BMP              358
FIND     BMP              358
FINDNEXT BMP              358
MDICHILD ICO            1,086
NEW      BMP              358
OPEN     BMP              358
PASTE    BMP              358
SAVE     BMP              358
TXT4MDI1 CPP              976
TXT4MDI1 H                909
TXT4MDIC CPP            4,768
TXT4MDIC H             1,362
TXTD4ABD CPP           4,745
TXTD4ABD H               910
TXTD4APP RC           14,009
```

TXTD4APP	RH	4,562
TXTD4APP	DEF	509
TXTD4APP	CPP	3,632
TXTD4APP	H	1,119
TXTED4	APX	24,490
TXTED4	IDE	56,182
TXTED4	DSW	262
UNDO	BMP	358

Build the TXTED4 project and run the TXTED4.EXE program. Experiment with this version of the text editor to develop a sense for the supported features. Figure 10.1 shows a sample session with the TXTED4.EXE application.

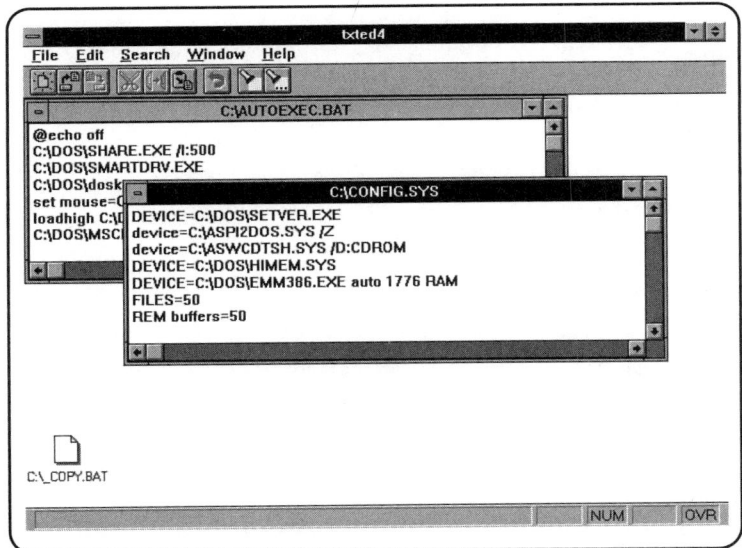

Figure 10.1. A sample session with the TXTED4.EXE application.

The preceding list of files shows the additional header and implementation files TXT4MDI1.H, TXT4MDIC.H, TXT4MDI1.CPP, and TXT4MDIC.CPP. Listing 10.1 shows the source code for the TXT4MDI1.H header file. This file contains the declaration of the MDI child window class txted4MDIChild. The class is declared as a descendant of the TMDIChild class and includes a constructor and a destructor.

LISTING 10.1. THE SOURCE CODE FOR THE TXT4MDI1.H HEADER FILE.

```
#if !defined(__txt4mdi1_h)              // Sentry, use file only if it's not
                                        already included.
#define __txt4mdi1_h

/*  Project txted4

    Copyright _ 1993. All Rights Reserved.

    SUBSYSTEM:    txted4.exe Application
    FILE:         txt4mdi1.h
    AUTHOR:


    OVERVIEW
    ========
    Class definition for txted4MDIChild (TMDIChild).
*/


#include <owl\owlpch.h>
#pragma hdrstop

#include <owl\editfile.h>
#include <owl\listbox.h>

#include "txtd4app.rh"            // Definition of all resources.


//{{TMDIChild = txted4MDIChild}}
class txted4MDIChild : public TMDIChild {
public:
    txted4MDIChild (TMDIClient &parent, const char far *title, TWindow
➡*clientWnd, BOOL shrinkToClient = FALSE, TModule* module = 0);
    virtual ~txted4MDIChild ();
};    //{{txted4MDIChild}}


#endif                                    // __txt4mdi1_h sentry.
```

Listing 10.2 shows the source code for the TXT4MDI1.CPP implementation file. The listing contains the implementation for the constructor and destructor of the txted4MDIChild class. The constructor invokes the constructor of the parent class. The destructor simply invokes the Destroy member function to remove the MDI child window. Both members include comments that indicate where to insert additional code.

LISTING 10.2. THE SOURCE CODE FOR THE TXT4MDI1.CPP IMPLEMENTATION FILE.

```
/*  Project txted4

    Copyright _ 1993. All Rights Reserved.

    SUBSYSTEM:      txted4.exe Application
    FILE:           txt4mdi1.cpp
    AUTHOR:


    OVERVIEW
    ========
    Source file for implementation of txted4MDIChild (TMDIChild).
*/


#include <owl\owlpch.h>
#pragma hdrstop

#include "txtd4app.h"
#include "txt4mdi1.h"

#include <stdio.h>


//{{txted4MDIChild Implementation}}


//////////////////////////////////////////////////////////////
// txted4MDIChild
// ==========
// Construction/Destruction handling.
txted4MDIChild::txted4MDIChild (TMDIClient &parent, const char far *title,
➡TWindow *clientWnd, BOOL shrinkToClient, TModule *module)
    : TMDIChild (parent, title, clientWnd == 0 ? new TEditFile(0, 0, 0) :
    ➡clientWnd, shrinkToClient, module)
{
    // INSERT>> Your constructor code here.

}


txted4MDIChild::~txted4MDIChild ()
{
    Destroy();

    // INSERT>> Your destructor code here.

}
```

Listing 10.3 shows the source code for the TXT4MDIC.H header file. This file contains the declaration of the MDI client window class `txted4MDIClient`, as a descendant of the `TMDIClient` class. The class declares the following members:

1. The public data member `ChildCount`, which stores the number of MDI child windows.

2. The public data member `FileData`, which is an instance of class `TOpenSaveDialog::TData`.

3. The constructor.

4. The destructor.

5. The `OpenFile` member function.

6. The private `LoadTextFile` member function.

7. The protected `SetupWindow` member function.

8. The protected member functions `CmFileNew` and `CmFileOpen`, which handle menu options.

LISTING 10.3. THE SOURCE CODE FOR THE TXT4MDIC.H HEADER FILE.

```
#if !defined(__txt4mdic_h)          // Sentry, use file only if it's not
                                    //   already included.

#define __txt4mdic_h

/*  Project txted4

    Copyright _ 1993. All Rights Reserved.

    SUBSYSTEM:    txted4.exe Application
    FILE:         txt4mdic.h
    AUTHOR:


    OVERVIEW
    ========
    Class definition for txted4MDIClient (TMDIClient).
*/


#include <owl\owlpch.h>
#pragma hdrstop

#include <owl\opensave.h>

#include "txtd4app.rh"          // Definition of all resources.
```

```
//{{TMDIClient = txted4MDIClient}}
class txted4MDIClient : public TMDIClient {
public:
    int ChildCount; // Number of child window created.
    TOpenSaveDialog::TData  FileData; // Data to control open/saveas standard
➥dialog.

    txted4MDIClient ();
    virtual ~txted4MDIClient ();

    void OpenFile (const char *fileName = 0);

private:
    void LoadTextFile ();

//{{txted4MDIClientVIRTUAL_BEGIN}}
protected:
    virtual void SetupWindow ();
//{{txted4MDIClientVIRTUAL_END}}

//{{txted4MDIClientRSP_TBL_BEGIN}}
protected:
    void CmFileNew ();
    void CmFileOpen ();
//{{txted4MDIClientRSP_TBL_END}}
DECLARE_RESPONSE_TABLE(txted4MDIClient);
};    //{{txted4MDIClient}}


#endif                                  // __txt4mdic_h sentry.
```

Listing 10.4 contains the source code for the TXT4MDIC.CPP implementation file. The listing contains the message response table macro and the definition of the various class members.

The message response table maps the messages for the support menu options. The class defines the following relevant members:

1. The constructor that invokes the constructor of the parent class and then assigns 0 to the ChildCount data member.

2. The destructor, which invokes the Destroy member function.

3. The SetupWindow member function initializes an MDI client window by performing the following tasks:

   - Invokes the SetupWindow of the parent class.

   - Assigns the bitwise ORed expression of OFN_xxxx constants to the Flags member of the FileData data member.

- Sends the C++ message `SetFilter` to the `FileData` data member. This message sets the file type filters used in the Open and Save File dialog boxes.

4. The `CmFileNew` member function creates a new MDI child window by performing the following tasks:

   - Generates the title of the new MDI child window.

   - Creates a new MDI child window object and assigns its address to the `child` local pointer.

   - Associates an icon with the MDI child window. This task involves sending the C++ message `SetIcon` to the MDI child window.

   - Maximizes the new MDI child window if the current MDI child window is also maximized.

   - Creates the visible MDI child window.

5. The `OpenFile` member function creates a new MDI child window and loads the text from the filename specified by the `fileName` parameter. The tasks of this function resemble those of `CmFileNew`. The main difference is that this function invokes the `LoadTextFile` member function after creating the MDI child window.

6. The `CmFileOpen` member function invokes the Open dialog box and then calls the `OpenFile` member function to process the selected file.

7. The `LoadTextFile` member function loads the text from the input file into the current MDI child window.

LISTING 10.4. THE SOURCE CODE FOR THE TXTD4MDIC.CPP IMPLEMENTATION FILE.

```
#if !defined(__txt4mdic_h)              // Sentry, use file only if it's not
                                        // already included.

#define __txt4mdic_h

/*  Project txted4

    Copyright _ 1993. All Rights Reserved.

    SUBSYSTEM:    txted4.exe Application
    FILE:         txt4mdic.h
    AUTHOR:
```

```
    OVERVIEW
    ========
    Class definition for txted4MDIClient (TMDIClient).
*/


#include <owl\owlpch.h>
#pragma hdrstop

#include <owl\opensave.h>

#include "txtd4app.rh"            // Definition of all resources.


//{{TMDIClient = txted4MDIClient}}
class txted4MDIClient : public TMDIClient {
public:
    int                     ChildCount;             // Number of child
                                                    // window created.
    TOpenSaveDialog::TData  FileData;               // Data to control open/
                                                    // saveas standard
                                                    // dialog.

    txted4MDIClient ();
    virtual ~txted4MDIClient ();

    void OpenFile (const char *fileName = 0);

private:
    void LoadTextFile ();

//{{txted4MDIClientVIRTUAL_BEGIN}}
protected:
    virtual void SetupWindow ();
//{{txted4MDIClientVIRTUAL_END}}

//{{txted4MDIClientRSP_TBL_BEGIN}}
protected:
    void CmFileNew ();
    void CmFileOpen ();
//{{txted4MDIClientRSP_TBL_END}}
DECLARE_RESPONSE_TABLE(txted4MDIClient);
};    //{{txted4MDIClient}}


#endif                                  // __txt4mdic_h sentry.
```

Listing 10.5 shows the source code for the TXTD4APP.H header file. This file contains the declaration of the application class txted4App. This declaration includes a constructor, a destructor, the InitMainWindow member function, and the SetupSpeedBar member function. Notice that the class declaration lacks the member functions that respond to the supported menu options. These functions are actually implemented in the MDI client class, and they are not the responsibility of the MDI-compliant application.

LISTING 10.5. THE SOURCE CODE FOR THE TXTD4APP.H HEADER FILE.

```
#if !defined(__txtd4app_h)              // Sentry, use file only if it's not
                                        // already included.

#define __txtd4app_h

/*  Project txted4

    Copyright _ 1993. All Rights Reserved.

    SUBSYSTEM:    txted4.exe Application
    FILE:         txtd4app.h
    AUTHOR:


    OVERVIEW
    ========
    Class definition for txted4App (TApplication).
*/


#include <owl\owlpch.h>
#pragma hdrstop

#include <owl\statusba.h>
#include <owl\controlb.h>
#include <owl\buttonga.h>

#include "txtd4app.rh"              // Definition of all resources.


//{{TApplication = txted4App}}
class txted4App : public TApplication {
private:

private:
    void SetupSpeedBar (TDecoratedMDIFrame *frame);
```

```
public:
    txted4App ();
    virtual ~txted4App ();

//{{txted4AppVIRTUAL_BEGIN}}
public:
    virtual void InitMainWindow();
//{{txted4AppVIRTUAL_END}}
//{{txted4AppRSP_TBL_BEGIN}}
protected:
    void CmHelpAbout ();
//{{txted4AppRSP_TBL_END}}
DECLARE_RESPONSE_TABLE(txted4App);
};    //{{txted4App}}


#endif                              // __txtd4app_h sentry.
```

Listing 10.6 shows the source code for the TXTD4APP.CPP implementation file. The listing contains the implementation for the constructor, the destructor, and the `SetupSpeedBar` and `InitMainWindow` member functions. The constructor simply invokes the constructor of the parent class. The destructor is a dummy member that contains no executable statements. The definitions of the `SetupSpeedBar` and `InitMainWindow` member functions resemble those in TXTD3APP.CPP in Listing 9.11.

LISTING 10.6. THE SOURCE CODE FOR THE TXTD4APP.CPP IMPLEMENTATION FILE.

```
/*  Project txted4

    Copyright _ 1993. All Rights Reserved.

    SUBSYSTEM:    txted4.exe Application
    FILE:         txtd4app.cpp
    AUTHOR:


    OVERVIEW
    ========
    Source file for implementation of txted4App (TApplication).
*/
```

continues

LISTING 10.6. CONTINUED

```cpp
#include <owl\owlpch.h>
#pragma hdrstop


#include "txtd4app.h"
#include "txt4mdic.h"
#include "txtd4abd.h"                          // Definition of about dialog.


//{{txted4App Implementation}}


//
// Build a response table for all messages/commands handled
// by the application.
//
DEFINE_RESPONSE_TABLE1(txted4App, TApplication)
//{{txted4AppRSP_TBL_BEGIN}}
    EV_COMMAND(CM_HELPABOUT, CmHelpAbout),
//{{txted4AppRSP_TBL_END}}
END_RESPONSE_TABLE;


//////////////////////////////////////////////////////////////
// txted4App
// =====
//
txted4App::txted4App () : TApplication("txted4")
{

    // INSERT>> Your constructor code here.

}


txted4App::~txted4App ()
{
    // INSERT>> Your destructor code here.

}


void txted4App::SetupSpeedBar (TDecoratedMDIFrame *frame)
{
    //
    // Create default toolbar New and associate toolbar buttons with commands.
    //
    TControlBar* cb = new TControlBar(frame);
    cb->Insert(*new TButtonGadget(CM_MDIFILENEW, CM_MDIFILENEW));
    cb->Insert(*new TButtonGadget(CM_MDIFILEOPEN, CM_MDIFILEOPEN));
```

```
    cb->Insert(*new TButtonGadget(CM_FILESAVE, CM_FILESAVE));
    cb->Insert(*new TSeparatorGadget(6));
    cb->Insert(*new TButtonGadget(CM_EDITCUT, CM_EDITCUT));
    cb->Insert(*new TButtonGadget(CM_EDITCOPY, CM_EDITCOPY));
    cb->Insert(*new TButtonGadget(CM_EDITPASTE, CM_EDITPASTE));
    cb->Insert(*new TSeparatorGadget(6));
    cb->Insert(*new TButtonGadget(CM_EDITUNDO, CM_EDITUNDO));
    cb->Insert(*new TSeparatorGadget(6));
    cb->Insert(*new TButtonGadget(CM_EDITFIND, CM_EDITFIND));
    cb->Insert(*new TButtonGadget(CM_EDITFINDNEXT, CM_EDITFINDNEXT));

    // Add fly-over help hints.
    cb->SetHintMode(TGadgetWindow::EnterHints);

    frame->Insert(*cb, TDecoratedFrame::Top);
}


//////////////////////////////////////////////////////////
// txted4App
// =====
// Application initialization.
//
void txted4App::InitMainWindow ()
{
    TDecoratedMDIFrame* frame = new TDecoratedMDIFrame(Name, MDI_MENU, *(new
 ➡txted4MDIClient), TRUE);

    nCmdShow = (nCmdShow != SW_SHOWMINNOACTIVE) ? SW_SHOWNORMAL : nCmdShow;

    //
    // Assign ICON w/ this application.
    //
    frame->SetIcon(this, IDI_MDIAPPLICATION);

    //
    // Menu associated with window and accelerator table associated with table.
    //
    frame->AssignMenu(MDI_MENU);

    //
    // Associate with the accelerator table.
    //
    frame->Attr.AccelTable = MDI_MENU;


    SetupSpeedBar(frame);

    TStatusBar *sb = new TStatusBar(frame, TGadget::Recessed,
                                    TStatusBar::CapsLock       ¦
```

continues

Listing 10.6. continued

```
                                    TStatusBar::NumLock       ¦
                                    TStatusBar::ScrollLock    ¦
                                    TStatusBar::Overtype);
    frame->Insert(*sb, TDecoratedFrame::Bottom);

    MainWindow = frame;

}


///////////////////////////////////////////////////////////
// txted4App
// ===========
// Menu Help About txted4.exe command
void txted4App::CmHelpAbout ()
{
    //
    // Show the modal dialog.
    //
    txted4AboutDlg(MainWindow).Execute();
}


int OwlMain (int , char* [])
{
    txted4App      App;
    int                result;

    result = App.Run();

    return result;
}
```

The TXTED5 Project

The TXTED5 project creates an MDI-compliant text editor that supports the drag-and-drop and printing features. When you invoke the AppExpert menu option, select the options for the MDI windows, the drag-and-drop feature, and the printing-related features. Clear the check marks for the other options. The AppExpert utility generates the following files:

APPLMDI	ICO	1,086
APXPREV	CPP	8,777
APXPREV	H	1,662
APXPRINT	CPP	5,617

```
APXPRINT H                     1,285
MDICHILD ICO                   1,086
NEXT     BMP                     322
PREVIEW1 BMP                     322
PREVIEW2 BMP                     322
PREVIOUS BMP                     322
TXT5MDI1 CPP                   5,118
TXT5MDI1 H                     1,225
TXT5MDIC CPP                   8,415
TXT5MDIC H                     1,535
TXTD5ABD CPP                   4,745
TXTD5ABD H                       910
TXTD5APP RC                   15,239
TXTD5APP RH                    5,501
TXTD5APP DEF                     509
TXTD5APP CPP                   7,355
TXTD5APP H                     2,203
TXTED5   APX                  36,375
TXTED5   IDE                  57,150
TXTED5   DSW                     262
```

The TXTED5 project files include a set of header and implementation files that are similar to those in the TXTED4 project.

Build the TXTED5 project and run the TXTED5.EXE program. Experiment with this version of the text editor to develop a sense for the supported features. Figure 10.2 shows a sample session with the TXTED5.EXE application.

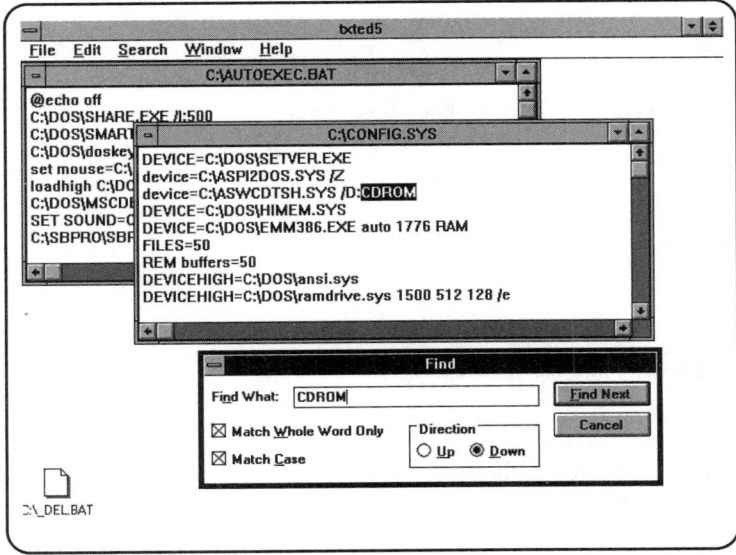

Figure 10.2. A sample session with the TXTED5.EXE application.

Listing 10.7 shows the source code for the APXPRINT.H header file. This file declares the APXPrintOut class (a descendant of the OWL class TPrintout), which supports printing. The class declares a constructor and the member functions GetDialogInfo, BeginPrinting, BeginPage, PrintPage, EndPage, SetBanding, and HasPage. The class also declares a set of protected data members to manage the printing process. The header file contains the definition of the constructor; the definition calls the constructor of the parent class and then assigns the arguments of its parameters to the related data members. The file APXPRINT.CPP file contains the implementation for the member functions of the APXPrintOut class.

LISTING 10.7. THE SOURCE CODE FOR THE APXPRINT.H HEADER FILE.

```
#if !defined(__apxprint_h)              // Sentry use file only if it's not
                                        // already included.

#define __apxprint_h

/*  Main txted5

    Copyright _ 1993. All Rights Reserved.

    SUBSYSTEM:    txted5.exe Application
    FILE:         APXPrint.H
    AUTHOR:


    OVERVIEW
    ========
    Class definition for APXPrintOut (TPrintOut).
*/



#include <owl\owlpch.h>
#pragma hdrstop

#include <owl\printer.h>


class APXPrintOut : public TPrintout {
public:
    APXPrintOut (TPrinter *printer, const char far *title, TWindow* window, BOOL
  ➥scale = TRUE) : TPrintout(title)
        { Printer = printer; Window = window; Scale = scale; MapMode =
          ➥MM_ANISOTROPIC; }

    void GetDialogInfo (int& minPage, int& maxPage, int& selFromPage, int&
  ➥selToPage);
```

```
        void BeginPrinting ();
        void BeginPage (TRect &clientR);
        void PrintPage (int page, TRect& rect, unsigned flags);
        void EndPage ();
        void SetBanding (BOOL b)          { Banding = b; }
        BOOL HasPage (int pageNumber);

protected:
        TWindow     *Window;
        BOOL        Scale;
        TPrinter    *Printer;
        int         MapMode;

        int         PrevMode;
        TSize       OldVExt, OldWExt;
        TRect       OrgR;
};


#endif           // __apxprint_h sentry.
```

Listing 10.8 shows the source code for the APXPREV.H header file. The file declares the PreviewWindow class (a descendant of the TDecoratedFrame class) that supports the print preview feature. The APXPREV.CPP file contains the implementation for the member functions of the PreviewWindow class. The class declares the following members:

1. The constructor.

2. The destructor.

3. The set of public members, which are mostly pointers to pages, control bars, printer devices, and printout objects.

4. The private member Client, which is a pointer to the layout window class TLayoutWindow.

5. The private member function SpeedBarState.

6. The protected member function SetupWindow.

7. The set of protected member functions PPR_xxxx, which respond to the speed bar buttons that support previewing the next and previous pages.

8. The set of protected member functions Evxxxx, which handle the speed bar buttons and close the preview page.

LISTING 10.8. THE SOURCE CODE FOR THE APXPREV.H HEADER FILE.

```
#if !defined(__apxprev_h)              // Sentry, use file only if it's not
                                          already included.

#define __apxprev_h

/*  Main txted5

    Copyright _ 1993. All Rights Reserved.

    SUBSYSTEM:    txted5.exe Application
    FILE:         APXPrev.H
    AUTHOR:


    OVERVIEW
    ========
    Class definition for PreviewWindow (Print Preview).
*/


#include <owl\owlpch.h>
#pragma hdrstop

#include <owl\controlb.h>
#include <owl\printdia.h>
#include <owl\preview.h>

#include "apxprint.h"
#include "txtd5app.rh"


//{{TDecoratedFrame = PreviewWindow}}
class PreviewWindow : public TDecoratedFrame {
public:
    PreviewWindow (TWindow *parentWindow, TPrinter *printer, TWindow*
  currWindow, const char far* title, TLayoutWindow* client);
    ~PreviewWindow ();

        int           PageNumber;

        TWindow       *CurrWindow;
        TControlBar   *PreviewSpeedBar;
        TPreviewPage  *Page1;
        TPreviewPage  *Page2;
        TPrinter      *Printer;

        TPrintDC      *PrnDC;
        TSize         *PrintExtent;
        APXPrintOut   *Printout;
```

```
private:
    TLayoutWindow    *Client;

    void SpeedBarState ();

//{{PreviewWindowVIRTUAL_BEGIN}}
protected:
    virtual void SetupWindow ();
//{{PreviewWindowVIRTUAL_END}}

//{{PreviewWindowRSP_TBL_BEGIN}}
protected:
    void PPR_Previous ();
    void PPR_Next ();
    void PPR_OneUp ();
    void PPR_TwoUp ();
    void EvNCLButtonDown (UINT wHitTestCode, TPoint & point);
    void EvClose ();
//{{PreviewWindowRSP_TBL_END}}
DECLARE_RESPONSE_TABLE(PreviewWindow);
};    //{{PreviewWindow}}


#endif      // __apxprev_h sentry.
```

Listing 10.9 shows the source code for the TXT5MDI1.H header file. This file contains the declaration for the MDI child class txted5MDIChild. The declaration includes the following members:

1. The public data member Printer, which is a pointer to the class TPrinter class.

2. The constructor.

3. The destructor.

4. The public member function Paint.

5. The protected member function EvGetMinMaxInfo.

LISTING 10.9. THE SOURCE CODE FOR THE TXT5MDI1.H HEADER FILE.

```
#if !defined(__txt5mdi1_h)         // Sentry, use file only if it's not
                                   //    already included.
#define __txt5mdi1_h
```

continues

LISTING 10.9. CONTINUED

```
/*  Project txted5

    Copyright _ 1993. All Rights Reserved.

    SUBSYSTEM:    txted5.exe Application
    FILE:         txt5mdi1.h
    AUTHOR:


    OVERVIEW
    ========
    Class definition for txted5MDIChild (TMDIChild).
*/


#include <owl\owlpch.h>
#pragma hdrstop

#include <owl\editfile.h>
#include <owl\listbox.h>

#include "txtd5app.rh"            // Definition of all resources.


//{{TMDIChild = txted5MDIChild}}
class txted5MDIChild : public TMDIChild {
public:
    txted5MDIChild (TMDIClient &parent, const char far *title, TWindow
➡ *clientWnd, BOOL shrinkToClient = FALSE, TModule* module = 0);
    virtual ~txted5MDIChild ();

//{{txted5MDIChildVIRTUAL_BEGIN}}
public:
    virtual void Paint (TDC& dc, BOOL erase, TRect& rect);
//{{txted5MDIChildVIRTUAL_END}}
//{{txted5MDIChildRSP_TBL_BEGIN}}
protected:
    void EvGetMinMaxInfo (MINMAXINFO far& minmaxinfo);
//{{txted5MDIChildRSP_TBL_END}}
DECLARE_RESPONSE_TABLE(txted5MDIChild);
};    //{{txted5MDIChild}}


#endif                                // __txt5mdi1_h sentry.
```

Listing 10.10 shows the source code for the TXT5MDI1.CPP implementation file. The listing defines the message response table to map the cm_*xxxx* printing-related constants with the appropriate CmFilePrint*xxxx* member functions.

The MDI child window class declares the following relevant members:

1. The constructor, which invokes the constructors of the parent class. The constructor contains comment-based placeholders for inserting additional class initialization statements.

2. The destructor, which destroys the MDI child window (by calling the inherited member function Destroy).

   - Increments the currentPage variable.

3. The Paint member function, which paints text for a window, printer, print preview, and edit clients. This function goes through an elaborate sequence of statements to prepare the resources and metrics for painting.

4. The member function EvGetMinMaxInfo returns the information about the window's maximum size and about the minimum and maximum tracking size. The function passes this information using the MINMAXINFO-type reference parameter minmaxinfo.

LISTING 10.10. THE SOURCE CODE FOR THE TXT5MDI1.CPP IMPLEMENTATION FILE.

```
/*  Project txted5

    Copyright _ 1993. All Rights Reserved.

    SUBSYSTEM:     txted5.exe Application
    FILE:          txt5mdi1.cpp
    AUTHOR:


    OVERVIEW
    ========
    Source file for implementation of txted5MDIChild (TMDIChild).
*/


#include <owl\owlpch.h>
#pragma hdrstop
```

continues

LISTING 10.10. CONTINUED

```
#include "txtd5app.h"
#include "txt5mdi1.h"

#include <stdio.h>


//{{txted5MDIChild Implementation}}


//
// Build a response table for all messages/commands handled
// by txted5MDIChild derived from TMDIChild.
//
DEFINE_RESPONSE_TABLE1(txted5MDIChild, TMDIChild)
//{{txted5MDIChildRSP_TBL_BEGIN}}
    EV_WM_GETMINMAXINFO,
//{{txted5MDIChildRSP_TBL_END}}
END_RESPONSE_TABLE;


//////////////////////////////////////////////////////////////
// txted5MDIChild
// ==========
// Construction/Destruction handling.
txted5MDIChild::txted5MDIChild (TMDIClient &parent, const char far *title,
➡TWindow *clientWnd, BOOL shrinkToClient, TModule *module)
    : TMDIChild (parent, title, clientWnd == 0 ? new TEditFile(0, 0, 0) :
  ➡clientWnd, shrinkToClient, module)
{
    // INSERT>> Your constructor code here.

}


txted5MDIChild::~txted5MDIChild ()
{
    Destroy();

    // INSERT>> Your destructor code here.

}


//
// Paint routine for Window, Printer, and PrintPreview for an TEdit client.
//
void txted5MDIChild::Paint (TDC& dc, BOOL, TRect& rect)
```

```
{
    txted5App *theApp = TYPESAFE_DOWNCAST(GetApplication(), txted5App);
    if (theApp) {
        // Only paint if we're printing and we have something to paint, other-
            wise do nothing.
        if (theApp->Printing && theApp->Printer && !rect.IsEmpty()) {
            // Use pageSize to get the size of the window to render into. For a
                Window it's the client area,
            // for a printer it's the printer DC dimensions and for print
                preview it's the layout window.
            TSize   pageSize(rect.right - rect.left,
                             rect.bottom - rect.top);

            HFONT   hFont = (HFONT)GetClientWindow()->GetWindowFont();
            TFont   font("Arial", -12);
            if (hFont == 0)
              dc.SelectObject(font);
            else
              dc.SelectObject(TFont(hFont));

            TEXTMETRIC  tm;
            int fHeight = (dc.GetTextMetrics(tm) == TRUE) ?
                          tm.tmHeight + tm.tmExternalLeading : 10;

            // How many lines of this font can we fit on a page.
            int linesPerPage = MulDiv(pageSize.cy, 1, fHeight);
            if (linesPerPage) {
                TPrintDialog::TData &printerData =
                          theApp->Printer->GetSetup();

                int maxPg = 1;

                // Get the client class window (this is the contents we're going
                    to print).
                TEdit *clientEditWindow = 0;
                TListBox *clientListWindow = 0;

                clientEditWindow = TYPESAFE_DOWNCAST(GetClientWindow(),
                              TEdit);
                if (clientEditWindow)
                    maxPg = ((clientEditWindow->GetNumLines() /
                            linesPerPage) + 1.0);
                else {
                    clientListWindow =
                          TYPESAFE_DOWNCAST(GetClientWindow(),
                                      TListBox);
                    if (clientListWindow)
                        maxPg = ((clientListWindow->GetCount() /
                            linesPerPage) + 1.0);
                }
```

continues

LISTING 10.10. CONTINUED

```
            // Compute the number of pages to print.
            printerData.MinPage = 1;
            printerData.MaxPage = maxPg;

            // Do the text stuff:
            int     fromPage = printerData.FromPage == -1 ?
                                 1 : printerData.FromPage;
            int     toPage = printerData.ToPage == -1 ?
                                 1 : printerData.ToPage;
            char    buffer[255];
            int     currentPage = fromPage;

            while (currentPage <= toPage) {
                int startLine = (currentPage - 1) * linesPerPage;
                int lineIdx = 0;
                while (lineIdx < linesPerPage) {
                    // If the string is no longer valid then there's nothing
                       more to display.
                    if (clientEditWindow) {
                        if (!clientEditWindow->GetLine(buffer,
                            sizeof(buffer), startLine + lineIdx))
                            break;
                    }
                    if (clientListWindow) {
                        if (clientListWindow->GetString(buffer,
                            startLine + lineIdx) < 0)
                            break;
                    }
                    dc.TabbedTextOut(TPoint(0, lineIdx * fHeight),
                        buffer, lstrlen(buffer), 0, NULL, 0);
                    lineIdx++;
                }
                currentPage++;
            }
        }
      }
    }
}


void txted5MDIChild::EvGetMinMaxInfo (MINMAXINFO far& minmaxinfo)
{
    txted5App *theApp = TYPESAFE_DOWNCAST(GetApplication(), txted5App);
    if (theApp) {
        if (theApp->Printing) {
            minmaxinfo.ptMaxSize = TPoint(32000, 32000);
```

```
            minmaxinfo.ptMaxTrackSize = TPoint(32000, 32000);
            return;
        }
    }
}
```

Listing 10.11 shows the source code for the TXT5MDIC.H header file. This listing declares the TFileDrop class and the MDI client window class txted5MDIClient. This declaration is similar to that of the txted4MDIClient class in the file TXT4MDIC.H in Listing 10.3. The main difference between the two classes is that the txted5MDIClient class declares the member functions CmFilePrint, CmFilePrintSetup, CmFilePrintPreview, CmPrintEnable, and EvDropFiles.

LISTING 10.11. THE SOURCE CODE FOR THE TXT5MDIC.H HEADER FILE.

```
#if !defined(__txt5mdic_h)           // Sentry, use file only if it's not
                                     // already included.

#define __txt5mdic_h

/*  Project txted5

    Copyright _ 1993. All Rights Reserved.

    SUBSYSTEM:    txted5.exe Application
    FILE:         txt5mdic.h
    AUTHOR:


    OVERVIEW
    ========
    Class definition for txted5MDIClient (TMDIClient).
*/


#include <owl\owlpch.h>
#pragma hdrstop

#include <owl\opensave.h>

#include "txtd5app.rh"           // Definition of all resources.


//{{TMDIClient = txted5MDIClient}}
class txted5MDIClient : public TMDIClient {
public:
```

continues

LISTING 10.11. CONTINUED

```
    int ChildCount;                  // Number of child window created.
    TOpenSaveDialog::TData  FileData; // Data to control open/saveas standard
                                     dialog.

    txted5MDIClient ();
    virtual ~txted5MDIClient ();

    void OpenFile (const char *fileName = 0);

private:
    void LoadTextFile ();

//{{txted5MDIClientVIRTUAL_BEGIN}}
protected:
    virtual void SetupWindow ();
//{{txted5MDIClientVIRTUAL_END}}

//{{txted5MDIClientRSP_TBL_BEGIN}}
protected:
    void CmFileNew ();
    void CmFileOpen ();
    void CmFilePrint ();
    void CmFilePrintSetup ();
    void CmFilePrintPreview ();
    void CmPrintEnable (TCommandEnabler &tce);
    void EvDropFiles (TDropInfo);
//{{txted5MDIClientRSP_TBL_END}}
DECLARE_RESPONSE_TABLE(txted5MDIClient);
};     //{{txted5MDIClient}}


#endif                              // __txt5mdic_h sentry.
```

Listing 10.12 shows the source code for the TXT5MDIC.CPP implementation file. The listing defines the following relevant members of the `txted5MDIClient` class:

1. The `SetupWindow` member function, which performs the following tasks to setup the MDI client window:

    - Invokes the `SetupWindow` of the parent class.

    - Assigns the bitwise ORed expression of `OFN_`*xxxx* constants to the `Flags` member of the `FileData` data member.

- Sends the C++ message SetFilter to the FileData data member. This message sets the file type filters used in the Open and Save File dialog boxes.

- Accepts files by the dragging or the dropping of a file in the client window. This task involves invoking the inherited member function DragAcceptFiles.

2. The CmFilePrint member function responds to the Print menu option. The function performs the following tasks:

- Assigns the address of the application to the theApp local pointer. The function performs the remaining tasks if the theApp pointer is not NULL.

- Creates a printer object (if the theApp->Printer pointer is NULL) and assigns the address of that object to the application member Printer.

- Creates the printout instance of the APXPrintOut class and assigns the printing characteristics.

- Assigns TRUE to the application's member Printing.

- Invokes the Print dialog box and prints the document. This task involves sending the C++ message Print to the printer object.

- Assigns FALSE to the application's member Printing.

3. The CmFilePrintSetup member function sets up the printer by performing the following tasks:

- Assigns the address of the application to the theApp local pointer. The function performs the remaining tasks if the theApp pointer is not NULL.

- Creates a printer object (if the theApp->Printer pointer is NULL) and assigns the address of that object to the application member Printer.

- Invokes the Print Setup dialog box by sending the C++ message Setup to the printer object.

4. The CmFilePrintPreview member function responds to the preview menu option. The function performs the following tasks:

- Assigns the address of the application to the local pointer `theApp`. The function performs the remaining tasks if the `theApp` pointer is not `NULL`.

- Creates a printer object (if the pointer `theApp->Printer` is `NULL`) and assigns the address of that object to the application's member `Printer`.

- Creates the `prevW` instance of the `PreviewWindow` class and assigns the printing preview aspects.

- Creates the print preview window by sending the C++ message `Create` to the preview window object.

- Invokes the preview window by sending the C++ message `BeginModal` to the application object.

- Destroys the preview window by sending it the C++ message `Destroy`.

- Removes the dynamic instance of the preview window.

- Assigns `TRUE` to the application's member `Printing`.

LISTING 10.12. THE SOURCE CODE FOR THE TXT5MDIC.CPP IMPLEMENTATION FILE.

```
/*  Project txted5

    Copyright _ 1993. All Rights Reserved.

    SUBSYSTEM:    txted5.exe Application
    FILE:         txt5mdic.cpp
    AUTHOR:


    OVERVIEW
    ========
    Source file for implementation of txted5MDIClient (TMDIClient).
*/


#include <owl\owlpch.h>
#pragma hdrstop

#include <dir.h>

#include "txtd5app.h"
#include "txt5mdic.h"
```

```
#include "txt5mdi1.h"
#include "apxprint.h"
#include "apxprev.h"


//{{txted5MDIClient Implementation}}


//
// Build a response table for all messages/commands handled
// by txted5MDIClient derived from TMDIClient.
//
DEFINE_RESPONSE_TABLE1(txted5MDIClient, TMDIClient)
//{{txted5MDIClientRSP_TBL_BEGIN}}
    EV_COMMAND(CM_MDIFILENEW, CmFileNew),
    EV_COMMAND(CM_MDIFILEOPEN, CmFileOpen),
    EV_COMMAND(CM_FILEPRINT, CmFilePrint),
    EV_COMMAND(CM_FILEPRINTERSETUP, CmFilePrintSetup),
    EV_COMMAND(CM_FILEPRINTPREVIEW, CmFilePrintPreview),
    EV_COMMAND_ENABLE(CM_FILEPRINT, CmPrintEnable),
    EV_COMMAND_ENABLE(CM_FILEPRINTERSETUP, CmPrintEnable),
    EV_COMMAND_ENABLE(CM_FILEPRINTPREVIEW, CmPrintEnable),
    EV_WM_DROPFILES,
//{{txted5MDIClientRSP_TBL_END}}
END_RESPONSE_TABLE;


///////////////////////////////////////////////////////////
// txted5MDIClient
// ===========
// Construction/Destruction handling.
 txted5MDIClient::txted5MDIClient ()
 : TMDIClient ()
{
    ChildCount = 0;

    // INSERT>> Your constructor code here.

}


 txted5MDIClient::~txted5MDIClient ()
{
    Destroy();

    // INSERT>> Your destructor code here.

}


///////////////////////////////////////////////////////////
```

continues

LISTING 10.12. CONTINUED

```
// txted5MDIClient
// ===========
// MDIClient site initialization.
void txted5MDIClient::SetupWindow ()
{
    // Default SetUpWindow processing.
    TMDIClient::SetupWindow ();

    // Common file file flags and filters for Open/Save As dialogs. Filename and
    // directory are computed in the member functions CmFileOpen, and
    // CmFileSaveAs.
    FileData.Flags = OFN_FILEMUSTEXIST | OFN_HIDEREADONLY | OFN_OVERWRITEPROMPT;
    FileData.SetFilter("All Files (*.*)|*.*|");

    // Accept files via drag/drop in the client window.
    DragAcceptFiles(TRUE);
}


/////////////////////////////////////////////////////////
// txted5MDIClient
// ===========
// Menu File New command
void txted5MDIClient::CmFileNew ()
{
    char    title[255];

    // Generate a title for the MDI child window.
    wsprintf(title, "%d", ChildCount++);

    txted5MDIChild* child = new txted5MDIChild(*this, title, 0);

    // Associate ICON w/ this child window.
    child->SetIcon(GetApplication(), IDI_DOC);

    // If the current active MDI child is maximize then this one should be also.
    txted5MDIChild *curChild = (txted5MDIChild *)GetActiveMDIChild();
    if (curChild && (curChild->GetWindowLong(GWL_STYLE) & WS_MAXIMIZE))
        child->Attr.Style |= WS_MAXIMIZE;

    child->Create();
}


void txted5MDIClient::OpenFile (const char *fileName)
{
    if (fileName)
        lstrcpy(FileData.FileName, fileName);

    //
```

```
    // Create a MDIChild window whose client is TEditFile.
    //
    txted5MDIChild* child = new txted5MDIChild(*this, "", new TEditFile(0, 0, 0,
0, 0, 0, 0, FileData.FileName));

    // Associate ICON w/ this child window.
    child->SetIcon(GetApplication(), IDI_DOC);

    // If the current active MDI child is maximize then this one should be also.
    txted5MDIChild *curChild = (txted5MDIChild *)GetActiveMDIChild();
    if (curChild && (curChild->GetWindowLong(GWL_STYLE) & WS_MAXIMIZE))
        child->Attr.Style |= WS_MAXIMIZE;

    child->Create();

    LoadTextFile();
}


///////////////////////////////////////////////////////////
// txted5MDIClient
// ===========
// Menu File Open command
void txted5MDIClient::CmFileOpen ()
{
    //
    // Display standard Open dialog box to select a file name.
    //
    *FileData.FileName = 0;
    if (TFileOpenDialog(this, FileData).Execute() == IDOK)
        OpenFile();
}


// Used by ListBox client to read a text file into the list box.
void txted5MDIClient::LoadTextFile ()
{
    char            buf[255+1];
    ifstream        *inStream;

    txted5MDIChild  *curChild = (txted5MDIChild *)GetActiveMDIChild();
    TListBox        *client = TYPESAFE_DOWNCAST(curChild->GetClientWindow(),
TListBox);

    // Only work if the client class is a TListBox.
    if (client) {
        client->ClearList();
        inStream = new ifstream(FileData.FileName);
        while (inStream->good()) {
            inStream->getline(buf, sizeof(buf) - 1);
```

continues

Listing 10.12. continued

```
            if (inStream->good())
                client->AddString(buf);
        }

        // Return an error message if we had a stream error and it wasn't the
          eof.
        if (inStream->bad() && !inStream->eof()) {
            string msgTemplate(*GetModule(), IDS_UNABLEREAD);
            char*  msg = new char[MAXPATH + msgTemplate.length()];
            wsprintf(msg, msgTemplate.c_str(), *FileData.FileName);
            MessageBox(msg, GetApplication()->GetName(), MB_ICONEXCLAMATION |
MB_OK);
            delete msg;
        }

        delete inStream;
    }
}


//////////////////////////////////////////////////////////
// txted5MDIClient
// ==========
// Menu File Print command
void txted5MDIClient::CmFilePrint ()
{
    //
    // Create Printer object if not already created.
    //
    txted5App *theApp = TYPESAFE_DOWNCAST(GetApplication(), txted5App);
    if (theApp) {
        if (!theApp->Printer)
            theApp->Printer = new TPrinter;

        //
        // Create Printout window and set characteristics.
        //
        APXPrintOut printout(theApp->Printer, Title, GetActiveMDIChild(), TRUE);

        theApp->Printing = TRUE;

        //
        // Bring up the Print dialog and print the document.
        //
        theApp->Printer->Print(GetActiveMDIChild()->GetClientWindow(), printout,
TRUE);

        theApp->Printing = FALSE;
```

```
    }
}


//////////////////////////////////////////////////////////
// txted5MDIClient
// ==========
// Menu File Print Setup command
void txted5MDIClient::CmFilePrintSetup ()
{
    txted5App *theApp = TYPESAFE_DOWNCAST(GetApplication(), txted5App);
    if (theApp) {
        if (!theApp->Printer)
            theApp->Printer = new TPrinter;

        //
        // Bring up the Print Setup dialog.
        //
        theApp->Printer->Setup(this);
    }
}


//////////////////////////////////////////////////////////
// txted5MDIClient
// ==========
// Menu File Print Preview command
void txted5MDIClient::CmFilePrintPreview ()
{
    txted5App *theApp = TYPESAFE_DOWNCAST(GetApplication(), txted5App);
    if (theApp) {
        if (!theApp->Printer)
            theApp->Printer = new TPrinter;

        theApp->Printing = TRUE;

        PreviewWindow *prevW = new PreviewWindow(Parent, theApp->Printer,
GetActiveMDIChild(), "Print Preview", new TLayoutWindow(0));
        prevW->Create();

        GetApplication()->BeginModal(GetApplication()->MainWindow);

        // We must destroy the preview window explicitly. Otherwise, the window
           will not be destroyed until
        // it's parent the MainWindow is destroyed.
        prevW->Destroy();
        delete prevW;

        theApp->Printing = FALSE;
```

continues

LISTING 10.12. CONTINUED

```
    }
}


//////////////////////////////////////////////////////////////
// txted5MDIClient
// ==========
// Menu enabler used by Print, Print Setup and Print Preview.
void txted5MDIClient::CmPrintEnable (TCommandEnabler &tce)
{
    if (GetActiveMDIChild()) {
        txted5App *theApp = TYPESAFE_DOWNCAST(GetApplication(), txted5App);
        if (theApp) {
            // If we have a Printer already created just test if all is okay.
            // Otherwise create a Printer object and make sure the printer
            // really exists and then delete the Printer object.
            if (!theApp->Printer) {
                theApp->Printer = new TPrinter;

                tce.Enable(theApp->Printer->GetSetup().Error == 0);
            } else
                tce.Enable(theApp->Printer->GetSetup().Error == 0);
        }
    } else
        tce.Enable(FALSE);
}


void txted5MDIClient::EvDropFiles (TDropInfo)
{
    Parent->ForwardMessage();
}
```

The files TXTD5APP.H and TXTD5APP.CPP are similar to the files TXTD4APP.H and TXTD4APP.CPP, respectively.

THE TXTED6 PROJECT

The TXTED6 project creates an MDI-compliant text editor that uses the document and view classes. The application contains no speed bar and no status line. It does not support printing, and it does not support the drag-and-drop feature. When you invoke the AppExpert menu option, select the options for the MDI windows and the Document/View feature. Clear the check marks for the other options. The AppExpert utility generates the following files:

```
APPLDOCV ICO              1,086
MDICHILD ICO              1,086
TXT6MDI1 CPP                934
TXT6MDI1 H                  909
TXT6MDIC CPP              1,345
TXT6MDIC H                1,208
TXTD6ABD CPP              4,745
TXTD6ABD H                 910
TXTD6APP RC             14,587
TXTD6APP RH              5,149
TXTD6APP DEF               509
TXTD6APP CPP             3,090
TXTD6APP H               1,156
TXTED6   APX            24,455
TXTED6   IDE            56,182
TXTED6   DSW               262
```

The header file TXT6MDI1.H is similar to the header file TXT4MDI1.H, and it declares a constructor, a destructor, and the message response table. The implementation file TXT6MDI1.CPP is similar to the file TXT4MDI1.CPP.

Build the TXTED6 project and run the TXTED6.EXE program. Experiment with this version of the text editor to develop a sense for the supported features. Figure 10.3 shows a sample session with the TXTED6.EXE application.

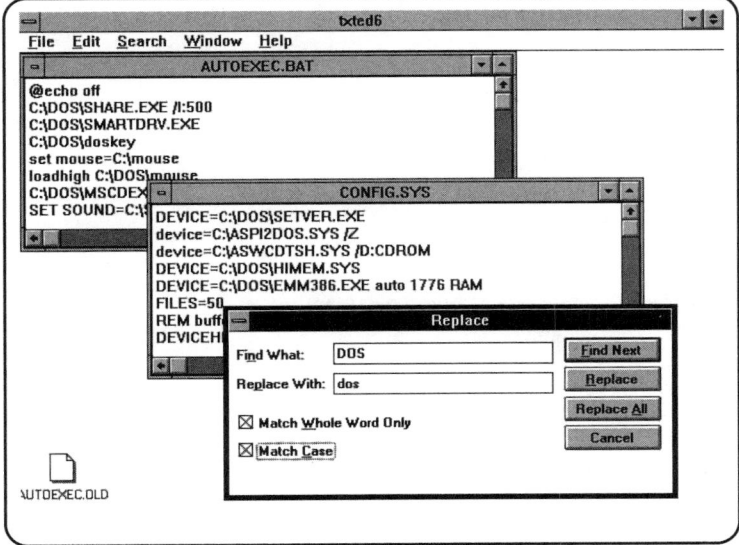

Figure 10.3. A sample session with the TXTED6.EXE application.

The header file TXT6MDI1.H is similar to the header file TXT4MDI1.H. The main difference is that file TXT6MDI1.H does not declare the CmFileNew and CmFileOpen functions as members of the MDI client window class.

The implementation file TXT6MDI1.CPP is similar to the implementation file TXT4MDI1.CPP. The main difference is that file TXT6MDI1.CPP does not define the functions CmFileNew and CmFileOpen and has no entries for these functions in the message response table.

Listing 10.13 shows the source code for the TXTD6APP.H header file. This file declares the application class txted6App. The class declaration includes the void constructor, the destructor, and the member functions InitMainWindow, EvNewView, EvCloseView, and CmHelpAbout. The last three member functions enable the application to handle creating a new view, closing a view, and responding to the Help menu option.

LISTING 10.13. THE SOURCE CODE FOR THE TXTD6APP.H HEADER FILE.

```
#if !defined(__txtd6app_h)              // Sentry, use file only if it's not
                                        //   already included.

#define __txtd6app_h

/*  Project txted6

    Copyright _ 1993. All Rights Reserved.

    SUBSYSTEM:     txted6.exe Application
    FILE:          txtd6app.h
    AUTHOR:


    OVERVIEW
    ========
    Class definition for txted6App (TApplication).
*/


#include <owl\owlpch.h>
#pragma hdrstop

#include <owl\editview.h>
#include <owl\listview.h>
#include <owl\docmanag.h>
#include <owl\filedoc.h>

#include "txtd6app.rh"            // Definition of all resources.
```

```
//{{TApplication = txted6App}}
class txted6App : public TApplication {
private:

public:
    txted6App ();
    virtual ~txted6App ();

//{{txted6AppVIRTUAL_BEGIN}}
public:
    virtual void InitMainWindow();
//{{txted6AppVIRTUAL_END}}

//{{txted6AppRSP_TBL_BEGIN}}
protected:
    void EvNewView (TView& view);
    void EvCloseView (TView& view);
    void CmHelpAbout ();
//{{txted6AppRSP_TBL_END}}
  DECLARE_RESPONSE_TABLE(txted6App);
};     //{{txted6App}}


#endif                              // __txtd6app_h sentry.
```

Listing 10.14 shows the source code for the TXTD6APP.CPP implementation file. The listing defines the following class members:

1. The constructor invokes the constructor of the parent class and creates a new document manager object. The member performs the latter task by creating a new instance of the TDocManager class.

2. The destructor has no executable statements.

3. The InitMainWindow member function initializes the main window by carrying out the following tasks:

   • Creates a new MDI decorated frame window by allocating an instance of the TDecoratedMDIFrame class. The function task assigns the address of this instance to the local pointer frame.

   • Assigns a value to the inherited data member nCmdShow so that the window appears in its normal state.

   • Assigns the application's icon using the icon resource IDI_MDIAPPLICATION. This task involves sending the C++ message SetIcon to the MDI window accessed by the frame pointer.

- Assigns the application's menu using the menu resource `MDI_MENU`. This task involves sending the C++ message `AssignMenu` to the MDI window accessed by the `frame` pointer.

- Assigns the accelerator table `MDI_MENU` to the `AccelTable` member of the `Attr` member.

- Assigns the address in the `frame` pointer to the inherited data member `MainWindow`.

4. The `EvNewView` member function creates a new MDI child window by performing the following steps:

    - Obtains the address of the MDI client window and assigns that address to the local pointer `mdiClient`.

    - Creates a new instance of the `txted6MDIChild` class and assigns the address of this instance to the local pointer `child`. This task invokes linking the new MDI child window with the MDI client window using the `mdiClient` pointer.

    - Sets the icon for the new MDI child window. This task sends the C++ message `SetIcon` to the new MDI child window.

    - Creates the visible part of the MDI child window. This task involves sending the C++ message `Create` to the new MDI child window.

5. The `EvCloseView` member function has no executable statements.

6. The member function creates an instance of the `txted6AboutDlg` class (which models the modal About dialog box) and sends it the C++ message `Execute`.

LISTING 10.14. THE SOURCE CODE FOR THE TXTD6APP.CPP IMPLEMENTATION FILE.

```
/*  Project txted6

    Copyright _ 1993. All Rights Reserved.

    SUBSYSTEM:    txted6.exe Application
    FILE:         txtd6app.cpp
    AUTHOR:


    OVERVIEW
    ========
```

```
        Source file for implementation of txted6App (TApplication).
*/


#include <owl\owlpch.h>
#pragma hdrstop


#include "txtd6app.h"
#include "txt6mdic.h"
#include "txt6mdi1.h"
#include "txtd6abd.h"                          // Definition of about dialog.


//{{txted6App Implementation}}

//{{DOC_VIEW}}
DEFINE_DOC_TEMPLATE_CLASS(TFileDocument, TEditView, DocType1);
//{{DOC_VIEW_END}}

//{{DOC_MANAGER}}
DocType1 __dvt1("All Files (*.*)", "*.*", 0, "TXT", dtAutoDelete | dtUpdateDir);
//{{DOC_MANAGER_END}}

//
// Build a response table for all messages/commands handled
// by the application.
//
DEFINE_RESPONSE_TABLE1(txted6App, TApplication)
//{{txted6AppRSP_TBL_BEGIN}}
    EV_OWLVIEW(dnCreate, EvNewView),
    EV_OWLVIEW(dnClose,  EvCloseView),
    EV_COMMAND(CM_HELPABOUT, CmHelpAbout),
//{{txted6AppRSP_TBL_END}}
END_RESPONSE_TABLE;


/////////////////////////////////////////////////////////
// txted6App
// =====
//
txted6App::txted6App () : TApplication("txted6")
{

    DocManager = new TDocManager(dmMDI | dmMenu);

    // INSERT>> Your constructor code here.

}
```

continues

LISTING 10.14. CONTINUED

```
txted6App::~txted6App ()
{
    // INSERT>> Your destructor code here.

}


///////////////////////////////////////////////////////////
// txted6App
// =====
// Application initialization.
//
void txted6App::InitMainWindow ()
{
    TDecoratedMDIFrame* frame = new TDecoratedMDIFrame(Name, MDI_MENU, *(new
txted6MDIClient), FALSE);

    nCmdShow = (nCmdShow != SW_SHOWMINNOACTIVE) ? SW_SHOWNORMAL : nCmdShow;

    //
    // Assign ICON w/ this application.
    //
    frame->SetIcon(this, IDI_MDIAPPLICATION);

    //
    // Menu associated with window and accelerator table associated with table.
    //
    frame->AssignMenu(MDI_MENU);

    //
    // Associate with the accelerator table.
    //
    frame->Attr.AccelTable = MDI_MENU;



    MainWindow = frame;

}


///////////////////////////////////////////////////////////
// txted6App
// =====
// Response Table handlers:
//
void txted6App::EvNewView (TView& view)
{
```

```
    TMDIClient *mdiClient = TYPESAFE_DOWNCAST(MainWindow->GetClientWindow(),
TMDIClient);
    if (mdiClient) {
        txted6MDIChild* child = new txted6MDIChild(*mdiClient, 0,
view.GetWindow());

        // Associate ICON w/ this child window.
        child->SetIcon(this, IDI_DOC);

        child->Create();
    }
}


void txted6App::EvCloseView (TView&)
{
}


/////////////////////////////////////////////////////////
// txted6App
// ===========
// Menu Help About txted6.exe command
void txted6App::CmHelpAbout ()
{
    //
    // Show the modal dialog.
    //
    txted6AboutDlg(MainWindow).Execute();
}


int OwlMain (int , char* [])
{
    txted6App      App;
    int            result;

    result = App.Run();

    return result;
}
```

THE TXTED7 PROJECT

The TXTED7 project creates an MDI-compliant text editor that uses the document and view classes, that offers the speed bar and status line, and that supports the printing-related and drag-and-drop features. When you invoke the AppExpert menu option, select the options for these features. The AppExpert utility generates the following files:

```
APPLDOCV ICO       1,086
APXPREV  CPP       8,777
APXPREV  H         1,662
APXPRINT CPP       5,617
APXPRINT H         1,285
COPY     BMP         358
CUT      BMP         358
FIND     BMP         358
FINDNEXT BMP         358
MDICHILD ICO       1,086
NEW      BMP         358
NEXT     BMP         322
OPEN     BMP         358
PASTE    BMP         358
PREVIEW  BMP         358
PREVIEW1 BMP         322
PREVIEW2 BMP         322
PREVIOUS BMP         322
PRINT    BMP         358
SAVE     BMP         358
TXT7MDI1 CPP       5,076
TXT7MDI1 H         1,225
TXT7MDIC CPP       5,010
TXT7MDIC H         1,381
TXTD7ABD CPP       4,745
TXTD7ABD H           910
TXTD7APP RC       16,705
TXTD7APP RH        6,088
TXTD7APP DEF         509
TXTD7APP CPP       9,789
TXTD7APP H         2,520
TXTED7   APX      36,327
TXTED7   IDE      57,150
TXTED7   DSW         262
UNDO     BMP         358
```

Build the TXTED7 project and run the TXTED7.EXE program. Experiment with this version of the text editor to develop a sense for the supported features. Figure 10.4 shows a sample session with the TXTED7.EXE application.

The class declaration of the MDI child window in the header file TXT7MDI1.H is similar to class declaration of TXT5MDI1.H in Listing 10.9. Likewise, the member function definitions of the implementation file TXT7MDI1.CPP are similar to those of TXT5MDI1.CPP in Listing 10.10.

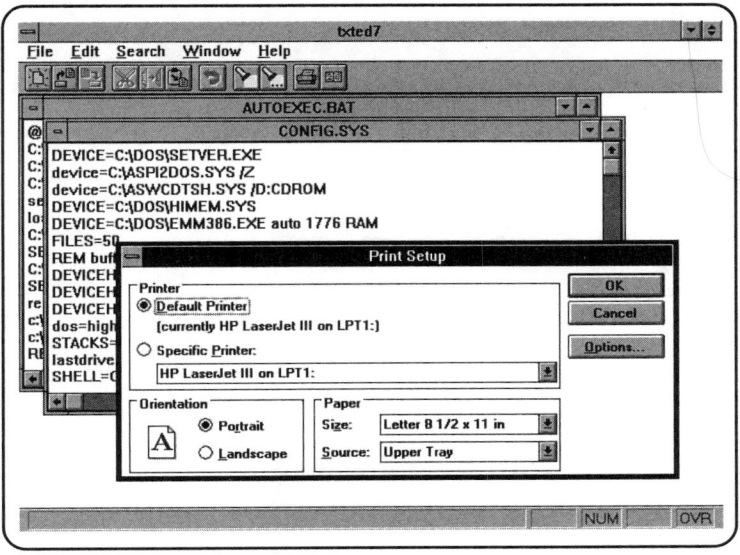

Figure 10.4. A sample session with the TXTED7.EXE application.

The header file TXT7MDIC.H contains declarations that are similar to those in the header file TXT5MDIC.H, shown in Listing 10.11. The contents of the implementation file TXT7MDIC.CPP are similar to those of file TXT5MDIC.CPP, shown in Listing 10.12.

The TXTD7APP.H header file declares the application class txted7APP. This declaration resembles that of the txted6App class, except that the txted7App class includes the following declaration of the additional member function:

```
void SetUpSpeedBar (TDecoratedMDIFrame *frame);
```

Listing 10.15 shows the source code for the TXTD7APP.H header file. The listing contains the definitions of the various member functions of the txted7App class. These definitions resemble ones presented in the last chapter and earlier in this chapter. Because the TXTED7 project combines all of the features mentioned earlier, it should be easy for you to examine the listing and see how the various pieces fit together. I leave this examination as an exercise for you.

LISTING 10.15. THE SOURCE CODE FOR THE TXTD7APP.H HEADER FILE.

```
#if !defined(__txtd7app_h)              // Sentry, use file only if it's not
                                        // already included.

#define __txtd7app_h

/*  Project txted7

    Copyright _ 1993. All Rights Reserved.

    SUBSYSTEM:    txted7.exe Application
    FILE:         txtd7app.h
    AUTHOR:


    OVERVIEW
    ========
    Class definition for txted7App (TApplication).
*/


#include <owl\owlpch.h>
#pragma hdrstop

#include <owl\statusba.h>
#include <owl\controlb.h>
#include <owl\buttonga.h>
#include <owl\editview.h>
#include <owl\listview.h>
#include <owl\docmanag.h>
#include <owl\filedoc.h>
#include <owl\printer.h>

#include <classlib\bags.h>


#include "txtd7app.rh"            // Definition of all resources.


// TFileDrop class Maintains information about a dropped file, its name, where
it was dropped,
// and whether or not it was in the client area
class TFileDrop {
public:
    operator == (const TFileDrop& other) const {return this == &other;}

    char*   FileName;
    TPoint  Point;
    BOOL    InClientArea;
```

```
    HICON     Icon;
    BOOL      DefIcon;

    TFileDrop (char*, TPoint&, BOOL, TModule* module);
    ~TFileDrop ();

    const char* WhoAmI ();
private:
    //
    // hidden to prevent accidental copying or assignment
    //
    TFileDrop (const TFileDrop&);
    TFileDrop & operator = (const TFileDrop&);
};

typedef TIBagAsVector<TFileDrop> TFileList;
typedef TIBagAsVectorIterator<TFileDrop> TFileListIter;


//{{TApplication = txted7App}}
class txted7App : public TApplication {
private:

private:
    void SetupSpeedBar (TDecoratedMDIFrame *frame);
    void AddFiles (TFileList* files);

public:
    txted7App ();
    virtual ~txted7App ();

    // Public data members used by the print menu commands and Paint routine in
        MDIChild.
    TPrinter      *Printer;                    // Printer support.
    BOOL          Printing;                    // Printing in progress.

//{{txted7AppVIRTUAL_BEGIN}}
public:
    virtual void InitMainWindow();
    virtual void InitInstance();
//{{txted7AppVIRTUAL_END}}

//{{txted7AppRSP_TBL_BEGIN}}
protected:
    void EvNewView (TView& view);
    void EvCloseView (TView& view);
    void CmHelpAbout ();
    void EvDropFiles (TDropInfo drop);
    void EvWinIniChange (char far* section);
```

continues

LISTING 10.15. CONTINUED

```
//{{txted7AppRSP_TBL_END}}
  DECLARE_RESPONSE_TABLE(txted7App);
};    //{{txted7App}}


#endif                              // __txtd7app_h sentry.
```

SUMMARY

This chapter presented the following MDI-compliant, minimally functioning text editors that are generated by the AppExpert utility:

- The TXTED4 project implements an editor with a speed bar and a status line.

- The TXTED5 project offers an editor that supports the printing-related and drag-and-drop features.

- The TXTED6 project provides an editor that uses the document and view classes.

- The TXTED7 project combines all of these features.

The chapter examines the differences and similarities between the header and implementation files for the projects named here. The information presented should make you familiar with the source code generated by AppExpert. This familiarity is the key for efficiently customizing AppExpert-generated source code files.

CHAPTER 11

USING THE CLASSEXPERT

In the last two chapters, I discussed using the AppExpert
utility in generating various kinds of SDI and MDI
editors. The ClassExpert utility complements AppExpert
by allowing you to declare new member functions and
classes. These additional items enable you to customize
and fine-tune the classes generated by AppExpert. In
this chapter, you will learn about the following topics:

- Invoking the ClassExpert utility

- Adding new member functions to a class created
  by AppExpert

- Adding a new class to the project created by
  AppExpert

INVOKING CLASSEXPERT

To use the ClassExpert, invoke the ClassExpert menu
option in the View menu selection. Figure 11.1 shows a
sample session with the ClassExpert utility in a project
created by AppExpert. The ClassExpert window contains three panes: the Classes pane, the Events pane,
and the editor pane. The Classes pane lists the classes in

the current project. If there are too many classes to fit in this pane, the ClassExpert window displays vertical scroll bars. The Events pane shows an outline of the various messages for the selected class in the Classes pane. These messages include command notifications, control notifications, virtual functions, and Windows messages. The thick + symbol signals that an outline item is hiding sub-items. The thick - symbol indicates that the item is expanded. The editor pane is supported by a BRIEF-like smart editor that enables you to type in, edit, and delete statements.

When you select a different class in the Class pane, the contents of the Events pane automatically change to reflect the events available for the newly selected class.

When you expand the outlines in the Events pane, you will notice check marks to the left of certain outline items. These check marks indicate that the event has a handler in the project's source code.

 The right mouse button offers versatile context-sensitive pop-up menus that enable you to perform various tasks. The pop-up menus are so context sensitive that they vary not only from one pane to another, but also between one type of selection and another in the same pane.

In the next sections I describe how to add new member functions and classes.

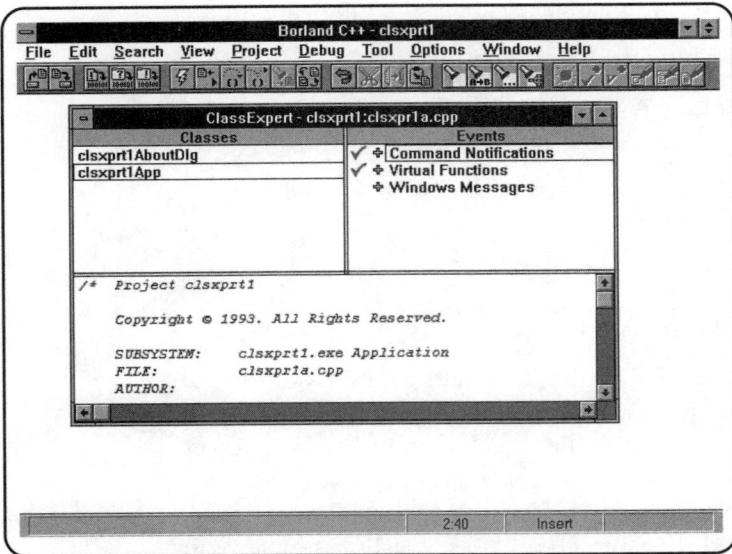

Figure 11.1. A sample session with the ClassExpert utility.

ADDING NEW MEMBER FUNCTIONS

Look at the example of a simple SDI-compliant text editor (very similar to program TXTED1.EXE in Chapter 9) with an additional menu. This menu supports the following features:

- Converting the selected text or the entire contents of the file (if there is no selected text) to lowercase characters

- Converting the selected text or the entire contents of the file (if there is no selected text) to uppercase characters

- Reversing the characters of the selected text or the entire contents of the file (if there is no selected text)

- Inserting the current date

- Inserting the current time

- Inserting the current date and time

Each of these features is supported by a menu option. Each menu option has an event handler member function.

To create the application, follow these general steps:

1. Use the AppExpert to create the new editor CLSXPRT1.EXE as an SDI-compliant application with no speed bar, no status line, no support for drag-and-drop, and no printing-related features.

2. Use the Resource Workshop to add the menu selection Special and its nested menu options Lowercase, Uppercase, Reverse, Insert Date, Insert Time, and Insert Date/Time. Use the identifiers CM_LOWERCASE, CM_UPPERCASE, CM_REVERSE, CM_INSDATE, CM_INSTIME, and CM_INSDATETIME, respectively, for these menu options. Insert a separator menu item between the first and last three menu options in the menu selection. The targeted menu resource is the one with the ID SDI_MENU. When you are finished with adding these menu items, save the updated resources.

3. Use the ClassExpert utility to add the member functions needed to handle the six new menu options. Click the Command Notifications item in the Events pane to expand that outline item.

4. Search for the CM_LOWERCASE identifier, which represents the commands for the new menu option Lowercase.

5. Click in the + symbol located to the left of the identifier CM_LOWERCASE. This action reveals the following two nested outline items: Command and Command Enable.

6. Select the Command outline and click the right mouse button to access the pop-up menu.

7. Select and invoke the Add handler menu option. This option prompts a simple input dialog box that requests that you type in the name of the handler member function. Enter CmLowercase and then click the OK button of the dialog box. The ClassExpert responds by creating the following:

   - The declaration of member function CmLowercase in the declaration of class clsxprt1App (located in the header file CLSXPR1A.H).

   - The response table macro that links the Windows command CM_LOWERCASE with the member function CmLowercase (located in the implementation file CLSXPR1A.CPP).

   - The empty definition of member function CmLowercase (located in the implementation file CLSXPR1A.CPP).

8. Repeat steps 4 through 7 for the other CM_xxxx constants that handle the remaining new menu options. Specify the member functions CmUppercase, CmInsertDate, CmInsertTime, CmInsertDateTime, and CmReverse to handle the Windows commands CM_UPPERCASE, CM_INSDATE, CM_INSTIME, CM_INSDATETIME, and CM_REVERSE, respectively.

9. Add the header files STDIO.H, STRING.H, and DOS.H, along with the statements for the member function Cmxxxx in file CLSXPR1AA.CPP. I will say more about these statements later.

Listing 11.1 shows the contents of the CLSXPR1A.DEF definition file. Listing 11.2 contains the source code for the CLSXPR1A.H header file. Listing 11.3 contains the source code for the CLSXPR1A.RH header file. Listing 11.4 shows the script of the CLSXPR1A.RC resource file. Listing 11.5 contains the source code for the CLSXPR1A.CPP implementation file.

LISTING 11.1. THE CONTENTS OF THE CLSXPR1A.DEF DEFINITION FILE.

```
;-------------------------------------------------
;    Main clsxprt1
;
;    Copyright _ 1993. All Rights Reserved.
;
;    SUBSYSTEM:     clsxprt1.exe Module Definition File
;    FILE:          clsxpr1a.def
;    AUTHOR:
;
;--------------------------------------------------

NAME clsxprt1

DESCRIPTION 'clsxprt1 Application - Copyright _ 1993. All Rights Reserved.'
EXETYPE     WINDOWS
CODE        PRELOAD MOVEABLE DISCARDABLE
DATA        PRELOAD MOVEABLE MULTIPLE
HEAPSIZE    4096
STACKSIZE   8192
```

LISTING 11.2. THE SOURCE CODE FOR THE CLSXPR1A.H HEADER FILE.

```
#if !defined(__clsxpr1a_h)          // Sentry, use file only if it's not
                                    //   already included.

#define __clsxpr1a_h

/*  Project clsxprt1

    Copyright _ 1993. All Rights Reserved.

    SUBSYSTEM:     clsxprt1.exe Application
    FILE:          clsxpr1a.h
    AUTHOR:


    OVERVIEW
    ========
    Class definition for clsxprt1App (TApplication).
*/


#include <owl\owlpch.h>
#pragma hdrstop
```

continues

Listing 11.2. continued

```
#include <owl\editfile.h>
#include <owl\opensave.h>

#include "clsxpr1a.rh"              // Definition of all resources.


//{{TApplication = clsxprt1App}}
class clsxprt1App : public TApplication {
private:
    TEditFile *Client;                          // Client window for the
                                                   frame.

    TOpenSaveDialog::TData FileData;            // Data to control open/
                                                   saveas standard
                                                   dialog.

public:
    clsxprt1App ();
    virtual ~clsxprt1App ();

    void OpenFile (const char *fileName = 0);
//{{clsxprt1AppVIRTUAL_BEGIN}}
public:
    virtual void InitMainWindow();
//{{clsxprt1AppVIRTUAL_END}}

//{{clsxprt1AppRSP_TBL_BEGIN}}
protected:
    void CmFileNew ();
    void CmFileOpen ();
    void CmFileClose ();
    void CmHelpAbout ();
    void CmUppercase ();
    void CmLowercase ();
    void CmInsertDate ();
    void CmInsertTime ();
    void CmInsertDateTime ();
    void CmReverse ();
//{{clsxprt1AppRSP_TBL_END}}
  DECLARE_RESPONSE_TABLE(clsxprt1App);
};      //{{clsxprt1App}}


#endif                                  // __clsxpr1a_h sentry.
```

Notice that the header file in Listing 11.2 contains the protected member
functions CmUppercase, CmLowercase, CmInsertDate, CmInsertTime, CmInsertDateTime,
and CmReverse that handle the Windows commands emitted by the new menu

options. The ClassExpert utility added these member functions. The remaining declarations are the product of AppExpert.

LISTING 11.3. THE SOURCE CODE FOR THE CLSXPR1A.RH HEADER FILE.

```
//#if !defined(__clsxpr1a_rh)              // Sentry use file only if it's not
                                           // already included.

//#define __clsxpr1a_rh

/*  Main clsxprt1

    Copyright _ 1993. All Rights Reserved.

    SUBSYSTEM:    clsxprt1.exe Application
    FILE:         clsxpr1a.rh
    AUTHOR:


    OVERVIEW
    ========
    Constant definitions for all resources defined in clsxpr1a.rc.
*/



//
// IDHELP BorButton for BWCC dialogs.
//
#define IDHELP              998           // Id of help button


//
// Application specific definitions:
//
#define IDI_SDIAPPLICATION    1001        // Application icon

#define SDI_MENU              100         // Menu resource ID and Accel-
erator IDs
#define CM_REVERSE      106
#define CM_INSDATETIME  105
#define CM_INSTIME      104
#define CM_INSDATE      103
#define CM_LOWERCASE    102
#define CM_UPPERCASE    101

//
// CM_FILEnnnn commands (include\owl\editfile.rh except for CM_FILEPRINTPREVIEW)
//
```

continues

LISTING 11.3. CONTINUED

```
#define CM_FILENEW          24331        // SDI New
#define CM_FILEOPEN         24332        // SDI Open
#define CM_FILECLOSE        24339
#define CM_FILESAVE         24333
#define CM_FILESAVEAS       24334


//
// Window commands (include\owl\windows.rh)
//
#define CM_EXIT             24310


//
// CM_EDITnnnn commands (include\owl\edit.rh)
//
#define CM_EDITUNDO         24321
#define CM_EDITCUT          24322
#define CM_EDITCOPY         24323
#define CM_EDITPASTE        24324
#define CM_EDITDELETE       24325
#define CM_EDITCLEAR        24326


//
// Search menu commands (include\owl\editsear.rh)
//
#define CM_EDITFIND         24351
#define CM_EDITREPLACE      24352
#define CM_EDITFINDNEXT     24353


//
// Help menu commands.
//
#define CM_HELPABOUT        24389


//
// About Dialogs
//
#define IDD_ABOUT       22000
#define IDC_VERSION     22001
#define IDC_COPYRIGHT   22002
#define IDC_DEBUG       22003


//
// OWL defined strings
//
```

```
// Statusbar
#define IDS_MODES              32530

// EditFile
#define IDS_UNTITLED           32550
#define IDS_UNABLEREAD         32551
#define IDS_UNABLEWRITE        32552
#define IDS_FILECHANGED        32553
#define IDS_FILEFILTER         32554

// EditSearch
#define IDS_CANNOTFIND         32540


//
// General & application exception messages (include\owl\except.rh)
//
#define IDS_UNKNOWNEXCEPTION   32767
#define IDS_OWLEXCEPTION       32766
#define IDS_OKTORESUME         32765
#define IDS_UNHANDLEDXMSG      32764
#define IDS_UNKNOWNERROR       32763
#define IDS_NOAPP              32762
#define IDS_OUTOFMEMORY        32761
#define IDS_INVALIDMODULE      32760
#define IDS_INVALIDMAINWINDOW  32759


//
// Owl 1 compatibility messages
//
#define IDS_INVALIDWINDOW      32756
#define IDS_INVALIDCHILDWINDOW 32755
#define IDS_INVALIDCLIENTWINDOW 32754


//
// TXWindow messages
//
#define IDS_CLASSREGISTERFAIL  32749
#define IDS_CHILDREGISTERFAIL  32748
#define IDS_WINDOWCREATEFAIL   32747
#define IDS_WINDOWEXECUTEFAIL  32746
#define IDS_CHILDCREATEFAIL    32745

#define IDS_MENUFAILURE        32744
#define IDS_VALIDATORSYNTAX    32743
#define IDS_PRINTERERROR       32742

#define IDS_LAYOUTINCOMPLETE   32741
#define IDS_LAYOUTBADRELWIN    32740
```

continues

LISTING 11.3. CONTINUED

```
//
// TXGdi messages
//
#define IDS_GDIFAILURE          32739
#define IDS_GDIALLOCFAIL        32738
#define IDS_GDICREATEFAIL       32737
#define IDS_GDIRESLOADFAIL      32736
#define IDS_GDIFILEREADFAIL     32735
#define IDS_GDIDELETEFAIL       32734
#define IDS_GDIDESTROYFAIL      32733
#define IDS_INVALIDDIBHANDLE    32732


// TInputDialog DIALOG resource (include\owl\inputdia.rh)
#define IDD_INPUTDIALOG         32514
#define ID_PROMPT               4091
#define ID_INPUT                4090


// TSlider bitmaps (horizontal and vertical) (include\owl\slider.rh)
#define IDB_HSLIDERTHUMB        32000
#define IDB_VSLIDERTHUMB        32001


// Validation messages (include\owl\validate.rh)
#define IDS_VALPXPCONFORM       32520
#define IDS_VALINVALIDCHAR      32521
#define IDS_VALNOTINRANGE       32522
#define IDS_VALNOTINLIST        32523


//#endif          // __clsxpr1a_rh sentry.
```

The resource header file in Listing 11.3 shows the CM_*xxxx* constants for the new menu options which were added by the Resource Workshop. The remaining statements are the product of AppExpert.

LISTING 11.4. THE SCRIPT OF THE CLSXPR1A.RC RESOURCE FILE.

```
/*  Main clsxprt1

    Copyright _ 1993. All Rights Reserved.
```

```
    SUBSYSTEM:     clsxprt1.exe Application
    FILE:          clsxpr1a.rc
    AUTHOR:


    OVERVIEW
    ========
    All resources defined here.
*/

#if !defined(WORKSHOP_INVOKED)
#include <windows.h>
#endif
#include "clsxpr1a.rh"

SDI_MENU MENU
{
 POPUP "&File"
 {
  MENUITEM "&New", CM_FILENEW
  MENUITEM "&Open...", CM_FILEOPEN
  MENUITEM "&Close", CM_FILECLOSE
  MENUITEM SEPARATOR
  MENUITEM "&Save", CM_FILESAVE, GRAYED
  MENUITEM "Save &As...", CM_FILESAVEAS, GRAYED
  MENUITEM SEPARATOR
  MENUITEM "E&xit\tAlt+F4", CM_EXIT
 }

 POPUP "&Edit"
 {
  MENUITEM "&Undo\tAlt+BkSp", CM_EDITUNDO, GRAYED
  MENUITEM SEPARATOR
  MENUITEM "Cu&t\tShift+Del", CM_EDITCUT, GRAYED
  MENUITEM "&Copy\tCtrl+Ins", CM_EDITCOPY, GRAYED
  MENUITEM "&Paste\tShift+Ins", CM_EDITPASTE, GRAYED
  MENUITEM SEPARATOR
  MENUITEM "Clear &All\tCtrl+Del", CM_EDITCLEAR, GRAYED
  MENUITEM "&Delete\tDel", CM_EDITDELETE, GRAYED
 }

 POPUP "&Search"
 {
  MENUITEM "&Find...", CM_EDITFIND, GRAYED
  MENUITEM "&Replace...", CM_EDITREPLACE, GRAYED
  MENUITEM "&Next\aF3", CM_EDITFINDNEXT, GRAYED
 }

 POPUP "S&pecial"
 {
```

continues

LISTING 11.4. CONTINUED

```
 MENUITEM "&Uppercase", CM_UPPERCASE
 MENUITEM "&Lowercase", CM_LOWERCASE
 MENUITEM "&Reverse", CM_REVERSE
 MENUITEM SEPARATOR
 MENUITEM "Insert &Date", CM_INSDATE
 MENUITEM "Insert &Time", CM_INSTIME
 MENUITEM "Insert D&ate/Time", CM_INSDATETIME
 }

 POPUP "&Help"
 {
  MENUITEM "&About...", CM_HELPABOUT
 }

 }


// Accelerator table for short-cut to menu commands. (include\owl\editfile.rc)
SDI_MENU ACCELERATORS
BEGIN
  VK_DELETE, CM_EDITCUT, VIRTKEY, SHIFT
  VK_INSERT, CM_EDITCOPY, VIRTKEY, CONTROL
  VK_INSERT, CM_EDITPASTE, VIRTKEY, SHIFT
  VK_DELETE, CM_EDITCLEAR, VIRTKEY, CONTROL
  VK_BACK,   CM_EDITUNDO, VIRTKEY, ALT
  VK_F3,     CM_EDITFINDNEXT, VIRTKEY
END


//
// Table of help hints displayed in the status bar.
//
STRINGTABLE
BEGIN
    -1,                     "File/document operations"
    CM_FILENEW,             "Creates a new window"
    CM_FILEOPEN,            "Opens a window"
    CM_FILECLOSE,           "Close this document"
    CM_FILESAVE,            "Saves this document"
    CM_FILESAVEAS,          "Saves this document with a new name"
    CM_EXIT,                "Quits clsxprt1App and prompts to save the
                             documents"
    CM_EDITUNDO-1,          "Edit operations"
    CM_EDITUNDO,            "Reverses the last operation"
    CM_EDITCUT,             "Cuts the selection and puts it on the Clip-
                             board"
    CM_EDITCOPY,            "Copies the selection and puts it on the
                             Clipboard"
```

```
        CM_EDITPASTE,                   "Inserts the clipboard contents at the insertion
                                         point"
        CM_EDITDELETE,                  "Deletes the selection"
        CM_EDITCLEAR,                   "Clear the document"
        CM_EDITFIND-1,                  "Search/replace operations"
        CM_EDITFIND,                    "Finds the specified text"
        CM_EDITREPLACE,                 "Finds the specified text and changes it"
        CM_EDITFINDNEXT,                "Finds the next match"
        CM_HELPABOUT-1,                 "Access About"
        CM_HELPABOUT,                   "About the clsxprt1 application"
END


//
// OWL string table
//

// EditFile (include\owl\editfile.rc and include\owl\editsear.rc)
STRINGTABLE LOADONCALL MOVEABLE DISCARDABLE
BEGIN
        IDS_CANNOTFIND,                 "Cannot find ""%s""."
        IDS_UNTITLED,                   "Untitled"
        IDS_UNABLEREAD,                 "Unable to read file %s from disk."
        IDS_UNABLEWRITE,                "Unable to write file %s to disk."
        IDS_FILECHANGED,                "The text in the %s file has changed.\n\nDo you
                                         want to save the changes?"
        IDS_FILEFILTER,                 "Text files (*.TXT)¦*.TXT¦AllFiles (*.*)¦*.*¦"
END


// Exception string resources (include\owl\except.rc)
STRINGTABLE LOADONCALL MOVEABLE DISCARDABLE
BEGIN
        IDS_OWLEXCEPTION,               "ObjectWindows Exception"
        IDS_UNHANDLEDXMSG,              "Unhandled Exception"
        IDS_OKTORESUME,                 "OK to resume?"
        IDS_UNKNOWNEXCEPTION,           "Unknown exception"

        IDS_UNKNOWNERROR,               "Unknown error"
        IDS_NOAPP,                      "No application object"
        IDS_OUTOFMEMORY,                "Out of memory"
        IDS_INVALIDMODULE,              "Invalid module specified for window"
        IDS_INVALIDMAINWINDOW,          "Invalid MainWindow"

        IDS_INVALIDWINDOW,              "Invalid window %s"
        IDS_INVALIDCHILDWINDOW,         "Invalid child window %s"
        IDS_INVALIDCLIENTWINDOW,        "Invalid client window %s"

        IDS_CLASSREGISTERFAIL,          "Class registration fail for window %s"
        IDS_CHILDREGISTERFAIL,          "Child class registration fail for window %s"
```

continues

LISTING 11.4. CONTINUED

```
    IDS_WINDOWCREATEFAIL,        "Create fail for window %s"
    IDS_WINDOWEXECUTEFAIL,       "Execute fail for window %s"
    IDS_CHILDCREATEFAIL,         "Child create fail for window %s"

    IDS_MENUFAILURE,             "Menu creation failure"
    IDS_VALIDATORSYNTAX,         "Validator syntax error"
    IDS_PRINTERERROR,            "Printer error"

    IDS_LAYOUTINCOMPLETE,        "Incomplete layout constraints specified in
                                  window %s"
    IDS_LAYOUTBADRELWIN,         "Invalid relative window specified in layout
                                  constraint in window %s"

    IDS_GDIFAILURE,              "GDI failure"
    IDS_GDIALLOCFAIL,            "GDI allocate failure"
    IDS_GDICREATEFAIL,           "GDI creation failure"
    IDS_GDIRESLOADFAIL,          "GDI resource load failure"
    IDS_GDIFILEREADFAIL,         "GDI file read failure"
    IDS_GDIDELETEFAIL,           "GDI object %X delete failure"
    IDS_GDIDESTROYFAIL,          "GDI object %X destroy failure"
    IDS_INVALIDDIBHANDLE,        "Invalid DIB handle %X"
END


// General Window's status bar messages. (include\owl\statusba.rc)
STRINGTABLE
BEGIN
    IDS_MODES                    "EXT¦CAPS¦NUM¦SCRL¦OVR¦REC"
    SC_SIZE,                     "Changes the size of the window"
    SC_MOVE,                     "Moves the window to another position"
    SC_MINIMIZE,                 "Reduces the window to an icon"
    SC_MAXIMIZE,                 "Enlarges the window to it maximum size"
    SC_RESTORE,                  "Restores the window to its previous size"
    SC_CLOSE,                    "Closes the window"
    SC_TASKLIST,                 "Opens task list"
    SC_NEXTWINDOW,               "Switches to next window"
END


// Validator messages (include\owl\validate.rc)
STRINGTABLE LOADONCALL MOVEABLE DISCARDABLE
BEGIN
    IDS_VALPXPCONFORM            "Input does not conform to picture:\n""%s"""
    IDS_VALINVALIDCHAR           "Invalid character in input"
    IDS_VALNOTINRANGE            "Value is not in the range %ld to %ld."
    IDS_VALNOTINLIST             "Input is not in valid-list"
END
```

```
//
// Misc application definitions
//

// Application ICON
IDI_SDIAPPLICATION ICON "applsdi.ico"


// About box.
IDD_ABOUT DIALOG 12, 17, 204, 65
STYLE DS_MODALFRAME ¦ WS_POPUP ¦ WS_CAPTION ¦ WS_SYSMENU
CAPTION "About clsxprt1"
FONT 8, "MS Sans Serif"
BEGIN
    CTEXT "Version", IDC_VERSION, 2, 14, 200, 8, SS_NOPREFIX
    CTEXT "My Application", -1, 2, 4, 200, 8, SS_NOPREFIX
    CTEXT "", IDC_COPYRIGHT, 2, 27, 200, 17, SS_NOPREFIX
    RTEXT "", IDC_DEBUG, 136, 55, 66, 8, SS_NOPREFIX
    ICON IDI_SDIAPPLICATION, -1, 2, 2, 16, 16
    DEFPUSHBUTTON "OK", IDOK, 88, 48, 28, 12
END


// TInputDialog class dialog box.
IDD_INPUTDIALOG DIALOG 20, 24, 180, 64
STYLE WS_POPUP ¦ WS_CAPTION ¦ DS_SETFONT
FONT 8, "Helv"
BEGIN
    LTEXT "", ID_PROMPT, 10, 8, 160, 10, SS_NOPREFIX
    CONTROL "", ID_INPUT, "EDIT", WS_CHILD ¦ WS_VISIBLE ¦ WS_BORDER ¦ WS_TABSTOP
➡ ¦ ES_AUTOHSCROLL, 10, 20, 160, 12
    DEFPUSHBUTTON "&OK", IDOK, 47, 42, 40, 14
    PUSHBUTTON "&Cancel", IDCANCEL, 93, 42, 40, 14
END


// Horizontal slider thumb bitmap for TSlider and VSlider
(include\owl\slider.rc)
IDB_HSLIDERTHUMB BITMAP PRELOAD MOVEABLE DISCARDABLE
BEGIN
    '42 4D 66 01 00 00 00 00 00 00 76 00 00 00 28 00'
    '00 00 12 00 00 00 14 00 00 00 01 00 04 00 00 00'
    '00 00 F0 00 00 00 00 00 00 00 00 00 00 00 00 00'
    '00 00 10 00 00 00 00 00 00 00 00 00 C0 00 00 C0'
    '00 00 00 C0 C0 00 C0 00 00 00 C0 00 C0 00 C0 C0'
    '00 00 C0 C0 C0 00 80 80 80 00 00 00 FF 00 00 FF'
    '00 00 00 FF FF 00 FF 00 00 00 FF 00 FF 00 FF FF'
    '00 00 FF FF FF 00 BB BB 0B BB BB BB B0 BB BB 00'
    '00 00 BB B0 80 BB BB BB 08 0B BB 00 00 00 BB 08'
```

continues

LISTING 11.4. CONTINUED

```
        'F8 0B BB B0 87 70 BB 00 00 00 B0 8F F8 80 BB 08'
        '77 77 0B 00 00 00 08 F8 88 88 00 88 88 87 70 00'
        '00 00 0F F7 77 88 00 88 77 77 70 00 00 00 0F F8'
        '88 88 00 88 88 87 70 00 00 00 0F F7 77 88 00 88'
        '77 77 70 00 00 00 0F F8 88 88 00 88 88 87 70 00'
        '00 00 0F F7 77 88 00 88 77 77 70 00 00 00 0F F8'
        '88 88 00 88 88 87 70 00 00 00 0F F7 77 88 00 88'
        '77 77 70 00 00 00 0F F8 88 88 00 88 88 87 70 00'
        '00 00 0F F7 77 88 00 88 77 77 70 00 00 00 0F F8'
        '88 88 00 88 88 87 70 00 00 00 0F F7 77 88 00 88'
        '77 77 70 00 00 00 0F F8 88 88 00 88 88 87 70 00'
        '00 00 0F F7 77 78 00 88 77 77 70 00 00 00 0F FF'
        'FF FF 00 88 88 88 80 00 00 00 B0 00 00 00 BB 00'
        '00 00 0B 00 00 00'
END


// Vertical slider thumb bitmap for TSlider and HSlider (include\owl\slider.rc)
IDB_VSLIDERTHUMB BITMAP PRELOAD MOVEABLE DISCARDABLE
BEGIN
        '42 4D 2A 01 00 00 00 00 00 00 76 00 00 00 28 00'
        '00 00 28 00 00 00 09 00 00 00 01 00 04 00 00 00'
        '00 00 B4 00 00 00 00 00 00 00 00 00 00 00 00 00'
        '00 00 10 00 00 00 00 00 00 00 00 00 C0 00 00 C0'
        '00 00 00 C0 C0 00 C0 00 00 00 C0 00 C0 00 C0 C0'
        '00 00 C0 C0 C0 00 80 80 80 00 00 00 FF 00 00 FF'
        '00 00 00 FF FF 00 FF 00 00 00 FF 00 FF 00 FF FF'
        '00 00 FF FF FF 00 B0 00 00 00 00 00 00 00 00 0B'
        'B0 00 00 00 00 00 00 00 0B 0F 88 88 88 88 88'
        '88 88 88 80 08 88 88 88 88 88 88 88 80 0F 77'
        '77 77 77 77 77 77 80 08 77 77 77 77 77 77 77'
        '77 80 0F 77 FF FF FF FF FF F7 80 08 77 FF FF'
        'FF FF FF FF F7 80 0F 70 00 00 00 00 00 77 80'
        '08 70 00 00 00 00 00 77 80 0F 77 77 77 77 77'
        '77 77 77 80 08 77 77 77 77 77 77 77 80 0F 77'
        '77 77 77 77 77 77 80 08 77 77 77 77 77 77 77'
        '77 80 0F FF FF FF FF FF FF FF F0 08 88 88 88'
        '88 88 88 88 88 80 B0 00 00 00 00 00 00 00 0B'
        'B0 00 00 00 00 00 00 00 0B'
END


// Version info.
//
#if !defined(__DEBUG_)
// Non-Debug VERSIONINFO
1 VERSIONINFO LOADONCALL MOVEABLE
FILEVERSION 1, 0, 0, 0
```

```
PRODUCTVERSION 1, 0, 0, 0
FILEFLAGSMASK 0
FILEFLAGS VS_FFI_FILEFLAGSMASK
FILEOS VOS__WINDOWS16
FILETYPE VFT_APP
BEGIN
    BLOCK "StringFileInfo"
    BEGIN
        // Language type = U.S. English (0x0409) and Character Set = Windows,
            Multilingual(0x04e4)
        BLOCK "040904E4"                              // Matches VarFileInfo
                                                         Translation hex value.
        BEGIN
            VALUE "CompanyName", "\000"
            VALUE "FileDescription", "clsxprt1 for Windows\000"
            VALUE "FileVersion", "1.0\000"
            VALUE "InternalName", "clsxprt1\000"
            VALUE "LegalCopyright", "Copyright _ 1993. All Rights Reserved.\000"
            VALUE "LegalTrademarks", "Windows /231 is a trademark of Microsoft
Corporation\000"
            VALUE "OriginalFilename", "clsxprt1.EXE\000"
            VALUE "ProductName", "clsxprt1\000"
            VALUE "ProductVersion", "1.0\000"
        END
    END

    BLOCK "VarFileInfo"
    BEGIN
        VALUE "Translation", 0x04e4, 0x0409        // U.S. English(0x0409)
                                                      & Windows
                                                      Multilingual(0x04e4) 1252
    END

END
#else

// Debug VERSIONINFO
1 VERSIONINFO LOADONCALL MOVEABLE
FILEVERSION 1, 0, 0, 0
PRODUCTVERSION 1, 0, 0, 0
FILEFLAGSMASK VS_FF_DEBUG ¦ VS_FF_PRERELEASE ¦ VS_FF_PATCHED ¦
VS_FF_PRIVATEBUILD ¦ VS_FF_SPECIALBUILD
FILEFLAGS VS_FFI_FILEFLAGSMASK
FILEOS VOS__WINDOWS16
FILETYPE VFT_APP
BEGIN
    BLOCK "StringFileInfo"
    BEGIN
        // Language type = U.S. English (0x0409) and Character Set = Windows,
            Multilingual(0x04e4)
```

continues

LISTING 11.4. CONTINUED

```
    BLOCK "040904E4"                                 // Matches VarFileInfo
                                                        Translation hex value.
    BEGIN
        VALUE "CompanyName", "\000"
        VALUE "FileDescription", "clsxprt1 for Windows\000"
        VALUE "FileVersion", "1.0\000"
        VALUE "InternalName", "clsxprt1\000"
        VALUE "LegalCopyright", "Copyright _ 1993. All Rights Reserved.\000"
        VALUE "LegalTrademarks", "Windows \231 is a trademark of Microsoft
        ➡Corporation\000"
        VALUE "OriginalFilename", "clsxprt1.EXE\000"
        VALUE "ProductName", "clsxprt1\000"
        VALUE "ProductVersion", "1.0\000"
        VALUE "SpecialBuild", "Debug Version\000"
        VALUE "PrivateBuild", "Built by \000"
    END
END

BLOCK "VarFileInfo"
BEGIN
    VALUE "Translation", 0x04e4, 0x0409          // U.S. English(0x0409)
                                                    & Windows
                                                    Multilingual(0x04e4) 1252

END

END
#endif
```

The resource file in Listing 11.4 shows the pop-up menu Special and its nested menu options. The Resource Workshop has inserted these script statements. The remaining script statements are the product of AppExpert.

LISTING 11.5. THE SOURCE CODE FOR THE CLSXPR1A.CPP IMPLEMENTATION FILE.

```
/*  Project clsxprt1

    Copyright _ 1993. All Rights Reserved.

    SUBSYSTEM:    clsxprt1.exe Application
    FILE:         clsxpr1a.cpp
    AUTHOR:


    OVERVIEW
    ========
```

```
        Source file for implementation of clsxprt1App (TApplication).
*/


#include <owl\owlpch.h>
#pragma hdrstop


#include "clsxpr1a.h"
#include "clsxp1ad.h"                        // Definition of about dialog.

#include <stdio.h>
#include <string.h>
#include <dos.h>

//{{clsxprt1App Implementation}}


//
// Build a response table for all messages/commands handled
// by the application.
//
DEFINE_RESPONSE_TABLE1(clsxprt1App, TApplication)
//{{clsxprt1AppRSP_TBL_BEGIN}}
    EV_COMMAND(CM_FILENEW, CmFileNew),
    EV_COMMAND(CM_FILEOPEN, CmFileOpen),
    EV_COMMAND(CM_FILECLOSE, CmFileClose),
    EV_COMMAND(CM_HELPABOUT, CmHelpAbout),
    EV_COMMAND(CM_UPPERCASE, CmUppercase),
    EV_COMMAND(CM_LOWERCASE, CmLowercase),
    EV_COMMAND(CM_INSDATE, CmInsertDate),
    EV_COMMAND(CM_INSTIME, CmInsertTime),
    EV_COMMAND(CM_INSDATETIME, CmInsertDateTime),
    EV_COMMAND(CM_REVERSE, CmReverse),
//{{clsxprt1AppRSP_TBL_END}}
END_RESPONSE_TABLE;


//
// FrameWindow must be derived to override Paint for Preview and Print.
//
class SDIDecFrame : public TDecoratedFrame {
public:
    SDIDecFrame (TWindow *parent, const char far *title, TWindow *clientWnd,
    ➥BOOL trackMenuSelection = FALSE, TModule *module = 0) :
            TDecoratedFrame(parent, title, clientWnd, trackMenuSelection,
            ➥module)
      {  }
    ~SDIDecFrame ()
      {  }
};
```

continues

LISTING 11.5. CONTINUED

```
////////////////////////////////////////////////////////////
// clsxprt1App
// =====
//
clsxprt1App::clsxprt1App () : TApplication("clsxprt1")
{

    // Common file file flags and filters for Open/Save As dialogs. Filename and
       directory are
    // computed in the member functions CmFileOpen, and CmFileSaveAs.
    FileData.Flags = OFN_FILEMUSTEXIST | OFN_HIDEREADONLY | OFN_OVERWRITEPROMPT;
    FileData.SetFilter("All Files (*.*)|*.*|");

    // INSERT>> Your constructor code here.

}


clsxprt1App::~clsxprt1App ()
{
    // INSERT>> Your destructor code here.

}


////////////////////////////////////////////////////////////
// clsxprt1App
// =====
// Application intialization.
//
void clsxprt1App::InitMainWindow ()
{
    Client = new TEditFile(0, 0, 0);
    SDIDecFrame *frame = new SDIDecFrame(0, GetName(), Client, FALSE);

    nCmdShow = nCmdShow != SW_SHOWMINIMIZED ? SW_SHOWNORMAL : nCmdShow;

    //
    // Assign ICON w/ this application.
    //
    frame->SetIcon(this, IDI_SDIAPPLICATION);

    //
    // Menu associated with window and accelerator table associated with table.
    //
    frame->AssignMenu(SDI_MENU);
```

```
    //
    // Associate with the accelerator table.
    //
    frame->Attr.AccelTable = SDI_MENU;


    MainWindow = frame;

}


////////////////////////////////////////////////////////
// clsxprt1App
// ===========
// Menu File New command
void clsxprt1App::CmFileNew ()
{
    Client->NewFile();
}


////////////////////////////////////////////////////////
// clsxprt1App
// ===========
// Menu File Open command
void clsxprt1App::CmFileOpen ()
{
    //
    // Display standard Open dialog box to select a file name.
    //
    *FileData.FileName = 0;
    if (Client->CanClose())
        if (TFileOpenDialog(MainWindow, FileData).Execute() == IDOK)
            OpenFile();
}


void clsxprt1App::OpenFile (const char *fileName)
{
    if (fileName)
        lstrcpy(FileData.FileName, fileName);

    Client->ReplaceWith(FileData.FileName);
}


////////////////////////////////////////////////////////
// clsxprt1App
// =====
```

continues

LISTING 11.5. CONTINUED

```cpp
// Menu File Close command
void clsxprt1App::CmFileClose ()
{
     if (Client->CanClose())
            Client->DeleteSubText(0, UINT(-1));
}


//////////////////////////////////////////////////////////////
// clsxprt1App
// ===========
// Menu Help About clsxprt1.exe command
void clsxprt1App::CmHelpAbout ()
{
    //
    // Show the modal dialog.
    //
    clsxprt1AboutDlg(MainWindow).Execute();
}


int OwlMain (int , char* [])
{
    clsxprt1App      App;
    int              result;

    result = App.Run();

    return result;
}

void clsxprt1App::CmUppercase ()
{
  UINT startPos, endPos;
  int numChars;
  char* pszStr;

  Client->GetSelection(startPos, endPos);
  // is there selected text
  if (startPos < endPos) {
    numChars = endPos - startPos + 1;
    pszStr = new char[numChars+1];
    Client->GetSubText(pszStr, startPos, endPos);
    strupr(pszStr);
    Client->Insert(pszStr);
    Client->SetSelection(startPos, endPos);
    delete [] pszStr;
  }
```

```
  else {
    numChars = Client->GetWindowTextLength();
    pszStr = new char[numChars+1];
    Client->GetSubText(pszStr, 0, (UINT)numChars);
    strupr(pszStr);
    Client->DeleteSubText(0, (UINT)numChars);
    Client->SetSelection(0, 0);
    Client->Insert(pszStr);
    delete [] pszStr;
  }
}


void clsxprt1App::CmLowercase ()
{
  UINT startPos, endPos;
  int numChars;
  char* pszStr;

  Client->GetSelection(startPos, endPos);
  // is there selected text
  if (startPos < endPos) {
    numChars = endPos - startPos + 1;
    pszStr = new char[numChars+1];
    Client->GetSubText(pszStr, startPos, endPos);
    strlwr(pszStr);
      Client->Insert(pszStr);
    Client->SetSelection(startPos, endPos);
    delete [] pszStr;
  }
  else {
    numChars = Client->GetWindowTextLength();
    pszStr = new char[numChars+1];
    Client->GetSubText(pszStr, 0, (UINT)numChars);
    strlwr(pszStr);
    Client->DeleteSubText(0, (UINT)numChars);
    Client->SetSelection(0, 0);
    Client->Insert(pszStr);
    delete [] pszStr;
  }
}


void clsxprt1App::CmInsertDate ()
{
  struct date dt;
  char szStr[41];

  getdate(&dt);
```

continues

LISTING 11.5. CONTINUED

```
  sprintf(szStr, "%02d/%02d/%4d",
          dt.da_mon, dt.da_day, dt.da_year);
  Client->Insert(szStr);
}


void clsxprt1App::CmInsertTime ()
{
  struct time tm;
  char szStr[41];

  gettime(&tm);
  sprintf(szStr, "%02d:%02d:%02d",
                  tm.ti_hour, tm.ti_min, tm.ti_sec);
  Client->Insert(szStr);
}


void clsxprt1App::CmInsertDateTime ()
{
  struct date dt;
  struct time tm;
  char szStr[41];

  getdate(&dt);
  sprintf(szStr, "%02d/%02d/%4d ",
          dt.da_mon, dt.da_day, dt.da_year);
  Client->Insert(szStr);

  gettime(&tm);
  sprintf(szStr, "%02d:%02d:%02d",
                  tm.ti_hour, tm.ti_min, tm.ti_sec);
  Client->Insert(szStr);
}


void clsxprt1App::CmReverse ()
{
  UINT startPos, endPos;
  int numChars;
  char* pszStr;
  char swapChar;

  Client->GetSelection(startPos, endPos);
  // is there selected text
  if (startPos < endPos) {
    numChars = endPos - startPos + 1;
    pszStr = new char[numChars+1];
```

```
    Client->GetSubText(pszStr, startPos, endPos);
    for (int i = 0, j = strlen(pszStr)-1; i < j ; i++, j—) {
      swapChar = pszStr[i];
      pszStr[i] = pszStr[j];
      pszStr[j] = swapChar;
    }
    Client->Insert(pszStr);
    Client->SetSelection(startPos, endPos);
    delete [] pszStr;
  }
  else {
    numChars = Client->GetWindowTextLength();
    pszStr = new char[numChars+1];
    Client->GetSubText(pszStr, 0, (UINT)numChars);
    for (int i = 0, j = strlen(pszStr)-1; i < j ; i++, j—) {
      swapChar = pszStr[i];
      pszStr[i] = pszStr[j];
      pszStr[j] = swapChar;
    }
    Client->DeleteSubText(0, (UINT)numChars);
    Client->SetSelection(0, 0);
    Client->Insert(pszStr);
    delete [] pszStr;
  }
}
```

The implementation file in Listing 11.5 shows the definitions of the Cm*xxxx* member functions that handle the new menu options. The file contains the #include statements which I added to include the header files STDIO.H, STRING.H, and DOS.H. In addition, notice the response table macros that were inserted by the ClassExpert utility. I added the code for the following member functions:

1. The member function CmUppercase responds to the Uppercase menu option by performing the following tasks:

   - Obtains the current selected text (if any). This task involves sending the C++ message GetSelection to the client window (accessed by the application's member Client). The arguments for this message are the local variables startPos and endPos.

   - Performs the following sequence of subtasks if the value in variable startPos is less than that in endPos (which indicates that there is selected text):

   - Calculates the number of characters in the selected text, and assigns this number to the local variable numChars.

- Creates a dynamic string with `numChars+1` characters and assigns the address of that string to the local pointer `pszStr`.

- Copies the selected text into the dynamic string. This task involves sending the C++ message `GetSubText` to the client window. The arguments for this message are `pszStr`, `startPos`, and `endPos`.

- Converts the characters of the dynamic string to uppercase by using the string function `strupr`.

- Replaces the selected text with the contents of the dynamic string. This task involves sending the C++ message `Insert` to the client window. The argument for this message is the pointer `pszStr`.

- Selects the newly inserted text by sending the C++ message `SetSelection` to the client window. The arguments for this message are the local variables `startPos` and `endPos`.

- Deletes the dynamic string accessed by pointer `pszStr`.

- If there is no selection, the function converts all the characters of the file to uppercase by performing the following subtasks:

  - Obtains the size of the edited text by sending the C++ message `GetWindowTextLength` to the client window. This task assigns the result of the message to the local variable `numChars`.

  - Creates a dynamic string with `numChars+1` characters and assigns the address of that string to the local pointer `pszStr`.

  - Obtains the entire edited text by sending the C++ message `GetSubText` to the client area. The arguments for this message are `pszStr` (the text copy buffer), 0, and `(UINT)numChars`.

  - Converts the characters of the dynamic string to uppercase by using the string function `strupr`.

  - Deletes the entire edited text by sending the C++ message `DeleteSubText` to the client window. The arguments for this message are 0 and `(UINT)numChars`.

  - Selects the start of the file as the insertion point by sending the C++ message `SetSelection` to the client window. The arguments for this message are the integers 0 and 0.

- Inserts the characters of the dynamic string into the client window. This task involves sending the C++ message Insert to the client area. The argument for this message is the pointer pszStr.

- Deletes the dynamic string accessed by pointer pszStr.

The program implements the various text edit operations using the data member client, which is a pointer to the class TEditFile. This class is a descendant of class TEditSearch, which in turn is a descendant of class TEdit. This lineage empowers the pointer client to receive a C++ editing message implemented by the member functions of class TEdit.

2. The member function CmLowercase responds to the menu option Lowercase. The function is similar to function CmUppercase and differs only by its use of string function strlwr instead of function strupr.

3. The member function CmInsertDate responds to the Insert Date menu option by performing the following options:

- Obtains the current system date by calling the function getdate (prototyped in the DOS.H header file). The argument for this function call is the address of the structured variable dt. This variable has the date structure.

- Creates a formatted string image of the month number, day number, and year number. This task uses the function sprintf and assigns the formatted string to the local string variable szStr.

- Inserts the string image into the client window by sending that window the C++ message Insert. The argument for this message is the variable szStr.

4. The member function CmInsertTime responds to the Insert Time menu option by performing the following options:

- Obtains the current system time by calling the function gettime (prototyped in the DOS.H header file). The argument for this function call is the address of the structured variable tm. This variable has the time structure.

- Creates a formatted string image of the hour, minute, and second. This task uses the function sprintf and assigns the formatted string to the local string variable szStr.

- Inserts the string image into the client window by sending that window the C++ message `Insert`. The argument for this message is the variable `szStr`.

5. The member function `CmInsertDateTime` responds to the Insert Date/Time menu option. This function combines the tasks of the member functions `CmInsertDate` and `CmInsertTime`.

6. The member function `Reverse` responds to the Reverse menu option. This function performs the following tasks:

   - Obtains the current selected text (if any). This task involves sending the C++ message `GetSelection` to the client window (accessed by the application's member `Client`). The arguments for this message are the local variables `startPos` and `endPos`.

   - Performs the following sequence of subtasks if the value in variable `startPos` is less than that in `endPos` (which indicates that there is selected text):

     - Calculates the number of characters in the selected text, and assigns this number to the local variable `numChars`.

     - Creates a dynamic string with `numChars+1` characters and assigns the address of that string to the local pointer `pszStr`.

     - Copies the selected text into the dynamic string. This task involves sending the C++ message `GetSubText` to the client window. The arguments for this message are `pszStr`, `startPos`, and `endPos`.

     - Reverses the characters in the dynamic string. This task involves using a `for` loop with two control variables `i` and `j`. The loop statements swap characters using the local variable `swapChar`. The loop initializes the variable `i` and `j` to 0 and `strlen(pszStr)-1`, respectively, and iterates until the variable `i` is equal to or is greater than variable `j`.

     - Replaces the selected text with the contents of the dynamic string. This task involves sending the C++ message `Insert` to the client window. The argument for this message is the pointer `pszStr`.

     - Selects the newly inserted text by sending the C++ message `SetSelection` to the client window. The arguments for this message are the local variables `startPos` and `endPos`.

- Deletes the dynamic string accessed by pointer pszStr.
- If there is no selection, the function converts all the characters of the file to uppercase by performing the following subtasks:
  - Obtains the size of the edited text by sending the C++ message GetWindowTextLength to the client window. This task assigns the result of the message to the local variable numChars.
  - Creates a dynamic string with numChars+1 characters and assigns the address of that string to the local pointer pszStr.
  - Obtains the entire edited text by sending the C++ message GetSubText to the client area. The arguments for this message are pszStr (the text copy buffer), 0, and (UINT)numChars.
  - Reverses the characters in the dynamic string. This task involves using a for loop with two control variables i and j. The loop statements swap characters using the local variable swapChar. The loop initializes the variables i and j to 0 and strlen(pszStr)-1, respectively, and iterates until the variable i is equal to or greater than variable j.
  - Deletes the entire edited text by sending the C++ message DeleteSubText to the client window. The arguments for this message are 0 and (UINT)numChars.
  - Selects the start of the file as the insertion point by sending the C++ message SetSelection to the client window. The arguments for this message are the integers 0 and 0.
  - Inserts the characters of the dynamic string into the client window. This task involves sending the C++ message Insert to the client area. The argument for this message is the pointer pszStr.
  - Deletes the dynamic string accessed by pointer pszStr.

Compile and run the program CLSXPRT1.EXE. Load a small text file and experiment with converting and reversing the characters of selected text and of the entire file. In addition, experiment with inserting the date, the time, or both. When you are done experimenting, exit the file without saving it. Figure 11.2 shows a sample session with the CLSXPRT1.EXE program.

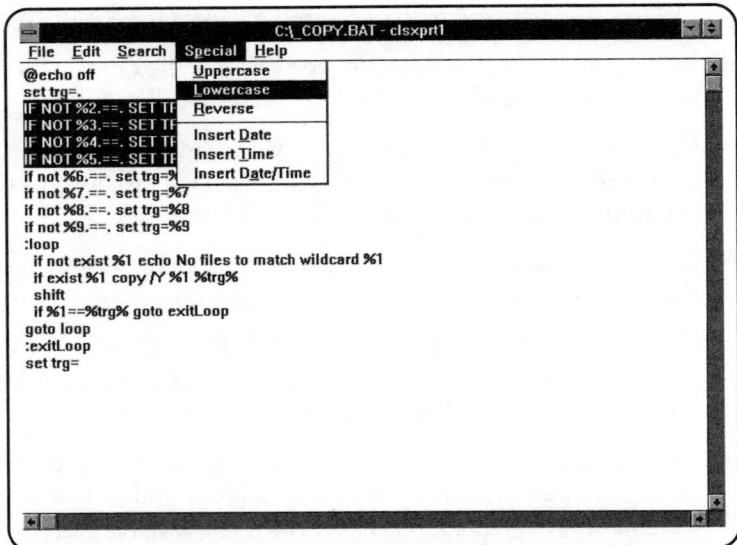

Figure 11.2. A sample session with the CLSXPRT1.EXE program.

Adding a Class

Now evolve the last programming project to create program CLSXPRT2.EXE by adding a new menu option in the Special menu selection. This option pops up a dialog box that enables you to select the date (MM/DD/YYYY, DD/MM/YYYY, and YYYY/MM/DD) and time formats (24 hours or AM/PM). The new program supports this dialog box by first creating its resource, then declaring its class, and finally adding the various member functions and declarations to breathe life into the new dialog box.

Here are the general steps to create the project files:

1. Create the files of project CLSXPRT2 using AppExpert as you did with project CLSXPRT1.

2. Use the Resource Workshop to add the menu selection Special and its menu options Lowercase, Uppercase, Reverse, Insert Date, Insert Time, Insert Date/Time, and Preferences.... The last menu option is the one that invokes the dialog box with the date and time format selection. Use the identifiers CM_LOWERCASE, CM_UPPERCASE, CM_REVERSE,

`CM_INSDATE`, `CM_INSTIME`, `CM_INSDATETIME`, and `CM_FORMATDATETIME`, respectively, for these menu options. Insert a separator menu item after the menu options Reverse and Insert Date/Time.

3. Use the Resource Workshop to create the new Borland-style dialog box resource `IDD_DATETIME_DLG` to contain the following controls:

   - The OK and Cancel pushbuttons, which are automatically inserted by the Resource Workshop.

   - The Date Format group box (with the ID `IDD_DATE_GRP`), which contains the following Borland-style radio buttons:

      - The mm/dd/yyyy radio button (with the ID `IDC_MMDDYY_RBT`)

      - The dd/mm/yyyy radio button (with the ID `IDC_DDMMYY_RBT`)

      - The yyyy/mm/dd radio button (with the ID `IDC_YYMMDD_RBT`)

   - The Time Format group box (with the ID `IDC_TIME_GRP`), which contains the following Borland-style radio buttons:

      - The 24 hour radio button (with the ID `IDC_24HR_RBT`)

      - The AM/PM radio button (with the ID `IDC_AMPM_RBT`)

4. Use the ClassExpert to add the member functions `CmLowercase`, `CmUppercase`, `CmReverse`, `CmInsertDate`, `CmInsertTime`, `CmInsertDateTime`, and `CmPreferences` to handle these new menu options, respectively.

5. Use the ClassExpert to create the new dialog box class `TFrmtDialog`. To perform this task, move the mouse to the Classes pane of the ClassExpert window, select the class `clsxprt2AboutDlg`, and then click the right mouse button to view the pop-up menu. Select the Create new class... menu option. This option brings up the Add New Class dialog box, which has the following controls:

   - The Base Class drop-down combo list that enables you to choose the base class for the new class. Accept the default selection of `TDialog` as the base class.

   - The Class Name edit box in which you enter the name of the new class. Enter `TFrmtDialog`.

   - The Source File edit box, which contains the name of the implementation file.

- The Header File edit box, which contains the name of the header file for the new class.

- The Dialog Id drop-down combo list, which enables you to choose the ID of the new dialog box.

When you type in the class name, the Add New Class dialog automatically forms the names of the implementation and header files. When you are done, click the OK pushbutton. Figure 11.3 shows a sample session with the Add New Class dialog box. It is worth pointing out that the Add New Class dialog box is context-sensitive. If you select the application class and then invoke it, you see slightly different controls, because ClassExpert assumes you wish to create a window or a control.

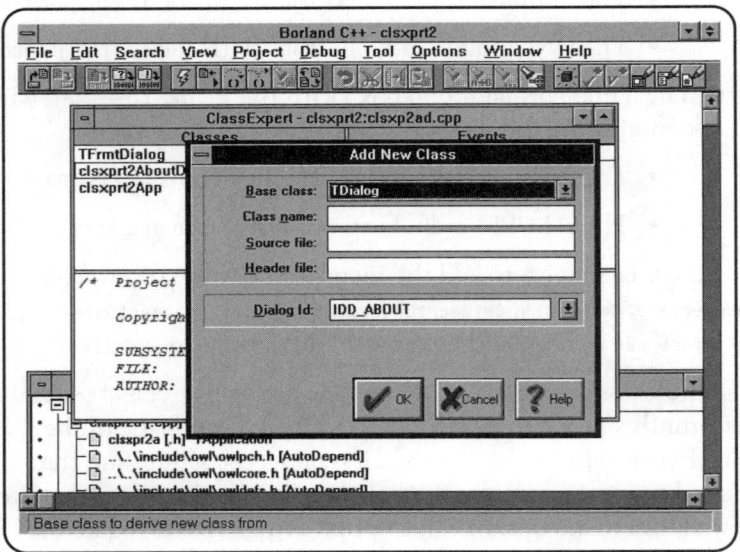

Figure 11.3. A sample session with the Add New Class dialog box.

Let me first indicate the relevant listings I want to present. I will discuss the customizing process for each listing later in this section. Listing 11.6 shows the contents of the CLSXPR2A.DEF definition file. Listing 11.7 contains the source code for the TFRMTDLG.H header file. Listing 11.8 contains the source code for the CLSXPR2A.H header file. Listing 11.9 contains the source code for the CLSXPR2A.RH header file. Listing 11.10 shows the script of the

CLSXPR2A.RC resource file. Listing 11.11 contains the source code for the TFRMTDLG.CPP implementation file. Listing 11.12 contains the source code for the CLSXPR2A.CPP implementation file.

Listing 11.6. The contents of the CLSXPR2A.DEF definition file.

```
;------------------------------------------------
;   Main clsxprt2
;
;   Copyright _ 1993. All Rights Reserved.
;
;   SUBSYSTEM:    clsxprt2.exe Module Definition File
;   FILE:         clsxpr2a.def
;   AUTHOR:
;
;------------------------------------------------

NAME clsxprt2

DESCRIPTION 'clsxprt2 Application - Copyright _ 1993. All Rights Reserved.'
EXETYPE     WINDOWS
CODE        PRELOAD MOVEABLE DISCARDABLE
DATA        PRELOAD MOVEABLE MULTIPLE
HEAPSIZE    4096
STACKSIZE   8192
```

Listing 11.7. The source code for the TFRMTDLG.H header file.

```
#if !defined(__tfrmtdlg_h)          // Sentry, use file only if it's not
                                    // already included.

#define __tfrmtdlg_h

/*  Project clsxprt2

    Copyright _ 1993. All Rights Reserved.

    SUBSYSTEM:    clsxprt2.exe Application
    FILE:         tfrmtdlg.h
    AUTHOR:


    OVERVIEW
    ========
    Class definition for TFrmtDialog (TDialog).
```

continues

LISTING 11.7. CONTINUED

```
*/

#include <owl\owlpch.h>
#pragma hdrstop

#include <owl\dialog.h>

#include "clsxpr2a.rh"            // Definition of all resources.
#include "clsxpr2a.h"

//{{TDialog = TFrmtDialog}}
class TFrmtDialog : public TDialog {
public:
    TFrmtDialog (TWindow* parent, TResId resId = IDD_ABOUT, TModule* module =
➡0);
    virtual ~TFrmtDialog ();
    BOOL IsAmPm;
    clsxprt2App::dateFormat df;

//{{TFrmtDialogVIRTUAL_BEGIN}}
public:
    virtual BOOL EvInitDialog (HWND hWndFocus);
    void CmOk();
//{{TFrmtDialogVIRTUAL_END}}

 // insert declaration of response table
 DECLARE_RESPONSE_TABLE(TFrmtDialog);
};     //{{TFrmtDialog}}


#endif                                   // __tfrmtdlg_h sentry.
```

Listing 11.7 shows the header file TFRMTDLG.H, which contains the declaration for the date/time format dialog box class TFrmtDialog. The ClassExpert utility generated this header file when I created the class TFrmtDialog. In addition, I used ClassExpert to add the member function EvInitDialog to handle initializing the dialog box. I manually added the following:

1. The #include "clsxprt2a.h", to allow the class TFrmtDialog to access a nested enumerated type in the application class.

2. The declaration of member function CmOk to handle pressing the OK button of the dialog box.

3. The Boolean data member IsAmPm, which stores the selection of the time format.

4. The enumerated data member df, which stores the date format. Notice that the enumerated type is clsxprt2App::dateFormat, an export of class clsxprt2App.

5. The declaration of the response table macro.

> **Listing 11.8. The source code for the CLSXPR2A.H header file.**

```
#if !defined(__clsxpr2a_h)          // Sentry, use file only if it's not
                                    already included.

#define __clsxpr2a_h

/*  Project clsxprt2

    Copyright _ 1993. All Rights Reserved.

    SUBSYSTEM:    clsxprt2.exe Application
    FILE:         clsxpr2a.h
    AUTHOR:


    OVERVIEW
    ========
    Class definition for clsxprt2App (TApplication).
*/


#include <owl\owlpch.h>
#pragma hdrstop

#include <owl\editfile.h>
#include <owl\opensave.h>

#include "clsxpr2a.rh"             // Definition of all resources.


//{{TApplication = clsxprt2App}}
class clsxprt2App : public TApplication {

  // declare friend class

private:
    TEditFile *Client;                        // Client window for the
                                              frame.
```

continues

LISTING 11.8. CONTINUED

```
    TOpenSaveDialog::TData FileData;                    // Data to control open
                                                        saveas standard
                                                        dialog.

public:
    // new nested enumerated type
    enum dateFormat { mmddyy, ddmmyy, yymmdd };

    clsxprt2App ();
    virtual ~clsxprt2App ();

    void OpenFile (const char *fileName = 0);
//{{clsxprt2AppVIRTUAL_BEGIN}}
public:
    virtual void InitMainWindow();
//{{clsxprt2AppVIRTUAL_END}}

//{{clsxprt2AppRSP_TBL_BEGIN}}
protected:
    BOOL IsAmPm;
    dateFormat df;

    void CmFileNew ();
    void CmFileOpen ();
    void CmFileClose ();
    void CmHelpAbout ();
    void CmInsertDateTime ();
    void CmInsertTime ();
    void CmLowercase ();
    void CmReverse ();
    void CmUppercase ();
    void CmDateTimeFormat ();
    void CmPreferences ();
    void CmInsertDate ();
//{{clsxprt2AppRSP_TBL_END}}
  DECLARE_RESPONSE_TABLE(clsxprt2App);
};    //{{clsxprt2App}}


#endif                                        // __clsxpr2a_h sentry.
```

Listing 11.8 shows the CLSXPR2A.H header file, which contains the declaration of the application class clsxprt2App. The AppExpert utility generated most of the statements in this file. The ClassExpert utility inserted the set of member functions Cm*xxxx*, which deal with the options of the Special menu selection. I manually added the following items:

1. The public declaration of the nested enumerated type `dateFormat`. This type models the three date formats.

2. The Boolean data member `IsAmPm`, which stores the time format.

3. The enumerated data member `df`, which stores the date format.

LISTING 11.9. THE PARTIAL SOURCE CODE FOR THE CLSXPR2A.RH HEADER FILE.

```
//#if !defined(__clsxpr2a_rh)              // Sentry use file only if it's not
                                           // already included.

//#define __clsxpr2a_rh

/*  Main clsxprt2

    Copyright _ 1993. All Rights Reserved.

    SUBSYSTEM:    clsxprt2.exe Application
    FILE:         clsxpr2a.rh
    AUTHOR:


    OVERVIEW
    ========
    Constant definitions for all resources defined in clsxpr2a.rc.
*/



//
// IDHELP BorButton for BWCC dialogs.
//
#define IDHELP               998           // Id of help button



//
// Application specific definitions:
//
#define IDI_SDIAPPLICATION   1001          // Application icon

#define SDI_MENU             100           // Menu resource ID and Accel-
                                           // erator IDs



//
// CM_FILEnnnn commands (include\owl\editfile.rh except for CM_FILEPRINTPREVIEW)
//
#define CM_FILENEW           24331         // SDI New
#define CM_FILEOPEN          24332         // SDI Open
```

continues

LISTING 11.9. CONTINUED

```
#define CM_FILECLOSE        24339
#define CM_FILESAVE         24333
#define CM_FILESAVEAS       24334


//
// Window commands (include\owl\windows.rh)
//
#define CM_EXIT             24310


//
// CM_EDITnnnn commands (include\owl\edit.rh)
//
#define CM_EDITUNDO         24321
#define CM_EDITCUT          24322
#define CM_EDITCOPY         24323
#define CM_EDITPASTE        24324
#define CM_EDITDELETE       24325
#define CM_EDITCLEAR        24326


//
// Search menu commands (include\owl\editsear.rh)
//
#define CM_EDITFIND         24351
#define CM_EDITREPLACE      24352
#define CM_EDITFINDNEXT     24353


//
// Special menu commands
//
#define CM_LOWERCASE        300
#define CM_UPPERCASE        301
#define CM_REVERSE          302
#define CM_INSDATE          303
#define CM_INSTIME          304
#define CM_INSDATETIME      305
#define CM_DATETIMEFORMAT   306

#define IDD_DATETIME_DLG    400
#define IDC_MMDDYY_RBT      401
#define IDC_DDMMYY_RBT      402
#define IDC_YYMMDD_RBT      403
#define IDC_24HR_RBT        404
#define IDC_AMPM_RBT        405
#define IDC_TIME_GRP        406
#define IDC_DATE_GRP        407
```

```
//
// Help menu commands.
//
#define CM_HELPABOUT            24389


//
// About Dialogs
//
.
.
.
//#endif          // __clsxpr2a_rh sentry.
```

The resource header file in Listing 11.9 (which is a *partial* listing) shows the CM_*XXXX*, IDD_DATETIME_DLG, and IDC_*XXXX*_RBT, and IDC_*XXXX*_GRP identifiers for the new menu options and the new dialog box resource. The Resource Workshop added these identifiers. The remaining statements are the product of AppExpert.

LISTING 11.10. THE PARTIAL SCRIPT OF THE CLSXPR2A.RC RESOURCE FILE.

```
/*  Main clsxprt2

    Copyright _ 1993. All Rights Reserved.

    SUBSYSTEM:    clsxprt2.exe Application
    FILE:         clsxpr2a.rc
    AUTHOR:


    OVERVIEW
    ========
    All resources defined here.
*/

#if !defined(WORKSHOP_INVOKED)
#include <windows.h>
#endif
#include "clsxpr2a.rh"

SDI_MENU MENU
{
 POPUP "&File"
 {
  MENUITEM "&New", CM_FILENEW
  MENUITEM "&Open...", CM_FILEOPEN
```

continues

LISTING 11.10. CONTINUED

```
 MENUITEM "&Close", CM_FILECLOSE
 MENUITEM SEPARATOR
 MENUITEM "&Save", CM_FILESAVE, GRAYED
 MENUITEM "Save &As...", CM_FILESAVEAS, GRAYED
 MENUITEM SEPARATOR
 MENUITEM "E&xit\tAlt+F4", CM_EXIT
}

POPUP "&Edit"
{
 MENUITEM "&Undo\tAlt+BkSp", CM_EDITUNDO, GRAYED
 MENUITEM SEPARATOR
 MENUITEM "Cu&t\tShift+Del", CM_EDITCUT, GRAYED
 MENUITEM "&Copy\tCtrl+Ins", CM_EDITCOPY, GRAYED
 MENUITEM "&Paste\tShift+Ins", CM_EDITPASTE, GRAYED
 MENUITEM SEPARATOR
 MENUITEM "Clear &All\tCtrl+Del", CM_EDITCLEAR, GRAYED
 MENUITEM "&Delete\tDel", CM_EDITDELETE, GRAYED
}

POPUP "&Search"
{
 MENUITEM "&Find...", CM_EDITFIND, GRAYED
 MENUITEM "&Replace...", CM_EDITREPLACE, GRAYED
 MENUITEM "&Next\aF3", CM_EDITFINDNEXT, GRAYED
}

POPUP "S&pecial"
{
 MENUITEM "&Uppercase", CM_UPPERCASE
 MENUITEM "&Lowercase", CM_LOWERCASE
 MENUITEM "&Reverse", CM_REVERSE
 MENUITEM SEPARATOR
 MENUITEM "Insert &Date", CM_INSDATE
 MENUITEM "Insert &Time", CM_INSTIME
 MENUITEM "Insert Date/Time", CM_INSDATETIME
 MENUITEM SEPARATOR
 MENUITEM "&Preferences...", CM_DATETIMEFORMAT
}

POPUP "&Help"
{
 MENUITEM "&About...", CM_HELPABOUT
}

}
```

```
// Accelerator table for short-cut to menu commands. (include\owl\editfile.rc)
SDI_MENU ACCELERATORS
BEGIN
  VK_DELETE, CM_EDITCUT, VIRTKEY, SHIFT
  VK_INSERT, CM_EDITCOPY, VIRTKEY, CONTROL
  VK_INSERT, CM_EDITPASTE, VIRTKEY, SHIFT
  VK_DELETE, CM_EDITCLEAR, VIRTKEY, CONTROL
  VK_BACK,   CM_EDITUNDO, VIRTKEY, ALT
  VK_F3,     CM_EDITFINDNEXT, VIRTKEY
END


//
// Table of help hints displayed in the status bar.
//
.
.
.
#endif

IDD_DATETIME_DLG DIALOG 55, 37, 189, 124
STYLE DS_MODALFRAME ¦ WS_POPUP ¦ WS_VISIBLE ¦ WS_CAPTION ¦ WS_SYSMENU
CLASS "bordlg"
CAPTION "Date & Time Formats"
FONT 8, "MS Sans Serif"
{
 CONTROL "", -1, "BorShade", BSS_HDIP ¦ BSS_LEFT ¦ WS_CHILD ¦
        WS_VISIBLE, 0, 83, 189, 3
 CONTROL "", IDOK, "BorBtn", BS_DEFPUSHBUTTON ¦ WS_CHILD ¦ WS_VISIBLE ¦
        WS_TABSTOP, 48, 92, 37, 25
 CONTROL "", IDCANCEL, "BorBtn", BS_PUSHBUTTON ¦ WS_CHILD ¦ WS_VISIBLE ¦
        WS_TABSTOP, 104, 92, 37, 25
 CONTROL "&mm/dd/yyyy", IDC_MMDDYY_RBT, "BorRadio", BS_AUTORADIOBUTTON ¦
         WS_CHILD ¦ WS_VISIBLE ¦ WS_TABSTOP,
          13, 27, 57, 12
 CONTROL "&dd/mm/yyyy", IDC_DDMMYY_RBT, "BorRadio", BS_AUTORADIOBUTTON ¦
        WS_CHILD ¦ WS_VISIBLE ¦ WS_TABSTOP,
        13, 44, 57, 12
 CONTROL "&yyyy/mm/dd", IDC_YYMMDD_RBT, "BorRadio", BS_AUTORADIOBUTTON ¦
        WS_CHILD ¦ WS_VISIBLE ¦ WS_TABSTOP, 13, 60, 57, 12
 GROUPBOX " Time Format", IDC_TIME_GRP, 97, 13, 63, 60, BS_GROUPBOX
 GROUPBOX " Date Format", IDC_DATE_GRP, 9, 9, 69, 73, BS_GROUPBOX
 CONTROL "24 Hour", IDC_24HR_RBT, "BorRadio", BS_AUTORADIOBUTTON ¦
        WS_CHILD ¦ WS_VISIBLE ¦ WS_TABSTOP, 108, 32, 44, 11
 CONTROL "AM/PM", IDC_AMPM_RBT, "BorRadio", BS_AUTORADIOBUTTON ¦
        WS_CHILD ¦ WS_VISIBLE ¦ WS_TABSTOP, 108, 55, 44, 11
}
```

Listing 11.10 shows the *partial* script statements of the resource file CLSXPR2A.RC. The listing shows the menu resource and the custom dialog box resource.

LISTING 11.11. THE SOURCE CODE FOR THE TFRMTDLG.CPP IMPLEMENTATION FILE.

```
/*  Project clsxprt2

    Copyright _ 1993. All Rights Reserved.

    SUBSYSTEM:    clsxprt2.exe Application
    FILE:         tfrmtdlg.cpp
    AUTHOR:


    OVERVIEW
    ========
    Source file for implementation of TFrmtDialog (TDialog).
*/

#include <owl\owlpch.h>
#pragma hdrstop

#include "tfrmtdlg.h"


//{{TFrmtDialog Implementation}}

DEFINE_RESPONSE_TABLE1(TFrmtDialog, TDialog)
    EV_COMMAND(IDOK, CmOk),
END_RESPONSE_TABLE;


TFrmtDialog::TFrmtDialog (TWindow* parent, TResId resId, TModule* module):
    TDialog(parent, resId, module)
{
    // INSERT>> Your constructor code here.

}


TFrmtDialog::~TFrmtDialog ()
{
    Destroy();

    // INSERT>> Your destructor code here.

}


BOOL TFrmtDialog::EvInitDialog (HWND hWndFocus)
{
    BOOL result;
```

```
    result = TDialog::EvInitDialog(hWndFocus);

    // INSERT>> Your code here.
    CheckRadioButton(IDC_MMDDYY_RBT, IDC_YYMMDD_RBT,
                     IDC_MMDDYY_RBT);
    CheckRadioButton(IDC_24HR_RBT, IDC_AMPM_RBT,
                     IDC_24HR_RBT);

    return result;
}

void TFrmtDialog::CmOk()
{
    // save date format
    if (IsDlgButtonChecked(IDC_MMDDYY_RBT))
      df = clsxprt2App::mmddyy;
    else if (IsDlgButtonChecked(IDC_DDMMYY_RBT))
      df = clsxprt2App::ddmmyy;
    else
      df = clsxprt2App::yymmdd;

    // save time format
    IsAmPm = (IsDlgButtonChecked(IDC_AMPM_RBT)) ?
                                    TRUE : FALSE;
    TDialog::CmOk();
}
```

Listing 11.11 shows the source code for the TFRMTDLG.CPP implementation file. The ClassExpert utility created this file and added the empty definition of member function EvInitDialog. I manually added the definition of the response table macro, the statements in function EvInitDialog, and the entire member function CmOk.

The member function EvInitDialog initializes the dialog box by performing the following tasks:

- Invokes the function EvInitDialog of the parent class and assigns its result to the local Boolean variable result.

- Clears the radio buttons in the Date Format group box and checks the mm/dd/yyyy radio button. This task uses the member function CheckRadioButton, which is inherited from class TWindow.

- Clears the radio buttons in the Time Format group box and checks the 24-hour radio button. This task uses the inherited member function CheckRadioButton.

- Returns the value in the local variable result.

The member function CmOk responds to clicking the OK pushbutton of the dialog box by performing the following tasks:

- Saves the date format in the data member df. This task uses a multiple-decision if statement to examine each radio button control in the Date Format group box. The if statement invokes the inherited member function IsDlgButtonChecked to determine which radio button is checked.

- Saves the time format in the data member IsAmPm. This task invokes the inherited member function IsDlgButtonChecked to determine if the AM/PM radio button is checked.

- Invokes the function CmOk of the parent class.

Listing 11.12. The source code for the CLSXPR2A.CPP implementation file.

```
/*  Project clsxprt2

    Copyright _ 1993. All Rights Reserved.

    SUBSYSTEM:    clsxprt2.exe Application
    FILE:         clsxpr2a.cpp
    AUTHOR:


    OVERVIEW
    ========
    Source file for implementation of clsxprt2App (TApplication).
*/


#include <owl\owlpch.h>
#pragma hdrstop


#include "clsxpr2a.h"
#include "clsxp2ad.h"                        // Definition of about dialog.

#include "tfrmtdlg.h"
#include <stdio.h>
#include <string.h>
#include <dos.h>

//{{clsxprt2App Implementation}}
```

```
//
// Build a response table for all messages/commands handled
// by the application.
//
DEFINE_RESPONSE_TABLE1(clsxprt2App, TApplication)
//{{clsxprt2AppRSP_TBL_BEGIN}}
    EV_COMMAND(CM_FILENEW, CmFileNew),
    EV_COMMAND(CM_FILEOPEN, CmFileOpen),
    EV_COMMAND(CM_FILECLOSE, CmFileClose),
    EV_COMMAND(CM_HELPABOUT, CmHelpAbout),
    EV_COMMAND(CM_INSDATETIME, CmInsertDateTime),
    EV_COMMAND(CM_INSTIME, CmInsertTime),
    EV_COMMAND(CM_LOWERCASE, CmLowercase),
    EV_COMMAND(CM_REVERSE, CmReverse),
    EV_COMMAND(CM_UPPERCASE, CmUppercase),
    EV_COMMAND(CM_DATETIMEFORMAT, CmPreferences),
    EV_COMMAND(CM_UPPERCASE, CmUppercase),
    EV_COMMAND(CM_REVERSE, CmReverse),
    EV_COMMAND(CM_LOWERCASE, CmLowercase),
    EV_COMMAND(CM_INSTIME, CmInsertTime),
    EV_COMMAND(CM_INSDATE, CmInsertDate),
    EV_COMMAND(CM_INSDATETIME, CmInsertDateTime),
//{{clsxprt2AppRSP_TBL_END}}
END_RESPONSE_TABLE;


//
// FrameWindow must be derived to override Paint for Preview and Print.
//
class SDIDecFrame : public TDecoratedFrame {
public:
    SDIDecFrame (TWindow *parent, const char far *title, TWindow *clientWnd,
    ➡BOOL trackMenuSelection = FALSE, TModule *module = 0) :
            TDecoratedFrame(parent, title, clientWnd, trackMenuSelection,
                ➡module)
        {  }
    ~SDIDecFrame ()
        {  }
};


//////////////////////////////////////////////////////////
// clsxprt2App
// =====
//
clsxprt2App::clsxprt2App () : TApplication("clsxprt2")
{

    // Common file file flags and filters for Open/Save As dialogs. Filename and
      directory are
```

continues

LISTING 11.12. CONTINUED

```
    // computed in the member functions CmFileOpen, and CmFileSaveAs.
    FileData.Flags = OFN_FILEMUSTEXIST ¦ OFN_HIDEREADONLY ¦ OFN_OVERWRITEPROMPT;
    FileData.SetFilter("All Files (*.*)¦*.*¦");

    // INSERT>> Your constructor code here.
    IsAmPm = FALSE;
    df = mmddyy;
}


clsxprt2App::~clsxprt2App ()
{
    // INSERT>> Your destructor code here.

}


/////////////////////////////////////////////////////////
// clsxprt2App
// =====
// Application initialization.
//
void clsxprt2App::InitMainWindow ()
{
    Client = new TEditFile(0, 0, 0);
    SDIDecFrame *frame = new SDIDecFrame(0, GetName(), Client, FALSE);

    nCmdShow = nCmdShow != SW_SHOWMINIMIZED ? SW_SHOWNORMAL : nCmdShow;

    //
    // Assign ICON w/ this application.
    //
    frame->SetIcon(this, IDI_SDIAPPLICATION);

    //
    // Menu associated with window and accelerator table associated with table.
    //
    frame->AssignMenu(SDI_MENU);

    //
    // Associate with the accelerator table.
    //
    frame->Attr.AccelTable = SDI_MENU;


    MainWindow = frame;

}
```

```
//////////////////////////////////////////////////////
// clsxprt2App
// ===========
// Menu File New command
void clsxprt2App::CmFileNew ()
{
    Client->NewFile();
}


//////////////////////////////////////////////////////
// clsxprt2App
// ===========
// Menu File Open command
void clsxprt2App::CmFileOpen ()
{
    //
    // Display standard Open dialog box to select a file name.
    //
    *FileData.FileName = 0;
    if (Client->CanClose())
        if (TFileOpenDialog(MainWindow, FileData).Execute() == IDOK)
            OpenFile();
}


void clsxprt2App::OpenFile (const char *fileName)
{
    if (fileName)
        lstrcpy(FileData.FileName, fileName);

    Client->ReplaceWith(FileData.FileName);
}


//////////////////////////////////////////////////////
// clsxprt2App
// =====
// Menu File Close command
void clsxprt2App::CmFileClose ()
{
    if (Client->CanClose())
            Client->DeleteSubText(0, UINT(-1));
}


//////////////////////////////////////////////////////
// clsxprt2App
// ===========
// Menu Help About clsxprt2.exe command
```

continues

LISTING 11.12. CONTINUED

```
void clsxprt2App::CmHelpAbout ()
{
    //
    // Show the modal dialog.
    //
    clsxprt2AboutDlg(MainWindow).Execute();
}


int OwlMain (int , char* [])
{
    clsxprt2App      App;
    int              result;

    result = App.Run();

    return result;
}

void clsxprt2App::CmInsertTime ()
{
  struct time tm;
  char szStr[41];

  gettime(&tm);
  if (IsAmPm) {
    if (tm.ti_hour == 12)
      sprintf(szStr, "12:%02d:%02d p.m.",
                     tm.ti_min, tm.ti_sec);
    else if (tm.ti_hour > 12)
      sprintf(szStr, "%2d:%02d:%02d p.m.",
                tm.ti_hour - 12, tm.ti_min, tm.ti_sec);
    else
        sprintf(szStr, "%2d:%02d:%02d a.m.",
                tm.ti_hour, tm.ti_min, tm.ti_sec);
  }
  else
    sprintf(szStr, "%2d:%02d:%02d",
                tm.ti_hour, tm.ti_min, tm.ti_sec);
  Client->Insert(szStr);

}


void clsxprt2App::CmLowercase ()
{
  UINT startPos, endPos;
  int numChars;
  char* pszStr;
```

```
  Client->GetSelection(startPos, endPos);
  // is there selected text
  if (startPos < endPos) {
    numChars = endPos - startPos + 1;
    pszStr = new char[numChars+1];
    Client->GetSubText(pszStr, startPos, endPos);
    strlwr(pszStr);
      Client->Insert(pszStr);
    Client->SetSelection(startPos, endPos);
    delete [] pszStr;
  }
  else {
    numChars = Client->GetWindowTextLength();
    pszStr = new char[numChars+1];
    Client->GetSubText(pszStr, 0, (UINT)numChars);
    strlwr(pszStr);
    Client->DeleteSubText(0, (UINT)numChars);
    Client->SetSelection(0, 0);
    Client->Insert(pszStr);
    delete [] pszStr;
  }
}


void clsxprt2App::CmReverse ()
{
  UINT startPos, endPos;
  int numChars;
  char* pszStr;
  char swapChar;

  Client->GetSelection(startPos, endPos);
  // is there selected text
  if (startPos < endPos) {
    numChars = endPos - startPos + 1;
    pszStr = new char[numChars+1];
    Client->GetSubText(pszStr, startPos, endPos);
    for (int i = 0, j = strlen(pszStr)-1; i < j ; i++, j-) {
      swapChar = pszStr[i];
      pszStr[i] = pszStr[j];
      pszStr[j] = swapChar;
    }
      Client->Insert(pszStr);
    Client->SetSelection(startPos, endPos);
    delete [] pszStr;
  }
  else {
    numChars = Client->GetWindowTextLength();
    pszStr = new char[numChars+1];
```

continues

LISTING 11.12. CONTINUED

```
    Client->GetSubText(pszStr, 0, (UINT)numChars);
    for (int i = 0, j = strlen(pszStr)-1; i < j ; i++, j—) {
      swapChar = pszStr[i];
      pszStr[i] = pszStr[j];
      pszStr[j] = swapChar;
    }
    Client->DeleteSubText(0, (UINT)numChars);
    Client->SetSelection(0, 0);
    Client->Insert(pszStr);
    delete [] pszStr;
  }
}


void clsxprt2App::CmUppercase ()
{
  UINT startPos, endPos;
  int numChars;
  char* pszStr;

  Client->GetSelection(startPos, endPos);
  // is there selected text
  if (startPos < endPos) {
    numChars = endPos - startPos + 1;
    pszStr = new char[numChars+1];
    Client->GetSubText(pszStr, startPos, endPos);
    strupr(pszStr);
    Client->Insert(pszStr);
    Client->SetSelection(startPos, endPos);
    delete [] pszStr;
  }
  else {
    numChars = Client->GetWindowTextLength();
    pszStr = new char[numChars+1];
    Client->GetSubText(pszStr, 0, (UINT)numChars);
    strupr(pszStr);
    Client->DeleteSubText(0, (UINT)numChars);
    Client->SetSelection(0, 0);
    Client->Insert(pszStr);
    delete [] pszStr;
  }
}

void clsxprt2App::CmPreferences ()
{
  TFrmtDialog* pDlg = new TFrmtDialog(Client,
                          TResID(IDD_DATETIME_DLG));
```

```
  pDlg->EnableTransfer();
  if (pDlg->Execute() == IDOK) {
    // save time format
    IsAmPm = pDlg->IsAmPm;
    // save date format
    df = pDlg->df;
  }
}


void clsxprt2App::CmInsertDateTime ()
{
  struct date dt;
  struct time tm;
  char szStr[41];

  getdate(&dt);
  switch (df) {
    case mmddyy:
        sprintf(szStr, "%2d/%02d/%4d ",
            dt.da_mon, dt.da_day, dt.da_year);
        break;
    case ddmmyy:
        sprintf(szStr, "%2d/%02d/%4d ",
            dt.da_day, dt.da_mon, dt.da_year);
        break;
    default:
        sprintf(szStr, "%4d/%02d/%02d ",
            dt.da_year, dt.da_day, dt.da_mon);
        break;
  }
  Client->Insert(szStr);

  gettime(&tm);
  if (IsAmPm) {
    if (tm.ti_hour == 12)
      sprintf(szStr, "12:%02d:%02d p.m.",
                    tm.ti_min, tm.ti_sec);
    else if (tm.ti_hour > 12)
      sprintf(szStr, "%2d:%02d:%02d p.m.",
                tm.ti_hour - 12, tm.ti_min, tm.ti_sec);
    else
        sprintf(szStr, "%2d:%02d:%02d a.m.",
                tm.ti_hour, tm.ti_min, tm.ti_sec);
  }
  else
    sprintf(szStr, "%2d:%02d:%02d",
                tm.ti_hour, tm.ti_min, tm.ti_sec);
  Client->Insert(szStr);
```

continues

Listing 11.12. continued

```
}

void clsxprt2App::CmInsertDate ()
{
  struct date dt;
  char szStr[41];

  getdate(&dt);
  switch (df) {
    case mmddyy:
        sprintf(szStr, "%2d/%02d/%4d",
            dt.da_mon, dt.da_day, dt.da_year);
        break;
    case ddmmyy:
        sprintf(szStr, "%2d/%02d/%4d",
            dt.da_day, dt.da_mon, dt.da_year);
        break;
    default:
        sprintf(szStr, "%4d/%02d/%02d",
            dt.da_year, dt.da_day, dt.da_mon);
        break;
  }
  Client->Insert(szStr);

}
```

Listing 11.12 shows the CLSXPR2AA.CPP implementation file. The AppExpert utility generated this file. The ClassExpert utility added the response table macro and the minimal definitions of the set of CmXXXX member functions that respond to the options of the Special menu selection. I inserted the statements in these member functions and added the #include directives to include files TFRMTDLG.H, STDIO.H, STRING.H, and DOS.H.

The member functions CmLowercase, CmUppercase, and CmReverse are identical to those in file CLSXPR1AA.CPP (in Listing 11.5). The member functions CmInsertTime, CmInsertDate, and CmInsertDateTime are expanded versions of their counterparts in Listing 11.5. This extension is due to the fact that these member functions use the data members IsAmPm and df to select the time and date format and create the string image of the date and/or time accordingly.

The most relevant member function in Listing 11.12 is function CmPreferences. This function performs the following tasks:

- Creates the instance pDlg of class TFrmtDialog. The parent window of this dialog box is the member client (which accesses the client window). The resource ID for this dialog box is IDD_DATETIME_FLG.

- Executes the dialog box instance by sending it the C++ message Execute and performs the subsequent tasks if the message returns IDOK.

- Copies the value of the dialog's data member IsAmPm to the application's data member IsAmPm.

- Copies the value of the dialog's data member df to the application's data member df.

Compile and run the CLSXPRT2.EXE program. Invoke the dialog box for selecting the date and time formats (see Figure 11.4). Then create a new text file and test inserting the date and/or time.

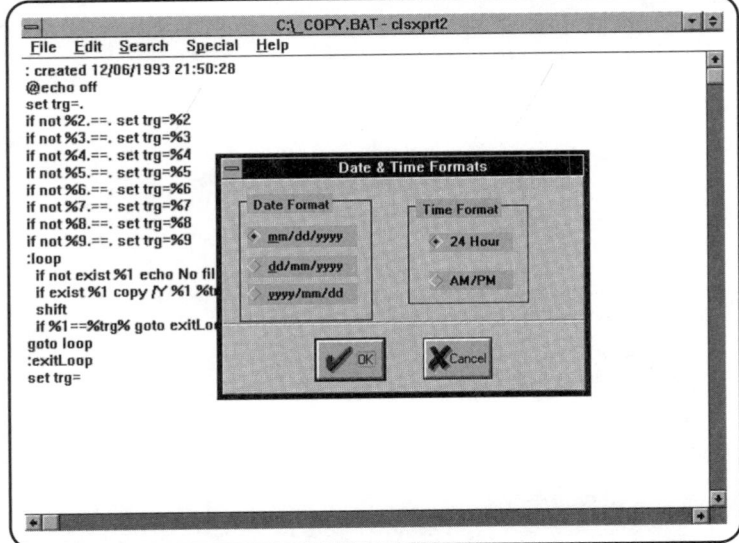

Figure 11.4. A sample session with program CLSXPRT2.EXE.

SUMMARY

This chapter presented the ClassExpert utility that enables you to fine-tune and customize OWL-based Windows applications generated by AppExpert.

You learned about the following topics:

- Invoking the ClassExpert utility from an option in the View menu selection. The ClassExpert displays a window with the Classes pane, Events pane, and the editor pane. The Classes pane lists the current project classes. The Events pane shows an outline for the various events related to the currently selected class. The editor pane lists the implementation file for the current class.

- ClassExpert allows you to add new member functions to a class created by AppExpert. This task involves adding the declaration of the member functions in the targeted class, adding the response table macros for the new functions, and inserting empty definitions of these functions.

- ClassExpert enables you to add a new class to the project created by AppExpert. This task involves creating the header and implementation files for the new class and placing the declaration and definition of the class in these files, respectively.

Windows Programming Tools

The Borland C++ 4.0 package contains several DOS-based and Windows-based programming tools. These tools assist in the various aspects of developing, debugging, and maintaining programs. This chapter presents the following Windows programming tools:

- The WinSight utility, which monitors the various kinds of Windows messages

- The WinSpector utility, which performs post-mortem analysis

- The Grep utility

THE WINSIGHT UTILITY

The WinSight utility is a debugging tool that acquires information related to windows, window classes (that is, categories of windows), and messages. It offers insights about how to create and use windows and window classes, as well as about the messages that the windows receive. WinSight intercepts and displays information about messages. Keep in mind that WinSight acts as a kind of spy; with WinSight you can look at information without changing it and without redirecting it away from its intended target.

WinSight can trace messages by window, by window class, by type of message, or by any combination of these three.

Getting Started

You can start the WinSight utility by clicking the WinSight icon located in the Borland C++ 4.0 folder. You can launch it also from within the IDE by selecting the WinSight menu option from the Tool menu selection. Finally, you can launch it also from the Windows File Manager (or any similar file managing shell). To view the main window in its default configuration, click twice on the WinSight icon. You will see all the currently active windows. Table 12.1 lists the mouse functions, along with the equivalent menu items and keyboard input.

TABLE 12.1. MOUSE FUNCTIONS WITH THEIR EQUIVALENT MENU ITEMS AND KEYBOARD INPUT.			
Action	Using the mouse	Using the keyboard	Using the menus
Choose item	Left click	↑ or ↓	
Move selection bar		Ctrl+↑ or Ctrl+↓	
Toggle highlighted item	Ctrl+Left click	Spacebar	
Display details of item	Left double-click	Enter	Spy I Open detail

Action	Using the mouse	Using the keyboard	Using the menus
Expand window tree		+	Tree | Expand one level
Expand branch	Right-click on <->	*	Tree | Expand branch
Collapse window tree	Left-click on <+>	-	Tree | Collapse branch
Fully expand tree		Ctrl+*	Tree | Expand all
Activate next pane		Tab or F6	
Activate previous pane		Shift+Tab or Shift+F6	

To exit the WinSight utility, close the WinSight icon the same way you close the icon of a minimized program.

Selecting a View

With WinSight, you can select from different views and levels of information for message tracing. The WinSight window can display up to three panes: a Window Tree pane, a Class List pane, and a Message Trace pane. You can choose to view any or all of these panes. Here is what each pane shows:

- The Window Tree pane displays the hierarchy of windows on the desktop. This is the default pane displayed by WinSight.

- The Class List pane shows all the currently registered window classes.

- The Message Trace pane displays the information regarding messages acquired by specific windows and window classes.

You can use the View menu display or you can hide these panes at your discretion. Hiding a pane does not make it lose its data, because that information still resides in memory.

You can arrange multiple panes either so they are stacked one on top of another or so they are side by side. The View menu selection contains the Split Vertical and Split Horizontal menu options to change back and forth between the vertical and horizontal arrangements, respectively.

With WinSight you can extract more detailed information within the Window Tree and the Class List panes. The Open Detail option in the Spy menu selection displays details on the selected windows or the selected classes.

To display more detailed information for the window tree, double-click an item or highlight it and press Enter. This action brings up the Window Detail window, which reveals detailed information regarding the targeted window and its class.

To display more detailed information for the class list, double-click an item or highlight it and press Enter. This action invokes the Class Detail window, which discloses more detailed information regarding the targeted window class.

Working with the Window Tree

The Window Tree pane displays, in an outline format, the hierarchy of all available windows. Using the displayed information, you may elect to carry out any one of the following tasks:

1. To select the windows whose messages you want to monitor.

2. To notice which windows are obtaining messages.

3. To monitor the status of both hidden and visible windows.

4. To conclude what windows actually exist.

A small diamond shape is associated with every Window Tree pane entry. This shape indicates whether a window has child windows. An empty diamond indicates that the window has no child windows. When the diamond contains a plus sign, the associated window has child windows that are currently hidden. By contrast, when the diamond contains a minus sign, the associated window has child windows that are visible.

The Format of the Window Tree Display

The Window Tree pane shows you the existing windows, along with their parent windows, child windows, and sibling windows. The Window Tree pane uses the following display format:

```
Tree Handle {Class} Module Position "Title"
```

The *Handle* item is the window handle. The *Class* item is the name of the window class. The *Module* item is the name of the executable module (either a .DLL file or an .EXE file) that creates the window. The *Position* item is a (xStart,yStart)-(xEnd,yEnd) set of coordinates when the window is visible; otherwise, it is *hidden* when the window is invisible. The *Title* item is the window's title or text.

Manipulating the Window Tree

The basic characteristics of an outline include the ability to expand and collapse nested outline items. The Window Tree is no exception. To reveal the immediate child windows, click the left mouse button on the diamond shape that appears immediately next to the targeted window; alternatively, you can press the + key. This action displays all of the child windows. To reveal all of the descendent child windows, click the diamond with the right mouse button. This action displays the immediate child windows, along with their own children and with their children's children, and so forth.

To collapse the Window Tree outline and hide all of the child windows for a particular window, click the diamond located next to the targeted window; alternatively, press the − key. This action hides the child windows and all of their descendent child windows.

Now test locating the window of the SECAPP.EXE program that I presented in Chapter 1. Figure 12.1 shows a sample Trace Message pane. The currently selected window belongs to the SECAPP.EXE program. To view the full information for a window, select that window and either press Enter or double-click the left mouse button. Figure 12.2 shows a sample window that contains the details for the window of the SECAPP.EXE program.

Finding a Window

WinSight supports a special operating mode for locating a window. This search mode works in two ways. You can highlight a selected window in the Window Tree, or you can distinguish the line in the Window Tree by moving the mouse over that window.

To locate a window, invoke the Find Window option in the Spy menu selection. This action puts WinSight in the window-locating mode. While WinSight is in this mode, move the mouse over any window in the desktop. The WinSight utility responds by displaying a thick border around the window below the mouse and by selecting that window's entry in the Window Tree pane.

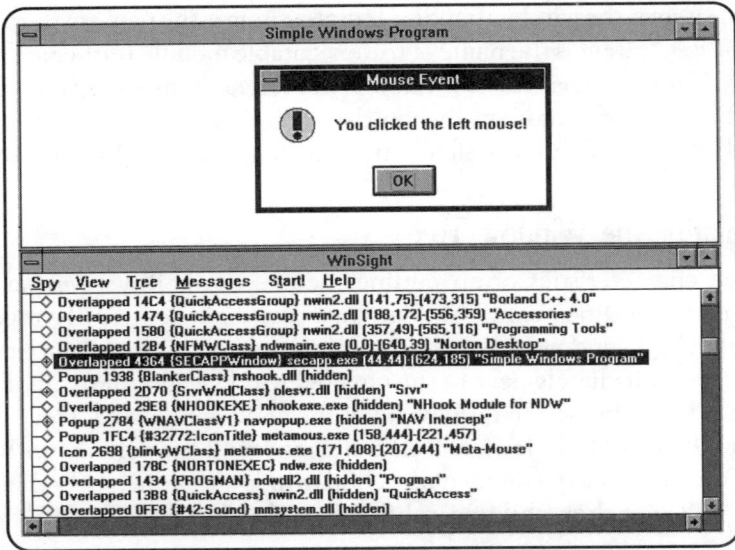

Figure 12.1. A sample Message Trace pane.

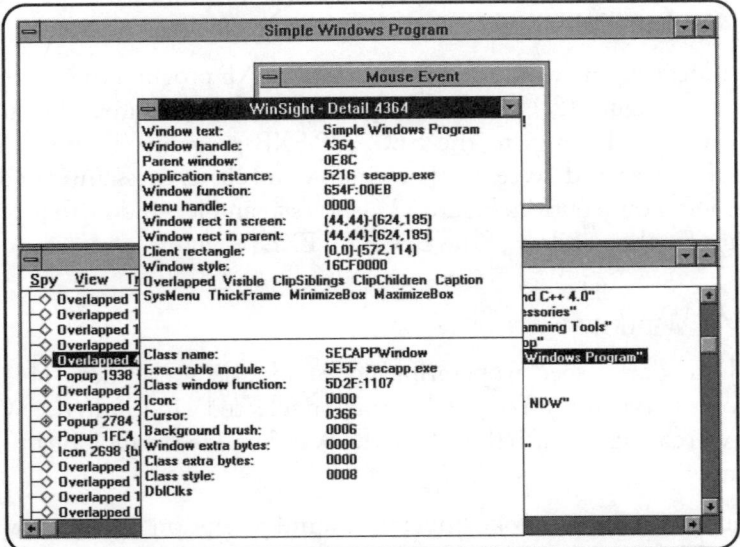

Figure 12.2. A sample detailed window for program SECAPP.EXE.

The alternate way for locating a window is to select a window in the Window Tree pane and then invoke the Find Window option in the Spy menu selection. The WinSight utility places a thick border around the frame of the selected window.

To exit the window-locating mode, you can use one of the following:

- Press the Esc key
- Press the Enter key
- Click the mouse button

Spying on Windows

With the WinSight utility, you can track the messages that are sent to a window. First, select that window and then choose the Selected Windows option in the Messages menu selection. If you choose another window in the Window Tree pane, WinSight starts tracing the newly selected window instead of the previously selected window. When you select a window to trace, the WinSight utility displays the Message Trace pane if it is not yet visible.

The WinSight utility offers the All Windows option in the Messages menu selection; with this option you can trace all the messages sent to all of the windows. When you choose to monitor a window, the WinSight utility shows the Message Trace pane if it is not yet visible.

To turn off tracing messages, select the menu option Trace off in the Messages menu selection. This option disables message tracing but maintains the visibility of the Message Trace pane.

Now trace all the messages sent to the window of the SECAPP.EXE program. Select the window of the SECAPP.EXE program in the Window Tree pane. Invoke Options... in the Messages menu selection. This option brings up the Message Trace Options dialog box. Check the All Messages check box to trace all of the messages. Exit the dialog box and click the Start! menu selection. Move the mouse to the window of the SECAPP.EXE program and click the left mouse button. This action invokes a simple message box with an OK button. Click the OK button. Now click the right mouse button. This action invokes a message box that asks you if you wish to close the application. Click the Yes button. Figure 12.3 shows part of the long list of traced messages. The top message shown in the figure is the Windows message WM_LBUTTONDOWN. The latter messages in the Message Trace pane deal with closing and destroying the window of the SECAPP.EXE program.

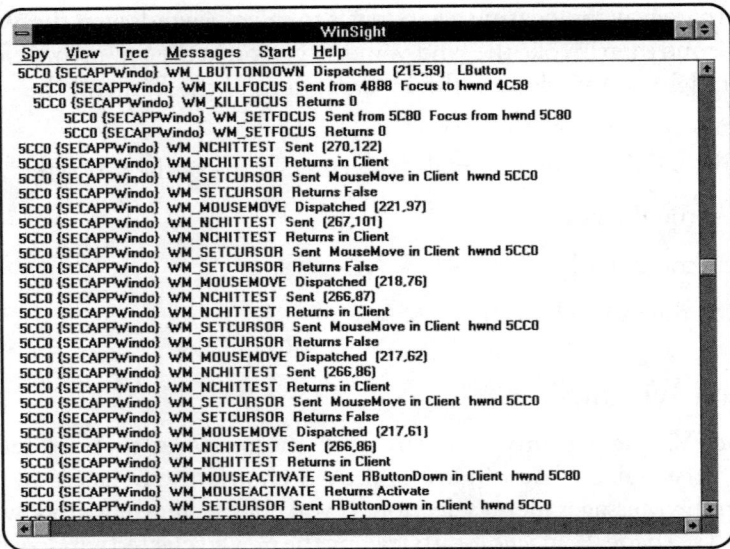

Figure 12.3. The sample messages sent to the window of program SECAPP.EXE.

Working with Classes

The WinSight utility provides the option of tracing messages to a particular class (read it as *category*) of windows, instead of to a specific window. This genre of message tracing employs the Class List pane.

The Class List pane appears similar to, but simpler than, the Window Tree pane. This simplicity is caused by the fact that the class list is not hierarchical like the Window List. Each entry in the Class List pane displays a currently registered window class. When you choose an entry, press Enter or double-click it to view the full details for that class. Each entry in the Class List pane has a diamond shape located to its left. This diamond symbol works the same as in the Window Tree pane.

Tracing the messages to a window class is quite simple. You can choose the Selected Classes menu option in the Messages menu selection to trace only those messages sent to a specific window class. When you elect to trace a window class, the WinSight utility displays the Message Trace pane if it is not yet visible.

When you choose a different window class, WinSight begins tracing the messages to the newly selected class instead of the previous selection.

The entries in the Class List pane have the following display format:

Class (Module) Function Styles

The *Class* item is the class name. This name is sometimes a numeric value. The *Module* item is the name of the executable module (a .DLL or an .EXE file) that registers the class. The *Function* item is the address of the class window function. The *Styles* item is a list of bitwise ORed cs_*xxxx* constants.

Figure 12.4 shows a sample Class List pane. To view the full information for a window class, select that window class and either press Enter or double-click the left mouse button. Figure 12.5 shows a sample window containing the details for a window.

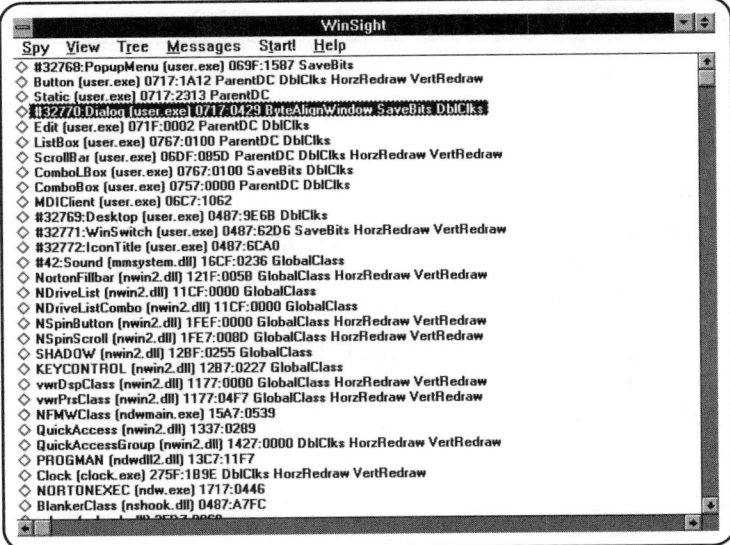

Figure 12.4. A sample Class List pane.

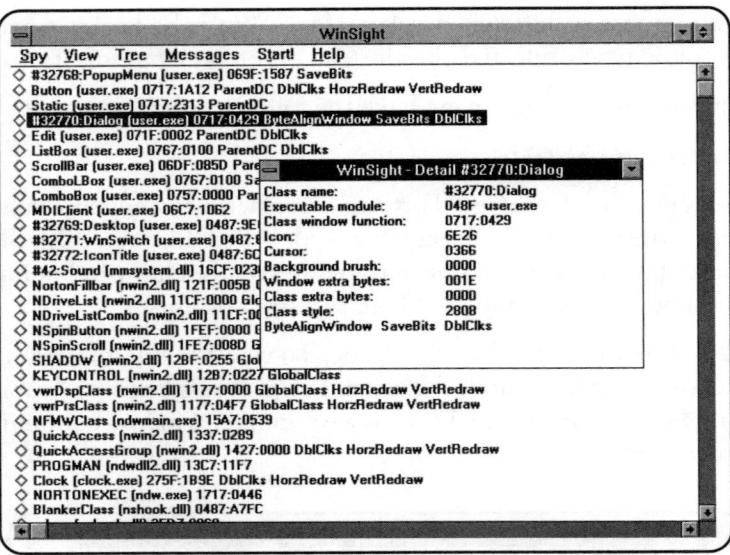

Figure 12.5. A sample detailed window class.

Selecting Traced Messages

The WinSight utility presents yet another versatile technique for tracing messages. With this technique you can choose a particular kind of message to trace, without being limited to a specific window or even a window class.

To select the category of messages to trace, invoke the menu option Options... in the menu selection Messages. This option brings up the Message Trace Options dialog box, shown in Figure 12.6. This dialog box enables you to select from any or all of the following kinds of messages:

- Mouse
- Window
- Input
- System
- Pen
- Initialization
- Clipboard

- DDE

- Nonclient

- Controls

- Multimedia

- Other

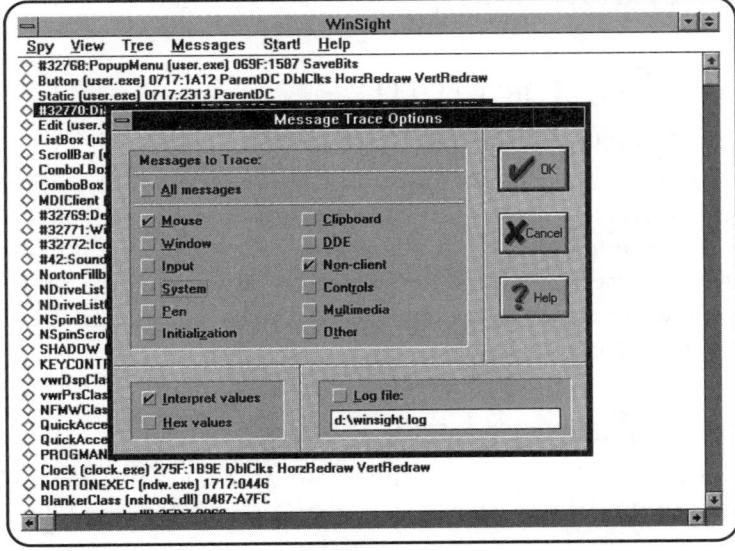

Figure 12.6. The Message Trace Options dialog box.

The dialog box has a check box that enables you to display the values of the wParam and lParam parameters as hexadecimal numbers. Another check box enables you to use a log file. The dialog box contains an edit box where you enter the path and name of the WinSight log file.

The Message Trace pane displays its entries using the following format:

```
Handle ["Title"} ¦ {Class}] Message Status
```

The *Handle* item is the handle of the window that receives the message. The *Title* item is the title or text of the window. If there is no title, the WinSight utility shows the class name, placed inside curly braces. The *Message* item is the message name as defined in the WINDOWS.H header file. The *Status* item is one of the following:

- *Dispatched*: this signals that the message was obtained via the Windows API function `DispatchMessage`.

- *Sent[from XXXX]*: this indicates that the message was obtained via the Windows API function `SendMessage`.

- *Returns*: this signals that the message was received via the `SendMessage` function and is now returning.

- Other information that is specific to each message.

THE WINSPECTOR UTILITY

The Borland C++ 4.0 package offers the WinSpector utility, which intercepts the unrecoverable applications errors (also known by the abbreviation UAE) or the general protected errors (GPE) and writes error-related data in a report log file. You can inquire about the case of the UAE or GPE using the information in the log file. When an exception occurs at runtime, the WinSpector utility shows in the Latest UAE Logged Dialog Box the date and time when the exception occurred.

Invoking the WinSpector Utility

You can invoke the WinSpector utility by using the IDE Tool menu selection or by clicking the WinSpector icon in the Borland C++ 4.0 folder. Once running, the utility shows its own icon on the desktop and may seem inactive. In reality, it is waiting to intercept the next UAE or general protection error. Double-clicking the WinSpector icon brings up the WinSpector dialog box, shown in Figure 12.7. The dialog box shows the current state of the last UAE. Figure 12.7 shows the typical appearance of the WinSpector dialog box with no prior UAE.

Figure 12.7. The WinSpector dialog box.

The Preferences Dialog Box

The Preferences dialog box, shown in Figure 12.8, has the following controls that influence the operations of the WinSpector utility:

- Directory edit box

- Viewer edit box

- Append New Reports diamond-shaped radio button

- Overwrite Previous Report diamond-shaped radio button

- System Information check box

- Summary of AUX check box

- PostMortem Dump check box

- Stack Frame Data check box

- User Comments check box

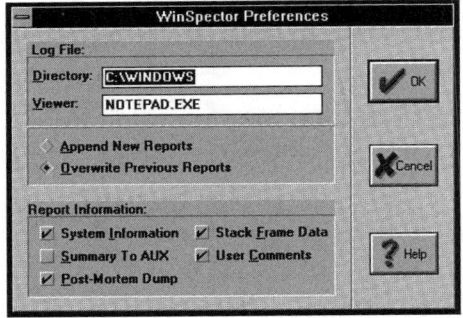

Figure 12.8. The Preferences dialog box.

Each one of these options has an entry in the WINSPCTR.INI file. Thus, you can alter the preferences by editing the WINSPCTR.INI file. The next subsections briefly discuss the features that these controls support.

The Directory Option

With the Directory option, you can determine the path of the log file WINSPCTR.LOG. By default, the log file directory is the Windows directory. In addition, this directory must also be the same one to contain the text editor that views the log file (more about this under Viewer Option).

The Viewer Option

The Viewer option selects the text editor employed in viewing the log file. By default, the Windows NOTEPAD.EXE editor is the viewing program. When you click the View Log pushbutton in the WinSpector dialog box, the file viewer you chose is invoked. This invocation passes the WINSPCTR.LOG filename as a command-line argument to the text editor.

The Append New Reports Option

With the Append New Reports option, you can append new WinSpector reports to the log file while maintaining the previous contents of the log file. When you select this option, WinSpector automatically turns off the Overwrite Previous Report option.

The Overwrite Previous Report Option

The Overwrite Previous Report option ensures that the log file contains only the new error reports. This option is the default setting. When you select this option, WinSight turns off the Append New Report option.

The System Information Option

The System Information option adds the Task List, the Module List, and the information about the USER and GDI heaps to the log file. By default, the setting for this option is checked.

The Summary to AUX Option

The Summary to AUX option signals to the WinSpector utility to generate a short version of the error report to the standard DOS file AUX (named STDAUX in the C library), in addition to writing the full report to the log file. This option needs a device driver that redirects AUX to a second monitor or redirects a terminal connect to AUX. By default, the setting for this option is unchecked.

The PostMortem Dump Option

The PostMortem Dump option creates the binary file WINSPCTR.BIN. The DFA utility (one of the Borland C++ programming utilities) combines the

WINSPCTR.BIN file and the Turbo Debugger .TDS files (which contain debugger information) to create more meaningful information. The DFA utility generates a file that has a stack trace similar to the one in the log file. The main difference is that the DFA utility output contains the names of functions, line numbers, local variables, and global variables.

The Stack Frame Data Option

The Stack Frame Data option generates a verbose stack trace display in the log file. The WinSpector carries out a hexadecimal dump for each stack frame that is 256 bytes or smaller in size. The hexadecimal dump begins at the SS:BP address for that frame. If more than 256 bytes are between two successive stack frames, the memory display is not included for that frame. This data may be used to obtain the values for the parameters that were passed to a function. By default, the setting for this option is unchecked.

The User Comments Option

The User Comments option helps you to type in a short message describing the conditions when the exception was raised. This option invokes a dialog box immediately after the exception log is written, and it enables you to type in your comments about the activities that led to the runtime error. The WinSpector utility then appends these comments to the log file.

Interpreting the Log File

I generated a sample WINSPCTR.LOG log file that contains the following sections:

- The first line
- The second line
- The Disassembly section
- The Stack Trace section
- The Register section
- The Message Queue section
- The Stack Frame Data section
- The Tasks section

- The Modules section
- The USER and GDI heap information section
- The System information section

Because the log file is long, I will present it piecewise when I discuss each section.

The First Line

The first line in the log file contains the date and time for the exception. My sample log file contains the following first line:

```
WinSpector failure report - 10/28/1993  15:12:20
```

The Second Line

The second line of the log file lists the following information:

- The kind of exception identified by a numeric code
- The name of the module that raised the exception
- The logical address
- The physical address
- The current task at the time of the exception

The second line in my sample log file is this:

```
Exception 13 at BC40RTL 0003:19B8 (2E67:19B8)  (TASK=DIALOG5)
```

This line indicates that exception number 13 took place in the BC40RTL module (runtime library) at the logical address 0003:19B8 (which is the physical address 2E67:19B8). The DISALOG5 task was the current task when the exception occurred.

The Disassembly Section

For assembly language gurus, WinSpector provides a collection of assembly language instructions to point out where the exception took place. The first assembly line instruction is the one that generated the error. The log file throws in more assembly line instructions to help you find the offending instruction using a disassembler. The assembly code in my sample log file is as follows:

```
Disassembly:
2E67:19B8  LES     BX,[BP+0A]
2E67:19BB  CMP     AX,WORD PTR ES:[BX+02]
2E67:19BF  JE      19C4
2E67:19C1  JMP     1A6D
2E67:19C4  LES     BX,[BP+06]
```

The first assembly language instruction generates an exception 13, because the value in register BX is greater than that of the segment limit referenced by register ES.

The Stack Trace Section

The first line of the Stack Trace section specifies the function that was executing when the exception took place. Every entry in the Stack Trace section includes the following information:

- The frame number

- The module name

- The name of the nearest function before the address of the error-generating function

- The logical and physical addresses for the stack frame

- The address where the program resumes after the call

Here is the Stack Trace section in my log file:

```
Stack Trace:
0  BC40RTL    <no info>
     CS:IP 0003:19B8 (2E67:19B8)    SS:BP 2287:198E
     C:\BC4\BIN\BC40RTL.DLL

1  BC40RTL    <no info>
     CS:IP 0003:4A80 (2E67:4A80)    SS:BP 2287:19B8
     C:\BC4\BIN\BC40RTL.DLL

2  OWL200     <no info>
     CS:IP 000B:06F6 (21CF:06F6)    SS:BP 2287:19FE
     C:\BC4\BIN\OWL200.DLL

3  USER       <no info>
     CS:IP 0019:039E (0717:039E)    SS:BP 2287:1A16
     C:\WINDOWS\SYSTEM\USER.EXE

4  USER       <no info>
     CS:IP 0019:045C (0717:045C)    SS:BP 2287:1A2E
     C:\WINDOWS\SYSTEM\USER.EXE
```

continues

continued

```
5   USER      <no info>
      CS:IP 0001:2817 (0487:2817)    SS:BP 2287:1A40
      C:\WINDOWS\SYSTEM\USER.EXE

6   OWL200    <no info>
      CS:IP 002C:1606 (20C7:1606)    SS:BP 2287:1A5E
      C:\BC4\BIN\OWL200.DLL

7   OWL200    <no info>
      CS:IP 002C:139F (20C7:139F)    SS:BP 2287:1A8C
      C:\BC4\BIN\OWL200.DLL

8   OWL200    <no info>
      CS:IP 002C:1480 (20C7:1480)    SS:BP 2287:1AB2
      C:\BC4\BIN\OWL200.DLL

9   OWL200    <no info>
      CS:IP 002C:1561 (20C7:1561)    SS:BP 2287:1ADC
      C:\BC4\BIN\OWL200.DLL

10  OWL200    <no info>
      CS:IP 002C:16FA (20C7:16FA)    SS:BP 2287:1B0C
      C:\BC4\BIN\OWL200.DLL

11  OWL200    <no info>
      CS:IP 002C:1928 (20C7:1928)    SS:BP 2287:1B34
      C:\BC4\BIN\OWL200.DLL

12  OWL200    <no info>
      CS:IP 002C:1A23 (20C7:1A23)    SS:BP 2287:1B6C
      C:\BC4\BIN\OWL200.DLL

13  OWL200    <no info>
      CS:IP 002C:196E (20C7:196E)    SS:BP 2287:1B84
      C:\BC4\BIN\OWL200.DLL

14  USER      <no info>
      CS:IP 0001:3AB4 (0487:3AB4)    SS:BP 2287:1BA4
      C:\WINDOWS\SYSTEM\USER.EXE

15  USER      <no info>
      CS:IP 001A:0A32 (071F:0A32)    SS:BP 2287:1BB4
      C:\WINDOWS\SYSTEM\USER.EXE

16  USER      <no info>
      CS:IP 001D:00E6 (0737:00E6)    SS:BP 2287:1BCC
      C:\WINDOWS\SYSTEM\USER.EXE

17  USER      <no info>
      CS:IP 001C:143B (072F:143B)    SS:BP 2287:1BE0
      C:\WINDOWS\SYSTEM\USER.EXE
```

```
18 USER      <no info>
   CS:IP 001A:0D66 (071F:0D66)   SS:BP 2287:1BF4
   C:\WINDOWS\SYSTEM\USER.EXE

19 USER      <no info>
   CS:IP 001A:001A (071F:001A)   SS:BP 2287:1C04
   C:\WINDOWS\SYSTEM\USER.EXE

20 USER      <no info>
   CS:IP 0001:2817 (0487:2817)   SS:BP 2287:1C16
   C:\WINDOWS\SYSTEM\USER.EXE

21 OWL200    <no info>
   CS:IP 002C:1606 (20C7:1606)   SS:BP 2287:1C34
   C:\BC4\BIN\OWL200.DLL

22 OWL200    <no info>
   CS:IP 002C:18BD (20C7:18BD)   SS:BP 2287:1C66
   C:\BC4\BIN\OWL200.DLL

23 OWL200    <no info>
   CS:IP 002C:1928 (20C7:1928)   SS:BP 2287:1C8E
   C:\BC4\BIN\OWL200.DLL

24 OWL200    <no info>
   CS:IP 002C:1A23 (20C7:1A23)   SS:BP 2287:1CC6
   C:\BC4\BIN\OWL200.DLL

25 OWL200    <no info>
   CS:IP 002C:196E (20C7:196E)   SS:BP 2287:1CDE
   C:\BC4\BIN\OWL200.DLL

26 USER      <no info>
   CS:IP 0001:3AB4 (0487:3AB4)   SS:BP 2287:1CFE
   C:\WINDOWS\SYSTEM\USER.EXE

27 USER      <no info>
   CS:IP 0001:19C3 (0487:19C3)   SS:BP 2287:1D12
   C:\WINDOWS\SYSTEM\USER.EXE

28 OWL200    <no info>
   CS:IP 0029:15FF (20DF:15FF)   SS:BP 2287:1D2E
   C:\BC4\BIN\OWL200.DLL

29 OWL200    <no info>
   CS:IP 002C:27AB (20C7:27AB)   SS:BP 2287:1D42
   C:\BC4\BIN\OWL200.DLL

30 OWL200    <no info>
   CS:IP 002C:0E4E (20C7:0E4E)   SS:BP 2287:1D5E
   C:\BC4\BIN\OWL200.DLL
```

continues

continued

```
31 OWL200    <no info>
   CS:IP 002C:2801 (20C7:2801)   SS:BP 2287:1D7C
   C:\BC4\BIN\OWL200.DLL

32 OWL200    <no info>
   CS:IP 002C:2842 (20C7:2842)   SS:BP 2287:1D92
   C:\BC4\BIN\OWL200.DLL

33 OWL200    <no info>
   CS:IP 002C:2750 (20C7:2750)   SS:BP 2287:1DCE
   C:\BC4\BIN\OWL200.DLL

34 OWL200    <no info>
   CS:IP 000B:0EC5 (21CF:0EC5)   SS:BP 2287:1DE6
   C:\BC4\BIN\OWL200.DLL

35 OWL200    <no info>
   CS:IP 000B:0E29 (21CF:0E29)   SS:BP 2287:1DFE
   C:\BC4\BIN\OWL200.DLL

36 OWL200    <no info>
   CS:IP 000B:0564 (21CF:0564)   SS:BP 2287:1E14
   C:\BC4\BIN\OWL200.DLL

37 OWL200    <no info>
   CS:IP 000B:0773 (21CF:0773)   SS:BP 2287:1E54
   C:\BC4\BIN\OWL200.DLL

38 USER      <no info>
   CS:IP 0019:039E (0717:039E)   SS:BP 2287:1E6C
   C:\WINDOWS\SYSTEM\USER.EXE

39 USER      <no info>
   CS:IP 0019:045C (0717:045C)   SS:BP 2287:1E84
   C:\WINDOWS\SYSTEM\USER.EXE

40 USER      <no info>
   CS:IP 0001:3AB4 (0487:3AB4)   SS:BP 2287:1EA4
   C:\WINDOWS\SYSTEM\USER.EXE

41 USER      <no info>
   CS:IP 0018:090A (070F:090A)   SS:BP 2287:1F80
   C:\WINDOWS\SYSTEM\USER.EXE

42 USER      <no info>
   CS:IP 0018:0080 (070F:0080)   SS:BP 2287:1FA6
   C:\WINDOWS\SYSTEM\USER.EXE

43 OWL200    <no info>
   CS:IP 000B:0A28 (21CF:0A28)   SS:BP 2287:1FC2
   C:\BC4\BIN\OWL200.DLL
```

```
44 OWL200    <no info>
   CS:IP 000B:094D (21CF:094D)   SS:BP 2287:2018
   C:\BC4\BIN\OWL200.DLL

45 DIALOG5   <no info>
   CS:IP 0002:0DF4 (2297:0DF4)   SS:BP 2287:2044
   C:\BC4\BC4SAMS\DIALOG5.EXE

46 OWL200    <no info>
   CS:IP 000D:0070 (21BF:0070)   SS:BP 2287:2054
   C:\BC4\BIN\OWL200.DLL

47 OWL200    <no info>
   CS:IP 0013:1353 (218F:1353)   SS:BP 2287:2072
   C:\BC4\BIN\OWL200.DLL

48 OWL200    <no info>
   CS:IP 002C:1473 (20C7:1473)   SS:BP 2287:20A2
   C:\BC4\BIN\OWL200.DLL

49 OWL200    <no info>
   CS:IP 002C:1561 (20C7:1561)   SS:BP 2287:20CC
   C:\BC4\BIN\OWL200.DLL

50 OWL200    <no info>
   CS:IP 0032:0811 (305F:0811)   SS:BP 2287:20E8
   C:\BC4\BIN\OWL200.DLL

51 OWL200    <no info>
   CS:IP 002C:16FA (20C7:16FA)   SS:BP 2287:2118
   C:\BC4\BIN\OWL200.DLL

52 OWL200    <no info>
   CS:IP 002C:1928 (20C7:1928)   SS:BP 2287:2140
   C:\BC4\BIN\OWL200.DLL

53 OWL200    <no info>
   CS:IP 002C:1A23 (20C7:1A23)   SS:BP 2287:2178
   C:\BC4\BIN\OWL200.DLL

54 OWL200    <no info>
   CS:IP 002C:196E (20C7:196E)   SS:BP 2287:2190
   C:\BC4\BIN\OWL200.DLL

55 USER      <no info>
   CS:IP 0001:27BB (0487:27BB)   SS:BP 2287:21AA
   C:\WINDOWS\SYSTEM\USER.EXE

56 OWL200    <no info>
   CS:IP 002E:0ABC (20B7:0ABC)   SS:BP 2287:21CE
   C:\BC4\BIN\OWL200.DLL
```

continues

continued

```
57 OWL200    <no info>
     CS:IP 002E:0F36 (20B7:0F36)    SS:BP 2287:2212
     C:\BC4\BIN\OWL200.DLL

58 OWL200    <no info>
     CS:IP 002E:0820 (20B7:0820)    SS:BP 2287:2266
     C:\BC4\BIN\OWL200.DLL

59 DIALOG5   <no info>
     CS:IP 0002:1061 (2297:1061)    SS:BP 2287:22D2
     C:\BC4\BC4SAMS\DIALOG5.EXE

60 DIALOG5   <no info>
     CS:IP 0003:0061 (228F:0061)    SS:BP 2287:22EC
     C:\BC4\BC4SAMS\DIALOG5.EXE

61 DIALOG5   <no info>
     CS:IP 0001:00B2 (227F:00B2)    SS:BP 2287:22FC
     C:\BC4\BC4SAMS\DIALOG5.EXE
```

The Register Section

The Register section presents the values in the CPU registers when the exception took place. The section also shows the limits and access rights for the CS, DS, ES, and SS registers. Here is the Register section that appears in my log file:

```
Registers:
AX    080F
BX    18F6
CX    1D00
DX    21FF
SI    1D00
DI    00CA
SP    197C
BP    198E
IP    19B8
FL    0203
CS    2E67    Limit: 4C3F   execute/read
DS    2E2F    Limit: 467F   read/write
ES    21FF    Limit: 1FFF   execute/read
SS    2287    Limit: 26FF   read/write
```

The Message Queue Section

The Message Queue section discloses the latest message obtained during processing. The section also contains any messages pending in the queue when the exception took place. The message information includes the following:

- The window handle
- The message ID number
- The `wParam` and `lParam` values that are passed along with the message

The Message Queue section in my sample log is as follows:

```
Message Queue:
Last message retrieved:
  hWnd: 227C  msg: 0111  wParam: 0065  lParam: 00000000
No waiting messages
```

This message queue contains only the last message retrieved.

The Stack Frame Data Section

The Stack Frame Data section shows the dumps of each stack frame that is 256 bytes or smaller. Here is the Stack Frame Data section in my log file:

```
Verbose Stack Trace:
0  BC40RTL    CS:IP 2E67:19B8  SS:BP 2287:198E
   <no info>

0000:    B9 19 80 4A 67 2E F6 18  FF 21 90 E9 76 FC CA 00
0010:    00 1D 00 00 00 00 87 C8  AE 02 4F 08 90 E9 76 FC
0020:    F6 18 FF 21 D9 0B 87 24  E7 2E

. . . . . . . . .

1  BC40RTL    CS:IP 2E67:4A80  SS:BP 2287:19B8
   <no info>

0000:    FF 19 F6 06 CF 21 FE 02  4F 08 4F 16 97 22 D9 0B
0010:    87 24 F6 18 FF 21 00 00  CA 00 00 1D 00 00 00 00
0020:    FE 02 4F 08 4A 1B 8F 36  67 2E 80 06 CF 21 CC 19
0030:    00 00 E7 2E 00 00 00 00  00 00 00 00 25 00 00 00
0040:    00 00 00 00 87 22

. . . . . . . . .

2  OWL200     CS:IP 21CF:06F6  SS:BP 2287:19FE
   <no info>

0000:    17 1A 9E 03 17 07 F8 1D  00 04 CA 00 11 01 00 1D
0010:    B7 07 00 1D 92 06 CF 21

. . . . . . . . .

3  USER       CS:IP 0717:039E  SS:BP 2287:1A16
   <no info>
```

continues

continued

```
0000:     2E 1A 5C 04 F8 1D 00 04  CA 00 11 01 00 1D 87 22
0010:     80 00 F8 1D 7C AF 00 00
```

```
4  USER    CS:IP 0717:045C  SS:BP 2287:1A2E
   <no info>
```

```
0000:     40 1A 17 28 87 04 F8 1D  00 04 CA 00 11 01 00 1D
0010:     E7 2E
```

```
5  USER    CS:IP 0487:2817  SS:BP 2287:1A40
   <no info>
```

```
0000:     5E 1A 06 16 C7 20 F8 1D  00 04 CA 00 11 01 00 1D
0010:     29 04 17 07 F8 1D 80 00  F8 1D 80 00 E7 2E
```

```
6  OWL200   CS:IP 20C7:1606  SS:BP 2287:1A5E
   <no info>
```

```
0000:     8D 1A 9F 13 C7 20 FE 02  4F 08 11 01 CA 00 F8 1D
0010:     00 04 F8 1D 80 00 00 00  CA 00 4F 08 9A 1A 00 00
0020:     00 00 C7 20 E7 2E B3 1A  8C 22 87 22 E7 2E
```

```
7  OWL200   CS:IP 20C7:139F  SS:BP 2287:1A8C
   <no info>
```

```
0000:     B3 1A 80 14 C7 20 FE 02  4F 08 F8 1D 80 00 00 04
0010:     CA 00 FE 02 4F 08 00 00  00 00 A1 10 C7 20 00 04
0020:     FE 02 4F 08 E7 2E
```

```
8  OWL200   CS:IP 20C7:1480  SS:BP 2287:1AB2
   <no info>
```

```
0000:     DD 1A 61 15 C7 20 A2 01  4F 08 F8 1D 80 00 00 04
0010:     FF FF A2 01 4F 08 00 00  00 00 A2 01 4F 08 00 00
0020:     00 00 00 04 A2 01 4F 08  E7 2E
```

```
9  OWL200   CS:IP 20C7:1561  SS:BP 2287:1ADC
   <no info>
```

```
0000:    0D 1B FA 16 C7 20 FE 02  4F 08 FF FF F8 1D 00 04
0010:    F8 1D 80 00 FE 23 7E 23  30 24 10 02 00 00 1F 0E
0020:    9C 03 54 1A 00 00 02 00  0A 17 00 00 22 1A E7 2E
```

- - - - - - - - -

10 OWL200   CS:IP 20C7:16FA SS:BP 2287:1B0C
   <no info>

```
0000:    35 1B 28 19 C7 20 FE 02  4F 08 11 01 CA 00 F8 1D
0010:    00 04 F8 1D 80 00 A2 01  4F 08 0C 00 00 00 5C 06
0020:    4F 08 0C 0E 01 00 E7 2E
```

- - - - - - - - -

11 OWL200   CS:IP 20C7:1928 SS:BP 2287:1B34
   <no info>

```
0000:    6D 1B 23 1A C7 20 FE 02  4F 08 11 01 CA 00 F8 1D
0010:    00 04 F8 1D 80 00 A4 1C  8F 36 67 2E E1 19 C7 20
0020:    42 1B 06 00 E7 2E 00 00  1B 0F 55 0C CE 20 25 00
0030:    00 00 00 00 BF 07 E7 2E
```

- - - - - - - - -

12 OWL200   CS:IP 20C7:1A23 SS:BP 2287:1B6C
   <no info>

```
0000:    85 1B 6E 19 C7 20 FE 02  4F 08 11 01 CA 00 F8 1D
0010:    00 04 F8 1D 80 00 87 22
```

- - - - - - - - -

13 OWL200   CS:IP 20C7:196E SS:BP 2287:1B84
   <no info>

```
0000:    A5 1B B4 3A 87 04 F8 1D  00 04 CA 00 11 01 00 1D
0010:    C8 00 7F 2D F8 1D 80 00  27 27 11 01 00 1D B4 A7
```

- - - - - - - - -

14 USER   CS:IP 0487:3AB4 SS:BP 2287:1BA4
   <no info>

```
0000:    B4 1B 32 0A 1F 07 F8 1D  00 04 CA 00 11 01 00 1D
```

- - - - - - - - -

15 USER   CS:IP 071F:0A32 SS:BP 2287:1BB4
   <no info>

continues

continued

```
0000:      CC 1B E6 00 37 07 00 04  80 00 80 00 0C 00 51 8C
0010:      0F 06 31 1C C3 2E 01 00

- - - - - - - -

16 USER      CS:IP 0737:00E6  SS:BP 2287:1BCC
   <no info>

0000:      E0 1B 3B 14 2F 07 5C 06  4F 08 80 00 80 00 F8 1D
0010:      04 2C 5F 06

- - - - - - - -

17 USER      CS:IP 072F:143B  SS:BP 2287:1BE0
   <no info>

0000:      F4 1B 66 0D 1F 07 5C 06  4F 08 00 00 0C 00 80 00
0010:      F8 1D 00 1D

- - - - - - - -

18 USER      CS:IP 071F:0D66  SS:BP 2287:1BF4
   <no info>

0000:      04 1C 1A 00 5C 06 4F 08  00 00 0C 00 F8 1D 87 22

- - - - - - - -

19 USER      CS:IP 071F:001A  SS:BP 2287:1C04
   <no info>

0000:      16 1C 17 28 87 04 5C 06  4F 08 00 00 0C 00 F8 1D
0010:      E7 2E

- - - - - - - -

20 USER      CS:IP 0487:2817  SS:BP 2287:1C16
   <no info>

0000:      34 1C 06 16 C7 20 5C 06  4F 08 00 00 0C 00 F8 1D
0010:      02 00 1F 07 F8 1D 00 1D  F8 1D 00 1D E7 2E

- - - - - - - -

21 OWL200    CS:IP 20C7:1606  SS:BP 2287:1C34
   <no info>

0000:      67 1C BD 18 C7 20 A2 01  4F 08 0C 00 00 00 5C 06
0010:      4F 08 F8 1D 00 1D 17 07  BA 0C 3F 27 08 00 0D 00
0020:      68 20 0C 00 00 00 A2 01  4F 08 00 00 00 00 05 00
0030:      E7 2E
```

```
- - - - - - - -

22 OWL200    CS:IP 20C7:18BD  SS:BP 2287:1C66
   <no info>

0000:     8F 1C 28 19 C7 20 A2 01  4F 08 0C 00 00 00 5C 06
0010:     4F 08 F8 1D 00 1D E6 06  4F 08 11 01 65 00 00 00
0020:     00 00 A8 1C B4 3A E7 2E

- - - - - - - -

23 OWL200    CS:IP 20C7:1928  SS:BP 2287:1C8E
   <no info>

0000:     C7 1C 23 1A C7 20 A2 01  4F 08 0C 00 00 00 5C 06
0010:     4F 08 F8 1D 00 1D A2 1D  8F 36 67 2E E1 19 C7 20
0020:     9C 1C 06 00 E7 2E 00 00  5F 06 F8 1D 00 1D 25 00
0030:     00 00 D8 1C AE 05 E7 2E

- - - - - - - -

24 OWL200    CS:IP 20C7:1A23  SS:BP 2287:1CC6
   <no info>

0000:     DF 1C 6E 19 C7 20 A2 01  4F 08 0C 00 00 00 5C 06
0010:     4F 08 F8 1D 00 1D 87 22

- - - - - - - -

25 OWL200    CS:IP 20C7:196E  SS:BP 2287:1CDE
   <no info>

0000:     FF 1C B4 3A 87 04 5C 06  4F 08 00 00 0C 00 F8 1D
0010:     BA 00 7F 2D F8 1D 00 1D  B7 07 6F 82 87 04 7E 81

- - - - - - - -

26 USER      CS:IP 0487:3AB4  SS:BP 2287:1CFE
   <no info>

0000:     12 1D C3 19 87 04 5C 06  4F 08 00 00 0C 00 F8 1D
0010:     AD 19 E7 2E

- - - - - - - -
27 USER      CS:IP 0487:19C3  SS:BP 2287:1D12
   <no info>

0000:     2E 1D FF 15 DF 20 5C 06  4F 08 F8 1D F8 1D 00 1D
0010:     5C 06 4F 08 CE 21 AE 0B  E7 2E E7 2E
```

continues

continued

```
28 OWL200    CS:IP 20DF:15FF  SS:BP 2287:1D2E
   <no info>

0000:    43 1D AB 27 C7 20 A2 01   4F 08 5C 06 4F 08 01 00
0010:    F8 1D 00 1D
```

```
29 OWL200    CS:IP 20C7:27AB  SS:BP 2287:1D42
   <no info>

0000:    5F 1D 4E 0E C7 20 A2 01   4F 08 74 1D 87 22 F8 1D
0010:    00 1D 1E 01 4F 08 A2 01   4F 08 E7 2E
```

```
30 OWL200    CS:IP 20C7:0E4E  SS:BP 2287:1D5E
   <no info>

0000:    7D 1D 01 28 C7 20 FE 02   4F 08 75 27 C7 20 74 1D
0010:    87 22 F8 1D 00 1D 5C 06   4F 08 01 00 E7 2E
```

```
31 OWL200    CS:IP 20C7:2801  SS:BP 2287:1D7C
   <no info>

0000:    93 1D 42 28 C7 20 FE 02   4F 08 5C 06 4F 08 01 00
0010:    F8 1D 00 1D E7 2E
```

```
32 OWL200    CS:IP 20C7:2842  SS:BP 2287:1D92
   <no info>

0000:    CF 1D 50 27 C7 20 FE 02   4F 08 01 00 F8 1D 00 1D
0010:    32 1E 8F 36 67 2E AD 26   C7 20 9A 1D 00 00 E7 2E
0020:    00 00 91 81 F0 80 EA 1D   25 00 00 00 F0 00 00 00
0030:    91 01 00 00 86 22 F8 1D   00 1D E7 2E
```

```
33 OWL200    CS:IP 20C7:2750  SS:BP 2287:1DCE
   <no info>

0000:    E7 1D C5 0E CF 21 FE 02   4F 08 AE 02 4F 08 FF FF
0010:    00 00 F8 1D 00 1D E7 2E
```

```
--------

34 OWL200    CS:IP 21CF:0EC5  SS:BP 2287:1DE6
   <no info>

0000:    FF 1D 29 0E CF 21 AE 02  4F 08 AE 02 4F 08 FE 02
0010:    4F 08 F8 1D 00 1D E7 2E

--------

35 OWL200    CS:IP 21CF:0E29  SS:BP 2287:1DFE
   <no info>

0000:    15 1E 64 05 CF 21 AE 02  4F 08 F8 1D F8 1D 00 1D
0010:    FC FF 00 1D E7 2E

--------

36 OWL200    CS:IP 21CF:0564  SS:BP 2287:1E14
   <no info>

0000:    55 1E 73 07 CF 21 AE 02  4F 08 10 01 F8 1D 00 00
0010:    00 00 F8 1D 00 1D AE 02  4F 08 00 00 00 00 D0 1F
0020:    8F 36 67 2E 80 06 CF 21  22 1E 06 00 E7 2E 00 00
0030:    B7 07 AC 20 57 00 25 00  00 00 A0 08 8F 06 87 22

--------

37 OWL200    CS:IP 21CF:0773  SS:BP 2287:1E54
   <no info>

0000:    6D 1E 9E 03 17 07 00 00  00 00 F8 1D 10 01 00 1D
0010:    B7 07 00 1D 92 06 CF 21

--------

38 USER      CS:IP 0717:039E  SS:BP 2287:1E6C
   <no info>

0000:    84 1E 5C 04 00 00 00 00  F8 1D 10 01 00 1D 87 22
0010:    00 1D 86 22 40 01 00 00

--------

39 USER      CS:IP 0717:045C  SS:BP 2287:1E84
   <no info>

0000:    A4 1E B4 3A 87 04 00 00  00 00 F8 1D 10 01 00 1D
0010:    29 04 17 07 86 22 00 1D  B7 07 10 01 00 1D B4 A7
```

continues

continued

```
40 USER        CS:IP 0487:3AB4   SS:BP 2287:1EA4
   <no info>

0000:     80 1F 0A 09 0F 07 00 00   00 00 F8 1D 10 01 00 1D
0010:     B7 07 90 00 00 00 00 00   00 00 B7 07 43 00 02 80
0020:     00 00 F8 1D 02 C3 00 00   2E 01 0F 22 D4 1E 9C 00
0030:     D2 00 01 00 2F 01 6A 1F   36 08 1F 01 B6 07 B6 07
0040:     0C 00 00 00 0E 22 BF 00   35 01 0F 22 28 00 00 00
0050:     3C 00 10 00 78 00 08 00   00 00 00 00 00 00 0E 22
0060:     00 00 0E 22 00 00 CA 3F   40 49 42 00 00 00 0E 22
0070:     0E 22 00 00 41 00 00 00   00 02 00 00 34 1F 00 00
0080:     00 00 3C 1F 19 2A D7 24   0F 22 29 2A 40 01 00 00
0090:     86 22 00 00 16 02 06 02   00 02 43 00 56 00 D5 01
00A0:     97 01 1D 00 0F 22 34 01   0F 22 FF FF 00 00 0A 03
00B0:     00 00 AC 20 00 24 00 00   01 50 2F 01 11 00 74 1F
00C0:     18 89 11 00 11 00 11 00   00 00 2F 01 78 1F D2 0F
00D0:     0F 22 87 22 8E 1F EC 87   17 01 0E 22
```

```
41 USER        CS:IP 070F:090A   SS:BP 2287:1F80
   <no info>

0000:     A6 1F 80 00 0F 07 00 00   00 00 92 06 CF 21 BC 22
0010:     00 00 0F 22 86 22 E7 2E   B8 21 B8 01 B8 21 0F 22
0020:     D1 0D 4D 0A 0E 22
```

```
42 USER        CS:IP 070F:0080   SS:BP 2287:1FA6
   <no info>

0000:     C2 1F 28 0A CF 21 00 00   00 00 92 06 CF 21 BC 22
0010:     91 01 00 00 86 22 B8 01   B8 21 E7 2E
```

```
43 OWL200      CS:IP 21CF:0A28   SS:BP 2287:1FC2
   <no info>

0000:     19 20 4D 09 CF 21 AE 02   4F 08 B8 01 B8 21 22 20
0010:     8F 36 67 2E 35 08 CF 21   C8 1F 00 00 E7 2E 00 00
0020:     3F 27 6A 0E 3F 27 25 00   00 00 7E 0F 3F 27 0A 0B
0030:     4F 08 26 0A 4F 08 12 00   4F 08 96 00 4F 08 1E 01
0040:     4F 08 A2 01 4F 08 2A 02   4F 08 87 22 45 20 A8 0D
0050:     97 22 AE 02 87 22
```

```
- - - - - - - -

44 OWL200    CS:IP 21CF:094D  SS:BP 2287:2018
   <no info>

0000:    45 20 F4 0D 97 22 AE 02  4F 08 56 21 8F 36 67 2E
0010:    30 0D 97 22 1E 20 06 00  87 22 00 00 7C 22 CF 00
0020:    7F 2D 25 00 00 00 AE 02  4F 08 E7 2E

- - - - - - - -

45 DIALOG5  CS:IP 2297:0DF4  SS:BP 2287:2044
   <no info>

0000:    55 20 70 00 BF 21 EE 05  4F 08 B8 01 B8 21 E7 2E

- - - - - - - -

46 OWL200    CS:IP 21BF:0070  SS:BP 2287:2054
   <no info>

0000:    73 20 53 13 8F 21 EE 05  4F 08 46 0D 97 22 00 00
0010:    00 00 65 00 00 00 00 00  B8 01 B8 21 E7 2E

- - - - - - - -

47 OWL200    CS:IP 218F:1353  SS:BP 2287:2072
   <no info>

0000:    A3 20 73 14 C7 20 AE 06  4F 08 8A 20 87 22 65 00
0010:    00 00 00 00 B8 01 B8 21  00 00 65 00 EE 05 4F 08
0020:    B6 00 87 22 00 00 00 00  65 00 EE 05 4F 08 E7 2E

- - - - - - - -

48 OWL200    CS:IP 20C7:1473  SS:BP 2287:20A2
   <no info>

0000:    CD 20 61 15 C7 20 DE 04  4F 08 B8 01 B8 21 00 00
0010:    65 00 DE 04 4F 08 00 00  00 00 00 00 00 00 00 00
0020:    00 00 65 00 DE 04 4F 08  E7 2E

- - - - - - - -

49 OWL200    CS:IP 20C7:1561  SS:BP 2287:20CC
   <no info>

0000:    E9 20 11 08 5F 30 DE 04  4F 08 65 00 00 00 00 00
0010:    B8 01 B8 21 DE 04 4F 08  44 23 E7 2E
```

continues

continued

```
- - - - - - - -

50 OWL200    CS:IP 305F:0811  SS:BP 2287:20E8
   <no info>

0000:    19 21 FA 16 C7 20 BA 06  4F 08 65 00 00 00 00 00
0010:    B8 01 B8 21 B8 01 A0 01  7F 2D 01 02 7C 22 B7 07
0020:    A1 00 00 00 E6 06 4F 08  E7 2E 4B 21 23 1A E7 2E

- - - - - - - -

51 OWL200    CS:IP 20C7:16FA  SS:BP 2287:2118

0000:    41 21 28 19 C7 20 E6 06  4F 08 11 01 65 00 00 00
0010:    00 00 B8 01 B8 21 00 00  00 00 00 00 00 00 00 00
0020:    00 00 00 00 00 00 E7 2E

- - - - - - - -

52 OWL200    CS:IP 20C7:1928  SS:BP 2287:2140

0000:    79 21 23 1A C7 20 E6 06  4F 08 11 01 65 00 00 00
0010:    00 00 B8 01 B8 21 E0 21  8F 36 67 2E E1 19 C7 20
0020:    4E 21 06 00 E7 2E 00 00  00 00 00 00 00 00 25 00
0030:    00 00 B8 01 A0 01 E7 2E

- - - - - - - -

53 OWL200    CS:IP 20C7:1A23  SS:BP 2287:2178

0000:    91 21 6E 19 C7 20 E6 06  4F 08 11 01 65 00 00 00
0010:    00 00 B8 01 B8 21 87 22

- - - - - - - -

54 OWL200    CS:IP 20C7:196E  SS:BP 2287:2190

0000:    AB 21 BB 27 87 04 00 00  00 00 65 00 11 01 7C 22
0010:    11 01 7C 22 E7 2E B8 01  A0 01

- - - - - - - -

55 USER      CS:IP 0487:27BB  SS:BP 2287:21AA

0000:    CE 21 BC 0A B7 20 CF 00  7F 2D B8 01 A0 01 7C 22
0010:    11 01 65 00 00 00 00 00  9B 03 01 00 65 00 4D 00
0020:    01 00 E7 2E
```

```
- - - - - - - -

56 OWL200    CS:IP 20B7:0ABC  SS:BP 2287:21CE

0000:     13 22 36 0F B7 20 8C 22   87 22 B8 01 A0 01 01 00
0010:     00 00 34 22 8F 36 67 2E   B6 0E B7 20 D4 21 06 00
0020:     E7 2E 00 00 B7 20 E2 21   00 00 25 00 00 00 00 00
0030:     00 00 B8 01 25 00 00 00   45 22 AC 08 5F 2E 9A 07
0040:     B8 01 E7 2E

- - - - - - - -

57 OWL200    CS:IP 20B7:0F36  SS:BP 2287:2212

0000:     67 22 20 08 B7 20 8C 22   87 22 B8 01 A0 01 A0 01
0010:     E0 0B E7 2E E0 0B E7 2E   41 22 D5 11 5F 22 00 00
0020:     C7 2D 70 22 8F 36 67 2E   A9 07 B7 20 18 22 06 00
0030:     E7 2E 00 00 8C 22 87 22   C2 22 25 00 00 00 87 22
0040:     00 00 00 00 86 22 80 00   67 22 B8 01 A0 01 87 22
0050:     D3 22 87 22

- - - - - - - -

58 OWL200    CS:IP 20B7:0820  SS:BP 2287:2266

0000:     D3 22 61 10 97 22 8C 22   87 22 FF FF 8F 36 67 2E
0010:     FA 0F 97 22 6C 22 06 00   87 22 00 00 87 22 B8 01
0020:     A0 01 20 00 00 00 D5 14   97 22 15 15 97 22 B2 07
0030:     4F 08 86 22 00 00 AA 07   4F 08 00 00 00 00 01 00
0040:     00 00 00 00 BA 06 4F 08   00 00 00 00 00 00 00 00
0050:     00 00 00 00 00 00 00 00   00 00 00 00 9A 07 4F 08
0060:     87 22 00 00 00 00 00 00   00 00 87 22

- - - - - - - -

59 DIALOG5   CS:IP 2297:1061  SS:BP 2287:22D2

0000:     ED 22 61 00 8F 22 01 00   16 08 4F 08 B8 01 A0 01
0010:     00 00 00 00 80 00 67 22   01 00

- - - - - - - -

60 DIALOG5   CS:IP 228F:0061  SS:BP 2287:22EC

0000:     FD 22 B2 00 7F 22 01 00   80 00 67 22 00 00 86 22   .

- - - - - - - -

61 DIALOG5   CS:IP 227F:00B2  SS:BP 2287:22FC
```

The Tasks Section

The Tasks section of the log file catalogs all of the programs that were executing when the exception took place. Every entry in this section includes the following information:

- The full path of the program's filename
- The name of the module
- The windows module handle
- The task handle
- The instance handle that specifies the value for the data segment

The Tasks section in my sample log file is as follows:

```
Tasks:
C:\NDW\NAVPOPUP.EXE
    Module: NAVPOPUP   hModule: 24DF   hTask: 241F   hInstance: 23F6
C:\NDW\NHOOKEXE.EXE
    Module: NHOOKEXE   hModule: 27C7   hTask: 27A7   hInstance: 2426
C:\BC4\BIN\WINSPCTR.EXE
    Module: WINSPCTR   hModule: 249F   hTask: 242F   hInstance: 2456
C:\WINDOWS\NDW.EXE
    Module: NDW        hModule: 0657   hTask: 0647   hInstance: 1706
C:\NDW\NDWMAIN.EXE
    Module: NDWMAIN    hModule: 15D7   hTask: 15C7   hInstance: 159E
C:\BC4\BC4SAMS\DIALOG5.EXE
    Module: DIALOG5    hModule: 24D7   hTask: 2667   hInstance: 2286
```

Notice that the last task in this list is the one that generated the exception.

The Modules Section

The Modules section catalogs the modules executing when the exception took place. Each entry in this section contains the following information:

- The path of the module's executing file
- The date stamp for the module's file
- The size of the file
- The name of the module
- The module handle
- The number of times the module is being used

The Modules section in my sample log file is as follows:

```
Modules:
C:\WINDOWS\SYSTEM\KRNL386.EXE        Date: 04/01/1992  Size: 75490
     Module: KERNEL    hModule: 010F  reference count: 32
C:\WINDOWS\SYSTEM\SYSTEM.DRV         Date: 04/01/1992  Size: 2304
     Module: SYSTEM    hModule: 013F  reference count: 23
C:\WINDOWS\SYSTEM\KEYBOARD.DRV       Date: 04/01/1992  Size: 7568
     Module: KEYBOARD  hModule: 0147  reference count: 25
C:\WINDOWS\SYSTEM\MOUSE.DRV          Date: 04/01/1992  Size: 10144
     Module: MOUSE     hModule: 015F  reference count: 21
C:\WINDOWS\SYSTEM\VGAPAL.DRV         Date: 04/07/1992  Size: 78176
     Module: DISPLAY   hModule: 01BF  reference count: 24
C:\WINDOWS\SYSTEM\SFSOUND.DRV        Date: 08/17/1992  Size: 15262
     Module: SOUND     hModule: 01D7  reference count: 21
C:\WINDOWS\SYSTEM\COMM.DRV           Date: 04/01/1992  Size: 9280
     Module: COMM      hModule: 0227  reference count: 21
C:\WINDOWS\SYSTEM\VGASYS.FON         Date: 04/01/1992  Size: 7280
     Module: FONTS     hModule: 0437  reference count: 2
C:\WINDOWS\SYSTEM\VGAOEM.FON         Date: 04/01/1992  Size: 5168
     Module: OEMFONTS  hModule: 046F  reference count: 2
C:\WINDOWS\SYSTEM\GDI.EXE            Date: 04/01/1992  Size: 220800
     Module: GDI       hModule: 047F  reference count: 21
C:\WINDOWS\SYSTEM\VGAFIX.FON         Date: 04/01/1992  Size: 5360
     Module: FIXFONTS  hModule: 0467  reference count: 1
C:\WINDOWS\SYSTEM\USER.EXE           Date: 01/07/1993  Size: 264016
     Module: USER      hModule: 048F  reference count: 20
C:\WINDOWS\SYSTEM\SFSAMPLE.DLL       Date: 06/14/1992  Size: 17888
     Module: SFSAMPLE  hModule: 0317  reference count: 1
C:\WINDOWS\SYSTEM\SSERIFE.FON        Date: 04/01/1992  Size: 64544
     Module: SSERIFE   hModule: 02BF  reference count: 1
C:\WINDOWS\SYSTEM\COURE.FON          Date: 04/01/1992  Size: 23408
     Module: COURE     hModule: 02AF  reference count: 1
C:\WINDOWS\SYSTEM\SERIFE.FON         Date: 04/01/1992  Size: 57936
     Module: SERIFE    hModule: 0337  reference count: 1
C:\WINDOWS\SYSTEM\SYMBOLE.FON        Date: 04/01/1992  Size: 56336
     Module: SYMBOLE   hModule: 033F  reference count: 1
C:\WINDOWS\SYSTEM\ROMAN.FON          Date: 04/01/1992  Size: 13312
     Module: ROMAN     hModule: 0297  reference count: 1
C:\WINDOWS\SYSTEM\SCRIPT.FON         Date: 04/01/1992  Size: 12288
     Module: SCRIPT    hModule: 02B7  reference count: 1
C:\WINDOWS\SYSTEM\MODERN.FON         Date: 04/01/1992  Size: 8704
     Module: MODERN    hModule: 02A7  reference count: 1
C:\WINDOWS\SYSTEM\SMALLE.FON         Date: 04/01/1992  Size: 26112
     Module: SMALLE    hModule: 032F  reference count: 1
C:\WINDOWS\SYSTEM\V1SP.FON           Date: 08/18/1992  Size: 52224
     Module: V1SP      hModule: 02C7  reference count: 1
C:\WINDOWS\SYSTEM\V2SP.FON           Date: 08/18/1992  Size: 48128
     Module: V2SP      hModule: 0307  reference count: 1
C:\WINDOWS\SYSTEM\V3SP.FON           Date: 08/18/1992  Size: 48128
     Module: V3SP      hModule: 17B7  reference count: 1
```

continues

continued

```
C:\WINDOWS\SYSTEM\V4SP.FON              Date: 08/18/1992  Size: 42496
    Module: V4SP       hModule: 17A7   reference count: 1
C:\WINDOWS\SYSTEM\V7SP.FON              Date: 08/18/1992  Size: 43008
    Module: V7SP       hModule: 1797   reference count: 1
C:\WINDOWS\SYSTEM\WINLD.FON             Date: 04/05/1993  Size: 17488
    Module: WINLD      hModule: 1787   reference count: 1
C:\WINDOWS\SYSTEM\VGALSB.FON            Date: 04/05/1993  Size: 64000
    Module: VGALSB     hModule: 178F   reference count: 1
C:\WINDOWS\SYSTEM\VGALSB1.FON           Date: 04/05/1993  Size: 63488
    Module: VGALSB1    hModule: 176F   reference count: 1
C:\WINDOWS\SYSTEM\VGALSB2.FON           Date: 04/05/1993  Size: 63488
    Module: VGALSB2    hModule: 175F   reference count: 1
C:\WINDOWS\SYSTEM\VGASB.FON             Date: 04/05/1993  Size: 10240
    Module: VGASB      hModule: 174F   reference count: 1
C:\WINDOWS\NDW.EXE                      Date: 03/30/1993  Size: 8112
    Module: NDW        hModule: 0657   reference count: 1
C:\WINDOWS\SYSTEM\MMSYSTEM.DLL          Date: 04/01/1992  Size: 61648
    Module: MMSYSTEM   hModule: 16F7   reference count: 9
C:\WINDOWS\SYSTEM\TIMER.DRV             Date: 04/01/1992  Size: 4192
    Module: TIMER      hModule: 16EF   reference count: 1
C:\WINDOWS\SYSTEM\SNDBLST2.DRV          Date: 03/10/1992  Size: 14464
    Module: SNDBLST2   hModule: 1697   reference count: 4
C:\WINDOWS\SYSTEM\MSADLIB.DRV           Date: 03/10/1992  Size: 22064
    Module: MSADLIB    hModule: 1637   reference count: 1
C:\WINDOWS\SYSTEM\MIDIMAP.DRV           Date: 04/01/1992  Size: 52784
    Module: MIDI       hModule: 162F   reference count: 1
C:\NDW\NDWMAIN.EXE                      Date: 03/30/1993  Size: 12288
    Module: NDWMAIN    hModule: 15D7   reference count: 1
C:\NDW\NDWDLL2.DLL                      Date: 03/30/1993  Size: 308576
    Module: NDWDLL2    hModule: 1597   reference count: 1
C:\NDW\NWIN2.DLL                        Date: 03/30/1993  Size: 477680
    Module: NWIN2      hModule: 12FF   reference count: 1
C:\NDW\NDLL2.DLL                        Date: 03/30/1993  Size: 65536
    Module: NDLL2      hModule: 1ED7   reference count: 1
C:\WINDOWS\SYSTEM\SHELL.DLL             Date: 04/01/1992  Size: 41600
    Module: SHELL      hModule: 1BA7   reference count: 3
C:\NDW\NHOOKDLL.DLL                     Date: 03/30/1993  Size: 9008
    Module: NHOOKDLL   hModule: 1ECF   reference count: 2
C:\WINDOWS\SYSTEM\WIN87EM.DLL           Date: 04/01/1992  Size: 12800
    Module: WIN87EM    hModule: 1B9F   reference count: 3
C:\NDW\NMAIL.DLL                        Date: 03/30/1993  Size: 9104
    Module: NMAIL      hModule: 12F7   reference count: 1
C:\NDW\NWRES2.DLL                       Date: 03/30/1993  Size: 355312
    Module: NWRES2     hModule: 1ABF   reference count: 1
C:\NDW\NTASTIC.DLL                      Date: 03/30/1993  Size: 6896
    Module: NTASTIC    hModule: 195F   reference count: 1
C:\DOS\MSTOOLS.DLL                      Date: 03/10/1993  Size: 13424
    Module: MSTOOLS    hModule: 18F7   reference count: 1
C:\NDW\NAVPOPUP.EXE                     Date: 01/03/1993  Size: 7344
    Module: NAVPOPUP   hModule: 24DF   reference count: 1
C:\NDW\NAVDLL.DLL                       Date: 01/03/1993  Size: 10208
```

```
        Module: NAVDLL     hModule: 23EF  reference count: 1
C:\NDW\NHOOKEXE.EXE                       Date: 03/30/1993  Size: 6176
        Module: NHOOKEXE   hModule: 27C7  reference count: 1
C:\BC4\BIN\WINSPCTR.EXE                   Date: 08/30/1993  Size: 46576
        Module: WINSPCTR   hModule: 249F  reference count: 1
C:\WINDOWS\SYSTEM\BWCC.DLL                Date: 08/24/1993  Size: 156496
        Module: BWCC       hModule: 245F  reference count: 1
C:\WINDOWS\SYSTEM\TOOLHELP.DLL            Date: 04/01/1992  Size: 14128
        Module: TOOLHELP   hModule: 2467  reference count: 1
C:\BC4\BC4SAMS\DIALOG5.EXE                Date: 10/28/1993  Size: 196899
        Module: DIALOG5    hModule: 24D7  reference count: 1
C:\BC4\BIN\OWL200.DLL                     Date: 08/30/1993  Size: 594960
        Module: OWL200     hModule: 229F  reference count: 1
C:\BC4\BIN\BIDS40.DLL                     Date: 08/30/1993  Size: 76800
        Module: BIDS40     hModule: 2EDF  reference count: 1
C:\BC4\BIN\BC40RTL.DLL                    Date: 08/30/1993  Size: 222568
        Module: BC40RTL    hModule: 2E7F  reference count: 1
C:\WINDOWS\SYSTEM\COMMDLG.DLL             Date: 04/01/1992  Size: 89248
        Module: COMMDLG    hModule: 2ED7  reference count: 1
```

The USER and GDI Heap Information Section

The USER and GDI heap information section consists of the percentage of free USER and GDI heaps accessible when the exception took place. Here is the heap information in my sample log file:

```
USER  Free  88%
GDI   Free  77%
```

The System Information Section

The System information section provides you with the following information:

- The Windows mode
- The Windows version
- The kind of CPU
- The biggest free contiguous memory block
- The total linear memory space in 14K pages
- The free linear memory space in 14K pages
- The number of 14K swap file pages and the size of the swap file

Here is the System Information section in my log file:

```
System info:
Running in enhanced mode under Windows 3.10 retail version
CPU: 80486
Largest free memory block: 40824832 bytes
Total linear memory space: 43504 K
Free linear memory space : 39892 K
Swap file Pages: 2a7c (43504 K)
```

The User Comments Section

The User Comments section includes the short memo included by the user. Here is the User Comments line for my sample log file:

```
Error in DIALOG5.EXE when attempting to invoke the dialog box from the menu
selection
```

THE GREP UTILITY

The Grep utility has its origin in UNIX and serves to search for text patterns using a special search string called *regular expressions*. The Grep utility is not new to Borland C++ 4.0; Borland included the DOS implementation of Grep in the early versions of its Turbo C package. What is new about Grep in Borland C++ 4.0 is that you can now use it from within the IDE *and also* exploit the results of the search from within the IDE.

The Regular Expressions of Grep

The Grep utility supports regular expressions used to search for nontrivial text patterns in files. The following characters play a special role in making up regular expressions:

- The ^ (circumflex) character that appears at the beginning of a string matches the start of the line. For example, the regular expression `^class` matches the lines that begin with the word `class`.

- The $ character at the end of the regular expression matches the end of the line. For example, the `calc()$` string matches the lines that end with `calc()`.

- The period character matches any character. For example, the regular expression `me.t` matches the words `meet` and `meat`.

- The * character specifies a match with zero or more characters that appear before the * character. For example, the regular expression to* matches the words to and too.

- The + character specifies a match with one or more characters that appear before the + character. For example, the regular expression 11+2 matches the strings 1112 and 11112, but not the string 12.

- The square brackets define a character set that matches any one character in that set. For example, the regular expression [the] matches the character t, h, or e.

- The ^ character at the start of a string in brackets matches any one character that is *not* in the character set. For example, the regular expression [^the] matches a, b, c, d, but not the character e, t, or h.

- The hyphen character inside a bracket defines a range of characters. For example, the regular expression [1-9] matches the digits 1 through 9. You can include the range of characters with other individual characters.

- The \ character enables you to tell the Grep utility to use the subsequent regular expression character as a normal character. For example, the string calc()\$ matches the string calc()$.

Invoking The Grep Utility

You invoke the Grep utility using the Grep option in the Tool menu selection. The option invokes a simple line input Program Arguments dialog box. This dialog box expects input that conforms to the following syntax:

```
[-rcnvidzuw] searchString file[s]
```

The first part is made up of options that fine-tune the operations of the Grep utility. Each option must have a – to its left and can be followed by a + or – to its right to turn it on or off, respectively. By default, an option is turned on. The options are as follows:

- The r option turns on regular expression search.

- The c option matches Count only.

- The v option displays nonmatching lines only.

- The d option searches subdirectories.

- The u option updates the default options.
- The l option displays the filenames that contain one or more matches.
- The n option displays line numbers that contain the matching string.
- The i option performs a non-case-sensitive search.
- The z option performs a verbose search.
- The w option performs a word search.

The searchString argument specifies the search string. The file[s] argument specifies one or more wildcard filenames.

Table 12.2 shows sample arguments for the Grep utility and the intended outcome.

TABLE 12.2. SAMPLE ARGUMENTS FOR THE GREP UTILITY AND THE INTENDED OUTCOME.

Argument	Purpose
-l- TMainWindow *.cpp	Searches for the verbatim string TMainWindow in the .CPP files of the current directory
-r+ -l- class.*TMainWindow *.cpp	Searches for a regular expression that matches the declaration of the TMainWindow class
-l- // *.h??	Locates C++ comments in .H, .HPP, and .HXX header files
-l- #define *.h *.rh	Locates the #define directives in .H and .RH files
-r+ -l- .*printf *.cpp	Searches for printf, sprintf, and wprintf in .CPP files

Figure 12.9 shows the Message window containing a sample set of matches for the Grep utility. I generated the set using the following arguments:

```
-r+ -l- class.*TMainWindow *.cpp
```

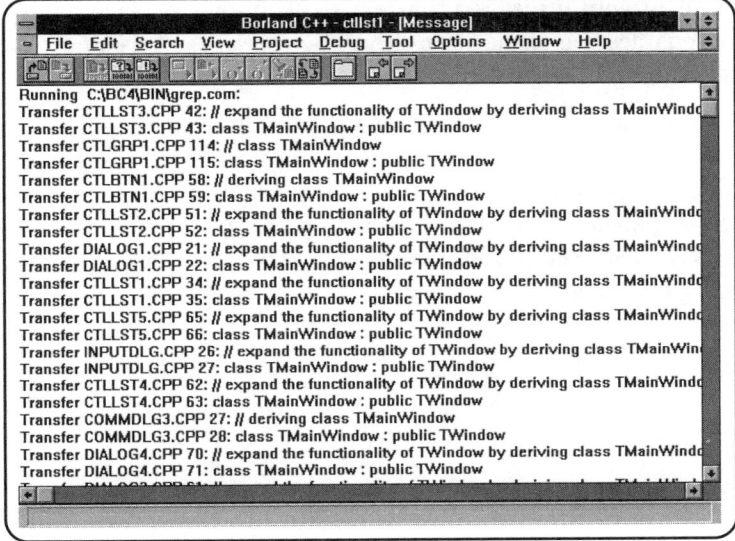

Figure 12.9. The Message window showing a sample set of matches for the Grep utility.

Invoking the Matching Lines

The results of the Grep utility appear in the Message window. If you click any Grep result, the IDE loads the source code file connected with that result and places the cursor at the matching line. This feature simplifies the process of examining the matching source code lines.

SUMMARY

In this chapter, you learned how to use the WinSpector, the WinSight, and the Grep utilities. These programs help you create professional code more quickly and easily. The following points were covered:

- The WinSpector is a postmortem utility that intercepts UAE and GPE errors and writes them to a log file. The log file contains much information about the tasks, modules, and other Windows components that were present when the runtime error occurred.

- The WinSight utility is a transparent Windows message spying tool that enables you to monitor either the messages to specific windows and to particular kinds of windows or else specific messages.

- The Grep utility offers an integrated tool for text and pattern search in source code files. The utility supports a versatile set of search wildcards. In addition, the Grep utility dumps its output in the Message window. You can use the Grep output in this window to load quickly the file containing the match and to zoom in on the matching source code line.

The Debugging Tools

Despite the evolution of programming languages, programs for debugging are still needed. Debugging Windows applications is generally more complex than debugging similar DOS applications. The Borland C++ 4.0 package includes the integrated debugger in the IDE, and the stand-alone Turbo Debugger for Windows (in both 16-bit and 32-bit versions). These separate debuggers are supersets of the integrated debugger. Nevertheless, the integrated debugger is still a valuable tool. This chapter presents ways of using this debugger and the browser. This chapter discusses the following topics:

- The menu options of the Debug menu selection

- Using the integrated debugger

- Using the IDE Browse symbol... option

THE DEBUG MENU SELECTION

The Debug menu selection provides you with several options that enable you to debug a program. Table 13.1 contains the summary of the options in the Debug menu selection.

TABLE 13.1. THE SUMMARY OF THE OPTIONS IN THE DEBUG MENU SELECTION.		
Menu Option	*Shortcut Keys*	*Function*
Run	Ctrl+F9	Executes the program of the currently selected target
Step over	F8	Single-steps through the next statement without tracing the statements of the called functions
Trace into	F7	Single-steps through the next statement and traces the statements of all called functions
Toggle **b**reakpoint	F5	Toggles an unconditional breakpoint at the line containing the insertion cursor
Find execution point		Places the cursor at the execution point in an edit window.
Pause program		Pauses the execution of an application
Terminate program	Ctrl+F2	Ends the debugging session
Add **w**atch...	Ctrl+F5	Brings up the Watch Properties dialog box to add a watched variable or expression
Add **b**reakpoint...		Brings up the Breakpoints dialog box to manage conditional or unconditional breakpoints

Menu Option	Shortcut Keys	Function
Evaluate/Modify…		Opens the Expression Evaluator dialog box to view, evaluate, and alter data
Inspect…	Alt+F5	Brings up the Data Inspector dialog box that enables you to enter a variable or expression
Load symbol table…		Opens the Load Symbol Table dialog box to view a symbol table

The Run Option

With the Run option, you can run the currently selected project target or shift from single-stepping through a program to full-speed execution. The program keeps running either until it encounters the next breakpoint or until it reaches the end. The IDE recompiles and links the files of the current target if needed, before running the target's program. The shortcut keys for this option are Ctrl+F9.

The Step Over Option

With the Step over option, you can single-step through the next executable statement. All the functions in that statement are executed at full speed. The shortcut key for this option is the F8 function key.

The Trace Into Option

With the Trace into option, you can single-step through the next executable statement and also through all the functions called in that statement. The shortcut key for this option is the F7 function key.

The Toggle Breakpoint Option

The Toggle breakpoint option toggles an unconditional breakpoint at the line containing the insertion cursor. An unconditional breakpoint causes the program to halt when it reaches that breakpoint, enabling you to inspect variables and expressions or even to single-step through subsequent statements. The shortcut key for this option is the F5 function key.

The Find Execution Point Option

The Find execution point option places the cursor at the execution point in an edit window. The IDE selects or opens the window that contains the source code at the execution point.

The Pause Program Option

The Pause program option stops the execution of a program in a debugging session.

The Terminate Program Option

The Terminate program option stops the current debugging session, releasing memory allocated by the debugged program and also closing any opened file. The shortcut keys for this option are Ctrl+F2.

The Add Watch Option

The Add watch... option invokes the Watch Properties dialog that enables you to set a watch variable or watch expression. The shortcut keys for this option are Ctrl+F5. Figure 13.1 shows the Watch Properties dialog box, which has the following options:

- A combo box that enables you to enter a variable or expression or to select a previous variable or expression.

- The choice of displaying integers in either decimal or hexadecimal format.

- The choice of displaying the contents of a variable or the result of an expression as a character, string, structure (showing the name of each member with its value), pointer, floating point, memory dump format, or default format.

- The size of the array to watch.

- The number of significant digits for watching a floating point. The range for this option is 2 to 18.

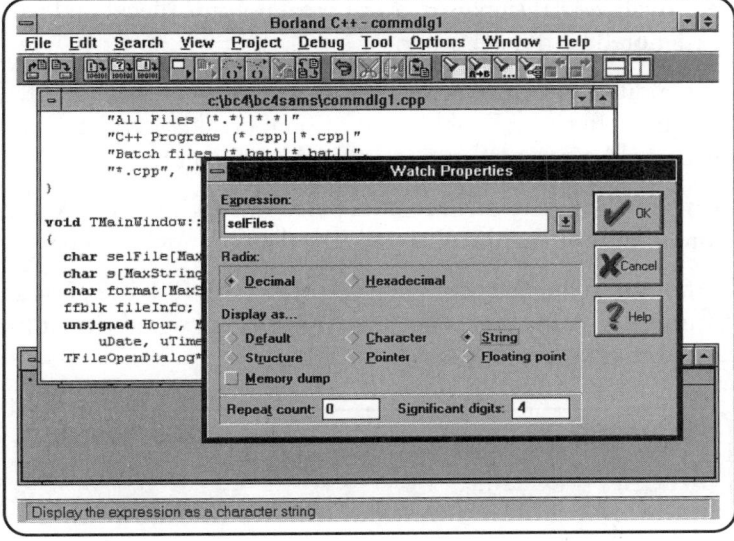

Figure 13.1. The Watch Properties dialog box.

Once you select or enter an item to watch, click the OK button. The IDE brings up the Watch window, shown in Figure 13.2. This window shows the list of watched items. Each item has an enabled-state check box control located to its left. Figure 13.2 shows the Watch window with two variables, `selFile` and `format`. The second variable is disabled.

The Add Breakpoint Option

The Add breakpoint... option brings up the Breakpoint Properties dialog box, shown in Figure 13.3. The dialog box contains various controls that present the following options:

- The full name of the file containing the breakpoint.
- The line number containing the breakpoint.
- The current state of the breakpoint. The state can be one of these three:
  - Verified: This indicates that the breakpoint is legal and was successfully created during the compilation process.
  - Unverified: This indicates that the breakpoint was added after the last time you compiled the program.

- Invalid: This signals that the breakpoint is illegal and will be ignored by the debugger.

- The conditional expression used with conditional breakpoint. The dialog box offers the Enabled conditional breakpoint check box, which enables you to set a conditional breakpoint.

- The number of times the program passes through the breakpoint before it halts at that breakpoint. The default number of passes is 1.

- The option to break at the breakpoint. You can ask the program to continue executing and to log an expression to signal that it has reached that breakpoint.

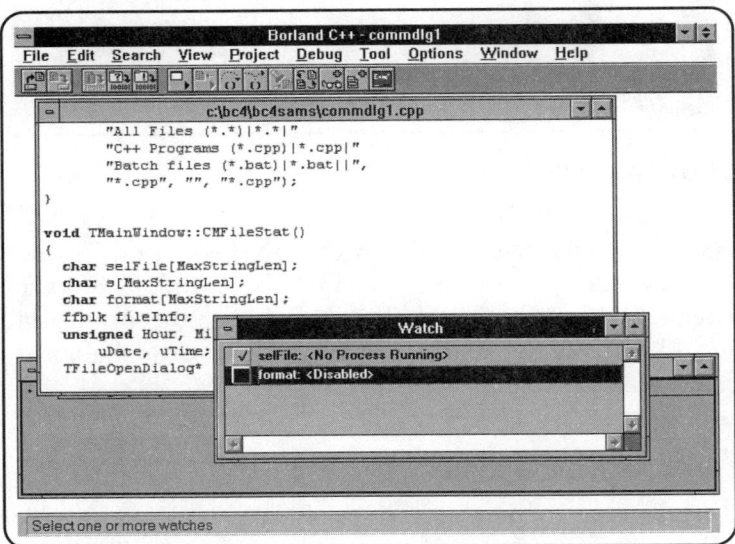

Figure 13.2. The Watch window.

The Evaluate/Modify Option

The Evaluate/Modify... option brings up the Expression Evaluator dialog box, shown in Figure 13.4. This dialog box has the following relevant controls:

- The Expression combo box, which enables you to enter or to select a previous variable or expression.

- The Result edit box, which displays the contents of the selected variable or the result of the specified expression.

- The New Value combo box, which enables you to enter the new value for the variable in the Expression combo box.

- The Eval pushbutton, which evaluates the expression or recalls the contents of the variable in the Expression combo box.

- The Modify pushbutton, which enables you to modify the contents of the variable that appears in the Expression combo box, using the value in the New Value combo box.

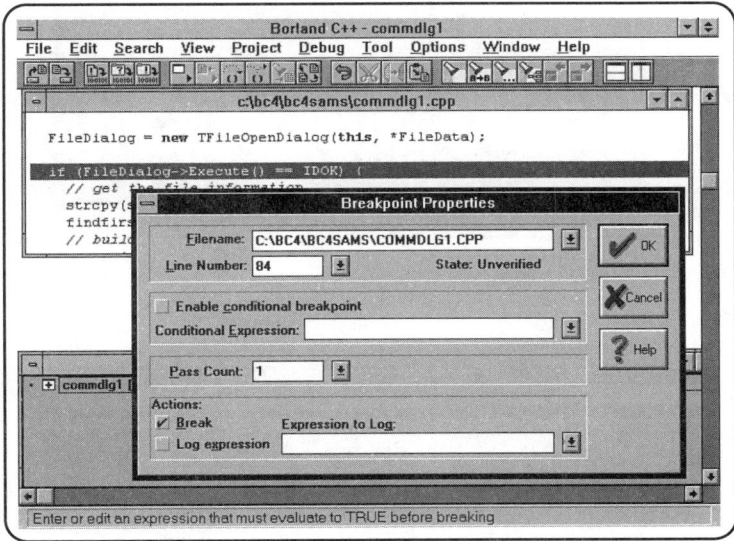

Figure 13.3. The Breakpoint Properties dialog box.

The Inspect Option

The Inspect... option invokes the Data Inspector dialog box, a simple dialog box that enables you to enter the name of the variable or expression you want to inspect. Once you enter the name of variable or expression, the option invokes the Inspect window. Figure 13.5 shows a sample Inspect window that enables you to look at the contents of the selFile variable (in the COMMDLG1.CPP file) as an array of characters. The window shows the index of each component, its type and contents as a character, decimal integer, and hexadecimal integer. The shortcut for this option is Alt+F5.

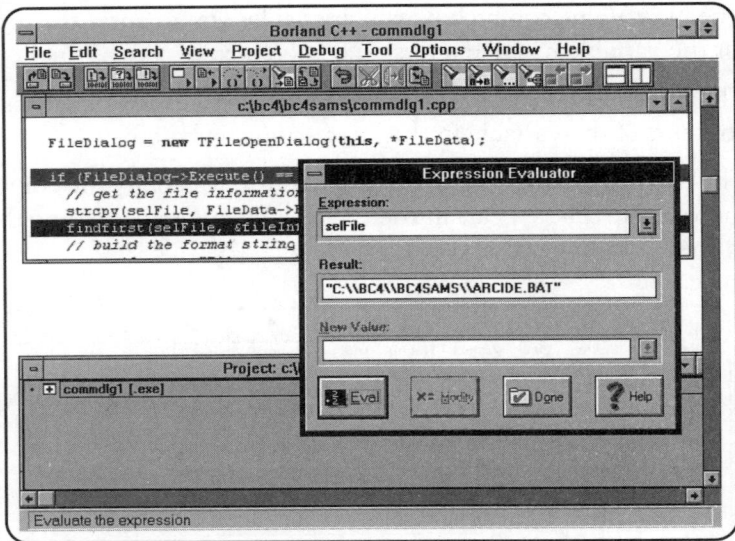

Figure 13.4. The Expression Evaluator dialog box.

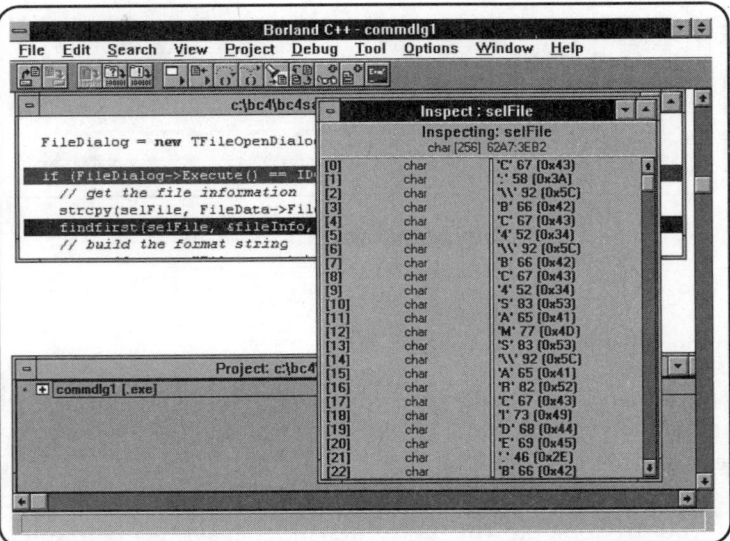

Figure 13.5. The Inspect window.

The Load Symbol Table Option

With the Load symbol table… option, you can view the name of the current symbol table, view the names of the other available tables, and load another table into the memory. Figure 13.6 shows a sample Load Symbol Table dialog box. You can use the Browse symbol… option in the Search menu selection to browse through the symbol table.

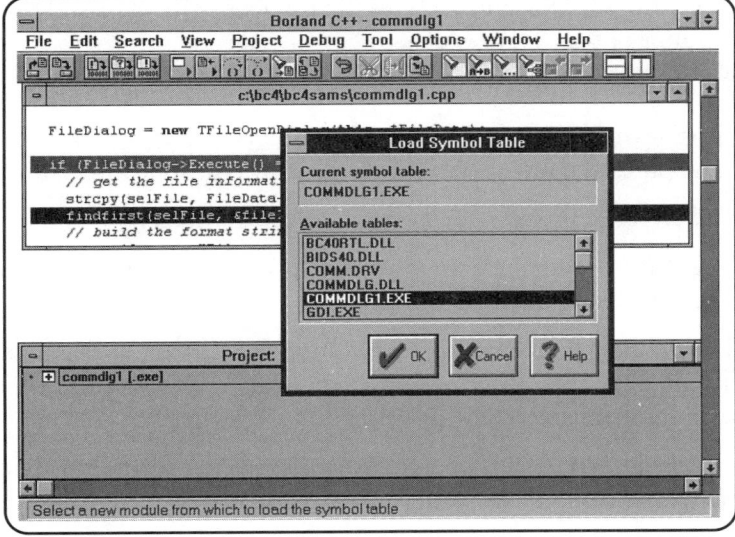

Figure 13.6. The Load Symbol Table dialog box.

USING UNCONDITIONAL BREAKPOINTS

The simplest and most common way to debug a program is to insert unconditional breakpoints. When the program stops at these breakpoints, you examine the current values of the watched variables. You can also single-step through the rest of the program or, more likely, through the next few statements.

The following presents the TIntArray class, which models a fixed array of integers. Listing 13.1 shows the line-numbered source code for the INTARR.HPP header file. This file contains the definition of constants, the declaration of the boolean type, and the declaration of the TIntArray class.

The constants declared in Listing 13.1 are these:

- The NO_ELEM_FOUND constant represents a numeric code used by the search member functions of the TIntArray class to signal that the search found no match.

- The BAD_VALUE constant is the default numeric code used for out-of-range indexing.

- The ARRAY_SIZE constant defines the number of integers stored in each instance of the TIntArray class.

- The HI_INDEX constant represents the value of the higher array index.

The listing also defines the enumerated type boolean. The TIntArray class defines public and protected members. The class defines the following data members:

- The arrData data member stores the array of integers.

- The badIndex data member is accessed when you supply the [] operator with an invalid index.

- The public data member isSorted stores the sort-order flag. I declared this member public because you may need to set it to false when writing to an array element using the [] operator.

The class declares a default constructor and a copy constructor. Because the class models a fixed-size array of integers, the implementation is simpler and easier for you to read.

The TIntArray class defines the following member functions:

1. The protected member function copy that copies the data from the srcArray to the target array instance.

2. The protected member function Qsort, which sorts the array elements using the recursive QuickSort method.

3. The [] operator, which enables you to access an element in the array of integers. Notice that the TIntArray class uses the unsigned type for indexing. This approach enables you to distinguish between the index of an array element and its value (of the int type).

4. The = operator enables you to assign one instance of the TIntArray class to another instance.

5. The fillArray member function, which fills the array elements with the argument of the fillValue parameter.

6. The shellSort member function, which sorts a specified range of array elements using the Shell-Metzner sorting method.

7. The CombSort member function, which sorts a specified range of array elements using the relatively new CombSort sorting method.

8. The QuickSort member function, which sorts a specified range of array elements using the recursive version of the QuickSort method. This function relies on the protected member function Qsort to perform the actual sorting.

9. The LinearSearch member function searches for a value in the array using the linear search method. You can apply this member function with both sorted and unsorted arrays.

10. The BinarySearch member function searches for a value in the array using the binary search method. You can apply this member function to sorted arrays only.

11. The StatisticalSearch member function searches for a value in the array using a scheme based on simple statistical assumptions. This method works best with randomly distributed data.

LISTING 13.1. THE LINE-NUMBERED SOURCE CODE FOR THE **INTARR.HPP** HEADER FILE.

```
 1:  #ifndef _INTARRAY_HPP
 2:  #define _INTARRAY_HPP
 3:
 4:  const unsigned NO_ELEM_FOUND = 0xffff;
 5:  const unsigned BAD_VALUE = 0xffff;
 6:  const unsigned ARRAY_SIZE = 15;
 7:  const unsigned HI_INDEX = ARRAY_SIZE - 1;
 8:
 9:  enum boolean { false, true };
10:
11:  class TIntArray
12:  {
13:
14:    protected:
15:      int arrData[ARRAY_SIZE];
16:      int badIndex;
17:      void copy(TIntArray& srcArray);
18:      void Qsort(unsigned first, unsigned last);
19:
20:    public:
```

continues

Listing 13.1. continued

```
21:
22:     boolean isSorted;
23:     TIntArray()
24:       { isSorted = false;
25:          badIndex = BAD_VALUE;
26:       }
27:     TIntArray(TIntArray& srcArray)
28:       { copy(srcArray); }
29:     int& operator[](unsigned index)
30:       { return (index < ARRAY_SIZE) ? arrData[index] : badIndex; }
31:     TIntArray& operator =(TIntArray& array)
32:     {
33:        copy(array);
34:        return *this;
35:     }
36:     void fillArray(int fillValue)
37:     {
38:       for (unsigned i = 0; i < ARRAY_SIZE; i++)
39:          arrData[i] = fillValue;
40:     }
41:
42:     //////////////////// Sort member functions ////////////////
43:     void ShellSort(unsigned last = HI_INDEX, unsigned first = 0);
44:     void CombSort(unsigned last = HI_INDEX, unsigned first = 0);
45:     void QuickSort(unsigned last = HI_INDEX, unsigned first = 0);
46:
47:     //////////////////// Search member functions ////////////////
48:     unsigned LinearSearch(int searchData,
49:                         unsigned last = HI_INDEX,
50:                         unsigned first = 0);
51:     unsigned BinarySearch(int searchData,
52:                         unsigned last = HI_INDEX,
53:                         unsigned first = 0);
54:
55:     unsigned StatisticalSearch(int searchData,
56:                         unsigned last = HI_INDEX,
57:                         unsigned first = 0);
58: };
59:
60: #endif
```

Listing 13.2 shows the line-numbered source code for the INTARR.CPP library file. The implementation is simple and easy to follow, because the class models fixed-size arrays of integers.

Listing 13.2. The line-numbered source code for the INTARR.CPP library file.

```
 1:   #include "intarr.hpp"
 2:
 3:   ////////////////////////////////////////////////////////////////////
 4:   //
 5:
 6:   void TIntArray::copy(TIntArray& srcArray)
 7:   //
 8:   // Purpose: copies the srcArray array to this instance.
 9:   //
10:   // Parameters:
11:   //
12:   //    input: srcArray - the source array to be copied.
13:   //
14:   //
15:   {
16:
17:     isSorted = srcArray.isSorted;
18:     badIndex = srcArray.badIndex;
19:     for (unsigned i = 0; i < ARRAY_SIZE; i++)
20:       arrData[i] = srcArray.arrData[i];
21:   }
22:
23:   ////////////////////////////////////////////////////////////////////
24:   //
25:
26:   void TIntArray::ShellSort(unsigned last, unsigned first)
27:   //
28:   // Purpose: sorts the array elements in the range [first..last]
29:   // using the Shell-Metzner sort method.
30:   //
31:   // Parameters:
32:   //
33:   //    input: first, last - the range of sorted array elements.
34:   //
35:   {
36:     unsigned i, j, offset, n;
37:     int swapElem;
38:
39:     if (first >= last ||
40:         first >= ARRAY_SIZE)
41:       return;
42:
43:     // adjust the parameter last?
44:     last = (last >= ARRAY_SIZE) ? ARRAY_SIZE - 1 : last;
45:     n = last - first + 1;
46:     offset = n;
47:     while (offset > 1) {
```

continues

Listing 13.2. continued

```
48:        // update offset and make sure it never goes below 1
49:        offset = (offset - 1) / 3;
50:        offset = (offset == 0) ? 1 : offset;
51:        // order neighbors that are offset elements apart
52:        do {
53:          isSorted = true;
54:          // compare neighbors that are offset elements apart
55:          for (i = first; i <= (last - offset); i++) {
56:            j = i + offset;
57:            // need to swap?
58:            if (arrData[i] > arrData[j]) {
59:              // swap elements i and j
60:              isSorted = false;
61:              swapElem = arrData[i];
62:              arrData[i] = arrData[j];
63:              arrData[j] = swapElem;
64:            }
65:          }
66:        } while (!isSorted);
67:     }
68: }
69:
70: ///////////////////////////////////////////////////////////////////////
71: //
72:
73: void TIntArray::CombSort(unsigned last, unsigned first)
74: //
75: // Purpose: sorts the array elements in the range [first..last]
76: // using the new Combsort method.
77: //
78: // Parameters:
79: //
80: //     input: first, last - the range of sorted array elements.
81: //
82: // Comments: The function exits if parameter first is greater than
83: // or equal to ARRAY_SIZE, or the parameter first is greater
84: // than or equal to the parameter last. If the parameter last is
85: // greater than or equal to ARRAY_SIZE, the function assigns the
86: // expression ARRAY_SIZE - 1 to the parameter last.
87: //
88: //
89: {
90:   unsigned i, j, n, offset;
91:   long k;
92:   int swapElem;
93:
94:   if (first >= ARRAY_SIZE || first >= last)
95:     return;
```

```
96:
97:     // adjust the argument for the parameter last ?
98:     last = (last >= ARRAY_SIZE) ? ARRAY_SIZE - 1 : last;
99:     // get the initial offset which is also
100:    // the number of sorted array elements.
101:    offset = last - first + 1; // get the initial offset
102:    // start loop to sort the array elements in the
103:    // range [first..last]
104:    do {
105:      // update the offset, making sure that it
106:      // does not become less than 1
107:      k = (offset * 8L) / 11;
108:      offset = (k == 0) ? 1 : (unsigned)k;
109:      isSorted = true;
110:      // start comparing array elements that are
111:      // offset members apart
112:      for (i = first; i <= (last - offset); i++) {
113:        j = i + offset;
114:        // need to swap elements i and j?
115:        if (arrData[i] > arrData[j]) {
116:          // swap the elements i and j
117:          isSorted = false;
118:          swapElem = arrData[i];
119:          arrData[i] = arrData[j];
120:          arrData[j] = swapElem;
121:        }
122:      }
123:    } while (!(isSorted && offset == 1));
124:  }
125:
126:  ///////////////////////////////////////////////////////////////////
127:  //
128:
129:  void TIntArray::QuickSort(unsigned last, unsigned first)
130:  //
131:  // Purpose: sorts the array elements in the range of [first..last]
132:  // using the QuickSort method. This function calls the recursive
133:  // (and protected) Qsort method to perform the actual sorting.
134:  //
135:  // Parameters:
136:  //
137:  //     input: first, last - the range of sorted array elements.
138:  //
139:  {
140:    if (first >= last ||
141:        first >= ARRAY_SIZE ||
142:        ARRAY_SIZE < 2)
143:        return;
144:
145:    // adjust the parameter last?
```

continues

Listing 13.2. continued

```
146:    last = (last >= ARRAY_SIZE) ? ARRAY_SIZE - 1 : last;
147:    Qsort(first, last);
148:    isSorted = true;
149:  }
150:
151:  ////////////////////////////////////////////////////////////////////
152:  //
153:
154:  void TIntArray::Qsort(unsigned first, unsigned last)
155:  //
156:  // Purpose: sorts the array elements in the range [first..last].
157:  //
158:  // Parameters:
159:  //
160:  //    input: first, last - the range of sorted array elements.
161:  //
162:  {
163:    unsigned i, j;
164:    int swapElem, median;
165:
166:    i = first;
167:    j = last;
168:    // get the median element
169:    median = arrData[(first + last) / 2];
170:    do {
171:      while (arrData[i] < median)
172:        i++;
173:      while (median < arrData[j])
174:        j—;
175:      if (i <= j) {
176:        swapElem = arrData[i];
177:        arrData[i++] = arrData[j];
178:        arrData[j—] = swapElem;
179:      }
180:    } while (i <= j);
181:
182:    if (first < j)
183:      Qsort(first, j);
184:
185:    if (i < last)
186:      Qsort(i, last);
187:  }
188:
189:  ////////////////////////////////////////////////////////////////////
190:  //
191:
192:  unsigned TIntArray::LinearSearch(int searchData,
193:                                   unsigned last,
194:                                   unsigned first)
```

```
195:    //
196:    // Purpose: performs a smart linear search in the range of first
197:    // to last.
198:    //
199:    // The function returns the index of the first
200:    // array member that matches the searchData. If no match is found,
201:    // the function yields NO_ELEM_FOUND.
202:    //
203:    // Parameters:
204:    //
205:    //    input: searchData - the data to search.
206:    //           first, last - the range of indices to search.
207:    //
208:    {
209:       boolean notFound = true;
210:       unsigned i;
211:
212:       // check the arguments
213:       if (first >= ARRAY_SIZE ¦¦ first > last)
214:         return NO_ELEM_FOUND;
215:
216:       // adjust the argument for parameter last
217:       last = (last < ARRAY_SIZE) ? last : ARRAY_SIZE - 1;
218:       // is search in the forward direction?
219:       i = first;
220:       // search from start to last
221:       while (i <= last && notFound)
222:         if (arrData[i] != searchData)
223:            i++;
224:         else
225:            notFound = false;
226:
227:       return (notFound == false) ? i : NO_ELEM_FOUND;
228:    }
229:
230:    ////////////////////////////////////////////////////////////////////
231:    //
232:
233:    unsigned TIntArray::StatisticalSearch(int searchData,
234:                                          unsigned last,
235:                                          unsigned first)
236:    //
237:    // Purpose: performs a linear search that starts at the median
238:    // array element and resumes toward the first and last members.
239:    // The function returns the index of the first array member that
240:    // matches the searchData. If no match is found, the function
241:    // yields NO_ELEM_FOUND.
242:    //
243:    // Parameters:
244:    //
```

continues

LISTING 13.2. CONTINUED

```
245:   //    input: searchData - the search data.
246:   //            first, last - the range of indices to search.
247:   //
248:   {
249:     unsigned n, m, i, j, k, count, shift;
250:     boolean notFound = true;
251:
252:     if (first > last ||
253:         first >= ARRAY_SIZE)
254:       return NO_ELEM_FOUND;
255:
256:     n = last - first + 1;
257:     m = n / 2;
258:     count = m;
259:     // is n an odd number?
260:     if ((n % 2) > 0) {
261:       // examine the median of an odd-number range
262:       if (arrData[m] == searchData)
263:         return m;
264:       shift = 1;
265:     }
266:     else
267:       shift = 0;
268:     k = 2 * m + shift;
269:     // search around the median value
270:     while (notFound && count > 0) {
271:       // search above the median
272:       j = k - count;
273:       // arrray[j] match search data ?
274:       if (arrData[j] == searchData) {
275:         k = j; // save matching index in k
276:         notFound = false;
277:       }
278:
279:       // still not found a match
280:       if (notFound) {
281:         // search below the median and also
282:         // decrement count
283:         i = count— - 1;
284:         // arrray[i] match search data ?
285:         if (arrData[i] == searchData) {
286:           k = i; // save matching index in k
287:           notFound = false;
288:         }
289:       }
290:     }
291:
```

```
292:     return (!notFound) ? k : NO_ELEM_FOUND;
293: }
294:
295: ////////////////////////////////////////////////////////////////
296: //
297:
298: unsigned TIntArray::BinarySearch(int searchData,
299:                                  unsigned last,
300:                                  unsigned first)
301: //
302: // Purpose: performs a simple binary search on the ordered elements
303: // of an array. You are responsible to ensure that the array elements
304: // in the range [first..last] are ordered.
305: //
306: // Parameters:
307: //
308: //    input: searchData - the search data.
309: //           first, last - the range of searched indices.
310: //
311: {
312:   int median;
313:   unsigned m;
314:
315:   do {
316:     m = (first + last) / 2;
317:     if (searchData < arrData[m])
318:       last = m - 1;
319:     else
320:       first = m + 1;
321:   } while (!(searchData == arrData[m] || first > last));
322:
323:   return (searchData == arrData[m]) ? m : NO_ELEM_FOUND;
324: }
325:
```

Listing 13.3 contains the line-numbered source code for TSARR1.CPP test program file. This file tests the ShellSort, LinearSearch, and BinarySearch member functions. The program creates the instances ar1 and ar2 and uses the ordinary array data to assign integers to these arrays. The program tests the member functions with the instance ar1. In addition, using the ShellSort function, the program sorts the elements of instance ar2 and applies the binary search method to that array.

```
 1:  /*
 2:    Program uses the class TIntArray to test unconditional breakpoints
 3:  */
 4:
 5:  #include <iostream.h>
 6:  #include "intarr.hpp"
 7:
 8:  // declare prototype
 9:  void displayArray(const char* msg, TIntArray& arr,
10:                    unsigned first, unsigned last);
11:  void pressEnterKey();
12:
13:  main()
14:  {
15:    int data[ARRAY_SIZE] = { 451, 927, 123, 675, 344,
16:                             210, 871, 655, 444, 368,
17:                             399, 545, 100, 888, 410 };
18:
19:    TIntArray ar1, ar2;
20:    unsigned i, n = ARRAY_SIZE - 1;
21:    unsigned idx1 = ARRAY_SIZE / 3;
22:    unsigned idx2 = 2 * idx1;
23:    int searchData;
24:
25:    // initialize the array ar1 with integers in the array data
26:    for (i = 0; i < ARRAY_SIZE; i++)
27:      ar1[i] = data[i];
28:
29:    displayArray("Unsorted array is:", ar1, 0, n);
30:    // search for data in the unordered array ar1
31:    searchData = ar1[idx1];
32:    i = ar1.LinearSearch(searchData);
33:    if (i != NO_ELEM_FOUND)
34:      cout << "Found match for " << searchData
35:           << " at index " << i << " of array ar1\n\n";
36:    else
37:      cout << "No match for " << searchData << " in array ar1\n\n";
38:    pressEnterKey();
39:
40:    ar2 = ar1;
41:    // test the ShellSort method
42:    ar2.ShellSort();
43:    displayArray("Array sorted using Shellsort is:", ar2, 0, n);
44:    // search for data in the ordered array ar2
45:    searchData = ar1[idx2];
46:    i = ar2.BinarySearch(searchData);
47:    if (i != NO_ELEM_FOUND)
48:      cout << "Found match for " << searchData
```

```
49:             << " at index " << i << " of array ar2\n\n";
50:    else
51:      cout << "No match for " << searchData << " of array ar2\n\n";
52:    pressEnterKey();
53:
54:    return 0;
55: }
56:
57:
58: void pressEnterKey()
59: {
60:    char c[3];
61:
62:    cout <<"press Enter to continue...";
63:    cin.getline(c, 2);
64: }
65:
66: void displayArray(const char* msg,
67:                   TIntArray& arr,
68:                   unsigned first,
69:                   unsigned last)
70: {
71:    cout << "\n\n\n\n" << msg << "\n\n";
72:    for (unsigned i = first; i <= last; i++) {
73:      cout.width(2);
74:      cout << i << " : " << arr[i] << '\n';
75:    }
76:    pressEnterKey();
77: }
```

Create the .IDE file INTARR as an EasyWin application and include the INTARR.CPP and TSARR1.CPP files in the TSARR1 target. Compile and link the files of the TSARR1 target. Run the TSARR1.EXE program to view the output, shown as follows:

```
Unsorted array is:

 0 : 451
 1 : 927
 2 : 123
 3 : 675
 4 : 344
 5 : 210
 6 : 871
 7 : 655
 8 : 444
 9 : 368
10 : 399
11 : 545
```

continues

continued

```
12 : 100
13 : 888
14 : 410
press Enter to continue...
Found match for 210 at index 5 of array ar1

press Enter to continue...

Array sorted using ShellSort is:


 0 : 100
 1 : 123
 2 : 210
 3 : 344
 4 : 368
 5 : 399
 6 : 410
 7 : 444
 8 : 451
 9 : 545
10 : 655
11 : 675
12 : 871
13 : 888
14 : 927
press Enter to continue...
Found match for 871 at index 12 of array ar2

press Enter to continue...
```

Now insert a few unconditional breakpoints in the following lines (the lines containing the breakpoints appear in bold):

1. In member function LinearSearch, insert a breakpoint at line 222:

```
219:     i = first;
220:     // search from start to last
221:     while (i <= last && notFound)
222:        if (arrData[i] != searchData)
223:           i++;
224:        else
225:           notFound = false;
```

2. In member function ShellSort, insert a breakpoint at line 53:

```
52:     do {
53:        isSorted = true;
```

```
54:          // compare neighbors that are offset elements apart
55:          for (i = first; i <= (last - offset); i++) {
```

3. In member function BinarySearch, insert a breakpoint at line 317:

```
315:    do {
316:      m = (first + last) / 2;
317:      if (searchData < arrData[m])
318:        last = m - 1;
319:      else
320:        first = m + 1;
321:    } while (!(searchData == arrData[m] ¦¦ first > last));
```

Now run the program again. The program stops at the first breakpoint (in member function LinearSearch). Table 13.2 shows the watched variables for the LinearSearch member function, as you single-step through the while loop in line 221.

TABLE 13.2. THE WATCHED VARIABLES FOR THE LINEARSEARCH MEMBER FUNCTION.					
Line Number	i	arrData[i]	searchData	last	notFound
222	0	451	210	14	1 /* true */
223	1	927	210	14	1 /* true */
221	1	927	210	14	1 /* true */
222	1	927	210	14	1 /* true */
223	2	123	210	14	1 /* true */
221	2	123	210	14	1 /* true */
222	2	123	210	14	1 /* true */
223	3	675	210	14	1 /* true */
221	3	675	210	14	1 /* true */
222	3	675	210	14	1 /* true */
223	4	344	210	14	1 /* true */
221	4	344	210	14	1 /* true */

continues

TABLE 13.2. CONTINUED

Line Number	i	arrData[i]	searchData	last	notFound
222	4	344	210	14	1 /* true */
223	5	210	210	14	1 /* true */
221	5	210	210	14	1 /* true */
222	5	210	210	14	1 /* true */
225	5	210	210	14	0 /* false */

Once you are out of the while loop, press the Ctrl+F9 keys to run the program at full speed until it waits for input and (or) reaches the next breakpoint. For the next breakpoint (in the ShellSort member function), remove the current watched variables and insert the offset and isSorted variables. In addition, use the Inspect... option to inspect the arrData member and watch its elements get sorted. Table 13.3 shows the value of the offset and isSorted variables, along with the contents of the arrData member. These are the values that appear at the breakpoint. To view subsequent table entries, press the Ctrl+F9 keys. In a sense, the information in Table 13.3 shows you snapshots of the array in arrData being sorted.

TABLE 13.3. THE WATCHED VARIABLES FOR THE SHELLSORT MEMBER FUNCTION.

offset	isSorted	arrData (in Inspect Window)
4	0 /* false*/	451 927 123 675 344 210 871 655 444 368 399 545 100 888 410
4	0 /* false*/	344 210 123 655 444 368 399 545 100 888 410 675 451 927 871
4	0 /* false*/	344 210 123 545 100 368 399 655 444 888 410 675 451 927 871
4	0 /* false*/	100 210 123 545 344 368 399 655 444 888 410 675 451 927 871
1	1 /* true */	100 210 123 545 344 368 399 655 444

offset	isSorted	arrData (in Inspect Window)
		888 410 675 451 927 871
1	0 /* false */	100 123 210 344 368 399 545 444 655 410 675 451 888 871 927
1	0 /* false */	100 123 210 344 368 399 444 545 410 655 451 675 871 888 927
1	0 /* false */	100 123 210 344 368 399 444 410 545 451 655 675 871 888 927
1	0 /* false */	100 123 210 344 368 399 410 444 451 545 655 675 871 888 927

When the program stops at the breakpoint in the BinarySearch member function, remove the current watched variables and close the Inspect window. Insert the variables m, arrData[m], searchData, first, and last in the Watch window. Table 13.4 shows the values of these watched variables each time the program stops at the breakpoint in the BinarySearch function. Notice that it takes three iterations of the efficient BinarySearch function to locate a match for the search value.

TABLE 13.4. THE WATCHED VARIABLES FOR THE BINARYSEARCH MEMBER FUNCTION.

m	arrData[m]	searchData	first	last
7	444	399	0	14
3	344	399	0	6
5	399	399	4	6

LOGGING EXPRESSIONS

Now use the breakpoint feature, which logs an expression at the breakpoints. The integrated debugger gives you the option of logging an expression (which appears in the Event Log window) with or without stopping at the breakpoint. First try the feature of logging an expression without stopping at the breakpoint. I'll use program TSARR2.CPP, appearing with line numbers in Listing 13.4.

The target TSARR2.EXE is also part of the INTARR.IDE project file. The source code in the TSARR2.CPP file is similar to that of TSARR1.CPP. The new program tests the CombSort member function instead of ShellSort, and it tests the StatisticalSearch member function instead of LinearSearch. The two programs emit the same output.

LISTING 13.4. THE LINE-NUMBERED SOURCE CODE FOR THE TSARR2.CPP PROGRAM FILE.

```
 1:   /*
 2:      Program uses the class TIntArray to test unconditional breakpoints
 3:   */
 4:
 5:   #include <iostream.h>
 6:   #include "intarr.hpp"
 7:
 8:   // declare prototype
 9:   void displayArray(const char* msg, TIntArray& arr,
10:                     unsigned first, unsigned last);
11:   void pressEnterKey();
12:
13:   main()
14:   {
15:     int data[ARRAY_SIZE] = { 451, 927, 123, 675, 344,
16:                              210, 871, 655, 444, 368,
17:                              399, 545, 100, 888, 410 };
18:
19:     TIntArray ar1, ar2;
20:     unsigned i, n = ARRAY_SIZE - 1;
21:     unsigned idx1 = ARRAY_SIZE / 3;
22:     unsigned idx2 = 2 * idx1;
23:     int searchData;
24:
25:     // initialize the array ar1 with integers in the array data
26:     for (i = 0; i < ARRAY_SIZE; i++)
27:       ar1[i] = data[i];
28:
29:     displayArray("Unsorted array is:", ar1, 0, n);
30:     // search for data in the unordered array ar1
31:     searchData = ar1[idx1];
32:     i = ar1.StatisticalSearch(searchData);
33:     if (i != NO_ELEM_FOUND)
34:       cout << "Found match for " << searchData
35:            << " at index " << i << " of array ar1\n\n";
36:     else
37:       cout << "No match for " << searchData << " in array ar1\n\n";
38:     pressEnterKey();
39:
40:     ar2 = ar1;
```

```
41:    // test the CombSort method
42:    ar2.CombSort();
43:    displayArray("Array sorted using CombSort is:", ar2, 0, n);
44:    // search for data in the ordered array ar2
45:    searchData = ar1[idx2];
46:    i = ar2.BinarySearch(searchData);
47:    if (i != NO_ELEM_FOUND)
48:      cout << "Found match for " << searchData
49:           << " at index " << i << " of array ar2\n\n";
50:    else
51:      cout << "No match for " << searchData << " of array ar2\n\n";
52:    pressEnterKey();
53:
54:    return 0;
55:  }
56:
57:
58:  void pressEnterKey()
59:  {
60:    char c[3];
61:
62:    cout <<"press Enter to continue...";
63:    cin.getline(c, 2);
64:  }
65:
66:  void displayArray(const char* msg,
67:                    TIntArray& arr,
68:                    unsigned first,
69:                    unsigned last)
70:  {
71:    cout << "\n\n\n\n" << msg << "\n\n";
72:    for (unsigned i = first; i <= last; i++) {
73:      cout.width(2);
74:      cout << i << " : " << arr[i] << '\n';
75:    }
76:    pressEnterKey();
77:  }
```

Insert three breakpoints to log expressions at lines 262, 274, and 286 of Listing 13.2. You enter the next messages in the Expression to Log combo box located in the Breakpoint Properties dialog box. Enter the message **Median search in StatisticalSearch()** for the breakpoint at line 262:

```
260:    if ((n % 2) > 0) {
261:      // examine the median of an odd-number range
262:      if (arrData[m] == searchData)
263:        return m;
264:      shift = 1;
```

Enter the message **Above-median search in StatisticalSearch()** for the breakpoint at line 274:

```
272:      j = k - count;
273:      // arrray[j] match search data ?
274:      if (arrData[j] == searchData) {
275:         k = j; // save matching index in k
276:         notFound = false;
277:      }
```

Enter the message **Below-median search in StatisticalSearch()** for the breakpoint at line 274:

```
283:      i = count— - 1;
284:      // arrray[i] match search data ?
285:      if (arrData[i] == searchData) {
286:         k = i; // save matching index in k
287:         notFound = false;
288:      }
```

Now run the program. Because the breakpoints you just set do not stop the program execution, the program runs at full speed. Once the program ends, invoke the Log Event option in the View menu selection. Figure 13.7 presents the Event Log window showing the results of the breakpoints, log expressions for the StatisticalSearch member function. The information in the Log Event window indicates that the StatisticalSearch function compared the search data with five array elements in order to find a match.

Another use for logging expressions is to count the number of operations, such as loops and data swapping (to name a few). Clear the breakpoints, in the StatisticalSearch member function and insert two new ones in the CombSort member function. The first breakpoint is at line 107 of Listing 13.2 and has the message Outer loop iteration:

```
104:   do {
105:      // update the offset, making sure that it
106:      // does not become less than 1
107:      k = (offset * 8L) / 11;
108:      offset = (k == 0) ? 1 : (unsigned)k;
109:      isSorted = true;
```

The second breakpoint is at line 117 of Listing 13.2 and has the message Swapping array elements:

```
114:         // need to swap elements i and j?
115:         if (arrData[i] > arrData[j]) {
```

```
116:              // swap the elements i and j
117:              isSorted = false;
118:              swapElem = arrData[i];
119:              arrData[i] = arrData[j];
120:              arrData[j] = swapElem;
121:          }
```

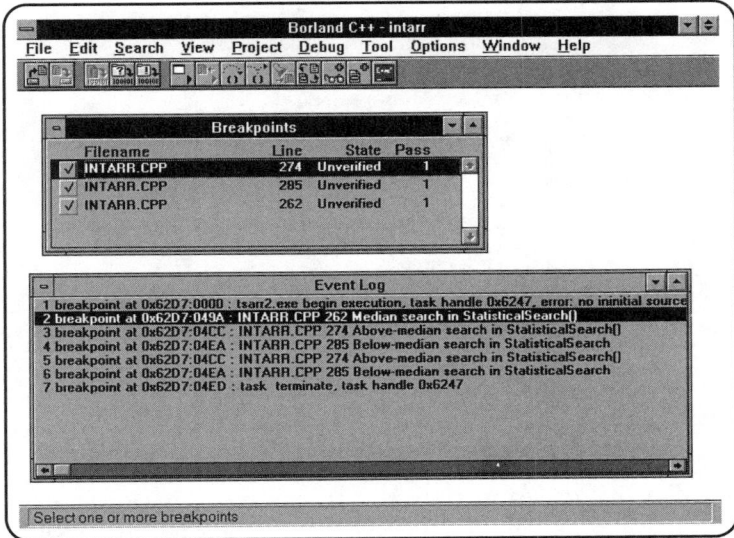

Figure 13.7. The Event Log window, showing the results of the breakpoints' log expressions for the StatisticalSearch member function.

Run the program with the two breakpoints. Again, the program executes in a normal fashion and logs the breakpoint expressions. Figure 13.8 shows the Log Event window with the logged expressions. The information in the Log Event indicates that the CombSort function executed the outer loop eight times. The sequence for the number of swapped elements is 3, 4, 2, 5, 4, 6, 2, and 0. This kind of information illustrates how to use logged expressions to track program flow without altering the source code itself. This approach prevents you from accidentally introducing errors in the source code when you modify it.

You can make the program stop at the breakpoint and also log an expression. With this approach you can keep track of both the number of times the program stopped and line numbers for these stops.

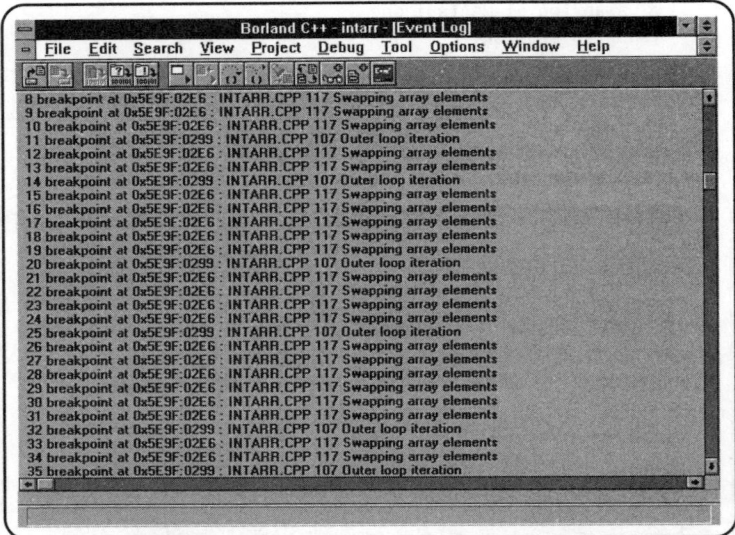

Figure 13.8. The Log Event window, showing the logged expression for the breakpoints in the CombSort function.

Tracking calls to recursive functions is another way of using logged expressions. Listing 13.5 shows the line-numbered source code for the TSARR3.CPP program file. This program is a scaled-down version of TSARR1.CPP that uses the QuickSort member function to sort the elements of array ar1 (the new program only declares one instance of the TIntArray class). To log the recursive calls to the protected member function QSort, insert a breakpoint at line 166 in Listing 13.2 and enter the expression "Call to QSort()":

```
166:    i = first;
167:    j = last;
168:    // get the median element
169:    median = arrData[(first + last) / 2];
```

Run the program and then view the Log Event window. Figure 13.9 shows the Log Event window containing the logged expressions for the breakpoints in the QSort function. The Log Event window indicates that the QSort function was called 12 times in all, of which 11 calls are recursive.

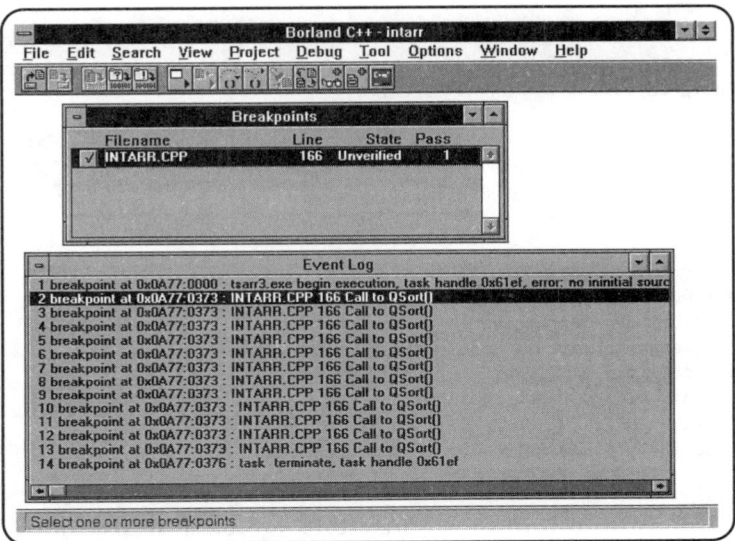

Figure 13.9. The Log Event window, showing the logged expressions for the breakpoints in the QSort function.

LISTING 13.5. THE LINE-NUMBERED SOURCE CODE FOR THE TSARR3.CPP PROGRAM FILE.

```
 1:  /*
 2:    Program uses the class TIntArray to test unconditional breakpoints
 3:  */
 4:
 5:  #include <iostream.h>
 6:  #include "intarr.hpp"
 7:
 8:  // declare prototype
 9:  void displayArray(const char* msg, TIntArray& arr,
10:                    unsigned first, unsigned last);
11:  void pressEnterKey();
12:
13:  main()
14:  {
15:    int data[ARRAY_SIZE] = { 451, 927, 123, 675, 344,
16:                             210, 871, 655, 444, 368,
17:                             399, 545, 100, 888, 410 };
18:
19:    TIntArray ar1;
20:    unsigned i, n = ARRAY_SIZE - 1;
```

continues

LISTING 13.5. CONTINUED

```
21:     unsigned idx1 = 2 * ARRAY_SIZE / 3;
22:     int searchData;
23:
24:     // initialize the array ar1 with integers in the array data
25:     for (i = 0; i < ARRAY_SIZE; i++)
26:       ar1[i] = data[i];
27:
28:     // test the QuickSort method
29:     ar1.QuickSort();
30:     displayArray("Array sorted using QuickSort is:", ar1, 0, n);
31:     // search for data in the ordered array ar1
32:     searchData = ar1[idx1;
33:     i = ar1.BinarySearch(searchData);
34:     if (i != NO_ELEM_FOUND)
35:       cout << "Found match for " << searchData
36:             << " at index " << i << " of array ar1\n\n";
37:     else
38:       cout << "No match for " << searchData << " of array ar1\n\n";
39:     pressEnterKey();
40:
41:     return 0;
42: }
43:
44:
45: void pressEnterKey()
46: {
47:   char c[3];
48:
49:   cout <<"press Enter to continue...";
50:   cin.getline(c, 2);
51: }
52:
53: void displayArray(const char* msg,
54:                   TIntArray& arr,
55:                   unsigned first,
56:                   unsigned last)
57: {
58:   cout << "\n\n\n\n" << msg << "\n\n";
59:   for (unsigned i = first; i <= last; i++) {
60:     cout.width(2);
61:     cout << i << " : " << arr[i] << '\n';
62:   }
63:   pressEnterKey();
64: }
```

USING COUNTED PASSES

Single-stepping through the statements of a loop can be tedious, time-consuming, and frustrating. To make matters worse, you may need to repeat the process to zoom in on the offending iteration. With the integrated debugger, you can specify the number of passes before the program stops at the breakpoint. This feature enables you to zoom in, at full speed, to the iteration you want to examine carefully.

Another use for specifying the number of passes deals with detecting and dealing with possible infinite loops. You set the number of passes to about (or beyond) the reasonable number of loop iterations. If the code of the loop makes it iterate indefinitely, the breakpoint enables you to stop the loop, detect and examine the offending variables and expression, and then make the required corrections.

Now work with the Pass Count combo box in the Breakpoint Properties dialog box. Insert a breakpoint at line 60 in Listing 13.2 and enter the number 7 in the Pass Count combo box:

```
58:             if (arrData[i] > arrData[j]) {
59:                 // swap elements i and j
60:                 isSorted = false;
61:                 swapElem = arrData[i];
62:                 arrData[i] = arrData[j];
63:                 arrData[j] = swapElem;
64:             }
```

To allow the program to stop at the breakpoint, mark the Break check box in the Breakpoint Properties dialog box. Clear any watched variables in the Watch window and insert the variables offset, i, j, arrData[i], and arrData[j]. Moreover, invoke the Inspect... option to inspect the elements of the arrData member. Run the TSARR1.EXE program. When the program starts sorting the elements of object ar2, it will stop after swapping every 7 elements, regardless of the value of control loops. Figures 13.10 through 13.12 present the snapshots of the Inspect and Watch windows for the three times the program stops. The figures show you the order of the array elements at each breakpoint. The Watch window gives you an idea of the progress in the sorting process. Thus, using counted passes, you can study the data in selected iterations instead of being overwhelmed by the data at every iteration.

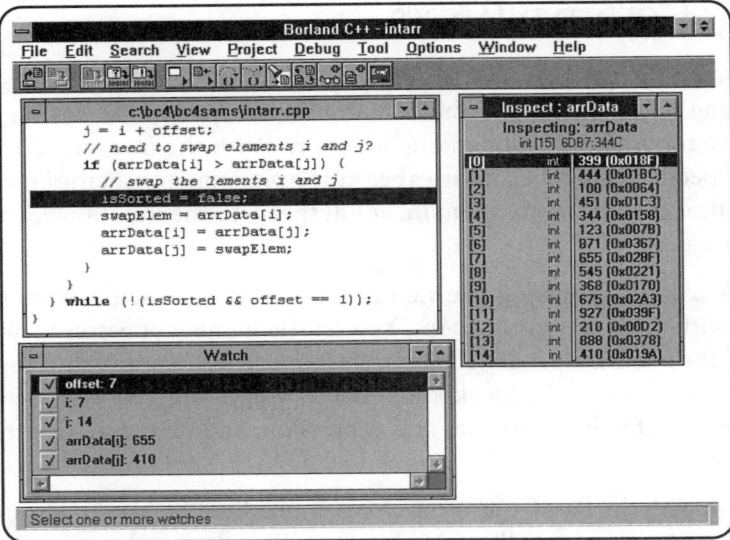

Figure 13.10. The counted passes for the TSARR1.EXE program the first time the program breaks.

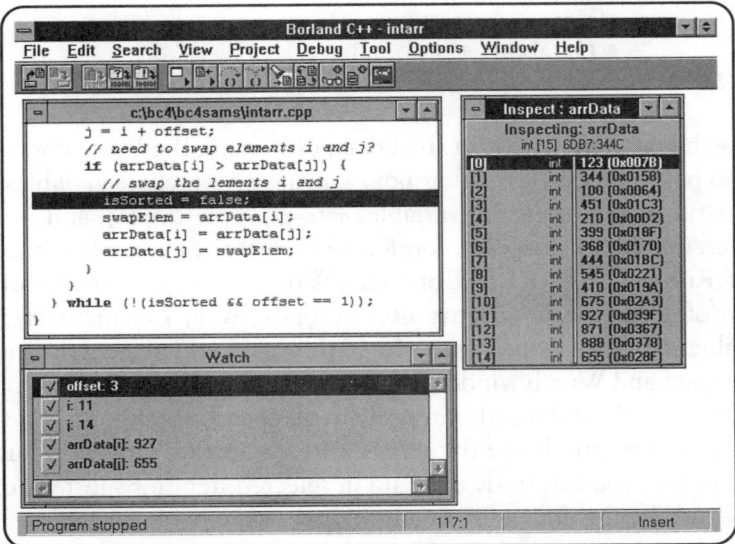

Figure 13.11. The counted passes for the TSARR1.EXE program the second time the program breaks.

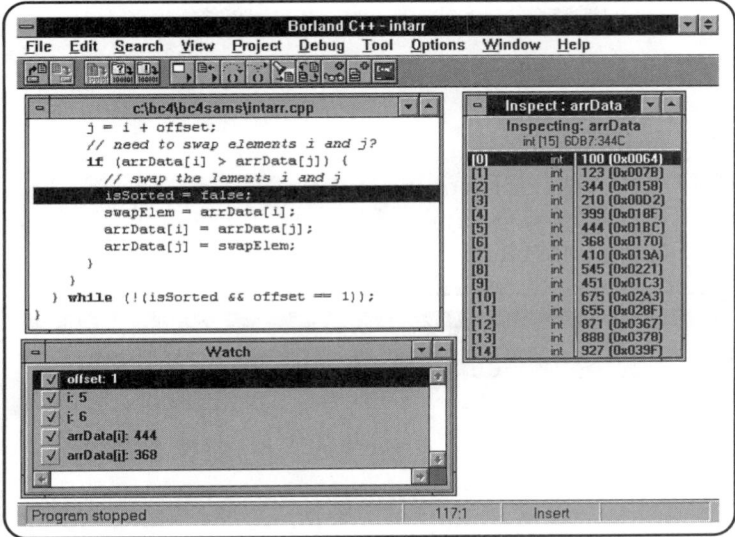

Figure 13.12. The counted passes for the TSARR1.EXE program the last time the program breaks.

USING CONDITIONAL BREAKPOINTS

Conditional breakpoints simplify and speed up debugging because they do not stop the program (or log an expression) unless a condition is true. The Breakpoint Properties dialog box offers controls to turn on conditional breakpoints and enter the conditional expression.

Look at a simple example of a conditional breakpoint. Assume that I want to get logged expressions for each do-while iteration in the BinarySearch function and for each iteration where the difference between the current values of the last and first parameters is less than 3. I first insert an unconditional breakpoint at line 316 in Listing 13.2 and supply it with the expression "Another iteration". Then, I insert a conditional breakpoint at line 317. The condition for this breakpoint is the expression (last - first) < 3. The accompanying expression is Narrow search range:

```
315:    do {
316:        m = (first + last) / 2;
317:        if (searchData < arrData[m])
318:            last = m - 1;
```

continues

continued

```
319:       else
320:           first = m + 1;
321:     } while (!(searchData == arrData[m] || first > last));
```

Run the TSARR2.EXE program to log the expressions of these breakpoints. Figure 13.13 shows the Log Event window after the program ends. The window shows the logged expression emitted by each breakpoint. The information shows how efficient the binary search algorithm is.

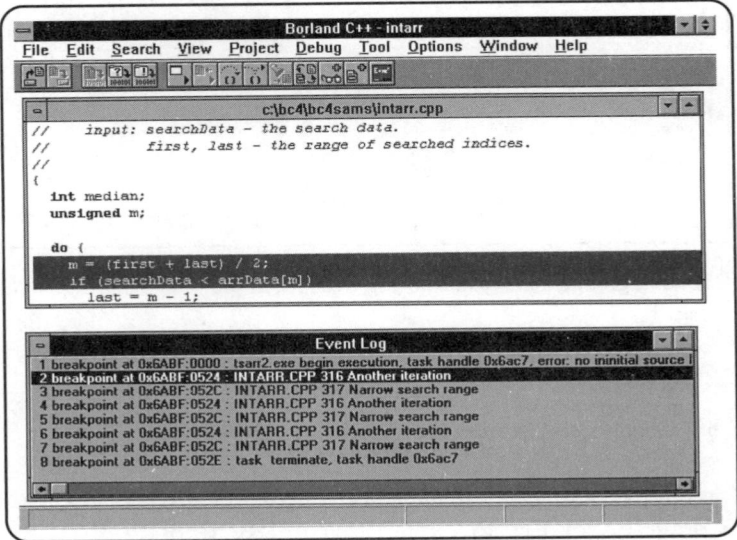

Figure 13.13. The Log Event window, showing logged expressions for conditional and unconditional breakpoints.

BROWSING AT SYMBOLS

The IDE provides you with the Browse symbol option in the View menu selection. With this option, you can list and examine the members of a class, including the inherited ones. Figure 13.14 presents the browsing window showing the members of the TIntArray class. The window includes symbol identifiers to the left of each member. The letter *v* indicates that the symbol is a data member. The letter *f* indicates that the member is a member function. The window shows the data type associated with the data members and also the parameter types and return type associated with the member functions. If you select a member function and double-click it, the IDE displays a list of the parameter types in a new window. Notice that all of the parameter lists end with the pointer this, an invisible parameter automatically included by the compiler. Figure 13.15 presents the browsing window that lists the parameters of the ShellSort member function.

With the browse option you can examine the makeup of classes, and you can focus especially on the inherited members.

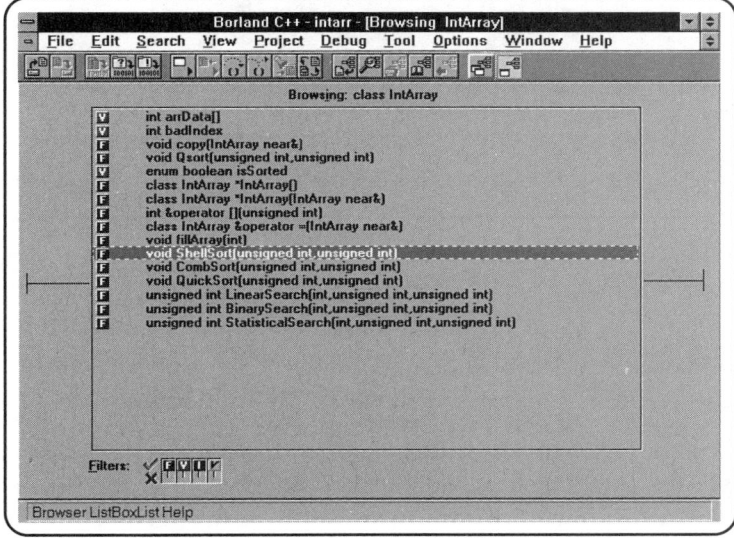

Figure 13.14. The browsing window showing the members of the TIntArray class.

SUMMARY

This chapter focused on working with the integrated debugger and using the browser. You learned about the following topics:

- The menu options of the Debug menu selection. These options support various aspects of debugging, such as single-stepping, setting different kinds of conditional and unconditional breakpoints, watching variables, evaluating expressions, and inspecting arrays.

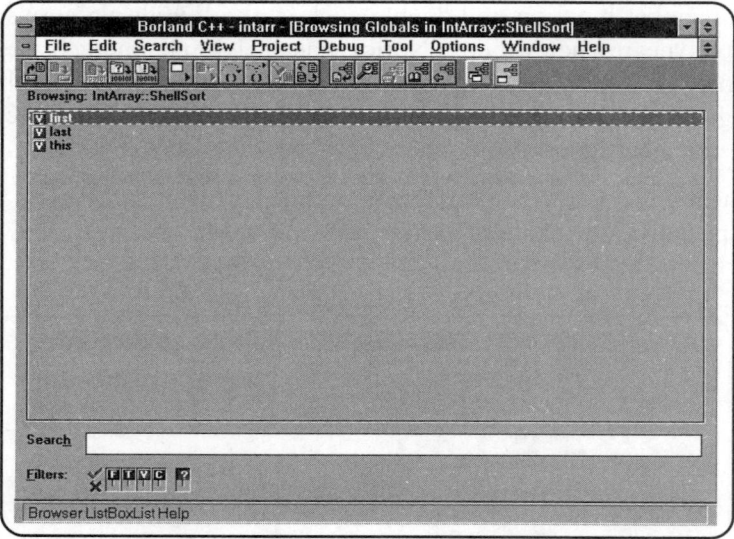

Figure 13.15. The browsing window showing the parameters of the ShellSort member function.

- How to use conditional and unconditional breakpoints, how to use logged expressions, and how to exploit multipass breakpoints.

- Using the IDE Browse symbol... option to view the declared and inherited data members and member functions of a class. With the IDE you also can focus on the parameter list of a member function.

OBJECT-ORIENTED PROGRAMMING AND C++ CLASSES

Classes provide C++ with object-oriented programming (OOP) constructs that you can use to encapsulate the characteristics and operations of an object. This appendix introduces you to building individual classes as well as class hierarchy. It covers the following topics:

- Basics of object-oriented programming

- Declaring base classes

- Constructors

- Destructors

- Declaring a class hierarchy

- Virtual functions

- Constant functions

- Friend functions

- Operators and friend operators

- Static data members

- Static member functions
- Multiple inheritance

BASICS OF OBJECT-ORIENTED PROGRAMMING

We live in a world of objects. Each object has its attributes and operations, and some objects are more animated than others. You can categorize objects into classes. For example, my CASIO Data Bank watch is an object that belongs to the class of the CASIO Data Bank watches. You can also relate individual classes in a class hierarchy. The class of CASIO Data Bank watches is part of the watch class hierarchy. Object-oriented programming (OOP) uses the notions of real-world objects to develop applications. The basics of OOP include classes, objects, messages, methods, inheritance, and polymorphism.

CLASSES AND OBJECTS

A *class* defines a category of objects. Each *object* is an instance of a class. An object shares the same attributes and functionality with other objects in the same class. Typically, an object has a unique state, defined by the current values of its attributes. The functionality of a class determines the operations that are possible for the class instances. C++ calls the attributes of a class *data members* and calls the operations of a class *member functions*. Classes encapsulate data members and member functions. Going back to the CASIO watch example, the buttons on the watch represent the member functions of the class of CASIO watches, whereas the display represents a data member. I can press certain buttons to edit the date and time. In OOP terms, the member functions alter the state of the object by changing its data members.

MESSAGES AND METHODS

Object-oriented programming models the interaction with objects as events where messages are sent to an object or between objects. The object receiving a message responds by invoking the appropriate method (that's the member function in C++). The *message* is **what** is done to an object. The *method* is **how** the object responds to the incoming message. C++ does not explicitly foster the notion of messages and methods as other OOP languages, such as SmallTalk, do. I find it easier, however, to use the term message when I discuss invoking member functions. The terms *methods* and *member functions* are equivalent.

INHERITANCE

In object-oriented languages, you can derive one class from another class. The derived class (also called the *descendant class*) inherits the data members and member functions of its *parent* and *ancestor classes*. The derived class represents a refinement of the parent class, because new attributes and new operations have been appended. The derived class typically declares new data members and new member functions. In addition, the derived class can also override inherited member functions when the operations of these functions are not suitable for the derived class.

To apply the concept of inheritance to the CASIO Data Bank watch, consider the following scenario. Suppose that the watch manufacturer decides to create a CASIO Data Bank watch that offers the same features as the CASIO Data Bank and also a beeper! Rather than redesign the new model (that is, the new class in OOP terms) from scratch, the CASIO engineers start with the existing design of the CASIO Data Bank and build on it. This process may well add new attributes and operations to the existing design and alter some existing operations to fit the new design. Thus, the enhanced CASIO Data Bank model inherits the attributes and the operations of the original CASIO Data Bank model. In OOP terms, the class of enhanced CASIO Data Bank watches is a descendant of the class of the original CASIO Data Bank watches.

POLYMORPHISM

Polymorphism is an OOP feature that allows the instances of different classes to react in a particular way to a message (or function invocation, in C++ terms). For example, in a hierarchy of graphical shapes (point, line, square, rectangle, circle, ellipse, and so on), each shape has a Draw function that is responsible for properly responding to a request to draw that shape.

DECLARING BASE CLASSES

With C++, you can declare a class that encapsulates data members and member functions. These functions alter and retrieve the values of the data members and perform related tasks.

The general syntax for declaring a base class is as follows:

```
class className
{
    private:
        <private data members>
        <private constructors>
        <private member functions>
    protected:
        <protected data members>
        <protected constructors>
        <protected member functions>
    public:
        <public data members>
        <public constructors>
        <public destructor>
        <public member functions>
};
```

Example:

```
class point
{
    protected:
        double x;
        double y;
    public:
        point(double xVal, double yVal);
        double getX();
        double getY();
        void assign(double xVal, double yVal);
        point& assign(point& pt);
};
```

THE SECTIONS OF A CLASS

The preceding syntax shows that the declaration involves the `class` keyword. C++ classes offers three levels of visibility for the various members (that is, both data members and member functions):

1. The private section: only the member functions of the class can access the private members. The class instances are denied access to private members.

2. The protected section: only the member functions of the class and its descendant classes can access protected members. The class instances are denied access to protected members.

3. The public section: specifies members that are visible to the member functions of the class, class instances, member functions of descendant classes, and their instances.

The following rules apply to the various class sections:

1. The class sections may appear in any order.

2. The class sections may appear more than once.

3. If no class section is specified, the C++ compiler treats the members as protected.

4. You should avoid placing data members in the public section, unless such a declaration simplifies the design significantly. Data members are typically placed in the protected section to allow their access by member functions of descendant classes.

5. Use member functions to set and query the values of data members. The members that set the data members assist in performing validation and updating other data members, if needed.

6. The class may have multiple constructors, typically located in the public section.

7. The class can have only one destructor, which must declared in the public section.

8. The member functions (as well as the constructors and destructors) that have multiple statements are defined outside the class declaration. The definition may reside in the same file that declares the class. In software libraries, the definition of the member functions typically resides in a separate source file. When you define a member function, you must qualify the function name with the class name. The syntax of such a qualification involves using the class name, followed by two colons (::), and then the name of a function. For example, consider the following class:

```
class point
{
    protected:
        double x;
        double y;
    public:
        point(double xVal, double yVal);
        double getX();
        // other member functions
};
```

The definitions of the constructor and member function are as follows:

```
point::point(double xVal, double yVal)
{
  // statements
}

double point::getX()
{
  // statements
}
```

After you declare a class, you can use the class name as a type identifier to declare class instances. The syntax resembles declaring variables.

Look at an example. Listing A.1 shows the source code for program CLASS1.CPP. The program prompts you to enter the length and width of a rectangle (which is an object). The program then displays the length, width, and area of the rectangle you specified.

LISTING A.1. THE SOURCE CODE FOR PROGRAM CLASS1.CPP.

```
// C++ program that illustrates a class

#include <iostream.h>

class rectangle
{
  protected:
    double length;
    double width;
  public:
    rectangle()
      { assign(0, 0); }
    rectangle(double len, double wide)
      { assign(len, wide); }
    double getLength() const
      { return length; }
```

```
        double getWidth() const
          { return width; }
        double getArea() const
          { return length * width; }
        void assign(double len, double wide);
};

void rectangle::assign(double len, double wide)
{
  length = len;
  width = wide;
}

main()
{
  rectangle rect;
  double len, wide;

  cout << "Enter length of rectangle : ";
  cin >> len;
  cout << "Enter width of rectangle : ";
  cin >> wide;
  rect.assign(len, wide);
  cout << "Rectangle length = " << rect.getLength() << "\n"
       << "          width  = " << rect.getWidth() << "\n"
       << "          area   = " << rect.getArea() << "\n";
  return 0;
}
```

Here is a sample session with the program in Listing A.1:

```
Enter length of rectangle : 10
Enter width of rectangle : 12
Rectangle length = 10
          width  = 12
          area   = 120
```

The program in Listing A.1 declares the rectangle class, which models a rectangle. The class has two double-type data members, length and width, that store the dimension of a rectangle. In addition, the class has two constructors: the default constructor, which creates an instance with 0 dimensions; and the non-default constructor, which creates an instance with non-zero dimension. The class also defines the getLength, getWidth, getArea, and assign member functions.

The getLength function, defined in the class declaration, simply returns the value in the length member. The getWidth function, also defined in the class declaration, merely returns the value in the width member. The getArea function, defined in the class declaration, simply returns the result of multiplying the length and width data members.

 Notice that the declarations of the getLength, getWidth, and getArea functions include the const keyword immediately after the parameter list. This keyword tells the compiler to make sure that none of these functions alters any data member. This programming feature is vital in creating constants that are instances of a class. Sending a message to a constant must use a member function that does not alter the data members of the constant object.

The assign member function, defined outside the class declaration, assigns the arguments for its len and wide parameters to the length and width data members, respectively. I simplified the implementation of this function by not checking for negative values.

The main function declares rect as the instance of the rectangle class and declares the double-typed len and wide variables. The first output statement prompts you to enter the length of the rectangle. The first input statement obtains your input and stores it in the len variable. The second output statement prompts you to enter the width of the rectangle. The second input statement obtains your input and stores it in the wide variable.

The main function assigns the input values to the rect instance using the assign member function. In OOP terms, I can say that the main function sends the assign message to the rect object. The arguments of the message are the len and wide variables. The rect object responds by invoking the method (that is, the member function) rectangle::assign(double, double).

The multiline output statement displays the length, width, and area of the rect object. This statement sends the getLength, getWidth, and getArea messages to the rect object. In turn, the rect object invokes the appropriate methods (or member functions, if you prefer) to respond to each one of these messages.

CONSTRUCTORS

C++ constructors and destructors work automatically to guarantee the appropriate creation and removal of class instances.

The general syntax for constructors is the following:

```
class className
{
    public:
        className(); // default constructor
        className(className& c); // copy constructor
        className(<parameter list>); // another
constructor
};
Example:
class point
{
    protected:
        double x;
        double y;
    public:
        point();
        point(double xVal, double yVal);
        point(point& pt);
        double getX() const;
        double getY() const;
        void assign(double xVal, double yVal);
        point& assign(point& pt);
};
```

C++ has the following features and rules regarding constructors:

1. The name of the constructor must be identical to the name of its class.

2. You must not include any return type, not even void.

3. A class can have any number of constructors, including none. In the latter case, the compiler automatically creates one for that class.

4. The default constructor is the one either that has no parameters or that possesses a parameter list where all the parameters use default arguments. Here are two examples:

```
// class use parameterless constructor
class point1
```

continues

continued

```
{
    protected:
        double x;
        double y;
    public:
        point1();
        // other member functions
};


// class uses constructor with default arguments

class point2
{
    protected:
        double x;
        double y;
    public:
        point(double xVal = 0, double yVal = 0);
        // other member functions
};
```

5. The copy constructor enables you to create a class instance using an existing instance. Here is an example:

```
class point
{
    protected:
        double x;
        double y;
    public:
        point();
        point(double xVal, double yVal);
        point(point& pt);
        // other member functions
};
```

 You should declare copy constructors, especially for classes that model dynamic data structures. These constructors perform what is called a *deep copy*, which includes the dynamic data. By default, the compiler creates what are called *shallow-copy* constructors, which copy the data members only. Don't rely on the shallow-copy constructor to copy instances for classes having members that are pointers.

6. The declaration of a class instance (which includes function parameters and local instances) involves a constructor. Which constructor is called? The answer depends on how many constructors you have declared for the class and how you declared the class instance. For example, consider the following instances of the last version of the `point` class:

```
point p1; // involves the default constructor
point p2(1.1, 1.3); // uses the second constructor
point p3(p2); // uses the copy constructor
```

Because the `p1` instance specifies no arguments, the compiler uses the default constructor. The `p2` instance specifies two floating-point arguments. Consequently, the compiler uses the second constructor. The `p3` instance has the `p2` instance as an argument. Therefore, the compiler uses the copy constructor to create the `p3` instance from the `p2` instance.

DESTRUCTORS

C++ classes may contain destructors that automatically remove class instances.

The general syntax for destructors is as follows:

```
class className
{
    public:
        className(); // default constructor
        // other constructors
        ~className();
        // other member function
};
```

Example:

```
class String
{
```

```
    protected:
        char *str;
        int len;


    public:
        String();
        String(String& s);
        ~String();
        // other member functions
};
```

C++ classes have the following features and rules regarding destructors:

1. The name of the destructor must begin with the tilde (~) character. The rest of the destructor name must be identical to the name of its class.

2. You must not include any return type, not even void.

3. A class can have no more than one destructor. In addition, if you omit the destructor, the compiler automatically creates one for you.

4. The destructor cannot have any parameters.

5. The runtime system automatically invokes a class destructor when the instance of that class is out of scope.

EXAMPLE OF CONSTRUCTORS AND DESTRUCTORS

Look now at a program that typifies the use of constructors and destructors. Listing A.2 contains the source code for the CLASS2.CPP program. The program performs the following tasks:

1. Creates a dynamic array (the object)

2. Assigns values to the elements of the dynamic array

3. Displays the values in the dynamic array

4. Removes the dynamic array

Listing A.2. The source code for the CLASS2.CPP program.

```cpp
// Program demonstrates constructors and destructors

#include <iostream.h>

const unsigned MIN_SIZE = 4;

class Array
{
   protected:
     double *dataPtr;
     unsigned size;

   public:
     Array(unsigned Size = MIN_SIZE);
     ~Array()
       { delete [] dataPtr; }
     unsigned getSize() const
       { return size; }
     void store(double x, unsigned index)
       { dataPtr[index] = x; }
     double recall(unsigned index) const
       { return dataPtr[index]; }
};

Array::Array(unsigned Size)
{
  size = (Size < MIN_SIZE) ? MIN_SIZE : Size;
  dataPtr = new double[size];
}

main()
{
  Array Ar1(10);
  double x;
  // assign data to array elements
  for (unsigned i = 0; i < Ar1.getSize(); i++) {
    x = double(i);
    x = x * x - 5 * x + 10;
    Ar1.store(x, i);
  }
  // display data in the array element
  cout << "Array Ar1 has the following values:\n\n";
  for (i = 0; i < Ar1.getSize(); i++)
    cout << "Ar1[" << i << "] = " << Ar1.recall(i) << "\n";
  return 0;
}
```

Here is a sample session with the program in Listing A.2:

```
Array Ar1 has the following values:

Ar1[0] = 10
Ar1[1] = 6
Ar1[2] = 4
Ar1[3] = 4
Ar1[4] = 6
Ar1[5] = 10
Ar1[6] = 16
Ar1[7] = 24
Ar1[8] = 34
Ar1[9] = 46
```

The program in Listing A.2 declares the MIN_SIZE global constant, which specifies the minimum size of dynamic arrays. The program also declares the Array class. The class has two data members, dataPtr and size. The dataPtr member is the pointer to the elements of the dynamically allocated array. The size member stores the number of elements in an instance of the Array class.

The class declares a default constructor (the constructor actually has a parameter with the default value MIN_SIZE; in general, a constructor whose entire parameter list has default arguments doubles as a default constructor). The program defines the constructor outside the class declaration. The arguments for the size parameter specify the number of array elements. The first statement assigns the greater value of the size parameter and the MIN_SIZE constant to the size data member. The second statement allocates the dynamic space for the array by using the new operator. The statement assigns the base address of the dynamic array to the dataPtr member.

The ~Array destructor removes the dynamic space of the array by applying the delete operator to the dataPtr member.

The getSize member function, defined in the class declaration, returns the value in the size data member.

The store function, defined in the class declaration, stores the value passed by the x parameter at the element number specified by the index parameter. I simplified the implementation of this function by eliminating the out-of-range index check.

The recall function, defined in the class declaration, returns the value in the element specified by the index parameter. I simplified the implementation of this function by eliminating the out-of-range index check.

The main function declares the Arr object as an instance of the Array class. The declaration specifies that the instance has 10 elements. The function also declares the double-typed x variable. The for loop stores values in the Arr instance. The loop uses the control variable i and iterates from 0 to Arr.getSize()-1, in increments of 1. The loop continuation condition sends the getSize message to the Arr instance to obtain the number of elements in the array. The statements inside the loop calculate the value to store in an element of the Arr instance, and then send the store message to the Arr instance. The arguments for this message are x and i. The Arr object saves the value in the x variable at the element number i.

The first output statement comments on the output of the second for loop in the main function. The loop uses the i control variable and iterates from 0 to Arr.getSize()-1, in increments of 1. The output statement in the loop displays the element in the Arr instance by sending the recall message to that instance. The message has the argument i.

DECLARING A CLASS HIERARCHY

The power of the OOP features of C++ comes from the fact that you can derive classes from existing ones. A descendant class inherits the members of its ancestor classes (that is, parent class, grandparent class, and so on) and can also override some of the inherited functions. Inheritance enables you to reuse code in descendant classes.

The general syntax for declaring a derived class is as follows:

```
class className : [public] parentClass
{
      <friend classes>


      private:
            <private data members>
            <private constructors>
            <private member functions>
```

```
        protected:
             <protected data members>
             <protected constructors>
             <protected member functions>
        public:
             <public data members>
             <public constructors>
             <public destructor>
             <public member functions>

             <friend functions and friend operators>
};
```

Example:

The following example shows the cRectangle class and its descendant, the cBox class:

```
class cRectangle
{
    protected:
         double length;
         double width;
    public:
         cRectangle(double len, double wide);
         double getLength() const;
         double getWidth(); const;
         double assign(double len, double wide);
         double calcArea() const;
};


class cBox : public cRectangle
{
    protected:
         double height;

    public:
         cBox(double len, double wide, double height);
         double getHeight() const;
```

```
        assign(double len, double wide, double height);
        double calcVolume() const;
};
```

The class lineage is indicated by a colon, followed by the optional keyword public, and then followed by the name of the parent class. When you include the public keyword, you allow the instances of the descendant class to access the public members of the parent and other ancestor classes. By contrast, when you omit the public keyword, you deprive the instance of the descendant class from accessing the members of the ancestor classes.

A descendant class inherits the data members of its ancestor classes. C++ has no mechanism for removing unwanted inherited data members; you are stuck with them. By contrast, in C++ you can override inherited member functions (you will see more about this topic later in this chapter). The descendant class declares new data members, new member functions, and overriding member functions. Again, you can place these members in the private, protected, or public sections as you see fit in your class design.

- Reduce the number of constructors by using default argument parameters.

- Use member functions to access the values in the data members. With these member functions you can control and validate the values in the data members.

- Don't declare all of the constructors of a class protected unless you want to force the client programmers to use the class by declaring its descendants with public constructors.

- Don't declare the data members in the public section unless it greatly simplifies the solution or unless it is the only way to implement a solution.

Look now at an example that declares a small class hierarchy. Listing A.3 shows the source code for the CLASS3.CPP program. This program declares classes that contain a hierarchy of two simple geometric shapes: a circle and a cylinder. The program requires no input. Instead, it uses internal data to create these two geometric shapes and to display their dimensions, areas, and volume.

```cpp
// Program demonstrates a small hierarchy of classes

#include <iostream.h>
#include <math.h>

const double pi = 4 * atan(1);

inline double sqr(double x)
{ return x * x; }

class cCircle
{
  protected:
    double radius;

  public:
    cCircle(double radiusVal = 0) : radius(radiusVal) {}
    void setRadius(double radiusVal)
      { radius = radiusVal; }
    double getRadius() const
      { return radius; }
    double area() const
      { return pi * sqr(radius); }
    void showData() const;
};

class cCylinder : public cCircle
{
  protected:
    double height;

  public:
    cCylinder(double heightVal = 0, double radiusVal = 0)
      : height(heightVal), cCircle(radiusVal) {}
    void setHeight(double heightVal)
      { height = heightVal; }
    double getHeight() const
      { return height; }
    double area() const
      { return 2 * cCircle::area() +
              2 * pi * radius * height; }
    void showData() const;
};

void cCircle::showData()
{
   cout << "Circle radius        = " << getRadius() << "\n"
        << "Circle area          = " << area() << "\n\n";
}
```

```
void cCylinder::showData()
{
   cout << "Cylinder radius      = " << getRadius() << "\n"
        << "Cylinder height      = " << getHeight() << "\n"
        << "Cylinder area        = " << area() << "\n\n";
}

main()
{
   cCircle Circle(1);
   cCylinder Cylinder(10, 1);

   Circle.showData();
   Cylinder.showData();
   return 0;
}
```

Here is a sample session with the program in Listing A.3:

```
Circle radius      = 1
Circle area        = 3.141593

Cylinder radius    = 1
Cylinder height    = 10
Cylinder area      = 69.115038
```

The program in Listing A.3 declares the cCircle and cCylinder classes. The cCircle class models a circle, whereas the cCylinder class models a cylinder.

The cCircle class declares a single data member, radius, to store the radius of the circle. The class also declares a constructor and a number of member functions. The constructor assigns a value to the radius data member when you declare a class instance. Notice that the constructor uses a new syntax to initialize the radius member. The setRadius and getRadius functions serve to set and query, respectively, the value in the radius member. The area function returns the area of the circle. The showData function displays the radius and area of a class instance.

The cCylinder class, a descendant of cCircle, declares a single data member, height, to store the height of the cylinder. The class inherits the radius member needed to store the radius of the cylinder. The cCylinder class declares a constructor and a number of member functions. The constructor assigns values to the radius and height members when creating a class instance. Notice the use of a new syntax to initialize the members: the height member is directly initialized, whereas the radius member is indirectly initialized by invoking the constructor of the cCircle class with the radiusVal argument. The functions getHeight and setHeight functions serve to set and to query, respectively, the value in member height. The class uses the inherited functions setRadius and getRadius to manipulate the inherited member radius. The area function, which overrides the inherited cCircle::area() function, returns the surface area of the cylinder. This function explicitly invokes the inherited function cCircle::area(). The showData function displays the radius, height, and area of a class instance.

The main function declares the circle instance of the cCircle class, and it assigns 1 to the circle's radius. In addition, the function also declares the cylinder instance of the cCylinder class, and it assigns 10 and 1 to the circle's height and radius, respectively. The function then sends the showData message to the circle and cylinder instances. Each object responds to this message by invoking the appropriate member function.

VIRTUAL FUNCTION

Polymorphic behavior is an important object-oriented programming feature. This feature allows the instances of different classes to respond to the same function in ways appropriate to each class. Consider the following simple classes and the main function:

```
#include <iostream.h>

class cA
{
    public:
        double A(double x) { return x * x; }
        double B(double x) { return A(x) / 2; }
};

class cB : public cA
{
    public:
        double A(double x) { return x * x * x; }
};

main()
{
    cB aB;
    cout << aB.B(3) << "\n";
    return 0;
    }
```

The cA class contains functions A and B, where function B calls function A. The cB class, a descendant of the cA class, inherits function B, but overrides function A. The intent here is that the inherited function cA::B call function cB::A in order to support polymorphic behavior. What is the program output? The answer is 4.5, *not* 13.5. This is because the compiler resolves the expression aB.B(3) by using the inherited function cA::B, which in turn calls function cA::A. Therefore, function cB::A is left out, and the program fails to support polymorphic behavior.

C++ supports polymorphic behavior by offering virtual functions. These functions, which are bound at runtime, are declared by placing the virtual keyword before each function's return type. Once you declare a function virtual, you can override it only with virtual functions in descendant classes. These overriding functions *must* have the same parameter list. Virtual functions can override nonvirtual functions in ancestor classes.

The general syntax for declaring virtual functions is as follows:

```
class className1
{
    // member functions
    virtual returnType functionName(<parameter list>);
};


class className2 : public className1
{
    // member functions
    virtual returnType functionName(<parameter list>);
};
```

The following example shows how virtual functions can successfully implement polymorphic behavior in the cA and cB classes.

```
#include <iostream.h>
class cA
{
    public:
        virtual double A(double x) { return x * x; }
        double B(double x) { return A(x) / 2; }
};
```

```
class cB : public cA
{
    public:
            virtual double A(double x) { return x * x * x; }
};

main()
{
    cB aB;
    cout << aB.B(3) << "\n";
    return 0;
}
```

The preceding example displays 13.5, the correct result, because the call to the inherited cA::B function is resolved at runtime by calling cB::A.

- Use virtual functions when you have a callable function that implements a behavior specific to a class. Declaring such a function as virtual ensures that it provides the correct response relevant to the associated class.

- Do not declare a member function as virtual by default. Virtual functions have some additional overhead.

Look at an example. Listing A.4 shows the source code for the program CLASS4.CPP. The program creates a square and a rectangle and displays their dimensions and areas. No input is required.

LISTING A.4. THE SOURCE CODE FOR THE CLASS4.CPP. PROGRAM.

```
// Program demonstrates virtual functions

#include <iostream.h>

class cSquare
{
  protected:
    double length;

  public:
    cSquare(double len)
```

```
      { length = len; }
    double getLength() const
      { return length; }
    virtual double getWidth() const
      { return length; }
    double getArea() const
      { return getLength() * getWidth(); }
};

class cRectangle : public cSquare
{
  protected:
    double width;

  public:
    cRectangle(double len, double wide) :
      cSquare(len), width(wide) {}
    virtual double getWidth() const
      { return width; }
};

main()
{
    cSquare square(10);
    cRectangle rectangle(10, 12);

    cout << "Square has length = " << square.getLength() << "\n"
         << "         and area   = " << square.getArea() << "\n";
    cout << "Rectangle has length = "
         << rectangle.getLength() << "\n"
         << "              and width  = "
         << rectangle.getWidth() << "\n"
         << "              and area   = "
         << rectangle.getArea() << "\n";
    return 0;
}
```

Here is a sample session of the program in Listing A.4:

```
Square has length = 10
        and area   = 100
Rectangle has length = 10
           and width  = 12
           and area   = 120
```

The program in Listing A.4 declares the cSquare and cRectangle classes to model squares and rectangles, respectively. The cSquare class declares a single data member, length, to store the length (and width) of the square. The class declares a constructor with the len parameter, which passes arguments to the length member. The class also declares the getLength, getWidth, and getArea functions. Both the getLength and getWidth functions return the value in the length member. Notice that the class declares the getWidth function as virtual. The getArea function returns the area of the rectangle, calculated by calling the getLength and getWidth functions. I chose to invoke these functions, rather than use the length data member, in order to demonstrate how the virtual function getWidth works.

The program declares the cRectangle class as a descendant of the cSquare class. The cRectangle class declares the width data member and inherits the length member. These members enable the class to store the basic dimensions of a rectangle. The class constructor has the parameters len and wide, which pass values to the members len and wide. The constructor invokes the cSquare constructor and supplies it with the len argument. The constructor initializes the width data member with the value of the wide parameter.

The cRectangle class declares the virtual function getWidth. This version returns the value in the width data member. The class inherits the member functions getLength and getArea, because their implementation is adequate for the cRectangle.

The main function declares the square object as an instance of the cSquare class. The square instance has a length of 10. The main function also declares the rectangle object as an instance of the cRectangle class. The rectangle instance has the length of 10 and the width of 12.

The first output statement displays the length and area of the square instance. The statement sends the getLength and getArea messages to this instance in order to obtain the sought values. The square instance invokes the function getArea, which in turn calls the functions cSquare::getLength and cSquare::getWidth.

The second output statement displays the length, width, and area of the rectangle instance. The statement sends the getLength, getWidth, and getArea messages to this instance. The instance responds by calling the inherited function cSquare::getLength, the virtual function cRectangle::getWidth, and the inherited function cSquare::getArea. The latter function calls the inherited function cSquare::getLength and the virtual function cRectange::getWidth to calculate correctly the area of the rectangle.

- Declare your destructor as virtual. This ensures polymorphic behavior in destroying class instances. In addition, it is highly recommended that you declare a copy constructor and an assignment operator for each class.

- Don't forget that you can inherit virtual functions and destructors when appropriate for the descendant class. You need not declare shell functions and destructors that simply call the corresponding member of the parent class.

RULES FOR VIRTUAL FUNCTIONS

The rule for declaring a virtual function is "once virtual, always virtual." In other words, once you declare a function to be virtual in a class, any subclass that overrides the virtual function must do so using another virtual function (one that has the same parameter list). The virtual declaration is mandatory for the descendant classes. At first, this rule seems to lock you in. This limitation is certainly true for object-oriented programming languages that support virtual functions but do not support overloaded functions. In the case of C++, the work-around is interesting. You can declare nonvirtual and overloaded functions that have the same name as the virtual function, but that bear a different parameter list. Moreover, you cannot inherit nonvirtual member functions that share the same name with a virtual function. Here is a simple example to demonstrate the point:

```
#include <iostream.h>
class cA
{
  public:
    cA() {}
    virtual void foo(char c)
      { cout << "virtual cA::foo() returns " << c << '\n'; }
};

class cB : public cA
{
  public:
    cB() {}
    void foo(const char* s)
      { cout << "cB::foo() returns " << s << '\n'; }
    void foo(int i)
      { cout << "cB::foo() returns " << i << '\n'; }
    virtual void foo(char c)
      { cout << "virtual cB::foo() returns " << c << '\n'; }
```

continues

```
continued
};

class cC : public cB
{
  public:
    cC() {}
    void foo(const char* s)
      { cout << "cC::foo() returns " << s << '\n'; }
    void foo(double x)
      { cout << "cC::foo() returns " << x << '\n'; }
    virtual void foo(char c)
      { cout << "virtual cC::foo() returns " << c << '\n'; }
};

main()
{
  int n = 100;
  cA Aobj;
  cB Bobj;
  cC Cobj;

  Aobj.foo('A');
  Bobj.foo('B');
  Bobj.foo(10);
  Bobj.foo("Bobj");
  Cobj.foo('C');
  // if you uncomment the next statement, program does not compile
  // Cobj.foo(n);
  Cobj.foo(144.123);
  Cobj.foo("Cobj");
  return 0;
}
```

The preceding code declares three classes—cA, cB, and cC—to form a linear hierarchy of classes. The cA class declares function foo(char) as virtual. The cB class also declares its own version of the virtual function foo(char). In addition, the cB class declares the nonvirtual, overloaded functions, respectively, foo(const char* s) and foo(int). The cC class, the descendant of class cB, declares the virtual function foo(char) and the nonvirtual and overloaded functions foo(const char*) and foo(double). Notice that the cC class *must* declare the foo(const char*) function if it needs the function, because it cannot inherit the cB::foo(const char*) member function. C++ supports a different function inheritance scheme when an overloaded and a virtual function are involved. The main function creates an instance for each of the three classes and involves the various versions of the foo member function.

FRIEND FUNCTIONS

C++ allows member functions to access all of the data members of a class. In addition, C++ grants the same privileged access to friend functions. *Friend* functions are ordinary functions that have access to all data members of one or more classes. The declaration of friend functions appears in the class and begins with the `friend` keyword. Other than using the special keyword, friend functions look very much like member functions (except that they cannot return a reference to the befriended class, because such a result requires returning the self-reference `*this`). However, when you define friend functions outside the declaration of their befriended class, you need not qualify the function names with the name of the class.

The general form of friend functions is as follows:

```
class className
{
    public:
        className();
        // other constructors

        friend returnType friendFunction(<parameter list>);
};
```

Example:

```
class String
{
    protected:
        char *str;
        int len;

    public:
        String();
        ~String();
        // other member functions
        friend String& append(String& str1, String& str2);
        friend String& append(const char* str1, String& str2);
        friend String& append(String& str1, const char* str2);
};
```

Friend classes can accomplish tasks that are awkward, difficult, and even impossible with member functions.

Look at a simple example of using friend functions. Listing A.5 contains the source code for the CLASS5.CPP program. This program internally creates two complex numbers, adds them, stores the result in another complex number, and then displays the operands and the resulting complex numbers.

LISTING A.5. THE SOURCE CODE FOR THE CLASS5.CPP PROGRAM.

```
// Program demonstrates friend functions

#include <iostream.h>

class Complex
{
   protected:
     double x;
     double y;

   public:
     Complex(double real = 0, double imag = 0);
     Complex(Complex& c) { assign(c); }
     void assign(Complex& c);
     double getReal() const
       { return x; }
     double getImag() const
       { return y; }
     friend Complex add(Complex& c1, Complex& c2);
};

Complex::Complex(double real, double imag)
{
  x = real;
  y = imag;
}

void Complex::assign(Complex& c)
{
  x = c.x;
  y = c.y;
}

Complex add(Complex& c1, Complex& c2)
{
  Complex result(c1);
```

```
    result.x += c2.x;
    result.y += c2.y;
    return result;
}

main()
{
  Complex c1(2, 3);
  Complex c2(5, 7);
  Complex c3;

  c3.assign(add(c1, c2));
  cout << "(" << c1.getReal() << " + i" << c1.getImag() << ")"
       << " + "
       << "(" << c2.getReal() << " + i" << c2.getImag() << ")"
       << " = "
       << "(" << c3.getReal() << " + i" << c3.getImag() << ")"
       << "\n\n";
  return 0;
}
```

Here is a sample session of the program in Listing A.5:

```
 (2 + i3) + (5 + i7) = (7 + i10)
```

The program in Listing A.5 declares the Complex class, which models complex numbers. This class declares two data members, two constructors, a friend function (the highlight of this example), and a set of member functions. The x and y data members store the real and imaginary components of a complex number, respectively.

The class has two constructors. The first constructor has two parameters (with default arguments) that enable you to build a class instance using the real and imaginary components of a complex. Because the two parameters have default arguments, the constructor doubles as the default constructor. The second constructor, Complex(Complex&), is the copy constructor that enables you to create a class instance by copying the data from existing instances.

The Complex class declares three member functions. The assign function copies a class instance into another instance. The getReal and getImag functions return the value stored in the real and imag members, respectively.

The `Complex` class declares the `add` friend function to add two complex numbers. To make the program short, I did not implement complementary friend functions that subtract, multiply, and divide class instances. What is so special about the `add` friend function? Why not use an ordinary member function to add a class instance? To answer these questions, let me present the declaration of the alternate `add` member function:

```
complex& add(complex& c)
```

The preceding declaration states that the function treats the `c` parameter as a second operand. Here is how the `add` member function works:

```
complex c1(3, 4), c2(1.2, 4.5);
c1.add(c2); // adds c2 to c1
```

First, the `add` member function works as an increment and not as an addition function. Second, the targeted class instance is always the first operand. Though this is not a problem for operations like addition and multiplication, it is a problem for subtraction and division. That is why the `add` friend function works better: it gives you the freedom of choosing how to add the class instances.

The `add` friend function returns a class instance. The function creates a local instance of the `Complex` class and returns that instance.

The `main` function uses the `assign` member function and the `add` friend function to perform plain complex operations. In addition, the `main` function invokes the `getReal` and `getImag` function with the various instances of the `Complex` class to display the components of each instance.

OPERATORS AND FRIEND OPERATORS

The last program uses a member function and a friend function to implement complex math operations. The approach is typical in C and Pascal, because these languages do not support user-defined operators. By contrast, in C++ you can declare operators and friend operators. These operators include +, -, *, /, %, ==, !=, <=, <, >=, >, +=, -=, *=, /=, %=, [], (), <<, and >>. Consult a C++ language reference book for more details on the rules for using these operators. C++ treats operators as special member functions and friend operators as friend functions.

The general syntax for declaring operators and friend operators is as follows:

```
class className
{
    public:
            // constructors and destructor
            // member functions

            // unary operator
            returnType operator operatorSymbol(operand);
            // binary operator
            returnType operator operatorSymbol(firstOperand,
                                               secondOperand);
            // unary friend operator
            friend returnType operator
operatorSymbol(operand);
            // binary operator
            friend returnType operator
                    operatorSymbol(firstOperand,
condOperand);
    };
```

Example:

```
class String
{
    protected:
        char *str;
        int len;

    public:
        String();
        ~String();
        // other member functions
        // assignment operator
        String& operator =(String& s);
        String& operator +=(String& s);
        // concatenation operators
        friend String& operator +(String& s1, String& s2);
        friend String& operator +(const char* s1, String& s2);
```

```
      friend String& operator +(String& s1, const char* s2);
      // relational operators
      friend int operator >(String& s1, String& s2);
      friend int operator =>(String& s1, String& s2);
      friend int operator <(String& s1, String& s2);
      friend int operator <=(String& s1, String& s2);
      friend int operator ==(String& s1, String& s2);
      friend int operator !=(String& s1, String& s2);
};
```

The client functions use the operators and friend operators like predefined operators. Therefore, you can create operators to support the operations of classes that model, for example, complex numbers, strings, arrays, and matrices. These operators enable you to write expressions that are far more readable than expressions that use named functions.

Look at an example. Listing A.6 contains the source code for the CLASS6.CPP program. I created this program by modifying and expanding Listing A.5. The new program performs more additions and displays two sets of operands and results.

LISTING A.6. THE SOURCE CODE FOR THE CLASS6.CPP PROGRAM.

```cpp
// Program demonstrates operators and friend operators

#include <iostream.h>

class Complex
{
   protected:
     double x;
     double y;

   public:
     Complex(double real = 0, double imag = 0)
       { assign(real, imag); }
     Complex(Complex& c);
     void assign(double real = 0, double imag = 0);
     double getReal() const
       { return x; }
     double getImag() const
       { return y; }
     Complex& operator =(Complex& c);
```

```cpp
    Complex& operator +=(Complex& c);
    friend Complex operator +(Complex& c1, Complex& c2);
    friend ostream& operator <<(ostream& os, Complex& c);
};

Complex::Complex(Complex& c)
{
  x = c.x;
  y = c.y;
}

void Complex::assign(double real, double imag)
{
  x = real;
  y = imag;
}

Complex& Complex::operator =(Complex& c)
{
  x = c.x;
  y = c.y;
  return *this;
}

Complex& Complex::operator +=(Complex& c)
{
  x += c.x;
  y += c.y;
  return *this;
}

Complex operator +(Complex& c1, Complex& c2)
{
  Complex result(c1);

  result.x += c2.x;
  result.y += c2.y;
  return result;
}

ostream& operator <<(ostream& os, Complex& c)
{
  os << "(" << c.x << " + i" << c.y << ")";
  return os;
}

main()
{

  Complex c1(3, 5);
  Complex c2(7, 5);
```

continues

LISTING **A.6.** CONTINUED

```
  Complex c3;
  Complex c4(2, 3);

  c3 = c1 + c2;
  cout << c1 << " + " << c2 << " = " << c3 << "\n";
  cout << c3 << " + " << c4 << " = ";
  c3 += c4;
  cout << c3 << "\n";
  return 0;
}
```

Here is a sample session of the program in Listing A.6:

```
(3 + i5) + (7 + i5) = (10 + i10)
(10 + i10) + (2 + i3) = (12 + i13)
```

The new class `Complex` replaces the `assign(Complex&)` member function with the `=` operator. The class also replaces the `add` friend function with the `+` friend operator:

```
Complex& operator =(Complex& c);
friend Complex operator +(Complex& c1, Complex& c2);
```

The `=` operator has one parameter—a reference to an instance of the `Complex` class—and returns a reference to the same class. The `+` friend operator has two parameters (both are references to instances of the `Complex` class) and yields a complex class type.

I also took the opportunity to add two new operators:

```
complex& operator +=(complex& c);
friend ostream& operator <<(ostream& os, complex& c);
```

 The `+=` operator is a member of the `Complex` class. This operator takes one parameter—a reference to an instance of the `Complex` class—and yields a reference to the same class. The other new operator is the `<<` friend operator, which illustrates how to write a stream extractor operator for a class. The friend operator has two parameters: a reference to the `ostream` class (the output stream class) and a reference to the `Complex` class. The `<<` operator returns a reference to the `ostream` class. This type of value enables you to chain stream output with other predefined types or with other classes (assuming that these classes have a << friend operator). The definition of the << friend operator has two statements. The first one outputs strings and the data members of the Complex class to the output stream parameter os. The friendship status of << operator allows it to access the real and imag data members of its Complex-typed parameter c. The second statement in the operator definition returns the first os parameter.

The main function declares four instances of the Complex class: c1, c2, c3, and c4. The c1, c2, and c4 instances are created with non-default values assigned to the real and imag data members. The function tests using the operators =, +, <<, and +=. The program illustrates that, using operators and friend operators, you can write code that is more readable and supports a higher level of abstraction.

STATIC DATA MEMBERS

Each instance of a class has its own copies of the data members declared in that class and inherited from the parent and ancestor classes. There are applications that require data members that are common to all instances of a class. Conceptually, these special data members belong to the class (which some OOP purists consider as a special object) and not to its instances. These data members play various roles, such as:

1. Keeping count of the number of instances. This task can also be used in special initialization that takes places immediately before the creation of the very first instance of a particular class. Likewise, you can use the number of instances to perform a special cleanup task, once all the class instances are removed.

2. Maintaining miniature databases commonly used by the various instances.

3. Managing the system's resources—such as the heap or virtual memory—that are commonly used by the instances of the host class.

C++ supports static data members declared in the class and initialized only outside the class declaration. The syntax for declaring a static data member requires placing the static keyword before the data type of the member. The initialization of a static data member must occur outside the class declaration and uses the following syntax:

```
dataType className::staticMember = initialValue;
```

Here is an example of a static member:

```
class Complex {

  protected:
    double real;
    double imag;
    static unsigned numInstances;

  public:
    // constructors, destructor, and other member declarations
};

// initialize the static member
unsigned Complex::numInstances = 0;
```

STATIC MEMBER FUNCTIONS

You can declare a static member function to access and manipulate static data members. The static functions must not contain the `this` pointer to avoid compile-time errors. To declare a static member function, place the `static` keyword before the return type of the function.

You can access public static data members and static member functions using a class instance, a pointer to the class, or directly. In using class instances, it does not matter which existing instances you use, because they all refer to the same static data member. You can directly access public static members before you create any instance of the host class. This is why a static member function must not use the `this` pointer. When you directly access a static member, you must qualify that access with the name of the accompanying class.

Look at an example that uses a static data member and a static member function. Listing A.7 shows the source code for the CLASS7.CPP program. I created this program by modifying program CLASS2.CPP in Listing A.2. The program displays the number of instances of the `Array` class at various locations in the `main` function.

LISTING A.7. THE SOURCE CODE FOR THE CLASS7.CPP PROGRAM.

```
// Program demonstrates static members

#include <iostream.h>

const unsigned MIN_SIZE = 4;
```

```
class Array
{
   protected:
     double *dataPtr;
     unsigned size;
     static unsigned numInstances;

   public:
     Array(unsigned Size = MIN_SIZE);
     ~Array();
     unsigned getSize() const
       { return size; }
     void store(double x, unsigned index)
       { dataPtr[index] = x; }
     double recall(unsigned index) const
       { return dataPtr[index]; }
     static unsigned getNumInstances()
       { return numInstances; }
};

Array::Array(unsigned Size)
{
  size = (Size < MIN_SIZE) ? MIN_SIZE : Size;
  dataPtr = new double[size];
  numInstances++;
}

Array::~Array()
{
  delete [] dataPtr;
  numInstances--;
}

// initialize the static data member
unsigned Array::numInstances = 0;

main()
{
  cout << "There are " << Array::getNumInstances()
       << " instances of class Array\n";
  Array Ar1(10), Ar2(10);
  cout << "There are " << Array::getNumInstances()
       << " instances of class Array\n";
  {
    Array Ar3(10);
    cout << "There are " << Array::getNumInstances()
      << " instances of class Array\n";    {
      Array Ar4(10);
      cout << "There are " << Array::getNumInstances()
        << " instances of class Array\n";    }
```

continues

LISTING A.7. CONTINUED

```
   cout << "There are " << Array::getNumInstances()
     << " instances of class Array\n";  }
  cout << "There are " << Array::getNumInstances()
     << " instances of class Array\n";  return 0;
}
```

Here is the output generated by the program in Listing A.7:

```
There are 0 instances of class Array
There are 2 instances of class Array
There are 3 instances of class Array
There are 4 instances of class Array
There are 3 instances of class Array
There are 2 instances of class Array
```

The program in Listing A.7 declares the Array class, as in Listing A.2. The new class contains the static data member numInstances, which keeps track of the number of class instances. In addition, the class declares the static member function getNumInstances to return the value in the protected member numInstances.

The class constructor and destructor, respectively, increment and decrement the static member numInstances. Thus, every time a program creates a new instance, the value in the numInstances member increases by 1. Likewise, every time an instance of the Array class is destroyed, the numInstances member decreases by 1.

The program initializes the value of the numInstances static member to zero, outside the class declaration.

The main function declares four instances of the Array class at various levels. The program displays the current number of instances before and after each function level. Notice that the output statements directly access the static member function getNumInstances. This direct access requires the accompanying class to qualify the static member function.

Multiple Inheritance

Multiple inheritance enables a class to have multiple parent classes. The relationship in this kind of class hierarchy is modeled by the HasA model or concept (the same as in containment). That is why some programmers prefer using containment over using multiple inheritance.

The parent classes may be part of either completely separate or intertwined hierarchies. In the latter case, the parent classes share a common ancestor class. Consider the following simple case. Class A is the parent of classes B and C. Class X is the subclass of both classes B and C. This means that class X has the same ancestor class A, because class A is the parent class of B and C. In this case, the C++ compiler requires you to use the virtual keyword in declaring classes B and C, shown as follows. The virtual keyword forewarns the compiler of the connected class hierarchies.

```
class A
{
  protected:
  // protected member declarations
  public:
  // constructor and other public members
  virtual void foo();
};

class B : virtual public A
{
  protected:
  // protected member declarations
  public:
  // constructor and other public members
  virtual void foo();
};

class C : virtual public A
{
  protected:
  // protected member declarations
  public:
  // constructor and other public members
  virtual void foo();
};

class X : public B, public C
{
  // member declarations
};
```

To add more complexity to the picture, consider the virtual functions that are declared in classes A, B, and C. The preceding code fragment specifies the virtual function foo as an example. The member functions of class X can specify which version of foo is the exact virtual function by qualifying it with the class name. Thus the A::foo(), B::foo(), and C::foo() calls specify the versions of the foo() functions in classes A, B, and C, respectively.

Look at an example of using multiple inheritance. Listing A.8 shows the source code for the CLASS8.CPP program. This program emulates a class that solves simultaneous equations (I say *emulates* because I use much shorter code to perform a simple matrix-array manipulation). The solution of simultaneous equations involves this equation,

```
A B = X
```

where A is the matrix of coefficients, B is the left-side vector (an array), and X is the solution vector (an array).

LISTING A.8. THE SOURCE CODE FOR THE CLASS8.CPP PROGRAM.

```cpp
#include <iostream.h>

class Array
{
  protected:
    unsigned arrSize;
    double *arrPtr;

  public:
    Array(unsigned ArraySize)
      { arrPtr = new double[arrSize = ArraySize]; }
    ~Array()
      { delete [] arrPtr; }

    void arrStore(double x, unsigned index)
      { arrPtr[index] = x; }
    void arrRecall(double& x, unsigned index)
      { x = arrPtr[index]; }
};

class Matrix
{
  protected:
    unsigned maxRows;
    unsigned maxCols;
    double *matPtr;
```

```cpp
  public:
    Matrix(unsigned Rows, unsigned Cols)
      { maxRows = Rows;
        maxCols = Cols;
        matPtr = new double[Rows * Cols];
      }
    ~Matrix()
      { delete [] matPtr; }

    void matStore(double x, unsigned row, unsigned col)
      { matPtr[row + maxRows * col] = x; }
    void matRecall(double& x, unsigned row, unsigned col)
      { x = matPtr[row + maxRows * col]; }
};

class SimultEqn : public Array, public Matrix
{
  protected:
    double *solnPtr;

  public:
    SimultEqn(unsigned Rows, unsigned Cols) :
      Array(Cols), Matrix(Rows, Cols)
    { solnPtr = new double[Rows]; }

    ~SimultEqn()
      { delete [] solnPtr; }
    void solve();
    void solnRecall(double& x, unsigned index)
      { x = solnPtr[index]; }

};

void SimultEqn::solve()
{
  double x, y;

  for (unsigned row = 0; row < maxRows; row++) {
    solnPtr[row] = 0;
    for (unsigned col = 0; col < maxCols; col++) {
      matRecall(x, row, col);
      arrRecall(y, col);
      solnPtr[row] += x * y;
    }
  }
}

main()
{
```

continues

LISTING A.8. CONTINUED

```
SimultEqn se(2,2);
double z;
for (unsigned i = 0; i < 2; i++)
  se.arrStore(1.0 + i, i);

for (i = 0; i < 2; i++)
  for (unsigned j = 0; j < 2; j++)
    se.matStore(2.5 + i + j, i, j);

se.solve();

cout << "Array B:\n";
for (i = 0; i < 2; i++) {
  se.arrRecall(z, i);
  cout << z << "\n";
}

cout << "\nMatrix A:\n";
for (i = 0; i < 2; i++) {
  for (unsigned j = 0; j < 2; j++) {
    se.matRecall(z, i, j);
    cout << z << " ";
  }
  cout << "\n";
}

cout << "\nArray X:\n";
for (i = 0; i < 2; i++) {
  se.solnRecall(z, i);
  cout << z << "\n";
}

return 0;
}
```

Here is the output for the program in Listing A.8:

```
Array B:
1
2
```

```
Matrix A:
2.5 3.5
3.5 4.5

Array X:
9.5
12.5
```

The listing declares the following classes:

1. The Array class models a dynamic numerical array.

2. The Matrix class models a dynamic numerical matrix.

3. The SimultEqn class is a child of the Array and Matrix classes and models a simultaneous-equations solver.

The SimultEqn class inherits the data members to support array B and matrix A from the Array and Matrix classes, respectively. To manage the dynamic array of solutions X, the class declares the protected pointer solnPtr. This pointer is similar to the arrPtr in the Array class. The SimultEqn class declares a constructor, a destructor, and a few functions.

The constructor for the SimultEqn class invokes the constructors of the Array and Matrix classes. In addition, the constructor allocates the dynamic space for the array X using the solnPtr member. The class destructor deletes the dynamic space accessed by the solnPtr member. The dynamic space for the matrix A and array B is deallocated by the destructors of the Matrix and Array classes, respectively.

The SimultEqn::solnRecall member function enables you to recall dynamic data for the solution array X. The solve function simulates solving the simultaneous equations. This function uses the array and matrix access functions inherited from the Array and Matrix classes.

The main function creates se, an instance of the SimultEqn class, with 2 rows and 2 columns. The function uses for loop statements to assign values to the array B and matrix A. Then the function calls the SimultEqn::solve function to manipulate the arrays and matrix. Finally, the main function uses another set of for loops to display the array B, the matrix A, and the array X.

SUMMARY

This chapter introduced you to C++ classes and discussed the following topics:

- Basics of object-oriented programming. These include classes, objects, messages, methods, inheritance, and polymorphism.

- Declaring base classes to specify the various private, protected, and public members. C++ classes contain data members and member functions. The data members store the state of a class instance, whereas the member functions query and manipulate that state.

- Constructors and destructors support the automatic creation and removal of class instances. Constructors are special members that must have the same name as the host class. You may declare any number of constructors or none at all. In the latter case, the compiler creates one for you. Each constructor enables you to create a class instance in a different way. There are two special kinds of constructors: the default constructor and the copy constructor. In contrast, in C++ you can declare only one parameterless destructor. The runtime system automatically invokes the constructor and destructor when a class instance comes into and goes out of its scope.

- Declaring a class hierarchy enables you to derive classes from existing ones. The descendant classes inherit the members of their ancestor classes. C++ classes are able to override inherited member functions by defining their own versions. If you override a nonvirtual function, you may declare the new version using a different parameter list. By contrast, you cannot alter the parameter list of an inherited virtual function.

- Virtual member functions enable your classes to support polymorphic behavior. Such behavior offers a response that is suitable for each class in a hierarchy. Once you declare a function virtual, you can override it only with a virtual function in a descendant class. All versions of a virtual function in a class hierarchy must have the same signature.

- Friend functions are special non-member functions that may access protected and private data members. These functions enable you to implement operations that are more flexible than those offered by member functions.

- Operators and friend operators enable you to support various operations, such as addition, assignment, and indexing. These operators enable you to offer a higher level of abstraction for your classes. In addition, they assist in making the expressions that manipulate class instances more readable and more intuitive.

- Constant functions are declared by placing the `const` keyword after the end of the parameter list. This kind of function must not modify a class data member.

- Static data members are, conceptually, a property of the class itself. Each class has only one copy of a static data member. By contrast, each instance has its own copy of the nonstatic data members. Static members assist in managing common aspects of the various instances of a class. These aspects include shared data and shared memory resources, to name a few.

- Static member functions access static data members. You can use static member functions before you create any class instance.

- Multiple inheritance allows a derived class to inherit from multiple classes. The parent classes may be part of either completely separate or intertwined hierarchies. In the latter case, the parent classes share a common ancestor class. Consequently, the C++ compiler requires you to use the `virtual` keyword in specifying the parent classes. The `virtual` keyword forewarns the compiler of the connected class hierarchies.

CONTROLS RESOURCE SCRIPT

This appendix presents the syntax for the menu resource script and the controls resource script. The resource script itself was defined by Microsoft long before it created the Microsoft Foundation Class hierarchy. However, as you saw in Chapter 5, dialog box instances are created using resources. You will learn about the following resources:

- The menu resources
- The dialog box resource
- The DIALOG option statements
- The general control resource
- The resources for the default controls

BUILDING MENU RESOURCES

The menu resource file (which is usually stored in a .RC file extension) may contain the following statements:

1. The MENU statement: defines the contents of a menu resource. The general syntax for the MENU statement is as follows:

```
menuID MENU [load options] [mem options]
BEGIN
        item definitions
END
```

The menuID is the unique name or integer ID of the menu resource. The keywords associated with a resource file appear in uppercase. This is optional, because they are not case-sensitive. I maintain the uppercase letters to make it easier to distinguish between resource keywords and non-keywords. The load options are these:

- PRELOAD: to load the resource immediately.

- LOADONCALL: to load the resource as needed. This is the default option.

The mem options are these:

- FIXED: to keep the resource in a fixed-memory location.

- MOVABLE: to move the resource when needed for the sake of memory compaction. This option is selected by default.

- DISCARDABLE: to discard the resource when no longer needed. This option is also selected by default.

2. The MENUITEM statement: defines the name and attributes of an actual menu item. The general syntax for the MENUITEM statement is this:

```
MENUITEM text, result [, option list]
```

The text field accepts a literal string (enclosed in double quotes) that designates the name of the menu item. To define a hot key for a menu item, place the ampersand character before the letter you want to designate as the hot key (the selection is case-insensitive). To display the ampersand as part of the menu name, use a sequence of two ampersand characters (that is, &&). You can also include the \t sequence to insert a tab in the menu item name. The \a sequence can be inserted to align all text that follows; the text is made flush to the right.

The result field contains an integer, usually a CM_xxxx constant, that represents the command emitted by the menu item.

The option list may contain the following items:

- CHECKED: displays a check mark next to the menu item.

- GRAYED: displays the menu item in a gray color to indicate that the menu item is not active.

- HELP: puts a vertical separator bar to the left of the menu item.

- INACTIVE: displays the menu item but prevents its selection. This option is usually combined with the GRAYED option to give a better visual indication that the menu item is inactive.

- MENUBARBREAK: places the menu item on a new line for static menu bar items. In the case of pop-up menu items, it separates the new and old columns with a vertical line.

- MENUBREAK: places the menu item on a new line for static menu bar items. For the pop-up menus (presented next), it places the menu item in a new column, without any dividing line between the columns.

3. The POPUP statement: defines the beginning of a pop-up menu. The general syntax for the POPUP statement is this:

```
POPUP text [,option list]
BEGIN
      item definitions
END
```

The text and option list fields are similar to their counterparts in the MENUITEM statement. The item definitions are made up of MENUITEM or other POPUP statements or both. The latter statements enable you to create nested menus.

4. The MENUITEM SEPARATOR statement: this is a special form of the MENUITEM statement that creates an inactive menu item and displays a dividing bar between two active menu items.

5. The ACCELERATORS statement: defines one or more accelerators for your Microsoft Foundation Class application. An accelerator is a keystroke defined to give the application user a quick way to select a menu item and carry out a specific task. The general syntax for the ACCELERATOR statement is this:

```
accTableName ACCELERATORS
BEGIN
    event, idValue, [type] [NOINVERT] [ALT] [SHIFT] [CONTROL]
END
```

The `accTableName` field defines a unique name or integer ID that distinguishes an accelerator resource from any other type of resource. The `event` field specifies the keystroke used as an accelerator and can be one of the following:

- A single ASCII character enclosed in double quotes. You can place a caret symbol before the character to signal that it is a control character. In this case, the type field is not required.

- An integer value that designates an ASCII code of a character. In this case, the type field must be the keyword `ASCII`.

- An integer value that represents a virtual key. In this case, the type field must be the keyword `VIRTKEY`.

The `idValue` field is an integer that identifies the accelerator. The `type` field is required only when the event field is an ASCII character code or a virtual key.

The `NOINVERT` option prevents a top-level menu item from being highlighted when the accelerator is used. The `ALT`, `SHIFT`, and `CONTROL` options activate the accelerator when the Alt, Shift, and Ctrl keys are pressed, respectively.

An example of an accelerators resource is as follows:

```
"EditKeys" ACCELERATORS
BEGIN
        "h",        IDDHEADING                      ; the H key
        "H",        IDDHOLD                         ; the Shift-H keys
        "^B",       IDDBOLD                         ; the Control-B keys
        64,         IDDADD                          ; The Shift-A keys
        97,         IDDAPPEND                       ; The A key
        "s",        IDDSEARCH, ALT                  ;  The Alt-S keys
        VK_F7,      IDDSAVE, VIRTKEY                ; The F7 function key
        VK_F2,      IDDLOAD, SHIFT, VIRTKEY        ; The Shift-F2 keys
        VK_F3,      IDDSAVEAS, CONTROL, VIRTKEY    ; The Control-F3
                                                    ; keys
        VK_F1,      IDDNEW, ALT, SHIFT, VIRTKEY    ; The Alt-Shift-F1
                                                    ; keys
END
```

DIALOG BOX RESOURCE

The `DIALOG` statement defines the resource that can be used in a Windows program to build dialog boxes. The general syntax for the `DIALOG` statement is this:

```
nameID DIALOG [load-option][mem-option] x, y, width, height
[option-statements]
BEGIN
     control-statements
END
```

The nameID is the unique name or integer ID of the dialog box resource. The keywords associated with resource files appear in uppercase. This is optional, because they are not case-sensitive. I maintain the uppercase letters to make it easier to distinguish between resource keywords and non-keywords. The *load options* are these:

- PRELOAD: to load the resource immediately.

- LOADONCALL: to load the resource as needed. This is the default option.

The *mem options* are these:

- FIXED: to keep the resource in a fixed-memory location.

- MOVABLE: to move the resource when needed for the sake of memory compaction. This option is selected by default.

- DISCARDABLE: to discard the resource when no longer needed. This option is also selected by default.

The x and y parameters specify the location of the upper-left corner of the dialog box. The width and height parameters define the dimensions of the dialog box.

An example of a dialog box resource definition is as follows :

```
#include <windows.h>
#include <afxres.h>

NEW DIALOG DISCARDABLE LOADONCALL PURE MOVEABLE 30, 50, 200, 100
STYLE WS_POPUP ¦ DS_MODALFRAME
CAPTION "Message"
BEGIN
  CTEXT "Exit the application?", 1, 10, 10, 170, 15
  CONTROL "OK", IDOK, "BUTTON", WS_CHILD ¦ WS_VISIBLE ¦
    WS_TABSTOP ¦ BS_DEFPUSHBUTTON, 20, 50, 70, 15
  CONTROL "Cancel", IDCANCEL, "BUTTON", WS_CHILD ¦ WS_VISIBLE ¦
    WS_TABSTOP ¦ BS_PUSHBUTTON, 110, 50, 70, 15
END
```

THE DIALOG OPTION STATEMENTS

The DIALOG option statements designate the special attributes of the dialog box, such as style, caption, and menu. These statements are optional. If you do not incorporate any option statements in your dialog box resource definition, you end up with a dialog box that has the default attributes. The DIALOG option statements include the following items:

- STYLE
- CAPTION
- MENU
- CLASS
- FONT

In the following subsections, I explain each of these dialog box attributes.

The STYLE Statement

The STYLE statement specifies the window style of the dialog box. This attribute indicates whether the dialog box is a child window or a pop-up window. The default style for the dialog box has the WS_POPUP, WS_BORDER, and WS_SYSMENU styles. The general syntax for the STYLE statement is this:

```
STYLE style
```

The *style* parameter takes an integer value made up of bitwise ORed style attributes. An example of the STYLE option statement is as follows:

```
STYLE WS_POPUP | DS_MODALFRAME
```

The CAPTION Statement

The CAPTION statement defines the title for the dialog box. This title appears in the caption bar of the dialog box, if the box has that bar. By default, the title is an empty string. The general syntax for the CAPTION statement is this:

```
CAPTION title
```

The *title* parameter is a literal string. An example of the CAPTION statement is given next:

```
CAPTION "Replace Text"
```

The MENU Statement

The MENU statement specifies the menu attached to the dialog box. By default, the dialog box has no menu. The general syntax for the MENU statement is this:

```
MENU menuName
```

The *menuName* parameter is the name or number of the menu resource. An example of the MENU statement is this:

```
#include <windows.h>
#include <owl\windows.h>

YesNo MENU LOADONCALL MOVEABLE PURE DISCARDABLE
BEGIN
    MENUITEM "&Ok", IDOK
    MENUITEM "&Cancel", IDCANCEL
END

NEW DIALOG DISCARDABLE LOADONCALL PURE MOVEABLE 30, 50, 200, 100
STYLE WS_POPUP ¦ DS_MODALFRAME
CAPTION "Message"
MENU YesNo
BEGIN
  CTEXT "Exit the application?", 1, 10, 10, 170, 15
  CONTROL "OK", IDOK, "BUTTON", WS_CHILD ¦ WS_VISIBLE ¦
    WS_TABSTOP ¦ BS_DEFPUSHBUTTON, 20, 50, 70, 15
  CONTROL "Cancel", IDCANCEL, "BUTTON", WS_CHILD ¦ WS_VISIBLE ¦
    WS_TABSTOP ¦ BS_PUSHBUTTON, 110, 50, 70, 15
END
```

The CLASS Statement

The CLASS statement specifies the Windows registration class (and not the MFC library class) of the dialog box. The general syntax for the CLASS statement is as follows:

```
CLASS className
```

The *className* parameter defines the integer or string name of the registration class. An example of the CLASS statement is as follows:

```
CLASS "ChitChat"
```

The FONT Statement

The FONT statement specifies the font used by Windows to draw text in the dialog box. The specified font must already be loaded, either from WIN.INI or from invoking the LoadFont API function. The general syntax for the FONT statement is this:

```
FONT pointSize, typeface
```

The *pointSize* parameter is an integer that specifies the size of the font in points. The *typeface* parameter is a string that indicates the name of the font. An example of using the FONT statement is given next:

```
FONT 10, "Helv"
```

The Dialog Box Control Resources

The resource script supports two types of controls resource. The first one is the CONTROL statement, which provides a general way for declaring the resource of a control. The other type of resource control is the modifiable default control resource. These resources use statements with keywords that are descriptive of the control they define. For example, the RADIOBUTTON statement defines the resource for a radio button. In the next section, I present the CONTROL statement. In the sections following that, I present the statements that define the resources for specific controls.

The General Control Resource

The CONTROL statement allows you to define the resource for any standard or user-defined control that is owned by a dialog box. The general syntax for the CONTROL statement is this:

```
CONTROL text, id, class, style, x, y, width, height
```

The `text` parameter specifies a string literal for the text that appears in the control.

The `id` parameter declares the control's unique ID.

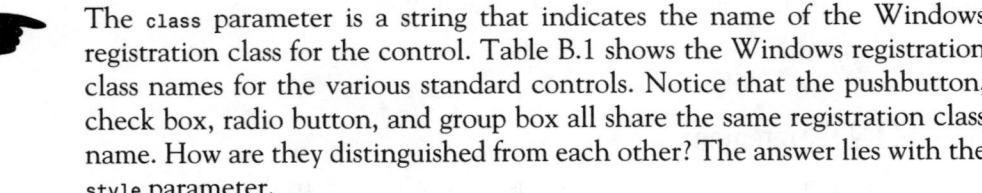 The `class` parameter is a string that indicates the name of the Windows registration class for the control. Table B.1 shows the Windows registration class names for the various standard controls. Notice that the pushbutton, check box, radio button, and group box all share the same registration class name. How are they distinguished from each other? The answer lies with the `style` parameter.

The `style` parameter, which is usually a bitwise ORed expression, sets all of the styles associated with the control. There are no default style values!

The x, y, width, and height parameters specify the location and dimensions of the control. These parameters are typically integer constants. You can also use the addition operator to build simple expressions.

TABLE B.1. THE WINDOWS REGISTRATION CLASS NAMES FOR THE VARIOUS STANDARD CONTROLS.	
Control	*Registration Class Name*
Check Box	BUTTON
Combo Box	COMBOBOX
Edit Box	EDIT
Group Box	BUTTON
List Box	LISTBOX
Push Button	BUTTON
Radio Button	BUTTON
Scroll Bar	SCROLLBAR
Static Text	STATIC

Examples of using the CONTROL statement to create dialog box controls are as follows:

```
ID_DIALOG DIALOG DISCARDABLE LOADONCALL PURE MOVEABLE 10, 10, 200, 150
STYLE WS_POPUP ¦ WS_CLIPSIBLINGS ¦ WS_CAPTION ¦ WS_SYSMENU ¦ DS_MODALFRAME
CAPTION "Controls Demo"
BEGIN
  CONTROL "Find", ID_FIND_TXT, "STATIC", WS_CHILD ¦ WS_VISIBLE ¦
    SS_LEFT, 20, 10, 100, 15

  CONTROL "", ID_FIND_CMB, "COMBOBOX", WS_CHILD ¦ WS_VISIBLE ¦
    WS_BORDER ¦ WS_TABSTOP ¦ CBS_DROPDOWN, 20, 25, 100, 50

  CONTROL "Replace", ID_REPLACE_TXT, "STATIC", WS_CHILD ¦ WS_VISIBLE ¦
    SS_LEFT, 20, 45, 100, 15

  CONTROL "", ID_REPLACE_CMB, "COMBOBOX", WS_CHILD ¦ WS_VISIBLE ¦
    WS_BORDER ¦ WS_TABSTOP ¦ CBS_DROPDOWN, 20, 60, 100, 50
```

continues

continued

```
  CONTROL " Scope ", ID_SCOPE_GRP, "BUTTON", WS_CHILD ¦ WS_VISIBLE
    ¦ WS_GROUP ¦ BS_GROUPBOX, 20, 80, 90, 50

  CONTROL "Global", ID_GLOBAL_RBT, "BUTTON", WS_CHILD ¦ WS_VISIBLE
    ¦ WS_TABSTOP ¦ BS_AUTORADIOBUTTON, 30, 90, 50, 15

  CONTROL "Selected Text", ID_SELTEXT_RBT, "BUTTON", WS_CHILD ¦
    WS_VISIBLE ¦ WS_TABSTOP ¦ BS_AUTORADIOBUTTON, 30, 105, 60, 15

  CONTROL "Case Sensitive", ID_CASE_CHK, "BUTTON", WS_CHILD ¦
    WS_VISIBLE ¦ WS_TABSTOP ¦ BS_AUTOCHECKBOX, 20, 130, 80, 15

  CONTROL "Whole Word", ID_WHOLEWORD_CHK, "BUTTON", WS_CHILD ¦
    WS_VISIBLE ¦ WS_TABSTOP ¦ BS_AUTOCHECKBOX, 100, 130, 80, 15

  CONTROL, "&OK", IDOK, "BUTTON", WS_CHILD ¦ WS_VISIBLE ¦ WS_TABSTOP
    ¦ BS_DEFPUSHBUTTON, 120, 90, 30, 20
  CONTROL "&Cancel", IDCANCEL, "BUTTON", WS_CHILD ¦ WS_VISIBLE ¦
    WS_TABSTOP, 160, 90, 30, 20
END
```

THE LTEXT STATEMENT

The LTEXT statement defines the resource of a static text control whose text is flushed left. The general syntax for the LTEXT statement is this:

```
LTEXT text, id, x, y, width, height [, style]
```

The text parameter specifies the static control text. This text may include an & character to underline a hot-key character. The id parameter defines the ID of the static control. The x, y, width, and height parameters specify the location and dimensions of the control. The optional style parameter specifies the additional styles for the resource. The default style is SS_LEFT and WS_GROUP. The style parameter can be the WS_TABSTOP style, or the WS_GROUP style, or both.

The characters of the text parameter are displayed left-justified. If the entire text does not fit in the specified width, the additional characters are wrapped to the beginning of the next line.

Examples of the LTEXT statement are shown next:

```
LTEXT "Current Drive:", ID_DRIVE_TXT, 10, 10, 50, 10

LTEXT "Current Dir:", ID_DIR_TXT, 10, 50, 50, 10, WS_TABSTOP
      ¦ WS_GROUP
```

THE RTEXT STATEMENT

The RTEXT statement defines the resource of a static text control whose text is flushed right. The general syntax for the RTEXT statement is this:

```
RTEXT text, id, x, y, width, height [, style]
```

The text parameter specifies the static control text. This text may include an & character to underline a hot-key character. The id parameter defines the ID of the static control. The x, y, width, and height parameters specify the location and dimensions of the control. The optional style parameter specifies the additional styles for the resource. The default style is SS_RIGHT and WS_GROUP. The style parameter can be the WS_TABSTOP style, or the WS_GROUP style, or both.

The characters of the text parameter are displayed right-justified. If the entire text does not fit in the specified width, the additional characters are wrapped to the next line and also appear right-justified.

An example of the RTEXT statement is shown next:

```
RTEXT "Current Drive:", ID_DRIVE_TXT, 70, 10, 50, 10
```

THE CTEXT STATEMENT

The CTEXT statement defines the resource of a static text control whose text is centered. The general syntax for the CTEXT statement is this:

```
CTEXT text, id, x, y, width, height [, style]
```

The text parameter specifies the static control text. This text may include an & character to underline a hot-key character. The id parameter defines the ID of the static control. The x, y, width, and height parameters specify the location and dimensions of the control. The optional style parameter specifies the additional styles for the resource. The default style is SS_CENTER and WS_GROUP. The style parameter can be the WS_TABSTOP style, or the WS_GROUP style, or both.

The characters of the text parameter are displayed centered. If the entire text does not fit in the specified width, the additional characters are wrapped to the next line and also appear centered.

An example of the CTEXT statement is shown next:

```
CTEXT "Current Drive:", ID_DRIVE_TXT, 10, 10, 50, 10
```

THE CHECKBOX STATEMENT

The CHECKBOX statement defines a check box control resource that has the BUTTON registration class. The general syntax for the CHECKBOX statement is this:

```
CHECKBOX text, id, x, y, width, height [, style]
```

The text parameter specifies the caption of the control. This text may include an & character to underline a hot-key character. The id parameter defines the ID of the check box control. The x, y, width, and height parameters specify the location and dimensions of the control. The optional style parameter specifies the additional styles for the resource. The default style is BS_CHECKBOX and WS_TABSTOP. The style parameter can be the WS_DISABLED style, or the WS_TABSTOP style, or both.

An example of the CHECKBOX statement is shown next:

```
CHECKBOX "Case-Sensitive", ID_CASE_CHK, 10, 10, 100, 10
```

THE PUSHBUTTON STATEMENT

The PUSHBUTTON statement defines a pushbutton control resource that has the BUTTON registration class. The general syntax for the PUSHBUTTON statement is this:

```
PUSHBUTTON text, id, x, y, width, height [, style]
```

The text parameter specifies the caption of the control. This text may include an & character to underline a hot-key character. The id parameter defines the ID of the pushbutton control. The x, y, width, and height parameters specify the location and dimensions of the control. The optional style parameter specifies the additional styles for the resource. The default style is BS_PUSHBUTTON and WS_TABSTOP. The style parameter can be the WS_TABSTOP style, or the WS_DISABLED style, or the WS_GROUP style, or any bitwise ORed combination of these styles.

An example of the PUSHBUTTON statement is shown next:

```
PUSHBUTTON "Calculate", ID_CALC_BTN, 10, 10, 100, 10, WS_DISABLED
```

THE DEFPUSHBUTTON STATEMENT

The DEFPUSHBUTTON statement defines a default pushbutton control resource that has the BUTTON registration class. The general syntax for the DEFPUSHBUTTON statement is this:

```
DEFPUSHBUTTON text, id, x, y, width, height [, style]
```

The text parameter specifies the caption of the control. This text may include an & character to underline a hot-key character. The id parameter defines the ID of the default pushbutton control. The x, y, width, and height parameters specify the location and dimensions of the control. The optional style parameter specifies the additional styles for the resource. The default style is BS_DEFPUSHBUTTON and WS_TABSTOP. The style parameter can be the WS_TABSTOP style, or the WS_DISABLED style, or the WS_GROUP style, or any bitwise ORed combination of these styles.

An example of the DEFPUSHBUTTON statement is shown next:

```
DEFPUSHBUTTON "Calculate", ID_CALC_BTN, 10, 10, 100, 10
```

The LISTBOX Statement

The LISTBOX statement defines a list box control resource that has the LISTBOX registration class. The general syntax for the LISTBOX statement is this:

```
LISTBOX id, x, y, width, height [, style]
```

The id parameter defines the ID of the list box control. The x, y, width, and height parameters specify the location and dimensions of the control. The optional style parameter specifies the additional styles for the resource. The default style is LBS_NOTIFY, WS_VSCROLL, and WS_BORDER. The style parameter can be the WS_BORDER style, or the WS_VSCROLL style, or both.

An example of the LISTBOX statement is shown next:

```
LISTBOX ID_OPERAND_LST, 10, 10, 100, 100
```

The GROUPBOX Statement

The GROUPBOX statement defines a group box control resource that has the BUTTON registration class. The general syntax for the GROUPBOX statement is this:

```
GROUPBOX text, id, x, y, width, height [, style]
```

The text parameter specifies the caption of the control. This text may include an & character to underline a hot-key character. The id parameter defines the ID of the group box control. The x, y, width, and height parameters specify the location and dimensions of the control. The optional style parameter specifies the additional styles for the resource. The default style is BS_GROUPBOX and WS_TABSTOP. The style parameter can be the WS_TABSTOP style, or the WS_DISABLED style, or both.

An example of the GROUPBOX statement is shown next:

```
GROUPBOX "Angle", ID_ANGLE_GRP, 10, 10, 200, 200
```

The RADIOBUTTON Statement

The RADIOBUTTON statement defines a radio button control resource that has the BUTTON registration class. The general syntax for the RADIOBUTTON statement is this:

```
RADIOBUTTON text, id, x, y, width, height [, style]
```

The text parameter specifies the caption of the control. This text may include an & character to underline a hot-key character. The id parameter defines the ID of the radio button control. The x, y, width, and height parameters specify the location and dimensions of the control. The optional style parameter specifies the additional styles for the resource. The default style is BS_RADIOBUTTON and WS_TABSTOP. The style parameter can be the WS_TABSTOP style, or the WS_GROUP style, or the WS_DISABLED style, or any bitwise ORed combination of these styles.

An example of the RADIOBUTTON statement is shown next:

```
RADIOBUTTON "Degrees", ID_DEGREES_RBT, 10, 10, 100, 10
```

The EDITTEXT Statement

The EDITTEXT statement defines an edit box control resource that has the EDIT registration class. The general syntax for the EDITTEXT statement is this:

```
EDITTEXT id, x, y, width, height [, style]
```

The id parameter defines the ID of the edit box control. The x, y, width, and height parameters specify the location and dimensions of the control. The optional style parameter specifies the additional styles for the resource. The default style is WS_TABSTOP, ES_EDIT, and WS_BORDER. The style parameter can be the WS_TABSTOP, or the WS_GROUP, or the WS_VSCROLL, or the WS_HSCROLL, or the WS_DISABLED styles, or any bitwise ORed combination of these styles.

An example of the EDITTEXT statement is shown next:

```
EDITTEXT ID_INPUT_BOX, 10, 10, 200, 200
```

THE COMBOBOX STATEMENT

The COMBOBOX statement defines a combo box control resource that has the COMBOBOX registration class. The general syntax for the COMBOBOX statement is this:

```
COMBOBOX id, x, y, width, height [, style]
```

The id parameter defines the ID of the combo box control. The x, y, width, and height parameters specify the location and dimensions of the control. The optional style parameter specifies the additional styles for the resource. The default style is WS_TABSTOP and CBS_SIMPLE. The style parameter can be the WS_TABSTOP, or the WS_GROUP, or the WS_VSCROLL, or the WS_DISABLED styles, or any bitwise ORed combination of these styles.

An example of the COMBOBOX statement is shown next:

```
COMBOBOX ID_INPUT_BOX, 10, 10, 200, 200
```

THE SCROLLBAR STATEMENT

The SCROLLBAR statement defines a scroll bar control resource that has the SCROLLBAR registration class. The general syntax for the SCROLLBAR statement is this:

```
SCROLLBAR id, x, y, width, height [, style]
```

The id parameter defines the ID of the scroll bar control. The x, y, width, and height parameters specify the location and dimensions of the control. The optional style parameter specifies the additional styles for the resource. The default style is SBS_HORZ. The style parameter can be the WS_TABSTOP, or the WS_GROUP, or the WS_GROUP, or the WS_DISABLED styles, or any bitwise ORed combination of these styles.

An example of the SCROLLBAR statement is shown next:

```
SCROLLBAR ID_INDEX_SCR, 10, 10, 20, 200
```

SUMMARY

This appendix briefly introduced you to the resource statements used to create the dialog box and its controls. You learned about the following topics:

- The DIALOG statement that defines a dialog box resource.

- The DIALOG option statements. This includes the STYLE, CAPTION, MENU, CLASS, and FONT statements.

- The CONTROL statement that defines the resources for both standard and user-defined controls.

- The LTEXT statement that defines the resource for a left-justified static text control.

- The RTEXT statement that defines the resource for a right-justified static text control.

- The CTEXT statement that defines the resource for a centered-text static text control.

- The CHECKBOX statement that defines the resource for check box control.

- The PUSHBUTTON statement that defines the resource for a pushbutton control.

- The DEFPUSHBUTTON statement that defines the resource for a default pushbutton control.

- The LISTBOX statement that defines the resource for a list box control.

- The GROUPBOX statement that defines the resource for a group box control.

- The RADIOBUTTON statement that defines the resource for a radio button control.

- The EDITTEXT statement that defines the resource for an edit box control.

- The COMBOBOX statement that defines the resource for a combo box control.

- The SCROLLBAR statement that defines the resource for a scroll bar control.

THE STRING CLASS

The Borland C++ 4.0 classes include the header file CSTRING.H, which contains the declaration and definition of the class string. What is special about this class is that it is compliant with the string class proposed by the ANSI C++ committee. This appendix discusses the following topics:

- The declaration of class string

- The kinds of public member functions in class string

- The TESTSTR.EXE Windows program, which is an interactive menu-driven program that permits you to test a selection of functions and operators declared in class string.

THE DECLARATION OF CLASS STRING

Listing C.1 shows the declaration of class string in the CSTRING.H header file. This file also contains the declaration and implementation (which uses many inline functions) of other classes, such as TSubString, TStringRef, and TRegexp (models regular expressions). Because of the limited space, I will only discuss the class string.

LISTING C.1. THE DECLARATION OF CLASS STRING IN THE CSTRING.H HEADER FILE.

```
class _EXPCLASS string
{

public:

    //
    // Exceptions
    //
    class outofrange : public xmsg
    {
    public:
        outofrange();
    };

    class lengtherror : public xmsg
    {
    public:
        lengtherror();
    };

    //
    // Constructors
    //

    string() throw(xalloc);

    string(const string _FAR &s) throw(xalloc);
    string(const string _FAR &s, size_t n) throw(xalloc);

    string(const char _FAR *cp) throw(xalloc, lengtherror);
    string(const char _FAR *cp, size_t n) throw(xalloc, lengtherror);

    string(char c) THROW_XALLOC_LENGTHERROR;
    string(char c, size_t n) THROW_XALLOC_LENGTHERROR;

    string(signed char c) THROW_XALLOC_LENGTHERROR;
    string(signed char c, size_t n) THROW_XALLOC_LENGTHERROR;

    string(unsigned char c) THROW_XALLOC_LENGTHERROR;
    string(unsigned char c, size_t n) THROW_XALLOC_LENGTHERROR;

    // non-standard constructors
    string(const TSubString _FAR &ss) throw(xalloc);

    // Special far string ctors for small & medium model
    #if defined(__TINY__) || defined(__SMALL__) || defined(__MEDIUM__)
    string(const char __far *cp) THROW_XALLOC_LENGTHERROR;
    string(const char __far *cp, size_t n) THROW_XALLOC_LENGTHERROR;
    #endif
```

```
// Ctor to make a string from a resource
#if defined(_Windows)
string(HINSTANCE instance, UINT id, int len = 255)
    throw(xalloc, lengtherror);
#endif

//
// Destructor
//
~string() throw();

//
// Assignment
//
string _FAR & operator = (const string _FAR &s) THROW_XALLOC;
string _FAR & assign(const string _FAR &s) THROW_XALLOC;
string _FAR & assign(const string _FAR &s, size_t n) throw(xalloc);

//
// Concatenation
//
string _FAR & operator += (const string _FAR &s)
    THROW_XALLOC_LENGTHERROR;
string _FAR & append(const string _FAR &s)
    THROW_XALLOC_LENGTHERROR;
string _FAR & append(const string _FAR &s, size_t n)
    throw(xalloc, lengtherror);

string _FAR & operator += (const char _FAR *cp)
    THROW_XALLOC_LENGTHERROR;
friend string _Cdecl _FARFUNC operator + (const string _FAR &s,
                                           const char _FAR *cp)
    THROW_XALLOC_LENGTHERROR;
string _FAR & append(const char _FAR *cp)
    throw(xalloc, lengtherror);
string _FAR & append(const char _FAR *cp, size_t n)
    throw(xalloc, lengtherror);

string _FAR &prepend(const string _FAR &s)
    THROW_XALLOC_LENGTHERROR;
string _FAR &prepend(const string _FAR &s, size_t n)
    THROW_XALLOC_LENGTHERROR;
string _FAR &prepend(const char _FAR *cp)
    THROW_XALLOC_LENGTHERROR;
string _FAR &prepend(const char _FAR *cp, size_t n)
    throw(xalloc, lengtherror);

//
// Comparison
//
```

continues

LISTING C.1. CONTINUED

```
int compare(const string _FAR &s) const throw();
int compare(const string _FAR &s, size_t n) const throw();

friend int operator == (const string _FAR &s1, const string _FAR &s2)
    THROW_NONE;

friend int operator != (const string _FAR &s1, const string _FAR &s2)
    THROW_NONE;

friend int operator == (const string _FAR &s, const char _FAR *cp)
    THROW_NONE;
friend int operator == (const char _FAR *cp, const string _FAR &s)
    THROW_NONE;

friend int operator != (const string _FAR &s, const char _FAR *cp)
    THROW_NONE;
friend int operator != (const char _FAR *cp, const string _FAR &s)
    THROW_NONE;

friend int operator <  (const string _FAR &s1, const string _FAR &s2)
    THROW_NONE;
friend int operator <  (const string _FAR &s, const char _FAR *cp)
    THROW_NONE;
friend int operator <  (const char _FAR *cp, const string _FAR &s)
    THROW_NONE;

friend int operator <= (const string _FAR &s1, const string _FAR &s2)
    THROW_NONE;
friend int operator <= (const string _FAR &s, const char _FAR *cp)
    THROW_NONE;
friend int operator <= (const char _FAR *cp, const string _FAR &s)
    THROW_NONE;

friend int operator >  (const string _FAR &s1, const string _FAR &s2)
    THROW_NONE;
friend int operator >  (const string _FAR &s, const char _FAR *cp)
    THROW_NONE;
friend int operator >  (const char _FAR *cp, const string _FAR &s)
    THROW_NONE;

friend int operator >= (const string _FAR &s1, const string _FAR &s2)
    THROW_NONE;
friend int operator >= (const string _FAR &s, const char _FAR *cp)
    THROW_NONE;
friend int operator >= (const char _FAR *cp, const string _FAR &s)
    THROW_NONE;
```

```
//
// Insertion at some position
//
string _FAR &insert(size_t pos, const string _FAR &s)
    throw(xalloc, outofrange, lengtherror);
string _FAR &insert(size_t pos, const string _FAR &s, size_t n)
    throw(xalloc, outofrange, lengtherror);

//
// Removal
//
string _FAR &remove(size_t pos) THROW_XALLOC_OUTOFRANGE;
string _FAR &remove(size_t pos, size_t n)
    throw(xalloc, outofrange);

//
// Replacement at some position
//
string _FAR &replace(size_t pos, size_t n, const string _FAR &s)
    THROW_XALLOC_RANGE_LENGTH;
string _FAR &replace(size_t pos, size_t n1,
                     const string _FAR &s, size_t n2)
    throw(xalloc, outofrange, lengtherror);

//
// Subscripting
//
char get_at(size_t pos) const THROW_OUTOFRANGE;
void put_at(size_t pos, char c) THROW_OUTOFRANGE;

char _FAR & operator[](size_t pos) THROW_OUTOFRANGE;
char _FAR & operator()(size_t pos) throw(outofrange);
TSubString operator()(size_t start, size_t len) THROW_NONE;
TSubString operator()(const TRegexp _FAR &re) THROW_NONE;
TSubString operator()(const TRegexp _FAR &re, size_t start) throw();

char operator[](size_t pos) const THROW_OUTOFRANGE;
char operator()(size_t pos) const THROW_OUTOFRANGE;
const TSubString operator()(size_t start, size_t len) const throw();
const TSubString operator()(const TRegexp _FAR &pat) const THROW_NONE;
const TSubString operator()(const TRegexp _FAR &pat, size_t start)
    const throw();

//
// Searching
//
size_t find(const string _FAR &s) const THROW_NONE;
size_t find(const string _FAR &s, size_t pos) const throw();
size_t rfind(const string _FAR &s) const THROW_NONE;
size_t rfind(const string _FAR &s, size_t pos) const throw();
```

continues

LISTING C.1. CONTINUED

```
int contains(const char _FAR *pat) const throw();
int contains(const string _FAR &s) const THROW_NONE;
size_t find(const TRegexp _FAR &pat, size_t i = 0) const throw();
size_t find(const TRegexp _FAR &pat, size_t _FAR *ext, size_t i = 0)
    const throw();

//
// Substring
//
string substr(size_t pos) const
    throw(xalloc, outofrange);
string substr(size_t pos, size_t n) const
    throw(xalloc, outofrange);

TSubString substring(const char _FAR *cp) THROW_NONE;
const TSubString substring(const char _FAR *cp)
    const THROW_NONE;
TSubString substring(const char _FAR *cp, size_t start) throw();
const TSubString substring(const char _FAR *cp, size_t start)
    const throw();

//
// Character set searching
//
size_t find_first_of(const string _FAR &s) const THROW_NONE;
size_t find_first_of(const string _FAR &s, size_t pos) const throw();
size_t find_first_not_of(const string _FAR &s) const THROW_NONE;
size_t find_first_not_of(const string _FAR &s, size_t pos)
    const throw();
size_t find_last_of(const string _FAR &s) const THROW_NONE;
size_t find_last_of(const string _FAR &s, size_t pos) const throw();
size_t find_last_not_of(const string _FAR &s) const THROW_NONE;
size_t find_last_not_of(const string _FAR &s, size_t pos)
    const throw();

//
// Miscellaneous
//
size_t length() const THROW_NONE;
size_t copy(char _FAR *cb, size_t n) throw(outofrange);
size_t copy(char _FAR *cb, size_t n, size_t pos) throw(outofrange);
const char _FAR *c_str() const THROW_XALLOC;
size_t reserve() const THROW_NONE;
void reserve(size_t ic) throw(xalloc, outofrange);

string copy() const throw(xalloc);     // Distinct copy of self.
```

```
        friend ipstream _FAR & _EXPFUNC operator >> (ipstream _FAR & is,
                                         string _FAR & str);

    // Static member functions:
    static int set_case_sensitive(int tf = 1);
    static int set_paranoid_check(int ck = 1);
    static int skip_whitespace(int sk = 1);
    static size_t initial_capacity(size_t ic = 63);
    static size_t resize_increment(size_t ri = 64);
    static size_t max_waste(size_t mw = 63);

    static int get_case_sensitive_flag();
    static int get_paranoid_check_flag();
    static int get_skip_whitespace_flag();
    static size_t get_initial_capacity();
    static size_t get_resize_increment();
    static size_t get_max_waste();

    enum StripType { Leading, Trailing, Both };

    // Non-static member functions:
    unsigned hash() const;
    int is_null() const;
    istream _FAR &read_file(istream _FAR &is);
    istream _FAR &read_string(istream _FAR &is);
    istream _FAR &read_line(istream _FAR &is);
    istream _FAR &read_to_delim(istream _FAR &is, char delim = '\n');
    istream _FAR &read_token(istream _FAR &is);
    void resize(size_t m);
    TSubString strip(StripType s = Trailing, char c = ' ');
    void to_lower();
    void to_upper();

    #if defined(_Windows)
    void ansi_to_oem() THROW_NONE;
    void oem_to_ansi() THROW_NONE;
    #endif

protected:

    int  valid_element(size_t pos) const THROW_NONE;
    int  valid_index(size_t pos) const THROW_NONE;

    void assert_element(size_t pos) const throw(outofrange);
    void assert_index(size_t pos) const throw(outofrange);

    string(const string _FAR &s, const char _FAR *cb);
    void cow();

private:
```

continues

LISTING C.1. CONTINUED

```
    TStringRef _FAR *p;

    static int case_sensitive;
    static int paranoid_check;
    static int skip_white;
    static size_t initial_capac;
    static size_t resize_inc;
    static size_t freeboard;

private:

    friend class _EXPCLASS TSubString;
    friend class _EXPCLASS TStringRef;

    void clone();
    size_t find_case_index(const char _FAR *cb,
                           size_t start,
                           size_t _FAR &patl) const;
    size_t rfind_case_index(const char _FAR *cb,
                            size_t start,
                            size_t _FAR &patl) const;
    size_t find_index(const char _FAR *,
                      size_t start,
                      size_t _FAR & patl) const;
    size_t rfind_index(const char _FAR *,
                       size_t start,
                       size_t _FAR & patl) const;
    unsigned hash_case() const;

};
```

The class string declares public, protected, and private members. The next section presents the public members. The remainder of this section briefly touches on the protected and private members. The protected member functions validate indices and assert the data. The private members include data members and member functions. The data members are as follows:

- The member p, which is a pointer to the class TStringRef. The dynamic instance of this class stores the characters of a string object.

- The static member case_sensitive stores the case-sensitivity flag used by the find functions.

- The static member `paranoid_check` stores the paranoid flag. The string class uses this flag to perform extra checking on the hash function values produced by member function `hash`.

- The static member `skip_white` stores the skip-whitespace flag used in reading strings.

- The static member `initial_capac` stores the initial capacity of string objects.

- The static member `resize_inc` stores the size increment used to expand the dynamic memory space which stores the characters.

- The static member `freeboard` stores the amount of free space available after a string is resized.

These static data members influence the behavior of all the `string` class instances. Why should you declare these members static? The answer lies in the need to make the instances of class `string` behave uniformly. Think of what might happen while evaluating a string expression if these static members where declared as ordinary data members: the various terms may lead to inconsistent results if each term had a string instance with a different set of flags!

The private member functions are mostly helper functions to the public member functions `find` and `rfind`.

The Class Member Functions

Let's focus on the public member functions. In the next subsections, I present these members by category.

The Constructors

The class `string` contains the following set of constructors:

```
string() throw(xalloc);

string(const string _FAR &s) throw(xalloc);
string(const string _FAR &s, size_t n) throw(xalloc);

string(const char _FAR *cp) throw(xalloc, lengtherror);
string(const char _FAR *cp, size_t n) throw(xalloc, lengtherror);
```

```
string(char c) THROW_XALLOC_LENGTHERROR;
string(char c, size_t n) THROW_XALLOC_LENGTHERROR;

string(signed char c) THROW_XALLOC_LENGTHERROR;
string(signed char c, size_t n) THROW_XALLOC_LENGTHERROR;

string(unsigned char c) THROW_XALLOC_LENGTHERROR;
string(unsigned char c, size_t n) THROW_XALLOC_LENGTHERROR;

// non-standard constructors
string(const TSubString _FAR &ss) throw(xalloc);

// Special far string ctors for small & medium model
#if defined(__TINY__) || defined(__SMALL__) || defined(__MEDIUM__)
string(const char __far *cp) THROW_XALLOC_LENGTHERROR;
string(const char __far *cp, size_t n) THROW_XALLOC_LENGTHERROR;
#endif

// Ctor to make a string from a resource
#if defined(_Windows)
string(HINSTANCE instance, UINT id, int len = 255)
    throw(xalloc, lengtherror);
#endif
```

These constructors allow you to build a nonempty string object from the following:

- An existing string object
- An ASCIIZ string (that is, a C-style string)
- A specified number of characters from an existing string object
- A character
- A sequence of the same characters
- A substring object (that is, an instance of class TSubString)
- A string resource

In addition, class string has a void constructor that permits you to create instances that have empty strings.

Here are a few examples of using some of the class constructors:

```
// create an empty string object
string emptyStringObject;

// creates the string object StrObj1 and initialize it
// with the ASCIIZ string literal "Hello World"
string StrObj1("Hello World");
```

```
// create the string object StrObj2 using StrObj1
string StrObj2(StrObj1);

// create the string object StrObj3 using the first 5 characters
// of StrObj1. The string object StrObj3 contains "Hello"
string StrObj3(StrObj1, 5);

// create the string object StrObj4 using a character
string StrObj4('+');

// create the string object StrObj5 using a sequence of the
// character '+'. The string object StrObj5 contains "+++++"
string StrObj5('+', 5);
```

Notice that the constructors lack parameters that define the initial capacity and size increment. These operational parameters are handled by other member functions that I present later in this section.

The Destructor

The string class declares the destructor that deletes the string instance and recuperates its memory.

The Assignment Functions

The class string offers one assignment operator and two overloaded assignment functions, shown next:

```
string _FAR & operator = (const string _FAR &s) THROW_XALLOC;
string _FAR & assign(const string _FAR &s) THROW_XALLOC;
string _FAR & assign(const string _FAR &s, size_t n) throw(xalloc);
```

The operator = and the first overloaded assign function copy a string object to another. The second overloaded assign function only assigns the first n characters of the string object s. Each of these member functions returns a reference to the resulting string object.

Here are examples of using the previously mentioned member functions:

```
string Str1("Hello");
string Str2, Str3, Str4;

Str2 = Str1; // use operator =
Str3.assign(Str1); // use first overloaded assign function
Str4.assign(Str1, 5); // use the second function assign
```

The Concatenation Functions

The class string provides the following member functions, friend functions, and operators to support concatenating strings to the target string object:

```
string _FAR & operator += (const string _FAR &s)
    THROW_XALLOC_LENGTHERROR;
string _FAR & append(const string _FAR &s)
    THROW_XALLOC_LENGTHERROR;
string _FAR & append(const string _FAR &s, size_t n)
    throw(xalloc, lengtherror);

string _FAR & operator += (const char _FAR *cp)
    THROW_XALLOC_LENGTHERROR;
friend string _Cdecl _FARFUNC operator + (const string _FAR &s,
                                          const char _FAR *cp)
    THROW_XALLOC_LENGTHERROR;
string _FAR & append(const char _FAR *cp)
    throw(xalloc, lengtherror);
string _FAR & append(const char _FAR *cp, size_t n)
    throw(xalloc, lengtherror);

string _FAR &prepend(const string _FAR &s)
    THROW_XALLOC_LENGTHERROR;
string _FAR &prepend(const string _FAR &s, size_t n)
    THROW_XALLOC_LENGTHERROR;
string _FAR &prepend(const char _FAR *cp)
    THROW_XALLOC_LENGTHERROR;
string _FAR &prepend(const char _FAR *cp, size_t n)
    throw(xalloc, lengtherror);
```

The operator += and the overloaded append functions serve to append a string to the target string object. The overloaded member functions prepend serve to prepend a string with the target string. The above overloaded functions use the following parameters:

- The parameter s represents a string object to be appended or prepended.

- The parameter cp represents an ASCIIZ string to be appended or prepended.

- The parameter n represents the number of characters to append or prepend.

Each of the overloaded append and prepend functions returns a reference to the resulting string object.

Here are examples of using these functions:

```
string Str1("Hello ");
string Str2("world!);
string Str3 = Str1 + Str2;

string Str4("I said ");
Str4.append(Str3); // contains "I said Hello world!"

string Str5("You said ");
Str5.append(Str3, 5); // contains "You said Hello"

string Str6(" How are you?");
Str6.prepend(Str3); // contains "Hello world! How are you?"

string Str7("I said ");
Str7.append("howdee!"); // contains "I said howdee!"

string Str8("You said ");
Str8.append("hello world!", 5); // contains "You said hello"
```

The Comparison Functions

The class string offers two overloaded versions of function compare and a set of friend operators that compare various combinations of string objects and ASCIIZ strings. The comparison functions are these:

```
int compare(const string _FAR &s) const throw();
int compare(const string _FAR &s, size_t n) const throw();
```

The first function compares the string object s with the target string object receiving the C++ message compare. The function returns the following:

- If the target string is greater than the argument of parameter s, the function returns a positive number.

- If the target string is less than the argument of parameter s, the function returns a negative number.

- If the target string is equal to the argument of parameter s, the function returns zero.

The parameter s represents the string object compared with the target string. The parameter n specifies the maximum number of characters in string object s to compare. Here are examples of using the compare functions:

```
string Str1("Meaning"), Str2("meaning");
int result;
```

continues

continued

```
result = Str1.compare(Str2);
cout << Str1.c_str();
if (result > 0)
  cout " < ";
else if (result < 0)
  cout " > ";
else
  cout " == ";
cout << Str2.c_str() << "\n";

result = Str1.compare(Str2, 2);
string Str1b(Str1, 2), Str2b(Str2, 2);
cout << Str1b.c_str();
if (result > 0)
  cout " < ";
else if (result < 0)
  cout " > ";
else
  cout " == ";
cout << Str2b.c_str() << "\n";
```

The friend relational operators are:

```
    friend int operator == (const string _FAR &s1,
                            const string _FAR &s2)
        THROW_NONE;

    friend int operator != (const string _FAR &s1,
                            const string _FAR &s2) THROW_NONE;

    friend int operator == (const string _FAR &s,
                            const char _FAR *cp) THROW_NONE;
    friend int operator == (const char _FAR *cp,
                            const string _FAR &s) THROW_NONE;

    friend int operator != (const string _FAR &s,
                            const char _FAR *cp) THROW_NONE;
    friend int operator != (const char _FAR *cp,
                            const string _FAR &s) THROW_NONE;

    friend int operator <  (const string _FAR &s1,
                            const string _FAR &s2) THROW_NONE;
    friend int operator <  (const string _FAR &s,
                            const char _FAR *cp) THROW_NONE;
    friend int operator <  (const char _FAR *cp,
                            const string _FAR &s) THROW_NONE;

    friend int operator <= (const string _FAR &s1,
                            const string _FAR &s2) THROW_NONE;
```

```
        friend int operator <= (const string _FAR &s,
                                const char _FAR *cp) THROW_NONE;
        friend int operator <= (const char _FAR *cp,
                                const string _FAR &s) THROW_NONE;

        friend int operator >  (const string _FAR &s1,
                                const string _FAR &s2) THROW_NONE;
        friend int operator >  (const string _FAR &s,
                                const char _FAR *cp) THROW_NONE;
        friend int operator >  (const char _FAR *cp,
                                const string _FAR &s) THROW_NONE;

        friend int operator >= (const string _FAR &s1,
                                const string _FAR &s2) THROW_NONE;
        friend int operator >= (const string _FAR &s,
                                const char _FAR *cp) THROW_NONE;
        friend int operator >= (const char _FAR *cp,
                                const string _FAR &s) THROW_NONE;
```

The parameters s, s1, and s2 represent string objects. The parameter cp represents an ASCIIZ string.

Here is an example of using the relational operators:

```
string Str1("Meaning"), Str2("meaning");

result = Str1.compare(Str2);
cout << Str1.c_str();
if (Str1 > Str2)
  cout " < ";
else if (Str1 < Str2)
  cout " > ";
else
  cout " == ";
cout << Str2.c_str() << "\n";
```

The Insertion Functions

The class string supports inserting string objects into other string objects by providing the overloaded insert functions:

```
string _FAR &insert(size_t pos, const string _FAR &s)
    throw(xalloc, outofrange, lengtherror);
string _FAR &insert(size_t pos, const string _FAR &s, size_t n)
    throw(xalloc, outofrange, lengtherror);
```

The parameter pos represents the index of the target string where insertion starts. The parameter s specifies the inserted string object. The parameter n indicates the number of characters to be inserted. Each of the overloaded functions returns a reference to the resulting string object.

Here are examples of using the overloaded insert functions:

```
string Str1("0123456789");
string Str2 = Str1;
string InsStr("+++++");
int pos = 4;
int n = 3;

Str1.insert(pos, InsStr);
cout << Str1.c_str() << "\n"; // displays string 0123+++++456789

Str2.insert(pos, InsStr, 2);
cout << Str2.c_str() << "\n"; // displays string 0123++456789
```

The Removal Functions

The class string supports removing characters from a string object by offering the following overloaded member functions:

```
string _FAR &remove(size_t pos) THROW_XALLOC_OUTOFRANGE;
string _FAR &remove(size_t pos, size_t n)
    throw(xalloc, outofrange);
```

The parameter pos specifies the index of the first deleted character in the target string object. The parameter n indicates the number of removed characters. The first overloaded version of the function removes the trailing characters in the target string object, starting with the character number pos. The second version of the function permits you to delete a set of characters inside the target string object. Each of the overloaded functions returns a reference to the resulting string object.

Here are examples of using the overloaded remove functions:

```
string Str1("0123456789);
string Str2(Str1);

Str1.remove(6);
cout << Str1.c_str() << "\n"; / displays the string 012345

Str2.remove(6, 2);
cout << Str2.c_str() << "\n"; / displays the string 01234589
```

The Replacement Functions

The string class offers the following member functions to replace the characters of a target string object:

```
string _FAR &replace(size_t pos, size_t n, const string _FAR &s)
    THROW_XALLOC_RANGE_LENGTH;
string _FAR &replace(size_t pos, size_t n1,
                        const string _FAR &s, size_t n2)
    throw(xalloc, outofrange, lengtherror);
```

The first version of the function deletes a specified number of characters and then inserts all the characters of the string parameter. The second version inserts only a specified number of characters.

The parameter pos specifies the index of the first character to be removed. The parameter s specifies the string object whose characters are inserted in the target string object. The parameters n (in the first overloaded function) and n1 (in the second overloaded function) specify the number of characters to delete from the target string object. The parameter n2 (in the second overloaded function) indicates the number of inserted characters.

Here are examples of using the overloaded functions replace:

```
string Str1("01234567890123456789");
string Str2(Str1);
string Str3("qwerty");

Str1.replace(10, 5, Str3);
cout << Str1.c_str() << "\n"; // shows 0123456789qwerty56789

Str2.replace(10, 5, 2, Str3);
cout << Str2.c_str() << "\n"; // shows 0123456789qw56789
```

The Subscripting Functions

The class string provides the following member functions and operators to access either individual characters or substrings:

```
char get_at(size_t pos) const THROW_OUTOFRANGE;
void put_at(size_t pos, char c) THROW_OUTOFRANGE;

char _FAR & operator[](size_t pos) THROW_OUTOFRANGE;
char _FAR & operator()(size_t pos) throw(outofrange);
TSubString operator()(size_t start, size_t len) THROW_NONE;
TSubString operator()(const TRegexp _FAR &re) THROW_NONE;
TSubString operator()(const TRegexp _FAR &re, size_t start) throw();

char operator[](size_t pos) const THROW_OUTOFRANGE;
char operator()(size_t pos) const THROW_OUTOFRANGE;
const TSubString operator()(size_t start, size_t len) const throw();
const TSubString operator()(const TRegexp _FAR &pat) const
                                        THROW_NONE;
const TSubString operator()(const TRegexp _FAR &pat, size_t start)
    const throw();
```

The member function get_at recalls a character at a specific index, pos. The member function put_at writes the character c at index pos. The first version of operator [] can replace both of the above member functions, because it returns the reference to the character at index pos. In addition, you can use the operator [] on either side of an assignment operator. The class provides a set of operator () to access individual characters and substrings. Some of the versions of operator () use the regular expression class TRegexp and the substring class TSubString.

Here are examples of using these member functions and operators:

```
string Str1("qWzErTy");
string Str2(Str1);
char c;

for (int i = 0; i < Str1.length(); i++) {
    c = Str1.get_at(i);
    if (c >= 'A' && c <= 'Z')
        Str1.put_at(i, c - 'A' + 'a');
    cout << Str1.get_at(i);
}

for (int i = 0; i < Str2.length(); i++) {
    if (Str2[i] >= 'A' && Str2[i] <= 'Z')
        Str2[i] = Str2[i] - 'A' + 'a';
    cout << Str2[i];
}
```

The Searching Functions

The class string offers two general sets of search functions. The first set searches for the occurrence of a string inside the target string object. The second set searches for character sets in the target string object. The first set of search functions are as follows:

```
size_t find(const string _FAR &s) const THROW_NONE;
size_t find(const string _FAR &s, size_t pos) const throw();
size_t rfind(const string _FAR &s) const THROW_NONE;
size_t rfind(const string _FAR &s, size_t pos) const throw();

int contains(const char _FAR *pat) const throw();
int contains(const string _FAR &s) const THROW_NONE;
```

The overloaded functions find searches for the first occurrence of the string object s in the target string object. The parameter pos, in the second version of function find, specifies the index of the first searched character. This function enables you to skip a specified number of leading characters in the target string.

The overloaded member function rfind searches for the last occurrence of the string object s in the target string object. The parameter pos in the second version of function rfind specifies the index of the first searched character. The arguments for this parameter are typically close to the index of the last character. The member function find and rfind return the index of the matching character or yield NPOS if no match is found.

The overloaded functions search for any occurrence of a string or character pattern in the target string object. These functions return 1 if the string or pattern exists, and 0 otherwise. The string class also declares the following versions of member function find that use regular expressions to search for text patterns in the target string object:

```
size_t find(const TRegexp _FAR &pat, size_t i = 0) const throw();
size_t find(const TRegexp _FAR &pat, size_t _FAR *ext, size_t i = 0)
    const throw();
```

Here are examples of using the member functions find and rfind:

```
string Str1("Saturday");
string Str2("Day");
string Str3("day");

// make search case-sensitive
Str1.set_case_sensitive(1);
cout << Str1.find(Str2) << "\n"; // displays 0
cout << Str1.find(Str3) << "\n"; // displays 5
cout << Str1.find(Str3, 3) << "\n"; // displays 5
cout << Str1.find(Str3, 7) << "\n"; // displays 0

// make search case-insensitive
Str1.set_case_sensitive(0);
cout << Str1.find(Str2) << "\n"; // displays 5
cout << Str1.rfind(Str2, 7) << "\n"; // displays 5
cout << Str1.rfind(Str3) << "\n"; // displays 5
```

Regarding the search for character sets, the string class offers the following member functions:

```
size_t find_first_of(const string _FAR &s) const THROW_NONE;
size_t find_first_of(const string _FAR &s, size_t pos)
                                            const throw();
size_t find_first_not_of(const string _FAR &s) const THROW_NONE;
size_t find_first_not_of(const string _FAR &s, size_t pos)
    const throw();
size_t find_last_of(const string _FAR &s) const THROW_NONE;
size_t find_last_of(const string _FAR &s, size_t pos) const throw();
size_t find_last_not_of(const string _FAR &s) const THROW_NONE;
size_t find_last_not_of(const string _FAR &s, size_t pos)
    const throw();
```

The parameter s represents the string object which contains the character set used in the search. The parameter pos designates the index of the first searched character in the target string object. The function find_first_of returns the index of the first character in the target string object which matches any character in parameter s. The function find_last_of returns the index of the last character in the target string object which matches any character in parameter s. The function find_first_not_of returns the index of the first character in the target string object which does not match any character in parameter s. The function find_last_not_of returns the index of the last character in the target string object which does not match any character in parameter s.

Here are a few examples of using the character set searching functions:

```
String Str1("0123456789");
String pat1("43210");
String pat2("98765");

cout << Str1.c_str().find_first_of(pat1) << "\n"; // displays 0
cout << Str1.find_first_of(pat2) << "\n"; // displays 6

cout << Str1.find_first_not_of(pat1) << "\n"; // displays 6
cout << Str1.find_first_not_of(pat2) << "\n"; // displays 0

cout << Str1.find_last_of(pat1) << "\n"; // displays 5
cout << Str1.find_last_of(pat2) << "\n"; // displays 10

cout << Str1.find_last_not_of(pat1) << "\n"; // displays 10
cout << Str1.find_last_not_of(pat2) << "\n"; // displays 5
```

The Substring Functions

The string class supplies the following member functions which extract a substring from the target string object:

```
string substr(size_t pos) const
    throw(xalloc, outofrange);
string substr(size_t pos, size_t n) const
    throw(xalloc, outofrange);

TSubString substring(const char _FAR *cp) THROW_NONE;
const TSubString substring(const char _FAR *cp)
    const THROW_NONE;
TSubString substring(const char _FAR *cp, size_t start) throw();
const TSubString substring(const char _FAR *cp, size_t start)
    const throw();
```

The overloaded functions substr return a string object. The parameter pos is the index of the first extracted character. The parameter n specifies the number of characters to extract. The first version of the overloaded function substr extracts to the end of the string, whereas the second version limits the number of extracted character to the argument of parameter n.

The class string also offers the member function substring which returns TSubString objects. The parameter cp represents the ASCIIZ string which is used to create the TSubString object. The parameter start is the index of the first character of parameter cp that makes up the function's returned value.

Here are examples of using the overloaded functions substr:

```
string Str1("0123456789");
string Str2, Str3;

Str2 = Str1.substr(2, 3);
cout << Str2.c_str() << "\n"; // displays string 234

Str3 = Str1.substr(2);
cout << Str3.c_str() << "\n"; // displays string 23456789
```

The Case Conversion Functions

The string class provides the following functions that perform in-place character-case conversion:

```
void to_lower();
void to_upper();
```

The functions to_lower and to_upper convert the characters of the target string object to lowercase and uppercase, respectively.

Here are examples of using these member functions:

```
string Str1("Hello");
string loCaseStr(Str1);
string upCaseStr(Str1);

loCaseStr.to_lower();
cout << loCaseStr.c_str() << "\n"; // displays string hello
upCaseStr.to_upper();
cout << upCaseStr.c_str() << "\n"; // displays string HELLO
```

The Query State Functions

The string class declares the following state query member functions:

```
size_t length() const THROW_NONE;
static int get_case_sensitive_flag();
static int get_paranoid_check_flag();
static int get_skip_whitespace_flag();
static size_t get_initial_capacity();
static size_t get_resize_increment();
static size_t get_max_waste();
int is_null() const;
const char _FAR *c_str() const THROW_XALLOC;
```

The function length returns the number of characters in the target string object. Keep in mind that because a string object may contain imbedded null characters, the result of the function aStr.length may be greater than that of strlen(aStr.c_str()). The static function get_case_sensitive_flag returns the value stored in the private data member case_sensitive. The static function get_paranoid_check_flag yields the value stored in the protected data member paranoid_check. The static function get_skip_whitespace_flag returns the value in the private data member skip_white. The static function get_initial_capacity yields the value in the private data member initial_capac. The static function get_resize_increment returns the value in the private data member resize_inc. The static function get_max_waste yields the value in the private data member freeboard. The member function is_null returns 1 if the target string object is not empty, and yields 0 if it is. The member function c_str returns the pointer to the characters in the target string object. Do not assign the result of function c_str to a pointer for subsequent character manipulation!

The Set State Functions

The string class provides the following member functions to assist you in setting the states of the various private data members:

```
static int set_case_sensitive(int tf = 1);
static int set_paranoid_check(int ck = 1);
static int skip_whitespace(int sk = 1);
static size_set initial_capacity(size_t ic = 63);
static size_t resize_increment(size_t ri = 64);
static size_t max_waste(size_t mw = 63);
void resize(size_t m);
```

The static function set_case_sensitive sets the value stored in the private data member case_sensitive. The default argument for this function is 1. The static function set_paranoid_check sets the value stored in the protected data member paranoid_check. The default argument for this function is 1. The static member function set_skip_whitespace sets the value in the private data member skip_white. The default argument for this function is 1. The static function set_initial_capacity sets the value in the private data member `initial_capac`. The default argument for this function is 63. The static function `resize_increment` sets the value in the private data member `resize_inc`. The default argument for this function is 64. The static function `max_waste` sets the value in the private data member `freeboard`. The default argument for this function is 63. The function `resize` sets the maximum number of character to the argument of parameter `m`.

The Stream I/O Functions

The `string` class offers the following member functions and operators to support input from streams:

```
friend ipstream _FAR & _EXPFUNC operator >> (ipstream _FAR & is,
                                             string _FAR & str);
istream _FAR &read_file(istream _FAR &is);
istream _FAR &read_string(istream _FAR &is);
istream _FAR &read_line(istream _FAR &is);
istream _FAR &read_to_delim(istream _FAR &is, char delim = '\n');
istream _FAR &read_token(istream _FAR &is);
```

The operator >> allows you to input the characters of the string object `str` from the input stream `is`. The member function read*xxxx* supports reading a token, a delimited string, a line, a string, and an entire file.

The Miscellaneous Functions

This last subsection contains the following miscellaneous functions of class `string`:

```
size_t copy(char _FAR *cb, size_t n) throw(outofrange);
size_t copy(char _FAR *cb, size_t n, size_t pos) throw(outofrange);
string copy() const throw(xalloc);    // Distinct copy of self.
size_t reserve() const THROW_NONE;
void reserve(size_t ic) throw(xalloc, outofrange);
// Non-static member functions:
unsigned hash() const;
TSubString strip(StripType s = Trailing, char c = ' ');
```

The first two overloaded `copy` functions support the task of copying a selected number of the ASCIIZ string `cb`. The parameter `n` specifies the number of copied characters. The parameter `pos` designates the index of the first copied character. The function `hash` returns a hash value for the target string object. The function `strip` removes leading characters, trailing character, or both from the target string object. The parameter `s` has the type `StripType` (this is an enumerated type declared within the `string` class) and determines the mode of character trimming. The default argument for this parameter specifies trimming the trailing characters. The parameter c specifies the trimmed characters. The default argument for this parameter is the space character.

Here are examples of using some of these functions:

```
string Str1;
char s[81] = "Hello World!";
Str1.copy(s, 0, 5);
cout << Str1.c_str() << "\n"; // displays string Hello

string Str2("+++++Hello+++++");
Str2.strip(StripType::Both, '+');
cout << Str2.c_str() << "\n"; // displays string Hello
```

THE TESTSTR PROJECT

Let's look at a program that tests a set of functions in the class string. Listing C.2 contains the source code for the TESTSTR.H header file. Listing C.3 shows the script for the TESTSTR.RC resource file. Listing C.4 contains the source code for the TESTSTR.CPP implementation file. The TESTSTR.EXE is a menu driven program which allows you to test using the following menu selections:

1. The Operators menu selection offers the options to test the following operators:

   - The operator =

   - The operator +

   - The operator [ ]

   - The operator ==

   - The operator !=

   - The operator <

   - The operator <=

   - The operator >

   - The operator >=

2. The Query menu selection contains options to test the following query functions:

- The member function `c_str`
- The member function `get_at`
- The member function `get_initial_capacity`
- The member function `get_max_waste`
- The member function `is_null`
- The member function `length`

3. The Find/Replace menu selection provides the following options to test the `find` and `replace` functions:

   - The member function `find(const string _FAR&, size_t)`
   - The member function `rfind(const string _FAR&, size_t)`
   - The member function `find_first_of(const string _FAR&, size_t)`
   - The member function `find_first_not_of(const string _FAR&, size_t)`
   - The member function `find_last_of(const string _FAR&, size_t)`
   - The member function `find_last_not_of(const string _FAR&, size_t)`
   - The member function `replace(size_t, size_t, const string _FAR&)`

4. The Case menu selection offers two options to manipulate the case of characters in a string object:

   - The member function `to_lower`
   - The member function `to_upper`

5. The SubStrings menu selection provides the following options to manipulate portions of a string:

   - The member function `insert(size_t, const string _FAR&, size_t)`
   - The member function `append(const string _FAR&)`
   - The member function `prepend(const string _FAR&)`
   - The member function `strip(StripType, char)`
   - The member function `substr(size_t, size_t)`

These menu options help you to select the function you want to test. They do not perform any test themselves.

Figure C.1 shows the initial window in a session with program TESTSTR.EXE. The main window has the following controls:

- The function name static text control. The program displays the name of the currently tested function using this control. The program updates the contents of this control as you select a new menu option.

- The main string static text control. This control maintains its text throughout the program.

- The main string edit box control. Use this control to enter the characters of the main string.

- The string argument static text control. The program alters the text of this control to represent the name of the string argument. When testing a function that does not require a string argument, the program assigns a null string to the text of this control.

- The string argument edit control. Use this control to enter a string argument. When the accompanying static text control shows no text, this control does not supply the tested function with any argument.

- The first index static text control. This control contains the text that labels and clarifies the role of the associated edit box control.

- The first index edit control. Use this control to enter an integer argument for the currently tested function. When the associated text control shows no text, this control does not supply the tested function with any argument.

- The second index static text control. This control contains the text that labels and clarifies the role of the associated edit box control.

- The second index edit control. Use this control to enter an integer argument for the currently tested function. When the associated text control shows no text, this control does not supply the tested function with any argument.

- The result static text control. This control clarifies the result shown in the result edit box control.

- The result edit box control shows the resulting string, character, or numeric value.

- The Apply pushbutton control. Use this control to carry out testing a function after entering the required arguments. The labeled strings and indices edit boxes are the ones that require input.

- The Exit pushbutton. This control permits you to exit the test program.

- The Case sensitive check box. Use this control to specify whether the *findxxxx* functions perform a case-sensitive search.

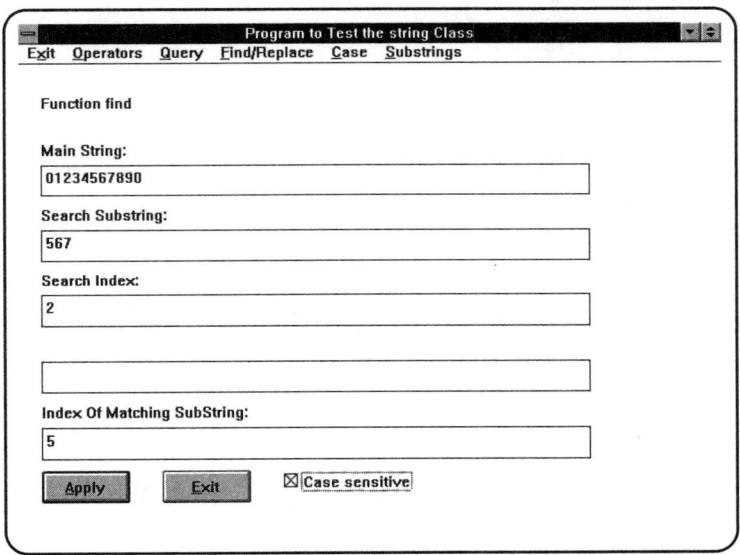

Figure C.1. The initial window in a session with program TESTSTR.EXE.

Build the TESTSTR.EXE program and run it. Experiment with testing the various functions.

LISTING C.2. THE SOURCE CODE FOR THE TESTSTR.H HEADER FILE.

```
#define ID_EXIT_BTN      101
#define CM_APPLY_BTN     102
#define ID_APPLY_BTN     103
#define CM_EXIT_BTN      104
#define IDR_BUTTONS      199
#define IDM_MAINMENU     200
```

continues

Listing C.2. continued

```
/* test operators */
#define CM_OP_EQL       201
#define CM_OP_ADD       202
#define CM_OP_APP       203
#define CM_OP_IDX       204
#define CM_OP_ISEQL     205
#define CM_OP_ISNEQL    206
#define CM_OP_ISLT      207
#define CM_OP_ISLTE     208
#define CM_OP_ISGT      209
#define CM_OP_ISGTE     210

/* test query functions */
#define CM_C_STR        211
#define CM_GET_AT       212
#define CM_GET_INICAP   213
#define CM_GET_MAXWST   214
#define CM_IS_NULL      215
#define CM_LENGTH       216

/* test find/replace functions */
#define CM_FIND         217
#define CM_RFIND        218
#define CM_FIND_FROF    219
#define CM_FIND_FRNOF   220
#define CM_FIND_LSOF    221
#define CM_FIND_LSNOF   222
#define CM_REPLACE      223

/* test string conversion functions */
#define CM_TO_LOWER     224
#define CM_TO_UPPER     225

/* test substring manipulation */
#define CM_INSERT       226
#define CM_APPEND       227
#define CM_PREPEND      228
#define CM_REMOVE       229
#define CM_STRIP        230
#define CM_SUBSTR       231
```

Listing C.3 shows the definitions for commands and resource ID used by the TESTSTR.EXE program. The listing shows the cm_*xxxx* command IDs grouped by the program's menu selections.

LISTING C.3. THE SCRIPT FOR THE TESTSTR.RC RESOURCE FILE.

```
#include <windows.h>
#include <owl\window.rh>
#include "teststr.h"

IDR_BUTTONS ACCELERATORS
BEGIN
  "a", CM_APPLY_BTN, ALT
  "e", CM_EXIT_BTN, ALT
END

IDM_MAINMENU MENU LOADONCALL MOVEABLE PURE DISCARDABLE
BEGIN

    MENUITEM "E&xit", CM_EXIT

    POPUP "&Operators"
    BEGIN
        MENUITEM "Operator =", CM_OP_EQL
        MENUITEM "Operator +", CM_OP_ADD
        MENUITEM "Operator +=", CM_OP_APP
        MENUITEM "Operator []", CM_OP_IDX
        MENUITEM "Operator ==", CM_OP_ISEQL
        MENUITEM "Operator !=", CM_OP_ISNEQL
        MENUITEM "Operator <", CM_OP_ISLT
        MENUITEM "Operator <=", CM_OP_ISLTE
        MENUITEM "Operator >", CM_OP_ISGT
        MENUITEM "Operator >=", CM_OP_ISGTE
    END

    POPUP "&Query"
    BEGIN
        MENUITEM "c_&str", CM_C_STR
        MENUITEM "get_&at", CM_GET_AT
        MENUITEM "get_initial_&capacity", CM_GET_INICAP
        MENUITEM "get_max_&waste", CM_GET_MAXWST
        MENUITEM "is_&null", CM_IS_NULL
        MENUITEM "&length", CM_LENGTH
    END

    POPUP "&Find/Replace"
    BEGIN
        MENUITEM "f&ind", CM_FIND
        MENUITEM "&rfind", CM_RFIND
        MENUITEM "find_&first_of", CM_FIND_FROF
        MENUITEM "find_first_&not_of", CM_FIND_FRNOF
        MENUITEM "find_&last_of", CM_FIND_LSOF
```

continues

LISTING C.3. CONTINUED

```
        MENUITEM "find_last_n&ot_of", CM_FIND_LSNOF
        MENUITEM "re&place", CM_REPLACE
    END

    POPUP "&Case"
    BEGIN
        MENUITEM "to_lower", CM_TO_LOWER
        MENUITEM "to_upper", CM_TO_UPPER
    END

    POPUP "&Substrings"
    BEGIN
        MENUITEM "&insert", CM_INSERT
        MENUITEM "&append", CM_APPEND
        MENUITEM "&prepend", CM_PREPEND
        MENUITEM "&remove", CM_REMOVE
        MENUITEM "stri&p", CM_STRIP
        MENUITEM "&substr", CM_SUBSTR
    END
END
```

Listing C.4. shows the accelerators and menu resource used by the TESTSTR.EXE program. The menu resource IDM_MAINMENU shows the program's menu selections and options.

LISTING C.4. THE SOURCE CODE FOR THE TESTSTR.CPP IMPLEMENTATION FILE.

```
/*
  Program to test the string class
*/

#include <owl\applicat.h>
#include <owl\framewin.h>
#include <owl\static.h>
#include <owl\edit.h>
#include <owl\button.h>
#include <owl\checkbox.h>
#include <owl\window.rh>
#include "teststr.h"
#include <stdlib.h>
#include <stdio.h>
#include <string.h>
#include <cstring.h>
```

```
// declare the constants that represent the sizes of the controls
const Wlbl = 100;
const WLonglbl = 500;
const Hlbl = 20;
const LblVertSpacing = 2;
const LblHorzSpacing = 40;
const Wbox = 500;
const Hbox = 30;
const BoxVertSpacing = 10;
const BoxHorzSpacing = 40;
const WLongbox = 4 * (Wbox + BoxHorzSpacing);
const Wvarbox = 2 * Wbox;
const Hvarbox = 3 * Hbox + 20;
const Hbtn = 30;
const Wbtn = 80;
const BtnHorzSpacing = 30;
const Hchk = 20;
const Wchk = 500;
const ChkVertSpacing = 30;
const MaxEditLen = 128;

// declare the ID_XXXX constants for the edit boxes
#define ID_FNNAME_TXT   111
#define ID_STRING1_TXT  112
#define ID_STRING2_TXT  113
#define ID_STRING3_TXT  114
#define ID_INDEX1_TXT   115
#define ID_INDEX2_TXT   116
#define ID_RESULT_TXT   117
#define ID_STRING1_EDIT 118
#define ID_STRING2_EDIT 119
#define ID_STRING3_EDIT 120
#define ID_INDEX1_EDIT  121
#define ID_INDEX2_EDIT  122
#define ID_RESULT_EDIT  123
#define ID_CASE_CHK     124

// declare the custom application class as
// a subclass of TApplication
class TWinApp : public TApplication
{
public:
  TWinApp() : TApplication() {}

protected:
  virtual void InitMainWindow();
};

// expand the functionality of TWindow by
// deriving class TMainWindow
```

continues

LISTING C.4. CONTINUED

```cpp
class TMainWindow : public TWindow
{
public:

  // declare nested enumerated type to index the various string
  // functions tested in this program
  enum fnType
    { enumNoFunction,
      enumOpEql, enumOpAdd, enumOpApp, enumOpIdx, enumOpIsEql,
      enumOpIsNEql, enumOpIsLT, enumOpIsLTE, enumOpIsGT,
      enumOpIsGTE, enumCStr, enum_get_at, enum_get_initial_capacity,
      enum_get_max_waste, enum_is_null, enum_length, enum_find,
      enum_rfind, enum_find_first_of, enum_find_first_not_of,
      enum_find_last_of, enum_find_last_not_of, enum_replace,
      enum_to_lower, enum_to_upper, enum_insert, enum_append,
      enum_prepend, enum_remove, enum_strip, enum_substr
    };

  TMainWindow();

protected:

  // pointers to the controls
  TStatic* FnNameTxt;
  TStatic* String1Txt;
  TStatic* String2Txt;
  TStatic* ResultTxt;
  TStatic* Index1Txt;
  TStatic* Index2Txt;
  TEdit* String1Box;
  TEdit* String2Box;
  TEdit* ResultBox;
  TEdit* Index1Box;
  TEdit* Index2Box;
  TButton* ApplyBtn;
  TButton* ExitBtn;
  TCheckBox* CaseChk;

  char Buffer[MaxEditLen+1];
  // declare the tested instances of class string
  string Str1;
  string Str2;
  string Result;
  int Index1;
  int Index2;
  fnType fnIdx;

  //--------------- member functions -----------------
```

```
// handle applying the currently selected function
void CmApplyBtn();

// handle the accelerator key for the Exit button
void CmExitBtn();

// handle closing the window
virtual BOOL CanClose();

// update the static text controls to match the arguments
// of the currently tested function
void updateText(const char* newFunName,
                const char* resultTitle,
                const char* string2Title = "",
                const char* index1Title = "",
                const char* index2Title = "");

// handle the menu options which test the operators
void CmOpEql();
void CmOpAdd();
void CmOpApp();
void CmOpIdx();
void CmOpIsEql();
void CmOpIsNEql();
void CmOpIsLT();
void CmOpIsLTE();
void CmOpIsGT();
void CmOpIsGTE();

// handle the menu options which test the query functions
void CmCStr();
void Cm_get_at();
void Cm_get_initial_capacity();
void Cm_get_max_waste();
void Cm_is_null();
void Cm_length();

// handle menu options that test the find and replace functions
void Cm_find();
void Cm_rfind();
void Cm_find_first_of();
void Cm_find_first_not_of();
void Cm_find_last_of();
void Cm_find_last_not_of();
void Cm_replace();

// handle menu options which test case conversion
void Cm_to_lower();
void Cm_to_upper();
```

continues

LISTING C.4. CONTINUED

```
// handle menu options which test substring manipulation
void Cm_insert();
void Cm_append();
void Cm_prepend();
void Cm_remove();
void Cm_strip();
void Cm_substr();

// the actual test functions
void DoOpEql();
void DoOpAdd();
void DoOpApp();
void DoOpIdx();
void DoOpIsEql();
void DoOpIsNEql();
void DoOpIsLT();
void DoOpIsLTE();
void DoOpIsGT();
void DoOpIsGTE();
void DoCStr();
void Do_get_at();
void Do_get_initial_capacity();
void Do_get_max_waste();
void Do_is_null();
void Do_length();
void Do_find();
void Do_rfind();
void Do_find_first_of();
void Do_find_first_not_of();
void Do_find_last_of();
void Do_find_last_not_of();
void Do_replace();
void Do_to_lower();
void Do_to_upper();
void Do_insert();
void Do_append();
void Do_prepend();
void Do_remove();
void Do_strip();
void Do_substr();

// declare the message map macro
DECLARE_RESPONSE_TABLE(TMainWindow);

};

DEFINE_RESPONSE_TABLE1(TMainWindow, TWindow)
  EV_COMMAND(CM_APPLY_BTN, CmApplyBtn),
```

```
  EV_COMMAND(ID_APPLY_BTN, CmApplyBtn),
  EV_COMMAND(ID_EXIT_BTN, CmExitBtn),
  EV_COMMAND(CM_EXIT_BTN, CmExitBtn),
  EV_COMMAND(CM_OP_EQL, CmOpEql),
  EV_COMMAND(CM_OP_ADD, CmOpAdd),
  EV_COMMAND(CM_OP_APP, CmOpApp),
  EV_COMMAND(CM_OP_IDX, CmOpIdx),
  EV_COMMAND(CM_OP_ISEQL, CmOpIsEql),
  EV_COMMAND(CM_OP_ISNEQL, CmOpIsNEql),
  EV_COMMAND(CM_OP_ISLT, CmOpIsLT),
  EV_COMMAND(CM_OP_ISLTE, CmOpIsLTE),
  EV_COMMAND(CM_OP_ISGT, CmOpIsGT),
  EV_COMMAND(CM_OP_ISGTE, CmOpIsGTE),
  EV_COMMAND(CM_C_STR, CmCStr),
  EV_COMMAND(CM_GET_AT, Cm_get_at),
  EV_COMMAND(CM_GET_INICAP, Cm_get_initial_capacity),
  EV_COMMAND(CM_GET_MAXWST, Cm_get_max_waste),
  EV_COMMAND(CM_IS_NULL, Cm_is_null),
  EV_COMMAND(CM_LENGTH, Cm_length),
  EV_COMMAND(CM_FIND, Cm_find),
  EV_COMMAND(CM_RFIND, Cm_rfind),
  EV_COMMAND(CM_FIND_FROF, Cm_find_first_of),
  EV_COMMAND(CM_FIND_FRNOF, Cm_find_first_not_of),
  EV_COMMAND(CM_FIND_LSOF, Cm_find_last_of),
  EV_COMMAND(CM_FIND_LSNOF, Cm_find_last_not_of),
  EV_COMMAND(CM_REPLACE, Cm_replace),
  EV_COMMAND(CM_TO_LOWER, Cm_to_lower),
  EV_COMMAND(CM_TO_UPPER, Cm_to_upper),
  EV_COMMAND(CM_INSERT, Cm_insert),
  EV_COMMAND(CM_APPEND, Cm_append),
  EV_COMMAND(CM_PREPEND, Cm_prepend),
  EV_COMMAND(CM_REMOVE, Cm_remove),
  EV_COMMAND(CM_STRIP, Cm_strip),
  EV_COMMAND(CM_SUBSTR, Cm_substr),
END_RESPONSE_TABLE;

TMainWindow::TMainWindow() :
        TWindow(0, 0, 0)
{
  char s[81];
  int x0 = 20;
  int y0 = 30;
  int x = x0, y = y0;

  // no function is selected by default
  fnIdx = enumNoFunction;
  // create the function name static text
  strcpy(s, "Function: none selected");
```

continues

Listing C.4. continued

```
FnNameTxt = new TStatic(this, ID_FNNAME_TXT, s, x, y,
                                    WLonglbl, Hlbl, strlen(s));
y += Hlbl + LblVertSpacing;

// create the controls for the main string
strcpy(s, "Main String:");
y += Hlbl + LblVertSpacing;
String1Txt = new TStatic(this, ID_STRING1_TXT, s, x, y,
                                    WLonglbl, Hlbl, strlen(s));
y += Hlbl + LblVertSpacing;
String1Box = new TEdit(this, ID_STRING1_EDIT, "", x, y,
                                Wbox, Hbox, 0, FALSE);

// create the controls for the argument string
strcpy(s, "String Argument:");
y += Hbox + BoxVertSpacing;
String2Txt = new TStatic(this, ID_STRING2_TXT, s, x, y,
                            WLonglbl, Hlbl, strlen(s));
y += Hlbl + LblVertSpacing;
String2Box = new TEdit(this, ID_STRING2_EDIT, "", x, y,
                            Wbox, Hbox, 0, FALSE);

// create the controls for the first index
strcpy(s, "First Index Argument:");
y += Hbox + BoxVertSpacing;
Index1Txt = new TStatic(this, ID_INDEX1_TXT, s, x, y,
                            WLonglbl, Hlbl, strlen(s));
y += Hlbl + LblVertSpacing;
Index1Box = new TEdit(this, ID_INDEX1_EDIT, "", x, y,
                            Wbox, Hbox, 0, FALSE);

// create the controls for the second index
strcpy(s, "Second Index Argument:");
y += Hbox + BoxVertSpacing;
Index2Txt = new TStatic(this, ID_INDEX2_TXT, s, x, y,
                                    WLonglbl, Hlbl, strlen(s));
y += Hlbl + LblVertSpacing;
Index2Box = new TEdit(this, ID_INDEX2_EDIT, "", x, y,
                            Wbox, Hbox, 0, FALSE);

// create the controls for the result string
strcpy(s, "Result:");
y += Hbox + BoxVertSpacing;
ResultTxt = new TStatic(this, ID_RESULT_TXT, s, x, y,
                            WLonglbl, Hlbl, strlen(s));
y += Hlbl + LblVertSpacing;
ResultBox = new TEdit(this, ID_RESULT_EDIT, "", x, y,
                            Wbox, Hbox, 0, FALSE);
```

```
    // create the Apply push button
    y += Hbox + BoxVertSpacing;
    ApplyBtn = new TButton(this, ID_APPLY_BTN, "&Apply",
                           x, y, Wbtn, Hbtn, FALSE);

    // Create the Exit Btn
    x += Wbtn + BtnHorzSpacing;
    ExitBtn = new TButton(this, ID_EXIT_BTN, "&Exit",
                    x, y, Wbtn, Hbtn, FALSE);

    // Create the Case sensitive check box
    x += Wbtn + BtnHorzSpacing;
    CaseChk = new TCheckBox(this, ID_CASE_CHK, "Case sensitive",
                               x, y, Wchk, Hchk, NULL);

    UpdateWindow();
}

void TMainWindow::CmExitBtn()
{
    // send a WM_CLOSE message to the parent window
    Parent->SendMessage(WM_CLOSE);
}

BOOL TMainWindow::CanClose()
{
    return MessageBox("Want to close this application?",
                "Query", MB_YESNO | MB_ICONQUESTION) == IDYES;
}

void TMainWindow::updateText(const char* newFunName,
                         const char* resultTitle,
                         const char* string2Title,
                         const char* index1Title,
                         const char* index2Title)
{
    // update the currently tested function name
    FnNameTxt->SetText(newFunName);
    // update the static text control for string argument
    String2Txt->SetText(string2Title);
    // erase the contents of the string argument edit box?
    if (string2Title[0] == '\0')
      String2Box->SetText("");
    // update the static text control for first index
    Index1Txt->SetText(index1Title);
    // erase the contents of the first index edit box?
    if (index1Title[0] == '\0')
      Index1Box->SetText("");
    // update the static text control for second index
    Index2Txt->SetText(index2Title);
```

continues

LISTING C.4. CONTINUED

```cpp
  // erase the contents of the second index edit box?
  if (index2Title[0] == '\0')
    Index2Box->SetText("");
  // update the static text control for result string
  if (resultTitle[0] == '\0')
      ResultTxt->SetText("Resulting String:");
  else
        ResultTxt->SetText(resultTitle);
  ResultBox->SetText("");
}
void TMainWindow::CmOpEql()
{
  fnIdx = enumOpEql;
  updateText("Operator =", "", "Assigned String:");
}

void TMainWindow::CmOpAdd()
{
  fnIdx = enumOpAdd;
  updateText("Operator +", "", "Added String:");
}

void TMainWindow::CmOpApp()
{
  fnIdx = enumOpApp;
  updateText("Operator +=", "", "Appended String:");
}

void TMainWindow::CmOpIdx()
{
  fnIdx = enumOpIdx;
  updateText("Operator []", "Indexed Character:",
             "", "Character Index:");
}

void TMainWindow::CmOpIsEql()
{
  fnIdx = enumOpIsEql;
  updateText("Operator ==",
             "Main String == String Argument?:",
             "String Argument:", "");
}

void TMainWindow::CmOpIsNEql()
{
  fnIdx = enumOpIsNEql;
```

```
    updateText("Operator !=",
                  "Main String != String Argument?:",
                      "String Argument:", "");
}

void TMainWindow::CmOpIsLT()
{
  fnIdx = enumOpIsLT;
  updateText("Operator <",
                  "Main String < String Argument?:",
                      "String Argument:", "");
}

void TMainWindow::CmOpIsLTE()
{
  fnIdx = enumOpIsLTE;
  updateText("Operator <=",
                      "Main String <= String Argument?:",
                      "String Argument:", "");
}

void TMainWindow::CmOpIsGT()
{
  fnIdx = enumOpIsGT;
  updateText("Operator >",
                  "Main String > String Argument?:",
                  "String Argument:", "");
}

void TMainWindow::CmOpIsGTE()
{
  fnIdx = enumOpIsGTE;
  updateText("Operator >=",
                  "Main String >= String Argument?:",
                      "String Argument:", "");
}

void TMainWindow::CmCStr()
{
  fnIdx = enumCStr;
  updateText("Function c_str", "String characters");
}

void TMainWindow::Cm_get_at()
{
  fnIdx = enum_get_at;
  updateText("Function get_at", "Indexed Character:",
                  "", "Character Index:");
}
```

continues

Listing C.4. continued

```cpp
void TMainWindow::Cm_get_initial_capacity()
{
  fnIdx = enum_get_initial_capacity;
  updateText("Function get_initial_capacity",
                      "Initial Capacity:");
}

void TMainWindow::Cm_get_max_waste()
{
  fnIdx = enum_get_max_waste;
  updateText("Function get_max_waste",
                  "Free Space:", "");
}

void TMainWindow::Cm_is_null()
{
  fnIdx = enum_is_null;
  updateText("Function is_null", "Is String Empty?:");
}

void TMainWindow::Cm_length()
{
  fnIdx = enum_length;
  updateText("Function length", "String Length:",
                  "String Argument:");
}
void TMainWindow::Cm_find()
{
  fnIdx = enum_find;
  updateText("Function find", "Index Of Matching SubString:",
                      "Search Substring:", "Search Index:");
}

void TMainWindow::Cm_rfind()
{
  fnIdx = enum_rfind;
  updateText("Function rfind", "Index Of Matching SubString:",
                  "Search Substring:", "Search Index:");
}

void TMainWindow::Cm_find_first_of()
{
  fnIdx = enum_find_first_of;
  updateText("Function find_first_of",
                  "Index Of Matching SubString:",
                      "Search Substring:", "Search Index:");
}
```

```
void TMainWindow::Cm_find_first_not_of()
{
  fnIdx = enum_find_first_not_of;
  updateText("Function find_first_not_of",
                  "Index Of Matching SubString:",
                  "Search Substring:", "Search Index:");
}

void TMainWindow::Cm_find_last_of()
{
  fnIdx = enum_find_last_of;
  updateText("Function find_last_of",
                  "Index Of Matching SubString:",
                  "Search Substring:", "Search Index:");
}

void TMainWindow::Cm_find_last_not_of()
{
  fnIdx = enum_find_last_not_of;
  updateText("Function find_last_not_of",
                  "Index Of Matching SubString:",
                      "Search Substring:", "Search Index:");
}

void TMainWindow::Cm_replace()
{
  fnIdx = enum_replace;
  updateText("Function replace",
                  "Update String:",
                      "Replacement String:",
                      "Index for First Replaced Character",
                      "Number of Removed Characters:");
}

void TMainWindow::Cm_to_lower()
{
  fnIdx = enum_to_lower;
  updateText("Function to_lower", "Lowercase String:");
}

void TMainWindow::Cm_to_upper()
{
  fnIdx = enum_to_upper;
  updateText("Function to_upper", "Uppercase String:");
}

void TMainWindow::Cm_insert()
{
  fnIdx = enum_insert;
```

continues

LISTING C.4. CONTINUED

```
  updateText("Function insert",
                "",
                "Inserted String:",
                "Insertion Index:",
                "Number of Inserted Characters:");
}

void TMainWindow::Cm_append()
{
  fnIdx = enum_append;
  updateText("Function append", "", "Appended String:");
}

void TMainWindow::Cm_prepend()
{
  fnIdx = enum_prepend;
  updateText("Function prepend", "", "Prepended String:");
}

void TMainWindow::Cm_remove()
{
  fnIdx = enum_remove;
  updateText("Function remove", "", "",
                    "Index of First Deleted Character:",
                "Number of Deleted Characters:");
}

void TMainWindow::Cm_strip()
{
  fnIdx = enum_strip;
  updateText("Function strip", "", "Stripped Character:");
}

void TMainWindow::Cm_substr()
{
  fnIdx = enum_substr;
  updateText("Function substr", "", "",
            "Index of First Extracted Character:",
            "Number of Extracted Characters:");
}

void TMainWindow::DoOpEql()
{
  // obtain the main string
  String1Box->GetText(Buffer, sizeof(Buffer));
  Str1 = Buffer;
  ResultBox->SetText(Str1.c_str());
}
```

```
void TMainWindow::DoOpAdd()
{
  // obtain the main string
  String1Box->GetText(Buffer, sizeof(Buffer));
  Str1 = Buffer;
  // obtain the string argument
  String2Box->GetText(Buffer, sizeof(Buffer));
  Str2 = Buffer;
  // concatenate Str1 and Str2 and assign the result in Result
  Result = Str1 + Str2;
  ResultBox->SetText(Result.c_str());
}

void TMainWindow::DoOpApp()
{
  // obtain the main string
  String1Box->GetText(Buffer, sizeof(Buffer));
  Str1 = Buffer;
  // obtain the string argument
  String2Box->GetText(Buffer, sizeof(Buffer));
  Str2 = Buffer;
  // append Str2 to Str1 using the operator +=
  Str1 += Str2;
  ResultBox->SetText(Str1.c_str());
}

void TMainWindow::DoOpIdx()
{
  char c;

  // obtain the main string
  String1Box->GetText(Buffer, sizeof(Buffer));
  Str1 = Buffer;
  // obtain the index
  Index1Box->GetText(Buffer, sizeof(Buffer));
  Index1 = atoi(Buffer);
  // is the index within range?
  if (Index1 >= 0 && Index1 < Str1.length()) {
    c = Str1[Index1];
    Result = c;
    ResultBox->SetText(Result.c_str());
  }
  else
    MessageBox("Index is out of range", "Error");
}

void TMainWindow::DoOpIsEql()
{
  // obtain the main string
  String1Box->GetText(Buffer, sizeof(Buffer));
```

continues

Listing C.4. continued

```
  Str1 = Buffer;
  // obtain the string argument
  String2Box->GetText(Buffer, sizeof(Buffer));
  Str2 = Buffer;
  // compare the strings Str1 and Str2
  if (Str1 == Str2)
    ResultBox->SetText("True");
  else
    ResultBox->SetText("False");
}

void TMainWindow::DoOpIsNEql()
{
  // obtain the main string
  String1Box->GetText(Buffer, sizeof(Buffer));
  Str1 = Buffer;
  // obtain the string argument
  String2Box->GetText(Buffer, sizeof(Buffer));
  Str2 = Buffer;
  // compare the strings Str1 and Str2
  if (Str1 != Str2)
    ResultBox->SetText("True");
  else
    ResultBox->SetText("False");
}

void TMainWindow::DoOpIsLT()
{
  // obtain the main string
  String1Box->GetText(Buffer, sizeof(Buffer));
  Str1 = Buffer;
  // obtain the string argument
  String2Box->GetText(Buffer, sizeof(Buffer));
  Str2 = Buffer;
  // compare the strings Str1 and Str2
  if (Str1 < Str2)
    ResultBox->SetText("True");
  else
    ResultBox->SetText("False");
}

void TMainWindow::DoOpIsLTE()
{
  // obtain the main string
  String1Box->GetText(Buffer, sizeof(Buffer));
  Str1 = Buffer;
  // obtain the string argument
  String2Box->GetText(Buffer, sizeof(Buffer));
```

```
  Str2 = Buffer;
  // compare the strings Str1 and Str2
  if (Str1 <= Str2)
     ResultBox->SetText("True");
  else
     ResultBox->SetText("False");
}

void TMainWindow::DoOpIsGT()
{
  // obtain the main string
  String1Box->GetText(Buffer, sizeof(Buffer));
  Str1 = Buffer;
  // obtain the string argument
  String2Box->GetText(Buffer, sizeof(Buffer));
  Str2 = Buffer;
  // compare the strings Str1 and Str2
  if (Str1 > Str2)
     ResultBox->SetText("True");
  else
     ResultBox->SetText("False");
}

void TMainWindow::DoOpIsGTE()
{
  // obtain the main string
  String1Box->GetText(Buffer, sizeof(Buffer));
  Str1 = Buffer;
  // obtain the string argument
  String2Box->GetText(Buffer, sizeof(Buffer));
  Str2 = Buffer;
  // compare the strings Str1 and Str2
  if (Str1 >= Str2)
     ResultBox->SetText("True");
  else
     ResultBox->SetText("False");
}

void TMainWindow::DoCStr()
{
  // obtain the main string
  String1Box->GetText(Buffer, sizeof(Buffer));
  Str1 = Buffer;
  // insert characters of Str1 in the result string edit box
  // using the tested function c_str
  ResultBox->SetText(Str1.c_str());
}

void TMainWindow::Do_get_at()
{
```

continues

LISTING C.4. CONTINUED

```
  DoOpIdx();
}

void TMainWindow::Do_get_initial_capacity()
{
  int n;

  // obtain the main string
  String1Box->GetText(Buffer, sizeof(Buffer));
  Str1 = Buffer;
  // obtain the initial string capacity
  n = Str1.get_initial_capacity();
  sprintf(Buffer, "%d", n);
  ResultBox->SetText(Buffer);
}

void TMainWindow::Do_get_max_waste()
{
  int n;

  // obtain the main string
  String1Box->GetText(Buffer, sizeof(Buffer));
  Str1 = Buffer;
  // obtain the maximum wasted space
  n = Str1.get_max_waste();
  sprintf(Buffer, "%d", n);
  ResultBox->SetText(Buffer);
}

void TMainWindow::Do_is_null()
{
  // obtain the main string
  String1Box->GetText(Buffer, sizeof(Buffer));
  Str1 = Buffer;
  ResultBox->SetText(Str1.is_null() ? "True" : "False");
}

void TMainWindow::Do_length()
{
  int n;

  // obtain the main string
  String1Box->GetText(Buffer, sizeof(Buffer));
  Str1 = Buffer;
  // get the number of characters in the Str1 object
  n = Str1.length();
  sprintf(Buffer, "%d", n);
  ResultBox->SetText(Buffer);
}
```

```
void TMainWindow::Do_find()
{
  int pos;
  int n;

  // obtain the main string
  String1Box->GetText(Buffer, sizeof(Buffer));
  Str1 = Buffer;
  // set the case sensitivity mode
  Str1.set_case_sensitive((CaseChk->GetCheck() == BF_CHECKED) ?
                                                     1 : 0);
  // obtain the string argument
  String2Box->GetText(Buffer, sizeof(Buffer));
  Str2 = Buffer;
  // obtain the search index
  Index1Box->GetText(Buffer, sizeof(Buffer));
  pos = atoi(Buffer);
  // search for the first occurence of Str2 in Str1,
  // starting at index pos
  n = Str1.find(Str2, pos);
  sprintf(Buffer, "%d", n);
  ResultBox->SetText(Buffer);
}

void TMainWindow::Do_rfind()
{
  int pos;
  int n;

  // obtain the main string
  String1Box->GetText(Buffer, sizeof(Buffer));
  Str1 = Buffer;
  // set the case sensitivity mode
  Str1.set_case_sensitive((CaseChk->GetCheck() == BF_CHECKED) ?
                                                     1 : 0);
  // obtain the string argument
  String2Box->GetText(Buffer, sizeof(Buffer));
  Str2 = Buffer;
  // obtain the search index
  Index1Box->GetText(Buffer, sizeof(Buffer));
  pos = atoi(Buffer);
  // search for the last occurence of Str2 in Str1,
  // starting at index pos
  n = Str1.rfind(Str2, pos);
  sprintf(Buffer, "%d", n);
  ResultBox->SetText(Buffer);
}

void TMainWindow::Do_find_first_of()
{
```

continues

LISTING C.4. CONTINUED

```cpp
  int pos;
  int n;

  // obtain the main string
  String1Box->GetText(Buffer, sizeof(Buffer));
  Str1 = Buffer;
  // set the case sensitivity mode
  Str1.set_case_sensitive((CaseChk->GetCheck() == BF_CHECKED) ?
                                                      1 : 0);
  // obtain the string argument
  String2Box->GetText(Buffer, sizeof(Buffer));
  Str2 = Buffer;
  // obtain the search index
  Index1Box->GetText(Buffer, sizeof(Buffer));
  pos = atoi(Buffer);
  // search for first occurrence of any character of Str2 in Str1,
  // starting at index pos
  n = Str1.find_first_of(Str2, pos);
  sprintf(Buffer, "%d", n);
  ResultBox->SetText(Buffer);
}

void TMainWindow::Do_find_first_not_of()
{
  int pos;
  int n;

  // obtain the main string
  String1Box->GetText(Buffer, sizeof(Buffer));
  Str1 = Buffer;
  // set the case sensitivity mode
  Str1.set_case_sensitive((CaseChk->GetCheck() == BF_CHECKED) ?
                                                      1 : 0);
  // obtain the string argument
  String2Box->GetText(Buffer, sizeof(Buffer));
  Str2 = Buffer;
  // obtain the search index
  Index1Box->GetText(Buffer, sizeof(Buffer));
  pos = atoi(Buffer);
  n = Str1.find_first_not_of(Str2, pos);
  // search for first occurrence of any character of Str2 not in
  // Str1, starting at index pos
  sprintf(Buffer, "%d", n);
  ResultBox->SetText(Buffer);
}

void TMainWindow::Do_find_last_of()
{
```

```
  int pos;
  int n;

  // obtain the main string
  String1Box->GetText(Buffer, sizeof(Buffer));
  Str1 = Buffer;
  // set the case sensitivity mode
  Str1.set_case_sensitive((CaseChk->GetCheck() == BF_CHECKED) ?
                                                   1 : 0);
  // obtain the string argument
  String2Box->GetText(Buffer, sizeof(Buffer));
  Str2 = Buffer;
  // obtain the search index
  Index1Box->GetText(Buffer, sizeof(Buffer));
  pos = atoi(Buffer);
  // search for last occurrence of any character of Str2 in
  // Str1, starting at index pos
  n = Str1.find_last_of(Str2, pos);
  sprintf(Buffer, "%d", n);
  ResultBox->SetText(Buffer);
}


void TMainWindow::Do_find_last_not_of()
{
  int pos;
  int n;

  // obtain the main string
  String1Box->GetText(Buffer, sizeof(Buffer));
  Str1 = Buffer;
  // set the case sensitivity mode
  Str1.set_case_sensitive((CaseChk->GetCheck() == BF_CHECKED) ?
                                                   1 : 0);
  // obtain the string argument
  String2Box->GetText(Buffer, sizeof(Buffer));
  Str2 = Buffer;
  // obtain the search index
  Index1Box->GetText(Buffer, sizeof(Buffer));
  pos = atoi(Buffer);
  n = Str1.find_last_not_of(Str2, pos);
  // search for last occurrence of any character of Str2 not in
  // Str1, starting at index pos
  sprintf(Buffer, "%d", n);
  ResultBox->SetText(Buffer);
}


void TMainWindow::Do_replace()
{
  int pos;
  int n;
```

continues

LISTING C.4. CONTINUED

```
  // obtain the main string
  String1Box->GetText(Buffer, sizeof(Buffer));
  Str1 = Buffer;
  // obtain the string argument
  String2Box->GetText(Buffer, sizeof(Buffer));
  Str2 = Buffer;
  // obtain the search index
  Index1Box->GetText(Buffer, sizeof(Buffer));
  pos = atoi(Buffer);
  // obtain the search index
  Index2Box->GetText(Buffer, sizeof(Buffer));
  n = atoi(Buffer);
  // replace characters of Str1 with those of Str2
  Str1.replace(pos, n, Str2);
  ResultBox->SetText(Str1.c_str());
}

void TMainWindow::Do_to_lower()
{
  // obtain the main string
  String1Box->GetText(Buffer, sizeof(Buffer));
  Str1 = Buffer;
  // convert to lowercase
  Str1.to_lower();
  ResultBox->SetText(Str1.c_str());
}

void TMainWindow::Do_to_upper()
{
  // obtain the main string
  String1Box->GetText(Buffer, sizeof(Buffer));
  Str1 = Buffer;
  // convert to uppercase
  Str1.to_upper();
  ResultBox->SetText(Str1.c_str());
}

void TMainWindow::Do_insert()
{
  int pos;
  int n;

  // obtain the main string
  String1Box->GetText(Buffer, sizeof(Buffer));
  Str1 = Buffer;
  // obtain the string argument
  String2Box->GetText(Buffer, sizeof(Buffer));
  Str2 = Buffer;
```

```
  // obtain the search index
  Index1Box->GetText(Buffer, sizeof(Buffer));
  pos = atoi(Buffer);
  // obtain the search index
  Index2Box->GetText(Buffer, sizeof(Buffer));
  n = atoi(Buffer);
  // insert n characters of Str2 in Str1, staring at index pos
  Result = Str1.insert(pos, Str2, n);
  ResultBox->SetText(Result.c_str());
}

void TMainWindow::Do_append()
{
  // obtain the main string
  String1Box->GetText(Buffer, sizeof(Buffer));
  Str1 = Buffer;
  // obtain the string argument
  String2Box->GetText(Buffer, sizeof(Buffer));
  Str2 = Buffer;
  // append strin Str2 to Str1
  Str1.append(Str2);
  ResultBox->SetText(Str1.c_str());
}

void TMainWindow::Do_prepend()
{
  // obtain the main string
  String1Box->GetText(Buffer, sizeof(Buffer));
  Str1 = Buffer;
  // obtain the string argument
  String2Box->GetText(Buffer, sizeof(Buffer));
  Str2 = Buffer;
  // prepend Str2 to Str1
  Str1.prepend(Str2);
  ResultBox->SetText(Str1.c_str());
}

void TMainWindow::Do_remove()
{
  int pos;
  int n;

  // obtain the main string
  String1Box->GetText(Buffer, sizeof(Buffer));
  Str1 = Buffer;
  // obtain the search index
  Index1Box->GetText(Buffer, sizeof(Buffer));
  pos = atoi(Buffer);
  // obtain the search index
  Index2Box->GetText(Buffer, sizeof(Buffer));
```

continues

LISTING C.4. CONTINUED

```
  n = atoi(Buffer);
  // remove n characters from Str1, starting at index pos
  Result = Str1.remove(pos, n);
  ResultBox->SetText(Result.c_str());
}

void TMainWindow::Do_strip()
{
  string::StripType s = string::Both;

  // obtain the main string
  String1Box->GetText(Buffer, sizeof(Buffer));
  Str1 = Buffer;
  // obtain the trimming character
  String2Box->GetText(Buffer, sizeof(Buffer));
  if (Buffer[0] != '\0') {
    // strip trailing characters of Str1
      Result = Str1.strip(s, Buffer[0]);
      ResultBox->SetText(Result.c_str());
  }
}

void TMainWindow::Do_substr()
{
  int pos;
  int n;

  // obtain the main string
  String1Box->GetText(Buffer, sizeof(Buffer));
  Str1 = Buffer;
  // obtain the search index
  Index1Box->GetText(Buffer, sizeof(Buffer));
  pos = atoi(Buffer);
  // obtain the search index
  Index2Box->GetText(Buffer, sizeof(Buffer));
  n = atoi(Buffer);
  // obtain a substring of Str1
  Result = Str1.substr(pos, n);
  ResultBox->SetText(Result.c_str());
}

void TMainWindow::CmApplyBtn()
{
  // select the tested function
  switch (fnIdx) {
    case enumOpEql :
        DoOpEql();
        break;
```

```
    case enumOpAdd :
        DoOpAdd();
        break;
    case enumOpApp :
        DoOpApp();
        break;
case enumOpIdx :
    DoOpIdx();
    break;
case enumOpIsEql :
    DoOpIsEql();
    break;
case enumOpIsNEql :
    DoOpIsNEql();
    break;
case enumOpIsLT :
    DoOpIsLT();
    break;
case enumOpIsLTE :
    DoOpIsLTE();
    break;
case enumOpIsGT :
    DoOpIsGT();
    break;
case enumOpIsGTE :
    DoOpIsGTE();
        break;
case enumCStr :
    DoCStr();
    break;
case enum_get_at :
    Do_get_at();
    break;
case enum_get_initial_capacity :
    Do_get_initial_capacity();
    break;
case enum_get_max_waste :
    Do_get_max_waste();
        break;
 case enum_is_null :
        Do_is_null();
        break;
 case enum_length :
        Do_length();
        break;
 case enum_find :
        Do_find();
        break;
```

continues

LISTING C.4. CONTINUED

```
        case enum_rfind :
            Do_rfind();
            break;
        case enum_find_first_of :
            Do_find_first_of();
            break;
        case enum_find_first_not_of :
            Do_find_first_not_of();
            break;
        case enum_find_last_of :
            Do_find_last_of();
            break;
        case enum_find_last_not_of :
            Do_find_last_not_of();
            break;
        case enum_replace :
            Do_replace();
            break;
        case enum_to_lower :
            Do_to_lower();
            break;
        case enum_to_upper :
            Do_to_upper();
            break;
        case enum_insert :
            Do_insert();
            break;
        case enum_append :
            Do_append();
            break;
        case enum_prepend :
            Do_prepend();
            break;
        case enum_remove :
            Do_remove();
            break;
        case enum_strip :
            Do_strip();
            break;
        case enum_substr :
            Do_substr();
            break;
        default:
            MessageBox("Please select a function", "Error");
    }
}
```

```
void TWinApp::InitMainWindow()
{
  MainWindow = new TFrameWindow(0,
          "Program to Test the string Class",
          new TMainWindow);
  // load the keystroke resources
  MainWindow->Attr.AccelTable = IDR_BUTTONS;
  // load the menu resource
  MainWindow->AssignMenu(TResID(IDM_MAINMENU));
  // enable the keyboard handler
  MainWindow->EnableKBHandler();
}

int OwlMain(int /* argc */, char** /*argv[] */)
{
  TWinApp app;
  return app.Run();
}
```

Listing C.4 shows the source code for the test program. Though this program is relatively long, it is not difficult to read. The source code contains the following sections:

- The #include section, which includes the required nested header files.

- The program's constants, most of which specify the sizes and locations of the various controls.

- The set of #define macros, which define the IDs for the various controls.

- The declaration of the application class TWinApp.

- The declaration of the main window class TMainWindow. This declaration contains the following subsections:

   - The nested enumerated type TMainWindow::fnType, which enumerates the 31 tested functions.

   - The set of data members which are pointers to the visual controls.

   - The instances of class string and other data members used in testing the string class functions.

   - The family of Cmxxxx event handling member functions. These functions respond to menu options and pushbutton control notification messages.

- The family of Do*xxxx* tester member functions. These functions contain the statements that actually test the string functions. The functions Do*xxxx* extract their arguments from the various edit controls and place them in the various data members that are instances of class `string`.

- The set of miscellaneous member functions that support the previously named sets of functions.

- The message response table macro with its message mapping entries.

- The constructor for the class `TMainWindow`. This member contains the statements that create and display the program's controls.

- The definition of the member functions Cm*xxxx*. The names of these functions are derived from the operator or function they select to test. For example, the function `Cm_get_at` selects the member function `string::get_at` for testing. Most of these functions handle the menu options. Such functions typically perform two simple tasks:

    Assign the enumerated value to the data member `fnIdx` (which has the `fnType` enumerated type).

    Invoke the member function `updateText` to update the text of the static controls in concert with the tested function. The function uses a smart feature that clears an edit box if the new text of the accompanying static control is a null string. The exception to this rule is the result box, which is systematically cleared.

- The set of Do*xxxx* member functions which perform the test. The names of these functions are derived from the operator or function they test. For example, the member function `Do_get_at` tests the member function `string::get_at`.

- The member function `CmApply` uses a `switch` statement and the enumerated data member `fnIdx` to invoke the appropriate Do*xxxx* member function to test the currently selected function.

- The member function `InitMainWindow` of the application class.

- The function `OwlMain`.

SUMMARY

This chapter presented the class string which models C++ string objects. This class complies with the ANSI C++ committee proposal and should therefore be used by various C++ compilers. This chapter discussed the following topics:

- The declaration of the class string. The text presented the public, protected, and private members of class string.

- The various kinds of public member functions for class string. These functions include the various constructors, the destructor, the assignment functions, the concatenation functions, the comparison functions, the insertion functions, the removal functions, the replacement functions, the substring functions, the searching functions, the substring functions, the case conversion functions, the query state functions, the set state functions, the stream I/O functions, and other miscellanous functions.

- The Windows program TESTSTR.EXE, which tests the various member functions of class string. The program uses the message dialog box to display the operands and results of using the tested member functions.

INDEX

M

Add to Your Sams Library Today with the Best Books for Programming, Operating Systems, and New Technologies

The easiest way to order is to pick up the phone and call

1-800-428-5331

between 9:00 a.m. and 5:00 p.m. EST.

For faster service please have your credit card available.

ISBN	Quantity	Description of Item	Unit Cost	Total Cost
0-672-30441-4		Borland C++ 4 Developer's Guide (book/disk)	$49.95	
0-672-30279-[illegible]		C++ Programming PowerPack (book/disk)	$24.95	
0-672-30177-6		Windows Programmer's Guide to Borland C++ Tools (book/disk)	$39.95	
0-672-30030-3		Windows Programmer's Guide to Serial Communications (book/disk)	$39.95	
0-672-30097-4		Windows Programmer's Guide to Resources (book/disk)	$34.95	
0-672-30226-8		Windows Programmer's Guide to OLE/DDE (book/disk)	$34.95	
0-672-30364-7		Win32 API Desktop Reference (book/CD)	$49.95	
0-672-30236-5		Windows Programmer's Guide to DLLs and Memory Management (book/disk)	$34.95	
0-672-30295-0		Moving into Windows NT Programming (book/disk)	$39.95	
0-672-30338-8		Inside Windows File Formats (book/disk)	$29.95	
0-672-30299-3		Uncharted Windows Programming (book/disk)	$34.95	
0-672-30239-X		Windows Developer's Guide [illegible] Application Design (book/disk)	$34.95	
		Shipping and Handling: See information below.		
		TOTAL		

❑ 3 ½" Disk

❑ 5 ¼" Disk

Shipping and [illegible], and $1.75 for each additional book. Floppy disk: add $1.75 for shipping and han[illegible] ship product to you in 24 hours for an additional charge of approximately [illegible] or in two days. Overseas shipping and handling: add $2.00 per book and [illegible]ge. Call for availability and pricing information on latest editions.

[illegible] Street, Indianapolis, Indiana 46290

[illegible]35-3202 — FAX 1-800-858-7674 — Customer Service

Book ISBN 0-672-30409-0